THE PSYCHOLOGY OF ENTREPRENEURSHIP

"This pathbreaking book makes clear the important inroads that psychology has contributed to the field of entrepreneurship. Not only does it contain state-of-the art research and thinking from a 'who's who' in the field, but it is a must read to anyone and everyone interested in entrepreneurship."

David Audretsch, *Indiana University, USA*

The Psychology of Entrepreneurship: New Perspectives is an update of the earlier landmark volume in the Society for Industrial and Organizational Psychology Organizational Frontiers Series. This new book takes stock of the advances in the field of the psychology of entrepreneurship with all new chapters and presents the latest findings on traditional topics, such as cognition, motivation, affect, personality, and action.

The Psychology of Entrepreneurship: New Perspectives compiles research of the most prolific scholars in the field to produce an overview of the most important psychological topics relevant to entrepreneurship. It includes novel insights into topics such as entrepreneurial cognition, intrapreneurship and innovation, leadership, entrepreneurial competencies, action theory, entrepreneurship training, and the process of entrepreneurship. Additionally, the updated volume presents new topics that have become more and more important in entrepreneurship research. These topics include affect, clinical psychology and disorders, biological correlates of entrepreneurship, entrepreneurial teams, culture, identity, starting capital, failure and exit, contextual factors, age and demographic change, evidence-based entrepreneurship, and entrepreneurs' well-being.

With a collection of authors comprising experts who have developed the field over the last decade, *The Psychology of Entrepreneurship: New Perspectives* is vital to all students, scholars, and instructors interested in staying abreast of the most current, novel research and insights into the psychology of entrepreneurship.

Michael M. Gielnik is Professor of HR Development at the Leuphana University of Lüneburg, Germany. His research focuses on entrepreneurship from a psychological perspective, in particular entrepreneurial learning and training. He has taken a special interest in entrepreneurship in developing countries.

Melissa S. Cardon is Haslam Professor of Entrepreneurship and Innovation at the University of Tennessee, Knoxville, USA. Her research focuses on unleashing human potential within entrepreneurial firms, including a dual interest in human resource practices that maximize employee potential, and the emotional, relational, and cognitive aspects of entrepreneurs that contribute to optimizing their behavior and performance.

Michael Frese has won many awards and is affiliated with the Asia School of Business (in collaboration with MIT Sloan Management), the Institute of Management and Organization at Leuphana University of Lüneburg, Germany, and the NUS Business School in Singapore (provost chair and former head of department). He bases his research on action theory and has developed the famous personal initiative training for entrepreneurs in developing countries. He was the editor of the last version of this important book and counts as one of the founding fathers of psychological approaches to entrepreneurship.

SIOP Organizational Frontiers Series

Series Editors

Angelo DeNisi
Tulane University, USA

Kevin Murphy
University of Limerick, Ireland
Editorial Board

Derek R. Avery
Wake Forest University, USA

Jill Ellingson
University of Kansas, USA

Franco Fraccaroli
University of Trento, Italy

Susan Jackson
Rutgers University, USA

Paul Sparrow
Lancaster University, UK

Hannes Zacher
Leipzig University, Germany

Jing Zhou
Rice University, USA

The Organizational Frontiers Series is sponsored by the Society for Industrial and Organizational Psychology (SIOP). Launched in 1983 to make scientific contributions accessible to the field, the series publishes books addressing emerging theoretical developments, fundamental and translational research, and theory-driven practice in the field of Industrial-Organizational Psychology and related organizational science disciplines including organizational behavior, human resource management, and labor and industrial relations.

Books in this series aim to inform readers of significant advances in research; challenge the research and practice community to develop and adapt new ideas; and promote the use of scientific knowledge in the solution of public policy issues and increased organizational effectiveness.

The Series originated in the hope that it would facilitate continuous learning and spur research curiosity about organizational phenomena on the part of both scientists and practitioners.

The Society for Industrial and Organizational Psychology is an international professional association with an annual membership of more than 8,000 industrial-organizational (I-O) psychologists who study and apply scientific principles to the workplace. I-O psychologists serve as trusted partners to business, offering strategically focused and scientifically rigorous solutions for a number of workplace issues. SIOP's mission is to enhance human well-being and performance in organizational and work settings by promoting the science, practice, and teaching of I-O psychology. For more information about SIOP, please visit www.siop.org.

The Psychology of Entrepreneurship
New Perspectives
Edited by Michael M. Gielnik, Melissa S. Cardon, and Michael Frese

For more information about this series, please visit www.routledge.com/SIOP-Organizational-Frontiers-Series/book-series/SIOP

THE PSYCHOLOGY OF ENTREPRENEURSHIP

New Perspectives

Edited by Michael M. Gielnik, Melissa S. Cardon and Michael Frese

Routledge
Taylor & Francis Group

NEW YORK AND LONDON

SOCIETY for INDUSTRIAL and ORGANIZATIONAL PSYCHOLOGY

ORGANIZATIONAL FRONTIERS SERIES

First published 2021
by Routledge
52 Vanderbilt Avenue, New York, NY 10017

and by Routledge
2 Park Square, Milton Park, Abingdon, Oxon, OX14 4RN

Routledge is an imprint of the Taylor & Francis Group, an informa business

Library of Congress Cataloging-in-Publication Data
Names: Gielnik, Michael M., editor. | Cardon, Melissa S., 1971- editor. | Frese, Michael, 1949- editor.
Title: The psychology of entrepreneurship : new perspectives / edited by Michael M. Gielnik, Melissa S. Cardon, Michael Frese.
Identifiers: LCCN 2020037352 (print) | LCCN 2020037353 (ebook) | ISBN 9780367684495 (hardback) | ISBN 9780367684471 (paperback) | ISBN 9781003137573 (ebook)
Subjects: LCSH: Entrepreneurship. | Entrepreneurship—Psychological aspects.
Classification: LCC HB615 .P7995 2021 (print) | LCC HB615 (ebook) | DDC 338/.04019—dc23
LC record available at https://lccn.loc.gov/2020037352
LC ebook record available at https://lccn.loc.gov/2020037353

ISBN: 978-0-367-68449-5 (hbk)
ISBN: 978-0-367-68447-1 (pbk)
ISBN: 978-1-003-13757-3 (ebk)

Typeset in Bembo
by Apex CoVantage, LLC

CONTENTS

ILLUSTRATIONS

Figures

Tables

Appendices

Exhibits

CONTRIBUTORS

Aaron H. Anglin Neeley School of Business, Texas Christian University, USA

Ted Baker Rutgers University, USA. University of Cape Town Graduate School of Business, South Africa

Robert Baron Spears School of Business, Oklahoma State University

James Bort Whitman School of Management, Syracuse University, USA

Nicola Breugst Technical University of Munich, Germany

Orla Byrne University College Dublin, Ireland

Melissa S. Cardon Haslam College of Business, University of Tennessee, USA

Michael P. Ciuchta Manning School of Business, UMass Lowell, USA

Per Davidsson Australian Centre for Entrepreneurship Research, QUT, Australia. Jönköping International Business School, Sweden

Samantha Elliott University of Oklahoma, USA

Maw-Der Foo Nanyang Technological University, Singapore

Michael Frese Leuphana University of Lüneburg, Germany

Michael M. Gielnik Leuphana University of Lüneburg, Germany

Yi Huang Nanyang Technological University, Singapore

Trevor Israelsen University of Victoria, Canada

Anna Jenkins University of Queensland, Australia

Daniel A. Lerner IE Business School, IE University, Spain

Chaim Letwin Suffolk University, USA

Robert W. Martin University of Oklahoma, USA

Mona Mensmann University of Warwick, England

J. Robert Mitchell Colorado State University, USA

Ronald K. Mitchell Texas Tech University, USA

Michael D. Mumford University of Oklahoma, USA

Charles Y. Murnieks University of Missouri-Kansas City, USA

Nicos Nicolaou Warwick Business School, England

Ahmed Maged Nofal Emlyon Business School, France

Holger Patzelt TUM School of Management, Germany

Jeffrey M. Pollack Poole College of Management, North Carolina State University, USA

E. Erin Powell North Carolina State University, USA

Rebecca Preller Technical University of Munich, Germany

Andreas Rauch The University of Sydney Business School, Australia

Shane W. Reid E.J. Ourso College of Business, Louisiana State University, USA

Scott Shane Weatherhead School of Management, USA

Dean A. Shepherd Mendoza College of Business, University of Notre Dame

Erik Stam Utrecht University School of Economics, Netherlands

Ute Stephan King's Business School, King's College London, England

Regan Stevenson Kelley School of Business Indiana University, USA

Marilyn A. Uy Nanyang Technological University, Singapore

Marco van Gelderen Vrije Universiteit Amsterdam, Netherlands

K. Jakob Weers Leuphana University of Lüneburg, Germany

Friederike Welter Institut für Mittelstandsforschung (IfM) Bonn, Germany. University of Siegen, Germany

Johan Wiklund Whitman School of Management, Syracuse University, USA

Hannes Zacher Leipzig University, Germany

SERIES FOREWORD

The phenomenon of entrepreneurship is ubiquitous. It can be observed taking place in most aspects of life, not just in new business venturing. It is international in scope and is transdisciplinary by nature. Its practitioners chose to deal with challenges or opportunities facing us today but which often have implications for the future. In this regard, *The Psychology of Entrepreneurship* edited by Michael M. Gielnik, Melissa S. Cardon, and Michael Frese is *a book for our times*. As I write the world is enduring a pandemic. Yet, in the face of all of the uncertainty, entrepreneurs continue to work their craft. Some have done so by "pivoting" and moving their operations to support such things as the production of "personal protection" equipment. Others are re-positioning existing products or services to support a society now requiring virtual teaching and learning, virtual living and virtual work arrangements. At the same time, entrepreneurs are looking toward the future. As an example, there are currently no fewer than 165 candidate vaccines being developed. The goal here is to quickly identify, test, and produce not just one but a set of vaccines that can address the complex nature of the virus and therefore truly protect the world's population. As implied, with very little effort one can find many examples of entrepreneurship in action. For those who want to go beyond the news headlines however, the chapters in this volume will allow you to develop a deep understanding of the entrepreneurial spirit. Here you will find a detailed and readable treatment of traditional topics associated with entrepreneurship such as action theory, entrepreneurial competencies, training, failure and exit, and the team work associated with successful new business venturing. But this volume also takes seriously the value of adopting a multidisciplinary approach. Toward this end, it offers original chapters covering recent discoveries on the potential role and impact of emotions, of human biology and of a variety of "clinical" conditions that are now thought to underlie entrepreneurial activities. Clearly, if one wants to know how entrepreneurial energy can come about and best be harnessed, there is no better way to do this than to engage in a close reading of this volume. It offers an up-to-date and visionary treatment of the personal and situational conditions that allow entrepreneurs to both enact their passion for innovation while contributing to a better world.

Rich Klimoski

1

INTRODUCTION TO THE PSYCHOLOGY OF ENTREPRENEURSHIP

New Perspectives

Michael M. Gielnik, Melissa S. Cardon & Michael Frese

Entrepreneurship involves "the processes of discovery, evaluation, and exploitation of opportunities; and the set of individuals who discover, evaluate, and exploit them" (Shane & Venkataraman, 2000, p. 218). This definition of entrepreneurship explicitly includes the role of the individual in entrepreneurship, and as such, "entrepreneurship is fundamentally personal" (Baum, Frese, Baron, & Katz, 2007, p. 1). Accordingly, the discipline of psychology, which deals with the human mind and behavior, provides a profound scientific base to understand and theorize about entrepreneurship. Indeed, the notion that psychology can make an important contribution to the domain of entrepreneurship has gained more and more traction in the last decade since the publication of the first edition of this book (Baron, 2008; Baum, Frese, & Baron, 2007; Frese & Gielnik, 2014; Gorgievski & Stephan, 2016; Shepherd, Souitaris, & Gruber, 2020).

Reviewing the research conducted over the last 10-plus years, the chapters in this book provide updates and novel insights into established topics and new developments in the field of the psychology of entrepreneurship. Figure 1.1 presents an overview of the chapters arranged in the framework of the action-characteristics model of entrepreneurship (Frese & Gielnik, 2014). Novel insights into established topics are presented in the chapters on entrepreneurial cognition (Chapter 2), intrapreneurship and innovation (Chapter 7), leadership (Chapter 9), entrepreneurial competencies (Chapter 12), action theory (Chapter 11), entrepreneurship training (Chapter 16), and the process of entrepreneurship (Chapter 20). Additionally, the psychology of entrepreneurship has identified new topics in terms of affect (Chapter 3), clinical psychology and disorders (Chapter 4), biological correlates of entrepreneurship (Chapter 5), entrepreneurial teams (Chapter 6), culture (Chapter 8), identity (Chapter 10), starting capital (Chapter 13), failure and exit (Chapter 14), contextual factors (Chapter 15), age and demographic

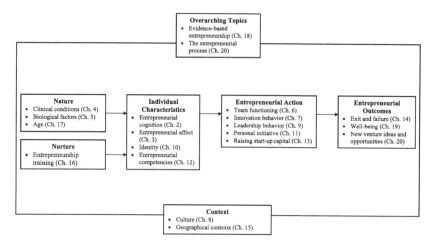

FIGURE 1.1 Overview of the Chapters in This Book Arranged According to the Action-Characteristics Model of Entrepreneurship

Source: Frese and Gielnik (2014)

change (Chapter 17), evidence-based entrepreneurship (Chapter 18), and entrepreneurs' well-being (Chapter 19).The diversity of topics demonstrates the variety of approaches from the discipline of psychology that can inform entrepreneurship research, and the variety of topics entrepreneurship researchers pursue related to the psychology of entrepreneurs.We believe that the diversity in topics has greatly enriched entrepreneurship research and contributed to its maturity.

Furthermore, we believe that the maturation of the field over the last 10 years provides a stable base to complement the diversity in topics with a similar diversity in opinions and a culture of controversy. In psychology, a culture of controversy and the resulting debates have oftentimes led to important scientific advancements. For example, the controversy about the primacy of affect or cognition has advanced the understanding of the interplay between emotions and cognition (Lazarus, 1984; Zajonc, 1984). More recently, the debate concerning whether self-efficacy positively or negatively influences performance has greatly enhanced our understanding of the motivational function of self-efficacy within and between persons (Bandura, 2012; Vancouver & Purl, 2017). In entrepreneurship, a controversial debate about the beneficial or detrimental effects of planning led to important theoretical advancements and empirical findings concerning when and under which conditions planning enhances entrepreneurial success (Brinckmann, Grichnik, & Kapsa, 2010; Frese, van Gelderen, & Ombach, 2000; Sarasvathy, 2001).

The chapters in this book provide an excellent starting point to engage in controversial debates over the next 10 years. For example, prior research has pondered the question of whether entrepreneurs are born with a certain disposition. Over the years, this research came to different conclusions, ranging from

"Who is an entrepreneur? is the wrong question" (Gartner, 1989, p. 47) to "Let's put the person back into entrepreneurship" (Rauch & Frese, 2007, p. 353). The chapter on "The Biology of Entrepreneurship" by Nofal, Nicolaou, and Shane (Chapter 5) provides a new theoretical approach to address the question by drawing from the discipline of biology to examine the genetic and physiological disposition of engaging in entrepreneurship. Accordingly, the question of whether entrepreneurs are born or made might be controversially debated and resolved by referring to and blending theories from psychology and biology. Similarly, the question of whether concepts from the field of clinical psychology are helpful to understand entrepreneurship can be subject to debate. On one hand, the chapter on "Clinical Psychology Constructs in Entrepreneurship Research: ADHD, Personality Disorders, and Others" by Lerner, Patzelt, and Wiklund (Chapter 4) provides strong arguments that examining clinical conditions might be advantageous in the context of entrepreneurship. On the other hand, it is counterintuitive to assume that disorders provide unique pathways to success because disorders are typically dysfunctional, by definition. Accordingly, engaging in a scholarly debate about the pros and cons might contribute to a deeper understanding of how and under which circumstances clinical conditions are beneficial or detrimental for entrepreneurship.

Finally, the readers of this book will realize that some chapters build strongly on theories from psychology and its subdisciplines, such as industrial–organizational (I/O) psychology and clinical psychology, whereas other chapters refer more strongly to theories specific to the field of entrepreneurship. We believe that the latter is a sign that the field of entrepreneurship, in general has developed substantially and become more mature. This is a positive development, which we fully endorse. It is important that the field of entrepreneurship cultivates its own theories and constructs to distinguish itself and solidify its position as a distinct discipline. Yet it is also important that scholars strike a balance between developing our own theories and adhering to the scientific principle of "standing on the shoulders of giants". According to this principle, research should build on prior work instead of reinventing the wheel, for example, by proliferating new constructs with a special entrepreneurial touch instead of building on general constructs that have strong roots in psychology. A critical debate therefore is to what extent the field of entrepreneurship requires its own theories and constructs or can rely on psychological theories without being mistaken as a subdiscipline of I/O psychology or other fields (e.g., strategy, management, or organizational behavior). However, we want to emphasize that the dictum is still correct that entrepreneurship research benefits from I/O psychology and vice versa (Baron, Frese, & Baum, 2007).

We hope that this book provides an interesting introduction to the fascinating field of the psychology of entrepreneurship and the various topics that it entails, and inspires scholars to reflect deeply about controversial theories and perspectives. We welcome and embrace diversity in topics and opinions, and we believe that controversial dialogues and debates will once again substantially move the field of the psychology of entrepreneurship forward over the next 10 years of research.

References

Bandura, A. (2012). On the functional properties of perceived self-efficacy revisited. *Journal of Management, 38*(1), 9–44.

Baron, R. A. (2008). The role of affect in the entrepreneurial process. *Academy of Management Review, 33*(2), 328–340.

Baron, R. A., Frese, M., & Baum, J. R. (2007). Research gains: Benefits of closer links between I/O psychology and entrepreneurship. In J. R. Baum, M. Frese, & R. A. Baron (Eds.), *The psychology of entrepreneurship* (pp. 347–373). Mahwah, NJ: Lawrence Erlbaum Associates.

Baum, J. R., Frese, M., & Baron, R. A. (2007). *The psychology of entrepreneurship.* Mahwah, NJ: Lawrence Erlbaum Associates.

Baum, J. R., Frese, M., Baron, R. A., & Katz, J. A. (2007). Entrepreneurship as an area of psychology study: An introduction. In J. R. Baum, M. Frese, & R. A. Baron (Eds.), *The psychology of entrepreneurship* (pp. 1–18). Mahwah, NJ: Lawrence Erlbaum Associates.

Brinckmann, J., Grichnik, D., & Kapsa, D. (2010). Should entrepreneurs plan or just storm the castle? A meta-analysis on contextual factors impacting the business planning-performance relationship in small firms. *Journal of Business Venturing, 25*(1), 24–40.

Frese, M., & Gielnik, M. M. (2014). The psychology of entrepreneurship. *Annual Review of Organizational Psychology and Organizational Behavior, 1*, 413–438.

Frese, M., van Gelderen, M., & Ombach, M. (2000). How to plan as a small scale business owner: Psychological process characteristics of action strategies and success. *Journal of Small Business Management, 38*(2), 1–18.

Gartner, W. B. (1989). "Who is an entrepreneur?" is the wrong question. *Entrepreneurship Theory and Practice, 13*(4), 47–68.

Gorgievski, M. J., & Stephan, U. (2016). Advancing the psychology of entrepreneurship: A review of the psychological literature and an introduction. *Applied Psychology: An International Review, 65*(3), 437–468.

Lazarus, R. S. (1984). On the primacy of cognition. *American Psychologist, 39*(2), 124–129.

Rauch, A., & Frese, M. (2007). Let's put the person back into entrepreneurship research: A meta-analysis on the relationship between business owners' personality traits, business creation, and success. *European Journal of Work and Organizational Psychology, 16*(4), 353–385.

Sarasvathy, S. D. (2001). Causation and effectuation: Toward a theoretical shift from economic inevitability to entrepreneurial contingency. *Academy of Management Review, 26*(2), 243–263.

Shane, S., & Venkataraman, S. (2000). The promise of entrepreneurship as a field of research. *Academy of Management Review, 25*(1), 217–226.

Shepherd, D. A., Souitaris, V., & Gruber, M. (in press). Creating new ventures: A review and research agenda. *Journal of Management.*

Vancouver, J. B., & Purl, J. D. (2017). A computational model of self-efficacy's various effects on performance: Moving the debate forward. *Journal of Applied Psychology, 102*(4), 599–616.

Zajonc, R. B. (1984). On the primacy of affect. *American Psychologist, 39*(2), 117–123.

2

ENTREPRENEURIAL COGNITION RESEARCH–AN UPDATE

J. Robert Mitchell, Trevor Israelsen &
Ronald K. Mitchell

Over the past twenty-five years, entrepreneurship research has been fundamentally transformed as a result of the extensive work on the topic of entrepreneurial cognition (Baron, 2004, 2007; Baron & Ward, 2004; Dew, Grichnik, Mayer-Haug, Read, & Brinckmann, 2015; Grégoire, Cornelissen, Dimov, & van Burg, 2015; J. R. Mitchell, R. K. Mitchell, & Randolph-Seng, 2014; Mitchell, Busenitz, Lant et al., 2002, 2004; Mitchell, Busenitz, Bird et al., 2007). This entrepreneurial cognition research has, for example, enabled an understanding of how entrepreneurs differ from non-entrepreneurs in terms of their thinking processes—including the use of heuristics (Busenitz & Barney, 1997) and self-efficacy (Chen, Greene, & Crick, 1998)—and their expertise (e.g., Mitchell, Smith, Seawright, & Morse, 2000). This research also has revealed what leads some individuals to be more likely than other individuals to identify entrepreneurial opportunities and start a venture, focusing on differentiators such as pattern recognition (Baron & Ensley, 2006), risk perception (Keh, Foo, & Lim, 2002; Simon, Houghton, & Aquino, 2000), structural alignment (Grégoire, Barr, & Shepherd, 2010), expertise (e.g., Mitchell et al., 2000) and self-image (Mitchell & Shepherd, 2010). Moreover, this research also has demonstrated how cognitive differences such as an entrepreneurs' optimism and self-efficacy (Hmieleski & Baron, 2008, 2009) and expertise (Reuber & Fischer, 1994) can also lead to differences in the performance of the entrepreneur's firm. As these examples illustrate, research on entrepreneurial cognition is now part of the mainstream of entrepreneurship research.

But it was not always this way. Most early entrepreneurship research focused primarily on an individual's response to economic inducements without regard to mediating variables internal to the entrepreneur. This lack of attention to mental processes reflected both the norms of entrepreneurship research that had roots in economic theory and was also supported by the strong emphasis on explaining observable behavior by psychologists of the time. However, beginning in the 1950s and 1960s, psychology research generally had begun to shift away from a behaviorist approach that saw action as being a direct result of stimuli in the environment and toward one that sought to understand the role of the individual in individual action (see Randolph-Seng, J. R. Mitchell, & R. K. Mitchell, 2014, for a detailed review). The work of Atkinson (1957, p. 360) contributed to this shift by explicitly addressing the role of cognition in the individual action that underlies entrepreneurship, by characterizing expectancy as a "cognitive anticipation, usually aroused in a situation, that performance of some act will be followed by a particular consequence." McClelland likewise contributed to the shift away from behaviorism (1955, 1961, 1965) by emphasizing, instead, the role of personality characteristics such as achievement motivation in explaining why some individuals are more likely to be entrepreneurs. Of the two, McClelland's approach was the one that took hold in the emerging entrepreneurship literature. Indeed, research that followed sought to explain how other characteristics such as autonomy (Hornaday & Aboud, 1971), risk-taking (Palmer, 1971), need for power (Winter, 1973), internal locus of control (Rotter, 1966; Timmons, 1978) and so forth could explain differences between entrepreneurs and non-entrepreneurs (see Carland, Hoy, Boulton, & Carland, 1984, for a more complete description).

Brockhaus and Horowitz (1986) noted that the results of prior research on the distinguishing characteristics of entrepreneurs were not sufficiently fine-grained to generalize distinctions between entrepreneurs and non-entrepreneurs. As they argued,

> the characteristics of the aspiring or successful entrepreneur vary depending upon the nature and scope of the business venture. Most entrepreneurial ventures result from a "push" from external factors. . . . [Thus,] it might be beneficial to concentrate research efforts on determining *why* entrepreneurs succeed or fail.
>
> *(1986, p. 44, emphasis added)*

This call, and similar ones (e.g., Gartner, 1988; Smith, Gannon, Grimm, & Mitchell, 1988; Shaver & Scott, 1991) led to research focusing more on entrepreneurial behavior and the processes underlying entrepreneurship. The quest towards understanding the *why* questions related to entrepreneurial processes paved the way for research on cognition to move toward the mainstream in entrepreneurship research. The work of Bird (1988, 1992) on entrepreneurial intentions represents an early example of entrepreneurship research that adopted the perspective of psychology and was indicative of the shift of entrepreneurial cognition research toward the mainstream. Shaver and Scott (1991) further articulated the behavior–psychology link, in suggesting that psychology can be distinguished from other behavioral sciences by its emphasis on the behavior of the individual person, which, in turn, is influenced by the way in which the external world is represented in the mind, and by the individual's exercise of choice.

(1991, p. 23)

They then asserted that "a psychological approach to new venture creation must involve cognitive processes that occur within the individual person" (1991, p. 26).

Research in entrepreneurship thus accelerated the study of the mental processes of entrepreneurs. *Entrepreneurship Theory and Practice* published a special issue on "Finding the Entrepreneur in Entrepreneurship" as a way "to encourage entrepreneurship researchers to re-conceptualize the nature of entrepreneurship by focusing on the individual and social/psychological processes involved in entrepreneurial activity" (Gartner, Shaver, Gatewood, & Katz, 1994, p. 5). The editors noted that cognition represents an essential part of explaining entrepreneurial processes, using "what entrepreneurs think about, and how they go about thinking about what they think about [being] critical to understanding much of what occurs during an entrepreneur's activities" (Gartner et al., 1994, p. 6). Other entrepreneurial cognition research soon followed.

Hisrich and Jankowicz (1990) investigated the cognitive complexity of venture capitalist funding decisions. Katz (1992) developed a psychosocial cognitive model of the decision to become self-employed versus wage-based employment. Krueger and Dickson (1994) sought to understand the effect of perceived self-efficacy on the risk-taking of entrepreneurs in the context of entrepreneurial opportunities. Mitchell and Chesteen (1995) and Mitchell (1996) worked to develop an understanding of the role of entrepreneurial expertise in entrepreneurial outcomes, especially in terms of its development. Gatewood, Shaver, and Gartner (1995) explored how certain cognitive factors influenced the persistence and success of entrepreneurs' start-ups. Jelinek and Litterer (1995) suggested that extant organization theory was based largely on static, deterministic assumptions about organizations and sought to develop a paradigm for understanding entrepreneurial organizations based on a dynamic, cognitive approach focused on individual sensemaking and collective decision processes. Busenitz and Lau (1996) developed a cross-cultural cognitive model of new venture creation. Likewise, Busenitz and Barney (1997) sought to understand cognitive differences in the decision-making biases and heuristics of managers in large organizations compared to those of entrepreneurs. Sarasvathy, Simon, and Lave (1998, p. 208) used "verbal protocol analyses to compare entrepreneurs with bankers in their cognitive approaches for solving problems involving a variety of risks." Importantly, Baron (1998, p. 275) seemed to cement the more mainstream status of the entrepreneurial cognition approach by "building additional conceptual bridges between entrepreneurship research and the large, extant literature on human cognition."

"Boxologies" and (Getting Back to) Socially Situated Cognition

As Baron's (1998) article argued, cognition research generally arose from the broader psychology literature on the role of human cognition in action. This research refocused attention toward mental processes as a cause of human action and away from behaviorism's basic conceptualization of human actions as a simple function of responses to environmental stimuli (Randolph-Seng et al., 2014). The emerging research on mental processes, however, drew heavily on a computer analogy that characterized the mind as a kind of "biological calculator," an "internal conduit with a lot of representational and computational operations created by smart and inventive thinkers" (Bandura, 2001, p. 2). The application of this analogy can be seen, for example, in the information processing approach to human cognition that is grounded in cognitive *scripts* (Abelson, 1981).

Such approaches have been recognized as valuable but insufficient. As Smith and Conrey (2009, p. 455) have noted, social cognition research, in general, has "frequently been formulated as abstract, disembodied stories about autonomous mental processes, expressed as 'boxologies' with little or no concern for adaptiveness in, or even interfaces with, real social environments." Social cognition researchers use the term "boxology" to refer to "seemingly static representations of abstract, disembodied cognitive structures [such as] biases, heuristics, scripts, etc." (R. K. Mitchell, Randolph-Seng, & J. R. Mitchell, 2011, p. 774). Given that entrepreneurship research on cognition has followed the broader field of psychology, it is no surprise that research in entrepreneurial cognition has faced the same challenge of being static and insufficiently situated in the broader social environment (Mitchell et al., 2011). Recent work in entrepreneurial cognition has begun to address these challenges (Mitchell, Randolph-Seng et al., 2011; J. R. Mitchell, R. K. Mitchell et al., 2014; Clarke & Cornelissen, 2011; Dew et al., 2015; Cacciotti, Hayton, Mitchell, & Giazitzoglu, 2016) by adopting a socially situated approach to the study of entrepreneurial cognition.

Interestingly, prior research in entrepreneurship might be said to have foreshadowed the socially situated approach to the study of entrepreneurial cognition. For example, Atkinson (1957) focused on the anticipation that was aroused in a situation as it related to some action and its consequences, but that pathway was not pursued until the more recent development of the entrepreneurial cognition research stream. Similarly, Brockhaus and Horowitz (1986) emphasized the possibility that entrepreneurs are heavily influenced by external factors, which idea was reiterated by Shaver and Scott (1991, p. 27), who argued that the psychology of entrepreneurship required an understanding of "how the individual's cognitive representations of the world get translated into action." Likewise, Jelinek and Litterer (1995) emphasized the importance of the role that the organizational context plays in influencing the processes of individual sensemaking and collective decision-making—this latter aspect also having been emphasized by Gartner et al.

(1994, p. 6) in the idea that the "'entrepreneur' in entrepreneurship is more likely to be plural, rather than singular." In this way, a move away from the static and disembodied "boxologies" evident in prior research on entrepreneurial cognition in some ways represents a return to, and more thorough treatment of, ideas that were present in the early work on cognition in entrepreneurship.

Socially Situated Entrepreneurial Cognition

The socially situated approach builds on the premise that cognition is (1) action-oriented, (2) embodied, (3) situated within and among specific social environments and (4) distributed across minds and tools (Smith & Semin, 2004). This approach suggests that the social world both shapes the content of thought and the processes underlying behavior. Hence, the foregoing four themes of socially situated cognition now are conceptualized in entrepreneurship research as being integrated (Mitchell et al., 2011). Each theme contributes to a gestalt and has been suggested to be applicable to entrepreneurial cognition research (*ibid*).

In more recent entrepreneurial cognition research, *action-oriented* mental representations may be observed, for example, in research on the metacognitive processing of entrepreneurs (Haynie, Shepherd, Mosakowski, & Earley, 2010), entrepreneurial behavior under time pressure (Mitchell & Shepherd, 2010), acting on what resources are available to effectuate new value (Sarasvathy, 2001) and research regarding entrepreneurial bricolage (Baker & Nelson, 2005)—each being subsumed under the overall notion of action-oriented, adaptive entrepreneurship (McMullen & Shepherd, 2006; Frese, 2007). But adaptive action also is enabled and constrained by the attributes of the brain and the physical body (Smith & Conrey, 2009). *Embodied* cognition may be observed in research connecting the physical being to the mental being. Such work has investigated, for example, how hormonal influences (such as higher testosterone levels) can help to explain willingness to venture (White, Thornhill, & Hampson, 2007), the importance of embodied affect and emotion in entrepreneurship (e.g., Baron, 2008; Cardon, Wincent, Singh, & Drnovsek, 2009) and the impact of physical movements (such as gesturing) and of speech in persuasion—as entrepreneurs "pitch" to potential investors (Clarke, Cornelissen, & Healey, 2019). The *situated* theme connects social objects, such as conversations, relationships with others and membership in social groups, to entrepreneurship through, for example, research on social networks (De Carolis & Saparito, 2006), mentorship (Ozgen & Baron, 2007) and a person-situation learning match (Dimov, 2007). And since cognition in a social situation occurs in many minds at once, the *distributed* theme suggests that cognition is "implemented by systems that link minds with aspects of the physical and social environment" (Smith & Conrey, 2009, p. 461). The distributed cognition theme is evident in entrepreneurial cognition research that explains, for example, the role of institutions and entrepreneurship (Lim, Morse, Mitchell, & Seawright, 2010), cross-cultural entrepreneurship (Mitchell et al., 2000), specific country profiles

(Busenitz, Gomez, & Spencer, 2000) and entreprenurial team cognition (Shepherd & Krueger, 2002; West, 2007).

Thus, when the foregoing four themes are viewed together, a dynamic conceptualization of entrepreneurial cognition becomes possible, and it is useful in interpretive terms especially as an ordering structure for entrepreneurial cognition research overall (Randolph-Seng et al., 2014). That is, while past entrepreneurial cognition research has been characterized separately, for example, in terms of heuristics, entrepreneurial alertness, expertise, effectuation, action and affect (Mitchell et al., 2007); the socially situated cognition approach enables researchers to "encompass and connect different approaches to entrepreneurial cognition research" (Randolph-Seng et al., 2015, p. 298). Thus.

> [h]euristics-based approaches can be positioned in terms of the situated theme, as they attempt to explain how individuals in certain situations (e.g., a complex situation) may rely on decision shortcuts. . . . Alertness approaches can be viewed in terms of the situated theme. Specifically, when individuals find themselves in different situations/contexts, those with certain entrepreneurial knowledge structures are expected to perceive their context differently than those who lack the same knowledge structures, enabling some individuals to better identify entrepreneurial opportunities. . . . Expertise approaches can be mapped at the intersection of distributed, situated, and action-oriented themes. That is, expertise can be viewed as both situated and action-oriented through its focus on deliberate practice (action-oriented) with experts (situated). . . . The effectuation approach can be seen as existing at the intersection between action-oriented and distributed themes, as it regularly emphasizes acting based on contingencies given the set of people and resources (minds and tools) at hand. . . . Action-centric approaches . . . can be placed in the intersection between situated and action-oriented themes, as taking action has been suggested to require at least two elements: the inner (goals as they influence thinking) and the outer (the situation) environment. . . . Finally, affect-centric approaches appear to operate at the intersection of situated, embodied, and action-oriented themes, given the potential role of the situation and the body on the potential for entrepreneurial action.
>
> *(Randolph-Seng et al., 2015, pp. 299–300)*

Consequently, with its capacity for enabling integration, the application of the socially situated cognition approach to many of the psychology-based arguments in entrepreneurship research enables researchers to have available a theoretical frame that permits the dynamism of previously elusive entrepreneurial phenomena (MacMillan & Katz, 1992) to become more tractable. But importantly, the integrative capacity of the socially situated approach also may open the study of mainstream entrepreneurial phenomena to new research possibilities.

Socially Situated Cognition Illustrated in Entrepreneurship Research

In this section, we draw on representative examples from entrepreneurship research to sketch some outlines of applicability of the socially situated entrepreneurial cognition approach to develop entrepreneurship research in general. In particular, we use the following research streams illustratively: entrepreneurial opportunity (action-oriented), entrepreneurial failure (embodied), family business (situated) and crowdfunding (distributed). We note that by "illustratively," we mean (1) that we observe in each stream used to illustrate the *predominance* of the theme within that stream as it currently stands and (2) that our use of these streams from entrepreneurship research is non-exhaustive (i.e., other streams could also illustrate these points, and each of these streams could receive much deeper treatment).

Our argument proceeds as follows: The socially situated cognition approach has four themes. The approach is integrative. Evidence of aspects for each of the four themes is prevalent within entrepreneurship research to date. However, the advantages from an integrative theory such as those from socially situated cognition are not yet realized. Hence, a helpful rationale for "updating" entrepreneurial cognition research is to offer potential pathways for deeper examination of questions within entrepreneurship research streams using a "what might be missing" lens motivated by socially situated cognition theory.

Entrepreneurial Opportunity (Action-Oriented)

Research on entrepreneurial opportunity has been described as being a central part of the entrepreneurship literature (Venkataraman, 1997). For example, Schumpeter (1934) discussed entrepreneurship as involving creative destruction and new combinations of resources. Kirzner (1973) highlighted the entrepreneur as one who is alert to entrepreneurial opportunity. Casson (1982) emphasized the function of the entrepreneur as the coordinator of resources that results in a return that is greater than the costs incurred by the entrepreneur. Action has been argued to be central to this research. Indeed, Frese (2007) asserts that "[e]ntrepreneurs' actions are important and should be a starting point for theorizing in entrepreneurship" (2007, p. 151). As McMullen and Shepherd (2006, p. 132) have described, "to be an entrepreneur is to act on the possibility that one has identified an opportunity worth pursuing." Much of the research reports either the study of "whether entrepreneurial action occurs" or "how prospective entrepreneurs go about acting" (*ibid*). And while prior research regarding opportunity and action is not necessarily universal in its answers to the question of how entrepreneurs go about acting, the majority of this research does emphasize the importance of action to conceptualizing entrepreneurial opportunity.

Aspects of the action-oriented theme in entrepreneurial opportunity research are illustrated in prior work, which has sought to develop explanations about "how opportunities to bring into existence 'future' goods and services are discovered, created, and exploited, by whom, and with what consequences" (Venkataraman, 1997, p. 120). Underlying this approach is the premise of adaptive action expressed in action terms such as discovery, creation and exploitation. In this literature, distinctions among these actions have been studied extensively. Alvarez and Barney (2007) cast the discovery of opportunity as mountain climbing and the creation of opportunity as mountain building. Each of these approaches has implications for understanding opportunity in terms of entrepreneurial action. Research adopting a creation perspective focuses on "the actions, reactions, and enactment of entrepreneurs exploring ways to produce new products or services" (2007, p. 15). Conversely, research adopting a discovery perspective focuses on the "different modes of action" that are used to exploit opportunities once they have been discovered by alert individuals (Shane & Venkataraman, 2000, p. 218). And while we cannot include all the research on entrepreneurial opportunity as it relates to adaptive action, we note that a large number of additional studies exist that frame entrepreneurial opportunity in terms of action (e.g., Dimov, 2010; Sarason, Dean, & Dillard, 2006; Sarasvathy, 2001). What we hope that we have demonstrated in this subsection is the importance of an adaptive, action-oriented approach, as a key theme to socially situated cognition, to entrepreneurship research more generally.

Entrepreneurial Failure (Embodied)

Research on failure in entrepreneurship has a long history in entrepreneurship research (e.g., Dickinson, 1981; Shepherd, 2003; McGrath, 1999), with failure being viewed as both positive (e.g., Cope, 2011; McGrath, 1999) and negative (e.g., Dickinson, 1981; Shepherd & Haynie, 2011). Specifically, entrepreneurial failure is sometimes viewed not only in terms of the learning and experience that can emerge from the process of failure (Cope, 2011) but also in terms of the effects of failure manifest in terms of monetary and emotional costs (e.g., loss and grief; Shepherd, 2003), as well as the prospective fear that a failure may occur (e.g., Cacciotti et al., 2016). In many treatments of failure in entrepreneurship research (Mantere, Aula, Schildt, & Vaara, 2013; Shepherd & Cardon, 2009), the focus is on the emotional and affective aspects of failure. Indeed, as Shepherd described, "business failure involves an involuntary change in both the ownership and management of the business owing to poor performance. . . [and] likely represents a personal loss, which, in turn, generates a negative emotional response" (2003, p. 319). This negative emotional response represents a kind of embodied affect that is physically experienced. And although not all research on entrepreneurial failure focuses on its affective and emotional aspects, much of it does.

Aspects of the embodied theme in entrepreneurial failure research are illustrated in prior work, which addresses the topic of entrepreneurial failure, for example, by adopting the lens of grief as a way of understanding how the emotions associated with a business failure can enable learning from that failure (Shepherd, 2003). This occurs, in part, by enabling the individual to understand that such emotions are normal and not something to be ashamed about in the entrepreneurial process. This also occurs as individuals realize that the emotions associated with failure can be both psychological and physiological, which is encompassed in the socially situated theme of entrepreneurial as being embodied and which can enable treatment of these physical effects. As a result, the individual can take the necessary steps to recover from the grief and begin to learn from the entrepreneurial failure. Similarly, Mantere et al. (2013) seek to understand the way that the stakeholders of a failed organization adopt narratives that help them better understand that entrepreneurial failure. This involves both the cognitive processing of the entrepreneurial failure and the emotional aspects of processing a failure. Their work captures the role of embodiment in cognition, as the physical act of speech is shown to influence embodied affect as a component of cognition. And while we cannot include all the research on fear of failure as it relates to embodied affect and emotion, we note that additional studies exist that frame entrepreneurial failure in terms of embodied affect and emotion (e.g., Morgan & Sisak, 2016; Ucbasaran, Shepherd, Lockett, & Lyon, 2013). What we hope that we have demonstrated in this subsection is the importance of an embodied approach to entrepreneurship research more generally.

Family Business (Situated)

Family has emerged as a salient context for understanding the emergence, perpetuation and decline of entrepreneurial behaviors over time (e.g., Dyer & Handler, 1994). This "family embeddedness perspective" (Aldrich & Cliff, 2003) suggests that entrepreneurial processes are enabled and constrained by personal relationships between entrepreneurs and their family members. As Aldrich and Cliff (2003, p. 577) suggest, individuals in family businesses "are implicated in networks of social relations. . . [and] do not decide to start a business in a vacuum; instead, they 'consult and are subtly influenced by significant others in their environment' (Aldrich & Zimmer, 1986, p. 6)." Accordingly, prior entrepreneurship research has examined how the social context of the family, such as the relationship between family members, influence an individual's propensity to become self-employed (Arregle et al., 2015). Similarly, in the family business literature, there is a growing interest in the ways in which some families enact social situations that foster "transgenerational entrepreneurship" (Nordqvist & Zellweger, 2010; Zellweger, Nason, & Nordqvist, 2012) and thereby increase the probability that the descendants of the founder of a family business will introduce new products, enter new markets or even establish new businesses (Jaskiewicz, Combs, & Rau, 2015; Erdogan, Rondi, & De Massis, 2020). Thus, although only some entrepreneurship can be explained in relation to the family context, because of the pervasive effect of the family on entrepreneurial behavior within and outside of established organizations (Anderson, Jack, & Dodd, 2005), we consider the family to be a particularly salient social situation for understanding entrepreneurship in general.

Aspects of the situated theme in family business research are illustrated in prior work, in which, the social situation of the multigenerational family firm has been shown to effect entrepreneurial processes. The descendants of entrepreneurs have been theorized to take inspiration from the "entrepreneurial legacies" of their forbearers as a source of inspiration for entrepreneurial behavior and a means of rationalizing a departure from outdated traditions (Jaskiewicz et al., 2015). Similarly, Erdogan et al. (2020) suggest that the relationship between tradition and innovation is more complex than previously thought and that "family firms can use innovation as a tool to protect or strengthen their tradition, and can revive their tradition to innovate" (2020, p. 25). In addition, intergenerational family ownership of a firm has been shown to increase tolerance for certain types of risk in the interest of continued family control while simultaneously increasing other types of risk aversion (Gómez-Mejía, Haynes, Núñez-Nickel, Jacobson, & Moyano-Fuentes, 2007). Thus, while we cannot include all the research on family business as it relates to the situated aspect of socially situated cognition (e.g., Matthews, Moore, & Fialko, 1999; Mitchell, Morse, & Sharma, 2003), what we hope to have demonstrated is that the work on family in entrepreneurship captures the essential, socially situated and historically embedded nature of entrepreneurial processes.

Crowdfunding (Distributed)

Crowdfunding research (see Letwin, Stevenson, & Ciuchta, this volume) has sought to develop explanations about how "an entrepreneur raises external financing from a large audience (the 'crowd'), in which each individual provides a very small amount, instead of soliciting a small group of sophisticated investors" (Belleflamme, Lambert, & Schwienbacher, 2014, p. 585). Drover et al. (2017) contextualized crowdfunding research by offering a road map for organizing entrepreneurial equity financing research, which includes accelerators, angel investment, venture capital and crowdfunding. The idea of pooling investor resources as a kind of coordinated investor behavior has a long research history—at least since such study began with the systematic examination of risk by scholars such as Fermat, Paccioli and Pascal (Bernstein, 1996) and with the pooling of investor resources in the joint-stock company (Mill, 1848). The notion of coordinated economic behavior thus is considered to be important in entrepreneurship research, in general, but especially important in the venture's ability to acquire necessary resources, as suggested for example by Brush, Greene and Hart (2001). As an illustration of how the theme of distributed cognition suffuses a substantive portion of the entrepreneurship literature, in terms of coordinated economic behavior, the phenomenon of crowdfunding is particularly apt.

Aspects of the distributed theme in crowdfunding research are illustrated in work that demonstrates, for example, how crowdfunding uses the connectivity of the internet to overcome obstacles from the broad geographic dispersion (e.g., average 3,000 miles) of investors in small, early-stage projects (Agrawal, Catalini, & Goldfarb, 2011). In this sense, crowdfunding research responds to the call by Suddaby, Bruton, and Si (2015, p. 9) for entrepreneurship research to examine "both empirically and conceptually, the various ways in which shared schemas or socially shared cognitions are created and diffused and how it is that some actors are able to overcome them." Furthermore, crowdfunding research has demonstrated that certain dispersed communication features such as narratives that create project legitimacy (e.g., "lower funding targets and shorter campaign durations . . . reward-levels as narrative tools that encourage funders to engage with the project . . . and visual pitches [that] transmit a broader sociocultural narrative, leveraging emotional rather than financial reasoning" (Frydrych, Bock, & Kinder, 2016, p. 99) affect the likelihood of funding. And while we cannot include all the research on crowdfunding as it relates to the distributed aspect of socially situated cognition (e.g., Manning & Bejarano, 2017; Parhankangas & Renko, 2017), we note that a substantial number of additional studies exist in the relatively recent body of crowdfunding research, which we hope will demonstrate the importance of a distributed approach to entrepreneurship research more generally.

Implied Opportunities for Future Entrepreneurial Cognition Research

In the previous section, we used entrepreneurial opportunity, entrepreneurial failure, family business, and crowdfunding research to illustrate separately how a socially situated approach to entrepreneurial cognition quite naturally maps onto entrepreneurship research in general. Our purpose in doing so, however, was not to classify each research stream as a type of entrepreneurial cognition. Indeed, such an approach would result in the same kind of "boxology" that a socially situated approach to entrepreneurial cognition seeks to remedy. Instead, our reason for doing so was to lay a foundation for explaining how entrepreneurial cognition research specifically can interpenetrate, integrate with and further animate future entrepreneurship research. In concluding this chapter, we thus extend our illustrations to other examples that represent further opportunities for the dynamism that can be captured by seeing the field through the socially situated entrepreneurial cognition lens.

Socially Situated Cognition and Entrepreneurial Opportunity Research Opportunities

As noted in the prior section, research on entrepreneurial opportunity has a predominant focus that can be captured by the action-oriented theme of socially situated cognition. We now extend this idea to suggest that research on entre-preneurial opportunity enables selective utilization of all the themes in research on this topic to offer a comprehensive and integrated understanding of entre-preneurial cognition as it relates to entrepreneurial opportunity. For example, Shane and Venkataraman (2000) and Alvarez and Barney (2007) each address the importance of action in entrepreneurial opportunity. But Shane and Venkatara-man (2000) also allude to the importance of "the tendency of certain people to respond to the situational cues of opportunities" (2000, pp. 218–219). What we find to be telling in terms of research on entrepreneurial opportunities as discov-ered versus opportunities as created is the possibility that the difference between the two approaches to entrepreneurial action place temporal preference on dif-ferent themes of socially-situated entrepreneurial cognition. That is, a discovery view of entrepreneurial opportunity seems to place precedence on the situated aspect of entrepreneurial cognition first and then on action. Conversely, a creation view seems to place precedence on the action-oriented aspect of entrepreneurial cognition and then on the situation. Both views can be explained in terms of socially situated entrepreneurial cognition, but with the additional explanatory granularity offered by the socially situated cognition approach, it can offer a the-ory to explain why one theme (e.g., situation) can take temporal precedence over another theme (e.g., action) in terms of entrepreneurial cognition or vice versa.

In this way, we note that although extensive research has been done on the action-oriented and situated aspects, future research on opportunities may explore how the situated, embodied and distributed elements effect the development of entrepreneurial opportunity. One promising avenue for research on this topic is in the area of co-working space. Indeed, understanding the underlying processes related to the development of opportunity in a co-working space would draw on the situated, embodied and distributed aspects of cognition by explaining how being located in a physical space that is shared by multiple individuals with dif-ferent perspectives on business may lead to the emergence of new opportunity. Further research along these lines could also look at the distributed aspects of such mechanisms to capture more fully the socially situated aspect of entrepreneurial cognition.

Socially Situated Cognition and Entrepreneurial Failure Research Opportunities

As also noted in the previous section, research on entrepreneurial failure has a predominant focus that can be captured, at least in part, by the embodied affect theme of socially situated cognition. We now extend this idea to suggest that all four themes are needed to offer a more comprehensive understanding of entre-preneurial failure. We see this, for example, in the work of Cardon, Stevens, and Potter (2011), who investigated through a lens of sensemaking, the accounts of failure provided by entrepreneurs. In adopting a sensemaking view to understand how entrepreneurs attributed failure—whether as mistakes or misfortune—the authors have captured how individuals base actions on the sensemaking process, as it relates to the "cognitive, affective, and behavioral responses" to a failure (2011, p. 82). Their approach relates to failure across a broader culture and implicitly integrates the key themes of socially situated cognition in a way that offers a richer understanding of the dynamic nature of entrepreneurial cognition. In their work on fear of failure, Cacciotti et al. (2016, p. 302) are more explicit in their articulation of fear of failure "in terms of socially-situated cognition by adopting an approach that captures a combination of cognition, affect and action as it relates to the challenging, uncertain, and risk-laden experience of entrepreneurship."

This forward-looking approach is consistent with earlier approaches to the interpretation of entrepreneurial failure but now using a socially situated lens. McGrath (1999) for example, has suggested that an approach to entrepreneurial failure based on real options reasoning, which "allows more of failure's possible benefits to be captured and the most egregious of its costs to be contained" (1999, p. 13). In her approach, McGrath captures the potential for dynamism in entrepreneurial cognition that offers new opportunities for explaining entrepreneurial failure using a cognitive lens. For example, in Table 5.1 (1999, pp. 17–19), she explains how action, emotion/embodiment, and the social situation and distribution of cognition, interweave to produce thinking errors, such as manipulation of metrics or diversion of resources (action to alter social perceptions), misattribution of success to the self and negative perception of events associated with failure (emotion/embodiment relating to the social situation) and oversampling success and under-sampling failure (the social situation and distribution of cognition). When seen through the more dynamic lens of the social-situation approach, we see possibilities for exploring the underlying mechanisms associated with entrepreneurial failure.

Socially Situated Cognition and Family Business Research Opportunities

As noted in the prior section, research on family business has a predominant focus that can be captured by the situated theme of socially situated cognition. We now extend this idea to suggest that, while the situated aspect has received extensive attention, the embodied aspect might warrant further attention with respect to family—who are similar in terms of their physical and affective embodiment as a result of a shared genetic and historical background. Indeed, we see the emerging research on socioemotional reference points in family business decision-making (see, e.g., Gomez-Mejia et al., 2007) and on reference point shifts (Nason, Mazzelli, & Carney, 2019) as early efforts to explain the role of embodied affect and action-oriented cognition in family business.

In addition, while family business is often treated as a context by entrepreneurship scholars, a socially situated approach to entrepreneurial cognition calls attention to the unique ways in which cognition not only is situated in families but also is distributed between and among family members. Such shared family cognition can be expected to evolve over time. Because families exist at the origins of both developmental and historical social interaction, they may also be an important site for understanding the gradual emergence of shared cognition between individuals. Family business scholars understand that such shared family cognition extends to both social and economic activities. This linkage between family and socially situated cognition suggests the need to extend our understanding of socio-cognitive mechanisms (such as memory) for the transmission of entrepreneurial thinking, behavior and values between individuals and across generations. We thus consider the relationship between family and entrepreneurship to be a fruitful line of inquiry that may provide a means of explaining heterogeneity in the underlying socio-cognitive mechanisms that enable and constrain entrepreneurial behaviors as well as the varying life circumstances in which individuals engage in entrepreneurship.

Socially Situated Cognition and Crowdfunding Research Opportunities

As noted in the prior section, research on crowdfunding in entrepreneurship has a predominant focus which can be captured by the distributed theme of entrepreneurial cognition. However, this is not the only potentially relevant theme for studying crowdfunding. Indeed, we further extend this idea to suggest that future research might explore in more detail the ways in which crowdfunding is situated from the perspective of both entrepreneurs and prospective stakeholders. How and in what circumstances might crowdfunding accelerate or constrain entrepreneurial processes? And, from the perspective of prospective stakeholders of a new venture, what heterogeneity exists in the manner in which new venture or product ideas are positioned within a broader sociohistorical context of prior (competing or noncompeting) ventures or products? In addition, how can online crowdfunding be better understood when it is situated within a broader historical context of alternative modes of resource acquisition?

In this sense, whereas crowdfunding has been treated predominantly as a more recent way for new ventures to be financed through a distributed approach, a socially situated approach to entrepreneurial cognition also calls attention to the ways in which cognition that is part of that financing not only is distributed but is also action-oriented. For instance, Block, Hornuf and Moritz (2018) found providing simple, informational updates to crowdfunding campaigns positively effects the investment of potential funders. In this way, the distributed component of crowdfunding is action-oriented in its effect. Similarly, Giudici, Guerini and Rossi-Lamastra (2018) found that even though the internet is a predominant enabler of crowdfunding, geography still plays a role in the altruistic (and likely affective) investment behavior of funders. From a socially situated cognition perspective, this research indirectly captures the situated space of geography, the extent to which cognition is distributed in that space, and the way that the affective elements of cognition drive actions. Future cognition research in the area of crowdfunding can thus further explore how the actions of the crowd emerge from affective elements that are distributed over and situated within geographic space.

Conclusion

What we hope to have demonstrated in this chapter is how a socially situated approach to entrepreneurial cognition both enables currently, and can yet enable, researchers to analyze a research stream according to the themes of socially situated cognition as a way of seeing potential research gaps that may exist. It has been argued that research streams develop, building both on prior work within that stream and on the importation of work from related disciplines (Shepherd & Wiklund, 2020). In this chapter, we have revisited entrepreneurial cognition research to suggest the latter: that entrepreneurship research can benefit from the extension of the integrative framework of socially situated cognition research into its various research streams, thereby enabling new ways of seeing research possibilities. It is our hope that the potential for new and refined explanations in all of our entrepreneurship research streams will be the result.

References

Abelson, R. P. (1981). Psychological status of the script concept. *American Psychologist, 36*(7), 715–729.

Agrawal, A. K., Catalini, C., & Goldfarb, A. (2011). *The geography of crowdfunding* (No. w16820). National Bureau of Economic Research.

Aldrich, H. E., & Cliff, J. E. (2003). The pervasive effects of family on entrepreneurship: Toward a family embeddedness perspective. *Journal of Business Venturing, 18*(5), 573–596.

Aldrich, H.E., & Zimmer, C. (1986). Entrepreneurship through social networks. In D. Sexton & R. Smilor (Eds.), *The art and science of entrepreneurship* (pp. 3–23). Cambridge, MA: Ballinger.

Alvarez, S. A., & Barney, J. B. (2007). Discovery and creation: Alternative theories of entrepreneurial action. *Strategic Entrepreneurship Journal, 1*(1), 11–26.

Anderson, A. R., Jack, S. L., & Dodd, S. D. (2005). The role of family members in entrepreneurial networks: Beyond the boundaries of the family firm. *Family Business Review, 18*(2), 135–154.

Arregle, J. L., Batjargal, B., Hitt, M. A., Webb, J. W., Miller, T., & Tsui, A. S. (2015). Family ties in entrepreneurs' social networks and new venture growth. *Entrepreneurship Theory and Practice, 39*(2), 313–344.

Atkinson, J. W. (1957). Motivational determinants of risk-taking behavior. *Psychological Review, 64*(6), 359–372.

Baker, T., & Nelson, R. E. (2005). Creating something from nothing: Resource construction through entrepreneurial bricolage. *Administrative Science Quarterly, 50*(3), 329–366.

Bandura, A. (2001). Social cognitive theory: An agentic perspective. *Annual Review of Psychology, 52*, 1–26.

Baron, R. A. (1998). Cognitive mechanisms in entrepreneurship: Why and when entrepreneurs think differently than other people. *Journal of Business Venturing, 13*(4), 275–294.

Baron, R. A. (2004). The cognitive perspective: A valuable tool for answering entrepreneurship's basic "why" questions. *Journal of Business Venturing, 19*(2), 221–239.

Baron, R. A. (2007). Behavioral and cognitive factors in entrepreneurship: Entrepreneurs as the active element in new venture creation. *Strategic Entrepreneurship Journal, 1*(1), 167–182.

Baron, R. A. (2008). The role of affect in the entrepreneurial process. *Academy of Management Review, 33*(2), 328–340.

Baron, R. A., & Ensley, M. D. (2006). Opportunity recognition as the detection of meaningful patterns: Evidence from comparisons of novice and experienced entrepreneurs. *Management Science, 52*(9), 1331–1344.

Baron, R. A., & Ward, T. B. (2004). Expanding entrepreneurial cognition's toolbox: Potential contributions from the field of cognitive science. *Entrepreneurship Theory and Practice, 28*(6), 553–573.

Belleflamme, P., Lambert, T., & Schwienbacher, A. (2014). Crowdfunding: Tapping the right crowd. *Journal of Business Venturing, 29*(5), 585–609.

Bernstein, P. L. (1996). *Against the gods: The remarkable story of risk*. New York: John Wiley & Sons.

Bird, B. (1988). Implementing entrepreneurial ideas: The case for intention. *Academy of Management Review, 13*(3), 442–453.

Bird, B. (1992). The operation of intentions in time: The emergence of the new venture. *Entrepreneurship Theory and Practice, 17*(1), 11–20.

Block, J., Hornuf, L., & Moritz, A. (2018). Which updates during an equity crowdfunding campaign increase crowd participation? *Small Business Economics, 50*(1), 3–27.

Brockhaus, R. H. S., & Horowitz, P. S. (1986). The psychology of the entrepreneur. In D. Sexton & R. Smilor (Eds.), *The art and science of entrepreneurship* (pp. 25–48). Cambridge, MA: Ballinger.

Brush, C. G., Greene, P. G., & Hart, M. M. (2001). From initial idea to unique advantage: The entrepreneurial challenge of constructing a resource base. *Academy of Management Executive, 15*(1), 64–78.

Busenitz, L. W., & Barney, J. B. (1997). Differences between entrepreneurs and managers in large organizations: Biases and heuristics in strategic decision making. *Journal of Business Venturing, 12*, 9–30.

Busenitz, L. W., Gomez, C., & Spencer, J. W. (2000). Country institutional profiles: Unlocking entrepreneurial phenomena. *Academy of Management Journal, 43*(5), 994–1003.

Busenitz, L. W., & Lau, C.-M. (1996). A cross-cultural cognitive model of new venture creation. *Entrepreneurship Theory and Practice, 20*(4), 25–39.

Cacciotti, G., Hayton, J. C., Mitchell, J. R., & Giazitzoglu, A. (2016). A reconceptualization of fear of failure in entrepreneurship. *Journal of Business Venturing, 31*(3), 302–325.

Cardon, M. S., Stevens, C. E., & Potter, D. R. (2011). Misfortunes or mistakes? Cultural sensemaking of entrepreneurial failure. *Journal of Business Venturing, 26*(1), 79–92.

Cardon, M. S., Wincent, J., Singh, J., & Drnovsek, M. (2009). The nature and experience of entrepreneurial passion. *Academy of Management Review, 34*(3), 511–532.

Carland, J. W., Hoy, F., Boulton, W. R., & Carland, J. A. C. (1984). Differentiating entrepreneurs from small business owners: A conceptualization. *Academy of Management Review, 9*(2), 354–359.

Casson, M. (1982). *The entrepreneur: An economic theory.* Totowa, NJ: Barnes and Noble.

Chen, C. C., Greene, P. G., & Crick, A. (1998). Does entrepreneurial self-efficacy distinguish entrepreneurs from managers? *Journal of Business Venturing, 13*(4), 295–316.

Clarke, J. S., & Cornelissen, J. P. (2011). Language, communication, and socially situated cognition in entrepreneurship (dialogue). *Academy of Management Review, 36*(4), 776–778.

Clarke, J. S., Cornelissen, J. P., & Healey, M. P. (2019). Actions speak louder than words: How figurative language and gesturing in entrepreneurial pitches influences investment judgments. *Academy of Management Journal, 62*(2), 335–360.

Cope, J. (2011). Entrepreneurial learning from failure: An interpretative phenomenological analysis. *Journal of Business Venturing, 26*(6), 604–623.

De Carolis, D. M., & Saparito, P. (2006). Social capital, cognition, and entrepreneurial opportunities: A theoretical framework. *Entrepreneurship Theory and Practice, 30*, 41–56.

Dew, N., Grichnik, D., Mayer-Haug, K., Read, S., & Brinckmann, J. (2015). Situated entrepreneurial cognition. *International Journal of Management Reviews, 17*(2), 143–164.

Dickinson, R. (1981). Business failure rate. *American Journal of Small Business, 6*(2), 17–25.

Dimov, D. (2007). From opportunity insight to opportunity intention: The importance of person-situation learning match. *Entrepreneurship Theory and Practice, 31*(4), 561–583.

Dimov, D. (2010). Nascent entrepreneurs and venture emergence: Opportunity confidence, human capital, and early planning. *Journal of Management Studies, 47*(6), 1123–1153.

Drover, W., Busenitz, L., Matusik, S., Townsend, D., Anglin, A., & Dushnitsky, G. (2017). A review and road map of entrepreneurial equity financing research: Venture capital, corporate venture capital, angel investment, crowdfunding, and accelerators. *Journal of Management, 43*(6), 1820–1853.

Dyer, W. G., & Handler, W. (1994). Entrepreneurship and family business: Exploring the connections. *Entrepreneurship Theory and Practice, 19*(1), 71–83.

Erdogan, I., Rondi, E., & De Massis, A. (2020). Managing the tradition and innovation paradox in family firms: A family imprinting perspective. *Entrepreneurship Theory and Practice, 44*(1), 20–54.

Frese, M. (2007). The psychological actions and entrepreneurial success: An action theory approach. In J. R. Baum, M. Frese, & R. A. Baron (Eds.), *The psychology of entrepreneurship* (pp. 151–188). Mahwah, NJ: Lawrence Earlbaum.

Frydrych, D., Bock, A. J., & Kinder, T. (2016). Creating project legitimacy - The role of entrepreneurial narrative in reward-based crowdfunding. In J. Méric, I. Maque, & J. Barbet (Eds.), *International perspectives on crowdfunding: Positive, normative and critical theory* (pp. 99–128). Bingley, UK: Emerald Group Publishing Limited.

Gartner, W. B. (1988). "Who is an entrepreneur?" is the wrong question. *Entrepreneurship Theory and Practice, 12*(4), 11–32.

Gartner, W. B., Shaver, K. G., Gatewood, E., & Katz, J. A. (1994). Finding the entrepreneur in entrepreneurship. *Entrepreneurship Theory and Practice, 18*(3), 5–9.

Gatewood, E., Shaver, K. G., & Gartner, W. B. (1995). A longitudinal study of cognitive factors influencing start-up behaviors and success at venture creation. *Journal of Business Venturing, 10*, 371–391.

Giudici, G., Guerini, M., & Rossi-Lamastra, C. (2018). Reward-based crowdfunding of entrepreneurial projects: The effect of local altruism and localized social capital on proponents' success. *Small Business Economics, 50*(2), 307–324.

Gómez-Mejía, L. R., Haynes, K. T., Núñez-Nickel, M., Jacobson, K. J., & Moyano-Fuentes, J. (2007). Socioemotional wealth and business risks in family-controlled firms: Evidence from Spanish olive oil mills. *Administrative Science Quarterly, 52*(1), 106–137.

Grégoire, D., Barr, P. S., & Shepherd, D. A. (2010). Cognitive processes of opportunity recognition: The role of structural alignment. *Organization Science, 21*(2), 413–431.

Grégoire, D., Cornelissen, J., Dimov, D., & van Burg, E. (2015). The mind in the middle: Taking stock of affect and cognition research in entrepreneurship. *International Journal of Management Reviews, 17*(2), 125–142.

Haynie, J. M., Shepherd, D. A., Mosakowski, E., & Earley, C. (2010). A situated metacognitive model of the entrepreneurial mindset. *Journal of Business Venturing, 25,* 217–229.

Hisrich, R. D., & Jankowicz, A. D. (1990). Intuition in venture capital decisions: An exploratory study using a new technique. *Journal of Business Venturing, 5,* 49–62.

Hmieleski, K. M., & Baron, R. A. (2008). When does entrepreneurial self-efficacy enhance versus reduce firm performance? *Strategic Entrepreneurship Journal, 2*(1), 57–72.

Hmieleski, K. M., & Baron, R. A. (2009). Entrepreneurs' optimism and new venture performance: A social cognitive perspective. *Academy of Management Journal, 52*(3), 473–488.

Hornaday, J. A., & Aboud, J. (1971). Characteristics of successful entrepreneurs. *Personnel Psychology, 24,* 141–153.

Jaskiewicz, P., Combs, J. G., & Rau, S. B. (2015). Entrepreneurial legacy: Toward a theory of how some family firms nurture transgenerational entrepreneurship. *Journal of Business Venturing, 30*(1), 29–49.

Jelinek, M., & Litterer, J. A. (1995). Toward entrepreneurial organizations: Meeting ambiguity with engagement. *Entrepreneurship Theory and Practice, 19*(3), 137–168.

Katz, J. A. (1992). A psychosocial cognitive model of employment status choice. *Entrepreneurship Theory and Practice, 17*(1), 29–37.

Keh, H. T., Foo, M.-D., & Lim, B. C. (2002). Opportunity evaluation under risky conditions: The cognitive processes of entrepreneurs. *Entrepreneurship Theory and Practice, 27*(2), 125–148.

Kirzner, I. M. (1973). *Competition and entrepreneurship.* Chicago: University of Chicago Press.

Krueger, N. F., & Dickson, P. R. (1994). How believing in ourselves increases risk taking: Perceived self-efficacy and opportunity recognition. *Decision Sciences, 25*(3), 385–400.

Letwin, C., Stevenson, R., & Ciuchta, M. P. (this volume). A psychological perspective on raising startup capital in the modern era. In M. M. Gielnik, M. Frese, & M. S. Cardon (Eds.), *The psychology of entrepreneurship* (2nd ed.). Abingdon, UK: Routledge.

Lim, D. S., Morse, E. A., Mitchell, R. K., & Seawright, K. K. (2010). Institutional environment and entrepreneurial cognitions: A comparative business systems perspective. *Entrepreneurship Theory and Practice, 34*(3), 491–516.

MacMillan, I. C., & Katz, J. A. (1992). Idiosyncratic milieus of entrepreneurial research: The need for comprehensive theories. *Journal of Business Venturing, 7,* 1–8.

Manning, S., & Bejarano, T. A. (2017). Convincing the crowd: Entrepreneurial storytelling in crowdfunding campaigns. *Strategic Organization, 15*(2), 194–219.

Mantere, S., Aula, P., Schildt, H., & Vaara, E. (2013). Narrative attributions of entrepreneurial failure. *Journal of Business Venturing, 28*(4), 459–473.

Matthews, C. H., Moore, T. W., & Fialko, A. S. (1999). Succession in the family firm: A cognitive categorization perspective. *Family Business Review, 12*(2), 159–170.

McClelland, D. C. (1955). Some social consequences of achievement motivation. In M. R. Jones (Ed.), *Nebraska symposium on motivation.* Lincoln, NE: University of Nebraska Press.

McClelland, D. C. (1961). *The achieving society.* Princeton, NJ: Van Nostrand.

McClelland, D. C. (1965). Need achievement and entrepreneurship: A longitudinal study. *Journal of Personality and Social Psychology, 1,* 389–392.

McGrath, R. G. (1999). Falling forward: Real options reasoning and entrepreneurial failure. *Academy of Management Review, 24*(1), 13–30.

McMullen, J. S., & Shepherd, D. A. (2006). Entrepreneurial action and the role of uncertainty in the theory of the entrepreneur. *Academy of Management Review, 31,* 132–152.

Mill, J. S. (1848). *Principles of political economy with some of their applications to social philosophy* (1st ed.). London, UK: John W. Parker.

Mitchell, J. R., Mitchell, R. K., & Randolph-Seng, B. (Eds.). (2014). *Handbook of entrepreneurial cognition*. Cheltenham, UK: Edward Elgar Publishing.

Mitchell, J. R., & Shepherd, D. A. (2010). To thine own self be true: Images of self, images of opportunity, and entrepreneurial action. *Journal of Business Venturing, 25*(1), 138–154.

Mitchell, R. K. (1996). Oral history and expert scripts: Demystifying the entrepreneurial experience. *Journal of Management History, 2*(3), 50–67.

Mitchell, R. K., Busenitz, L., Bird, B., Gaglio, C. M., McMullen, J. S., Morse, E. A., & Smith, J. B. (2007). The central question in entrepreneurial cognition research. *Entrepreneurship Theory and Practice, 31*(1), 1–27.

Mitchell, R. K., Busenitz, L., Lant, T., McDougall, P. P., Morse, E. A., & Smith, B. (2002). Toward a theory of entrepreneurial cognition: Rethinking the people side of entrepreneurship research. *Entrepreneurship Theory and Practice, 27*(2), 93–104.

Mitchell, R. K., Busenitz, L., Lant, T., McDougall, P. P., Morse, E. A., & Smith, B. (2004). The distinctive and inclusive domain of entrepreneurial cognition research. *Entrepreneurship Theory and Practice, 28*(6), 505–518.

Mitchell, R. K., & Chesteen, S. A. (1995). Enhancing entrepreneurial expertise: Experiential pedagogy and the entrepreneurial expert script. *Simulation & Gaming, 26*(3), 288–306.

Mitchell, R. K., Morse, E. A., & Sharma, P. (2003). The transacting cognitions of nonfamily employees in the family businesses setting. *Journal of Business Venturing, 18*(4), 533–551.

Mitchell, R. K., Randolph-Seng, B., & Mitchell, J. R. (2011). Socially situated cognition: Imagining new opportunities for entrepreneurship research (dialogue). *Academy of Management Review, 36*(4), 774–776.

Mitchell, R. K., Smith, B., Seawright, K. W., & Morse, E. A. (2000). Cross-cultural cognitions and the venture creation decision. *Academy of Management Journal, 43,* 974–993.

Morgan, J., & Sisak, D. (2016). Aspiring to succeed: A model of entrepreneurship and fear of failure. *Journal of Business Venturing, 31*(1), 1–21.

Nason, R. S., Mazzelli, A., & Carney, M. (2019). The ties that unbind: Socialization and business-owning family reference point shift. *Academy of Management Review, 44*(4), 846–870.

Nordqvist, M., & Zellweger, T. (Eds.). (2010). *Transgenerational entrepreneurship: Exploring growth and performance in family firms across generations*. Cheltenham, UK: Edward Elgar Publishing.

Ozgen, E., & Baron, R. A. (2007). Social sources of information in opportunity recognition: Effects of mentors, industry networks, and professional forums. *Journal of Business Venturing, 22,* 174–192.

Palmer, M. (1971). The application of psychological testing to entrepreneurial potential. *California Management Review, 13*(3), 32–38.

Parhankangas, A., & Renko, M. (2017). Linguistic style and crowdfunding success among social and commercial entrepreneurs. *Journal of Business Venturing, 32*(2), 215–236.

Randolph-Seng, B., Mitchell, J. R., & Mitchell, R. K. (2014). Introduction: Historical context, present trends and future directions in entrepreneurial cognition research. In J. R.

Mitchell, R. K. Mitchell, & B. Randolph-Seng (Eds.), *Handbook of entrepreneurial cognition* (pp. 1–60). Cheltenham, UK: Edward Elgar Publishing.

Randolph-Seng, B., Mitchell, R. K., Vahidnia, H., Mitchell, J. R., Chen, S., & Statzer, J. (2015). The microfoundations of entrepreneurial cognition research: Toward an integrative approach. *Foundations and Trends in Entrepreneurship*, *11*(4), 207–335.

Reuber, A. R., & Fischer, E. M. (1994). Entrepreneurs' experience, expertise, and the performance of technology-based firms. *IEEE Transactions on Engineering Management*, *41*(4), 365–374.

Rotter, J. B. (1966). Generalized expectations for internal versus external control of reinforcement. *Psychological Monographs*, *80*, 609.

Sarason, Y., Dean, T., & Dillard, J. F. (2006). Entrepreneurship as the nexus of individual and opportunity: A structuration view. *Journal of Business Venturing*, *21*(3), 286–305.

Sarasvathy, S. D. (2001). Causation and effectuation: Toward a theoretical shift from economic inevitability to entrepreneurial contingency. *Academy of Management Review*, *26*, 243–288.

Sarasvathy, D. K., Simon, H. A., & Lave, L. (1998). Perceiving and managing business risks: Differences between entrepreneurs and bankers. *Journal of Economic Behavior and Organization*, *33*(2), 207–225.

Schumpeter, J. (1934). *The theory of economic development*. Boston, MA: Harvard University Press.

Shane, S., & Venkataraman, S. (2000). The promise of entrepreneurship as a field of research. *Academy of Management Review*, *25*(1), 217–226.

Shaver, K. G., & Scott, L. R. (1991). Person, process, choice: The psychology of new venture creation. *Entrepreneurship Theory and Practice*, *16*(2), 23–45.

Shepherd, D. A. (2003). Learning from business failure: Propositions of grief recovery for the self-employed. *Academy of Management Review*, *28*(2), 318–328.

Shepherd, D. A., & Cardon, M. S. (2009). Negative emotional reactions to project failure and the self-compassion to learn from the experience. *Journal of Management Studies*, *46*(6), 923–949.

Shepherd, D. A., & Haynie, J. M. (2011). Venture failure, stigma, and impression management: A self-verification, self-determination view. *Strategic Entrepreneurship Journal*, *5*(2), 178–197.

Shepherd, D. A., & Krueger, N. F. (2002). An intentions-based model of entrepreneurial teams' social cognition. *Entrepreneurship Theory and Practice*, *27*(2), 167–185.

Shepherd, D. A., & Wiklund, J. (2020). Simple rules, templates, and heuristics! An attempt to deconstruct the craft of writing an entrepreneurship paper. *Entrepreneurship Theory and Practice*, *44*(3), 371–390.

Simon, M., Houghton, S. M., & Aquino, K. (2000). Cognitive biases, risk perception, and venture formation: How individuals decide to start companies. *Journal of Business Venturing*, *15*(2), 113–134.

Smith, E. R., & Conrey, F. R. (2009). The social context of cognition. In P. Robbins & M. Aydede (Eds.), *The Cambridge handbook of situated cognition* (pp. 454–466). Cambridge, UK: Cambridge University Press.

Smith, E. R., & Semin, G. R. (2004). Socially situated cognition: Cognition in its social context. In M. Zanna (Ed.), *Advances in experimental social psychology* (pp. 53–117). London, UK: Academic Press.

Smith, K. G., Gannon, M. J., Grimm, C., & Mitchell, T. R. (1988). Decision making behavior in smaller entrepreneurial and larger professionally managed firms. *Journal of Business Venturing*, *3*(3), 223–232.

Suddaby, R., Bruton, G. D., & Si, S. X. (2015). Entrepreneurship through a qualitative lens: Insights on the construction and/or discovery of entrepreneurial opportunity. *Journal of Business Venturing, 30*(1), 1–10.

Timmons, J. A. (1978). Characteristics and role demands of entrepreneurship. *Entrepreneurship Theory and Practice, 3,* 5–17.

Ucbasaran, D., Shepherd, D. A., Lockett, A., & Lyon, S. J. (2013). Life after business failure: The process and consequences of business failure for entrepreneurs. *Journal of Management, 39*(1), 163–202.

Venkataraman, S. (1997). The distinctive domain of entrepreneurship research. In J. A. Katz (Ed.), *Advances in entrepreneurship, firm emergence and growth* (Vol. 3, pp. 119–138). Oxford: JAI Press.

West, G. P., III. (2007). Collective cognition: When entrepreneurial teams, not individuals, make decisions. *Entrepreneurship Theory and Practice, 31*(1), 77–102.

White, R. E., Thornhill, S., & Hampson, E. (2007). A biosocial model of entrepreneurship: The combined effects of nurture and nature. *Journal of Organizational Behavior, 28,* 451–466.

Winter, D. G. (1973). *The power motive.* New York: The Free Press.

Zellweger, T. M., Nason, R. S., & Nordqvist, M. (2012). From longevity of firms to transgenerational entrepreneurship of families: Introducing family entrepreneurial orientation. *Family Business Review, 25*(2), 136–155.

3

MAPPING THE HEART

Trends and Future Directions for Affect Research in Entrepreneurship

Yi Huang, [1]Maw-Der Foo, [1]Charles Y. Murnieks & [1]Marilyn A. Uy

Introduction

Interest in affect and how it influences the entrepreneurial process is burgeoning (Cardon, Foo, Shepherd, & Wiklund, 2012). As one of the earliest proponents for studying affect in the context of entrepreneurship, Baron (2008) offers two major reasons for why entrepreneurship is an emotional journey. First, the environment surrounding new enterprises is highly unpredictable, which amplifies the influence of affect on individual decisions and actions. Second, affect exerts a strong influence on the range of tasks entrepreneurs perform, including creative thinking, persuasion, decision-making, and forming work relationships with others. Studying affect in entrepreneurial contexts effectively complements psychology, organizational behavior, and management research by providing evidence concerning the role affect plays in small, nascent organizations operating in uncertain environments (Cardon et al., 2012).

As research surrounding affect in entrepreneurship has grown and evolved, several literature reviews have emerged that address various aspects of the role of affect in the entrepreneurial process. For instance, Foo, Murnieks, and Chan (2014) reviewed articles regarding how affect influences entrepreneurial cognition, with a particular emphasis on the differential effects of two dimensions of affect—valence (hedonic tone) and activation (energy). In addition, Frese and Gielnik's (2014) annual review article on the psychology of entrepreneurship had a dedicated section on affect research in entrepreneurship which featured research papers that examined entrepreneurs' positive affect, negative affect, and entrepreneurial passion. Notwithstanding the contributions of these articles, extant research on affect in entrepreneurship remains fragmented. We lack a holistic perspective for the role of affect in entrepreneurship that presents what we already know and what knowledge gaps still persist. As such, in this review, we provide a model that synthesizes extant literature by summarizing the antecedents, outcomes, and moderators of entrepreneurial affect. We also discuss knowledge gaps and directions for future research.

In contrast to previous reviews, our review covers a broader range of affective elements that influence the wide spectrum of entrepreneurial processes. In addition, we synthesize conceptual and empirical work on the antecedents, outcomes, and moderators of entrepreneurs' affect. Our review makes the following contributions: First, we provide a comprehensive portrayal of the role of affect in entrepreneurship. Not only do we consider the dimension of affective valence (i.e., positive and negative valence), but we also include the dimension of activation. Both dimensions are necessary because affect's influence on thoughts and actions depends not only on whether affect is positive or negative (valence) but also on whether affect is high or low in activation or arousal. Second, we incorporate boundary conditions involved in the relationships surrounding entrepreneurs' affect. In each section, we review individual moderators (e.g., prior failure experiences) and contextual moderators (e.g., the life-cycle stage of a venture) that shape the antecedent-to-affect and affect-to-outcome relationships. Incorporating boundary conditions offers a more holistic and complete account of affect in entrepreneurship research. Finally, and perhaps most importantly, our review summarizes knowledge gaps on entrepreneurs' affect. For instance, our review shows that even though both valence and activation are key dimensions of affect, empirical research on affect in entrepreneurship has paid more attention to valence, and as a result, we know little about the role played by activation. We discuss these knowledge gaps in the concluding section and provide a roadmap for future research.

Concepts Used in This Chapter

To facilitate the conversation going forward, we briefly explain the definitions utilized in this review.

First, we distinguish experienced affect from displayed affect. In entrepreneurship, experienced affect includes the actual feelings of entrepreneurs, while displayed affect involves entrepreneurs' affective expressions to stakeholders, such as angel investors and firm employees. For example, investors might perceive an entrepreneur as being excited regardless of what the entrepreneur actually feels. This differentiation between experienced and displayed affect is demonstrated in the conceptualization and operationalization of affect in a number of entrepreneurship articles (e.g., Breugst, Domurath, Patzelt, & Klaukien, 2012; Li, Chen, Kotha, & Fisher, 2017; Mitteness, Sudek, & Cardon, 2012).

Furthermore, we consider entrepreneurs' experienced affect as a construct that is not just limited to valence, that is, positive or negative affect (Larsen & Diener, 1992; Russell & Barrett, 1999; Watson & Tellegen, 1985). According to Russell and Barrett (1999), affect comprises two primary dimensions: valence and activation. Specifically, valence refers to positivity and negativity while activation refers to "a sense of mobilization of energy" (Russell & Barrett, 1999, p. 809). Several scholars have acknowledged the dimensionality of affect in entrepreneurship research (e.g., Baron, Hmieleski, & Henry, 2012; Foo, Uy, & Murnieks, 2015). To give an example, nervous entrepreneurs and depressed entrepreneurs both experience unpleasant feelings (i.e., negative valence), but nervous entrepreneurs experience a higher level of activation than depressed ones.

In addition, affect includes dispositional affect, that is, trait, and event-generated affect, that is, state (Brief & Weiss, 2002). Trait affect is more stable and not directed at a specific stimulus (Fleeson & Gallagher, 2009), while state affect is subject to changes typically in response to events (Weiss & Cropanzano, 1996). State affect could be further differentiated into emotions and moods (Weiss & Cropanzano, 1996), which are distinguished by three features: intensity, duration, and diffuseness (Russell & Barrett, 1999; Weiss & Cropanzano, 1996). More specifically, emotions refer to intense feelings that often last for a short duration and are directed at a particular stimulus. Moods refer to relatively mild feelings that often last for an extended period and are not directed at a specific target. Throughout this chapter, our use of the term *affect* refers to both dispositional and event-generated feelings. We specify trait, state, emotion, and mood where appropriate.

Scope of the Review

Our review includes articles focusing on entrepreneurs' affect that have been published in mainstream general management (the *Academy of Management Journal*, the *Academy of Management Review*, *Administrative Science Quarterly*, the *Journal of International Business Studies*, the *Journal of Management*, the *Journal of Management Studies*, the *Journal of Organizational Behavior*, *Management Science*, *Organizational Behavior and Human Decision Processes*, *Organization Science*, *Organization Studies*, the *Strategic Management Journal*), entrepreneurship (*Entrepreneurship Theory and Practice*, the *International Small Business Journal: Researching Entrepreneurship*, the *Journal of Business Venturing*, the *Journal of Small Business Management*, *Small Business Economics*, the *Strategic Entrepreneurship Journal*), and psychology journals (*Applied Psychology: An International Review*, the *Journal of Applied Psychology*, *Personnel Psychology*).

In the first step, we searched using multiple key words associated with entrepreneurship (e.g., "entrepreneurship", "entrepreneurs", "start-up") and associated with affect (e.g., "affect", "emotion", "feeling", "mood", "passion") over the most recent 10-year period (2008–2018). We started with 2008 because this is the year Baron's (2008) seminal article on the role of affect in entrepreneurship was published. A total of 449 articles met this initial search criterion. In the second step, we reviewed each article to determine whether it concentrates on entrepreneurs' affect. This process resulted in 71 journal articles from 13 journals.

To summarize our literature search results, first, the past 10 years have witnessed a surge in interest around affect in entrepreneurship. The number of articles published in this space have increased in each period reviewed and continued to grow. Second, based on the articles we have collected and included in this review, there are significantly more empirical (81.7%) than conceptual articles (18.3%). Third, there is an apparent imbalance in terms of the type of entrepreneurs' affect being studied: the vast majority of studies (95.8%) focused on differences in valence (i.e., positive versus negative affect) while a disproportionately smaller number of studies addressed activation (4.2%).

What We Know About Entrepreneurs' Affect

To organize the vast literature across both experienced and displayed affect, we categorized the articles in this review according to their focus (see Figure 3.1). Namely, we separated the articles by their focus on the predictors, outcomes, or moderators of affective relationships within the entrepreneurial process.

As proposed by Cacciotti, Hayton, Mitchell, and Giazitzoglu (2016), affect experienced by entrepreneurs involves a dynamic and situational process which includes appraising internal cognitive evaluations and externally situated social cues. Extending their framework, we classified predictors of entrepreneurs' affect as (1) individual predictors and (2) external social cues and events. Examples of individual predictors are psychological capital and entrepreneurial self-efficacy. Examples of external social cues and events are new venture progress and financial

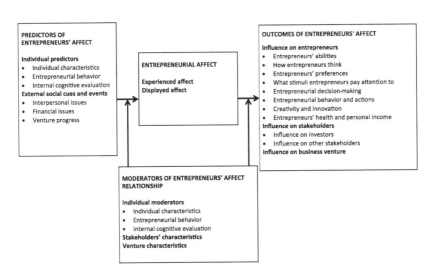

FIGURE 3.1 Summary of Entrepreneurial Affect: Predictors, Outcomes, and Moderators

strain. Regarding individual predictors, we further classified them into (1) individual characteristics, (2) entrepreneurial behaviors, and (3) internal cognitive evaluations. Regarding external social cues and events, we differentiated them into (1) interpersonal issues, (2) financial issues, and (3) venture progress.

We grouped the outcomes of entrepreneurs' affect into those that influence (1) the entrepreneur him- or herself, (2) the stakeholders (i.e., key actors other than entrepreneurs, such as investors and employees), and (3) the business venture. To further differentiate the influence on the self, we classified the articles based on affective influences on (1) entrepreneurs' abilities, (2) how entrepreneurs think, (3) entrepreneurs' preferences, (4) what stimuli entrepreneurs pay attention to, (5) entrepreneurial decision-making, (6) entrepreneurial behavior and actions, (7) creativity and innovation, and (8) entrepreneur's health and personal income.

We separated the first-stage moderators (i.e., moderators influencing the relationship between antecedents and affect) and the second-stage moderators (i.e., moderators influencing the relationship between affect and outcomes). Then, we classified the moderators of entrepreneurs' affect into three categories: (1) individual-level moderators, (2) stakeholders' characteristics, and (3) venture characteristics. For example, entrepreneurial feedback-seeking behavior can be a moderator at the individual level, business angels' entrepreneurial experience can be a moderator of stakeholders' characteristics, and firm size can be a moderator of venture characteristics. Regarding individual moderators, we further grouped them into (1) individual characteristics, (2) entrepreneurial behaviors, and (3) internal cognitive evaluations. Examples of individual characteristic moderators are openness to feedback and commitment. Examples of entrepreneurial behavior moderators are feedback-seeking behavior and problem-coping behavior. An example of internal cognitive evaluation is the level of satisfaction with the team.

Based on the preceding classification, we integrated and synthesized key findings of entrepreneurial affect into the model in Figure 3.1. Although this model is not exhaustive, it serves as a guiding framework to understand the diverse body of entrepreneurial affect literature. In addition, Figure 3.1 can be expanded to include concepts that can be added in the future.

Entrepreneurs' Positive Affect

According to Watson, Clark, and Tellegen (1988, p. 1063), "positive affect (PA) reflects the extent to which a person feels enthusiastic, active, and alert". A large number of conceptual and empirical studies have theorized about, and examined, the influence of positive affective states (e.g., Foo, Uy, & Baron, 2009; Hayton & Cholakova, 2012), traits (e.g., Baron et al., 2012; Baron & Tang, 2011; Baron, Tang, & Hmieleski, 2011; Delgado-García, Rodríguez-Escudero, & Martín-Cruz, 2012), and general positive affect (e.g., Ahsan, Zheng, DeNoble, & Musteen, 2018; Baron, 2008; Foo et al., 2015; Stanley, 2010) in entrepreneurship. In this section, we have also included articles on entrepreneurial passion since the content of "passion" includes intense positive emotions (Cardon, Wincent, Singh, & Drnovsek, 2009). At the individual level, researchers have also studied more specific, discrete positive entrepreneurial emotions such as hope (Foo, 2011).

Predictors

The papers we reviewed suggest that entrepreneurs' positive affect can originate from individual characteristics, cognitive evaluation, behavior, and external social cues. We highlight two particular antecedents of entrepreneurs' positive affect that have received much attention in the literature: self-efficacy and positive entrepreneurial events.

Regarding self-efficacy, scholars consistently find that entrepreneurs who hold a more affirmative belief in their ability to perform venture-relevant tasks experience higher levels of positive affect. Individuals enjoy engaging in activities in which they have a strong belief of success, as confidence can increase one's feelings of safety and security (Cardon & Kirk, 2015; Hayward, Forster, Sarasvathy, & Fredrickson, 2010). Regarding positive entrepreneurial events, research confirms that positive affect can be generated by certain entrepreneurial behaviors or events. For example, new venture effort heightens entrepreneurial passion through new venture progress (Gielnik, Spitzmuller, Schmitt, Klemann, & Frese, 2015). Two theoretical perspectives help explain this mechanism. First, following self-regulation theory (Bandura, 1997; Carver & Scheier, 1990), greater effort tends to lead toward goal achievement, which produces positive emotions such as happiness and excitement (Carver & Scheier, 1982). Second, according to goal setting theory and social cognitive theory (Locke & Latham, 2002), entrepreneurs making faster progress tend to experience positive emotions. In sum, making progress toward one's entrepreneurial goals predicts an increase in entrepreneurs' positive affect.

Outcomes

In general, research indicates that positive affect delivers beneficial outcomes to entrepreneurs and their businesses. For example, positive affective traits can increase satisfaction with business performance (Delgado-García et al., 2012) and increase a firm's creativity and innovation (Baron & Tang, 2011). In addition, entrepreneurial passion can inspire greater effort (Murnieks, Mosakowski, & Cardon, 2014), enhance self-efficacy (Baum & Locke, 2004; Huyghe, Knockaert, & Obschonka, 2016; Murnieks et al., 2014), and bolster start-up and spin-off intentions (Huyghe et al., 2016). Interestingly, while the majority of studies show that positive affect improves the chances of entrepreneurial survival and enhanced venture growth (Baum & Locke, 2004; Drnovsek, Cardon, & Patel, 2016; Stenholm & Renko, 2016), some research warned about the "too-much-of-a-good-thing" effect of positive affect among entrepreneurs. Baron et al. (2011) cautioned that extreme positive affect can result in detrimental outcomes such as biased information recall and reduced effort. Indeed, they found a curvilinear relationship between dispositional positive affect and sales growth because overwhelming positive affect interfered with cognitive flexibility and resilience. They argued and demonstrated that although positive affect is beneficial, too much positive affect may not yield favorable outcomes.

Notably, our review indicates that scholars have drawn on various theoretical lenses to explain how positive affect drives entrepreneurial outcomes. For example, Foo et al. (2009) used affect-as-information theory, which suggests that individuals tend to rely on their affective states as a source of information when evaluating and making decisions on tasks, objects, and alternatives at hand (Schwarz, 1999). They found that positive affect had a positive relationship with the entrepreneur's future temporal focus because positive affect signaled that all is well in the present environment, and thus, one can switch attention to the future and expand one's scope of attention to areas beyond current venture demands (Foo et al., 2009). Consequently, entrepreneurs with positive affect increased effort on venture tasks beyond what was immediately required. Some scholars also employed the broaden-and-build theory, which argues that positive emotions broaden one's awareness and encourage novel thoughts and actions (Fredrickson, 2001). Specifically, researchers proposed that the positive emotional element in entrepreneurial passion can drive the setting of more challenging goals, goal commitment, and goal striving (Cardon et al., 2009; Drnovsek et al., 2016). Another prominent theoretical lens is the affective congruency perspective, which implies that individuals with higher positive affective traits evaluate situations more positively (Rusting, 1998). Following this perspective, Delgado-García et al. (2012) argued that positive entrepreneurial affective traits led to higher satisfaction with business performance because of an optimistic interpretation bias. In sum, our review indicates that researchers have employed a variety of affective theories to analyze and forecast outcomes resulting from positive affect.

Moderators

Scholars have tested moderators of affective relationships at both the individual and the venture level. Regarding individual-level moderators, one factor that frequently emerges is the importance of sense of control. Specifically, Gielnik, Uy, Funken, and Bischoff (2017) found that entrepreneurial self-efficacy sustains the positive effect of entrepreneurial training on entrepreneurial passion because people are more likely to be passionate when they perceive a sense of control. Similarly, as feedback-seeking behavior can increase the sense of control and self-determination, Collewaert, Anseel, Crommelinck, De Beuckelaer, and Vermeire (2016) found that more feedback-seeking behavior mitigated the negative effect of entrepreneurs' role ambiguity on entrepreneurial passion. In addition, self-perception theory implied that one's process of inferring emotions depends on whether the behavior is voluntary (Bem, 1972). Drawing on this theory, Gielnik et al. (2015) found that entrepreneurial effort only influences entrepreneurial passion through venture progress when entrepreneurs had free choice or a sense of autonomy over their behavior.

In addition to moderators at the individual level, affective relationships are also moderated by venture-level variables and environmental factors. For example, firm size negatively moderated the influence of entrepreneurial dispositional positive affect on sales growth (Baron et al., 2011). Moreover, the relationship between positive affect and creativity is stronger in environments with high rather than low dynamism and uncertainty, because entrepreneurs are more likely to experience a higher level of affect activation in dynamic rather than stable environments (Baron & Tang, 2011). In sum, scholars need to be mindful of the fact that in addition to individual-level factors, the influence of entrepreneurs' positive affect is also contingent on venture-related contextual factors.

Entrepreneurs' Negative Affect

Besides positive affect, entrepreneurship research has paid attention to negative affect (Breugst & Shepherd, 2017), which refers to "a general dimension of subjective distress and unpleasurable engagement" (Watson et al., 1988, p. 1063). In addition to negative affect in general (e.g., Foo et al., 2009; Patzelt & Shepherd, 2011), previous studies focusing on the entrepreneurs' experienced negative affect have addressed some discrete negative emotions regarding socially situated events. One of the most widely analyzed catalysts in this category is entrepreneurial failure. Researchers have investigated both entrepreneurial fear of failure (e.g., Cacciotti et al., 2016; Kollmann, Stöckmann, & Kensbock, 2017) and entrepreneurial affective reactions to failure (e.g., Rauter, Weiss, & Hoegl, 2018; Shepherd, Covin, & Kuratko, 2009; Shepherd, Wiklund, & Haynie, 2009).

Scholars have looked at stress as a form of discrete negative emotion typically experienced by entrepreneurs. Interestingly, there are contradictory perspectives surrounding whether entrepreneurs experience more stress than people in other occupations. Specifically, Baron, Franklin, and Hmieleski (2016) argued that entrepreneurs report equivalent or lower levels of stress than comparable, non-entrepreneur professionals. They posit that investors tended to favor entrepreneurs who can perform well under pressure (i.e., environmental selection) and that nascent entrepreneurs understood the role requirements associated with entrepreneurship and that they self-selected into this occupation, which helped them cope with the associated stress. In addition, Patzelt and Shepherd (2011) argued that entrepreneurs' job autonomy could counterbalance their demanding tasks, thus diminishing their negative emotions from work. On the contrary, Cardon and Patel (2015) argued that entrepreneurs would experience greater levels of stress than employees because of entrepreneurs' demanding work tasks, ambiguous role, and uncertain environment. Murnieks et al. (2020) argued along the same lines and proposed that entrepreneurs will experience higher levels of perceived exhaustion than professional workers in other occupations. Empirical results from both Cardon and Patel (2015) and Murnieks et al. (2020) supported their arguments. One potential pathway to reconciling these equivocal findings is to consider the venture stage in which the entrepreneurs are currently operating. The vast majority of the studies we reviewed do not control for venture stage. As asserted by Uy, Foo, and Song (2013), entrepreneurs whose ventures are in early stages could be facing greater stress due to uncertainty, limited resources and control over their work, and high failure rates. In comparison, entrepreneurs running established or relatively mature ventures could be experiencing less stress as they tend to experience more stability and control over their work and the environment.

Predictors

The sources of entrepreneurs' negative affect can be attributed to both internal cognitive evaluations (e.g., social esteem) and externally situated social cues (e.g., financial security) (Cacciotti et al., 2016). We classify the latter antecedents of negative affect into three groups: interpersonal issues, financial issues, and venture progress. Examples of interpersonal issues are conflict (Breugst & Shepherd, 2017; Breugst & Preller, in press) and being coerced to maintain a subordinate position in social interactions with state officials (Doern & Goss, 2014). Studies on financial issues and venture progress corroborate that negative affect can be activated when external social cues signal that failure is possible or imminent (Kollmann et al., 2017). Examples of financial issues that resulted in negative affect include financial security (Cacciotti et al., 2016) and financial strain (Jenkins, Wiklund, & Brundin, 2014). Examples of venture progress issues that resulted in negative affect include the venture's inability to execute (Cacciotti et al., 2016) and project termination (Shepherd, Patzelt, Williams, & Warnecke, 2014).

Outcomes

Extant research shows that entrepreneurs' negative affect generates unfavorable outcomes for both the individual entrepreneur and the business venture. For example, researchers find that entrepreneurs' stress is negatively related to their subjective well-being (Baron et al., 2016) and their physical health (Cardon & Patel, 2015). In addition to the deleterious effects on health, entrepreneurs' negative affect generates other negative outcomes. For example, Baron (2008) argues that entrepreneurs' negative affect decreases their capacity for acquiring financial and human resources, hampers their ability to respond to dynamic environments, and impedes their expansion of skills and social networks, which are all critical to the entrepreneurial process. Empirical studies have substantiated some of the purported detrimental impact. For example, when entrepreneurs experience negative affect, research shows they tend to undertake narrower and less ambitious goals (Delgado-García et al., 2012).

Intriguingly, negative entrepreneurial affect is desirable, at times. According to affect-as-information theory, negative affect indicates that progress toward goals is inadequate and as such, drives increased effort (Foo et al., 2009). Relatedly, at the individual level, Cardon and Patel (2015) find that entrepreneurial stress predicts higher personal income because of the additional motivation and effort arising from stress. In addition, regarding failure experiences, Shepherd, Covin et al. (2009) propose that learning from project failure and commitment to subsequent projects increases with grief (to a certain point) for individuals with high coping self-efficacy. In a case study involving eight entrepreneurial narratives, Byrne and Shepherd (2015) find that entrepreneurs who express higher levels of negative emotions are more motivated to make sense of their business failures. Similarly, at the team level, Rauter et al. (2018) find that together with team reflexivity, negative affective reactions to experienced setbacks trigger a team learning response because reflexive teams tend to see their negative reactions as a warning signal for potential problems. In sum, despite the widespread negative influences generated by entrepreneurs' negative affect, there are also positive outcomes for entrepreneurs as well.

Moderators

Scholars have investigated individual and contextual moderators to explain the variance in intensity and outcomes of negative affect. Entrepreneurship researchers have studied a wide variety of factors that mitigate the unfavorable consequences of negative affect. For example, when encountering business setbacks, entrepreneurs can protect themselves and offset negative affect through the employment of a number of different wellness mindsets including self-kindness (i.e., understanding oneself rather than engaging in harsh self-criticism), common humanity (i.e., perceiving one's experience as part of the common human experience), mindfulness (i.e., holding painful thoughts and confining them to a particular stimulus rather than over-identifying with them), problem-focused coping, and emotion-focused coping (Byrne & Shepherd, 2015; Patzelt & Shepherd, 2011; Shepherd & Cardon, 2009). In addition, research shows that entrepreneurs who experience greater contact with members of their social network are less likely to suffer from venture pressure because they receive more empathy and comfort from the realization that they are not alone in their struggles (Pollack, Vanepps, & Hayes, 2012). To sum up, although negative affect is oftentimes unavoidable in the entrepreneurial process, a number of individual characteristics, cognitive evaluations, and behaviors can alleviate its intensity and/or mitigate its negative impact.

Entrepreneurs' Affect Activation

Our review reveals that a paucity of studies have tried to disentangle the effects of affective valence versus activation in entrepreneurship research (Foo et al., 2015). We found two conceptual articles and one empirical piece focusing on entrepreneurial affect activation. It is important to separate activation and valence, as they exert different influences on outcomes. For example, the meta-analysis by Baas, De Dreu, and Nijstad (2008) showed that positive affect that was high in activation (e.g., excited) was positively related to increased creativity, while positive affect that was low in activation (e.g., relaxed) was not. This highlights the importance of taking into account the dimension of activation beyond the focus on valence.

Regarding conceptual models, Morris, Kuratko, Schindehutte, and Spivack (2012) proposed that ongoing processing of experiential events tends to influence entrepreneurs' affective states and that when the impacted affective state is more positive and intense, entrepreneurs tend to experience a higher level of satisfaction and engage in more improvisational behavior that includes innovation and risk-taking. In another conceptual paper, Foo et al. (2015) theorized how affective valence and affective activation interact to influence opportunity recognition. They argued that activation impacts opportunity recognition by providing energy that prompts individuals to devote greater effort. In addition to these two conceptual articles, an empirical paper by Perry-Smith and Coff (2011) found that activated-pleasant group mood enhanced the number of unique entrepreneurial ideas generated and deactivated-pleasant group mood increased the novelty of the selected entrepreneurial ideas. Based on their findings, higher activation seemed to provide the drive to produce a large number of ideas while lower activation left the teams more open to novel selections. In sum, these studies on affective activation shed light on the importance of studying activation as a separate dimension as experienced by entrepreneurs.

Entrepreneurs' Displayed Affect

We close our review of affect research by discussing displayed affect. Most of the papers reviewed study affect as experienced by the entrepreneur which concerns what the entrepreneur actually feels; in comparison, displayed affect involves outward affective expressions as perceived by relevant others. These two conceptualizations are related but different, as not all experienced affect is displayed and what is displayed may or may not be congruent with actual feelings and emotions. In this segment, we briefly discuss displayed affect, noting that there are limited studies in this area.

Articles focusing on entrepreneurs' displayed affect addressed the affect perceived by stakeholders such as investors (e.g., Li et al., 2017) and employees (e.g., Breugst et al., 2012) rather than the affect experienced by entrepreneurs. This subtle but important distinction matters because stakeholders' perceptions can be different from entrepreneurs' experiences. Research on impression management has shown that individuals are able to shape the message they convey by displaying certain types of affect, even if they do not experience them (Bolino, Kacmar, Turnley, & Gilstrap, 2008). Prior research suggests that entrepreneurs actively employ impression-management tactics (e.g., Artinger, Vulkan, & Shem-Tov,

2015; Mason & Harrison, 2003) so that they can achieve favorable evaluations from their stakeholders. Given the paucity of research on predictors of displayed affect (only two articles to date) we revisit this in the section on future directions.

Outcomes

Compared to experienced affect, entrepreneurial displayed affect has a potentially wider range of influence on stakeholders such as investors, employees, and innovators. Regarding the influence on investors, past studies reveal inconsistent findings regarding investors' funding potential when they perceive entrepreneurs' positive emotions such as passion (Murnieks, Cardon, Sudek, White, & Brooks, 2016). Although investors tend to react favorably to displays of passion, this finding is not conclusive. Although some researchers found that displayed positive affect increased investor interest (e.g., Mitteness et al., 2012; Warnick, Murnieks, McMullen, & Brooks, 2018), other studies did not (e.g., Cardon, Mitteness, & Sudek, 2017; Chen, Yao, & Kotha, 2009). For example, according to Chen et al. (2009), preparedness, rather than displayed passion, positively impacted investors' funding decisions. A possible explanation for these equivocal findings is the existence of moderation effects, as discussed later.

Apart from investors, researchers proposed other stakeholders such as employees and innovators are significantly influenced by perceiving entrepreneurs' positive emotions. Specifically, Breugst et al. (2012) found that both perceived passion for inventing and perceived passion for developing positively influenced employees' positive affect at work and affective commitment. However, Breugst et al. (2012) also found that entrepreneurs' perceived passion for founding negatively influences employees' positive affect. In another study analyzing the accounts of interactions in entrepreneurship, J. E. Jennings, Edwards, P. D. Jennings, and Delbridge (2015) found that entrepreneurs' displayed emotions led to stakeholders' emotional arousal (i.e., positive emotion or negative emotion) and identity cognitions (i.e., identity resonance or identity dissonance). Taken together, this body of work suggests that entrepreneurs' displayed affect influences stakeholders in a myriad of ways.

Moderators

The relationships between entrepreneurs' displayed affect and outcomes vary primarily due to moderating effects related to the individual entrepreneur, projects, and perceivers. Regarding entrepreneurs, their tenacity (Murnieks et al., 2016) and openness to feedback (Warnick et al., 2018) led to a stronger relationship between perceived passion and positive outcomes. Surprisingly, Cardon, Mitteness, et al. (2017) found that if entrepreneurs displayed personal commitment by investing their own money and spending a long time pursuing the venture, they actually received lower evaluations of funding potential when they displayed high enthusiasm. Based on the escalation of commitment literature, Cardon, Mitteness, et al. (2017) speculated that high levels of commitment signaled a potential problem where entrepreneurs continued to allocate funds to a losing venture despite the negative feedback. Regarding entrepreneurial crowdfunding, Li et al. (2017) found that perceived innovativeness moderated the positive relationships between displayed entrepreneurial passion and funding amount as well as social-media exposure, such that perceived innovativeness strengthened the effects of entrepreneurs' displayed passion.

Regarding professional investors, Murnieks et al. (2016) found that the entrepreneurial experience of business angels positively moderated the interaction effect of entrepreneurial passion and tenacity on investors' evaluations. They argued that investors with greater entrepreneurial experience understood the uncertainty of entrepreneurship and as a result, these investors attached even more importance to founders' passion and tenacity. In addition, Mitteness et al. (2012) proposed and found that perceived passion related positively to evaluations of funding potential, especially for business angels who were older, more open, rely on intuition, and had stronger motivations to mentor. Contrary to their predictions, these relationships weakened for extraverted business angels. A possible explanation for this unexpected finding is that extraverted business angels are more careful in evaluating whether entrepreneurs are truly passionate versus just enthusiastic in general. In addition, they found that the relationship weakened for angels who had a promotion-dominated regulatory focus. To account for this unexpected moderation effect, they speculate that business angels with a promotion-dominated focus felt more certain while angels with a prevention-dominated regulatory focus perceived higher risks, which makes passion even more important. Overall, the influence of entrepreneurs' displayed affect is contingent on entrepreneurs' characteristics, venture characteristics, and perceivers' characteristics.

Future Directions

We have summarized the predictors, outcomes, and moderators of entrepreneurial affect in Figure 3.1 Based on our review, we have identified several knowledge gaps in the entrepreneurial affect literature. Below we describe these gaps and offer several suggestions for future research.

First, a gap surrounds the study of affective activation. Extant studies on entrepreneurial affect have overwhelmingly focused on affective valence, that is, whether feelings are pleasurable (Russell & Barrett, 1999), but neglected activation. This is an important oversight because affective activation and valence have differential outcomes. To give an example, highly activated affect such as feeling nervous and excited is different from deactivated feelings such as fatigue (Russell & Barrett, 1999) and would consequently exert different influences on entrepreneurs' cognitions, attitudes, and behaviors. We speculate that activated affect, of both positive and negative valence, would predict entrepreneurial actions more so than deactivated affected. By providing evidence about the existence of this gap, we join the chorus advocating for the need to investigate entrepreneurs' affective activation (Foo et al., 2014; Foo et al., 2015). Based on the suggestions from Foo et al. (2015), one possible area of future exploration could involve entrepreneurs' risk evaluations, since affect influences risk evaluations (Mittal & Ross Jr, 1998; Nygren, Isen, Taylor, & Dulin, 1996). We conjecture that activated affect, by virtue of its energizing effects, could shape these evaluations more so than deactivated affect. Researchers could expand current studies by considering the effects of activation alongside valence among entrepreneurs. Analogously, researchers may include considerations of affective activation and affective valence when exploring other entrepreneurship topics such as resource acquisition, social network development, and innovation. In addition, besides the different outcomes from affective activation, researchers may further investigate the sources of different levels of activation as well. There may be important nuances in the effects that emerge from moderately versus highly activated affect.

Second, much of the extant empirical research on entrepreneurial affect has focused on the individual level, while little attention has been paid to entrepreneurial affect in teams (for a review on entrepreneurial teams, please refer to Breugst & Preller in this book). Given that most ventures are started by teams of entrepreneurs rather than individuals (Cardon, Post, & Forster, 2017; Klotz, Hmieleski, Bradley, & Busenitz, 2014), investigating entrepreneurial affect at the team level is needed to improve our understanding of new ventures. To address this gap, a few scholars have begun to investigate affect at the team level (e.g., Cardon, Post, et al., 2017; Hmieleski, Cole, & Baron, 2012). For example, Hmieleski et al. (2012) examine positive team affective tone, which is the degree to which positive emotions are commonly experienced among top management team members. They found that positive team affective tone mediates the positive relationship between shared authentic leadership and firm performance. In addition, Santos and Cardon (2019) conducted an empirical examination of team entrepreneurial passion. Their findings showed that teams vary considerably in the existence and the specific type of team entrepreneurial passion. Such heterogeneity further corroborated the importance of studying entrepreneurial affect at the team level.

Some interesting research on entrepreneurs' affect at the team level explored the affect contagion process among team members. Through emotional contagion (Barsade, 2002), team members can all experience similar types and levels of affect. Notably, team affect should not be considered as a simple extension of individual affect (Perry-Smith & Coff, 2011); these two types of affect can generate different outcomes. For example, consistent with team polarization (Myers & Lamm, 1975), team members experiencing collective affect can make more extreme decisions than individual entrepreneurs do (Foo et al., 2014). Research on the causes and consequences of team affective tone can help us better understand the entrepreneurial process and business survival, as teams rather than individuals found and run the majority of high growth ventures (Klotz et al., 2014).

Third, we conclude from our review that little is known about key elements of entrepreneurs' affective expressions. We only found two studies exploring the predictors of entrepreneurs' displayed affect. In a qualitative study, Clarke (2011) demonstrated that more experienced entrepreneurs use a wider range of visual symbols to regulate emotions. In addition, Artinger et al. (2015) found that in negotiations, entrepreneurs expressed emotions more frequently than non-entrepreneurs as a means of persuasion. More research on the antecedents and consequences of entrepreneurs' displayed affect is needed. Future research can consider exploring the impact of these manifestations on venture outcomes (Clarke, 2011). In addition, research can look into how displayed emotions can influence entrepreneurial well-being. Entrepreneurs are expected to remain positive, upbeat, and optimistic about their ventures even when things are not going well. Yet, while displayed emotions can be a useful tool to create favorable impressions or interactions with others (Tan, Foo, & Kwek, 2004), burnout occurs when displayed emotions are incongruent with experienced emotions (Zapf, 2002).

Fourth, following the suggestions from previous scholars (Foo et al., 2014), our review calls for research to investigate complex, nonlinear relationships (e.g., Baron et al., 2012; Baron et al., 2011; Cardon et al., 2009; Foo et al., 2015; Shepherd, Wiklund, et al., 2009), which could more accurately illustrate how these affective mechanisms unfold and explain some inconsistent empirical findings. For example, the equivocal findings regarding investors' funding potential and the perception of entrepreneurs' positive emotions might be explained by the "too-much-of-a-good-thing" effect (Pierce & Aguinis, 2013, p. 313). We conjecture that an entrepreneur who expresses excessive positive emotions could be viewed as being insufficiently informed of the risks and dangers faced in the entrepreneurial process, leading to more unfavorable perceptions of the entrepreneur and/or of the venture.

Fifth, besides trait and state affect, researchers can explore other properties of entrepreneurs' affect. For example, Uy, Sun, and Foo (2017) examined entrepreneurs' affect spin, which is defined as "an individual difference construct that captures intraindividual fluctuations of positive and negative affect over time" (p. 445; please refer to Beal, Trougakos, Weiss, and Dalal [2013] for more in-depth explanation of affect spin), and demonstrated that over and above trait and state affect, affect spin shaped the entrepreneurs' psychological well-being and venture goal progress, and large fluctuations of affect—for both positive and negative affect—resulted in lower venture progress and wellbeing. Affect spin consumes psychological resources (hurting wellbeing) and uses up resources that would otherwise be used to operate the venture. Besides affect spin, future researchers can also explore the effects of affect variability (the range of one's affect across time), affect instability (the magnitude of consecutive affect changes), and affect inertia (the intensity of previous affect predicting the following affect) (Houben, Van Den Noortgate, & Kuppens, 2015; Kuppens, Allen, & Sheeber, 2010).

Sixth, researchers may find it interesting to explore the impact of anticipated emotions, which can be critical for entrepreneurs. For example, Neneh (2019) found that anticipated regret positively moderated the relationship between entrepreneurial intentions and actions. The emotions literature has acknowledged differences between current emotions and anticipated emotions (Baumeister, Vohs, Nathan DeWall, & Zhang, 2007; Baumgartner, Pieters, & Bagozzi, 2008; Brown & McConnell, 2011). According to the emotion-as-feedback perspective, anticipated emotions also guide human behavior (Baumeister et al., 2007). A meta-analysis supports this theoretical perspective: anticipated emotions reliably influenced behavior and judgement; in fact, the predictive power of current emotions could be less than that of anticipated emotions (DeWall, Baumeister, Chester, & Bushman, 2016). By separating the influence of current emotions and anticipated emotions, we can develop a more fine-grained understanding on the role of affect in entrepreneurship. Finally, researchers who study entrepreneurship can take advantage of recent advances regarding measurement, research design, and data-analytic approaches. We call for more objective measurements to complement existing approaches to gathering data. For example, Cardon and Patel (2015) combined self-reported stress measures with more objective blood pressure measures. When studying entrepreneurs' affect, researchers may also consider physiological measures such as skin conductance responses which is a well-established and robust method of measuring peripheral (bodily) signals (Christopoulos, Uy, & Yap, 2016).

In terms of research design, we advocate longitudinal studies so as to capture nuanced changes in entrepreneurs' states. We highlight the use of experience sampling methodology in entrepreneurship research. According to Uy, Foo, and Aguinis (2010), by requiring participants to report their feelings multiple times in a field setting, researchers could better capture dynamic person-by-situation interactions over time, enhance ecological validity, examine between-person and within-person variability, and mitigate memory biases. We refer readers to Uy et al. (2010), where they elaborate the implementation of applying experience sampling methodology to advance entrepreneurship theory and research.

Furthermore, researchers could begin to apply "big data" analytics in entrepreneurial emotion research (Wiklund, Nikolaev, Shir, Foo, & Bradley, 2019). These techniques can handle a large number of data and provide researchers immense opportunities to study the heterogeneity of entrepreneurs' psychology. For example, Abreu, Oner, Brouwer, and van Leeuwen (2018) used the UK Household Longitudinal Study (UKHLS), which tracks almost 50,000 individuals across seven waves, to study entrepreneurial well-being across geographic locations. Ryff (2019) drew from the Midlife in the United States (MIDUS), a national longitudinal study of health and well-being, to provide insights on the interface between eudaemonic well-being and entrepreneurship. Future researchers may use massive data sets with fine-grained information in studying entrepreneurial affect across different venture stages, industries, and socioeconomic contexts.

Conclusion

Our review comes at a time when scholarly interest in entrepreneurs' affect is growing. To spur the development of this research stream, we provide an overall framework of the antecedents and consequences of entrepreneurial affect, along with the moderators of the key relationships. Based on the identified knowledge gaps, we highlighted future research opportunities that may guide researchers to develop a more in-depth understanding of entrepreneurial affect.

Note

1. The last three authors contributed equally to the manuscript.

References

Abreu, M., Oner, O., Brouwer, A., & van Leeuwen, E. (2018). Well-being effects of self-employment: A spatial inquiry. *Journal of Business Venturing, 34*(4), 589–607.

Ahsan, M., Zheng, C., DeNoble, A., & Musteen, M. (2018). From student to entrepreneur: How mentorships and affect influence student venture launch. *Journal of Small Business Management, 56*(1), 76–102.

Artinger, S., Vulkan, N., & Shem-Tov, Y. (2015). Entrepreneurs' negotiation behavior. *Small Business Economics, 44*(4), 737–757.

Baas, M., De Dreu, C. K., & Nijstad, B. A. (2008). A meta-analysis of 25 years of mood-creativity research: Hedonic tone, activation, or regulatory focus? *Psychological Bulletin, 134*(6), 779.

Bandura, A. (1997). *Self-efficacy: The exercise of control.* New York, NY: Freeman.

Baron, R. A. (2008). The role of affect in the entrepreneurial process. *Academy of Management Review, 33*(2), 328–340.

Baron, R. A., Franklin, R. J., & Hmieleski, K. M. (2016). Why entrepreneurs often experience low, not high, levels of stress: The joint effects of selection and psychological capital. *Journal of Management, 42*(3), 742–768.

Baron, R. A., Hmieleski, K. M., & Henry, R. A. (2012). Entrepreneurs' dispositional positive affect: The potential benefits-and potential costs-of being "up". *Journal of Business Venturing, 27*(3), 310–324.

Baron, R. A., & Tang, J. (2011). The role of entrepreneurs in firm-level innovation: Joint effects of positive affect, creativity, and environmental dynamism. *Journal of Business Venturing, 26*(1), 49–60.

Baron, R. A., Tang, J., & Hmieleski, K. M. (2011). The downside of being "up": Entrepreneurs' dispositional positive affect and firm performance. *Strategic Entrepreneurship Journal, 5*(2), 101–119.

Barsade, S. G. (2002). The ripple effect: Emotional contagion and its influence on group behavior. *Administrative Science Quarterly, 47*(4), 644–675.

Baum, J. R., & Locke, E. A. (2004). The relationship of entrepreneurial traits, skill, and motivation to subsequent venture growth. *Journal of Applied Psychology, 89*(4), 587.

Baumeister, R. F., Vohs, K. D., Nathan DeWall, C., & Zhang, L. (2007). How emotion shapes behavior: Feedback, anticipation, and reflection, rather than direct causation. *Personality and Social Psychology Review, 11*(2), 167–203.

Baumgartner, H., Pieters, R., & Bagozzi, R. P. (2008). Future-oriented emotions: Conceptualization and behavioral effects. *European Journal of Social Psychology*, *38*(4), 685–696.

Beal, D. J., Trougakos, J. P., Weiss, H. M., & Dalal, R. S. (2013). Affect spin and the emotion regulation process at work. *Journal of Applied Psychology*, *98*(4), 593.

Bem, D. J. (1972). Self-Perception Theory. In L. Berkowitz (Ed.), *Advances in experimental social psychology* (pp. 1–63). New York, NY: Academic Press.

Bolino, M. C., Kacmar, K. M., Turnley, W. H., & Gilstrap, J. B. (2008). A multi-level review of impression management motives and behaviors. *Journal of Management*, *34*(6), 1080–1109.

Breugst, N., Domurath, A., Patzelt, H., & Klaukien, A. (2012). Perceptions of entrepreneurial passion and employees' commitment to entrepreneurial ventures. *Entrepreneurship: Theory and Practice*, *36*(1), 171–192.

Breugst, N., & Preller, R. (in press). Where the magic happens: Opening the black box of entrepreneurial team functioning. In M. M. Gielnik, M. S. Cardon, & M. Frese (Eds.), *The psychology of entrepreneurship: The next decade*. New York, NY: Informa UK Limited.

Breugst, N., & Shepherd, D. A. (2017). If you fight with me, I'll get mad! A social model of entrepreneurial affect. *Entrepreneurship Theory and Practice*, *41*(3), 379–418.

Brief, A. P., & Weiss, H. M. (2002). Organizational behavior: Affect in the workplace. *Annual Review of Psychology*, *53*(1), 279–307.

Brown, C. M., & McConnell, A. R. (2011). Discrepancy-based and anticipated emotions in behavioral self-regulation. *Emotion*, *11*(5), 1091.

Byrne, O., & Shepherd, D. A. (2015). Different strokes for different folks: Entrepreneurial narratives of emotion, cognition, and making sense of business failure. *Entrepreneurship Theory and Practice*, *39*(2), 375–405.

Cacciotti, G., Hayton, J. C., Mitchell, J. R., & Giazitzoglu, A. (2016). A reconceptualization of fear of failure in entrepreneurship. *Journal of Business Venturing*, *31*(3), 302–325.

Cardon, M. S., Foo, M.-D., Shepherd, D., & Wiklund, J. (2012). Exploring the heart: Entrepreneurial emotion is a hot topic. *Entrepreneurship Theory and Practice*, *36*(1), 1–10.

Cardon, M. S., & Kirk, C. P. (2015). Entrepreneurial passion as mediator of the self–efficacy to persistence relationship. *Entrepreneurship Theory and Practice*, *39*(5), 1027–1050.

Cardon, M. S., Mitteness, C., & Sudek, R. (2017). Motivational cues and angel investing: Interactions among enthusiasm, preparedness, and commitment. *Entrepreneurship Theory and Practice*, *41*(6), 1057–1085.

Cardon, M. S., & Patel, P. C. (2015). Is stress worth it? Stress-related health and wealth trade-offs for entrepreneurs. *Applied Psychology*, *64*(2), 379–420.

Cardon, M. S., Post, C., & Forster, W. R. (2017). Team entrepreneurial passion: Its emergence and influence in new venture teams. *Academy of Management Review*, *42*(2), 283–305.

Cardon, M. S., Wincent, J., Singh, J., & Drnovsek, M. (2009). The nature and experience of entrepreneurial passion. *Academy of Management Review*, *34*(3), 511–532.

Carver, C. S., & Scheier, M. F. (1982). Control theory: A useful conceptual framework for personality-social, clinical, and health psychology. *Psychological Bulletin*, *92*(1), 111.

Carver, C. S., & Scheier, M. F. (1990). Origins and functions of positive and negative affect: A control-process view. *Psychological Review*, *97*(1), 19.

Chen, X.-P., Yao, X., & Kotha, S. (2009). Entrepreneur passion and preparedness in business plan presentations: A persuasion analysis of venture capitalists' funding decisions. *Academy of Management Journal*, *52*(1), 199–214.

Christopoulos, G. I., Uy, M. A., & Yap, W. J. (2016). The body and the brain: Measuring skin conductance responses to understand the emotional experience. *Organizational Research Methods*, 1094428116681073.

Clarke, J. (2011). Revitalizing entrepreneurship: How visual symbols are used in entrepreneurial performances. *Journal of Management Studies*, *48*(6), 1365–1391.

Collewaert, V., Anseel, F., Crommelinck, M., De Beuckelaer, A., & Vermeire, J. (2016). When passion fades: Disentangling the temporal dynamics of entrepreneurial passion for founding. *Journal of Management Studies*, *53*(6), 966–995.

Delgado-García, J. B., Rodríguez-Escudero, A. I., & Martín-Cruz, N. (2012). Influence of affective traits on entrepreneur's goals and satisfaction. *Journal of Small Business Management*, *50*(3), 408–428.

DeWall, C. N., Baumeister, R. F., Chester, D. S., & Bushman, B. J. (2016). How often does currently felt emotion predict social behavior and judgment? A meta-analytic test of two theories. *Emotion Review*, *8*(2), 136–143.

Doern, R., & Goss, D. (2014). The role of negative emotions in the social processes of entrepreneurship: Power rituals and shame-related appeasement behaviors. *Entrepreneurship Theory and Practice*, *38*(4), 863–890.

Drnovsek, M., Cardon, M. S., & Patel, P. C. (2016). Direct and indirect effects of passion on growing technology ventures. *Strategic Entrepreneurship Journal*, *10*(2), 194–213.

Fleeson, W., & Gallagher, P. (2009). The implications of Big Five standing for the distribution of trait manifestation in behavior: Fifteen experience-sampling studies and a meta-analysis. *Journal of Personality and Social Psychology*, *97*(6), 1097.

Foo, M.-D. (2011). Emotions and entrepreneurial opportunity evaluation. *Entrepreneurship Theory and Practice*, *35*(2), 375–393.

Foo, M.-D., Murnieks, C. Y., & Chan, E. T. (2014). Feeling and thinking: The role of affect in entrepreneurial cognition. In J. R. Mitchell, R. K. Mitchell, & B. Randolph-Seng (Eds.), *Handbook of entrepreneurial cognition* (pp. 154–181). Cheltenham, UK: Edward Elgar Publishing Ltd.

Foo, M.-D., Uy, M. A., & Baron, R. A. (2009). How do feelings influence effort? An empirical study of entrepreneurs' affect and venture effort. *Journal of Applied Psychology*, *94*(4), 1086.

Foo, M.-D., Uy, M. A., & Murnieks, C. (2015). Beyond affective valence: Untangling valence and activation influences on opportunity identification. *Entrepreneurship Theory and Practice*, *39*(2), 407–431.

Fredrickson, B. L. (2001). The role of positive emotions in positive psychology: The broaden-and-build theory of positive emotions. *American Psychologist*, *56*(3), 218.

Frese, M., & Gielnik, M. M. (2014). The psychology of entrepreneurship. *Annual Review of Organizational Psychology and Organizational Behavior*, *1*(1), 413–438.

Gielnik, M. M., Spitzmuller, M., Schmitt, A., Klemann, D. K., & Frese, M. (2015). "I put in effort, therefore I am passionate": Investigating the path from effort to passion in entrepreneurship. *Academy of Management Journal*, *58*(4), 1012–1031.

Gielnik, M. M., Uy, M. A., Funken, R., & Bischoff, K. M. (2017). Boosting and sustaining passion: A long-term perspective on the effects of entrepreneurship training. *Journal of Business Venturing*, *32*(3), 334–353.

Hayton, J. C., & Cholakova, M. (2012). The role of affect in the creation and intentional pursuit of entrepreneurial ideas. *Entrepreneurship Theory and Practice*, *36*(1), 41–67.

Hayward, M. L., Forster, W. R., Sarasvathy, S. D., & Fredrickson, B. L. (2010). Beyond hubris: How highly confident entrepreneurs rebound to venture again. *Journal of Business Venturing*, *25*(6), 569–578.

Hmieleski, K. M., Cole, M. S., & Baron, R. A. (2012). Shared authentic leadership and new venture performance. *Journal of Management*, *38*(5), 1476–1499.

Houben, M., Van Den Noortgate, W., & Kuppens, P. (2015). The relation between short-term emotion dynamics and psychological well-being: A meta-analysis. *Psychological Bulletin, 141*(4), 901.

Huyghe, A., Knockaert, M., & Obschonka, M. (2016). Unraveling the "passion orchestra" in academia. *Journal of Business Venturing, 31*(3), 344–364.

Jenkins, A. S., Wiklund, J., & Brundin, E. (2014). Individual responses to firm failure: Appraisals, grief, and the influence of prior failure experience. *Journal of Business Venturing, 29*(1), 17–33.

Jennings, J. E., Edwards, T., Jennings, P. D., & Delbridge, R. (2015). Emotional arousal and entrepreneurial outcomes: Combining qualitative methods to elaborate theory. *Journal of Business Venturing, 30*(1), 113–130.

Klotz, A. C., Hmieleski, K. M., Bradley, B. H., & Busenitz, L. W. (2014). New venture teams: A review of the literature and roadmap for future research. *Journal of Management, 40*(1), 226–255.

Kollmann, T., Stöckmann, C., & Kensbock, J. M. (2017). Fear of failure as a mediator of the relationship between obstacles and nascent entrepreneurial activity - An experimental approach. *Journal of Business Venturing, 32*(3), 280–301.

Kuppens, P., Allen, N. B., & Sheeber, L. B. (2010). Emotional inertia and psychological maladjustment. *Psychological Science, 21*(7), 984–991.

Larsen, R. J., & Diener, E. (1992). Promises and problems with the circumplex model of emotion. In M. S. Clark (Ed.), *Review of personality and social psychology, No. 13. Emotion* (pp. 25–59). Newbury Park, CA: Sage.

Li, J. J., Chen, X.-P., Kotha, S., & Fisher, G. (2017). Catching fire and spreading it: A glimpse into displayed entrepreneurial passion in crowdfunding campaigns. *Journal of Applied Psychology, 102*(7), 1075.

Locke, E. A., & Latham, G. P. (2002). Building a practically useful theory of goal setting and task motivation: A 35-year odyssey. *American Psychologist, 57*(9), 705.

Mason, C., & Harrison, R. T. (2003). Auditioning for money: What do technology investors look for at the initial screening stage? *Journal of Private Equity*, 1–27.

Mittal, V., & Ross Jr, W. T. (1998). The impact of positive and negative affect and issue framing on issue interpretation and risk taking. *Organizational Behavior and Human Decision Processes, 76*(3), 298–324.

Mitteness, C., Sudek, R., & Cardon, M. S. (2012). Angel investor characteristics that determine whether perceived passion leads to higher evaluations of funding potential. *Journal of Business Venturing, 27*(5), 592–606.

Morris, M. H., Kuratko, D. F., Schindehutte, M., & Spivack, A. J. (2012). Framing the entrepreneurial experience. *Entrepreneurship Theory and Practice, 36*(1), 11–40.

Murnieks, C. Y., Arthurs, J. D., Cardon, M. S., Farah, N., Stornelli, J., & Haynie, J. M. (2020). Close your eyes or open your mind: Effects of sleep and mindfulness exercises on entrepreneurs' exhaustion. *Journal of Business Venturing, 35*(2), 105918.

Murnieks, C. Y., Cardon, M. S., Sudek, R., White, T. D., & Brooks, W. T. (2016). Drawn to the fire: The role of passion, tenacity and inspirational leadership in angel investing. *Journal of Business Venturing, 31*(4), 468–484.

Murnieks, C. Y., Mosakowski, E., & Cardon, M. S. (2014). Pathways of passion: Identity centrality, passion, and behavior among entrepreneurs. *Journal of Management, 40*(6), 1583–1606.

Myers, D. G., & Lamm, H. (1975). The polarizing effect of group discussion. *American Scientist, 63*(3), 297–303.

Neneh, B. N. (2019). From entrepreneurial intentions to behavior: The role of anticipated regret and proactive personality. *Journal of Vocational Behavior, 112*, 311–324.

Nygren, T. E., Isen, A. M., Taylor, P. J., & Dulin, J. (1996). The influence of positive affect on the decision rule in risk situations: Focus on outcome (and especially avoidance of loss) rather than probability. *Organizational Behavior and Human Decision Processes, 66*(1), 59–72.

Patzelt, H., & Shepherd, D. A. (2011). Negative emotions of an entrepreneurial career: Self-employment and regulatory coping behaviors. *Journal of Business Venturing, 26*(2), 226–238.

Perry-Smith, J. E., & Coff, R. W. (2011). In the mood for entrepreneurial creativity? How optimal group affect differs for generating and selecting ideas for new ventures. *Strategic Entrepreneurship Journal, 5*(3), 247–268.

Pierce, J. R., & Aguinis, H. (2013). The too-much-of-a-good-thing effect in management. *Journal of Management, 39*(2), 313–338.

Pollack, J. M., Vanepps, E. M., & Hayes, A. F. (2012). The moderating role of social ties on entrepreneurs' depressed affect and withdrawal intentions in response to economic stress. *Journal of Organizational Behavior, 33*(6), 789–810.

Rauter, S., Weiss, M., & Hoegl, M. (2018). Team learning from setbacks: A study in the context of start-up teams. *Journal of Organizational Behavior, 39*(6), 783–795.

Russell, J. A., & Barrett, L. F. (1999). Core affect, prototypical emotional episodes, and other things called emotion: Dissecting the elephant. *Journal of Personality and Social Psychology, 76*(5), 805.

Rusting, C. L. (1998). Personality, mood, and cognitive processing of emotional information: Three conceptual frameworks. *Psychological Bulletin, 124*(2), 165.

Ryff, C. D. (2019). Entrepreneurship and eudaimonic well-being: Five venues for new science. *Journal of Business Venturing, 34*(4), 646–663.

Santos, S. C., & Cardon, M. S. (2019). What's love got to do with it? Team entrepreneurial passion and performance in new venture teams. *Entrepreneurship Theory and Practice, 43*(3), 475–504.

Schwarz, N. (1999). Self-reports: How the questions shape the answers. *American Psychologist, 54*(2), 93.

Shepherd, D. A., & Cardon, M. S. (2009). Negative emotional reactions to project failure and the self-compassion to learn from the experience. *Journal of Management Studies, 46*(6), 923–949.

Shepherd, D. A., Covin, J. G., & Kuratko, D. F. (2009). Project failure from corporate entrepreneurship: Managing the grief process. *Journal of Business Venturing, 24*(6), 588–600.

Shepherd, D. A., Patzelt, H., Williams, T. A., & Warnecke, D. (2014). How does project termination impact project team members? Rapid termination, "creeping death", and learning from failure. *Journal of Management Studies, 51*(4), 513–546.

Shepherd, D. A., Wiklund, J., & Haynie, J. M. (2009). Moving forward: Balancing the financial and emotional costs of business failure. *Journal of Business Venturing, 24*(2), 134–148.

Stanley, L. J. (2010). Emotions and family business creation: An extension and implications. *Entrepreneurship Theory and Practice, 34*(6), 1085–1092.

Stenholm, P., & Renko, M. (2016). Passionate bricoleurs and new venture survival. *Journal of Business Venturing, 31*(5), 595–611.

Tan, H. H., Foo, M.-D., & Kwek, M. H. (2004). The effects of customer personality traits on the display of positive emotions. *Academy of Management Journal, 47*(2), 287–296.

Uy, M. A., Foo, M.-D., & Aguinis, H. (2010). Using experience sampling methodology to advance entrepreneurship theory and research. *Organizational Research Methods, 13*(1), 31–54.

Uy, M. A., Foo, M.-D., & Song, Z. (2013). Joint effects of prior start-up experience and coping strategies on entrepreneurs' psychological well-being. *Journal of Business Venturing, 28*(5), 583–597.

Uy, M. A., Sun, S., & Foo, M.-D. (2017). Affect spin, entrepreneurs' well-being, and venture goal progress: The moderating role of goal orientation. *Journal of Business Venturing, 32*(4), 443–460.

Warnick, B. J., Murnieks, C. Y., McMullen, J. S., & Brooks, W. T. (2018). Passion for entrepreneurship or passion for the product? A conjoint analysis of angel and VC decision-making. *Journal of Business Venturing, 33*(3), 315–332.

Watson, D., Clark, L. A., & Tellegen, A. (1988). Development and validation of brief measures of positive and negative affect: The PANAS scales. *Journal of Personality and Social Psychology, 54*(6), 1063.

Watson, D., & Tellegen, A. (1985). Toward a consensual structure of mood. *Psychological Bulletin, 98*(2), 219.

Weiss, H. M., & Cropanzano, R. (1996). Affective events theory: A theoretical discussion of the structure, causes and consequences of affective experiences at work. In B. M. Staw & L. L. Cummings (Eds.), *Research in organizational behavior: An annual series of analytical essays and critical reviews* (Vol. 18, pp. 1–74). Greenwich, CT: Elsevier Science/ JAI Press.

Wiklund, J., Nikolaev, B., Shir, N., Foo, M.-D., & Bradley, S. (2019). Entrepreneurship and well-being: Past, present, and future. *Journal of Business Venturing, 34*(4), 579–588.

Zapf, D. (2002). Emotion work and psychological well-being: A review of the literature and some conceptual considerations. *Human Resource Management Review, 12*(2), 237–268.

4

CLINICAL PSYCHOLOGY CONSTRUCTS IN ENTREPRENEURSHIP RESEARCH

ADHD, Personality Disorders, and Others

Daniel A. Lerner, Holger Patzelt & Johan Wiklund

Introduction

Why should entrepreneurship scholars care about clinical psychology? Entrepreneurship research has advanced in the past 40-plus years by engaging several psychology literatures—yet neglected clinical psychology and abnormal psychological phenomena. This is unfortunate, because leveraging clinical psychology in entrepreneurship research stands to make contributions to entrepreneurship, clinical psychology, and practice. In this chapter, we introduce a number of clinical conditions (attention-deficit/hyperactivity disorder [ADHD], depression, bipolar disorder, and personality disorders), followed by associated constructs (impulsivity, disinhibition, the dark triad of personality), and explore their roles in entrepreneurial activity. Particular attention is given to ADHD since it is quite frequent and its very symptoms (hyperactivity/impulsivity) appear to be positively linked to engagement and performance in entrepreneurship (e.g., Wiklund, Yu, & Patzelt, 2018; Yu, Wiklund, & Pérez-Luño, 2019).

As noted elsewhere (Wiklund, Hatak, Patzelt, & Shepherd, 2018), there are several reasons why entrepreneurship scholars should care about these conditions and constructs. First and most important, what is functional and dysfunctional in terms of human characteristics and behavior is often a matter of context—and there is reason to believe that entrepreneurship is a unique work context where otherwise problematic traits can be leveraged. Symptoms and traits associated with certain disorders or pathologies may be advantageous when unspecified actions under uncertainty are needed, as when responding to entrepreneurial opportunities (Lerner, Hunt, & Dimov, 2018; Lerner, Alkærsig,

Fitza, Lomberg, & Johnson, 2020). The practical and theoretical implications for entrepreneurship are important because potentially positive implications of clinical conditions have been almost completely overlooked within the mainstream clinical literature.

Second, entrepreneurs craft their jobs to fit their own idiosyncratic needs and abilities (Miner, 1994; Baron, 2010). Thus, when they show clinical or subclinical symptoms, they are able to design their own work to overcome personal limitations; they may also capitalize on their personal strengths that may come along with their clinical symptoms. The high flexibility to shape their own work and task environment may render entrepreneurship to be a better option than traditional employment for people with such symptoms.

Third, prior entrepreneurship research has largely overlooked dark-side characteristics of entrepreneurs as well as the potential for unproductive and destructive entrepreneurship. Fourth, to a large extent, prior work on entrepreneurial psychology has established that certain psychological characteristics that benefit people in many walks of life are also beneficial in entrepreneurship. Thus, based on such findings, there seems to be little need for domain-specific psychological theory in entrepreneurship. Findings that clinical psychology constructs such as ADHD, which are generally dysfunctional by definition, may be positive for venturing suggest that entrepreneurship is a unique context. The fact that variable relationships may be different or even opposite of what has been established in other fields suggests that entrepreneurship is in need of unique theorizing. A broader and deeper understanding of the connection between the potentially clinical and entrepreneurship offers nuanced insights into various phenomena and theories and many future research possibilities.

Clinical Psychology, Related Psychological Constructs, and Entrepreneurship

Defining, diagnosing, and treating mental disorders are central parts of clinical psychology. The *Diagnostic and Statistical Manual of Mental Disorders, 5th Edition* (*DSM-5*; American Psychiatric Association, 2013) and the World Health Organization's International Classification of Diseases provide definitions of a wide range of diagnoses. For example, the *DSM-5*, in its 947 pages, lists no less than 153 distinct disorders. Importantly, diagnoses are based on syndromes, that is, clusters of behavioral symptoms, rather than on underlying etiology (causes of the condition which are often unknown). Thus, the causal order is that person X has diagnosis Y because he or she displays behaviors Z, *not* that person X displays behaviors Y because he or she has diagnosis Z. Furthermore, many symptoms (e.g., impulsivity) are shared across a range of disorders. One such common disorder is ADHD.

Attention-Deficit/Hyperactivity Disorder

ADHD is a clinical diagnosis and condition. It is defined by "a persistent pattern of inattention and/or hyperactivity-impulsivity that interferes with functioning or development" (American Psychiatric Association, 2013, p. 59). The *DSM-5* delineates nine possible symptoms for *inattention* and for *hyperactivity/impulsivity* respectively, that "must have [been present] for at least 6 months to a degree that is inconsistent with developmental [age] level" (American Psychiatric Association, 2013, p. 59). For ADHD in adults, at least five (of nine) *inattention* symptoms or five (of nine) *hyperactivity/impulsivity* symptoms must apply. Additionally, the diagnostic criteria explicitly note that "[s]everal inattentive or hyperactive-impulsive symptoms are present in two or more settings", "[clearly] interfere with, or reduce the quality of, social, academic, or occupational functioning", "were present prior to age 12", and "are not better explained by another mental disorder" (American Psychiatric Association, 2013, p. 60). Underlying the *DSM-5*'s explicit consideration of ADHD in adults, research has shown that it often persists beyond adolescence (Biederman, Petty, Evans, Small, & Faraone, 2010; Faraone, Biederman, & Mick, 2006). Its prevalence in the adult population is noteworthy—estimated to affect hundreds of millions of workers worldwide, with significant costs of inadequately treated ADHD (de Graaf et al., 2008; Halbesleben, Wheeler, & Shanine, 2013).

The fact that there are many clinical psychology and epidemiological studies finding adverse effects of ADHD in traditional employment is not just expected but axiomatic; by definition, symptoms must have a clear adverse effect on "social [and or] occupational functioning" (academic functioning is no longer applicable once out of school). In terms of entrepreneurship, however, questions arise. A number of recent studies have suggested a potential positive link between ADHD *symptoms* and various aspects of venturing—for example, opportunity recognition (Lerner, Hunt, & Verheul, 2018; Wiklund, Patzelt, & Dimov, 2016), entrepreneurial intention (Lerner, Verheul, & Thurik, 2019; Verheul et al., 2015), entrepreneurial behavior (Lerner et al., 2019; Verheul et al., 2016; Wiklund et al., 2016), entrepreneurial orientation (Yu et al., 2019), and performance (Yu et al., 2019). These prior studies typically suggest the hyperactivity/impulsivity symptoms appear responsible for these positive relationships. In terms of verified clinical ADHD diagnosis, a recent unpublished study sampling the whole Danish population of entrepreneurs suggests that on average those with an ADHD diagnosis perform *worse* than those without the diagnosis—yet if either married or university-educated, they actually *outperformed* their peers without the diagnosis (Wiklund, Lomberg, Alkærsig, & Miller, 2019).

These recent studies provide a solid basis for subsequent research.[1] Additionally, given the limitations of the entrepreneurship studies to date, recent works demonstrate the need for future research, which we later discuss.

Depression and Bipolar Disorder

Depression is the most frequently diagnosed mental disorder, with an estimated 264 million people being clinically depressed at any given time (GBD, 2018). Symptoms of depression include negative emotions (including low feelings of self-worth, loss of pleasure, sadness), impaired physical functioning (including lack of appetite and fatigue), and diminished cognitive abilities (including problems with memory and concentration), which can severely impact functioning at work. In contrast to unipolar depression, bipolar depression leads to large mood-swings from deep depression to episodes of (hypo)mania; the latter often affords high energy levels, little sleep, doing many things in parallel, and engaging in risky behaviors. Current estimates state that between 2% and 7% of people in the United States suffer from bipolar disorder (Burgess, 2006).

Although unipolar depression and bipolar depression are common, extant studies on linkages to entrepreneurship are rare. Freeman and colleagues (2019) find that "[e]ntrepreneurs reported experiencing more depression (30%), ... and bipolar disorder (11%) than comparison participants" (Freeman, Staudenmaier, Zisser, & Andresen, 2019, p. 323). Johnson and colleagues' (2018) literature review suggests a potential positive link between entrepreneurship and mania. Specifically, these authors present "a model in which some specific personality traits tied to mania risk might also be related to entrepreneurial intent and entry" (Johnson, Freeman, & Madole, 2018, p. 207).

Other Disorders

Other clinical psychological conditions, as organized by the *DSM-5* (American Psychiatric Association, 2013), include personality disorders, obsessive–compulsive and related disorders, and substance-related and addictive disorders, among others. While generally beyond what can be reviewed in this chapter, personality disorders provide a brief illustration. The *DSM-5* defines a personality disorder as "an enduring pattern of inner experience and behavior that deviates markedly from the expectations of the individual's culture, is pervasive and inflexible, has an onset in adolescence or early adult-hood, is stable over time, and leads to distress or impairment" (American Psychiatric Association, 2013, p. 645). This general definition applies to the *DSM-5*'s specification of 10 particular personality disorders (e.g., antisocial personality disorder; borderline personality disorder; histrionic personality disorder). For further details on particular clinical conditions, diagnostic criteria, and various nuances, the current *DSM* and associated clinical literature should be consulted (American Psychiatric Association, 2013).

In terms of connections to entrepreneurship, at present, there are only a few studies considering clinical conditions other than ADHD. For example, Wolfe and Patel (2017) found obsessive-compulsive personality disorder to be positively linked to self-employment. Freeman and colleagues (2019) found that entrepreneurs were significantly higher in reporting substance use disorders than non-entrepreneurs. While not tied to clinical diagnosis, other scholars suggest the relevance of addiction in entrepreneurship (Spivack, McKelvie, & Haynie, 2014; Spivack & McKelvie, 2018). Also, discussed later in this chapter, entrepreneurship scholars have considered narcissism and other parts of the dark triad, associated with personality disorders.

Associated General Factors

Disinhibition figures in many clinical conditions (Nigg, 2000). Insufficient inhibition undermines prudent decision-making and complex behavioral integration, while excessive inhibition yields inaction and rigidity (Carver, 2005). Trait impulsivity, as well as associated underlying psychophysiological systems are studied extensively across the psychology literature (Sharma, Markon, & Clark, 2014).

Impulsivity

Impulsivity has received much conceptual and empirical attention in the clinical literature, leading to a good understanding of the mechanisms relating it to behavior, as well as to well-validated measurement scales. Also, impulsivity figures prominently in many psychiatric diagnoses, suggesting that it can have greater generality than individual diagnoses. The negative connotations associated with impulsivity are generally strong (e.g., Ainslie, 1975). Trait impulsivity represents a multifaceted super-construct (Evenden, 1999) consisting of independent dimensions that need not covary. Impulsivity dimensions include sensation-seeking, a lack of premeditation, a lack of perseverance, and urgency (Whiteside & Lynam, 2001).

Of the four impulsivity dimensions, prior entrepreneurship research has examined aspects of the sensation-seeking dimension under rubrics such as *risk-taking propensity* or *tolerance of uncertainty* (e.g., Brockhaus, 1980; Forlani & Mullins, 2000; Teoh & Foo, 1997). These concepts have been considered positive in entrepreneurship. Furthermore, in their theoretical model, Wiklund, Yu, and Patzelt (2018) outline how all four dimensions of impulsivity relate to the entrepreneurship process. Their theorizing suggests that impulsivity dimensions influence different stages of the entrepreneurial process in complex ways such that there is no uniformly positive or negative impact of impulsivity on entrepreneurial action. Finally, to date, research has found that the dimensions of impulsivity mediate the relationship between ADHD symptoms and entrepreneurial action (Wiklund, Yu, Tucker, & Marino, 2017). As anticipated by the conceptual models (Wiklund, Yu, et al., 2018; Lerner, Hunt, & Verheul, 2018), some relationships are positive and others negative. Much more research is needed however to definitively and comprehensively understand when and how impulsivity affects venturing.

For example, we speculate that impulsivity and its subdimensions have a stronger effect on the likelihood of exploiting opportunities that are less complex, are more risky (due to impulsive entrepreneurs' sensation-seeking), and do not require co-founders or investors (which might counteract fast, impulsive decisions). We encourage future studies to explore these and other potential contingencies of the relationship between impulsivity and various entrepreneurial outcomes.

Disinhibition and Behavioral Inhibition System and Behavioral Activation System

Conceptually closely related to impulsivity is disinhibition (e.g. Nigg, 2000). Disinhibition can originate from relatively asymmetric sensitivity/reactivity of two psychophysiological systems—the behavioral inhibition system (BIS) and the behavioral activation system (BAS) (Gray, 1970, 1982, 1994). "Behavioral disinhibition refers broadly to unrestrained behavior, from cognitive and hedonic motivational origins (Carver & White, 1994; Nigg, 2000)" (Lerner, 2016, p. 237).

In terms of entrepreneurship, individual differences in BIS/BAS sensitivity may be at the root of other linkages recently established (e.g., of impulsivity and entrepreneurship). A number of recent empirical studies have also directly considered potential linkages. Geenen, Urbig, Muehlfeld, van Witteloostuijn, and Gargalianou (2016) found differential BAS subdimensions being linked to entrepreneurial intentions. Lerner, Hatak, and Rauch (2018) found that differences in BIS/BAS sensitivity affect entrepreneurial action and performance. Lerner (2016) suggests disinhibition should facilitate acting on opportunities and finds that behavioral disinhibition by an entrepreneur negatively affects potential resource providers' interest in supporting the venture. Additional research suggests disinhibition as a potential basis for and driver of entrepreneurial action (Lerner, Hunt, & Dimov, 2018).

The Dark Triad (of Personality)

The dark triad refers to three distinguishable but related and often connected constructs—*narcissism, psychopathy,* and *Machiavellianism* (Jonason & Webster, 2010). Akin to constructs such as impulsivity and disinhibition, they are not clinical disorders as they do not represent any specific clinical condition.[2] They are, however, the basis for some personality disorders (e.g. narcissistic personality disorder, antisocial personality disorder) and are generally considered undesirable. As reviewed by Hmieleski and Lerner (2016, pp. 10–11), individuals high in narcissism are typically self-centered, looking to attract others' attention and admiration, engage in grandiose thinking, and expect others to follow them. Those high in psychopathy are unable to experience affective empathy and tend to take advantage of others. They often perform well under conditions of high stress, seek sensation, and challenge the status quo. Finally, Machiavellianism is associated with a strong need for money, power, and competition, as well as the belief that ends justify the means, yielding deviant behaviors such as lying, stealing, and cheating. Hmieleski and Lerner (2016) elaborate potential theoretical linkages between these three constructs and entrepreneurship. In an empirical study with two samples, they found that narcissism was positively linked to entrepreneurial intention; all facets of the triad positively were linked to unproductive entrepreneurial motives; psychopathy was negatively linked to productive entrepreneurial motives; and found mixed results between narcissism and productive entrepreneurial motives (a positive relationship in one sample, null in another).

In relation to the dark triad and its three individual components, it warrants reminding the following. While narcissism, psychopathy, and Machiavellianism are related to personal disorders (and at very high levels likely coincide with a diagnosable disorder), each is simply a construct of personality. Just as individuals vary in degree of other personality constructs like extraversion, so too do individuals vary in their degrees of the three dark-triad components.

Considerations for Future Research

As noted at the outset, what is functional and dysfunctional in terms of human characteristics and behavior is often a matter of context. Symptoms and traits associated with clinical conditions may be advantageous in the performance of some entrepreneurial tasks. Entrepreneurs can, more than others, craft their jobs to fit their own idiosyncratic needs and abilities (Miner, 1994; Baron, 2010). To ignore individual differences that are often problematic (e.g., impulsivity, narcissism) is to ignore something that may often be present, that might facilitate or (also) undermine entrepreneurial efforts. Furthermore, to presume entrepreneurial action is necessarily good and that all venturing is productive is naïve. Examining and understanding the dark, unproductive, and even destructive is as relevant for entrepreneurship theory and practice as is understanding the positive.

In terms of future research, there are many potentially important considerations. We can only offer a selection here, as follows. While largely framed/illustrated in relation to ADHD, something analogous in relation to the other constructs could also apply.

First, future entrepreneurship studies need to be clear as to whether they study diagnosed disorders, specified symptoms of clinical disorders, or constructs related to disorders (e.g., impulsivity). These are not the same. For example, is a particular research study on ADHD (the clinical condition) or something related such as *ADHD-type* behavior or level of *ADHD-symptoms/traits*? The very term *ADHD* is an acronym, abbreviating attention-deficit/hyperactivity disorder. Yet, as popular and nonclinical uses of the term (and presumed understandings) vary greatly, extra effort is necessary on behalf of scholars to avoid misunderstandings (e.g., see Wiklund, Hatak, Lerner, Verheul, Thurik, & Antshel, 2020). This applies not only to the discussion of ADHD but also to general constructs such as impulsivity (e.g., see Wiklund, 2019; Hunt & Lerner, 2018). Certainly, future research considering both clinical conditions (e.g. ADHD, depression, and bipolar disorder) as well as (sub)clinical symptoms/behavior/dispositions in entrepreneurship in needed. Challenges remain to effectively handle the language/communication/ definitional matters, thus representing an important area for future entrepreneurship research.

Second, through decades of research, research has established that those with ADHD on average perform worse in many walks of life and that many with the condition face extensive problems. As with other clinical conditions, dysfunction/ pathology is logically built into the definition of ADHD itself. Because extant research on ADHD has all but recently been dominated by the medical profession, it has logically focused on the psychopathology. However, very little effort has been expended to study the full range of the distribution of outcomes. For example, while the *occupational outcomes* for those with ADHD appear to be lower on average (lower mean), the distribution may also be different, with a higher proportion of those with ADHD doing really well and really poorly, at least in entrepreneurship ADHD symptoms seem to positively influence an entrepreneurial orientation (EO) in terms of innovativeness, risk-taking, and proactiveness (e.g., Yu et al., 2019), and EO is associated with a wider distribution in performance outcomes (Wiklund & Shepherd, 2011).

On average having ADHD is a bad thing. But a small group of people with ADHD may do very well in competitive environments such as risky sports and entrepreneurship. For example, it would be interesting to study how an entrepreneur with ADHD could be complemented by a co-founder or spouse that has very different personality characteristics. The entrepreneurial cases of Richard Branson, Paul Orfaela, and others suggest that it may be a potential recipe for success. Of course, it must not be forgotten that there are very serious potential costs to entrepreneurial missteps. For example, impulsivity not only facilities quick action but also increases the chances of making otherwise foreseeable errors and missteps. Thus, continued research requires endeavoring to take a broad and comprehensive consideration of the potential effects of the clinical or related psychological construct. Whenever examining the implications of clinical or otherwise atypical personality characteristics, it is important to consider the full range of implications, including both positive and negative outcomes (e.g., Lerner, Hunt, & Verheul, 2018). This applies not just to ADHD but also suggests fruitful ground for related inquires based on other clinical conditions and constructs.

Third, the aforementioned also indicates a need to grapple with challenges related to studying how *atypical* individuals cope with the complex entrepreneurial process. Clinical conditions and associated constructs could be expected to have varying connections and impacts across different activities and stages of the entrepreneurial process. Taking ADHD as an example, it presents dualisms across, and even within, particular venturing activities/stages. Lerner, Hunt and Verheul (2018) and Lerner, Hunt and Dimov (2018) illustrate how the ambivalent characteristics and behaviors of entrepreneurs may have to be balanced by characteristics and activities (e.g., from other individuals). For example, in relation to just opportunity recognition, ADHD may enhance opportunity perception but undermine the perception of relevant threats and opportunity costs, yielding imbalanced perception and under-regulated approach behavior. This not only relates to "perceived opportunity X" in face of its risks and opportunity costs but also in relation to suboptimal behavioral integration (e.g., maintaining attention and behavior on opportunity X long enough before moving on to newly perceived opportunity Y or Z). Considering how dualisms interact and play out across time, and how they can be productively channeled, is both challenging and valuable.

In terms of balancing or harnessing an individual's potential, Wiklund and colleagues (2018) suggest that entrepreneurs' domestic partners and their work–life balance can influence the extent to which entrepreneurs are able to manage the entrepreneurial process despite mental disorders. Importantly, however, these studies provide a rather general assessment of the phenomenon, such that there are ample opportunities for both conceptual and empirical studies to link specific mental disorders or characteristics to specific steps of the entrepreneurial process and the outcomes of this process. Such detailed investigation might have substantial implications for entrepreneurs with particular diagnoses or symptoms because it might help them to best navigate through the specific challenges they face in founding, building, and or running their venture.

Finally, we believe that there are major opportunities for future research centering on the design and testing of interventions, programs, curricula, and policies associated with (sub)clinical conditions and entrepreneurship. Although effective pharmacological interventions exist for a variety of disorders, including ADHD, people vary considerably in their use of these medications—either across individuals or across time. For understanding the impact of ADHD on the entrepreneurial process, for example, researchers could compare not only entrepreneurs with ADHD to those without but also how the same ADHD individual accomplishes entrepreneurial tasks in periods when they take medication and in periods when they do not. To identify such periods, researchers might use apps by which people with ADHD register their medication uptake and their moods, sleep, and anxieties. If such data are combined with insights into entrepreneurs' actions, behaviors, progress, and so on, scholars can gain detailed insights into the link between ADHD or other disorders, their symptoms, and how they affect the entrepreneurial process.

Scholars can also explore how it is possible to develop entrepreneurship coaching programs and course curricula that are tailored to those with mental conditions or otherwise high in clinical constructs. Moreover, research could investigate how such programs and curricula can address those aspects of the disorder that can be developed into an asset for the entrepreneur and which strategies can be taught to compensate for the specific disorder's weaknesses (e.g., finding a complementary business or domestic partner, design of appropriate business policy for the venture).

Finally, from a policy perspective, it would be interesting to better understand the impact these programs could have beyond the (potential) entrepreneur—namely, what is the (potential) societal and economic impact of better training and coaching individuals with mental disorders to pursue an entrepreneurial career. Based on the findings, such research could inform policy makers whether/how to allocate resources toward novel and potentially highly impactful ways of not only helping those with mental conditions but also the society and economy at large.

To conclude, mental disorders are prevalent in today's society. Although research on the link between clinical psychology and entrepreneurship is just beginning to emerge, there is hope that the gloomy picture often depicted can at least partly be augmented by one that considers the positive and valued. We encourage future researchers to continue the emerging research avenue engaging such links.

Notes

1. At the time of this writing, additional forthcoming studies are expected involving entrepreneurship and ADHD, as well as other clinical conditions and constructs.
2. For example, there is no recognized narcissist or psychopath condition or diagnosis. Also, for example, psychopathy here is not the same as in forensic psychology.

References

Ainslie, G. (1975). Specious reward: A behavioral theory of impulsiveness and impulse control. *Psychological Bulletin, 82*(4), 463.

American Psychiatric Association. (2013). *Diagnostic and statistical manual of mental disorders (DSM-5)*. Washington, DC: American Psychiatric Association.

Baron, R. A. (2010). Job design and entrepreneurship: Why closer connections = mutual gains. *Journal of Organizational Behavior, 31*(2-3), 370–378.

Biederman, J., Petty, C. R., Evans, M., Small, J., & Faraone, S. V. (2010). How persistent is ADHD? A controlled 10-year follow-up study of boys with ADHD. *Psychiatry Research, 177*(3), 299–304.

Brockhaus, R. H. (1980). Risk taking propensity of entrepreneurs. *Academy of Management Journal, 23*(3), 509–520.

Burgess, W. (2006). *The bipolar handbook: Real-life questions with up-to-date answers*. New York: Penguin.

Carver, C. S. (2005). Impulse and constraint: Perspectives from personality psychology, convergence with theory in other areas, and potential for integration. *Personality and Social Psychology Review, 9,* 312–333.

Carver, C. S., & White, T. (1994). Behavioral inhibition, behavioral activation, and affective responses to impending reward and punishment: The BIS/BAS scales. *Journal of Personality and Social Psychology, 67,* 319–333.

de Graaf, R., Kessler, R. C., Fayyad, J., Ten Have, M., Alonso, J., Angermeyer, M., . . . Posada-Villa, J. (2008). The prevalence and effects of adult attention deficit/hyperactivity disorder (ADHD) on the performance of workers: Results from the WHO World Mental Health Survey Initiative. *Occupational and Environmental Medicine, 65,* 835–842.

Evenden, J. L. (1999). Varieties of impulsivity. *Psychopharmacology, 146*(4), 348–361.

Faraone, S. V., Biederman, J., & Mick, E. (2006). The age-dependent decline of attention deficit hyperactivity disorder: A meta-analysis of follow-up studies. *Psychological Medicine, 36*(2), 159–165.

Forlani, D., & Mullins, J. W. (2000). Perceived risks and choices in entrepreneurs' new venture decisions. *Journal of Business Venturing, 15*(4), 305–322.

Freeman, M. A., Staudenmaier, P. J., Zisser, M. R., & Andresen, L. A. (2019). The prevalence and co-occurrence of psychiatric conditions among entrepreneurs and their families. *Small Business Economics, 53*(2), 323–342. doi:10.1007/s11187-018-0059-8

GBD. (2018). Global, regional, and national incidence, prevalence, and years lived with disability for 354 diseases and injuries for 195 countries and territories, 1990–2017: A systematic analysis for the Global Burden of Disease Study 2017. *Lancet, 392*(10159), 1789–1858.

Geenen, N., Urbig, D., Muehlfeld, K., van Witteloostuijn, A., & Gargalianou, V. (2016). BIS and BAS: Biobehaviorally rooted drivers of entrepreneurial intent. *Personality and Individual Differences, 95*, 204–213.

Gray, J. A. (1970). The psychophysiological basis of introversion-extraversion. *Behaviour Research and Therapy, 8*(3), 249–266.

Gray, J. A. (1982). *The neuropsychology of anxiety: An enquiry into the functions of the septo-hippocampal system.* Oxford: Oxford University Press.

Gray, J. A. (1994). Personality dimensions and emotion systems. In P. Ekman & R. J. Davidson (Eds.), *The nature of emotion* (pp. 329–331). New York: Oxford University Press.

Halbesleben, J. R. B., Wheeler, A. R., & Shanine, K. K. (2013). The moderating role of attention-deficit/hyperactivity disorder in the work engagement-performance process. *Journal of Occupational Health Psychology, 18*(2), 132–143.

Hmieleski, K., & Lerner, D. (2016). The dark triad and nascent entrepreneurship: An examination of unproductive versus productive entrepreneurial motives. *Journal of Small Business Management, 54*(S1), 7–32. doi:10.1111/jsbm.12296

Hunt, R., & Lerner, D. (2018). Entrepreneurial action as human action: Sometimes judgment-driven, sometimes not. *Journal of Business Venturing Insights,* 10c e00102.

Johnson, S., Freeman, M., & Madole, J. (2018). Mania risk and entrepreneurship: Overlapping personality traits. *Academy of Management Perspectives, 32*(2), 207–227. doi:10.5465/amp.2016.0165

Jonason, P. K., & Webster, G. D. (2010). The dirty dozen: A concise measure of the dark triad. *Psychological Assessment, 22*, 420–432.

Lerner, D. (2016). Behavioral disinhibition & nascent venturing: Relevance and initial effects on potential resource providers. *Journal of Business Venturing, 31*(2), 234–252.

Lerner, D., Alkærsig, L., Fitza, M., Lomberg, C., & Johnson, S. (2020). Nothing ventured, nothing gained: Parasite infection is associated with entrepreneurial initiation, engagement and performance. *Entrepreneurship Theory and Practice.* Retrieved from https://doi.org/10.1177/1042258719890992

Lerner, D., Hatak, I., & Rauch, A. (2018). Deep roots? Behavioral inhibition and behavioral activation system (BIS/BAS) sensitivity and entrepreneurship. *Journal of Business Venturing Insights, 9*, 107–115.

Lerner, D., Hunt, R., & Dimov, D. (2018). Action! Moving beyond the intendedly-rational logics of entrepreneurship. *Journal of Business Venturing, 33*(1), 52–69. Retrieved from https://doi.org/10.1016/j.jbusvent.2017.10.002

Lerner, D., Hunt, R., & Verheul, I. (2018). Dueling banjos: Harmony and discord between ADHD and entrepreneurship. *Academy of Management Perspectives, 32*(2), 266–286. Retrieved from https://doi.org/10.5465/amp.2016.0178

Lerner, D., Verheul, I., & Thurik, R. (2019). Entrepreneurship & attention deficit/hyperactivity disorder: A large-scale study involving the clinical condition of ADHD. *Small Business Economics, 53*(2), 381–392. Retrieved from https://doi.org/10.1007/s11187-018-0061-1

Miller, D., & Le Brenton-Miller, I. (2017). Underdog entrepreneurs: A model of challenge-based entrepreneurship. *Entrepreneurship Theory & Practice, 41*(1), 7–17.

Miner, J. B. (1994). *Role motivation theories*. New York: Routledge.

Nigg, J. T. (2000). On inhibition/disinhibition in developmental psychopathology: Views from cognitive and personality psychology and a working inhibition taxonomy. *Psychological Bulletin, 126*(2), 220–246.

Sharma, L., Markon, K. E., & Clark, L. A. (2014). Toward a theory of distinct types of "impulsive" behaviors: A meta-analysis of self-report and behavioral measures. *Psychological Bulletin, 140*(2), 374–408. doi:10.1037/a0034418

Spivack, A., & McKelvie, A. (2018). Entrepreneurship addiction: Shedding light on the manifestation of the "dark side" in work-behavior patterns. *Academy of Management Perspectives, 32*(3), 358–378.

Spivack, A., McKelvie, A., & Haynie, J. M. (2014). Habitual entrepreneurs: Possible cases of entrepreneurship addiction? *Journal of Business Venturing, 29*(5), 651–667.

Teoh, H. Y., & Foo, S. L. (1997). Moderating effects of tolerance for ambiguity and risk taking propensity on the role conflict-perceived performance relationship: Evidence from Singaporean entrepreneurs. *Journal of Business Venturing, 12*(1), 67–81.

Verheul, I., Block, J., Burmeister-Lamp, K., Thurik, R., Tiemeier, H., & Turturea, R. (2015). ADHD-like behavior and entrepreneurial intentions. *Small Business Economics*. Retrieved from https://doi.org/10.1007/s11187-015-9642-4

Verheul, I., Rietdijk, W., Block, J., Franken, I., Larsson, H., & Thurik, R. (2016). The association between attention-deficit/hyperactivity symptoms and self-employment. *European Journal of Epidemiology*. doi:10.1007/s10654-016-0159-1

Whiteside, S. P., & Lynam, D. R. (2001). The five factor model and impulsivity: Using a structural model of personality to understand impulsivity. *Personality and Individual Differences, 30*(4), 669–689.

Wikipedia. (2019). Clinical psychology. Retrieved from https://en.wikipedia.org/wiki/Clinical_psychology, on June 8, 2019.

Wiklund, J. (2019). Entrepreneurial impulsivity is not rational judgment. *Journal of Business Venturing Insights, 11*, e00105.

Wiklund, J., Hatak, I., Lerner, D., Verheul, I., Thurik, R., & Antshel, K. (2020). Entrepreneurship, clinical psychology and mental health: An exciting and promising new field of research. *Academy of Management Perspectives*. Retrieved from doi.org/10.5465/amp.2019.0085

Wiklund, J., Hatak, I., Patzelt, H., & Shepherd, D. (2018). Mental disorders in the entrepreneurship context: When being different can be an advantage. *Academy of Management Perspectives, 32*, 2.

Wiklund, J., Lomberg, C., Alkærsig, L., & Miller, D. (2019). When ADHD helps and harms in entrepreneurship: An epidemiological approach. In *Academy of management proceedings* (Vol. 2019, No. 1, p. 17481). Briarcliff Manor, NY: Academy of Management.

Wiklund, J., Patzelt, H., & Dimov, D. (2016). Entrepreneurship and psychological disorders: How ADHD can be productively harnessed. *Journal of Business Venturing Insights, 6*, 14–20.

Wiklund, J., & Shepherd, D. A. (2011). Where to from here? EO-as-experimentation, failure, and distribution of outcomes. *Entrepreneurship Theory and Practice, 35*(5), 925–946.

Wiklund, J., Yu, W., & Patzelt, H. (2018). Impulsivity and entrepreneurial action. *Academy of Management Perspectives, 32*(3), 379–403.

Wiklund, J., Yu, W., Tucker, R., & Marino, L. (2017). ADHD, impulsivity and entrepreneurship. *Journal of Business Venturing, 32*(6), 627–656.

Wolfe, M., & Patel, P. (2017). Persistent and repetitive: Obsessive-compulsive personality disorder and self-employment. *Journal of Business Venturing Insights, 8*, 125–137.

Yu, W., Wiklund, J., & Pérez-Luño, A. (2019). ADHD symptoms, entrepreneurial orientation (EO), and firm performance. *Entrepreneurship Theory and Practice*. Retrieved from https://doi.org/10.1177/1042258719892987

5

THE BIOLOGY OF ENTREPRENEURSHIP

Ahmed Maged Nofal, Nicos Nicolaou & Scott Shane

The Biology of Entrepreneurship

Historically, research in entrepreneurship has largely ignored biological factors. However, recently researchers have begun to explore the ways in which human biology affects this phenomenon. This literature has been fragmented, scattered across various outlets, making it difficult for entrepreneurship scholars to aggregate the findings and develop a broad theoretical perspective to describe how biology relates to entrepreneurship (Nofal, Nicolaou, Symeonidou, & Shane, 2018).

In this chapter, we provide a systematic review of the biological perspective in entrepreneurship. Specifically, we systematically review research linking the three biological strands of genetics, physiology, and neuroscience to entrepreneurship. We discuss the findings of this growing literature and how incorporating biology into the study of entrepreneurship can enhance our understanding of various entrepreneurial outcomes. We then discuss the mechanisms through which biology affects entrepreneurship. Finally, we conclude with directions for future research.

Systematic Review

The review strategy is designed to provide a systematic and explicit method for reviewing the research on genetics, physiology, and neuroscience in entrepreneurship.

It adopts the same approach that Nofal et al. (2018) have previously used in their review of the biology of management. First, it uses the same keywords used by Nofal et al. (2018) that are related to the three biological areas (see Table 5.1). Second, it follows the protocols of Tranfield, Denyer, and Smart (2003) for undertaking systematic reviews in the field of management.

Using these protocols, we searched the databases of Thomson ISI Web of Knowledge and Google Scholar. We then reviewed all studies published in journals listed in the Chartered Association of Business Schools' list. We included all papers that were written through the end of July 2019, the stop point for this review. We transferred all the papers to Endnote and screened all the papers using title and abstract analysis to identify the studies that might be relevant to the review. This process resulted in a total of 200 articles. Of these articles, 151 were then excluded according to the exclusion criteria of Nofal et al. (2018) (see Table 5.2), leaving us with a total of 49 articles. We also approached two experts in the area and employed a backward and forward snowballing procedure by manually searching the reference lists of all included studies to make sure that we included all the necessary articles—the approach that yielded 13 more papers on genetics, 8 more papers on physiology, and 11 more papers on neuroscience.[1] After validating the retrieved papers, our overall search shows a total number of 81 papers and 5 books/book chapters (see Table 5.3).

The articles that result from the systematic review are listed in Table 5.3. The journals that make the biggest contribution to the review are the *Journal of Business Venturing*, the *Journal of Applied Psychology*, *Organizational Behavior and Human Decision Processes*, and *Applied Psychology*. We next review the papers in each of the three biological strands. Afterward, we discuss the mechanisms through which biology influences entrepreneurship.

Research on Genetics and Entrepreneurship

Research in the genetics strand has examined the influence of DNA on the propensity to engage in entrepreneurship, the propensity to recognize entrepreneurial opportunities, entrepreneurial intentions, and entrepreneurial performance (Nicolaou & Shane, 2009, p. 2). Two methods are used to examine whether genetics affects entrepreneurship. The first method is called "quantitative genetics", while the second is called "molecular genetics". The former builds on natural experiments of twins and adoptees to separate the influences of genes from the effects of environmental factors in an entrepreneurial phenotype. The latter attempts to identify the specific genetic variants that influence entrepreneurial propensities, using candidate gene and genome-wide association studies.

To date, quantitative genetics research has received more attention than molecular genetics research, as evidenced by the number of publications. This research shows that genetic factors explain 48% of the variance in self-employment (Nicolaou, Shane, Cherkas, Hunkin, & Spector, 2008; Zhang, Ilies, et al., 2009), 40%

TABLE 5.1 Keywords and Search Terms

	Genetics	Physiology	Neuroscience
Business	✓ Biology and business ✓ Gene and business	✓ Biology and business ✓ Hormone and business ✓ Testosterone and business ✓ Dopamine and business ✓ Cortisol and business ✓ Oxytocin and business ✓ Serotonin and business ✓ Physiology and business	✓ Biology and business, ✓ Neuroscience and business
Management	✓ Biology and management ✓ Gene and management	✓ Biology and management ✓ Hormone and management ✓ Testosterone and management ✓ Dopamine and management ✓ Cortisol and management ✓ Oxytocin and management ✓ Serotonin and management ✓ Physiology and management	✓ Biology and management ✓ Neuroscience and management
Leadership	✓ Biology and leadership ✓ Gene and leadership	✓ Biology and leadership ✓ Hormone and leadership ✓ Testosterone and leadership ✓ Dopamine and leadership ✓ Cortisol and leadership ✓ Oxytocin and leadership ✓ Serotonin and leadership ✓ Physiology and leadership	✓ Biology and leadership ✓ Neuroscience and leadership

(Continued)

TABLE 5.1 (Continued)

	Genetics	Physiology	Neuroscience
Entrepreneurship	✓ Biology and entrepreneurship ✓ Gene and entrepreneurship	✓ Biology and entrepreneurship ✓ Hormone and entrepreneurship ✓ Testosterone and entrepreneurship ✓ Dopamine and entrepreneurship ✓ Cortisol and entrepreneurship ✓ Oxytocin and entrepreneurship ✓ Serotonin and entrepreneurship ✓ Physiology and leadership	✓ Biology and entrepreneurship ✓ Neuroscience and entrepreneurship
Organizational Behavior	✓ Biology and organizational behavior ✓ Gene and organizational behavior	✓ Biology and organizational behavior ✓ Hormone and organizational behavior ✓ Testosterone and organizational behavior ✓ Dopamine and organizational behavior ✓ Cortisol and organizational behavior ✓ Oxytocin and organizational behavior ✓ Serotonin and organizational behavior ✓ Physiology and organizational behavior	✓ Biology and organizational behavior ✓ Neuroscience and organizational behavior
Strategy	✓ Biology and strategy ✓ Gene and strategy	✓ Biology and strategy ✓ Hormone and strategy ✓ Testosterone and strategy ✓ Dopamine and strategy ✓ Cortisol and strategy ✓ Oxytocin and strategy ✓ Serotonin and strategy ✓ Physiology and strategy	✓ Biology and strategy ✓ Neuroscience and strategy
Occupational Health and Safety	✓ Biology and occupational health and safety ✓ Gene and occupational health and safety	✓ Biology and occupational health and safety ✓ Hormone and occupational health and safety ✓ Testosterone and occupational health and safety ✓ Dopamine and occupational health and safety ✓ Cortisol and occupational health and safety ✓ Oxytocin and occupational health and safety ✓ Serotonin and occupational health and safety ✓ Physiology and occupational health and safety	✓ Biology and occupational health and safety ✓ Neuroscience and occupational health and safety

TABLE 5.2 Exclusion Criteria

N	Criteria	Reason for Exclusion
1	Organizational evolution papers	Examine how organizations evolve but do not look at the relationships between biology and entrepreneurship
2	Metaphor papers	Compare organizational activities to biology only metaphorically and do not look at the relationships between biology and entrepreneurship
3	Biological contexts papers	Examine the relationships between different management variables in biology-related contexts such as hospitals, pharmacies, biotech companies but do not look at the relationships between biology and entrepreneurship
4	Proxy papers	Use proxies such as age, gender, and ethnicity for biology
5	Marketing papers	Do not capture entrepreneurship-related phenotypes
6	Accounting, Economics and Finance papers	Do not capture entrepreneurship-related phenotypes

Source: Adapted from Nofal et al. (2018)

of the variance in starting a new business, and 43% of the variance in engaging in the firm start-up process (Lindquist, Sol, & Van Praag, 2015; Nofal et al., 2018; Zunino, 2016). The majority of those papers used self-employment and business ownership as proxies to measure entrepreneurship, which are less likely to capture the explorative dimensions of entrepreneurship (Henrekson & Sanandaji, 2014). Attempting to address this issue, other studies have examined the influence of genes on other entrepreneurial outcomes, such as opportunity recognition and entrepreneurial intentions. For instance, there is evidence that genetics contribute to 45% of the variance in opportunity recognition (Shane & Nicolaou, 2015b) and 42% of the variance in entrepreneurial intentions (Nicolaou & Shane, 2010).

While research shows that genetic factors explain a significant part of the variance in entrepreneurship, research trying to detect the specific genes influencing the tendency to engage in entrepreneurship has been less informative compared to quantitative genetics research. In this regard, Nicos Nicolaou et al. (2011) found a single nucleotide polymorphism in the dopamine receptor genes to be associated with entrepreneurship using a candidate-gene study.

However, candidate gene studies (in most settings) have suffered from a lack of replication (Duncan, Ostacher, & Ballon, 2019; van der Loos et al., 2011) and have been superseded by genome-wide association studies (GWAS). GWAS

TABLE 5.3 Publications Included in the Systematic Review (sorted by year)

Genetics	Physiology	Neuroscience
1. Nicolaou, Shane, Cherkas, Hunkin, et al. (2008)	1. White, Thornhill, & Hampson (2006)	1. Frank et al. (2009)
2. Nicolaou, Shane, Cherkas, & Spector (2008)	2. Tomasino (2007)	2. Collins & Karasek (2010); Shane (2009)
3. Frank, Doll, Oas-Terpstra, & Moreno (2009)	3. Weis, Firker, & Hennig (2007)	3. Laureiro-Martínez, Brusoni, & Zollo (2010)
4. W. Johnson (2009)	4. White, Thornhill, & Hampson (2007)	4. Arvey & Zhen (2012)
5. Nicolaou & Shane (2009)	5. Shane (2009)	5. de Holan (2013)
6. Nicolaou, Shane, Cherkas, & Spector (2009)	6. Unger, Rauch, Narayanan, Weis, & Frese (2009)	6. Nejati & Shahidi (2013)
7. Shane (2009)	7. Sundararajan (2010)	7. Nicolaou & Shane (2013)
8. Zhang, Ilies, & Arvey (2009)	8. Trahms, Coombs, & Barrick (2010)	8. Tracey & Schluppeck (2013)
9. (Zhang, Zyphur, et al., 2009)	9. Guiso & Rustichini (2011b)	9. Krueger & Welpe (2014)
10. Koellinger et al. (2010)	10. Guiso & Rustichini (2011a)	10. McMullen, Wood, & Palich (2014)
11. Nicolaou & Shane (2010)	11. Arvey & Zhen (2012)	11. Laureiro-Martinez et al. (2014)
12. (Shane, 2010)	12. van der Loos, Haring, et al. (2013)	12. Arvey & Zhang (2015)
13. Shane, Nicolaou, Cherkas, & Spector (2010b)	13. Alrajih & Ward (2014)	13. Laureiro-Martínez, Brusoni, Canessa, & Zollo (2015a)
14. Shane, Nicolaou, Cherkas, & Spector (2010a)	14. Greene, Han, Martin, Zhang, & Wittert (2014)	14. Laureiro-Martínez, Venkatraman, Cappa, Zollo, & Brusoni (2015)
15. van der Loos, Koellinger, Groenen, & Thurik (2010)	15. Rietveld, van Kippersluis, & Thurik (2014)	15. Massaro (2015)
16. Nicolaou & Shane (2011)	16. Arvey & Zhang (2015)	16. Shane & Nicolaou (2015a)
17. Nicolaou, Shane, Adi, Mangino, & Harris, (2011); van der Loos et al. (2010)	17. (Bönte, Procher, & Urbig (2015)	17. de holan & Couffe (2017)
	18. Shane & Nicolaou (2015a)	18. Nofal et al. (2017)
	19. Unger, Rauch, Weis, & Frese (2015)	19. Pérez-Centeno (2017)
	20. Nofal et al. (2017)	20. Nofal et al. (2018)
	21. Wolfe & Patel, (2017)	21. S. K. Johnson et al. (2018)

18. van der Loos et al. (2011)
19. Arvey & Zhen (2012)
20. Quaye, Nicolaou, Shane, & Harris (2012)
21. Quaye, Nicolaou, Shane, & Mangino (2012)
22. Wernerfelt, Rand, Dreber, Montgomery, & Malhotra (2012)
23. Shane & Nicolaou (2013)
24. van der Loos, Rietveld, et al. (2013)
25. Arvey & Zhang (2015)
26. Lindquist et al., 2015)
27. Shane & Nicolaou (2015a)
28. Schermer, Johnson, Jang, & Vernon (2015)
29. Shane & Nicolaou (2015b)
30. Arvey, Li, & Wang (2016)
31. Zunino (2016)
32. Nofal, Nicolaou, & Symeonidou (2017)
33. Nofal et al. (2018)
34. Guedes, Nicolaou, & Patel (2019)
35. Kuechle (2019)

22. Nicolaou, Patel, & Wolfe (2017)
23. Nofal et al. (2018)
24. Diallo (2019)
25. Patel & Wolfe (in press)
26. Wolfe & Patel (2018)

22. Pérez-Centeno (2018)
23. Lahti, Halko, Karagozoglu, & Wincent (2019)
24. Nicolaou, Lockett, Ucbasaran, & Rees (2019)
25. Shane, Drover, Clingingsmith, & Cerf (2019)

Note: Some papers span more than one category and accordingly appear in more than one column.

aim to identify small effect–size genes influencing entrepreneurial phenotypes by examining the entire genome without the need for a priori hypotheses.

GWAS suffer from their own limitations. In particular, GWAS require very large samples (Koellinger et al., 2010; van der Loos et al., 2010) and genome-wide significance levels of 5×10^{-8}. In other words, due to the large number of statistical tests conducted, a Bonferroni correction is needed to adjust the alpha values from $p < 0.05$ to $p < (0.05/\text{number of statistical tests})$. For GWAS, the adjusted Bonferroni correction corresponds to $p < 5 \times 10^{-8}$. Meanwhile, the highest significance values achieved for GWAS in entrepreneurship were 6×10^{-7} for the rs10791283 of the OPCML gene (Quaye, Nicolaou, Shane, & Mangino, 2012), and 1.25×10^{-7} for the rs6738407 located in the HECW2 gene (van der Loos, Rietveld, et al., 2013). As a result, the GWAS are largely inconclusive. There might be a very large number of genes involved in entrepreneurship, each with such a small individual effect size that the effects are difficult to detect.

Research on Physiology and Entrepreneurship

Physiology is the second strand in the literature on the biology of entrepreneurship. This strand has mainly focused on the influence of hormones. Among the key findings are that testosterone influences the tendency of people to engage in self-employment (White et al., 2006; Greene et al., 2014). Testosterone is suggested to influence risk-taking which in turn affects the tendency to become self-employed (Bönte et al., 2015; White et al., 2006). Nicos Nicolaou, Patel, and Wolfe (2018) utilized three different studies using serum testosterone levels, prenatal testosterone exposure using the 2D:4D ratio, and testosterone transfer in opposite-sex and same-sex twins to show that testosterone is associated with a higher propensity of engaging in entrepreneurship. Jens M. Unger et al. (2015) also found a significant interactive effect between prenatal testosterone and need for achievement on the number of jobs created by an entrepreneur.

Testosterone is not the only hormone examined. Other research shows a significant interactive effect of the stress hormone "cortisol" and epinephrine on the tendency to become an entrepreneur (Wolfe & Patel, 2017). Individuals with elevated epinephrine levels are more likely to engage in risky decision-making when their cortisol levels are low.

Research on Neuroscience and Entrepreneurship

The third strand of the biological theory of entrepreneurship examines the relationship between neuroscience and entrepreneurship (de Holan, 2013; Nicolaou & Shane, 2013). Examining neural activity in the brain can help us better understand how human beings function (Hannah, Balthazard, Waldman, Jennings, & Thatcher, 2013; Lee, Butler, & Senior, 2008). For instance, incorporating neuroscience methods into the study of entrepreneurship has allowed "researchers to obtain more truthful data" about numerous "psychological functions such as brain reward systems and judgement" (Lahti, Halko, Karagozoglu, & Wincent, 2018, p. 17). Capturing the neural activity has also helped in revealing various neuropsychological antecedents to individuals' strategic decisions, including emotions and cognitions (Laureiro-Martínez et al., 2015).

Nicos Nicolaou et al. (2019) propose four complementary mechanisms through which neuroscience can enhance our understanding of entrepreneurship: (1) capturing hidden mental processes that are unlikely to be revealed using other techniques, (2) confirming discriminant and convergent validity of entrepreneurship constructs, (3) investigating the underlying antecedents and temporal ordering of variables, and (4) refining theoretical perspectives.

Unfortunately, to date, most of the work on the neuroscience of entrepreneurship is conceptual (Nicos Nicolaou et al., 2019). Nevertheless, the few empirical papers in this area have uncovered some patterns for the study of entrepreneurship. For example, Lahti et al. (2018) argue that entrepreneurs' bonding with their ventures activates the same brain regions as parents' bonding with children, suggesting that entrepreneurs exhibit strong bonding, intimacy, caregiving dispositions, and affective emotions when thinking about their ventures—which resembles the relationship between parents and their children. Laureiro-Martinez et al. (2014) show that entrepreneurs have greater decision-making efficiency than managers and stronger activation in the frontopolar cortex, which has been associated with exploration. In a recent functional magnetic resonance imaging study Shane et al. (2019) found that founders with high passion trigger investors' neural engagement by 39% and investors' interest in the venture by 26% compared to founders with low passion.

Mechanisms Explaining the Biological Basis of Entrepreneurship

An understanding of the mechanisms relating biology to entrepreneurship can augment our ability to understand various entrepreneurial outcomes (Colarelli & Arvey, 2015; Nicolaou & Shane, 2011). As (Shane et al., 2019, p. 6) explain, understanding the mechanisms relating biology to entrepreneurship is novel, but not easy, and "human beings are too complex biologically for there to be a single mechanism". Research has presented a number of mechanisms to explain how biology impacts the tendency of people to engage in entrepreneurship.

First, biology may impact the tendency of people to engage in entrepreneurship through psychological characteristics. Prior work shows, for instance, that agreeableness, openness to experience, and extraversion mediate the relationship between genetic factors and entrepreneurial performance (Shane & Nicolaou, 2013). Extant literature also shows that testosterone affects entrepreneurial intentions through risk-taking (Bönte et al., 2015).

Second, biology may moderate the relationship between environmental factors and the tendency to engage in entrepreneurship. Empirical evidence, for example, indicates that genetics and social environments play an interactive role in influencing the propensity toward entrepreneurship (Zhang, Ilies, & Arvey, 2010; Zhang, Zyphur, et al., 2009). Further work proposes an interactive influence of genetic factors and education on the likelihood of self-employment (Quaye, Nicolaou, Shane, & Harris, 2012).

Third, biology may influence the propensity towards entrepreneurship by affecting the likelihood of people to select certain environments that, in turn, affect their likelihood of engaging in entrepreneurship. For instance, the genetic makeup of individuals may enable them to self-select environments that give them better access to business angels and venture capitalists which in turn increases the likelihood that they engage in entrepreneurship (Shane & Nicolaou, 2015a).

Fourth, interactions between biological factors may affect the tendency of people to become entrepreneurs. Research shows, for instance, that cortisol and epinephrine have an interactive effect on the probability of becoming self-employed (Wolfe & Patel, 2017). Cortisol has been commonly labeled as the stress hormone, and epinephrine is widely known as adrenaline—which triggers the decision to fight rather than withdraw. Bringing these arguments to entrepreneurship, Wolfe and Patel (2017) propose that individuals who have high levels of epinephrine (i.e., adrenaline) are more likely to fight and engage in entrepreneurship provided that they possess low levels of stress as expressed by their decreased levels of cortisol.

In the same line, studies show that the anterior cingulate cortex interacts with the orbitofrontal cortex and the locus coeruleus to affect exploration and exploitation (Aston-Jones & Cohen, 2005; Laureiro-Martínez et al., 2010; Nofal et al., 2018). This evidence shows that exploration and exploitation are associated with interactions between the two brain regions that are responsible for reward-seeking and attentional control (Laureiro-Martínez, Brusoni, Canessa, & Zollo, 2015b). While showing the complexity of entrepreneurial behavior, those interactive influences of biological factors on entrepreneurship could also partly explain why prior studies have failed to detect the specific genetic variants influencing the tendency to engage in entrepreneurship. For example, there could be interactions between genetic factors contributing to the variance of who engages in entrepreneurship.

Future Research

There are a number of research gaps that future studies need to address. For instance, further entrepreneurship variables need to be examined, such as the influence of biology on entrepreneurial biases, entrepreneurs' thinking styles, and their fear of failure. Researchers are also urged to provide further empirical evidence on how biology and environmental factors interact to influence the tendency of people to engage in entrepreneurship (Quaye, Nicolaou, Shane, & Harris, 2012). More empirical work is also needed on how people's biological makeup can drive them to self-select into certain environments to engage in entrepreneurship (Nicolaou & Shane, 2009).

Research pertaining to the specific biological strands is also needed. For example, extant work trying to identify specific genes influencing entrepreneurship has been less successful, with detected genes explaining a very low percentage of the variance of entrepreneurship (Quaye, Nicolaou, Shane, & Mangino, 2012; van der Loos, Rietveld, et al., 2013). These unsuccessful attempts are believed to be due to a number of reasons. First, genes can influence entrepreneurship by interacting with other biological and environmental factors (Nicolaou & Shane, 2009). Second, the effect of genes on complex variables, such as entrepreneurial outcomes, is characterized by being polygenic in nature (Plomin, DeFries, Knopik, & Neiderhiser, 2012). It is unlikely that a single gene would have a large effect on entrepreneurial outcomes but rather that a combination of genes each of a small effect size combine to affect the tendency of people to engage in entrepreneurial outcomes (Quaye, Nicolaou, Shane, & Massimo, 2012). Research on polygenic risk scores may be a useful avenue in this endeavor (e.g. Belsky et al., 2016)).

In addition, empirical studies on hormones and entrepreneurship have only focused on a few hormones, such as testosterone, cortisol, and epinephrine (Nofal et al., 2018; Wolfe & Patel, 2017). Researchers are encouraged to examine the influence of serotonin, dopamine, and oxytocin on entrepreneurship. Serotonin and dopamine contribute to the formation of various personality traits and psychological attitudes, which have been previously related to entrepreneurship, such as sensation-seeking, risk-taking, novelty-seeking, and job satisfaction (Song, Li, & Arvey, 2011). Oxytocin is commonly known as the social bonding and/or the trust hormone as it promotes social networking abilities, with people high in oxytocin more likely to establish trusted social networks and bonds (Algoe, Kurtz, & Grewen, 2017), and therefore more likely to engage in entrepreneurship (Shane & Nicolaou, 2015a). Oxytocin is also famous for its impact on stress regulation (Olff et al., 2013).

Additional research on the neural correlates of entrepreneurship is also required. For instance, although studies have reported that entrepreneurs exhibit distinctive activity in certain regions of the brain relative to their counterparts, we need to know more about the implications of this neural activity for entrepreneurship (Laureiro-Martinez et al., 2014; Nofal et al., 2018; Shane et al., 2019).

Discussion

The goal of this chapter is to bring together research examining the role of genetics, physiology, and neuroscience in entrepreneurship. This literature has been highly fragmented, limiting our ability to comprehensively understand the mechanisms governing the relationship between biology and entrepreneurship (Nofal et al., 2018). Our systematic review shows that the past decade has witnessed a significant rise in work examining the influence of biology on entrepreneurship as well as calls for research in this area. For instance, our review shows that six journals in the past 10 years have called for special issues on the role of biology and/or mental conditions in management: *Academy of Management Perspectives* (Phan & Wright, 2018), *Applied Psychology* (Arvey & Zhen, 2012; Arvey & Zhang, 2015), the *Journal of Business Venturing* (Wiklund, Nikolaev, Shir, Foo, & Bradley, 2019), *Entrepreneurship Theory & Practice* (Nicolaou, Phan, & Stephan, in press), *Leadership Quarterly* (Lee, Senior, & Butler, 2012), and *Organizational Behavior and Human Decision Process* (Shane, 2009). There have also been some special issues calls in nonmanagement journals, such as *Frontiers in Human Neuroscience* (Waldman, 2013).

Studies on the biology of entrepreneurship demonstrate that entrepreneurship is a function not only of environmental factors but also of biological factors. In fact, as researchers argue, "we are all biological creatures and our biology affects all aspects of our behavior, including our work" (Nofal et al., 2018, p. 23). Entrepreneurial outcomes, such as opportunity recognition (Shane et al., 2010a), entrepreneurial intentions, entrepreneurial performance (Patel & Wolfe, in press; Shane & Nicolaou, 2013; Wolfe, Patel, & Drover, 2018), crowdfunding performance (Anglin, Wolfe, Short, McKenny, & Pidduck, 2018), business ownership (Nicolaou, Shane, Cherkas, Hunkin et al., 2008), self-employment. and the tendency to engage in entrepreneurship (Shane & Nicolaou, 2015b; Wolfe & Patel, 2017), have all been shown to be influenced by both biological and environmental factors. These biological factors often play a role in affecting people's psychological traits and attitudes, which, in turn, affect their tendencies to engage in entrepreneurship. These traits include sensation-seeking, openness to experience, creativity, and extraversion.

Moreover, our systematic review shows that different biological strands can jointly play a role in entrepreneurship, such as evidence of gene–gene interactions, gene–hormone interactions (Frank et al., 2009; Quaye, Nicolaou, Shane, & Harris, 2012), and hormone–psychological variables interactions (Unger et al., 2015). Furthermore, evidence of the influence of biology on entrepreneurship suggests that the effect of biology on entrepreneurship is less likely to be direct but likely to partially manifest through other psychological factors and attitudes, such as risk-taking, openness to experience, and sensation-seeking (Bönte et al., 2015; Nicolaou, Shane, Cherkas, & Spector, 2008; Shane et al., 2010a; White et al., 2006).

Conclusion

The biological theory of entrepreneurship is becoming an increasingly important area in the field. This chapter has examined how genetics, physiology, and neuroscience influence the tendencies of people who become entrepreneurs.

This growth is parallel to the growth in the biological perspective in management, where more than 133 journals worldwide have published at least one article on the biological perspective in management during the past few years (Nofal et al., 2018). Yet many gaps still exist and further research is required to boost our understanding of the biological underpinnings of entrepreneurship.

Acknowledgment

We are grateful to Michael Frese and Michael M. Gielnik for their most helpful comments on an earlier version of the paper.

Note

1. Some articles and book chapters are included in more than one biological strand because they examine more than one biological factor.

References

Algoe, S. B., Kurtz, L. E., & Grewen, K. (2017). Oxytocin and social bonds: The role of oxytocin in perceptions of romantic partners' bonding behavior. *Psychological Science*, *28*(12), 1763–1772.

Alrajih, S., & Ward, J. (2014). Increased facial width-to-height ratio and perceived dominance in the faces of the UK's leading business leaders. *British Journal of Psychology*, *105*(2), 153–161. doi:10.1111/bjop.12035

Anglin, A. H., Wolfe, M. T., Short, J. C., McKenny, A. F., & Pidduck, R. J. (2018). Narcissistic rhetoric and crowdfunding performance: A social role theory perspective. *Journal of Business Venturing*, *33*(6), 780–812. Retrieved from https://doi.org/10.1016/j.jbusvent.2018.04.004

Arvey, R. D., Li, W.-D., & Wang, N. (2016). Genetics and organizational behavior. *Annual Review of Organizational Psychology and Organizational Behavior*, *3*(1), 167–190. doi:10.1146/annurev-orgpsych-032414-111251

Arvey, R. D., & Zhang, Z. (2015). Biological factors in organizational behavior and I/O psychology: An introduction to the special section. *Applied Psychology*, *64*(2), 281–285. doi:10.1111/apps.12044

Arvey, R. D., & Zhen, Z. (2012). Applied psychology: An international review special issue; biological factors in organizational behavior and I/O psychology. *Applied Psychology*, *61*(1), 174–176. doi:10.1111/j.1464-0597.2011.00466.x

Aston-Jones, G., & Cohen, J. D. (2005). An integrative theory of locus coeruleus-norepinephrine function: Adaptive gain and optimal performance. *Annual Review of Neuroscience*, *28*, 403–450.

Belsky, D. W., Moffitt, T. E., Corcoran, D. L., Domingue, B., Harrington, H., Hogan, S., . . . Williams, B. S. (2016). The genetics of success: How single-nucleotide polymorphisms associated with educational attainment relate to life-course development. *Psychological Science*, *27*(7), 957–972.

Bönte, W., Procher, V. D., & Urbig, D. (2015). Biology and selection into entrepreneurship: The relevance of prenatal testosterone exposure. *Entrepreneurship Theory and Practice*, *40*(5), 1121–1148. doi:10.1111/etap.12165

Colarelli, S. M., & Arvey, R. D. (2015). *The biological foundations of organizational behavior.* Chicago: University of Chicago Press.

Collins, S., & Karasek, R. (2010). Reduced vagal cardiac control variance in exhausted and high strain job subjects. *International Journal of Occupational Medicine and Environmental Health, 23*(3), 267–278. doi:10.2478/v10001-010-0023-6

de Holan, P. M. (2013). It's all in your head: Why we need neuroentrepreneurship. *Journal of Management Inquiry, 23*(1), 93–97. doi:10.1177/1056492613485913

de Holan, P. M., & Couffe, C. (2017). Unpacking neuroentrepreneurship: Conducting entrepreneurship research with EEG technologies. In *Handbook of research methodologies and design in neuroentrepreneurship.* Cheltenham, UK: Edward Elgar Publishing.

Diallo, B. (2019). Entrepreneurship and genetics: New evidence. *Journal of Business Venturing Insights, 11*, e00123. Retrieved from https://doi.org/10.1016/j.jbvi.2019.e00123

Duncan, L. E., Ostacher, M., & Ballon, J. (2019). How genome-wide association studies (GWAS) made traditional candidate gene studies obsolete. *Neuropsychopharmacology: Official Publication of the American College of Neuropsychopharmacology, 44*(9), 1518–1523.

Frank, M. J., Doll, B. B., Oas-Terpstra, J., & Moreno, F. (2009). Prefrontal and striatal dopaminergic genes predict individual differences in exploration and exploitation. *Nature Neuroscience, 12*(8), 1062–1068. doi:10.1038/nn.2342

Greene, F. J., Han, L., Martin, S., Zhang, S., & Wittert, G. (2014). Testosterone is associated with self-employment among Australian men. *Economics and Human Biology, 13*, 76–84. doi:10.1016/j.ehb.2013.02.003

Guedes, M. J., Nicolaou, N., & Patel, P. C. (2019). Genetic distance and the difference in new firm entry between countries. *Journal of Evolutionary Economics.* doi:10.1007/s00191-019-00613-2

Guiso, L., & Rustichini, A. (2011a). Understanding the size and profitability of firms: The role of a biological factor. *CEPR Discussion Paper* (DP8205). Retrieved from SSRN: https://ssrn.com/abstract=1749846

Guiso, L., & Rustichini, A. (2011b). What drives women out of entrepreneurship? The joint role of testosterone and culture. Paper presented at the *CEPR Discussion Paper.*

Hannah, S. T., Balthazard, P. A., Waldman, D. A., Jennings, P. L., & Thatcher, R. W. (2013). The psychological and neurological bases of leader self-complexity and effects on adaptive decision-making. *Journal of Applied Psychology, 98*(3), 393–411. doi:10.1037/a0032257

Henrekson, M., & Sanandaji, T. (2014). Small business activity does not measure entrepreneurship. *Proceedings of the National Academy of Sciences, 111*(5), 1760–1765.

Johnson, S. K., Fitza, M. A., Lerner, D. A., Calhoun, D. M., Beldon, M. A., Chan, E. T., & Johnson, P. T. (2018). Risky business: Linking toxoplasma gondii infection and entrepreneurship behaviours across individuals and countries. *Proceedings of the Royal Society B: Biological Sciences, 285*(1883), 20180822.

Johnson, W. (2009). So what or so everything? Bringing behavior genetics to entrepreneurship research. *Journal of Business Venturing, 24*(1), 23–26. doi:10.1016/j.jbusvent.2007.11.002

Koellinger, P. D., van der Loos, M. J. H. M., Groenen, P. J. F., Thurik, A. R., Rivadeneira, F., van Rooij, F. J. A., ... Hofman, A. (2010). Genome-wide association studies in economics and entrepreneurship research: Promises and limitations. *Small Business Economics, 35*(1), 1–18. doi:10.1007/s11187-010-9286-3

Krueger, N., & Welpe, I. (2014). Neuroentrepreneurship: What can entrepreneurship learn from neuroscience? *Annals of entrepreneurship education and pedagogy.* Cheltenham, UK: Edward Elgar Publishing.

Kuechle, G. (2019). The contribution of behavior genetics to entrepreneurship: An evolutionary perspective. *Journal of Evolutionary Economics,* 1–22.

Lahti, T., Halko, M.-L., Karagozoglu, N., & Wincent, J. (2018). Why and how do founding entrepreneurs bond with their ventures? Neural correlates of entrepreneurial and parental bonding. *Journal of Business Venturing.* Retrieved from https://doi.org/10.1016/j.jbusvent.2018.05.001

Lahti, T., Halko, M.-L., Karagozoglu, N., & Wincent, J. (2019). Why and how do founding entrepreneurs bond with their ventures? Neural correlates of entrepreneurial and parental bonding. *Journal of Business Venturing, 34*(2), 368–388. Retrieved from https://doi.org/10.1016/j.jbusvent.2018.05.001

Laureiro-Martínez, D., Brusoni, S., Canessa, N., & Zollo, M. (2015a). Understanding the exploration-exploitation dilemma: An fMRI study of attention control and decision-making performance. *Strategic Management Journal, 36*(3), 319–338. doi:10.1002/smj.2221

Laureiro-Martínez, D., Brusoni, S., Canessa, N., & Zollo, M. (2015b). Understanding the exploration-exploitation dilemma: An fMRI study of attention control and decision-making performance. *Strategic Management Journal, 36*(3), 319–338. doi:10.1002/smj.2221

Laureiro-Martínez, D., Brusoni, S., & Zollo, M. (2010). The neuroscientific foundations of the exploration–exploitation dilemma. *Journal of Neuroscience, Psychology, and Economics, 3*(2), 95–115. doi:10.1037/a0018495

Laureiro-Martinez, D., Canessa, N., Brusoni, S., Zollo, M., Hare, T., Alemanno, F., & Cappa, S. F. (2014). Frontopolar cortex and decision-making efficiency: Comparing brain activity of experts with different professional background during an exploration-exploitation task. *Frontiers in Human Neuroscience, 7*, 927. doi:10.3389/fnhum.2013.00927

Laureiro-Martínez, D., Venkatraman, V., Cappa, S., Zollo, M., & Brusoni, S. (2015). Cognitive neurosciences and strategic management: Challenges and opportunities in tying the knot. In *Cognition and strategy* (Vol. 32, pp. 351–370). Bingley, UK: Emerald Group Publishing Limited.

Lee, N., Butler, M. J., & Senior, C. (2008). The brain in business: The case for organizational cognitive neuroscience? *Nature Precedings.* Retrieved from https://doi.org/10.1038/npre.2008.2159.1.

Lee, N., Senior, C., & Butler, M. (2012). Leadership research and cognitive neuroscience: The state of this union. *The Leadership Quarterly, 23*(2), 213–218. Retrieved from http://dx.doi.org/10.1016/j.leaqua.2011.08.001

Lindquist, M. J., Sol, J., & Van Praag, M. (2015). Why do entrepreneurial parents have entrepreneurial children? *Journal of Labor Economics, 33*(2), 269–296. doi:10.1086/678493

Massaro, S. (2015). Neuroscientific methods for strategic management. *Research Methods for Strategic Management*, 253.

McMullen, J. S., Wood, M. S., & Palich, L. E. (2014). Entrepreneurial cognition and social cognitive neuroscience. *Handbook of Entrepreneurial Cognition, 29*, 723–740.

Nejati, V., & Shahidi, S. (2013). Does the ability to make a new business need more risky choices during decisions? Evidences for the neurocognitive basis of entrepreneurship. *Basic and Clinical Neuroscience, 4*(4), 287–290.

Nicolaou, N., Lockett, A., Ucbasaran, D., & Rees, G. (2019). Exploring the potential and limits of a neuroscientific approach to entrepreneurship. *International Small Business Journal: Researching Entrepreneurship, 37*(6), 557–580. doi:10.1177/0266242619843234

Nicolaou, N., Patel, P. C., & Wolfe, M. T. (2017). Testosterone and tendency to engage in self-employment. *Management Science, 64*(4).

Nicolaou, N., Patel, P. C., & Wolfe, M. T. (2018). Testosterone and tendency to engage in self-employment. *Management Science, 64*(4), 1825–1841. doi:10.1287/mnsc.2016.2664

Nicolaou, N., Phan, P., & Stephan, U. (in press). Entrepreneurship and biology. *Entrepreneurship Theory and Practice*.

Nicolaou, N., & Shane, S. (2009). Can genetic factors influence the likelihood of engaging in entrepreneurial activity? *Journal of Business Venturing, 24*(1), 1–22. doi:10.1016/j.jbusvent.2007.11.003

Nicolaou, N., & Shane, S. (2010). Entrepreneurship and occupational choice: Genetic and environmental influences. *Journal of Economic Behavior & Organization, 76*(1), 3–14. doi:10.1016/j.jebo.2010.02.009

Nicolaou, N., & Shane, S. (2011). The genetics of entrepreneurship. In *Handbook of research on innovation and entrepreneurship*. Cheltenham, UK: Edward Elgar Publishing, Inc.

Nicolaou, N., & Shane, S. (2013). Biology, neuroscience, and entrepreneurship. *Journal of Management Inquiry, 23*(1), 98–100. doi:10.1177/1056492613485914

Nicolaou, N., Shane, S., Adi, G., Mangino, M., & Harris, J. (2011). A polymorphism associated with entrepreneurship: Evidence from dopamine receptor candidate genes. *Small Business Economics, 36*(2), 151–155. doi:10.1007/s11187-010-9308-1

Nicolaou, N., Shane, S., Cherkas, L., Hunkin, J., & Spector, T. D. (2008). Is the tendency to engage in entrepreneurship genetic? *Management Science, 54*(1), 167–179. doi:10.1287/mnsc.1070.0761

Nicolaou, N., Shane, S., Cherkas, L., & Spector, T. D. (2008). The influence of sensation seeking in the heritability of entrepreneurship. *Strategic Entrepreneurship Journal, 2*(1), 7–21. doi:10.1002/sej.37

Nicolaou, N., Shane, S., Cherkas, L., & Spector, T. D. (2009). Opportunity recognition and the tendency to be an entrepreneur: A bivariate genetics perspective. *Organizational Behavior and Human Decision Processes, 110*(2), 108–117. doi:10.1016/j.obhdp.2009.08.005

Nofal, A. M., Nicolaou, N., & Symeonidou, N. (2017). Biology and entrepreneurship. In G. Ahmetoglu, T. Chamorro-Premuzic, B. Klinger, & T. Karcisky (Eds.), *The Wiley handbook of entrepreneurship*. New York: John Wiley & Sons.

Nofal, A. M., Nicolaou, N., Symeonidou, N., & Shane, S. (2018). Biology and management: A review, critique, and research agenda. *Journal of Management, 44*(1), 7–31. doi:10.1177/0149206317720723

Olff, M., Frijling, J. L., Kubzansky, L. D., Bradley, B., Ellenbogen, M. A., Cardoso, C., . . . van Zuiden, M. (2013). The role of oxytocin in social bonding, stress regulation and mental health: An update on the moderating effects of context and interindividual differences. *Psychoneuroendocrinology, 38*(9), 1883–1894. Retrieved from https://doi.org/10.1016/j.psyneuen.2013.06.019

Patel, P. C., & Wolfe, M. T. (in press). In the eye of the beholder? The returns to beauty and IQ for the self-employed. *Strategic Entrepreneurship Journal*. doi:10.1002/sej.1323

Pérez-Centeno, V. (2017). Brain-driven entrepreneurship research: A review and research agenda. In *Handbook of research methodologies and design in neuroentrepreneurship*. Cheltenham, UK: Edward Elgar Publishing.

Pérez-Centeno, V. (2018). Brain-driven entrepreneurship research: Expanded review and research agenda towards entrepreneurial enhancement. *Working Paper*.

Phan, P., & Wright, M. (2018). Advancing the science of human cognition and behavior. *Academy of Management Perspectives, 32*(3), 287–289. doi:10.5465/amp.2018.0058

Plomin, R., DeFries, J. C., Knopik, V. S., & Neiderhiser, J. M. (2012). *Behavioral genetics*. New York: Worth Publishers.

Quaye, L., Nicolaou, N., Shane, S., & Harris, J. (2012). A study of gene-environment interactions in entrepreneurship. *Entrepreneurship Research Journal, 2*(2). doi:10.1515/2157-5665.1053

Quaye, L., Nicolaou, N., Shane, S., & Mangino, M. (2012). A discovery genome-wide association study of entrepreneurship. *International Journal of Developmental Science, 6,* 127–135.

Quaye, L., Nicolaou, N., Shane, S., & Massimo, M. (2012). A discovery genome-wide association study of entrepreneurship. *International Journal of Developmental Science, 6,* 127–135.

Rietveld, C. A., van Kippersluis, H., & Thurik, A. R. (2014). Self-employment and health: Barriers or benefits? *Health Economics.* doi:10.1002/hec.3087

Schermer, J. A., Johnson, A. M., Jang, K. L., & Vernon, P. A. (2015). Phenotypic, genetic, and environmental relationships between self-reported talents and measured intelligence. *Twin Research and Human Genetics, 18*(1), 36–42. doi:10.1017/thg.2014.80

Shane, S. (2009). Introduction to the focused issue on the biological basis of business. *Organizational Behavior and Human Decision Processes, 110*(2), 67–69. doi:10.1016/j. obhdp.2009.10.001

Shane, S. (2010). *Born entrepreneurs, born leaders: How your genes affect your work life.* New York: Oxford University Press.

Shane, S., Drover, W., Clingingsmith, D., & Cerf, M. (2019). Founder passion, neural engagement and informal investor interest in startup pitches: An fMRI study. *Journal of Business Venturing,* 105949.

Shane, S., & Nicolaou, N. (2013). The genetics of entrepreneurial performance. *International Small Business Journal: Researching Entrepreneurship, 31*(5), 473–495. doi:10.1177/0266242613485767

Shane, S., & Nicolaou, N. (2015a). The biological basis of entrepreneurship. In S. M. Colarelli & R. D. Arvey (Eds.), *The biological foundations of organizational behavior.* Chicago: University of Chicago Press.

Shane, S., & Nicolaou, N. (2015b). Creative personality, opportunity recognition and the tendency to start businesses: A study of their genetic predispositions. *Journal of Business Venturing, 30*(3), 407–419. doi:10.1016/j.jbusvent.2014.04.001

Shane, S., Nicolaou, N., Cherkas, L., & Spector, T. D. (2010a). Do openness to experience and recognizing opportunities have the same genetic source? *Human Resource Management, 49*(2), 291–303. doi:10.1002/hrm.20343

Shane, S., Nicolaou, N., Cherkas, L., & Spector, T. D. (2010b). Genetics, the Big Five, and the tendency to be self-employed. *Journal of Applied Psychology, 95*(6), 1154–1162. doi:10.1037/a0020294

Song, Z., Li, W., & Arvey, R. D. (2011). Associations between dopamine and serotonin genes and job satisfaction: Preliminary evidence from the Add Health Study. *Journal of Applied Psychology, 96*(6), 1223–1233. Retrieved from http://dx.doi.org/10.1037/a0024577

Sundararajan, M. (2010). Physiological emotions and entrepreneurial decisions. *Global Business and Management Research: An International Journal, 2*(4), 310–322.

Tomasino, D. (2007). The psychophysiological basis of creativity and intuition: Accessing "the zone" of entrepreneurship. *International Journal of Entrepreneurship and Small Business, 4*(5), 528–542. doi:10.1504/ijesb.2007.014388

Tracey, P., & Schluppeck, D. (2013). Neuroentreprenuership: "Brain pornography" or new frontier in entrepreneurship research? *Journal of Management Inquiry, 23*(1), 101–103. doi:10.1177/1056492613485915

Trahms, C. A., Coombs, J. E., & Barrick, M. (2010). Does biology matter? How prenatal testosterone, entrepreneur risk propensity, and entrepreneur risk perceptions influence venture performance. [Aufsatz im Buch, Article in book]. *Frontiers of Entrepreneurship Research 2010: Proceedings of the Thirtieth Annual Entrepreneurship Research Conference,* 217–229.

Tranfield, D., Denyer, D., & Smart, P. (2003). Towards a methodology for developing evidence-informed management knowledge by means of systematic review. *British Journal of Management, 14*(3), 207–222. doi:10.1111/1467-8551.00375

Unger, J. M., Rauch, A., Narayanan, J., Weis, S., & Frese, M. (2009). Does prenatal testosterone predict entrepreneurial success? Relationships of 2D: 4D and business success (summary). *Frontiers of Entrepreneurship Research, 29*(5), 15.

Unger, J. M., Rauch, A., Weis, S. E., & Frese, M. (2015). Biology (prenatal testosterone), psychology (achievement need) and entrepreneurial impact. *Journal of Business Venturing Insights, 4,* 1–5. Retrieved from http://dx.doi.org/10.1016/j.jbvi.2015.05.001

van der Loos, M. J. H. M., Haring, R., Rietveld, C. A., Baumeister, S. E., Groenen, P. J. F., Hofman, A., . . . Thurik, A. R. (2013). Serum testosterone levels in males are not associated with entrepreneurial behavior in two independent observational studies. *Physiology and Behavior, 119,* 110–114. doi:10.1016/j.physbeh.2013.06.003

van der Loos, M. J. H. M., Koellinger, P. D., Groenen, P. J. F., Rietveld, C. A., Rivadeneira, F., van Rooij, F. J. A., . . . Thurik, A. R. (2011). Candidate gene studies and the quest for the entrepreneurial gene. *Small Business Economics, 37*(3), 269–275. doi:10.1007/s11187-011-9339-2

van der Loos, M. J. H. M., Koellinger, P. D., Groenen, P. J. F., & Thurik, A. R. (2010). Genome-wide association studies and the genetics of entrepreneurship. *European Journal of Epidemiology, 25*(1), 1–3.

van der Loos, M. J. H. M., Rietveld, C. A., Eklund, N., Koellinger, P. D., Rivadeneira, F., Abecasis, G. R., . . . Thurik, A. R. (2013). The molecular genetic architecture of self-employment. *PLoS One, 8*(4), e60542. doi:10.1371/journal.pone.0060542

Waldman, D. A. (2013). Interdisciplinary research is the key. *Frontiers in Human Neuroscience, 7,* 562. doi:10.3389/fnhum.2013.00562

Weis, S. E., Firker, A., & Hennig, J. (2007). Associations between the second to fourth digit ratio and career interests. *Personality and Individual Differences, 43*(3), 485–493. doi:10.1016/j.paid.2006.12.017

Wernerfelt, N., Rand, D. G., Dreber, A., Montgomery, C., & Malhotra, D. K. (2012). Arginine Vasopressin 1a Receptor (AVPR1a) RS3 repeat polymorphism associated with entrepreneurship. Retrieved from SSRN: https://ssrn.com/abstract=2141598 or http://dx.doi.org/10.2139/ssrn.2141598

White, R. E., Thornhill, S., & Hampson, E. (2006). Entrepreneurs and evolutionary biology: The relationship between testosterone and new venture creation. *Organizational Behavior and Human Decision Processes, 100*(1), 21–34. doi:10.1016/j.obhdp.2005.11.001

White, R. E., Thornhill, S., & Hampson, E. (2007). A biosocial model of entrepreneurship: The combined effects of nurture and nature. *Journal of Organizational Behavior, 28*(4), 451–466. doi:10.1002/job.432

Wiklund, J., Nikolaev, B., Shir, N., Foo, M.-D., & Bradley, S. (2019). Entrepreneurship and well-being: Past, present, and future. *Journal of Business Venturing, 34*(4), 579–588. Retrieved from https://doi.org/10.1016/j.jbusvent.2019.01.002

Wolfe, M. T., & Patel, P. C. (2017). Two are better than one: Cortisol as a contingency in the association between epinephrine and self-employment. *Journal of Business Venturing Insights, 8,* 78–86. Retrieved from https://doi.org/10.1016/j.jbvi.2017.07.002

Wolfe, M. T., & Patel, P. C. (2018). Racing to get self-employed? Life history models and self-employment. *Journal of Business Venturing Insights, 10,* e00093. Retrieved from https://doi.org/10.1016/j.jbvi.2018.e00093

Wolfe, M. T., Patel, P. C., & Drover, W. (2018). The influence of hypomania symptoms on income in self-employment. *Entrepreneurship Theory and Practice*, 1042258718807175. doi:10.1177/1042258718807175

Zhang, Z., Ilies, R., & Arvey, R. D. (2009). Beyond genetic explanations for leadership: The moderating role of the social environment. *Organizational Behavior and Human Decision Processes*, *110*(2), 118–128. Retrieved from http://dx.doi.org/10.1016/j.obhdp.2009.06.004

Zhang, Z., Ilies, R., & Arvey, R. D. (2010). Moderating effects of earlier family environment on genetic influences on entrepreneurship. *Behavior Genetics*, *40*(6), 821.

Zhang, Z., Zyphur, M. J., Narayanan, J., Arvey, R. D., Chaturvedi, S., Avolio, B. J., . . . Larsson, G. (2009). The genetic basis of entrepreneurship: Effects of gender and personality. *Organizational Behavior and Human Decision Processes*, *110*(2), 93–107. Retrieved from http://dx.doi.org/10.1016/j.obhdp.2009.07.002

Zunino, D. (2016). Are genetics and environment substitutes or complements in affecting entrepreneurial choice? *Academy of Management Proceedings*, *2016*(1), 12173. doi:10.5465/ambpp.2016.12173abstract

6

WHERE THE MAGIC HAPPENS

Opening the Black Box of Entrepreneurial Team Functioning

Nicola Breugst & Rebecca Preller

Introduction

While entrepreneurship research has traditionally implied that a new venture is founded by a 'lonely hero,' (i.e., a solo entrepreneur leading and developing his or her venture), research has started to acknowledge that many new ventures are founded by entrepreneurial teams rather than individuals (Klotz, Hmieleski, Bradley, & Busenitz, 2014; Lazar et al., 2020). For example, Wasserman (2012) reports that in his sample, only 17.5% of technology ventures and 11.7% of life sciences ventures were founded by solo entrepreneurs. Entrepreneurial teams are formed by "two or more individuals who pursue a new business idea, are involved in its subsequent management, and share ownership" (Lazar et al., 2020, p. 29). Importantly, entrepreneurial teams can form via different paths: Lead entrepreneurs might recruit teammates for their idea or teams can jointly develop an idea for their venture (Lazar et al., 2020). Independent of the presence of a strong lead entrepreneur, these teams work in a highly interdependent way (Blatt, 2009; A. de Jong, M. Song, & L. Z. Song, 2013). Since teams are "chiefly responsible for the strategic decision making and ongoing operations of a new venture" (Klotz et al., 2014, p. 227), it is crucial to understand how entrepreneurial teams function to understand new venture development.

To date, research on entrepreneurial teams has mainly taken an upper echelons perspective, focusing on team members' characteristics and their impact on ventures (Jin et al., 2017). Inspired by research on top management teams (Carpenter, Geletkanycz, & Sanders, 2004), this stream of research focuses on a range of demographic and 'observable' factors of entrepreneurial teams (Jin et al., 2017; Klotz et al., 2014). For example, previous research has addressed the question of how venture outcomes are shaped by various types of prior experience, such as functional experience (e.g., Amason, Shrader, & Tompson, 2006), educational background (e.g., Foo, Sin, & Yiong, 2006; Hmieleski & Ensley, 2007), and entrepreneurial experience (e.g., Brannon, Wiklund, & Haynie, 2013). Moreover, beyond focusing on aggregated characteristics, this stream of research includes different experience constellations within teams, such as heterogeneity in characteristics (e.g., Souitaris & Maestro, 2010; Tzabbar & Margolis, 2017) and shared (i.e., jointly made) experiences (e.g., Zheng, 2012; Zheng, DeVaughn, & Zellmer-Bruhn, 2016). Entrepreneurial team research includes not only broad human capital–related measures but also more specific capabilities, such as teamwork capabilities and relational capabilities (Brinckmann & Hoegl, 2011), which are also linked to venture performance. Furthermore, research analyzes which competence sets entrepreneurial team members prefer in potential cofounders depending on their own experience (Kollmann, Häsel, & Breugst, 2009) as well as product characteristics (Häsel, Kollmann, & Breugst, 2010). Following the same tradition, research also explores entrepreneurial team characteristics appreciated by investors, such as team experience and prior affiliations (Beckman, Burton, & O'Reilly, 2007).

While this research provides crucial insights into entrepreneurial team composition by connecting inputs to important venture outcomes, it creates a "black box" (Klotz et al., 2014, p. 248) because we do not sufficiently understand how entrepreneurial teams translate these inputs into outcomes. Consequently, findings on team member characteristics and their effects on performance outcomes are equivocal. For example, Jin et al. (2017) review 47 studies on the relationship between team members' aggregated human capital and venture performance, finding positive, nonsignificant, and even negative effects. Across these studies, the meta-analysis reveals a positive relationship. Yet, the authors note that the lack of more nuanced insights limits our detailed understanding of the relationship between team member characteristics and performance. Extending this research tradition, an increasing number of studies relying on primary data promise a finer-grained understanding of *how* team characteristics are translated into venture outcomes. This 'translation' is the focus of this chapter and clearly demonstrates how (social) psychology can contribute to entrepreneurial team research.

Prior work in social psychology as well as in organizational behavior has offered two main categories to understand this translation: team processes and team emergent states (Ilgen, Hollenbeck, Johnson, & Jundt, 2005; Mathieu, Maynard, Rapp, & Gilson, 2008). Team processes (Mathieu et al., 2008) refer to "members' interdependent acts that convert inputs to outcomes through cognitive, verbal, and behavioral activities" (Marks, Mathieu, & Zaccaro, 2001, p. 357). In contrast, emergent states "represent member attitudes, values, cognitions, and motivations . . . that are typically dynamic in nature" (Marks et al., 2001, p. 357). The relevance of these two categories is also echoed in entrepreneurial team research (de Mol, Khapova, & Elfring, 2015; Klotz et al., 2014), which provides a rich theoretical basis for understanding how entrepreneurial team members work together and how they think about and feel toward their teams. Specifically, *entrepreneurial team functioning*—teams' processes, emergent states, and outcomes (Ilgen et al., 2005)—has great potential for entrepreneurship research. Given these opportunities, this chapter focuses on entrepreneurial team functioning and consolidates current (still-fragmented) insights to develop a research agenda on entrepreneurial team functioning.

Methodology

We followed a formal review process, including compiling a comprehensive collection of previous studies, synthesizing them, and outlining future research (Short, 2009). We included all papers on entrepreneurial teams that were published between January 2008 and December 2019 and were either listed in previous reviews[1] (Bolzani, Fini, Napolitano, & Toschi, 2019; de Mol et al., 2015; Klotz et al., 2014) or identified by searching in databases for relevant articles in leading management, entrepreneurship, and organizational behavior journals.[2] This search resulted in 83 articles. Next, together with two research assistants, we coded these articles to determine whether they focus on entrepreneurial team functioning and analyzed further aspects (e.g., key constructs). For the inclusion decision, we relied on a comprehensive assessment of the articles' content. To ensure accuracy, we discussed codes intensively until we reached full agreement. Finally, we agreed to include 26 articles in the review. We further coded these articles into task-related and interpersonal processes, on one hand, and cognitive and affective emergent states, on the other hand.

Entrepreneurial Team Functioning

When developing a venture, entrepreneurial team members need to interact continuously and interdependently (A. de Jong et al., 2013). While our understanding of entrepreneurial team functioning is still limited, an increasing number of studies provides important insights on this topic. These articles can be categorized with respect to their focus: task-related and interpersonal processes, on one hand, and cognitive and affective emergent states, on the other hand.

Entrepreneurial Team Processes

Team processes can be differentiated into task-related and interpersonal processes. While task-related processes describe teams' interactions with their tasks, including executing and monitoring them, teams use interpersonal processes to manage intrateam relationships (Marks et al., 2001). Extant research on entrepreneurial teams mainly investigates task-related processes in terms of decision-making and learning as well as on interpersonal processes in terms of conflict within teams.

Task-Related Processes

An important task-related process in entrepreneurial team research is entrepreneurial learning. Chandler and Lyon (2009) distinguish between different types of learning and link them to venture performance. They find that experiential learning (i.e., based on prior experience) as well as vicarious learning (i.e., based on observing others) is positively related to venture performance. They also show that these effects are stronger when environmental dynamism is high, consistent with the increasing cognitive demands arising from a quickly changing environment. Focusing on knowledge transfer in academic spinoffs, Knockaert, Ucbasaran, Wright, and Clarysse (2011) highlight that tacit knowledge transfer works better for teams in which the original scientists play a major role but individuals with a commercial mindset are also represented. Importantly, between both groups (i.e., scientists and individuals with commercial knowledge), cognitive distance should be rather small (Knockaert et al., 2011). Other studies investigate entrepreneurial learning as an outcome. For example, Sardana and Scott-Kemmis (2010) reveal that entrepreneurs learn most when they take on a challenging role outside of the scope of their prior experience but the entrepreneurial team possesses the necessary knowledge and thus provides a rich learning context. Furthermore, Rauter, Weiss, and Hoegl (2018) show that teams' negative affective reactions to setbacks have a complex relationship with their self-assessed team learning: If teams engage in high levels of reflexivity, they learn after a setback, whereas learning is reduced if they engage in low levels of reflexivity.

Taking a broader perspective on entrepreneurial teams and entrepreneurial action, Harper's classic theoretical paper (2008) describes entrepreneurial teams as actors that discover, evaluate, and exploit opportunities. However, despite his call for empirical research, his propositions have not been tested systematically along the process from opportunity recognition to exploitation. Thus, with respect to entrepreneurship-specific tasks, research mainly studies initial opportunity recognition investigating the role of team experience (Gruber, MacMillan, & Thompson, 2012, 2013) and affect (Perry-Smith & Coff, 2011). The study by Preller, Patzelt, and Breugst (2020) identifies differences in how entrepreneurial teams develop opportunities, contrasting focused and comprehensive opportunity-development paths. Specifically, team members' congruent visions lead teams to develop their opportunities in small and infrequent steps, whereas team members' incongruent visions are connected to substantial changes in their opportunities.

Entrepreneurial decision-making has been extensively studied at the individual level (Shepherd, Williams, & Patzelt, 2015). While some early work on entrepreneurial teams has shed light on the process of entrepreneurial team decision-making (e.g., Bourgeois & Eisenhardt, 1988; Eisenhardt, 1989; Eisenhardt & Schoonhoven, 1990), the studies in the period covered in this review mainly focus on the link between team composition and decision-making. For example, Chaganti, Watts,

Chaganti, and Zimmerman-Treichel (2008) find that teams that include ethnic immigrants are more likely to make more aggressive decisions than teams with non-ethnic/non-immigrant team members. Specifically, ethnically diverse teams tend to seek more opportunities for growth. The study by Souitaris and Maestro (2010) links team composition and venture outcomes by including team processes. They focus on polychronicity among team members—that is, "the extent to which TMT [top management team] members mutually prefer and tend to engage in multiple tasks simultaneously or intermittently instead of one at a time and believe that this is the best way of doing things" (Souitaris & Maestro, 2010, p. 653). Higher levels of polychronicity increase venture performance, and this relationship is partially mediated by decision speed and comprehensiveness.

While all these studies have significantly contributed to our understanding of how entrepreneurial teams' activities transform inputs into outcomes, there are many task-related processes in team research that have not received sufficient attention in entrepreneurial team research, such as coordination (Harrison & Rouse, 2014) and monitoring (B. A. de Jong & Elfring, 2010). Further, although a plethora of individual-level work has focused on the role of business planning (Brinckmann, Grichnik, & Kapsa, 2010) and action planning (Frese et al., 2007; Gielnik, Barabas et al., 2014), there are no insights into the role of teamwork planning—that is, "the development of alternative courses of action for mission accomplishment" (Marks et al., 2001, p. 365)—despite its important role as a team process (Fisher, 2014).

Interpersonal Processes

Research on interpersonal processes in entrepreneurial teams mainly focuses on conflict within teams and the associated consequences. In line with the general literature on team conflict (de Wit, Greer, & Jehn, 2012), research on conflict in entrepreneurial teams highlights that (1) cognitive conflict positively influences venture performance outcomes[3] (A. de Jong et al., 2013; Vanaelst et al., 2006), (2) affective conflict negatively affects venture performance (A. de Jong et al., 2013; Ensley, Pearson, & Amason, 2002), and (3) affective conflict promotes team member exit (Vanaelst et al., 2006). Studying entrepreneurial affect as a more proximal outcome of team conflict, Breugst and Shepherd (2017) show that in a field setting, both types of conflict increase entrepreneurial team members' negative affect, whereas in a lab setting, affective conflict increases and cognitive conflict reduces team members' negative affect. Consistent with attribution theory (Weiner, 1985), uncertainty buffers these affective reactions, while satisfaction with the team intensifies them. Other work investigates entrepreneurial team conflict as an outcome of venture-related events (Forbes, Korsgaard, & Sapienza, 2010), showing that financial devaluations of ventures result in increased affective conflict compared to up-round financings. Finally, the study by Breugst, Patzelt, and Rathgeber (2015) identifies not only negative, conflict-laden team interaction spirals but also positive spirals increasing intrateam attraction triggered by the perceived (in)justice of equity distribution. In turn, these spirals shape team and venture performance.

Unfortunately, research on interpersonal processes in entrepreneurial teams is rather limited. This lack of research is surprising because entrepreneurial teams working without organizational boundaries and supervisors need to define and manage their intrateam relationships by themselves. For example, research on self-managing teams studies the role of team charters—namely, "a formal document written by team members at the outset of a team's life cycle that specifies acceptable behaviors in the team" (Courtright, McCormick, Mistry, Jiexin, & Wang, 2017, p. 1462)—as a way of helping teams manage and structure their teamwork. Courtright et al. (2017) find that high-quality team charters have a positive effect on team performance via cohesion, particularly in teams with members scoring low in conscientiousness. In the field of leadership, supportive leaders can help teams translate their team cohesion into more innovative outcomes (Janssen, Kostopoulos, Mihalache, & Papalexandris, 2016). But insights on intrateam management, mutual support, and social processes within entrepreneurial teams are sparse. A recent study exploring social motivation in entrepreneurial teams and the contagion of entrepreneurial effort demonstrates that teammates' effort can indeed be contagious if entrepreneurial team members are confronted with threats, specifically low venture performance and high environmental hostility (Breugst, Patzelt, & Shepherd, in press). Beyond these findings inside and outside of entrepreneurial team research, we need a better understanding how entrepreneurial team members mutually support and motivate each other and how they provide rewards as well as sanctions to each other.

Entrepreneurial Team Emergent States

While team processes describe teams' activities, emergent states refer to "member attitudes, values, cognitions, and motivations" (Marks et al., 2001, p. 357). The entrepreneurial team literature mainly explores cognitive and affective emergent states. We highlight the key insights from these streams of research in the following sections.

Entrepreneurial Team Cognitive States

Extant research on cognition in the entrepreneurial context has mainly taken an individual-level perspective, with only a few studies investigating the link between team cognition and performance (Grégoire, Corbett, & McMullen, 2011). Based on a comprehensive literature review of entrepreneurial team cognition, de Mol et al. (2015, p. 243) define entrepreneurial team cognition as

> an emergent state that refers to the manner in which knowledge is mentally organized, represented and distributed within the team and allows

entrepreneurial team members to approach problem-solving and make assessments, judgments or decisions concerned with milestones and outcomes relevant to the entrepreneurial process, such as identifying and evaluating different opportunities, or defining and implementing launch and growth strategies.

Importantly, entrepreneurial team cognition does not emerge as the sum of individual cognitions held by team members but "arises from complex interactions among (cognitions) of individual members of an entrepreneurial team" and "varies as a function of team context, inputs, processes, and outcomes" (de Mol et al., 2015, p. 240).

Entrepreneurial team cognition has been studied using many different concepts, such as strategic consensus (Vissa & Chacar, 2009), team creative cognition (Shalley & Perry-Smith, 2008), and transactive memory systems (Zheng, 2012; Zheng & Mai, 2013). For example, the theoretical paper by Shalley and Perry-Smith (2008) proposes that individual team members' diverse networks shape how teams collectively address problems in a creative way. The study by Vissa and Chacar (2009) focuses on the interplay between entrepreneurial teams' network characteristics and team members' consensus and the resulting effect on ventures' strategies and goals. Studies on transactive memory systems not only show their positive effects on team (Zheng & Mai, 2013) and venture outcomes (Dai, Roundy, Chok, Ding, & Byun, 2016; Zheng, 2012) but also suggest that these relationships are contingent on the task and venture context. While all these studies provide specific and interesting insights, the different constructs subsumed under entrepreneurial team cognition and their different operationalizations limit the comparability of results and prevent us from developing a more abstract pattern (de Mol et al., 2015).

Another interesting challenge arising in research on entrepreneurial team cognition is its dynamic nature (Lewis & Herndon, 2011; Shalley & Perry-Smith, 2008). While previous research has mainly taken a static perspective when studying entrepreneurial team cognition, the study by Perry-Smith and Coff (2011) highlights the importance of studying entrepreneurial team cognition over time. The authors demonstrate that for different stages in the entrepreneurial process (i.e., idea generation and selection), different moods are conducive to the process (Perry-Smith & Coff, 2011).

While an individual's identity is partly based on his or her social cognition (Ellemers, Spears, & Doosje, 2002; Hogg & Terry, 2000), we have hardly any insights into entrepreneurial team identity despite the growing number of studies on entrepreneurial identity at the individual level (e.g., Fauchart & Gruber, 2011; Grimes, 2018; Mathias & Williams, 2018). This lack of research is surprising given that "individual cognitions about identity ("I think") facilitate the emergence of shared cognitions ("we think")" (Ashforth, Rogers, & Corley, 2011, p. 1146). As an exception, the inductive study by Powell and Baker (2017) analyzes how entrepreneurial team members' identities flow into a prototype of a collective identity that shapes team and venture development. Importantly, the entrepreneurial team members and ventures in their sample all have a community-oriented purpose. Thus, future research could complement these insights and explore how team identity forms and shapes a venture's vision or mission in other contexts.

Entrepreneurial Team Affective States

Typically, research on entrepreneurial teams focuses more on team cognition and less on teams' affective states. According to a review by Mathieu et al. (2008, p. 428) on general team research, one of the most studied affective emergent states is team cohesion—"the commitment of team members to the team's overall task or to each other." Consistent with cohesion's importance for team research, early studies on entrepreneurial teams also explore team cohesion, showing its positive consequences for ventures (Ensley & Hmieleski, 2005; Ensley et al., 2002). Moreover, cohesion helps teams benefit from individual members' resources (Vissa & Chacar, 2009).

Further entrepreneurial team research related to affect typically builds on work at the individual level, bringing it to the team level. For example, while entrepreneurs' passion is extensively studied at the individual level (Cardon & Kirk, 2015; Gielnik, Spitzmuller, Schmitt, Klemann, & Frese, 2014; Ho & Pollack, 2014; Murnieks, Mosakowski, & Cardon, 2012) and in relation to employees (Breugst, Domurath, Patzelt, & Klaukien, 2012; Cardon, 2008; Hubner, Baum, & Frese, 2019), surprisingly little is known about entrepreneurial passion in the context of entrepreneurial teams. In a theoretical paper, Cardon, Post, and Forster (2017, p. 286) conceptualize team entrepreneurial passion as "the level of shared intense positive feelings for a collective team identity that is high in identity centrality" for an entrepreneurial team. The first empirical articles (Boone, Andries, & Clarysse, 2020; de Mol, Cardon, de Jong, Khapova, & Elfring, 2020; Santos & Cardon, 2019) studying team entrepreneurial passion highlight the complexity of the construct with a multifaceted conceptualization of passion at the team level. Unsurprisingly, the relationship between team entrepreneurial passion and team performance is highly complex, stressing the need to take into account the domain of passion as well as the specific constellations within teams (Santos & Cardon, 2019).

These first theoretical and empirical insights show how important research at the team level is for a more complete understanding of the role of affect in the entrepreneurial process. Importantly, the picture can become even more complex when temporal dynamics of affect are considered that are more frequently included in individual-level studies (Collewaert, Anseel, Crommelinck, De Beuckelaer, & Vermeire, 2016; Gielnik, Uy, Funken, & Bischoff, 2017; Uy, Sun, & Foo, 2017). First insights based on an experimental setting that clearly distinguishes entrepreneurial idea generation and selection suggest that distinct collective moods (measured as average individual moods) are needed for different stages of the entrepreneurial process (Perry-Smith & Coff, 2011). While research including all aspects of dynamic changes is certainly methodologically challenging, it would be insightful to understand how individual team members' affect and attitudes interact and collectively shape the highly 'messy' and iterative entrepreneurial process over longer periods.

Future Research

As entrepreneurial team research only starts to explore the black box of team functioning (Klotz et al., 2014), future research is needed to provide more systematic insights into entrepreneurial team processes and emergent states. While we have already presented ideas for the individual blocks of entrepreneurial team functioning above, adopting a broader perspective on entrepreneurial team functioning opens up promising avenues for future research. On one hand, entrepreneurial team research could gain additional insights by studying interactions between entrepreneurial team processes and emergent states. On the other hand, the explicit integration of entrepreneurial tasks will broaden our understanding of entrepreneurial teams as well as the entrepreneurial process.

Interactions Between Entrepreneurial Team Processes and Emergent States

Whereas team research generally analyzes the role of team processes and emergent states separately (Ilgen et al., 2005), they can substantially influence each other and jointly impact entrepreneurial team functioning. For example, it could be highly interesting to study the role of cohesion in entrepreneurial team learning. While prior research has explained how entrepreneurial team members learn from each other based on teammates' experience (Knockaert et al., 2011; Sardana & Scott-Kemmis, 2010), we do not sufficiently understand the role of team members' affective attitudes toward their teams in providing a conducive or unconducive climate for learning. Although cohesion is related to more openness within teams and more information sharing (Mesmer-Magnus & DeChurch, 2009), it might also limit critical thinking and thus prevent teams from carefully exchanging ideas (Ellis et al., 2003). Thus, for entrepreneurial teams that need to process a plethora of information to benefit from team members' perspectives (Fern, Cardinal, & O'Neill, 2012), cohesion could play a decisive role in learning. Moreover, it is also possible that positive learning experiences within teams can contribute to higher levels of team cohesion.

Also, studies at the individual level show that passion infuses entrepreneurial decisions, such as the decision to start or spin off a venture (Huyghe, Knockaert, & Obschonka, 2016) or to persist in tasks (Cardon & Kirk, 2015). However, it is unclear how team entrepreneurial passion shapes team decision-making. Differences in the foci of passion will also have an impact on team members' preferences in strategic decisions. Thus, team entrepreneurial passion has the potential to shed light on decision-making processes (e.g., Is decision-making speed higher for teams with a singular passion focus compared to multiple foci? Is decision-making comprehensiveness highest in teams representing all foci?) and on the outcomes of strategic decisions (e.g., Can a singular focus on inventing inspire teams to spend substantial time and effort on product development and thus prolong time to market?).

As a final example, we suggest exploring the role of identity in entrepreneurial team conflict. Fauchart and Gruber (2011) already suggest that incompatibilities among individual team members' identities can represent a source of conflict. Additionally, it would be interesting to understand the role of collective entrepreneurial team identity in the emergence and management of conflict. As collective entrepreneurial team identity captures not only "who we are" but also "how we do things" (Powell & Baker, 2017, p. 2383), it might also provide the team with an implicit understanding of how it should behave in case of conflict. Some teams might believe they are harmonious and conflict-free, making it more difficult to deal with controversial ideas and interests. Also, experiencing conflict could shape the collective entrepreneurial team identity. For example, frequent and harsh episodes of conflict could prevent the development of a positive entrepreneurial team identity.

Explicitly Including Entrepreneurial Tasks

Individual-level entrepreneurship research often explicitly includes entrepreneurial tasks, such as opportunity recognition, evaluation, and exploitation (McMullen & Shepherd, 2006). In contrast, at the team level, research mainly focuses on opportunity recognition (Gruber et al., 2012, 2013). These findings complement prior work on team innovation analyzing team-level antecedents, such as team composition and processes (for an overview, see the meta-analysis by Huelsheger, Anderson, & Salgado, 2009). However, entrepreneurial team research does not sufficiently include the specific features of other entrepreneurial tasks. This gap is surprising because a clearly described task environment is likely to lead to more precise research questions and thus contribute to a better understanding of entrepreneurial team functioning.

Importantly, research on entrepreneurial team cognition suffers from a lack of clarity in the individual constructs (de Mol et al., 2015). One avenue to develop more specific research questions is to explicitly connect team cognition to entrepreneurial tasks. For example, instead of trying to understand the overall effects of a team's transactive memory system for venture performance, studies could analyze its impact on opportunity recognition. As individuals' opportunity recognition is described as connecting the dots of their prior experiences (Baron & Ensley, 2006), a well-established transactive memory system might help team members bring their experiences together to collectively discover an opportunity.

Later, during opportunity evaluation, strategic consensus among team members might be necessary to move from individual team members' judgments and beliefs to a collective judgment and belief.

Consistent with the influence of affect at the individual level, teams' affective tone might influence their work on specific entrepreneurial tasks, such as opportunity evaluation (Foo, 2011) and exploitation (Van Gelderen, Kautonen, & Fink, 2015). However, affect at the team level can take even more complex forms if team members experience emotions of different valence (e.g., fear vs. hope) or of different activation level (e.g., fear vs. resignation) in the face of challenges. Indeed, interesting questions on this topic arise: Are some team members' negative emotions more dominant than their teammates' positive emotions, causing teams to be more careful when evaluating new opportunities? Can one team member's fear shape the risk assessment of the entire team? Are highly activating emotions (e.g., enthusiasm or fear; Larsen & Diener, 1992) contagious in a team setting, and can they trigger team action? Future research could help us to understand how entrepreneurial teams jointly master the emotional experiences of the entrepreneurial journey.

Finally, changes in the opportunities entrepreneurial teams pursue in terms of 'pivots' based on customer feedback (Grimes, 2018), significant growth (Wasserman, 2012), or investor involvement (Hellmann & Puri, 2002) give rise to very specific tasks that teams face. For example, if entrepreneurial team members are confronted with different feedback from customers, they need to find ways to integrate diverging information, which represents an important learning process. Rapid growth is likely to necessitate role (re)allocation, thereby changing not only important team processes but also teams' transactive memory systems. Finally, after significant financing rounds, venture capital firms take firm equity and serve on ventures' boards of directors. Consequently, entrepreneurial teams no longer have complete control over their ventures, which may change their approach to team decision-making.

Practical Implications

While individual studies on entrepreneurial team functioning provide specific practical implications, there is not (yet) a comprehensive roadmap for entrepreneurial team members or entrepreneurship educators to follow given the early stage of research on this topic. However, taking a broader perspective on entrepreneurial team functioning is likely to support successful collaboration in entrepreneurial teams. While popular startup methods (e.g., Lean Startup; Ries, 2011) emphasize the complexity of the *outside* world (e.g., gathering and acting upon diverse feedback from various stakeholders), research on entrepreneurial team functioning highlights the immense complexity *within* entrepreneurial teams. Thus, for entrepreneurial teams, understanding their *specific* complexity in terms of task-related and interpersonal processes as well as team emergent states is crucial. By understanding this complexity, teams will be better able to realize when they need to prioritize interpersonal processes compared to task-related processes. Despite the overwhelmingly high workload and stress inherent in founding new ventures (Cardon & Patel, 2015), teams need to balance their different tasks and opportunities to reflect, learn, and solve potential conflict. Developing team emergent states might take some time, and these states also need to be adjusted on a continual basis. The complexity of the outside world is likely to shape individual team members' knowledge, so teammates should find ways to update each other and bring these insights to the collective level. Throughout a team's entrepreneurial journey, affective states could serve as important team-internal feedback that can substantially facilitate or hamper collaboration. Thus, teams should not only acknowledge their existing affective states but also try to shape them to support entrepreneurial team functioning as well as individual members' well-being.

Conclusion

Our literature review focuses on entrepreneurial team functioning and highlights the important insights provided by prior research. Compared to research on entrepreneurial team composition, these insights represent only the first, but crucial, steps to developing a better understanding of how entrepreneurial teams translate their members' inputs into outcomes. Because this translation is a core part of the entrepreneurial process, we hope that our review contributes to entrepreneurship research by opening up a fruitful agenda for future research on entrepreneurial team functioning.

Notes

1. While we focus on articles published after January 2008, these reviews also include earlier studies.
2. See Klotz et al. (2014) for the detailed journal list.
3. There has been some debate in general team research on conflict regarding whether cognitive conflict is indeed connected to positive outcomes. Importantly, the meta-analysis by de Wit et al. (2012) shows an overall nonsignificant relationship between cognitive conflict and performance. However, for top management teams, the cognitive conflict–performance relationship is more positive.

References

Amason, A. C., Shrader, R. C., & Tompson, G. H. (2006). Newness and novelty: Relating top management team composition to new venture performance. *Journal of Business Venturing*, *21*(1), 125–148.

Ashforth, B. E., Rogers, K. M., & Corley, K. G. (2011). Identity in organizations: Exploring cross-level dynamics. *Organization Science*, *22*(5), 1144–1156.

Baron, R. A., & Ensley, M. D. (2006). Opportunity recognition as the detection of meaningful patterns: Evidence from comparisons of novice and experienced entrepreneurs. *Management Science*, *52*(9), 1331–1344.

Beckman, C. M., Burton, M. D., & O'Reilly, C. (2007). Early teams: The impact of team demography on VC financing and going public. *Journal of Business Venturing, 22*(2), 147–173.

Blatt, R. (2009). Tough love: How communal schemas and contracting practices build relational capital in entrepreneurial teams. *Academy of Management Review, 34*(3), 533–551.

Bolzani, D., Fini, R., Napolitano, S., & Toschi, L. (2019). Entrepreneurial teams: An input-process-outcome frame-work. *Foundations and Trends in Entrepreneurship, 15*(2), 56–258.

Boone, S., Andries, P., & Clarysse, B. (2020). Does team entrepreneurial passion matter for relationship conflict and team performance? On the importance of fit between passion focus and venture development stage. *Journal of Business Venturing, 35*(5), 105984.

Bourgeois, L. J., III, & Eisenhardt, K. M. (1988). Strategic decision process in high velocity environments: Four cases in the microcomputer industry. *Management Science, 34*(7), 816–835.

Brannon, D. L., Wiklund, J., & Haynie, J. M. (2013). The varying effects of family relationships in entrepreneurial teams. *Entrepreneurship: Theory and Practice, 37*(1), 107–132.

Breugst, N., Domurath, A., Patzelt, H., & Klaukien, A. (2012). Perceptions of entrepreneurial passion and employees' commitment to entrepreneurial ventures. *Entrepreneurship: Theory and Practice, 36*(1), 171–192.

Breugst, N., Patzelt, H., & Rathgeber, P. (2015). How should we divide the pie? Equity distribution and its impact on entrepreneurial teams. *Journal of Business Venturing, 30*(1), 66–94.

Breugst, N., Patzelt, H., & Shepherd, D. A. (in press). When is effort contagious in new venture management teams? Understanding the contingencies of social motivation theory. *Journal of Management Studies.*

Breugst, N., & Shepherd, D. A. (2017). If you fight with me, I'll get mad! A social model of entrepreneurial affect. *Entrepreneurship Theory and Practice, 41*(3), 379–418.

Brinckmann, J., Grichnik, D., & Kapsa, D. (2010). Should entrepreneurs plan or just storm the castle? A meta-analysis on contextual factors impacting the business planning-performance relationship in small firms. *Journal of Business Venturing, 25*(1), 24–40.

Brinckmann, J., & Hoegl, M. (2011). Effects of initial teamwork capability and initial relational capability on the development of new technology-based firms. *Strategic Entrepreneurship Journal, 5*(1), 37–57.

Cardon, M. S. (2008). Is passion contagious? The transference of entrepreneurial passion to employees. *Human Resource Management Review, 18*, 77–86.

Cardon, M. S., & Kirk, C. P. (2015). Entrepreneurial passion as mediator of the self-efficacy to persistence relationship. *Entrepreneurship Theory and Practice, 39*(5), 1027–1050.

Cardon, M. S., & Patel, P. C. (2015). Is stress worth it? Stress-related health and wealth trade-offs for entrepreneurs. *Applied Psychology, 64*(2), 379–420.

Cardon, M. S., Post, C., & Forster, W. R. (2017). Team entrepreneurial passion: Its emergence and influence in new venture teams. *Academy of Management Review, 42*(2), 283–305.

Carpenter, M. A., Geletkanycz, M. A., & Sanders, W. G. (2004). Upper echelons research revisited: Antecedents, elements, and consequences of top management team composition. *Journal of Management, 30*(6), 749–778.

Chaganti, R. S., Watts, A. D., Chaganti, R., & Zimmerman-Treichel, M. (2008). Ethnic-immigrants in founding teams: Effects on prospector strategy and performance in new Internet ventures. *Journal of Business Venturing, 23*(1), 113–139.

Chandler, G. N., & Lyon, D. W. (2009). Involvement in knowledge-acquisition activities by venture team members and venture performance. *Entrepreneurship Theory and Practice, 33*(3), 571–592.

Collewaert, V., Anseel, F., Crommelinck, M., De Beuckelaer, A., & Vermeire, J. (2016). When passion fades: Disentangling the temporal dynamics of entrepreneurial passion for founding. *Journal of Management Studies, 53*(6), 966–995.

Courtright, S. H., McCormick, B. W., Mistry, S., Jiexin, W., & Wang, J. (2017). Quality charters or quality members? A control theory perspective on team charters and team performance. *Journal of Applied Psychology, 102*(10), 1462–1470.

Dai, Y., Roundy, P. T., Chok, J. I., Ding, F., & Byun, G. (2016). "Who knows what?" in new venture teams: Transactive memory systems as a micro-foundation of entrepreneurial orientation. *Journal of Management Studies, 53*(8), 1320–1347.

de Jong, A., Song, M., & Song, L. Z. (2013). How lead founder personality affects new venture performance: The mediating role of team conflict. *Journal of Management, 39*(7), 1825–1854.

de Jong, B. A., & Elfring, T. (2010). How does trust affect the performance of ongoing teams? The mediating role of reflexivity, monitoring, and effort. *Academy of Management Journal, 53*(3), 535–549.

de Mol, E., Cardon, M. S., de Jong, B., Khapova, S. N., & Elfring, T. (2020). Entrepreneurial passion diversity in new venture teams: An empirical examination of short-and long-term performance implications. *Journal of Business Venturing, 35(4)*, 105965.

de Mol, E., Khapova, S. N., & Elfring, T. (2015). Entrepreneurial team cognition: A review. *International Journal of Management Reviews, 17*(2), 232–255.

de Wit, F. R., Greer, L. L., & Jehn, K. A. (2012). The paradox of intragroup conflict: A meta-analysis. *Journal of Applied Psychology, 97*(2), 360.

Eisenhardt, K. M. (1989). Making fast strategic decisions in high-velocity environments. *Academy of Management Journal, 32*(3), 543–576.

Eisenhardt, K. M., & Schoonhoven, C. B. (1990). Organizational growth: Linking founding team, strategy, environment, and growth among U.S. semiconductor ventures, 1978–1988. *Administrative Science Quarterly, 35*(3), 504–529.

Ellemers, N., Spears, R., & Doosje, B. (2002). Self and social identity. *Annual Review of Psychology, 53*(1), 161–186.

Ellis, A. P. J., Hollenbeck, J. R., Ilgen, D. R., Porter, C. O. L. H., West, B. J., & Moon, H. (2003). Team learning: Collectively connecting the dots. *Journal of Applied Psychology, 88*(5), 821–835.

Ensley, M. D., & Hmieleski, K. M. (2005). A comparative study of new venture top management team composition, dynamics and performance between university-based and independent start-ups. *Research Policy, 34*(7), 1091–1105.

Ensley, M. D., Pearson, A. W., & Amason, A. C. (2002). Understanding the dynamics of new venture top management teams: Cohesion, conflict, and new venture performance. *Journal of Business Venturing, 17*(4), 365–386.

Fauchart, E., & Gruber, M. (2011). Darwinians, communitarians and missionaries: The role of founder identity in entrepreneurship. *Academy of Management Journal, 54*(5), 935–957.

Fern, M. J., Cardinal, L. B., & O'Neill, H. M. (2012). The genesis of strategy in new ventures: Escaping the constraints of founder and team knowledge. *Strategic Management Journal, 33*(4), 427–447.

Fisher, D. M. (2014). Distinguishing between taskwork and teamwork planning in teams: Relations with coordination and interpersonal processes. *Journal of Applied Psychology, 99*(3), 423–436.

Foo, M.-D. (2011). Emotions and entrepreneurial opportunity evaluation. *Entrepreneurship Theory and Practice, 35*(2), 375–393.

Foo, M.-D., Sin, H. P., & Yiong, L. P. (2006). Effects of team inputs and intrateam processes on perceptions of team viability and member satisfaction in nascent ventures. *Strategic Management Journal*, 27(4), 389–399.

Forbes, D. P., Korsgaard, M. A., & Sapienza, H. J. (2010). Financing decisions as a source of conflict in venture boards. *Journal of Business Venturing*, 25(6), 579–592.

Frese, M., Krauss, S. I., Keith, N., Escher, S., Grabarkiewicz, R., Luneng, S. T., . . . Friedrich, C. (2007). Business owners' action planning and its relationship to business success in three African countries. *Journal of Applied Psychology*, 92(6), 1481–1498.

Gielnik, M. M., Barabas, S., Frese, M., Namatovu-Dawa, R., Scholz, F. A., Metzger, J. R., & Walter, T. (2014). A temporal analysis of how entrepreneurial goal intentions, positive fantasies, and action planning affect starting a new venture and when the effects wear off. *Journal of Business Venturing*, 29(6), 755–772.

Gielnik, M. M., Spitzmuller, M., Schmitt, A., Klemann, D., & Frese, M. (2014). I put in effort, therefore I am passionate: Investigating the path from effort to passion in entrepreneurship. *Academy of Management Journal*, 58(4), 1012–1031.

Gielnik, M. M., Uy, M. A., Funken, R., & Bischoff, K. M. (2017). Boosting and sustaining passion: A long-term perspective on the effects of entrepreneurship training. *Journal of Business Venturing*, 32(3), 334–353.

Grégoire, D. A., Corbett, A. C., & McMullen, J. S. (2011). The cognitive perspective in entrepreneurship: An agenda for future research. *Journal of Management Studies*, 48(6), 1443–1477.

Grimes, M. G. (2018). The pivot: How founders respond to feedback through idea and identity work. *Academy of Management Journal*, 61(5), 1692–1717.

Gruber, M., MacMillan, I. C., & Thompson, J. D. (2012). From minds to markets: How human capital endowments shape market opportunity identification of technology start-ups. *Journal of Management*, 38(5), 1421–1449.

Gruber, M., MacMillan, I. C., & Thompson, J. D. (2013). Escaping the prior knowledge corridor: What shapes the number and variety of market opportunities identified before market entry of technology start-ups? *Organization Science*, 24(1), 280–300.

Harper, D. A. (2008). Towards a theory of entrepreneurial teams. *Journal of Business Venturing*, 23(6), 613–626.

Harrison, S. H., & Rouse, E. D. (2014). Let's dance! Elastic coordination in creative group work: A qualitative study of modern dancers. *Academy of Management Journal*, 57(5), 1256–1283.

Häsel, M., Kollmann, T., & Breugst, N. (2010). IT competence in internet founder teams. *Business & Information Systems Engineering*, 2(4), 209–217.

Hellmann, T., & Puri, M. (2002). Venture capital and the professionalization of start-up firms: Empirical evidence. *The Journal of Finance*, 57(1), 169–197.

Hmieleski, K. M., & Ensley, M. D. (2007). A contextual examination of new venture performance: Entrepreneur leadership behavior, top management team heterogeneity, and environmental dynamism. *Journal of Organizational Behavior*, 28(7), 865–889.

Ho, V. T., & Pollack, J. M. (2014). Passion isn't always a good thing: Examining entrepreneurs' network centrality and financial performance with a dualistic model of passion. *Journal of Management Studies*, 51(3), 433–459.

Hogg, M. A., & Terry, D. I. (2000). Social identity and self-categorization processes in organizational contexts. *Academy of Management Review*, 25(1), 121–140.

Hubner, S., Baum, M., & Frese, M. (2019). Contagion of entrepreneurial passion: Effects on employee outcomes. *Entrepreneurship Theory and Practice*, 44(6), 1112–1140.

Huelsheger, U. R., Anderson, N., & Salgado, J. F. (2009). Team-level predictors of innovation at work: A comprehensive meta-analysis spanning three decades of research. *Journal of Applied Psychology, 94*(5), 1128–1145.

Huyghe, A., Knockaert, M., & Obschonka, M. (2016). Unraveling the "passion orchestra" in academia. *Journal of Business Venturing, 31*(3), 344–364.

Ilgen, D. R., Hollenbeck, J. R., Johnson, M., & Jundt, D. (2005). Teams in organizations: From input-process-output models to IMOI models. *Annual Review of Psychology, 56*(1), 517–543.

Janssen, J. J. P., Kostopoulos, K. C., Mihalache, O. R., & Papalexandris, A. (2016). A socio-psychological perspective on team ambidexterity: The contingency role of supportive leadership behaviours. *Journal of Management Studies, 53*(6), 939–965.

Jin, L., Madison, K., Kraiczy, N. D., Kellermanns, F. W., Crook, T. R., & Xi, J. (2017). Entrepreneurial team composition characteristics and new venture performance: A meta-analysis. *Entrepreneurship: Theory and Practice, 41*(5), 743–771.

Klotz, A. C., Hmieleski, K. M., Bradley, B. H., & Busenitz, L. W. (2014). New venture teams: A review of the literature and roadmap for future research. *Journal of Management, 40*(1), 226–255.

Knockaert, M., Ucbasaran, D., Wright, M., & Clarysse, B. (2011). The relationship between knowledge transfer, top management team composition, and performance: The case of science-based entrepreneurial firms. *Entrepreneurship Theory and Practice, 35*(4), 777–803.

Kollmann, T., Häsel, M., & Breugst, N. (2009). Competence of IT professionals in e-business venture teams: The effect of experience and expertise on preference structure. *Journal of Management Information Systems, 25*(4), 51–79.

Larsen, R. J., & Diener, E. (1992). Promises and problems with the circumplex model of emotion. In M. S. Clark (Ed.), *Review of personality and social psychology: Emotion* (pp. 25–59). Newbury Park, CA: Sage.

Lazar, M., Miron-Spektor, E., Agarwal, R., Erez, M., Goldfarb, B., & Chen, G. (2020). Entrepreneurial team formation. *Academy of Management Annals, 14*(1), 29–59.

Lewis, K., & Herndon, B. (2011). Transactive memory systems: Current issues and future research directions. *Organization Science, 22*(5), 1254–1265.

Marks, M. A., Mathieu, J., & Zaccaro, S. J. (2001). A temporally based framework and taxonomy of team processes. *Academy of Management Review, 26*(3), 356–376.

Mathias, B. D., & Williams, D. W. (2018). Giving up the hats? Entrepreneurs' role transitions and venture growth. *Journal of Business Venturing, 33*(3), 261–277.

Mathieu, J., Maynard, M. T., Rapp, T., & Gilson, L. (2008). Team effectiveness 1997–2007: A review of recent advancements and a glimpse into the future. *Journal of Management, 34*(3), 410–476.

McMullen, J. S., & Shepherd, D. A. (2006). Entrepreneurial action and the role of uncertainty in the theory of the entrepreneur. *Academy of Management Review, 31*(1), 132–152.

Mesmer-Magnus, J. R., & DeChurch, L. A. (2009). Information sharing and team performance: A meta-analysis. *Journal of Applied Psychology, 94*(2), 535–546.

Murnieks, C. Y., Mosakowski, E., & Cardon, M. S. (2012). Pathways of passion: Identity centrality, passion, and behavior among entrepreneurs. *Journal of Management, 40*(6), 1583–1606.

Perry-Smith, J. E., & Coff, R. W. (2011). In the mood for entrepreneurial creativity? How optimal group affect differs for generating and selecting ideas for new ventures. *Strategic Entrepreneurship Journal, 5*(3), 247–268.

Powell, E., & Baker, T. (2017). In the beginning: Identity processes and organizing in multi-founder nascent ventures. *Academy of Management Journal, 60*(6), 2381–2414.

Preller, R., Patzelt, H., & Breugst, N. (2020). Entrepreneurial visions in founding teams: Conceptualization, emergence, and effects on opportunity development. *Journal of Business Venturing*, *35*(2), 105914.

Rauter, S., Weiss, M., & Hoegl, M. (2018). Team learning from setbacks: A study in the context of start-up teams. *Journal of Organizational Behavior*, *39*(6), 783–795.

Ries, E. (2011). *The lean startup: How today's entrepreneurs use continuous innovation to create radically successful businesses*. New York: Crown Business.

Santos, S. C., & Cardon, M. S. (2019). What's love got to do with it? Team entrepreneurial passion and performance in new venture teams. *Entrepreneurship Theory and Practice*, *43*(3), 475–504.

Sardana, D., & Scott-Kemmis, D. (2010). Who learns what? A study based on entrepreneurs from biotechnology new ventures. *Journal of Small Business Management*, *48*(3), 441–468.

Shalley, C. E., & Perry-Smith, J. E. (2008). The emergence of team creative cognition: The role of diverse outside ties, sociocognitive network centrality, and team evolution. *Strategic Entrepreneurship Journal*, *2*(1), 23–41.

Shepherd, D. A., Williams, T. A., & Patzelt, H. (2015). Thinking about entrepreneurial decision making: Review and research agenda. *Journal of Management*, *41*(1), 11–46.

Short, J. (2009). The art of writing a review article. *Journal of Management*, *35*(6), 1312–1317.

Souitaris, V., & Maestro, B. M. M. (2010). Polychronicity in top management teams: The impact on strategic decision processes and performance of new technology ventures. *Strategic Management Journal*, *31*(6), 652–678.

Tzabbar, D., & Margolis, J. (2017). Beyond the startup stage: The founding team's human capital, new venture's stage of life, founder–CEO duality, and breakthrough innovation. *Organization Science*, *28*(5), 857–872.

Uy, M. A., Sun, S., & Foo, M.-D. (2017). Affect spin, entrepreneurs' well-being, and venture goal progress: The moderating role of goal orientation. *Journal of Business Venturing*, *32*(4), 443–460.

Vanaelst, I., Clarysse, B., Wright, M., Lockett, A., Moray, N., & S'Jegers, R. (2006). Entrepreneurial team development in academic spinouts: An examination of team heterogeneity. *Entrepreneurship Theory and Practice*, *30*(2), 249–271.

Van Gelderen, M., Kautonen, T., & Fink, M. (2015). From entrepreneurial intentions to actions: Self-control and action-related doubt, fear, and aversion. *Journal of Business Venturing*, *30*(5), 655–673.

Vissa, B., & Chacar, A. S. (2009). Leveraging ties: The contingent value of entrepreneurial teams' external advice networks on Indian software venture performance. *Strategic Management Journal*, *30*(11), 1179–1191.

Wasserman, N. (2012). *Founder's dilemmas: Anticipating and avoiding the pitfalls that can sink a startup*. Princeton, NJ: Princeton University Press.

Weiner, B. (1985). An attributional theory of achievement motivation and emotion. *Psychological Review*, *92*(4), 548–573.

Zheng, Y. (2012). Unlocking founding team prior shared experience: A transactive memory system perspective. *Journal of Business Venturing*, *27*(5), 577–591.

Zheng, Y., DeVaughn, M. L., & Zellmer-Bruhn, M. (2016). Shared and shared alike? Founders' prior shared experience and performance of newly founded banks. *Strategic Management Journal*, *37*(12), 2503–2520.

Zheng, Y., & Mai, Y. (2013). A contextualized transactive memory system view on how founding teams respond to surprises: Evidence from China. *Strategic Entrepreneurship Journal*, *7*(3), 197–213.

7

INTRAPRENEURSHIP AND FIRM INNOVATION

Conditions Contributing to Innovation

Michael D. Mumford, Samantha Elliott &
Robert W. Martin

Intrapreneurship may be considered critical to the development of innovative new products and processes in established firms. In the present effort, we argue that firms can structure themselves to support intrapreneurship. Seven key skills needed for intrapreneurs to do innovative work are discussed, including affordance recognition, idea evaluation, constraint analysis, planning, forecasting, wisdom, and championing. Subsequently, we examine the policies and practices of firms that would contribute to the development and application of these skills. To understand the factors supportive of intrapreneurship, it is first critical to discuss the nature of creative work and the translation of creative ideas into innovative products.

Innovation, the development and deployment of new products and services is considered critical to both economic growth and perhaps, more centrally, to the growth and survival of firms (Audretsch, Coad, & Segarra, 2014; Goedhuys, 2007). People typically assume innovation is a property of entrepreneurial firms. In fact, the best evidence available indicates that the initial development and deployment of innovative new products and services typically occur in large firms (Chandy & Tellis, 1998). Although this observation may seem counterintuitive, remember it was Xerox, not Apple, a small start-up at the time, which developed graphical user interfaces. It was Bell Labs, not Fairchild Semiconductor, that developed silicon chip technology. It was DuPont that developed Kevlar.

These observations pose a question, why do innovations flow from large firms—even if these innovations are often deployed by smaller, entrepreneurial, firms (Fischer et al., 2014)? One answer to this question is larger firms have the capital to invest in the research and development efforts that often provide the basis for the development of innovative new products (Bernstein & Nadiri, 1989). Large firms often have more human capital available (Ballot, Fakhfakh, &

Taymaz, 2001), and large firms often place more value on institutional learning and the diversity of institutional learning initiatives (Chen & Miller, 2007). Taken together, these forces all would lead one to expect that it is large firms that will typically be the source of innovative new products and services.

Innovation, of course, ultimately depends on the creative work, the production of high quality (i.e., the overall quality of the participant's campaign, including how coherent and useful it is), original (i.e., the extent to which the plan is unique and unexpected), and elegant (i.e., the degree to which the participant's plan is articulately arranged in a succinct way) solutions to complex, novel, ill-defined, or poorly structured problems by individuals or teams (Besemer & O'Quin, 1999; Mumford & Gustafson, 2007; Reiter-Palmon & Paulus, in press). Creative problem solutions, however, are, to firms, something of a risk. Creative efforts do not always work out—in fact, they often fail (Huber, 2000). Managers often do not see the potential value in innovative new ideas (Licuanan, Dailey, & Mumford, 2007). And new ways of work, or new methods of production, may prove so disruptive that the firm may find it necessary to refuse to pursue creative ideas (Jelinek & Schoonhoven, 1990).

These pressures have led many scholars to argue creative ideas, and the innovations flowing from creative thought, will die in firms unless intrapreneurs actively advocate the pursuit of new ideas, new technologies, or new products and services (Ahmad, Nasurdin, & Zainal, 2011; Blanka, 2018; Burgelman, 1983). Although definitions of exactly what is meant by the term *intrapreneurship* are ambiguous, advocacy of innovative efforts within the firm is almost always viewed as crucial (Amo, 2010; Gupta & Srivastava, 2013; Campos et al., 2017).

As advocates for creative efforts, the creative work giving rise to new products and services, scholars tend to see the intrapreneur acting in opposition to the firms standing norms and business practices (Ahmad et al., 2011; Gündoğdu, 2012). In the present effort, we will argue this need not always be the case. We, in the present effort, argue that intrapreneurship relies on seven key skills, affordance recognition, idea evaluation, constraint analysis, forecasting, planning, championing, and wisdom. And firms may take actions to encourage effective execution of these skills—actions likely to contribute to intrapreneurial behavior in firms.

Skills and Intrapreneurship

As noted earlier, intrapreneurship is held to be based on innovative behavior, or actions, in firms (Antoncic & Hisrich, 2003). Thus, intrapreneurs are held to create new business ideas to be pursued by a firm or creative new ways of doing things in firms. This observation led Ahmad et al. (2011) to argue the basis for intrapreneurship in firms is idea generation and idea application or the development and deployment of ideas. Essentially, these observations imply that intrapreneurship is based on creative thinking.

Creative thinking, however, is not a new concept and has been widely studied for many years. For example, creative thinking has been found to depend on intelligence and divergent thinking abilities (Runco, in press). People's ability to produce creative ideas has been found to depend, in part, on their personality—with creative ideas emerging from achievement-oriented, autonomous, energetic people, who are curious and open to new approaches (Feist & Gorman, 1998; Fischer et al., 2014). Creative people believe in their capability to produce creative ideas, creative self-efficacy, (Tierney & Farmer, 2002) and are motivated to pursue creative efforts based on both intrinsic and extrinsic concerns (Eisenburger & Shanock, 2003). What should be noted here is that many of the same characteristics characterize those who adopt intrapreneurial roles in firms (Antoncic & Hisrich, 2003).

Criticism about the relationship between individual differences (e.g., personality) and intrapreneurial work is expected given some controversy in the entrepreneurship literature (Rauch & Frese, 2007a, 2007b). For example, although arguments exist that personality is not strongly related to entrepreneurial and intrapreneurial work, meta-analytic evidence provided by Rauch and Frese (2007b) shows that entrepreneurial performance was significantly related to a number of individual differences, including need for achievement, self-efficacy, innovativeness, need for autonomy, and proactive personality—characteristics also seen in creative people. Given these findings, one would expect intrapreneurs, who must think creatively, to hold these characteristics.

Although many variables influence people's creative performance, their ability to solve the kind of complex, novel, ill-defined problems that call for creative thought, raises a fundamental question. How do people go about solving creative problems? Put differently, what are the key cognitive processes to be executed by those working on creative problems? Over the years, a number of such process models have been proposed (e.g., Dewey, 1910; Parnes & Noller, 1972; Sternberg, 1986). In a review of these models, Mumford, Mobley, Reiter-Palmon, Uhlman, and Doares (1991) identified eight core processes commonly held to be involved in incidents of creative thought: (1) problem definition, (2) information gathering, (3) concept/case selection, (4) conceptual combination, (5) idea generation, (6) idea evaluation, (7) implementation planning, and (8) adaptive monitoring. These processes are held to operate in an interdependent fashion where the products produced through the execution of one process are used in the next processing operation. More centrally, effective execution of these processes was held to depend on domain-specific knowledge or expertise.

Over the years, a variety of evidence has been accrued that indicates Mumford et al.'s (1991) model provides an adequate description of creative thought. For example, effective execution of each process has been shown to impact creative performance in multiple domains such as business consulting, marketing, education, and public policy (e.g., Baughman & Mumford, 1995). Effective execution of each process has been shown to depend on use of viable strategies in process execution such as search for key facts and anomalies in information gathering (Mumford, Baughman, Supinski, & Maher, 1996) or concept mapping in conceptual combination (Scott, Lonergan, & Mumford, 2005). Effective execution of all these processes has been proved to be a powerful predictor of creative performance across multiple domains (Mumford, Supinski, Baughman, Costanza, & Threlfall, 1997). And errors have been shown to flow through process execution such that errors made in problem definition disrupts subsequent information gathering (Friedrich & Mumford, 2009).

Mumford, Medeiros, and Partlow (2012) argued that in creative problem-solving, it is not fully sufficient simply to be able to execute each process. In addition, people must possess certain thinking skills—cross-process skills contributing to the effective execution of multiple creative thinking processes. For example, Marcy and Mumford (2007, 2010) argued that causal analysis skills contribute to the execution of multiple creative thinking processes. They found that training people in causal analysis skills contributed to better performance in solving social innovation problems calling for creative thought and better performance on a managerial simulation exercise requiring creative thought. In another study along these lines, Robledo et al. (2012) argued error analysis skill might contribute to the effective execution of each of these processes. And, in fact, they found that skill in error analysis contributed to better performance on creative problem-solving tasks.

Mumford, Antes, Caughron, Connelly, and Beeler (2010), however, examined how creative thinking skills were applied in solving problems drawn from different work domains. Their findings indicated that all these processes and skills were used as people, early-career professionals, sought to solve the kinds of problems presented to them in the health sciences (e.g., medicine) biological sciences (e.g., microbiology), and social sciences (e.g., social work). That said, some processes, and some skills, were found to be more important in some domains than others. This observation broaches a new question. What are the key skills needed by intrapreneurs?

A model of the key skills contributing to the performance of intrapreneurs is presented in Figure 7.1. This model assumes intrapreneurs must be able to recognize significant, noteworthy, problems being encountered by the firm or opportunities opened up by the activities of competitors, technology, or the activities of the firm. The need to recognize *both* opportunities and problems led us to label this skill affordance recognition (Zaccaro, Green, DuBrow, & Kolze, 2018). Affordance recognition may cause the intrapreneur to engage in creative problem-solving. However, it is not always the case that intrapreneurs, themselves, need to engage in creative idea generation, although at times they may. Often intrapreneurs may encourage others to engage in idea generation, or, alternatively, adopt the ideas of others.

What is clear is that intrapreneurs must be able to evaluate or appraise the ideas they, or others, have generated. Thus, intrapreneurs are held to need substantial

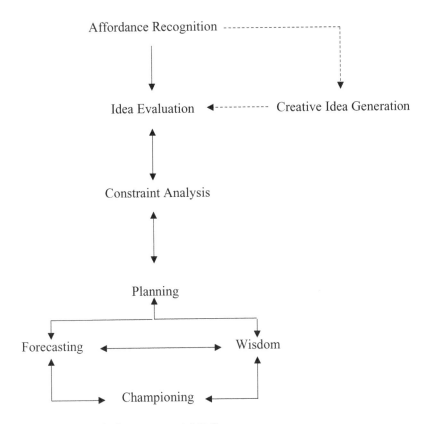

FIGURE 7.1   Model of Intrapreneurial Skills

idea evaluation skills. In evaluating ideas, however, constraints on idea development, or idea potential, must be taken into account. More centrally, intrapreneurs must be able to analyze and work within, or work around, constraints imposed by the firm, its people, or its technology. Following idea evaluation and analysis of constraints, intrapreneurs must plan how ideas will be resourced, developed, and deployed—ideas for a new business, new technology, or new processes. Plans are noteworthy because they provide intrapreneurs with a basis for forecasting the outcomes of actions being contemplated. Wisdom, an appraisal of the viability of actions in a social context (Connelly et al., 2000), contributes to the evaluation of forecasted outcomes for a given idea. And, if a wise evaluation of forecasted outcomes proves promising, then other people will begin to champion the ideas across the firm establishing a context where ideas can be developed, fielded, and implemented.

Thus, this model suggests seven skills will prove crucial to the success of intrapreneurs, (1) affordance recognition, (2) idea evaluation, (3) constraint analysis, (4) planning, (5) forecasting, (6) wisdom, and (7) championing. Identification of these skills is noteworthy because each skill points to actions that might be taken by the firm to encourage intrapreneurship by creating conditions facilitating the application of these skills. In the following sections, we consider some of the available evidence bearing on the importance of each of these intrapreneurship skills along with the institutional conditions likely to encourage, or inhibit, effective application of these skills.

Affordance Recognition

Affordance recognition can be viewed generally as the identification, understanding, and integration of environmental factors that contribute to the interactions which occur in any given situation (Greeno, 1994). It is closely related to a key creative thinking process, problem definition, found to consistently influence performance on creative problem-solving tasks (Reiter-Palmon & Robinson, 2009). Affordance recognition, however, should not be arbitrarily equated with problem definition. It requires a broader appraisal of the opportunities and risks evident in the environment and, as a result, may be more closely related to an older concept of mess finding (Parnes & Noller, 1972)—although affordance recognition represents a more localized skill than mess finding.

Redmond, Mumford, and Teach (1993) examined affordance recognition. In this study, undergraduates were asked to formulate an advertising campaign for a new product—the three-dimensional (3D) holographic television. Participants were asked to provide a written description of a television advertisement and a magazine advertisement. Senior working marketing executives appraised the quality and originality of these advertisements. Affordance recognition was manipulated by asking, or not asking, participants to formulate a marketing survey before starting work on the advertising task. Note that the formation of a marketing survey required participants to think about the kind of affordances that might be operating in this low-fidelity simulation exercise. It was found both the quality and originality of the resulting television and magazine advertisements were strongly influenced by this affordance recognition manipulation. Thus, there is reason to suspect affordance recognition might be critical for intrapreneurship.

In the Redmond et al (1993) study, however, grades in marketing classes and marketing knowledge were also assessed. Not only was it found that marketing expertise enhanced task performance, but the affordance recognition manipulation was also more impactful when examining the interaction effect between expertise and affordance recognition. This observation is consistent with Bjornali and Støren (2012) study of intrapreneurship which found intrapreneurship requires substantive expertise. These findings are noteworthy because they point to the need for firms to encourage ongoing professional development if they wish to encourage affordance recognition and intrapreneurship.

Affordance recognition also depends on intrapreneurs having access to information bearing on the opportunities and threats relevant to the firm. One way such information might be acquired is through personal social networks—both networks within the firm and networks outside the firm. Prior research on intrapreneurship, moreover, indicates that intrapreneurs have both broader and more diverse networks of contacts both within and outside the firm (Bicknell, Francis-Smythe, & Arthur, 2010; Urbano & Turro, 2013) as well as stronger networking skills (Whittle & Mueller, 2008). What should be recognized here is firms might take many actions to encourage the acquisition of stronger networks—actions ranging from cross-functional assignments to encouragement to attend professional conferences to sitting on the boards of relevant institutions.

Of course, information access is not just a matter of personal networks. At least three other actions can be taken by firms likely to encourage affordance recognition. First, firm information systems should distribute, widely distribute, information bearing on competitors, and key technological developments. Second, firms should consider initiating actions likely to ensure active analysis of relevant affordances. For example, firms might require mandatory meetings in key work groups, where emerging opportunities and threats are assessed—with the results of this analysis being fed back to senior management. Third, firms should clarify, through ongoing communication, key strategic objectives by asking staff to appraise, and report, risks and opportunities they see with respect to the attainment of those objectives. Thus, in firms seeking to encourage intrapreneurship strategy analysis may become a collective activity (Friedrich, Vessey, Schuelke, Ruark, & Mumford, 2009), not simply a prerogative of senior management.

Idea Evaluation

Regardless of whether an intrapreneur has generated an idea or whether the idea has come from elsewhere, either inside or outside the firm, the idea must be evaluated. In fact, given the high failure rate of creative ideas, intrapreneurs must be risk-tolerant, and the firm must establish a climate that supports the risk tolerance of intrapreneurs (Hagedorn & Jamieson, 2014). By the same token, the risk involved in pursuing creative ideas implies idea evaluation and skill in idea evaluation will prove critical to intrapreneurial success.

Traditionally, idea evaluation has been understood as a rather passive activity. A go, no-go decision was to be made based on the development of the idea and its potential contribution to firm performance. Typically, such decisions were held to be made based solely on economic appraisals. More recent research, however, indicates idea evaluation is a far more complex activity.

In one study along these lines, Lonergan, Scott, and Mumford (2004) asked participants to assume the role of a manager in a marketing firm reviewing proposals for advertising a new product—the 3D holographic television. After reading through this proposal, they were asked to provide a written evaluation of the idea presented and then provide their own written plan for advertising this product. In one manipulation, participants were presented with either high-quality ideas or highly original ideas as defined by senior marketing executives in the Redmond et al. (1993) study. In addition, participants were asked to appraise ideas and recommend revisions in the idea using either efficiency or innovative standards. It was found the highest quality and most original advertising campaigns emerged when participants evaluated high-quality ideas with respect to the potential for innovation *or* when they evaluated highly original ideas with respect to efficiency. Thus, idea evaluation is not a passive activity rather idea evaluation requires creative thinking as the evaluator seeks to improve ideas by addressing perceived weaknesses.

One implication of these observations is that intrapreneurship can be improved by asking managers to evaluate ideas from multiple perspectives. For example, requiring people to consider both the strengths and the weaknesses of ideas. Moreover, firms might ask people in proposing ideas to lay out both the strengths and weaknesses of ideas and prepare plans for addressing the weaknesses of ideas.

More broadly, the findings obtained in the Longergan, Scott, and Mumford (2004) study suggest creative thinking is required in idea evaluation. Given the need for intrapreneurs to think creatively in idea evaluation, one approach that might be used by firms to encourage intrapreneurship is to provide staff with training in creative thinking skills. Indeed, prior meta-analytic work by Scott, Leritz, and Mumford (2004) has shown creativity training programs are often quite effective especially when they focus on the core creative thinking processes (e.g., problem definition, conceptual combination, idea generation) identified by Mumford et al. (1991).

In addition, establishing a climate, which encourages creative thinking with respect to ideas is also likely to have some value. Hunter, Bedell, and Mumford (2007) conducted a meta-analysis of the relationship between climate perceptions and creativity finding that climate perceptions were strongly related to creative thinking. In the four climate dimensions, exerting the strongest effects were task challenges, intellectual stimulation, positive interpersonal exchange, and risk-taking. Thus, a supportive trusting work environment where challenging high-risk tasks are presented seems to contribute to creativity, and likely intrapreneurship given findings by Rigtering and Weitzel (2013), which show that highly specialized work activities and trust in management are influential to intrapreneurial behavior. What should be recognized here is that many actions of the firm, and firm managers, contribute to the development of these climate perceptions, such as encouraging participation, rewarding initiative, and calling for active, supportive peer exchange (Isaksen, 2017).

What should be recognized here, however, is that people are generally quite bad at idea evaluation. For example, Blair and Mumford (2007) asked undergraduates to assume the role of members of a foundation's proposal review panel and evaluate ideas for potential funding. What is of note is the attributes of the ideas presented were systematically varied. It was found people preferred to fund ideas that were easy to understand provided short-term benefits to many and were consistent with prevailing social norms. They tended to discount risky, time-consuming original ideas.

This bias to safe, as opposed to original, risky, ideas clearly will act to undermine both creative thinking and intrapreneurship in firms. Thus, the question arises as to how this bias might be offset. In one study along these lines, Gibson and Mumford (2013) found that if people think deeply in idea evaluation, these biases are minimized and creative thinking improves. In another study along these lines, Licuanan et al. (2007) found that active analysis of ideas presented contributes to creative thought. These findings are noteworthy because they suggest that intrapreneurs must not only think actively and deeply about the ideas presented to them but also that firms should take actions to encourage active, deep analysis of ideas. One way this might be accomplished is by asking intrapreneurs to write reports—reports detailing when and how an idea might, or might not, workout downstream. Another way such active deep analysis might be encouraged is by encouraging intrapreneurs to benchmark ideas against similar ideas pursued in the past.

Constraint Analysis

Earlier we noted the traditional view of intrapreneurship held that intrapreneurship was inhibited by the structure, norms, and extant processes of the firm. Thus, the intrapreneur was held to be, at least to some extent, in conflict with the firm. This same view is evident in traditional conceptions of creative thought where external constraints were seen as inhibitors with respect to the generation of multiple new ideas. An alternative view, however, holds that constraints on pursuing new ideas might serve as a stimulus for creative problem-solving as people seek ways to work with, or work around, these constraints.

Some support for this alternative view of the role of constraints has been provided in a study by Medeiros, Partlow, and Mumford (2014). In this study, undergraduates were asked to provide written advertising campaigns for a new product, a high-energy root beer. Judges were asked to appraise the resulting campaign proposals for quality, originality, and elegance. Prior to starting work on their campaign, the description of the firm and product were used to impose constraints with respect to marketing fundamentals, marketing themes, market information, or task objectives. It was found that the imposition of these constraints led to the production of higher quality, more original, and more elegant problem solutions than when constraints were not imposed and the constraints were malleable. In another study along these lines, Medeiros, Steele, Watts, and Mumford (2018) introduced constraints on a restaurant business development task where the resulting business development plans were appraised for quality, originality, and elegance. Again, it was found that the induction of constraints resulted in business development plans of higher quality, originality, and elegance, especially when people thought about operative constraints early in their cycle of problem-solving activities.

Thus, the available evidence suggests that the constraints imposed by firms may not inhibit creative thought, and intrapreneurship, at least when people think about constraints early on and seek to work around, or work within, these constraints. Some support for this argument has been provided in a study by Peterson and colleagues (2013). In this study, participants were asked to provide solutions to an educational leadership problem—providing a curriculum plan for a new experimental secondary school where they had recently been appointed as principal. Curriculum plans were appraised by judges for quality, originality, and elegance. Prior to preparing these plans, however, participants were, or were not, asked to complete a set of self-paced instructional modules. These instructional modules provided participants with strategies for identifying and working around (1) resource constraints, (2) system capability constraints, (3) user skill constraints, and (4) goal constraints. It was found this training in constraint analysis resulted in the production of higher quality, more original, and more elegant curriculum plans.

The studies described earlier are noteworthy for two reasons. First, firms impose constraints and, through firm norms, leave people to assume that constraints are absolutely fixed and unmalleable. Thus, to encourage intrapreneurship, firms should make clear and communicate exactly which, to what degree, and by whom any given constrain is malleable. Thus firms, if they seek intrapreneurship, should clarify the nature and manipulability of the constraints they impose.

Second, intrapreneurship requires thinking about how to work within, or work around, these constraints. The Peterson et al. (2013) study suggests that training intrapreneurs in strategies for identifying, analyzing, and finding ways of working around constraints might prove of value in enhancing intrapreneurship. Alternatively, or in addition, firms might task intrapreneurs to identify key constraints impacting on their ideas and provide an analysis of how they, or the firm, might act to minimize the impact of these constraints. Indeed, firms seeking intrapreneurship might apply systematic procedures where constraints bearing on new ideas are discussed and analyzed in teams to provide legitimation for the strategies selected to work within and around these constraints.

Planning

Prior research on intrapreneurship indicates that one way intrapreneurs differ from entrepreneurs is they are more likely to engage in planning activities (Blanka, 2018). Indeed, prior research indicates that constraints, and the need to manage constraints, encourages planning (Mumford & Frese, 2015). Intrapreneurial activities must be embedded in ongoing firm activities—a set of constraints. And, again, the need to integrate intrapreneurial activities within firm constraints points to the need for planning.

Although the significance of planning for intrapreneurs may seem obvious, the need for planning has historically been discounted (Sarasvathy, 2001). Some argue that planning can be problematic as the future is unpredictable (Mintzberg, 1994), and that successful entrepreneurial efforts require effectuation (Sarasvathy, 2001), or logic that states the future is not predicted but controlled through action (Wiltbank, Read, Dew, & Sarasvathy, 2009). That said, the effectuation theory has received criticism in the literature for lack of empirical support (Arend, Sarooghi, & Burkemper, 2015). Given evidence that intrinsically motivated individuals perceive uncertainty (e.g., the future) as an exploration activity where they identify business opportunities (Schmitt, Rosing, Zhang, & Leatherbee, 2018), it appears planning may actually improve performance in firms fostering intrapreneurship. In fact, it is known through expertise and implementation intentions (i.e., intentions to implement the forecasts) that individuals are better, and more accurate, at predicting future trends (i.e., forecasting) (Dailey & Mumford, 2006). In other words, when people have the experience they need and fully intend on implementing their forecasts, the accuracy of said forecasts improves. With expertise and motivation to implement creative ideas, intrapreneur forecasts should be more accurate and lead to more successful innovative efforts.

Additionally, work by Marta, Leritz, and Mumford (2005) suggests that planning skills may be critical to intrapreneurs innovative efforts. In this study, undergraduate participants were asked to work in teams as consultants formulating a plan for turning around a failing automotive firm. After teams had formulated their plan, they were asked to nominate their leader and judges appraised the turnaround plans produced by teams for quality, originality, and elegance. Prior to starting work on this task, all participants were asked to complete a measure examining business planning skills such as the identification of key causes, identification of restrictions, identification of downstream consequences, use of opportunistic implementation strategies, and viable environmental scanning. In addition, leader initiation, structure, and consideration were assessed. It was found that leader structuring behavior was a powerful influence on the quality, originality, and elegance of teams' turnaround plans. More centrally, effective leader structuring behavior was largely determined by leader planning skills. Thus, the ability of intrapreneurs to produce viable, creative products depends on structuring behavior with effective structuring depending on planning skills.

In another study along those lines, Giorgini and Mumford (2013) asked undergraduates to work on plans for restructuring a firm. Final plans provided by these undergraduates were appraised by judges for quality, originality, and elegance. Prior to preparing their final plans, however, participants were asked to formulate an initial plan and backup plans that might be executed if certain restrictions or constraints were encountered. It was found the detail and depth of participant's initial plans, and their backup plans, contributed to the production of higher quality, more original, and more elegant turnaround plans. Thus, planning skills are not just critical to team-level innovation but also individual-level innovation— innovation held to be crucial to the performance of intrapreneurs.

These findings point to the impact of planning skills on intrapreneurship are noteworthy because they suggest a number of actions firms might take to improve intrapreneurship. As O'Connor (1998) notes, asking people to anticipate how ideas might unfold over time and the critical roadblocks likely to be encountered in pursuing these ideas may contribute to intrapreneurship behavior. Furthermore, asking people to spend time thinking deeply about roadblocks that might be encountered in developing and implementing new ideas can be expected to contribute to intrapreneurship. In fact, work by Osburn and Mumford (2006) suggests that providing training in planning skills will not only improve planning, but results in people producing ideas of higher quality, originality, and elegance— especially when such training is provided to people who have a propensity for pursuing creative, new ideas, such as intrapreneurs.

Forecasting

Action theory suggests that planning is critical to intrapreneurial efforts, as these efforts require proactive steps to problem-solve or develop a product (Frese, 2007). Planning is significant, in part, because plans allow intrapreneurs to forecast the implications of pursuing new ideas and appraising and adapting their plans for developing these ideas. Byrne, Shipman, and Mumford (2010) and Shipman, Byrne, and Mumford (2010) have examined the impact of forecasting skills on the development of creative ideas. In the Byrne et al. (2010) study, undergraduate participants were asked to assume the role of a manager in an advertising firm and formulate a campaign to market a new product. In the Shipman et al. (2010) study, undergraduate participants were asked to formulate a plan for leading a new experimental secondary school. Final marketing campaigns and school leadership plans were appraised by judges for quality, originality, and elegance. Prior to preparing these plans, however, participants reviewed emails from a consulting firm hired to help them in their work—one email asked them to provide their initial idea whereas the second email asked them to forecast the outcomes of pursuing this idea.

Written responses to the forecasting email were appraised by judges on twenty-seven attributes such as number of positive outcomes forecasted, number of negative outcomes forecasted, anticipating changes in resources, and anticipating changes in restrictions. Subsequently, these ratings were factored with four dimensions emerging: (1) forecasting extensiveness, (2) forecasting over longer time frames, (3) forecasting resources, and (4) forecasting negative outcomes. More centrally, in both the Byrne et al. (2010) and Shipman et al. (2010) studies, it was found that extensiveness of forecasting and the time frame of forecasting was strongly related (R ≅ .45) to the quality, originality, and elegance of final plans. In another study along these lines, McIntosh, Mulhearn, and Mumford (in press) asked undergraduates to assume the role of a restaurant consultant and provide a plan for a new restaurant concept—plans appraised by judges for quality, originality, and elegance. Not only was extensiveness of forecasting found to be strongly related to performance on this task, but it was also found that people's best solutions emerged when they forecasted both positive and negative outcomes.

These studies are noteworthy because they indicate forecasting skill might be critical to intrapreneurship. This observation, however, broaches the question, How might firms encourage more extensive forecasting and forecasting over longer time frames? One way this might be accomplished is suggested by McIntosh et al. (in press) study. Firms should ask people to anticipate both the risks and benefits of ideas as they will unfold over progressively longer periods and provide an appraisal of alternative strategies for managing both risks and benefits. Another approach firms might take to encourage more extensive, longer term forecasting is to encourage people to set aside current firm operations and forecast how an idea might play out for the firm or the industry over a ten-year period (O'Connor, 1998). Yet another approach might include asking review teams to provide intrapreneurs with feedback concerning downstream risks and benefits and ask intrapreneurs to provide responses to this forecasting feedback.

Wisdom

What should be recognized here is that forecasts may not always suggest how ideas should be pursued by a firm. A new idea, however viable, might prove so disruptive to current firm operations, pursuit of this idea is simply not feasible. Alternatively, a new idea being contemplated by an intrapreneur may exceed the adaptive capacity of the firm. These observations are noteworthy because they imply that intrapreneurs must evaluate ideas and forecasts within the context of the firm—pursuing only those ideas likely to prove workable in this context. The contextual appraisal of ideas has traditionally been subsumed under the rubric of wisdom. Wisdom may be defined as expert knowledge providing insight and judgment, or guidance, about complicated and uncertain matters (Baltes, Staudinger, Maercker, & Smith, 1995; Kunzmann & Baltes, 2005) and may be seen as a skill integrating tacit and experiential knowledge for problem-solving efforts (Sternberg, 1990). Although the importance of wisdom in a firm's decision-making, including the decision-making of intrapreneurs, has been recognized for some time (McKenna, Rooney, & Boal, 2009), little research has examined the impact of wisdom on the pursuit of new and/or innovative ideas in firms.

In a study by Connelly et al. (2000) creative thinking and the performance of leaders in a highly bureaucratic institution, the U.S. Army, was examined. Some 2,000 army officers, ranging in grade from second lieutenant to full colonel, were asked to work through a series of military problems calling for creative thought where the quality and originality of problem solutions were assessed. In addition, officer performance in resolving critical incidents was assessed along with institutional appraisals of the success of such efforts—reflected in medals won.

Officers were asked to complete a measure of wisdom, developed by the researchers. On this measure, officers were presented with a series of complex, ambiguous scenarios emerging from the business domain where they were asked to indicate why this situation emerged, the contextual mistake made by the key actor in this scenario, and how they would respond if they were placed in this situation. Judges rated written responses to these questions on key attributes of wise decision-making such as systems perception, self-reflection, objectivity, sensitivity to solution fit, judgment under uncertainty, and systems commitment. It was found that these attributes of wisdom were strongly ($r \cong .40$) related to officer's production of creative problem solutions, their management of critical incidents, and institutional evaluation of their performance in managing critical incidents. Three attributes of wisdom were found to prove especially effective predictors of officer creativity and performance: (1) sensitivity to solution fit, (2) objectivity, and (3) self-reflection. Indeed, other studies (e.g., Strange & Mumford, 2005) have provided evidence pointing to the criticality of these skills in creative thinking in firms. From these findings, one can see that contextual appraisal, or the analysis of environmental, social, personal, and other relevant factors, is vital in understanding how a solution will fit in a given environment, remaining objective in decision-making, and reflecting on one's own actions and goals. These skills allow the individual to better navigate their environment and make sensible, wise decisions.

One implication of these observations is firms should seek to build wisdom in intrapreneurs through exposure to a wide range of firm operations through briefings, rotational assignments, or assignments to action planning teams (Mumford, Marks, Connelly, Zaccaro, & Reiter-Palmon, 2000). Firms might also encourage intrapreneurs to reflect on the implications of ideas and forecast for their work team or potential impacts on the growth of the firm. Finally, firms might highlight the value of sustained, objective thought by successful intrapreneurs as a means for encouraging objectivity on the part of intrapreneurs as they appraise ideas and forecast outcomes for the firm of pursuing ideas.

Championing

Our argument that intrapreneurs must remain objective with respect to ideas, and in their evaluation of ideas, may strike one as contradicting a key quality we commonly ascribe to both entrepreneurs and intrapreneurs. More specifically, we assume that intrapreneurs, like entrepreneurs, must sell, or champion, their ideas to the firm especially top management. In fact, a variety of work suggests that when firms pursue new ideas these ideas are actually championed by certain advocates (Markham & Smith, 2017). In this regard, it is important to ask exactly how the "sales" of new ideas occur in firms (Anderson & Bateman, 2000).

A study by Howell and Boies (2004) provides evidence for how the "sale" of ideas occurs in firms. They identified matched pairs of nineteen new product champions and non-champions by asking top management teams to identify those who championed, or did not champion, innovative new products fielded by some eighty-eight large Canadian firms. Interviews concerning the development and fielding of these innovative new products were conducted with champions and non-champions. A content analysis was then used to identify the key variables distinguishing champions from non-champions. It was found that idea generation led to idea promotion. Thus, champions do sell ideas. However, idea promotion was based on appropriate packaging and selling of ideas with respect to both knowledge of firm strategy and knowledge of firm norms.

These findings are noteworthy for three reasons. First, they suggest that firms, or people, who seek to bring new ideas to fruition in organizations cannot remain in the world of their idea—they must sell or promote the idea within the firm. Second, to sell or promote ideas within firms, people must know and understand the nature and significance of the norms of the firm. Thus, champions, intrapreneurs, are not outsiders. They must be insiders in the firm and have enough experience to understand, and work within, firm norms. Third, and perhaps most important, champions must know and understand firm strategy.

Our third observation is especially noteworthy because it points to one way firms might encourage intrapreneurship. Firms that seek intrapreneurship should make the business strategy of the firm, and its competitors, available to all employees. And firms should explicitly say where and why new ideas might contribute to the execution of this strategy. Not only will widespread dissemination of firm strategy encourage intrapreneurship, but the dissemination of the firm strategy will also prove especially useful if ambiguities in firm plans for executing this strategy are expressly noted. If firms disseminate strategy appropriately and allow intrapreneurs the access needed to promote new ideas vis-à-vis this strategy, many more people may be willing to adopt intrapreneurial roles.

Conclusion

Before turning to the broader implications of the present effort, certain limitations should be noted. To begin, we have not, in the present effort, examined all individual-level characteristics that might contribute to intrapreneurship. For example, little has been said in the present effort about what motivates intrapreneurs or the personality characteristics exhibited by intrapreneurs (Blanka, 2018). By the same token, we should note these motivational and dispositional characteristics are largely consistent with what is known about creative people in general (e.g., Feist & Gorman, 1998). Along related lines, little was said in the present effort about the kind of abilities that might be needed by intrapreneurs. Finally, in the present effort, we have focused on the skills intrapreneurs must possess largely using evidence derived from a set of low-fidelity simulation exercises (i.e., participants in a paper-and-pencil study design) examining creative performance in organizational settings—typically on tasks similar to those likely to be presented to intrapreneurs. Nonetheless, the question remains as to whether similar findings concerning the impact of these skills on performance would be obtained if intrapreneurs acting in real-world settings had been examined.

Even bearing these caveats in mind, we believe the present effort is noteworthy because it defines a set of key skills needed by intrapreneurs. We have provided some evidence that seven distinct skills contribute to the success of intrapreneurial efforts in firms: (1) affordance recognition, (2) idea evaluation, (3) constraint analysis, (4) planning, (5) forecasting, (6) wisdom, and (7) championing. Hopefully future research will provide additional evidence bearing on the impact of all these skills on the emergence of intrapreneurs and their performance in intrapreneurial roles.

Although other researchers have provided frameworks for analyzing and measuring intrapreneurship (see Ireland, Covin, & Kuratko, 2009; Narayanan, Yang, & Zahra, 2009; Gawke, Gorgievski, & Bakker, 2019), this piece explains a unique view that focuses on the cognitive processes involved in creative problem-solving, an inherent activity involved in any intrapreneurial endeavors of an organization. We present ways that firms can foster intrapreneurial activities by promoting and maintaining these cognitive processes. And although it is important to synthesize and integrate the literature within this domain at a macro level (see Narayanan et al., 2009), it is also critical to analyze how firms can promote the aforementioned skills necessary for organizational intrapreneurship.

Further work along these lines is noteworthy for two reasons. First, well-developed measures of intrapreneurial skill may provide a basis for assessing people's potential to engage in intrapreneurial activity. Second, such measures, along with viable developmental programs may allow people to pursue intrapreneurial ventures more effectively. Indeed, at least some studies, for example, Osburn and Mumford (2006) and Peterson et al. (2013), suggest that many of these skills can, in fact, be developed through appropriate training interventions.

More broadly, our observations with regard to these skills point to a broader conclusion with regard to intrapreneurship. Traditionally, intrapreneurs have been viewed as being in conflict with the firm as they seek to move the firm into new business areas or new production processes. Our observations regarding these skills, however, suggest that conflict between the intrapreneurs and the firm is not a given. Firms can take actions likely to encourage the application of intrapreneurial skills. For example, firms can broadly disseminate firm business strategy to encourage championing. Firms can encourage intrapreneurship by requiring managers to not simply evaluate ideas but also to seek to improve these ideas—actions that contribute to more effective idea evaluation. Firms can establish information systems that allow for ready recognition of affordances or key risks and opportunities. Although other examples might be cited, our foregoing examples seem sufficient to make our basic point. Firms can create conditions likely to encourage intrapreneurship. We hope the present effort provides an impetus for future research intended to establish exactly how firms might encourage the application of the skills needed by intrapreneurs.

References

Ahmad, N. H., Nasurdin, A. M., & Zainal, S. R. (2011). The role of organizational internal ecosystem in fostering intrapreneurship spirit. *World Review of Business Research, 1,* 38–51.

Amo, B. W. (2010). Corporate entrepreneurship and intrapreneurship related to innovation behaviour among employees. *International Journal of Entrepreneurial Venturing, 2,* 144–158.

Anderson, L. M., & Bateman, T. S. (2000). Individual environmental initiative: Championing natural environmental issues in US business organizations. *Academy of Management Journal, 43,* 548–570.

Antoncic, B., & Hisrich, R. D. (2003). Clarifying the intrapreneurship concept. *Journal of Small Business and Enterprise Development, 10,* 7–24.

Arend, R., Sarooghi, H., & Burkemper, A. (2015). Effectuation as ineffectual? Applying the 3E theory-assessment framework to a proposed new theory of entrepreneurship. *Academy of Management Review, 40,* 630–651.

Audretsch, D. B., Coad, A., & Segarra, A. (2014). Firm growth and innovation. *Small Business Economics, 43,* 743–749.

Ballot, G., Fakhfakh, F., & Taymaz, E. (2001). Firms' human capital, R&D and performance: A study on French and Swedish firms. *Labour Economics, 8,* 443–462.

Baltes, P. B., Staudinger, U. M., Maercker, A., & Smith, J. (1995). People nominated as wise: A comparative study of wisdom-related knowledge. *Psychology and Aging, 10,* 155–166.

Baughman, W. A., & Mumford, M. D. (1995). Process-analytic models of creative capacities: Operations influencing the combination-and-reorganization process. *Creativity Research Journal, 8,* 37–62.

Bernstein, J. I., & Nadiri, M. I. (1989). Research and development and intra-industry spillovers: An empirical application of dynamic duality. *The Review of Economic Studies, 56,* 249–267.

Besemer, S. P., & O'Quin, K. (1999). Confirming the three-factor creative product analysis matrix model in an American sample. *Creativity Research Journal, 12,* 287–296.

Bicknell, A., Francis-Smythe, J., & Arthur, J. (2010). Knowledge transfer: De-constructing the entrepreneurial academic. *International Journal of Entrepreneurial Behavior & Research, 16,* 485–501.

Bjornali, E. S., & Anne Støren, L. (2012). Examining competence factors that encourage innovative behaviour by European higher education graduate professionals. *Journal of Small Business and Enterprise Development, 19,* 402–423.

Blair, C. S., & Mumford, M. D. (2007). Errors in idea evaluation: Preference for the unoriginal? *The Journal of Creative Behavior, 41,* 197–222.

Blanka, C. (2018). An individual-level perspective on intrapreneurship: A review and ways forward. *Review of Managerial Science, 12,* 1–43.

Burgelman, R. A. (1983). Corporate entrepreneurship and strategic management: Insights from a process study. *Management Science, 29,* 1349–1364.

Byrne, C. L., Shipman, A. S., & Mumford, M. D. (2010). The effects of forecasting on creative problem-solving: An experimental study. *Creativity Research Journal, 22,* 119–138.

Campos, F., Frese, M., Goldstein, M., Iacovone, L., Johnson, H., McKenzie, D., & Mensmann, M. (2017). Teaching personal initiative beats traditional business training in boosting small business in West Africa. *Science, 357,* 1287–1290.

Chandy, R. K., & Tellis, G. J. (1998). Organizing for radical product innovation: The overlooked role of willingness to cannibalize. *Journal of Marketing Research, 35,* 474–487.

Chen, W. R., & Miller, K. D. (2007). Situational and institutional determinants of firms' R&D search intensity. *Strategic Management Journal, 28*, 369–381.

Connelly, M. S., Gilbert, J. A., Zaccaro, S. J., Threlfall, K. V., Marks, M. A., & Mumford, M. D. (2000). Exploring the relationship of leadership skills and knowledge to leader performance. *The Leadership Quarterly, 11*, 65–86.

Dailey, L., & Mumford, M. D. (2006). Evaluative aspects of creative thought: Errors in appraising the implications of new ideas. *Creativity Research Journal, 18*, 385–390.

Dewey, J. (1910). Science as subject-matter and as method. *Science, 31*, 121–127.

Eisenberger, R., & Shanock, L. (2003). Rewards, intrinsic motivation, and creativity: A case study of conceptual and methodological isolation. *Creativity Research Journal, 15*, 121–130.

Feist, G. J., & Gorman, M. E. (1998). The psychology of science: Review and integration of a nascent discipline. *Review of General Psychology, 2*, 3–47.

Fischer, S., Frese, M., Mertins, J. C., Hardt, J. V., Flock, T., Schauder, J., . . . Wiegel, J. (2014). Climate for personal initiative and radical and incremental innovation in firms: A validation study. *Journal of Enterprising Culture, 22*, 91–109.

Frese, M. (2007). The psychological actions and entrepreneurial success: An action theory approach. In J. R. Baum, M. Frese, & R. A. Baron (Eds.), *The psychology of entrepreneurship* (pp. 151–188). Mahwah, NJ: Lawrence Erlbaum Associates.

Friedrich, T. L., & Mumford, M. D. (2009). The effects of conflicting information on creative thought: A source of performance improvements or decrements? *Creativity Research Journal, 21*, 265–281.

Friedrich, T. L., Vessey, W. B., Schuelke, M. J., Ruark, G. A., & Mumford, M. D. (2009). A framework for understanding collective leadership: The selective utilization of leader and team expertise within networks. *The Leadership Quarterly, 20*, 933–958.

Gawke, J. C., Gorgievski, M. J., & Bakker, A. B. (2019). Measuring intrapreneurship at the individual level: Development and validation of the Employee Intrapreneurship Scale (EIS). *European Management Journal.* Retrieved from https://doi.org/10.1016/j.emj.2019.03.001

Gibson, C., & Mumford, M. D. (2013). Evaluation, criticism, and creativity: Criticism content and effects on creative problem solving. *Psychology of Aesthetics, Creativity, and the Arts, 7*, 314.

Giorgini, V., & Mumford, M. D. (2013). Backup plans and creative problem-solving: Effects of causal, error, and resource processing. *The International Journal of Creativity and Problem Solving, 23*, 121–147.

Goedhuys, M. (2007). Learning, product innovation, and firm heterogeneity in developing countries: Evidence from Tanzania. *Industrial and Corporate Change, 16*, 269–292.

Greeno, J. G. (1994). Gibson's affordances. *Psychological Review, 101*, 336–342.

Gündoğdu, M. Ç. (2012). Re-thinking entrepreneurship, intrapreneurship, and innovation: A multi-concept perspective. *Procedia-Social and Behavioral Sciences, 41*, 296–303.

Gupta, A., & Srivastava, N. (2013). An exploratory study of factors affecting intrapreneurship. *International Journal of Innovative Research and Development, 2*, 1–8.

Hagedorn, R. A., & Jamieson, D. W. (2014). Intrapreneurial sensemaking: The case of a reenvisioned school of professional studies. *International Journal of Entrepreneurship and Innovation Management, 18*, 425–437.

Howell, J. M., & Boies, K. (2004). Champions of technological innovation: The influence of contextual knowledge, role orientation, idea generation, and idea promotion on champion emergence. *The Leadership Quarterly, 15*, 123–143.

Huber, J. C. (2000). A statistical analysis of special cases of creativity. *The Journal of Creative Behavior, 34,* 203–225.

Hunter, S. T., Bedell, K. E., & Mumford, M. D. (2007). Climate for creativity: A quantitative review. *Creativity Research Journal, 19,* 69–90.

Ireland, R. D., Covin, J. G., & Kuratko, D. F. (2009). Conceptualizing corporate entrepreneurship strategy. *Entrepreneurship Theory and Practice, 33,* 19–46.

Isaksen, A. (2017). Regional clusters building on local and non-local relationships: A European comparison. In *Proximity, distance and diversity* (pp. 137–160). London, UK: Routledge.

Jelinek, M., & Schoonhoven, C. B. (1990). *The innovation marathon: Lessons learned from high technology firms.* Oxford: Blackwell.

Kunzmann, U., & Baltes, P. B. (2005). The psychology of wisdom: Theoretical and empirical challenges. In R. J. Jordan (Ed.), *A handbook of wisdom: Psychological perspectives* (pp. 110–135). New York: Cambridge University Press.

Licuanan, B. F., Dailey, L. R., & Mumford, M. D. (2007). Idea evaluation: Error in evaluating highly original ideas. *The Journal of Creative Behavior, 41,* 1–27.

Lonergan, D. C., Scott, G. M., & Mumford, M. D. (2004). Evaluative aspects of creative thought: Effects of appraisal and revision standards. *Creativity Research Journal, 16,* 231–246.

Marcy, R. T., & Mumford, M. D. (2007). Social innovation: Enhancing creative performance through causal analysis. *Creativity Research Journal, 19,* 123–140.

Marcy, R. T., & Mumford, M. D. (2010). Leader cognition: Improving leader performance through causal analysis. *The Leadership Quarterly, 21,* 1–19.

Markham, S. E., & Smith, J. W. (2017). How can we advise Achilles? A rehabilitation of the concept of the champion for leadership. In M. D. Mumford & S. Hemlin (Eds.), *Handbook of research on leadership and creativity* (pp. 59–81). London, UK: Edward Elgar Publishing.

Marta, S., Leritz, L. E., & Mumford, M. D. (2005). Leadership skills and the group performance: Situational demands, behavioral requirements, and planning. *The Leadership Quarterly, 16,* 97–120.

McIntosh, T., Mulhearn, T., & Mumford, M. D. (in press). Taking the good with the bad: The impact of forecasting timing and valence on idea evaluation and creativity. *Psychology of Aesthetics, Creativity, and the Arts.*

McKenna, B., Rooney, D., & Boal, K. B. (2009). Wisdom principles as a meta-theoretical basis for evaluating leadership. *The Leadership Quarterly, 20,* 177–190.

Medeiros, K. E., Partlow, P. J., & Mumford, M. D. (2014). Not too much, not too little: The influence of constraints on creative problem solving. *Psychology of Aesthetics, Creativity, and the Arts, 8,* 198–210.

Medeiros, K. E., Steele, L. M., Watts, L. L., & Mumford, M. D. (2018). Timing is everything: Examining the role of constraints throughout the creative process. *Psychology of Aesthetics, Creativity, and the Arts, 12,* 471–488.

Mintzberg, H. (1994). The fall and rise of strategic planning. *Harvard Business Review, 72,* 107–114.

Mumford, M. D., Antes, A. L., Caughron, J. J., Connelly, S., & Beeler, C. (2010). Cross-field differences in creative problem-solving skills: A comparison of health, biological, and social sciences. *Creativity Research Journal, 22,* 14–26.

Mumford, M. D., Baughman, W. A., Supinski, E. P., & Maher, M. A. (1996). Process-based measures of creative problem-solving skills: II: Information encoding. *Creativity Research Journal, 9,* 77–88.

Mumford, M. D., & Frese, M. (Eds.). (2015). *The psychology of planning in organizations: Research and applications.* New York: Routledge.

Mumford, M. D., & Gustafson, S. B. (2007). Creative thought: Cognition and problem solving in a dynamic system. *Creativity Research Handbook, 2,* 33–77.

Mumford, M. D., Marks, M. A., Connelly, M. S., Zaccaro, S. J., & Reiter-Palmon, R. (2000). Development of leadership skills: Experience and timing. *The Leadership Quarterly, 11,* 87–114.

Mumford, M. D., Medeiros, K. E., & Partlow, P. J. (2012). Creative thinking: Processes, strategies, and knowledge. *The Journal of Creative Behavior, 46,* 30–47.

Mumford, M. D., Mobley, M. I., Reiter-Palmon, R., Uhlman, C. E., & Doares, L. M. (1991). Process analytic models of creative capacities. *Creativity Research Journal, 4,* 91–122.

Mumford, M. D., Supinski, E. P., Baughman, W. A., Costanza, D. P., & Threlfall, K. V. (1997). Process-based measures of creative problem-solving skills: V: Overall prediction. *Creativity Research Journal, 10,* 73–85.

Narayanan, V. K., Yang, Y., & Zahra, S. A. (2009). Corporate venturing and value creation: A review and proposed framework. *Research Policy, 38,* 58–76.

O'Connor, G. C. (1998). Market learning and radical innovation: A cross case comparison of eight radical innovation projects. *Journal of Product Innovation Management, 15,* 151–166.

Osburn, H. K., & Mumford, M. D. (2006). Creativity and planning: Training interventions to develop creative problem-solving skills. *Creativity Research Journal, 18,* 173–190.

Parnes, S. J., & Noller, R. B. (1972). Applied creativity: The creative studies project: Part results of a two year study. *Journal of Creative Behavior, 6,* 164–186.

Peterson, D. R., Barrett, J. D., Hester, K. S., Robledo, I. C., Hougen, D. F., Day, E. A., & Mumford, M. D. (2013). Teaching people to manage constraints: Effects on creative problem-solving. *Creativity Research Journal, 25,* 335–347.

Rauch, A., & Frese, M. (2007a). Born to be an entrepreneur? Revisiting the personality approach to entrepreneurship. In M. Frese, J. R. Baum, & R. A. Baron (Eds.), *The psychology of entrepreneurship* (pp. 41–66). Mahwah, NJ: Lawrence Erlbaum Associates.

Rauch, A., & Frese, M. (2007b). Let's put the person back into entrepreneurship research: A meta-analysis on the relationship between business owners' personality traits, business creation, and success. *European Journal of Work & Organizational Psychology, 16,* 353–385.

Redmond, M. R., Mumford, M. D., & Teach, R. (1993). Putting creativity to work: Effects of leader behavior on subordinate creativity. *Organizational Behavior and Human Decision Processes, 55,* 120–151.

Reiter-Palmon, R., & Paulus, P. B. (in press). Cognitive and social processes in team creativity. In M. D. Mumford & E. M. Todd (Eds.), *Creativity and innovation in organizations.* New York: Taylor & Francis.

Reiter-Palmon, R., & Robinson, E. J. (2009). Problem identification and construction: What do we know, what is the future? *Psychology of Aesthetics, Creativity, and the Arts, 3,* 43.

Rigtering, J. P. C., & Weitzel, U. (2013). Work context and employee behaviour as antecedents for intrapreneurship. *International Entrepreneurship and Management Journal, 9,* 337–360.

Robledo, I. C., Hester, K. S., Peterson, D. R., Barrett, J. D., Day, E. A., Hougen, D. P., & Mumford, M. D. (2012). Errors and understanding: The effects of error-management training on creative problem-solving. *Creativity Research Journal, 24,* 220–234.

Runco, M. A. (in press). Abilities. In M. D. Mumford & E. M. Todd (Eds.), *Creativity and innovation in organizations*. New York: Taylor & Francis.

Sarasvathy, S. D. (2001). Causation and effectuation: Toward a theoretical shift from economic inevitability to entrepreneurial contingency. *Academy of Management Review, 26*, 243–263.

Schmitt, A., Rosing, K., Zhang, S. X., & Leatherbee, M. (2018). A dynamic model of entrepreneurial uncertainty and business opportunity identification: Exploration as a mediator and entrepreneurial self-efficacy as a moderator. *Entrepreneurship Theory and Practice, 42*, 835–859.

Scott, G., Leritz, L. E., & Mumford, M. D. (2004). The effectiveness of creativity training: A quantitative review. *Creativity Research Journal, 16*, 361–388.

Scott, G. M., Lonergan, D. C., & Mumford, M. D. (2005). Contractual combination: Alternative knowledge structures, alternative heuristics. *Creativity Research Journal, 17*, 21–36.

Shipman, A. S., Byrne, C. L., & Mumford, M. D. (2010). Leader vision formation and forecasting: The effects of forecasting extent, resources, and timeframe. *The Leadership Quarterly, 21*, 439–456.

Sternberg, R. J. (1986). Critical thinking: Its nature, measurement, and improvement. In F. R. Link (Ed.), *Essays on the intellect* (pp. 45–65). Alexandria, VA: Association for Supervision and Curriculum Development.

Sternberg, R. J. (Ed.). (1990). *Wisdom: Its nature, origins, and development*. Cambridge, UK: Cambridge University Press.

Tierney, P., & Farmer, S. M. (2002). Creative self-efficacy: Its potential antecedents and relationship to creative performance. *Academy of Management Journal, 45*, 1137–1148.

Urbano, D., & Turró, A. (2013). Conditioning factors for corporate entrepreneurship: An in (ex) ternal approach. *International Entrepreneurship and Management Journal, 9*, 379–396.

Whittle, A., & Mueller, F. (2008). Intra-preneurship and enrollment: Building networks of ideas. *Organization, 15*, 445–462.

Wiltbank, R., Read, S., Dew, N., & Sarasvathy, S. D. (2009). Prediction and control under uncertainty: Outcomes in angel investing. *Journal of Business Venturing, 24*, 116–133.

Zaccaro, S. J., Green, J. P., Dubrow, S., & Kolze, M. (2018). Leader individual differences, situational parameters, and leadership outcomes: A comprehensive review and integration. *The Leadership Quarterly, 29*, 2–43.

8

CULTURE AND ENTREPRENEURSHIP

A Cross-Cultural Perspective

Ute Stephan

Introduction

Entrepreneurial activity—from start-up to entrepreneurial failure—differs substantially across countries. These country differences tend to persist over time (Appendix 8.1). Some but not all of these differences can be attributed to formal institutions such as business regulations or the rule of law (Estrin, Mickiewicz, Stephan, & Wright, 2018; Terjesen, Hessels, & Li, 2016). Another complementary explanation is that such stable differences are rooted in culture, which is the focus of this chapter.

Culture refers to the shared values, norms, and practices of societies "that differentiate collectives from each other in meaningful ways" (House, Javidan, Hanges, & Dorfman, 2002, p. 5). The idea that culture influences entrepreneurship goes back to the work by sociologist Max Weber (1930), who suggested that the values, norms, and practices associated with the Protestant work ethic stimulated individuals to engage in enterprise and supported the success of capitalism in those societies. Moreover, the concept of 'entrepreneurial culture' has intuitive appeal and face validity, for instance, for policy makers who seek to enhance it.[1]

Two reviews have summarized research on culture and entrepreneurship (Hayton & Cacciotti, 2013; Hayton, George, & Zahra, 2002). The last review concluded that research on culture and entrepreneurship has resulted in mixed findings and sheds doubt on the existence of an entrepreneurial culture (Hayton & Cacciotti, 2013). Should we abandon research for the cultural roots of entrepreneurship? I do not think so, but we need to be more rigorous, both theoretically and empirically, in how we conduct culture and entrepreneurship research. This requires clarity about cultural concepts, about the theoretical mechanisms linking culture and entrepreneurship, and about the nature and type of entrepreneurship under investigation.

Figure 8.1 illustrates the structure of this chapter. I first define culture and then give an overview of the main cultural frameworks used in entrepreneurship research to date. These frameworks capture aspects of culture in distinct ways, yet sometimes they are applied indiscriminately, which can give rise to an impression of mixed findings. Thereafter, I review the theoretical mechanisms through which culture and entrepreneurship are thought to be linked. These mechanisms entail different and sometimes opposing predictions for how culture influences entrepreneurship. I close by reflecting on how entrepreneurship is measured and how different measures may again lead to different findings. Throughout this chapter, I highlight seminal work and give examples of research on culture and entrepreneurship from the past 10 years. The chapter offers an overview of culture and entrepreneurship research that is selective in its focus on recent research and on trying to understand when and how what aspects of culture matter for entrepreneurship.

Understanding Culture: Definitions, Perspectives and Its Multilevel Nature

There are countless definitions of culture reflecting the long tradition of research on culture in disciplines such as psychology, anthropology, economics, and sociology. Two perspectives of culture receive the most attention. Both see culture as something that differentiates collectives of individuals (e.g. countries) and which is stable, because it has evolved to enable societies to adapt to their environments, coordinate individuals as part of collectives, and ensure individuals' basic physiological and survival needs are met (Berry, 1993; Schwartz, 2006). The two perspectives of culture differ in where they 'locate' culture and its measurement.

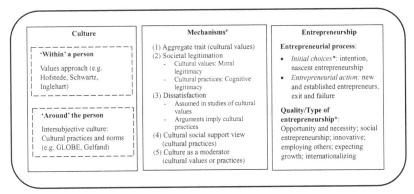

Note: ª suggested links of mechanisms with cultural values and practices in brackets
*indicates aspects of entrepreneurship likely influenced by cultural values because they reflect personal choices, in addition to influences of cultural practices driven by cognitive legitimacy, dissatisfaction and cultural social support

FIGURE 8.1 Overview of the Chapter

The first perspective sees culture as residing *'in' individuals* or "the collective programming of the mind" (Hofstede, 2001, p. 596). Culture is expressed and assessed through individuals' personal values. The mean aggregated values of individuals in a country are taken to represent that country's culture. Examples of this approach are the cultural values theories of Geert Hofstede (2001); Shalom Schwartz (2006) and Ronald Inglehart (1997).

In the second perspective, culture is socially constructed and 'intersubjective' resting on the *shared* perceptions of what individuals of a collective perceive to exist 'around them' (Chiu, Gelfand, Yamagishi, Shteynberg, & Wan, 2010). Culture resides in the "shared motives, values, beliefs, identities, and interpretations or meanings of significant events that result from common experiences of members of collectives and are transmitted across age generations" (House et al., 2002, p. 5). In this approach, the measurement of culture requires the assessment of sharedness or agreement of values, practices, or norms that members of a collective perceive to be prevalent within their society (House, Hanges, Javidan, Dorfman, & Gupta, 2004). Examples are the work of the Global Leadership and Organizational Behavior Effectiveness (GLOBE) project (House et al., 2004) and Michele Gelfand's theory of cultural tightness (Gelfand et al., 2011). Within entrepreneurship research, shared perceptions of the legitimacy of entrepreneurs within a country also fall under this perspective of culture.

The 'collective' typically considered in research on culture and entrepreneurship is the country and thus national culture. Some research on other levels of analyses also exists, for instance, considering regions, communities, or urban versus rural locations within one country (Davidsson, 1995; Garcia-Cabrera & Garcia-Soto, 2008; Hopp & Stephan, 2012; Rooks, Sserwanga, & Frese, 2016). Over the past decade, culture and entrepreneurship research has been influenced by multilevel theory (Kozlowski & Klein, 2000) and multilevel studies are now common. Multilevel studies include culture as a construct at a higher level of aggregation (e.g. country) and allow to model its influence on entrepreneurship at the individual level (e.g., individuals starting or leading a new business), while controlling for confounding factors at both the higher and individual levels of analyses.

Multilevel studies help to overcome biases: the ecological fallacy and the reverse ecological fallacy, also termed disaggregation and aggregation bias (Hofstede, 2001; Smith, 2002). The ecological fallacy cautions to generalize from relationships found at a higher level of analyses to individuals, while the reverse ecological fallacy warns against inferring culture effects from individual-level relationships. An example of the reverse ecological fallacy is to assume that entrepreneurship thrives in individualistic cultures solely on the basis of individual-level research that identifies entrepreneurs as individuals holding individualistic values such as emphasizing personal achievement and independence (Gorgievski, Stephan, Laguna, & Moriano, 2018; McGrath et al., 1992; Noseleit, 2010). Multilevel studies also offer more statistically valid conclusions than single-level research (e.g., due to incorrect estimates of standard errors and therefore significance levels in single-level research; Peterson, Arregle, & Martin, 2012).[2] They also entail new opportunities such as testing cross-level interactions and frog-pond models (see the section on mechanisms).

An Overview of Cultural Theories and Entrepreneurship

This section gives an overview of the dominant cultural theories and empirical research that relates them to entrepreneurship. I discuss in turn, Hofstede and the work of the GLOBE project that built on Hofstede, followed by Schwartz's and Inglehart's value theories, and Gelfand's theory on cultural norms of tightness–looseness.

Hofstede, GLOBE and Entrepreneurship

Past research on entrepreneurship and culture considered almost entirely Hofstede's (2001) theory of culture (Hayton & Cacciotti, 2013). Although Hofstede's measurement instrument includes a mix of questions about values, individual beliefs, and some practices, his theory is widely treated as a theory of cultural values. The main dimensions describe whether people are seen primarily as individuals or as members of a group (individualism–collectivism); the extent to which unpredictability, ambiguity, and lack of structure are intolerable (uncertainty–avoidance); the degree of gender differentiation and assertiveness (masculinity–femininity); and acceptance of status, hierarchy, and power differences (power distance). An entrepreneurial culture was thought to consistent of high individualism, low uncertainty avoidance, masculinity, and low power distance (Hayton et al., 2002), reflecting a drive to take autonomous action in the face of uncertainty; being assertive ('masculine') while doing so, and enabled by an egalitarian (rather than power distant) culture. The fifth dimension in Hofstede's framework is the emphasis on the past versus future (long-term orientation) but so far has found little interest in the entrepreneurship literature.

Hofstede Versus GLOBE

The GLOBE study (House et al., 2004; Javidan, House, Dorfman, Hanges, & Sully De Luque, 2006) developed Hofstede's dimensions of culture further in terms of content and by introducing separate measures of shared cultural values in a country ('should be' measures) and of observed shared cultural practices ('as is' measures). Cultural practices are a type of cultural descriptive norm whereby a particular behavior is seen as legitimate because it is frequently enacted and observed by individuals in that culture (Stephan & Uhlaner, 2010). Often researchers explain the effect of culture in terms of practices, that is, what people do and how that supports entrepreneurs, but rely on cultural value measures to test their prediction. The difference is not trivial as most dimensions of cultural practices and values are negatively related (House et al., 2004). For instance, uncertainty avoidance practices and values correlate at $r = -.62$ (House et al., 2004, p. 736).

In terms of the content of cultural dimensions, GLOBE built on Hofstede's work and features similar dimensions such as uncertainty avoidance, power distance, future orientation (long-term orientation in the Hofstede framework). GLOBE includes more refined measures of individualism–collectivism that distinguish institutional collectivism (risk sharing in society) from in-group or family collectivism. The masculinity–femininity dimension was partitioned into four dimensions: performance orientation, gender egalitarianism, assertiveness, and humane orientation.

Critically, although the labels of the dimensions appear very similar in Hofstede's and GLOBE's work, the relationships among the dimensions with the same label are sometimes unexpected and reveal important conceptual differences (Javidan et al., 2006). For instance, Hofstede's uncertainty avoidance is chiefly a measure of individual stress and anxiety resulting from uncertainty (Sully De Luque & Javidan, 2004), whereas in the GLOBE study the emphasis is on rule orientation in society as a means of avoiding uncertainty (Venaik & Brewer, 2010). Moreover, Hofstede's uncertainty avoidance, although presumed to be a value, correlates strongly negatively with GLOBE uncertainty avoidance cultural practices and more weakly positively with the corresponding GLOBE value[3] (Venaik & Brewer, 2010, Appendix 8.2 illustrates these correlations). Similar item-level analyses led Brewer and Venaik (2011) to suggest that Hofstede's individualism measure would be more appropriately labeled self- versus work orientation, which they found correlated strongly with GLOBE in-group/family collectivism practices and moderately strong with GLOBE institutional collectivism values. Hofstede's power distance measure also mixes cultural practices and values items but correlates more closely with GLOBE practices. Further analyses are beyond the scope of this chapter. Appendix 8.2 should help the reader to see differences between the dimensions whilst also noticing that GLOBE offers insights into culture that are not captured through Hofstede's dimensions.

Hofstede's Theory of Culture and Entrepreneurship

As mentioned earlier, Hayton and Cacciotti (2013) summarized research based on Hofstede's framework. Yet most of the country-level studies included in their review investigated culture's impact on national rates of innovation (and rarely on entrepreneurship). With regard to entrepreneurship, Wennekers, Thurik, Van Stel, and Noorderhaven (2007) found that Hofstede's uncertainty avoidance rather than uncertainty tolerance was positively associated with national rates of business ownership across developed economies. Hofstede et al. (2004) report a similar positive relationship of uncertainty avoidance as well as of power distance with national rates of business ownership in bivariate correlation analyses across a similar set of developed countries (in particular, Organisation for Economic Co-operation and Development (OECD) member countries). Pinillos and Reyes (2011) report that the relationship of Hofstede's individualism depends on the national wealth of countries. In richer developed countries individualism related positively to entrepreneurship, whereas in poorer emerging economies collectivism showed a positive relationship with national entrepreneurship rates. This was true for entrepreneurship that is voluntarily pursued to take advantage of an opportunity (opportunity entrepreneurship) and for entrepreneurship out of necessity, that is, due to lack of alternative employment (necessity entrepreneurship).

Hofstede's cultural indices rely on data collected from IBM employees in the 1960s and 1970s and partly on updated data from diverse samples (Hofstede, 2001). Taras, Steel, and Kirkman (2012) conducted a meta-analysis summarizing research on Hofstede's dimension from 451 empirical studies and over 2,000 samples. Their analyses suggest that meaningful changes over time took place in several cultural dimensions.[4] One study used these updated meta-analytically derived culture scores. This nation-level study found that across a diverse set of countries, individualism was positively and uncertainty avoidance negatively related to entrepreneurship (measured as the national rate of new entrepreneurs; Harms & Groen, 2017). Relationships with power distance and masculinity were not significant. None of the four dimensions related significantly to the national rate of social entrepreneurs, who pursue businesses to help others, or entrepreneurs with expectations to create jobs for others in the future (growth-oriented entrepreneurship; Harms & Groen, 2017). In sum, evidence on culture and entrepreneurship using Hofstede's framework is not as voluminous as one might expect and it is partly contradicting (e.g., negative vs. positive relationship with uncertainty avoidance). Yet the underlying studies used different measures of entrepreneurship (self-employed vs. Global Entrepreneurship Monitor [GEM]–based indicators) and spanned different sets of countries (rich OECD vs. a more mixed set of countries participating in GEM).

GLOBE's Theory of Culture and Entrepreneurship

Due to the negative cultural value–practice relationships, many researchers focus on the cultural practice dimensions of GLOBE as they see the common lived practices around the entrepreneur as the main influence on entrepreneurial behavior. GLOBE cultural practices are also more strongly and consistently correlated with a wide range of objective indicators, whereas GLOBE values correlated with attitudinal measures (Gupta, Sully de Luque, & House, 2004).

If all cultural practice dimensions are considered jointly, multicollinearity arises due to the intercorrelations among them. Hence, Stephan and Uhlaner (2010) followed Peterson and Castro (2006) and conducted a second-order factor analysis that resulted in two higher-order dimensions of cultural practices. The first, *performance-based culture* describes "a culture that rewards individual accomplishments (vs collective membership, family relationships or position) and in which systematic, future-oriented planning is viewed as a key way to achieve high performance" (Stephan & Uhlaner, 2010, p. 1351). It combines high future and performance orientation with uncertainty avoidance, low power distance, and low in-group collectivism practices.[5] The second, *socially supportive culture*, features high humane orientation and low assertiveness and reflects "a positive societal climate in which people support each other" (Stephan & Uhlaner, 2010, p. 1351). Several studies report positive relationships of socially supportive culture with different types of commercial entrepreneurship rates both in country-level and multilevel studies (e.g., Autio et al., 2013; Stephan & Uhlaner, 2010; Thai & Turkina, 2014) as well as with social entrepreneurship (Stephan, Uhlaner, & Stride, 2015). A performance-based culture appears to be related to formal entrepreneurship (i.e. the rate of registered businesses) and the quality of institutions supporting entrepreneurship, but not to other indicators of entrepreneurship (Stephan & Uhlaner, 2010; Thai & Turkina, 2014).

Studies have sought to determine mechanisms through which cultural practices influence entrepreneurship such as enhancing the legitimacy of entrepreneurs, entrepreneurial self-efficacy, and motivation (Hopp & Stephan, 2012; Stephan & Uhlaner, 2010). A study of 3,411 new ventures across 24 countries related socially supportive and performance-based culture positively to new venture performance (Laskovaia, Shirokova, & Morris, 2017). Furthermore, the two types of cultural practices were related to different decision-making logics. The relationship of socially supportive culture on venture performance was mediated by increased effectuation, whereas entrepreneurs used more causation in performance-based cultures (Laskovaia et al., 2017).

Other studies consider practice dimensions they see particularly aligned with entrepreneurship. In a nation-level study, Bullough, Renko, and Abdelzaher (2017) found that gender-egalitarian practices related positively to the rate of women's entrepreneurship, as did medium levels of institutional and in-group collectivism practices in interaction. In their multilevel study, Autio and colleagues (2013) found that performance orientation positively and uncertainty avoidance and institutional collectivism negatively relate to the likelihood that individuals will start a business. Only institutional collectivism related positively to entrepreneurs' growth expectations. Autio and colleagues also examined several GLOBE's cultural values (in-group and institutional collectivism, uncertainty avoidance, performance orientation, and assertiveness) but did not find relationships with entrepreneurship. A further multilevel study (Stephan & Pathak, 2016) found that cultural practices related directly to entrepreneurship but that cultural values (such as in-group collectivism and uncertainty avoidance) should be seen as a more distal antecedent of entrepreneurship. Cultural values were indirectly related to entrepreneurship through shaping cultural ideals of leaders, which help legitimize emerging entrepreneurs as leaders (Stephan & Pathak, 2016).

Shalom Schwartz's Theory of Culture and Entrepreneurship

Schwartz's proposed two value theories which are based on a variety of samples, including population-representative samples collected in the 1990s and 2000. His individual-level theory (Schwartz, 1992) differentiates 10 value types which are clustered along two dimensions. The first, openness to change versus conservation, reflects a focus on new experiences (openness to change) as opposed to fitting into society and abiding by norms and traditions (conservation). The second self-enhancement versus self-transcendence is concerned with advancing the self and obtaining power and influence (self-enhancement) as opposed to caring about and benefiting others (self-transcendence). Individual-level studies find that openness to change and self-enhancement correlate with entrepreneurial intentions and being an entrepreneur (Gorgievski et al., 2018; Liñán, Moriano, & Jaén, 2015; Noseleit, 2010).

Schwartz's theory of cultural values (Schwartz, 2006) differentiates cultural value orientations along three dimensions. *Mastery versus harmony values* reflect the desirability of taking charge and initiating change in contrast to fitting harmoniously into existing structures. *Autonomy versus embeddedness* reflects view of individuals as autonomous entities in a society or chiefly as members of existing groups. *Egalitarianism versus hierarchy* reflects whether individuals are seen as equal or whether the distribution of power and resources is expected to be hierarchically and unequally organized in a society (Schwartz, 2006).

Research using Schwartz's cultural value theory in entrepreneurship is surprisingly scarce. A multilevel study across 28 European countries found that mastery and egalitarianism related positively to entrepreneurship (Morales, Holtschlag, Masuda, & Marquina, 2019). The authors argued that high mastery values in societies would lead to greater appreciation and rewards for beings self-staring, ambitious and assertive (all characteristics associated with entrepreneurs) whereas cultural egalitarianism would allow individuals in those cultures to pursue their own path through entrepreneurship rather than having to seek to fit into established organizations. Another multilevel study, spanning 32 counties from different continents, reported similar effects (De Clercq, Lim, & Oh, 2013). In this study hierarchy and embeddedness (termed conservation) were both negatively related to being a start-up entrepreneur, suggesting (again) that egalitarian cultures, as well as those cultures that value autonomy, support entrepreneurship. Both studies also investigated cross-level interaction effects which are discussed in the section on mechanisms.

Ronald Ingelhart's Theory of Culture and Entrepreneurship

The third value theory has its roots in political science. The theory of *postmaterialism* values (Inglehart, 1997) describes an emphasis on self-expression and freedom of speech rather than on material goods and concerns with survival. Inglehart's (1997) analysis suggests that the latter values are more common in resource-constrained context, but as societies become richer, they start to appreciate non-material values. Inglehart expanded the index of postmaterialism values to a scale of *survival versus self-expression values*, which includes the postmaterialism index as well as questions on generalized trust, happiness, and attitudes towards signing a petition and homosexuality (Inglehart & Baker, 2000). He also introduced a second dimension of *traditional versus secular-rational values*. Traditional values reflect the importance of religion, obedience, respect for authority, national pride, and the disapproval of abortion, and secular-rational values emphasize the opposite (Inglehart & Baker, 2000).

In line with the notion that entrepreneurs pursue entrepreneurship to secure income and thus out of materialistic motivations, postmaterialism values correlated negatively with national rates of entrepreneurship across 27 countries (Uhlaner & Thurik, 2007) and across 17 regions in Spain (Pinillos, 2011). Considering survival versus self-expression and traditional versus secular-rational values, Hechavarria and Reynolds (2009) found that self-expression values were positively associated with national rates of opportunity but not necessity entrepreneurship across 38 countries. Traditional values were associated with higher national rates of both opportunity and necessity entrepreneurship. These findings suggest that culture may matter differently for different types of entrepreneurship. Research on social entrepreneurship further supports this notion. Social entrepreneurship was positively related to postmaterialism values in a multilevel study of 26 countries (Stephan, Uhlaner, & Stride, 2015) and to high secular-rational and high self-expression values in a national-level study across 53 countries (Hechavarría, 2016). In a multilevel study across 48 countries, postmaterialism values related positively to entrepreneurs' social and negatively to economic goals they had for their business (Hechavarría et al., 2016).

Michele Gelfand's Theory of Tightness–Looseness and Entrepreneurship

Cultural tightness–looseness describes "the difference between nations that are "tight"—have strong norms and a low tolerance of deviant behavior—and those that are "loose"—have weak norms and a high tolerance of deviant behavior" (Gelfand et al., 2011, p. 1100, also Harrington & Gelfand, 2014). Considering that a minority of a country's working population are entrepreneurs, one could see entrepreneurship as a type of deviant behavior that may flourish in loose cultures. Only one national-level study so far investigated this and found no significant relationships with the rate of new business owners, social entrepreneurs, or entrepreneurs with growth expectations (Harms & Groen, 2017). Moreover, the researchers had expected but found no support for cultural tightness as a moderator of the relationships of Hofstede's value dimension with entrepreneurship.

Cultural tightness might be an important moderator of cultural practices—in tight cultures, individuals might be more guided by cultural practices than in loose cultures. It might also be that cultural tightness has a paradoxical relationship with entrepreneurship whereby cultural looseness may support creativity and opportunity recognition, but cultural tightness might be necessary to mobilize support and start a business successfully. This calls for more research on mechanisms that mediate the effect of culture on entrepreneurship.

Insights From Research on Cultural Theories and Entrepreneurship

The insights so far may be summarized as follows: Research building on *value-based* cultural theories suggests broadly support for positive relationships of individualism and the related cultural values of autonomy and egalitarianism with entrepreneurship—but this relationship seems to hold chiefly for developed countries (and may flip if developing countries are considered). Similarly, the relationship of Hofstede's uncertainty avoidance with entrepreneurship is positive in samples consisting of richer OECD countries but negative when more diverse countries of different development stages are considered. Masculinity and power distance seem to be less relevant. However, the relationship of postmaterialism and self-expression values with entrepreneurship is consistent and differs predictably for different types of entrepreneurship.

In terms of *cultural practices and norms*, socially supportive cultural practices are positively linked to entrepreneurship including different types of entrepreneurship, whereas the effects of performance-based cultural practice depend on the type of entrepreneurship under investigation. Similarly, effects of individual practice dimensions underlying performance-based cultures on entrepreneurship tend to be variable. Cultural tightness seems to be largely overlooked to date, although one study reports no significant relationship with entrepreneurship. So far, the discussion focused on the type and content of specific cultural dimensions. Next, I review the mechanisms of how culture may influence entrepreneurship.

How Does Culture Impact Entrepreneurship? Five Mechanisms

A robust understanding of the theoretical mechanisms that link culture and entrepreneurship is important for progress in this area of research. Often, studies provide only brief explanations of how they expect culture to shape entrepreneurship. Next, I elaborate on what I deem the five most frequently discussed mechanisms in the literature. They are often referred to as (1) the aggregate trait view, (2) the societal legitimation view, (3) the dissatisfaction view, (4) the social support view, and (5) the culture as a moderator perspective. Not all studies label these mechanisms clearly and often more than one mechanism is argued to underlie the same effect (e.g. of individualism on entrepreneurship). For instance, the aggregate trait and societal legitimation views, which are the earliest views noted in the entrepreneurship literature (Davidsson, 1995; Davidsson & Wiklund, 1997), are often discussed together as mechanisms that both 'pull' individuals into entrepreneurship due to 'culture-entrepreneurship-fit' or alignment (Tung, Walls, & Frese, 2007). I now discuss each mechanism, mention seminal sources, and give examples of recent studies.

In the *aggregate trait view*, entrepreneurial cultures are those where a greater number of individuals have the traits or values predisposing them for entrepreneurial action and thus there is a greater supply of potential entrepreneurs (Davidsson, 1995). The aggregate trait view goes back to the works of Weber (1930) and McClelland (1961). They respectively argued that the source of societies' competitiveness and entrepreneurship lies in the values aligned with Protestantism (Weber, 1930) or the achievement motivation of its citizens (McClelland, 1961). Empirical studies building on the aggregate trait perspective often focus on the individual level of analysis and compare the personality traits and values of entrepreneurs across cultures. Such studies were frequent up to about 2010. They demonstrate similarity in traits and values for entrepreneurs across cultures, especially if studies draw on larger and matched samples (McGrath, MacMillan, & Scheinberg, 1992; Noseleit, 2010). The same does not hold for studies of student samples (Mueller & Thomas, 2001; Thomas & Mueller, 2000). Again, generalizing these individual-level relationships to describe culture would constitute the reverse ecological fallacy (Hofstede, 2001).

More recently, studies drawing on the aggregate trait view started to adopt multilevel designs. An example is research based on cultural values theories (reviewed earlier) that relates cultural values of postmaterialism to entrepreneurship. The aggregate trait view is also underpinning research that relates regional entrepreneurship rates to regional entrepreneurship-prone Big Five profiles. The latter are computed at the individual level and then aggregated to state or regional levels (Obschonka, Schmitt-Rodermund, Silbereisen, Gosling, & Potter, 2013). However, while specific traits such as self-efficacy or personal initiative are clearly associated with entrepreneurship, the relevance of the broad Big Five traits for a specific behavior such as entrepreneurship is subject to debate (Rauch & Frese, 2007).

In the *societal legitimation view*, the moral approval of entrepreneurs in a society encourages people to engage in entrepreneurship because entrepreneurship is viewed as desirable and socially approved career (Etzioni, 1987). The legitimation perspective can draw on established theories in management and sociology to understand when and how behaviors become legitimate, that is accepted and approved of (Suddaby, Bitektine, & Haack, 2017). Both value-based cultural theories and practice-based cultural concepts fit legitimation-based explanations. Value-based accounts can be understood as injunctive norms that confer legitimacy judgments of what is morally good, or moral legitimacy. Practice-based cultural theories align with descriptive norms, that is norms arising from observing what others do and which can powerfully guide behavior even outside of awareness (see Frese, 2015; Stephan & Uhlaner, 2010). Thus, prevalent cultural practices can confer so-called cognitive legitimacy, whereby legitimacy arises from the taken-for-granted character (Suchman, 1995), in this instance, of commonly occurring practices and behaviors in a culture.

One popular direct measure of the societal legitimacy of entrepreneurs is provided by GEM. It is often used as a three-item index of judgments by the general adult population whether starting a business is a desirable career choice, whether the media feature stories about successful new businesses, and whether those successful starting a new business have a high level of status and respect (Reynolds, Bygrave, & Autio, 2004). The index relates positively to entrepreneurship and has been found to mediate the effects of socially supportive cultural practices on entrepreneurship (Stephan & Uhlaner, 2010). Others also find positive relationships with entrepreneurship for a slightly different measure of societal legitimacy of entrepreneurship (Kibler & Kautonen, 2014). While these studies investigate the legitimacy of entrepreneurship among a country's population, other work looks specifically at the legitimacy of social enterprises as perceived by national experts (e.g. policy makers, investors, entrepreneurship researchers; Kibler, Salmivaara, Stenholm, & Terjesen, 2018). This work suggests a positive relationship with the prevalence of social entrepreneurship, although based on a small sample of 11 countries (Kibler et al., 2018).

In contrast to emphasizing a 'pull' into entrepreneurship in the aggregate trait and societal legitimation views, the *dissatisfaction view* states that individuals are 'pushed' into entrepreneurship because they differ from mainstream culture. The first studies offering tests of this perspective established positive relationships of the aggregate life dissatisfaction (and dissatisfaction with democracy) of a country's population with national entrepreneurship rates (Hofstede et al., 2004; Noorderhaven, Thurik, Wennekers, & van Stel, 2004).

The dissatisfaction perspective has also been used to explain why despite predictions from the aggregate trait and societal legitimation perspectives, Hofstede's cultural uncertainty avoidance related positively to national rates of entrepreneurship (Wennekers et al., 2007). Individuals with entrepreneurial traits presumably seek to escape the uncertainty avoidant, inflexible and planning oriented organizations that employ them by creating their own businesses. Thus, instead of the alignment of the individual with the wider culture, it is the misalignment, misfit, or distance from the dominant culture that motivates entrepreneurial action. Multilevel theory offers a template for testing such models, so-called frog-pond models, by considering the distance of a person's score from the national average (Kozlowski & Klein, 2000).

In a multilevel study across 28 European countries, Morales and colleagues (2019) provide a test of the ideas behind the dissatisfaction view by using both Schwartz's individual and cultural value theories. Testing cross-level interactions, this study finds that individual entrepreneurial values (high openness to change and self-enhancement) tend to matter more in cultural environments stacked against entrepreneurship (low mastery and low egalitarianism). In a complementing individual-level study across seven Spanish regions, entrepreneurial intentions were highest for individuals who held openness to change and self-enhancement values that exceeded the regional mean of those values (Liñán et al., 2015).

The *cultural social support view* draws inspiration from a long research tradition on cultural social capital (Beugelsdijk & van Schaik, 2005; Westlund & Adam, 2010). This tradition emphasizes how widespread social capital in a culture—the "instantiated informal norm that promotes cooperation" (Fukuyama, 2001, p. 7)—facilitates information exchange that helps entrepreneurs' to discover opportunities and mobilize informal financial, instrumental, and social support (Kwon & Arenius, 2010; Stephan & Uhlaner, 2010).

Several studies found a positive link of socially supportive cultures that enable cooperation with different types of entrepreneurship rates. These studies were reviewed earlier when discussing GLOBE research and cultural practices. The findings parallel those that relate other forms of social capital to entrepreneurship. For instance, Kwon and Arenius (2010) document that across countries, social capital (especially generalized trust) related positively to the perceptions of entrepreneurial opportunities among individuals' in that country as well as the likelihood to invest in an entrepreneur. Across communities in the US, generalized trust was positively related to the rate of incorporated and unincorporated businesses (Kwon, Heflin, & Ruef, 2013). Both studies accounted for clustering effects in the data, through robust standard errors—similar to multilevel modeling. A further country-level study, found positive associations of social capital (especially general trust but also indicators of social norms of honesty) with entrepreneurship (Kim & Kang, 2014).

Finally, *the culture as moderator perspective* describes research that tests whether established relationships are contingent on the cultural context in which they are embedded. Such research helps establish the generalizability of individual or firm-level relationships across cultures (e.g. of the effect of human capital on starting a business or innovation on the performance of entrepreneurial firms). I discuss first relationships at the individual level before turning to firm-level relationships.

Few studies have examined how culture may shape *individual-level relationships* to date. Example studies investigated gender, the entrepreneurial intention-behavior link, and the relevance of specific personality traits. With regard to gender, a 48 country multilevel study found that women entrepreneurs are more likely to espouse social and less likely to espouse economic goals for their ventures compare to male entrepreneurs (Hechavarría et al., 2016). Cultural postmaterialism values moderated this relationship such that the gender gap in value creation goals was more pronounced in countries where citizens value postmaterialism more strongly. The authors suggest that in such cultures, women can more freely express their social orientations in their business, because these motivations are more culturally legitimate.

In a multilevel study across 65 regions in Finland and Austria, higher legitimacy of entrepreneurship in a region strengthened the effect of entrepreneurial intention on behavior (as well as of entrepreneurial attitudes on intention; Kibler, Kautonen, & Fink, 2014). The higher legitimacy of entrepreneurship is likely to make it easier for entrepreneurs to follow their intentions and mobilize support from others when starting their business.

Several studies investigate the moderating effect of culture on the relationship of specific traits and entrepreneurship although they often focus on intentions (e.g. Schmutzler, Andonova, & Diaz-Serrano, 2018). Two example studies investigated individuals likelihood to start a business: A 32-country multilevel study found that the positive effect of entrepreneurial self-efficacy[6] on individual's likelihood to start a business is stronger in more egalitarian and individualistic cultures (i.e. cultures low in hierarchy and embeddedness in Schwartz's cultural value theory; De Clercq et al., 2013). There were no significant moderating effects of culture for other individual-level variables (knowing entrepreneurs and financial capital). In a 42-country multilevel study, Wennberg, Pathak, and Autio (2013) found that institutional collectivism, uncertainty avoidance, and performance orientation strengthened the positive relationship of entrepreneurial self-efficacy with an individual's likelihood to start a business. Similar moderating effects were not or weakly significant when fear of failure instead of self-efficacy was considered (Wennberg et al., 2013).

The findings by De Clercq et al. (2013) and Wennberg et al. (2013) appear conflicting. It is unclear which cultural aspect is the most relevant moderator. Neither paper offered joint analyses that considered all moderations simultaneously, and the cultural dimensions under consideration are known to intercorrelate. Moreover, the underpinning causal relationships may be more complex. Other research suggests that certain cultural practices may support the development of self-efficacy in the first place, for instance through enabling experimentation and mitigating the stigma of failure (Hopp & Stephan, 2012; Stephan & Uhlaner, 2010).

Research investigating culture as a moderator of *firm-level relationships* is growing. In sum, it suggests that collectivist cultural contexts can help firms to reap the benefits of variance-inducing strategies (entrepreneurial orientation and innovation) because it enables collaboration in the firm. The findings for other cultural dimensions are more mixed.

For example, Saeed, Yousafzai, and Engelen (2014) conducted a meta-analysis of entrepreneurial orientation and firm performance. They found that the EO-firm performance was stronger in more in-group collectivist, less rule-oriented (uncertainty tolerant), and less power distant cultures (measured through GLOBE cultural practices; Saeed et al., 2014). Another meta-analysis on innovation and firm performance found that this relationship is stronger in collectivist cultures (measured as Hofstede individualism; Rosenbusch, Brinckmann, & Bausch, 2011). Finally, a five-country study reported a similar finding (Rauch et al., 2013).

Innovation was more closely related to small firm growth in collectivist and non-assertive cultures (measured through GLOBE practices). Although in contrast to Saeed et al. (2014), more uncertainty-avoidant cultures also strengthened the innovation–firm growth relationship. The higher rule orientation and planning in more uncertainty avoidant cultures may lead to better implementation of innovations and thus strengthened the innovation–firm growth relationship (Rauch et al., 2013). Rauch et al. (2013) considered the cultural orientations of the entrepreneurs separately from country cultural practices and found distinct effects. This reiterates the importance of differentiating levels of analysis in research on culture.

The Nature and Type of Entrepreneurship in Cultural and Entrepreneurship Research

In this final section, I reflect on the definitions and indicators of entrepreneurship used in culture and entrepreneurship research, which may yield different association with culture. Most studies rely on data from GEM (Bosma, 2013; Reynolds et al., 2005) and use indicators of entrepreneurship that are consistent with the definition of entrepreneurship as 'new entry' through the creation of an organization. In this sense, GEM indicators capture the 'flow' of individuals into entrepreneurship. Other research relies on 'static' indicators of self-employment. These are widely available in different types of surveys as most household surveys ask respondents about their occupational status. Self-employment is consistent with an occupational definition of entrepreneurship, that is working for one's own account and risk. For both measures, authors have attempted to capture the quality of entrepreneurial activity, for instance by differentiating the motivation for starting the business (out of necessity, to pursue an opportunity, expectations of job creation, innovative, social entrepreneurship) or being self-employed with and without employees. Yet research rarely specifies the comparison group of non-entrepreneurs. Typically, this group encompasses all others who are not entrepreneurs, although a comparison with those in employment could be more informative.

GEM is based on population-representative samples of at least 2,000 working-age adults (18 to 64) per country. GEM measures are harmonized across countries, are provided annually since 1999, and cover a substantive number of countries. By asking individuals directly about their engagement in entrepreneurship, GEM captures both formal and informal entrepreneurship. Many entrepreneurs especially in emerging economies never register their activities (Williams, Martinez-Perez, & Kedir, 2017), and even in developed economies, a large number of entrepreneurs start their business and trade before registering officially (Reynolds & Curtin, 2008). Thus, GEM offers a unique view on entrepreneurship compared to administrative databases, which may also contain 'zombie-businesses' such as businesses registered for tax-evasion purposes.

GEM defines an entrepreneur as someone who at least part-owns and manages a business, that is, as business-owner managers. A business is considered started if it has a continuous cash flow for at least 3 months (to avoid capturing one-off transactions; Reynolds et al., 2005). This results in indicators of *nascent entrepreneurs*, who have started a business but who have not traded yet beyond 3 months; *new entrepreneurs* (or new business-owner managers), who have traded for at least 3 months and up to a maximum of 3.5 years; and *established entrepreneurs* (or established business-owner managers) who have traded longer than 3.5 years. GEM also captures intentions to start a business in the next 3 years as well as disengagement/exit from a business within the past 12 months—both of which have not yet been explored in culture and entrepreneurship research.

The different indicators provided by GEM can be used to proxy entrepreneurship as a process—also termed the entrepreneurial ladder (Van Der Zwan, Verheul, Thurik, & Grilo, 2011, also Mickiewicz, Nyakudya, Theodorskopoulos & Hart, 2017). In line with action regulation theories (Frese, 2020), intention is the first step of considering entrepreneurship as a personal occupational choice (a so-called first-person opportunity; McMullen & Shepherd, 2006), whereas nascent entrepreneurship is reflective of, first, more serious engagement with limited action (e.g. nascent entrepreneurs may have crafted a business plan). New entrepreneurs by contrast have clearly successfully engaged in entrepreneurial action and managed to create positive cash flow.

Often, nascent and new entrepreneurs are combined into one 'total entrepreneurial activity' (TEA) indicator, and this indicator is frequently and widely used in entrepreneurship and culture research. TEA obscures important information (Bergmann & Stephan, 2013). The same TEA rate might be composed of relatively high rates of nascent and low rates of new entrepreneurs or vice versa. These different compositions have different conceptual and policy implications, which separate analysis of nascent and new entrepreneurs overcome. TEA composed of high rates of nascent relative to new entrepreneurs implies difficulties for entrepreneurs to convert their ideas into sustainable entrepreneurial activities, whereas the opposite (high new entrepreneurship, low nascent entrepreneurship) would indicate a highly efficient business creation process (Bergmann & Stephan, 2013).

Appendix 8.1 shows the stability (yearly and over a decade) of different GEM-based indicators of the entrepreneurial process. Most have very high year-on-year as well as longer-term stabilities, suggesting that culture may well play a role. Other indicators such as business angels, high growth expectations, and successful firm exit appear to be more susceptible to time-varying processes (e.g. their long-term stabilities are lower). Notably, the exit phase is entirely overlooked in current research, even though there is first evidence for cultural variation in how entrepreneurial failure is seen and potentially stigmatized (Cardon, Stevens, & Potter, 2011). Also scarce is research on business angels, who are the main source of informal finance for entrepreneurs in most of the world (for an exception, see De Clercq, Meuleman, & Wright, 2012).

In terms of cultural concepts, there is no research that directly tests whether cultural practices or values are more important for different types or phases of entrepreneurship. The evidence reviewed earlier in this chapter suggests that cultural practices are especially likely to shape actual behavior and thus relate to indicators such as new entrepreneurship and entrepreneurial exit. These phases of the entrepreneurial process require the entrepreneur to interact with their environment and to elicit the cooperation of others (customers, funders, supplies); and such interactions will be shaped by prevalent cultural practices. Consistent with this notion, a recent study on regional social capital found it to impact the transition from the intention to the new entrepreneur phase but not the intention formation phase (Kleinhempel, Beugelsdijk, & Klasing, 2020). By comparison, values may be particularly useful to understand individual's intention and willingness to take the first steps to start a business. Values act as decision-making standards and help us evaluate what choices are 'good' or 'bad' (Schwartz, 1992). Thus, they are likely to impact the decision to engage in entrepreneurship in the first place, as well as support choices such as whether to create a social or commercial enterprise. The latter fits with the evidence reviewed on postmaterialism values.

Conclusion and Future Research

Although research on culture and entrepreneurship has flourished, many open questions and opportunities for future research remain. I highlighted cultural frameworks and how they may relate differently to entrepreneurship (especially cultural practices and values). There is a scope for future research to explore how culture shapes the entrepreneurial process by testing the different and potentially competing theoretical mechanisms involved (see Figure 8.1). Future research may also examine whether specific cultural concepts and dimensions may influence certain phases of the entrepreneurial process more strongly than others. For instance, cultural values may be particularly helpful to understand choices such as the initial engagement in entrepreneurship and choices for different types of entrepreneurship. Cultural practices, although likely relevant for multiple phases, may have the strongest effects on entrepreneurial action—that is, for phases where the behavior of others around the entrepreneur and their willingness to interact and support entrepreneurs is critical for the entrepreneurs' success. Future research on culture and entrepreneurship should also avoid the biases that come with single-level studies and embrace multilevel methods. Researchers should be mindful that the diversity or homogeneity of country samples (e.g., only developed nations) can lead to opposing findings by enhancing or restricting the range of variation in cultural dimensions. Due to data limitations, not all of these recommendations can be implemented by relying on secondary survey data, which are the method of choice to date. Thus, simulations and experiments could be useful methods to further advance our understanding of culture and entrepreneurship.

Disclaimer

I have no known conflicts of interest to disclose. The chapter has benefited from comments and reviews by Michael Frese and Michael M. Gielnik as well as from discussions with Lorraine Uhlaner, Andreana Drencheva, Emma Folmer, and Ian Macdonald. All errors are my own.

Notes

1. For instance, the European Commission's Entrepreneurship 2020 Action Plan is a commitment to grow entrepreneurship in part through "revolutioniz[ing] the culture of entrepreneurship in the EU". Retrieved from https://ec.europa.eu/growth/smes/promoting-entrepreneurship/action-plan_en
2. In contrast to multilevel studies, national-level studies work with aggregated data and relate national culture scores to national rates of entrepreneurship. They are often limited by small sample sizes. Although aggregation can lead to more reliable scores, it can also inflate estimates of relationships. Individual-level studies disaggregate data by assigning everyone in a country the same score on their national culture. They thereby artificially enhance sample size and increase the chance of significant findings.
3. Hofstede's uncertainty avoidance measure includes one practice item (asking about stress at work), a value item about rule orientation, and an item about employment stability. The index correlates positively with national indicators of stress, worry, alcoholism, and neuroticism, whereas GLOBE uncertainty avoidance practices correlate highly with rule-based indicators such as the strength of the rule of law and national governance and control of corruption (see Venaik & Brewer, 2010 for a summary, also Hofstede, 2001; Sully De Luque & Javidan, 2004). Considering that rule orientation and good governance create predictability that help alleviate stress, the high negative correlation between Hofstede's stress uncertainty avoidance and GLOBEs rule-orientation uncertainty avoidance practices makes sense.
4. Other empirical work also suggests change in Hofstede's dimensions yet indicates that the relative position of countries remains relatively stable (Beugelsdijk, Maseland, & van Hoorn, 2015; Beugelsdijk & Welzel, 2018).
5. Performance-based culture correlates in expected ways with Hofstede's power distance, uncertainty avoidance and individualism, whereas socially supportive culture has no complement in Hofstede's dimensions, see Appendix 8.2. It does not significantly correlate with four of the five Hofstede dimensions, and is weakly negative with uncertainty avoidance. This correlation appears consistent with the notion that more assertive cultures (low socially supportive cultures) are experienced as more stressful (high uncertainty avoidant cultures).
6. In the study, the measure was referred to as "human capital".

References

Autio, E., Pathak, S., & Wennberg, K. (2013). Consequences of cultural practices for entrepreneurial behaviors. *Journal of International Business Studies*, 44(4), 334–362. Retrieved from https://doi.org/10.1057/jibs.2013.15

Bergmann, H., & Stephan, U. (2013). Moving on from nascent entrepreneurship: Measuring cross-national differences in the transition to new business ownership. *Small Business Economics*, 41(4), 945–959. Retrieved from https://doi.org/10.1007/s11187-012-9458-4

Berry, J. W. (1993). An ecological approach to understanding cognition across cultures. In *Advances in psychology* (Vol. 103, pp. 361–375). Amsterdam: Elsevier.

Beugelsdijk, S., Maseland, R., & van Hoorn, A. (2015). Are scores on Hofstede's dimensions of national culture stable over time? A cohort analysis. *Global Strategy Journal*, *5*(3), 223–240. Retrieved from https://doi.org/10.1002/gsj.1098

Beugelsdijk, S., & van Schaik, T. (2005). Social capital and growth in European regions: An empirical test. *European Journal of Political Economy*, *21*(2), 301–324. Retrieved from https://doi.org/10.1016/J.EJPOLECO.2004.07.004

Beugelsdijk, S., & Welzel, C. (2018). Dimensions and dynamics of national culture: Synthesizing Hofstede with Inglehart. *Journal of Cross-Cultural Psychology*, *49*(10), 1469–1505. Retrieved from https://doi.org/10.1177/0022022118798505

Bosma, N. (2013). The global entrepreneurship monitor (GEM) and its impact on entrepreneurship research. *Foundations and Trends® in Entrepreneurship*, *9*(2), 143–248. Retrieved from https://doi.org/10.1561/0300000033

Brewer, P., & Venaik, S. (2011). Individualism–collectivism in Hofstede and GLOBE. *Journal of International Business Studies*, *42*(3), 436–445. Retrieved from https://doi.org/10.1057/jibs.2010.62

Bullough, A., Renko, M., & Abdelzaher, D. (2017). Women's business ownership: Operating within the context of institutional and in-group collectivism. *Journal of Management*, *43*(7), 2037–2064. Retrieved from https://doi.org/10.1177/0149206314561302

Cardon, M. S., Stevens, C. E., & Potter, D. R. (2011). Misfortunes or mistakes? *Journal of Business Venturing*, *26*(1), 79–92. Retrieved from https://doi.org/10.1016/j.jbusvent.2009.06.004

Chiu, C.-Y., Gelfand, M. J., Yamagishi, T., Shteynberg, G., & Wan, C. (2010). Intersubjective culture. *Perspectives on Psychological Science*, *5*(4), 482–493. Retrieved from https://doi.org/10.1177/1745691610375562

Davidsson, P. (1995). Culture, structure and regional levels of entrepreneurship. *Entrepreneurship and Regional Development*, *7*(1), 41–62. Retrieved from https://doi.org/10.1080/08985629500000003

Davidsson, P., & Wiklund, J. (1997). Values, beliefs and regional variations in new firm formation rates. *Journal of Economic Psychology*, *18*(2–3), 179–199. Retrieved from https://doi.org/10.1016/S0167-4870(97)00004-4

De Clercq, D., Lim, D. S. K., & Oh, C. H. (2013). Individual-level resources and new business activity: The contingent role of institutional context. *Entrepreneurship Theory and Practice*, *37*(2), 303–330. Retrieved from https://doi.org/10.1111/j.1540-6520.2011.00470.x

De Clercq, D., Meuleman, M., & Wright, M. (2012). A cross-country investigation of micro-angel investment activity: The roles of new business opportunities and institutions. *International Business Review*, *21*(2), 117–129.

Estrin, S., Mickiewicz, T., Stephan, U., & Wright, M. (2018). Entrepreneurship in emerging markets. In R. Grosse & K. E. Meyer (Eds.), *The Oxford handbook of management in emerging markets* (Vol. 1, pp. 23–39). Retrieved from https://doi.org/10.1093/oxfordhb/9780190683948.013.21

Etzioni, A. (1987). Entrepreneurship, adaptation and legitimation: A macro-behavioral perspective. *Journal of Economic Behavior & Organization*, *8*(2), 175–189. Retrieved from https://doi.org/10.1016/0167-2681(87)90002-3

Frese, M. (2015). Cultural practices, norms, and values. *Journal of Cross-Cultural Psychology*, *46*(10), 1327–1330. Retrieved from https://doi.org/10.1177/0022022115600267

Frese, M. (2020). An action theory (AT) approach to the psychology of entrepreneurial actions and entrepreneurial success. In *The psychology of entrepreneurship: The next decade* (Chapter 11). Routledge.

Fukuyama, F. (2001). Social capital, civil society and development. *Third World Quarterly*, *22*(1), 7–20. Retrieved from https://doi.org/10.1080/0143659002002254

Garcia-Cabrera, A. M., & Garcia-Soto, M. G. (2008). Cultural differences and entrepreneurial behaviour: An intra-country cross-cultural analysis in Cape Verde. *Entrepreneurship Regional Development*, *20*(5), 451–483. Retrieved from https://doi.org/10.1080/08985620801912608

Gelfand, M. J., Raver, J. L., Nishii, L., Leslie, L. M., Lun, J., Lim, B. C., . . . Yamaguchi, S. (2011). Differences between tight and loose cultures: A 33-nation study. *Science*, *332*(6033), 1100–1104. Retrieved from https://doi.org/10.1126/science.1197754

Gorgievski, M. J., Stephan, U., Laguna, M., & Moriano, J. A. (2018). Predicting entrepreneurial career intentions. *Journal of Career Assessment*, *26*(3), 457–475. Retrieved from https://doi.org/10.1177/1069072717714541

Gupta, V., Sully de Luque, M. F., & House, R. J. (2004). Multisource construct validity of GLOBE scales. In R. J. House, P. J. Hanges, M. Javidan, P. W. Dorfman, & V. Gupta (Eds.), *Culture leadership and organizations: The GLOBE study of 62 societies* (pp. 152–177). Thousand Oaks, CA: Sage.

Harms, R., & Groen, A. (2017). Loosen up? Cultural tightness and national entrepreneurial activity. *Technological Forecasting and Social Change*, *121*, 196–204. Retrieved from https://doi.org/10.1016/j.techfore.2016.04.013

Harrington, J. R., & Gelfand, M. J. (2014). Tightness-looseness across the 50 united states. *Proceedings of the National Academy of Sciences*, *111*(22), 7990–7995. Retrieved from https://doi.org/10.1073/pnas.1317937111

Hayton, J. C., & Cacciotti, G. (2013). Is there an entrepreneurial culture? A review of empirical research. *Entrepreneurship & Regional Development*, *25*(9–10), 708–731. Retrieved from https://doi.org/10.1080/08985626.2013.862962

Hayton, J. C., George, G., & Zahra, S. A. (2002). National culture and entrepreneurship: A review of behavioral research. *Entrepreneurship: Theory and Practice*, *26*(4), 33.

Hechavarria, D. M. (2016). The impact of culture on national prevalence rates of social and commercial entrepreneurship. *International Entrepreneurship and Management Journal*, *12*(4), 1025–1052. Retrieved from https://doi.org/10.1007/s11365-015-0376-1

Hechavarria, D. M., & Reynolds, P. D. (2009). Cultural norms & business start-ups: The impact of national values on opportunity and necessity entrepreneurs. *International Entrepreneurship and Management Journal*, *5*(4), 417–437. Retrieved from https://doi.org/10.1007/s11365-009-0115-6

Hechavarría, D. M., Terjesen, S. A., Ingram, A. E., Renko, M., Justo, R., & Elam, A. (2016). Taking care of business: The impact of culture and gender on entrepreneurs' blended value creation goals. *Small Business Economics*, 1–33. Retrieved from https://doi.org/10.1007/s11187-016-9747-4

Hofstede, G. (2001). *Culture's conseqences: Comparing values, behaviors, institutions, and organisations across nations*. Thousand Oaks, CA: Sage. Retrieved from https://doi.org/10.1177/0022022110388567

Hofstede, G., Noorderhaven, N., Thurik, A. R., Uhlaner, L., Wennekers, S., & Wildeman, R. E. (2004). Culture's role in entrepreneurship. In J. Ulijn & T. Brown (Eds.), *Innovation, entrepreneurship and culture* (pp. 162–203). Cheltenham, UK: Edward Elgar Publishing.

Hopp, C., & Stephan, U. (2012). The influence of socio-cultural environments on the performance of nascent entrepreneurs: Community culture, motivation, self-efficacy and start-up success. *Entrepreneurship and Regional Development*, *29*(9–19), 1–29. Retrieved from https://doi.org/10.1080/08985626.2012.742326

House, R. J., Hanges, P. J., Javidan, M., Dorfman, P. W., & Gupta, V. (2004). *Culture, leadership, and organizations: The GLOBE study of 62 societies*. Thousand Oaks, CA: Sage.

House, R. J., Javidan, M., Hanges, P., & Dorfman, P. (2002). Understanding cultures and implicit leadership theories across the globe: An introduction to project GLOBE. *Journal of World Business, 37*(1), 3–10. Retrieved from https://doi.org/10.1016/S1090-9516(01)00069-4

Inglehart, R. (1997). *Modernization and postmodernization: Cultural, economic, and political change in 43 societies* (Vol. 19). Cambridge, UK: Cambridge University Press.

Inglehart, R., & Baker, W. E. (2000). Modernization, cultural change, and the persistence of traditional values. *American Sociological Review, 65*(1), 19–51.

Javidan, M., House, R. J., Dorfman, P., Hanges, P. J., & Sully De Luque, M. (2006). Conceptualizing and measuring cultures and their consequences: A comparative review of GLOBE's and Hofstede's approaches. *Journal of International Business Studies, 37*(6), 897–914. Retrieved from https://doi.org/10.1057/palgrave.jibs.8400234

Kibler, E., & Kautonen, T. (2014). The moral legitimacy of entrepreneurs: An analysis of early-stage entrepreneurship across 26 countries. *International Small Business Journal: Researching Entrepreneurship.* Retrieved from https://doi.org/10.1177/0266242614541844

Kibler, E., Kautonen, T., & Fink, M. (2014). Regional social legitimacy of entrepreneurship: Implications for entrepreneurial intention and start-up behaviour. *Regional Studies, 48*(6), 995–1015. Retrieved from https://doi.org/10.1080/00343404.2013.851373

Kibler, E., Salmivaara, V., Stenholm, P., & Terjesen, S. (2018). The evaluative legitimacy of social entrepreneurship in capitalist welfare systems. *Journal of World Business, 53*(6), 944–957. Retrieved from https://doi.org/10.1016/j.jwb.2018.08.002

Kim, B.-Y., & Kang, Y. (2014). Social capital and entrepreneurial activity: A pseudo-panel approach. *Journal of Economic Behavior & Organization, 97*, 47–60. Retrieved from https://doi.org/10.1016/J.JEBO.2013.10.003

Kleinhempel, J., Beugelsdijk, S., & Klasing, M. J. (2020). The changing role of social capital during the venture creation process: A multilevel study. *Entrepreneurship Theory and Practice*, 1042258720913022. Retrieved from https://doi.org/10.1177/1042258720913022

Kozlowski, S. W. J., & Klein, K. J. (2000). A multilevel approach to theory and research in organizations: Contextual, temporal, and emergent processes. In *Multilevel theory, research and methods in organizations: Foundations, extensions, and new directions* (pp. 3–90). San Francisco, CA: Jossey-Bass.

Kwon, S.-W., & Arenius, P. (2010). Nations of entrepreneurs: A social capital perspective. *Journal of Business Venturing, 25*(3), 315–330. Retrieved from https://doi.org/10.1016/j.jbusvent.2008.10.008

Kwon, S.-W., Heflin, C., & Ruef, M. (2013). Community social capital and entrepreneurship. *American Sociological Review, 78*(6), 980–1008. Retrieved from https://doi.org/10.1177/0003122413506440

Laskovaia, A., Shirokova, G., & Morris, M. H. (2017). National culture, effectuation, and new venture performance: Global evidence from student entrepreneurs. *Small Business Economics*, 1–23. Retrieved from https://doi.org/10.1007/s11187-017-9852-z

Liñán, F., Moriano, J. A., & Jaén, I. (2015). Individualism and entrepreneurship: Does the pattern depend on the social context? *International Small Business Journal: Researching Entrepreneurship.* Retrieved from https://doi.org/10.1177/0266242615584646

McClelland, D. C. (1961). *Achieving society.* New York, NY: Simon & Schuster.

McGrath, R. G., MacMillan, I. C., & Scheinberg, S. (1992). Elitists, risk-takers, and rugged individualists? An exploratory analysis of cultural differences between entrepreneurs and non-entrepreneurs. *Journal of Business Venturing, 7*(2), 115–135. Retrieved from https://doi.org/10.1016/0883-9026(92)90008-F

McMullen, J. S., & Shepherd, D. A. (2006). Entrepreneurial action and the role of uncertainty in the theory of the entrepreneur. *Academy of Management Review, 31*(1), 132–152. Retrieved from https://doi.org/10.5465/AMR.2006.19379628

Mickiewicz, T., Nyakudya, F. W., Theodorakopoulos, N., & Hart, M. (2017). Resource endowment and opportunity cost effects along the stages of entrepreneurship. *Small Business Economics, 48*(4), 953–976. Retrieved from https://doi.org/10.1007/s11187-016-9806-x

Morales, C., Holtschlag, C., Masuda, A. D., & Marquina, P. (2019). In which cultural contexts do individual values explain entrepreneurship? An integrative values framework using Schwartz's theories. *International Small Business Journal: Researching Entrepreneurship, 37*(3), 241–267. Retrieved from https://doi.org/10.1177/026624 2618811890

Mueller, S., & Thomas, A. S. (2001). Culture and entrepreneurial potential: A nine country study of locus of control and innovativeness. *Journal of Business Venturing, 16*(1), 51–75. Retrieved from https://doi.org/10.1016/S0883-9026(99)00039-7

Noorderhaven, N., Thurik, R., Wennekers, S., & van Stel, A. (2004). The role of dissatisfaction and per capita income in explaining self-employment across 15 European countries. *Entrepreneurship-Theory and Practice, 28*(5), 447–466. Retrieved from https://doi.org/10.1111/j.1540-6520.2004.00057.x

Noseleit, F. (2010). The entrepreneurial culture: Guiding principles of the self-employed. In A. Freytag & R. Thurik (Eds.), *Entrepreneurship and culture* (pp. 41–54). Retrieved from https://doi.org/10.1007/978-3-540-87910-7_3

Obschonka, M., Schmitt-Rodermund, E., Silbereisen, R. K., Gosling, S. D., & Potter, J. (2013). The regional distribution and correlates of an entrepreneurship-prone personality profile in the United States, Germany, and the United Kingdom: A socioecological perspective. *Journal of Personality and Social Psychology, 105*(1), 104–122. Retrieved from https://doi.org/10.1037/a0032275

Peterson, M. F., Arregle, J.-L., & Martin, X. (2012). Multilevel models in international business research. *Journal of International Business Studies, 43*, 451–457. Retrieved from https://doi.org/10.1057/jibs.2011.59

Peterson, M. F., & Castro, S. L. (2006). Measurement metrics at aggregate levels of analysis: Implications for organization culture research and the GLOBE project. *The Leadership Quarterly, 17*(5), 506–521. Retrieved from https://doi.org/10.1016/j.leaqua.2006.07.001

Pinillos, M.-J., & Reyes, L. (2011). Relationship between individualist-collectivist culture and entrepreneurial activity: Evidence from global entrepreneurship monitor data. *Small Business Economics, 37*(1), 23–37. Retrieved from https://doi.org/10.1007/s11187-009-9230-6

Pinillos Costa, M. J. (2011). Cultura postmaterialista y variaciones en el espíritu emprendedor. *Investigaciones Europeas de Dirección de La Empresa (IEDEE), 17*(1), 37–55.

Rauch, A., & Frese, M. (2007). Let's put the person back into entrepreneurship research: A meta-analysis on the relationship between business owners' personality traits, business creation, and success. *European Journal of Work and Organizational Psychology, 16*(4), 353–385. Retrieved from https://doi.org/10.1080/13594320701595438

Rauch, A., Frese, M., Wang, Z.-M., Unger, J., Lozada, M., Kupcha, V., & Spirina, T. (2013). National culture and cultural orientations of owners affecting the innovation-growth relationship in five countries. *Entrepreneurship and Regional Development, 25*, 732–755. Retrieved from https://doi.org/10.1080/08985626.2013.862972

Reynolds, P. D., Bosma, N., Autio, E., Hunt, S., De Bono, N., Servais, I., . . . Chin, N. (2005). Global entrepreneurship monitor: Data collection design and implementation 1998–2003. *Small Business Economics, 24*(3), 205–231. Retrieved from https://doi.org/10.1007/s11187-005-1980-1

Reynolds, P. D., Bygrave, W. D., & Autio, E. (2004). *Global entrepreneurship monitor 2003 executive report.* Babson Park; London; Kansas City: GERA research consortium.

Reynolds, P. D., & Curtin, R. T. (2008). Business creation in the United States: Panel study of entrepreneurial dynamics II Initial Assessment. *Foundations and Trends in Entrepreneurship, 4*(3), 155–307. Retrieved from https://doi.org/10.1561/0300000022

Rooks, G., Sserwanga, A., & Frese, M. (2016). Unpacking the personal initiative–performance relationship: A multi-group analysis of innovation by Ugandan rural and urban entrepreneurs. *Applied Psychology, 65*(1), 99–131. Retrieved from https://doi.org/10.1111/apps.12033

Rosenbusch, N., Brinckmann, J., & Bausch, A. (2011). Is innovation always beneficial? A meta-analysis of the relationship between innovation and performance in SMEs. *Journal of Business Venturing, 26*(4), 441–457.

Saeed, S., Yousafzai, S.Y., & Engelen, A. (2014). On cultural and macroeconomic contingencies of the entrepreneurial orientation–performance relationship. *Entrepreneurship Theory and Practice, 38*(2), 255–290. Retrieved from https://doi.org/10.1111/etap.12097

Schmutzler, J., Andonova, V., & Diaz-Serrano, L. (2018). How context shapes entrepreneurial self-efficacy as a driver of entrepreneurial intentions: A multilevel approach. *Entrepreneurship Theory and Practice, 43*(5), 880–920. Retrieved from https://doi.org/10.1177/1042258717753142

Schwartz, S. H. (1992). Universals in the content and structure of values: Theoretical advances and empirical tests in 20 countries. *Advances in Experimental Social Psychology, 25*, 1–65. Retrieved from https://doi.org/10.1016/S0065-2601(08)60281-6

Schwartz, S. H. (2006). A theory of cultural value orientations: Explication and applications. *Comparative Sociology, 5*(2), 137–182. Retrieved from https://doi.org/10.1163/156913306778667357

Smith, P. B. (2002). Culture's consequences: Something old and something new. *Human Relations, 55*(1), 119–135.

Stephan, U., & Pathak, S. (2016). Beyond cultural values? Cultural leadership ideals and entrepreneurship. *Journal of Business Venturing, 31*(5), 505–523. Retrieved from https://doi.org/10.1016/j.jbusvent.2016.07.003

Stephan, U., & Uhlaner, L. M. (2010). Performance-based vs socially supportive culture: A cross-national study of descriptive norms and entrepreneurship. *Journal of International Business Studies, 41*(8), 1347–1364. Retrieved from https://doi.org/10.1057/jibs.2010.14

Stephan, U., Uhlaner, L. M., & Stride, C. (2015). Institutions and social entrepreneurship: The role of institutional voids, institutional support, and institutional configurations. *Journal of International Business Studies, 46*(3), 308–331. Retrieved from https://doi.org/10.1057/jibs.2014.38

Suchman, M. C. (1995). Managing legitimacy: Strategic and institutional approaches. *Academy of Management Review, 20*(3), 571–610. Retrieved from https://doi.org/10.5465/AMR.1995.9508080331

Suddaby, R., Bitektine, A., & Haack, P. (2017). Legitimacy. *Academy of Management Annals, 11*(1), 451–478. Retrieved from https://doi.org/10.5465/annals.2015.0101

Sully De Luque, M., & Javidan, M. (2004). Uncertainty avoidance. In R. J. House, P. J. Hanges, M. Javidan, P. Dorfman, & V. Gupta (Eds.), *Culture leadership and organizations: The GLOBE study of 62 societies* (pp. 592–653). Thousand Oaks, CA: Sage.

Taras, V., Steel, P., & Kirkman, B. L. (2012). Improving national cultural indices using a longitudinal meta-analysis of Hofstede's dimensions. *Journal of World Business, 47*(3), 329–341. Retrieved from https://doi.org/10.1016/J.JWB.2011.05.001

Terjesen, S., Hessels, J., & Li, D. (2016). Comparative international entrepreneurship. *Journal of Management, 42*(1), 299–344. Retrieved from https://doi.org/10.1177/0149206313486259

Thai, M. T. T., & Turkina, E. (2014). Macro-level determinants of formal entrepreneurship versus informal entrepreneurship. *Journal of Business Venturing, 29*(4), 490–510. Retrieved from https://doi.org/10.1016/j.jbusvent.2013.07.005

Thomas, A. S., & Mueller, S. L. (2000). A case for comparative entrepreneurship: Assessing the relevance of culture. *Journal of International Business Studies, 31*(2), 287–301. Retrieved from https://doi.org/10.1057/palgrave.jibs.8490906

Tung, R. L., Walls, J., & Frese, M. (2007). Cross-cultural entrepreneurship: The case of China. In J. R. Baum, M. Frese, & R. A. Baron (Eds.), *The psychology of entrepreneurship* (pp. 265–286). Mahwah, NJ: Lawrence Erlbaum Associates.

Uhlaner, L., & Thurik, R. (2007). Postmaterialism influencing total entrepreneurial activity across nations. *Journal of Evolutionary Economics, 17*(2), 161–185. Retrieved from https://doi.org/10.1007/s00191-006-0046-0

Van Der Zwan, P., Verheul, I., Thurik, R., & Grilo, I. (2011). Entrepreneurial progress: Climbing the entrepreneurial ladder in Europe and the United States. *Regional Studies, 47*(5), 803–825. Retrieved from https://doi.org/10.1080/00343404.2011.598504

Venaik, S., & Brewer, P. (2010). Avoiding uncertainty in Hofstede and GLOBE. *Journal of International Business Studies, 41*(8), 1294–1315. Retrieved from https://doi.org/10.1057/jibs.2009.96

Weber, M. (1930). *The protestant ethic and the spirit of capitalism.* New York: Citadel Press.

Wennberg, K., Pathak, S., & Autio, E. (2013). How culture moulds the effects of self-efficacy and fear of failure on entrepreneurship. *Entrepreneurship & Regional Development, 25*(9–10), 756–780. Retrieved from https://doi.org/10.1080/08985626.2013.862975

Wennekers, S., Thurik, A. R., Van Stel, A., & Noorderhaven, N. (2007). Uncertainty avoidance and the rate of business ownership across 21 OECD countries, 1976–2004. *Journal of Evolutionary Economics, 17*(2), 133–160.

Westlund, H., & Adam, F. (2010). Social capital and economic performance: A meta-analysis of 65 studies. *European Planning Studies, 18*(6), 893–919. Retrieved from https://doi.org/10.1080/09654311003701431

Williams, C. C., Martinez-Perez, A., & Kedir, A. M. (2017). Informal entrepreneurship in developing economies: The impacts of starting up unregistered on firm performance. *Entrepreneurship Theory and Practice, 41*(5), 773–799. Retrieved from https://doi.org/10.1111/etap.12238

APPENDIX 8.1

Overview Stability of Entrepreneurship Rates

Average year-to-year and 10-year stabilities of different measures of entrepreneurship (own computations based on publicly available data from the Global Entrepreneurship Monitor, www.gemconsortium.org). Averages are based on r-to-Z averaged stability correlations, N refers to the average number of countries.

Indicator	Year-to year stability					10-year stability		
	r	*Min*	*Max*	*Average N*	*Averaged over time period of:*	*r*	*Average N*	*Number of 10-year periods averaged*
Entrepreneurial intention	**0.91**	0.81	0.97	40	16 years 2002–2018	**0.83**	28	7
Nascent entrepreneurship	**0.88**	0.79	0.93	40.5	16 years 2002–2018	**0.72**	28	7
New entrepreneurship	**0.88**	0.75	0.93	40.5	16 years 2002–2018	**0.75**	28	7
Total Entrepreneurial Activity (TEA)	**0.91**	0.82	0.97	40.5	16 years 2002–2018	**0.78**	28	7
Established entrepreneurship	**0.84**	0.65	0.94	40.5	16 years 2002–2018	**0.79**	28	7
Failure: Exited a business in past year, business did not continue	**0.88**	0.65	0.97	46	11 years 2007–2018	**0.77**	26.5	2
Exit: Existed a business in past year, business continued	**0.76**	0.5	0.94	46	11 years 2007–2018	**0.39**	26.5	2

Indicator	Year-to year stability					10-year stability		
	r	Min	Max	Average N	Averaged over time period of:	r	Average N	Number of 10-year periods averaged
Nascent necessity	**0.85**	0.7	0.93	41	15 years 2003–2018	**0.62**	28	6
Nascent opportunity	**0.84**	0.69	0.93	41	15 years 2003–2018	**0.72**	28	6
TEA any employment (now or 5 years)	**0.88**	0.68	0.96	41	15 years 2003–2018	**0.76**	28	6
TEA high growth	**0.76**	0.27	0.89	40.5	16 years 2002–2018	**0.56**	28	7
Business angel	**0.84**	0.64	0.96	40.5	16 years 2002–2018	**0.55**	28	7

APPENDIX 8.2

Correlations Among Hofstede and GLOBE Cultural Dimensions

Hofstede	Uncertainty Avoidance	Individua-lism	Power distance	Masculi-nity	Long-term orientation
GLOBE practices					
Uncertainty Avoidance	−.637★★	.472★★	−.519★★	−.123	.231
Institutional collectivism	−.464★★	.248	−.251	−.187	.360★
Ingroup collectivism	.315★	−.726★★	.739★★	.138	−.127
Power Distance	.509★★	−.239	.411★★	.210	−.057
Performance orientation	−.590★★	.247	−.287	.095	.233
Future orientation	−.596★★	.361★	−.385★★	−.094	.211
Assertiveness	.240	.245	−.162	.278	−.040
Humane orientation	−.389★★	−.022	.033	−.095	−.375★★
Gender egalitarianism	.067	.310★	−.075	−.176	−.074
Performance based culture	−.629★★	.565★★	−.626★★	−.125	.213
Socially supportive culture	−.367★	−.135	.101	−.198	−.230
GLOBE values					
Uncertainty Avoidance	.388★★	−.659★★	.692★★	.033	−.248
Institutional collectivism	.399★★	−.364★	.255	.000	−.323★
Ingroup collectivism	.200	.076	−.037	−.237	−.459★★
Power Distance	−.297★	.301★	−.120	.092	−.055
Performance orientation	.086	.250	−.138	.013	−.446★★
Future orientation	.299★	−.286	.454★★	.107	−.381★★
Assertiveness	−.358★	−.108	.251	.175	.070
Humane orientation	−.074	.453★★	−.286	−.053	.167
Gender egalitarianism	.076	.566★★	−.549★★	−.056	−.023

Source: Hofstede, data released 2015: https://geerthofstede.com/research-and-vsm/dimension-data-matrix/, Globe: response bias corrected scores from House et al., (2004). Performance-based and socially supportive culture from Stephan and Uhlaner (2010) based on House et al. (2004)

Note. Correlations based on own computations; $N = 46$ countries, except for correlations with long-term orientation, $N = 50$ countries. ★ $p < .05$, ★★$p < .01$, ★★★$p < .001$

9

LEADING ENTREPRENEURIAL VENTURES

A Psychology-Based Approach to Stakeholder Engagement

Shane W. Reid, Aaron H. Anglin & Jeffrey M. Pollack

Introduction

This chapter summarizes emerging research that has embraced a psychological perspective to better understand the leadership processes individuals (or teams) must undertake to effectively lead entrepreneurial ventures. To explain how the new venture context shapes leadership actions and outcomes, we explore how the differing circumstances ventures face in pre-legitimacy compared to post-legitimacy necessitate distinct leadership actions. To better condense the breadth and depth of the extant literature, we organize the insights captured here around four distinct aspects scholars have identified as central to both effective leadership and entrepreneurship: (1) crafting a *vision* to communicate important goals or objectives, (2) exhibiting *influence* on others, (3) leveraging *creativity and innovation* to impact performance outcomes, and (4) utilizing a *plan* to guide current and future action (e.g., Cogliser & Brigham, 2004; Reid, Anglin, Baur, Short, & Buckley, 2018). Although not exhaustive of the actions and behaviors required to navigate the new venture process, each aspect broadly captures, and can help explain, how entrepreneurs overcome other specific challenges related to launching a new venture such as networking, resource acquisition, and stakeholder engagement. Here, we consider how inter- and intrapersonal factors might facilitate stakeholder engagement, and overall, we highlight the substantial advancements that have been achieved thus far and draw attention to several areas where more research is still needed.

Background

Entrepreneurs are "those individuals or groups, who are responsible for the discovery, evaluation, and exploitation of opportunities to create some form of new value" (Reid et al., 2018, p. 151). However, successful entrepreneurship does not occur in isolation but rather requires that "entrepreneurs interact with different types of individuals who have different expectancies of the outcomes of interaction in an emerging venture" (Gartner, Bird, & Starr, 1992, p. 25). Indeed, one of the primary functions of leading nascent ventures is to identify, contact, and align the key stakeholders needed for venture survival and growth (Pollack, Barr, & Hanson, 2017). In this capacity, perhaps the most challenging obstacle entrepreneurs face when launching a new venture is how to effectively motivate and involve different stakeholder groups in the organizing process (Gartner et al., 1992).

If leadership is the process of influencing others and facilitating efforts towards shared objectives (Yukl, 2013), then effective leadership is critical to new venture survival as entrepreneurs must be able to successfully organize efforts around an opportunity (e.g., Renko, El Tarabishy, Carsrud, & Brännback, 2015). Given this central role leadership plays in the new venture process, it is tempting, and perhaps intuitively appealing, to consider the topics of "entrepreneurial leadership" and "leading entrepreneurial ventures" as two sides of the same coin. However, subtle differences exist.

Traditional perspectives consider entrepreneurial leadership as simply the application of leadership principles in new venture settings (Vecchio, 2003). Here, what defines entrepreneurial leadership is generally limited to only those specific actions and approaches entrepreneurs might take to influence, motivate, and manage stakeholders towards the venture's goals and objectives (Renko et al., 2015). Accordingly, research on entrepreneurial leadership tends to focus on how the entrepreneur might act as a leader as well as the dynamics of the entrepreneur–stakeholder relationship (e.g., Haynes, Hitt, & Campbell, 2015; Vecchio, 2003).

In contrast to this approach, some scholars argue the high degree of environmental volatility, inherent risk, information asymmetry, and stakeholder uncertainty that uniquely characterize the new venture creation process necessitate that specific leadership actions be taken if such complexities are to be navigated successfully (e.g., Kuratko, 2007; Leitch & Volery, 2017). In this way, leading entrepreneurial ventures is concerned with more than just viewing the entrepreneur in a leadership role. Rather, it also requires further examination of specific leadership behaviors entrepreneurs must undertake to navigate the unique aspects of entrepreneurship. As such, research examining leading new ventures should not just investigate the social dynamics between entrepreneurs and stakeholders but also consider how environmental or situational factors might dictate what types of social interactions are necessary to successfully exploit entrepreneurial opportunities. Thus, we contend that what differentiates "entrepreneurial leadership" from "leading entrepreneurial ventures" is how *context* shapes the specific type of "leadership" required in new and emerging ventures.

Context, as it relates to entrepreneurial ventures, refers to the conditions under which new ventures first develop and emerge (W. B. Gartner, W. C. Gartner,

Shaver, Carter, & Reynolds, 2004). For instance, specific actions are often required of entrepreneurs if the venture is to overcome stakeholder doubts that hinder the venture's ability to grow (e.g., Fisher, Kotha, & Lahiri, 2016; Stinchcombe, 1965). Here, the *vision* for the future of the venture resides with an individual or small group, and it is through *creativity* and *innovation* this individual or group must develop the *plan* to proceed and *influence* key stakeholders to take actions that enable the venture to survive and grow (Reid et al., 2018). Although such efforts are vital and common in any entrepreneurial venture, the unique challenges and obstacles imposed by the conditions surrounding the emergence of a *new* venture tend to be more profound than those faced by more established ventures (Gartner et al., 1992; Leitch & Volery, 2017).

Leading Entrepreneurial Ventures During Pre-Legitimacy

Legitimacy occurs when ventures achieve initial acceptance from various stakeholders who consider the venture to be a viable and worthy opportunity in which to further engage and allow resource access (Fisher, Kuratko, Bloodgood, & Hornsby, 2017; Zimmerman & Zeitz, 2002). Ventures in pre-legitimacy (before legitimacy is granted) are characterized as those in the earliest stages of development, often existing simply as an idea yet to achieve the acceptance needed to establish itself as a functioning organizational entity (e.g., Tost, 2011; Überbacher, 2014). New ventures gain legitimacy only if granted by various sets of influential stakeholders. To do so, entrepreneurs must make the case that their venture idea presents an acceptable risk: for investors to commit money or resources, for potential employees to leave established careers, or for customers to change their consumption behaviors (e.g., Choi & Shepherd, 2005). Accordingly, perhaps the primary challenge for entrepreneurs leading ventures in pre-legitimacy is persuading others on the merits and potential of the venture and its related opportunity (Rutherford & Buller, 2007).

Here, leading entrepreneurial ventures begins to offer unique challenges compared to more general leadership contexts. Whereas any leader is tasked with influencing others towards a common goal or shared objective (Yukl, 2013), most tend operate within existing organizational or well-defined institutional structures (e.g., DeRue & Ashford, 2010). This provides a point of reference for the leader's motives to be, at least, partially understood and where leader and follower interactions are somewhat defined (e.g., Hogg, van Knippenberg, & Rast, 2012). Having this established starting point from which to operate allows leaders to better engage followers who might be predisposed towards supporting a leader's message based on factors such as alignment of personal beliefs (e.g., political ideology) or professional considerations (e.g., employee–employer; e.g., Hogg et al., 2012).

Comparatively, the new venture context is often marked by the high degree of ambiguity and uncertainty where institutional structures, market dynamics, and social norms might not yet be established or are poorly defined and understood (e.g., McKelvie, Haynie, & Gustavsson, 2011). Issues related to 'liability of newness' mean the new venture's anticipated outcomes, structures, practices, and behaviors might not align with prevailing institutions in the environment in which the venture hopes to operate (e.g., Stinchcombe, 1965; Tolbert, David, & Sine, 2011). Entrepreneurs must not only convince external audiences that the entrepreneur's goals and objectives align with their own values and beliefs but also that the related opportunity offers a valid, feasible, and plausible outcome worth committing resources towards (Fisher et al., 2017). Furthermore, because new ventures fail at a rate much higher than established organizations, stakeholders are often resistant to commit the resources needed to establish and grow the venture (e.g., Morse, Fowler, & Lawrence, 2007; Stinchcombe, 1965). Accordingly, leadership in the earliest stages of a venture tends to take an external focus—towards customers and financiers—as entrepreneurs need to effectively galvanize the initial support and acceptance in order to legitimize their ideas as a viable venture.

Articulating the Vision

To make an entrepreneur's vision a reality, scholars have emphasized that entrepreneurs benefit from a transformational, rather than transactional, leadership approach with potential stakeholders (e.g., Engelen, Gupta, Strenger, & Brettel, 2015; Ensley, Pearce, & Hmieleski, 2006). Transformational leadership inspires a sense of confidence and competence that inspires a belief in others that the vision is important and attainable (Antonakis & Autio, 2007). Not surprisingly, Ensley and colleagues (2006) find entrepreneurs who exhibit transformational, rather than transactional, characteristics find more success gaining stakeholder acceptance. Here, they note that stakeholders are better able to make sense of the uncertainty and often disjointed activities associated with early-stage ventures. Consequently, stakeholders tend to be more open to, and willing to, further engage in the pursuit of innovation and new opportunities (Engelen et al., 2015).

An entrepreneur's vision offers insight into the entrepreneur's motivations and intended strategy for the venture (e.g., Ruvio, Rosenblatt, & Hertz-Lazarowitz, 2010; Waddock & Steckler, 2016), and stakeholders look to see that the vision facilitates alignment between this motivation, intended strategy, and what type of venture is emerging. For example, an entrepreneur's prosocial motivation to stimulate social change or promote general welfare should be clear in the vision for nonprofit or social ventures. Such visions are most effective when they come across as inspirational and realistic (Ruvio & Shoham, 2011). Conversely, stakeholders would expect visions of for-profit ventures to highlight the competitive intentions aimed at maximizing financial return. If properly aligned, the motivation–vision–strategy relationship signals goal congruency to potential stakeholders and instills confidence in how the venture will proceed. If not aligned, stakeholders may question the entrepreneur's authenticity and ability to deliver on the vision (Ruvio et al., 2010).

Influencing Other's Perceptions

A fundamental influence mechanism for pre-legitimacy entrepreneurs is to communicate a sense of authenticity and convey information that lets others know 'who the entrepreneur is' as a potential leader. Communicating personal attributes reduces unknowns concerning the entrepreneur and inspires confidence in the entrepreneur's abilities. For example, conveying positive psychological capital (i.e., hope, optimism, resilience, and confidence) leads to greater acceptance of a company's offering from resource providers in crowdfunding, particularly when the entrepreneur also provides evidence of human capital alongside psychological capital (Anglin, Short, et al., 2018). Seeking to establish a group identification with potential stakeholders may foster affective commitment among stakeholders (Allison, Davis, Webb, & Short, 2017), while telling stories about the venture may serve to enhance perceived legitimacy (Lounsbury & Glynn, 2001). Furthermore, establishing commonalities between themselves and others enables entrepreneurs to convince partners that their vision for the firm is a viable one (Powell & Baker, 2017). The effectiveness of conveying personal attributes has key boundary conditions—notably the gender of the entrepreneur (Anglin, Wolfe, Short, McKenny, & Pidduck, 2018). For example, stakeholders may expect and even reward displays of narcissism from entrepreneur to a point, although women are not rewarded nearly as strongly as men when displaying narcissism (Anglin, Wolfe, et al., 2018). Overall, here, the evidence points to the conclusion that—when legitimacy is lacking—entrepreneurs may be able to share personal qualities, and enhance similarity perceptions, to influence others.

Taking the Creative and Innovative Approach

In pre-legitimacy, entrepreneurs who demonstrate an intuitive innovative capability and creative approach to leadership can better engage potential stakeholders. Doing so indicates a willingness to take the risks and seek out the information needed to effectively operate within the uncertainty inherent to new ventures. Several studies highlight that a departure from more traditional, linear leadership—that is more analytical and rational in approach than intuitive and creative—allows entrepreneurs to be viewed as less susceptible to status quo bias and capable of navigating uncertainty (Dyer, Gregersen, & Christensen, 2008; Groves, Vance, & Choi, 2011). As Fisher (2012) notes, behaviors associated with effectuation (affordable loss, experimentation) instill the creative flexibility that allows the venture to land on the right competitive strategy for launch and growth. Related, in turbulent environments (e.g., high-tech industries) findings show that displayed innovativeness and creativity can enable entrepreneurs to be better able to exploit market opportunities and maximize available resources (Chen, 2007). Taken together, the collective research points to the need for entrepreneurs to outwardly express an openness to thinking differently and a willingness to operate outside of current industry norms and 'best' practices (e.g., Gielnik, Frese, Graf, & Kampschulte, 2012).

Planning for the Future

Although the dynamic and rapidly changing environments common in entrepreneurship might suggest formal planning to be a futile effort, scholars find planning to be important to the overall perception of an entrepreneur's leadership capability. Adopting formal planning and utilizing financial projections can lead to overconfidence and leave entrepreneurs prone to overestimating future sales and the likelihood of venture survival (Cassar, 2010); however, planning may also allow entrepreneurs to mitigate this bias through setting realistic and attainable goals (Forbes, 2005). Effective planning also allows entrepreneurs to demonstrate the ability to work within the resource and information availability constraints of their environment, minimizing possible stakeholder perceptions that the entrepreneur will act irrationality as a result of overconfidence and hubris (Chwolka & Raith, 2012). Planning is also seen as an opportunity to provide stakeholders insight into how the entrepreneur intends to manage uncertainty and identify potential critical flaws that may prohibit launch (Dimov, 2010). Furthermore, a formal plan supplements an entrepreneur's vision for the venture in providing stakeholders more specific details concerning intended strategies. As a result, the formal planning process offers stakeholders assurances that the entrepreneur is prepared to, and capable of, effectively leading the venture towards the established goals (Burke, Fraser, & Greene, 2010).

Managing Entrepreneurial Ventures Post-Legitimacy

Ventures attain legitimacy at different points of time in the new venture process, depending on both the set of stakeholders granting it and the criteria used to do so (Fisher et al., 2017). For example, potential co-founders or employees who join the venture might be the first stakeholders to legitimize the venture when they deem the venture to be a viable employment opportunity and acceptable career risk (e.g., Moser, Tumasjan, & Welpe, 2017; Tornikoski & Newbert, 2007). Having an established management team and employees is often a key criterion external investors look for before legitimizing the venture by providing financial capital or coming onboard as equity partners (e.g., Rutherford, Tocher, Pollack, & Coombes, 2016). As legitimacy is granted by different stakeholder groups (i.e., post-legitimacy), the leadership focus of the entrepreneur will shift from engaging external audiences to engaging internal stakeholders responsible for enacting the entrepreneur's vision (Gupta, MacMillan, & Surie, 2004; Rutherford & Buller, 2007). Thus, leading entrepreneurial ventures post-legitimacy centers on how to best direct and motivate those now responsible (e.g., employees) for enacting the entrepreneur's vision and the venture's objectives (e.g., Renko et al., 2015).

Sharing a Collective Vision

Entrepreneurs who effectively articulate their vision, and pass that vision on to employees, tend to inspire greater employee commitment and engagement (Renko et al., 2015). Specifically, a vision-centric leadership approach can instill a belief that the entrepreneur(s) will act in the best interests of the firm (e.g., Gupta et al., 2004). Building a shared vision for the venture among a broader group of stakeholders is necessary for venture growth. Here, Ensley and colleagues (2006) find lone entrepreneurs are less effective at leading new ventures than are entrepreneurial teams who share a collective vision. This shared leadership approach creates a distribution of resources, roles, and responsibilities that enables venture leadership to be more responsive to stakeholder needs. Moreover, ventures become better equipped to address problems likely to emerge during venture growth that can stagnate performance (Hmieleski, Cole, & Baron, 2012). As such, Carland and Carland (2012) perhaps best articulate the collective agreement within the extant literature that if entrepreneurs are to achieve the levels of success they envision for their venture, they must be willing to abandon the tendency to take on a self-centered, individualistic approach to leadership in favor of a more collective one.

Exerting Influence on Venture Outcomes

Perhaps the most important leadership approach entrepreneurs must adopt is to cultivate a sense of authenticity with regards to any leadership action or approach they choose to take. Authentic leadership, the result of inner self-awareness and self-regulation on the part of the leader, represents an optimistic, hopeful, and transparent approach that prioritizes the development of followers (Luthans & Avolio, 2003). Such an approach can be particularly relevant in newer and emerging ventures where the inherent uncertainty creates challenges for employees to find a sense of purpose and meaning (Jensen & Luthans, 2006). Furthermore, employees can also trust that authentic leaders will act in positive and ethical ways and that their values align with social norms. For example, in underdeveloped and emerging environments that lack institutional rules and norms, the belief that an entrepreneur will act with integrity and can be trusted to do the right thing plays a critical role in shaping stakeholder relationships (Welter & Smallbone, 2006). Additionally, entrepreneurs viewed as ethical are seen by stakeholders as being better able to acquire resources needed to continue to grow the venture (Harris, Sapienza, & Bowie, 2009). Taken together, employees' perception of an entrepreneur's authenticity in leading the venture perhaps has the single strongest influence on employee job satisfaction, organizational commitment, work happiness, and performance (e.g., Hmieleski et al., 2012; Jensen & Luthans, 2006).

Inspiring Creativity and Innovation

Although creativity and innovation are hallmarks of effective leadership in any organizational setting (e.g., Carmeli, Gelbard, & Gefen, 2010), such efforts are particularly critical in new ventures that often still lack, or are in the process of still, accruing the resources needed (e.g., financing, human capital) to grow and compete. Research into effectuation and bricolage highlights the need for entrepreneurs to exhibit improvisational and novelty-seeking behaviors. Doing so allows entrepreneurs to make effective use of the limited resources at hand (e.g., financing, human capital) as they continue to seek legitimacy from additional resource providers post-legitimacy (e.g., Baker & Nelson, 2005; Welter, Mauer, & Wuebker, 2016). In such instances, engaging in creative problem solving that departs from traditional decision-making approaches can similarly inspire greater creativity and innovativeness in stakeholders (both external and internal) needed to overcome the initial resource disadvantages (financial and human capital) new ventures experience relative to more established firms.

Research on ambidextrous leadership also highlights the need for entrepreneurs to be flexible in allowing stakeholders to take risks and think independently to foster the innovation needed to grow the venture. Innovation takes two distinct forms in organizations, characterized by contradictory features and associated with different behaviors (e.g., Bledow, Frese, Anderson, Erez, & Farr, 2009; Leonidou, Christofi, Vrontis, & Thrassou, 2018). Exploration innovation is the seeking out of creative and novel products, processes, and possibilities that can lead to 'radical' innovation and is fostered by opening leadership behaviors, which are sets of actions leaders take designed to break up routines and encourage thinking in new directions. Here, entrepreneurs afford employees the freedom and latitude to take risks, cultivate their own ideas, challenge the status quo, and work through their errors as part of the learning process (Rosing, Frese, & Bausch, 2011). In situations marked by high rates of change and uncertainty, such as the early stages of a new venture, employees tend to be more receptive to a leadership approach that increases and encourages variance in ideas and outcomes (e.g., Jansen, Vera, & Crossan, 2009).

However, entrepreneurs must take caution not to overly focus on exploration innovation as doing so can limit the venture's ability to grow. Specifically, opening leadership behaviors might not provide the structure and direction to turn creative ideas and assignments into value-adding organizational processes and outcomes (Bledow, Frese, & Mueller, 2011). As such, entrepreneurs must be able to balance and readily switch from an opening leadership approach to closing leadership behaviors defined by establishing routines, monitoring goal attainment, and taking corrective action (Rosing et al., 2011). Closing leadership behaviors encourage exploitative innovation in others, reducing variance in behaviors, and align actions towards producing commercial goods or services (Rosing et al., 2011). Whereas exploration innovation and opening leadership behaviors might be critical for getting newly established ventures out of the starting gate, exploitative innovation and closing leadership behaviors can ensure the venture remains a viable commercial enterprise. Accordingly, research suggests that ventures that are most likely to maximize performance and chances of survival through creativity and innovation require entrepreneurs to undertake an ambidextrous leadership approach (e.g., Zacher & Rosing, 2015).

How entrepreneurs effectively manage and mitigate the conflicting perspectives, goals, and tensions that arise in new ventures still seeking stability (e.g., competing demands of internal and external stakeholders, family vs. nonfamily) can either inhibit or foster innovation (e.g., Ingram, Lewis, Barton, & Gartner, 2016; McMullen & Bergman, 2017). For example, a substantial leadership challenge entrepreneurs face in social ventures is how to reconcile the social mission of the venture with its commercial demands (Smith, Besharov, Wessels, & Chertok, 2012). Such tensions can stymie innovation unless entrepreneurs adopt a paradoxical leadership approach. Here, research suggests that entrepreneurs must strike a balance with their approach to stakeholder management. Specifically, it may be necessary to maintain a level of power and control that moves the venture towards the overarching objectives of the venture while still allowing for individualization and proactiveness in stakeholders (Lewis, Andriopoulos, & Smith, 2014; Zhang, Waldman, Han, & Li, 2015). To do so, entrepreneurs must avoid having a singular focus in their approach to the venture. Instead, entrepreneurs should be holistic in their thinking, consider the 'whole picture', and be open or willing to acknowledge competing perspectives on the same issue (Zhang et al., 2015). Doing so empowers stakeholders to pursue those ideas and opportunities that offer real possibilities for innovation and creativity while not deviating too far from the path needed to grow the venture (e.g., Ingram et al., 2016; Smith et al., 2012).

Knowing When to Change the Plan

Having a specific plan can often give reluctant stakeholders assurances that the entrepreneur will be able to effectively manage the often-turbulent new venture creation process (e.g., Chwolka & Raith, 2012; Dimov, 2010). However, most new ventures rarely start out with an optimal strategy and often must pivot from their initial plans to maximize chances for growth and survival (e.g., Furr, Cavarretta, & Garg, 2012). Here, effective leadership requires entrepreneurs to actively balance an open, flexible, and opportunistic approach against expectations to be persistent, tenacious, and committed (Crilly, 2018). Early stakeholders often remain steadfastly committed to an entrepreneur's initial plan for the venture, expecting future strategic and operational decisions to align accordingly. As such, any deviation or strategic reorientation may be met with a loss of legitimacy (e.g., Pontikes, 2012). To mitigate such issues, McDonald and Gao (2019) suggest that entrepreneurs evoke several rhetorical strategies to best prepare stakeholders for anticipated changes to the plan. Specifically, their work highlights the importance of staging strategic transitions across several phases that allow for a more gradual and effective pacing of change that enables a greater potential for stakeholder acceptance of the entrepreneur's course of action than a single, quick change of direction might (McDonald & Gao, 2019).

Conversely, entrepreneurs must also be aware of their own proclivity to remain fixated on their initial plan when emerging opportunities and changing market dynamics suggest the need for a revised approach (e.g., Sio, Kotovsky, & Cagan, 2015). These strong feelings of 'psychological ownership', the degree to which entrepreneurs feel the venture is truly theirs alone that can create an emotional attachment that can overwhelm cognitive evaluations (Pierce, Kostova, & Dirks, 2003), can have adverse effects such as risk aversion, overconfidence, and dysfunctional persistence that can stifle an entrepreneur's ability to effectively lead the venture through strategic change (e.g., Grimes, 2012; Pierce et al., 2003). In such instances, stakeholders might lose confidence that the entrepreneur is the right person to continue to lead the venture. To counteract such effects, entrepreneurs should focus on exercising caution around expertise, achieving the right balance of resources, and defining the venture on what has been achieved rather than how it was achieved (Crilly, 2018). Taken together, research suggests entrepreneurs need to not only be adaptable when it comes to the strategic direction of the venture but also must be adaptable in how they manage stakeholder expectations of what the venture intended to do and what it now needs to do.

Next Steps in Future Research

Although research concerning the leading of entrepreneurial ventures has seen considerable advancements in recent years, opportunities remain for future research. Contemporary leadership research has seen new theoretical perspectives and themes emerge as scholars seek to be more holistic in how the dynamics of the leadership process are captured and explained (Lord, Day, Zaccaro, Avolio, & Eagly, 2017). While some have been applied to entrepreneurial settings to better understand what entrepreneurs must do to effectively lead new ventures, the entrepreneurship literature has been slow to embrace other contemporary leadership theories that might further inform what entails leading entrepreneurial ventures.

Leader–member exchange (LMX) theory, in particular, has potential applications to new venture settings given its focus on the relationship dynamics that develop between leaders and followers. LMX suggests that leaders treat individual followers or sets of followers differently than others within the same group or organization (e.g., Day & Miscenko, 2016). In doing so, leaders develop strong trust-, emotional-, and respect-based relationships with certain individuals but not others, creating an in-group/out-group dynamic that has implications for organizational performance outcomes (e.g., Martin, Guillaume, Thomas, Lee, & Epitropaki, 2016). Applied to an entrepreneur's relationships with various stakeholder groups, it might be beneficial to explore how prioritization of relationships affects stakeholders' relationships with the firm. For example, entrepreneurs often prioritize relationships with investors in the earliest stages of the venture given the critical need for financial capital (Huang & Knight, 2017), and it is possible that investors' concerns may not align with employees' concerns. To investigate the impact of such situations, researchers could use semi-structured interviews to uncover how entrepreneurs prioritize relationships as well as survey employees concerning their relationships with the entrepreneurs. Such data could be compared to performance data (e.g., sales growth, employee retention, stakeholder satisfaction) to understand how the management of these relationships is related to performance.

Today's shifting sociopolitical trends have pushed organizational leaders to consider more than a venture's financial returns and to be more cognizant of the social, moral, and ethical implications of their decisions. For example, an organization's social stance on potentially controversial moral issues can influence the ability to attract important resources such as human capital (Turner, McIntosh, Reid, & Buckley, 2019). Moving forward, the moral and ethical values exhibited by entrepreneurs might hold greater sway compared to traditional strategic leadership actions when influencing stakeholders (e.g., Becker, 2018; Mai, Zhang, & Wang, 2019). As such, more work is needed to examine how the expressed values of entrepreneurs may influence the actions of stakeholders. For instance, scholars might examine the prevalence of moral or social values in pitch competitions to uncover how potential resource providers rate entrepreneurs who place a higher emphasis on social concerns.

Factors out of leaders' or entrepreneurs' control, such as their gender or race, also shape perceptions of leadership effectiveness and entrepreneurial ability (Younkin & Kuppuswamy, 2017). Recently, social scientists in psychology and sociology have questioned whether the typical category-based emphasis on race creates a complete picture of how racial or skin color differences influence perceptions of others. As such, these scholars have called for investigations of colorism, which refers to preferences or biases based on an individual's skin tone irrespective of category of race or ethnicity (Dixon & Telles, 2017). For instance, manipulating photographs of Barak Obama where his skin was lightened and darkened resulted in lower evaluations of him as a leader when his skin was darkened (Nevid & McClelland, 2010). Entrepreneurship research could draw inspiration from such work to examine how skin color affects perceptions of entrepreneurs and the ability to influence others. For example, scholars could manipulate the skin tone of White, Black, or Hispanic entrepreneurs in pictures or in online funding pitches and assess evaluations of leadership or entrepreneurial ability. Such research would provide a more nuanced understanding of how implicit biases may influence the perception of leaders as well as provide guidance on how to reduce such biases.

Another notable area deficient of research is how entrepreneurs develop and refine their leadership skills. Work in this area has often focused on university settings (e.g., Bagheri & Pihie, 2011). However, questions remain as to whether universities are effective in developing an entrepreneur's leadership skills compared to more practical, real-world experiences (Davey, Hannon, & Penaluna, 2016). Thus, more work is needed to investigate where and how entrepreneurs learn and acquire leadership skills. One interesting line of inquiry may center on military training. Military veterans often score high in entrepreneurial passion and are more likely to launch their business than nonveterans after completing education programs (Kerrick, Cumberland, & Choi, 2016). Service members often undergo intensive leadership training as a part of their military service. Yet, the mechanism(s) underlying the link between such training and leadership in entrepreneurial ventures remains unclear. Future research could investigate how a veteran's worldview, experience, and skills learned in the military relate to the ability to lead entrepreneurial ventures.

The leadership literature has noted that the leadership of virtual teams may be fundamentally different from leading teams face-to-face (e.g., Hoch & Dulebohn, 2017; Purvanova & Bono, 2009). For example, the influence of transformational leadership has shown to be stronger in virtual contexts than in face-to-face contexts (Purvanova & Bono, 2009). As the entrepreneurship landscape continues to evolve, evidence suggests leading virtually may become increasingly important. Notably, the emergence of crowdfunding, initial coin offerings, and online angel investor platforms allows entrepreneurs to obtain resources from potential stakeholders virtually, with some evidence suggesting that leadership qualities drive funding outcomes (e.g., Anglin, Short, et al., 2018).

However, such contexts have more limited interactions between entrepreneurs and stakeholders than traditional virtual teams, where the majority of virtual leadership research has been conducted. Here, entrepreneurs have limited opportunities in interpersonal interactions to inspire and influence stakeholders in crowdfunding contexts. This likely means that the limited exchanges between entrepreneurs and crowdfunding supporters, via project updates and response to supporter comments, play a highly salient role in maintaining firm support. Future research might investigate the content of these exchanges using serial crowdfunders to determine how such exchanges influence the success of future campaigns. Because one's individual characteristics often shape their ability to lead, researchers might go one step further and investigate how indications of an entrepreneur's narcissism, psychological capital, or Big Five personality traits mediate the exchange between entrepreneurs' responses to backers and future funding success.

Leadership scholars might also seek to leverage entrepreneurial settings and the new venture context to further explore how leaders manage situations that involve high levels of risk and adapt in environments characterized by high degrees of uncertainty. Given that contemporary organizations must contend with an ever-increasing pace of change and the environments in which they compete are becoming more dynamic, leaders are being asked to adopt an entrepreneurial mindset to navigate such challenges. As such, because entrepreneurial contexts require leaders to adopt certain behaviors and approaches, how that translates to more traditional organizational settings has potential implications for how we understand and define leadership moving forward. Consequently, the leadership literature might unlock new insights into leaders' actions and behaviors by applying entrepreneurship theory and utilizing new venture settings to conduct mainstream leadership research.

As one example, the discovery and creation perspectives provide two theoretical mechanisms by which an entrepreneur will act on opportunities that could be used by leadership scholars. The discovery perspective argues that opportunities exist exogenously, are the result of market imperfections, and must be discovered by entrepreneurs through environmental analyses and making judgments about the future environment (Alvarez & Barney, 2007). The creation perspective suggests that opportunities are created in the minds of entrepreneurs and only exist once acted on as the entrepreneur constructs the future environment (Alvarez & Barney, 2007).

These perspectives, while different, should not be viewed in competition of one another as both theories have merit in explaining the paths by which opportunities emerge (Edelman & Yli–Renko, 2010). Because leaders must evaluate and plan for the future, it is likely these perspectives may have implications for how leaders engage followers in preparing for the future (Reid et al., 2018). Leaders who view the world from a discovery perspective may encourage followers to conduct a systematic analysis of the environment and present evidence-based plans for assessing future opportunities or threats. In contrast, leaders adopting a creation perspective may encourage a more intuitive approach to the future, where followers should form ideas, act on them, and then assess the results of their actions. Given the potential these perspectives have to help explain leadership approaches and followers' actions in broad organizational settings, it is surprising that research here remains contained to the entrepreneurship literature. Accordingly, we see the discovery and creation perspectives as the next natural extension of the entrepreneurship literature into the broader leadership domain.

Concluding Thoughts

It is intuitively appealing, and common in the academic literature as well as the popular press, to conflate the processes of 'entrepreneurial leadership' with 'leading entrepreneurial ventures.' However, a conflation of these two topics fails to account for the complexities and distinct challenges of the new venture creation process. Here, what is required of entrepreneurs as leaders, we contend, is shaped by the circumstances surrounding two critical periods unique within the life span of entrepreneurial ventures—pre-legitimacy and post-legitimacy. Put simply, in the pre-legitimacy phase of the entrepreneurial venture there is a struggle for survival and the success of the venture is based on leadership in terms of relationships with external stakeholders. In contrast, the post-legitimacy phase sees the leadership focus shift to internal stakeholders as the newly established venture seeks to establish itself and grow.

Our aim in this chapter was to outline what we already know as well as what we do not yet know about leading entrepreneurial ventures throughout these two phases. Although the literature has grown quickly, there are multiple relationships that have yet to be explored and replicated, and the area of inquiry related to leading entrepreneurial ventures promises to be a fruitful domain of research for decades to come.

References

Allison, T. H., Davis, B. C., Webb, J. W., & Short, J. C. (2017). Persuasion in crowdfunding: An elaboration likelihood model of crowdfunding performance. *Journal of Business Venturing, 32*(6), 707–725.

Alvarez, S. A., & Barney, J. B. (2007). Discovery and creation: Alternative theories of entrepreneurial action. *Strategic Entrepreneurship Journal, 1*(1-2), 11–26.

Anglin, A. H., Short, J. C., Drover, W., Stevenson, R. M., McKenny, A. F., & Allison, T. H. (2018). The power of positivity? The influence of positive psychological capital language on crowdfunding performance. *Journal of Business Venturing*. Retrieved from https://doi.org/10.1016/j.jbusvent.2018.03.003

Anglin, A. H., Wolfe, M. T., Short, J. C., McKenny, A. F., & Pidduck, R. J. (2018). Narcissistic rhetoric and crowdfunding performance: A social role theory perspective. *Journal of Business Venturing*. Retrieved from doi.org/10.1016/j.jbusvent.2018.04.004

Antonakis, J., & Autio, E. (2007). Entrepreneurship and leadership. In J. R. Baum, M. Frese, & R. A. Baron (Eds.), *The psychology of entrepreneurship* (pp. 189–207). East Sussex, UK: Psychology Press.

Bagheri, A., & Pihie, Z. A. L. (2011). Entrepreneurial leadership: Towards a model for learning and development. *Human Resource Development International, 14*(4), 447–463.

Baker, T., & Nelson, R. E. (2005). Creating something from nothing: Resource construction through entrepreneurial bricolage. *Administrative Science Quarterly, 50*(3), 329–366.

Becker, G. K. (2018). Moral leadership in business. *Contemporary Issues in Leadership*, 237–257.

Bledow, R., Frese, M., Anderson, N., Erez, M., & Farr, J. (2009). A dialectic perspective on innovation: Conflicting demands, multiple pathways, and ambidexterity. *Industrial and Organizational Psychology, 2*(3), 305–337.

Bledow, R., Frese, M., & Mueller, V. (2011). Ambidextrous leadership for innovation: The influence of culture. In *Advances in global leadership* (pp. 41–69). Bingley, UK: Emerald Group Publishing Limited.

Burke, A., Fraser, S., & Greene, F. J. (2010). The multiple effects of business planning on new venture performance. *Journal of Management Studies, 47*(3), 391–415.

Carland, J. C., & Carland Jr, J. W. (2012). A model of shared entrepreneurial leadership. *Academy of Entrepreneurship Journal, 18*(2), 71.

Carmeli, A., Gelbard, R., & Gefen, D. (2010). The importance of innovation leadership in cultivating strategic fit and enhancing firm performance. *The Leadership Quarterly, 21*(3), 339–349.

Cassar, G. (2010). Are individuals entering self-employment overly optimistic? An empirical test of plans and projections on nascent entrepreneur expectations. *Strategic Management Journal, 31*(8), 822–840.

Chen, M. H. (2007). Entrepreneurial leadership and new ventures: Creativity in entrepreneurial teams. *Creativity and Innovation Management, 16*(3), 239–249.

Choi, Y. R., & Shepherd, D. A. (2005). Stakeholder perceptions of age and other dimensions of newness. *Journal of Management, 31*(4), 573–596.

Chwolka, A., & Raith, M. G. (2012). The value of business planning before start-up – A decision-theoretical perspective. *Journal of Business Venturing, 27*(3), 385–399.

Cogliser, C. C., & Brigham, K. H. (2004). The intersection of leadership and entrepreneurship: Mutual lessons to be learned. *The Leadership Quarterly, 15*(6), 771–799.

Crilly, N. (2018). "Fixation" and "the pivot": Balancing persistence with flexibility in design and entrepreneurship. *International Journal of Design Creativity and Innovation, 6*(1–2), 52–65.

Davey, T., Hannon, P., & Penaluna, A. (2016). Entrepreneurship education and the role of universities in entrepreneurship: Introduction to the special issue. *Industry and Higher Education, 30*(3), 171–182.

Day, D. V., & Miscenko, D. (2016). Leader-member exchange (LMX): Construct evolution, contributions, and future prospects for advancing leadership theory. In T. N. Bauer & B. Erdogan (Eds.), *Oxford library of psychology. The Oxford handbook of leader-member exchange* (pp. 9–28). New York, NY: Oxford University Press.

DeRue, D. S., & Ashford, S. J. (2010). Who will lead and who will follow? A social process of leadership identity construction in organizations. *Academy of Management Review, 35*(4), 627–647.

Dimov, D. (2010). Nascent entrepreneurs and venture emergence: Opportunity confidence, human capital, and early planning. *Journal of Management Studies, 47*(6), 1123–1153.

Dixon, A. R., & Telles, E. E. (2017). Skin color and colorism: Global research, concepts, and measurement. *Annual Review of Sociology, 43*, 405–424.

Dyer, J. H., Gregersen, H. B., & Christensen, C. (2008). Entrepreneur behaviors, opportunity recognition, and the origins of innovative ventures. *Strategic Entrepreneurship Journal, 2*(4), 317.

Edelman, L., & Yli-Renko, H. (2010). The impact of environment and entrepreneurial perceptions on venture-creation efforts: Bridging the discovery and creation views of entrepreneurship. *Entrepreneurship Theory and Practice, 34*(5), 833–856.

Engelen, A., Gupta, V., Strenger, L., & Brettel, M. (2015). Entrepreneurial orientation, firm performance, and the moderating role of transformational leadership behaviors. *Journal of Management, 41*(4), 1069–1097.

Ensley, M. D., Pearce, C. L., & Hmieleski, K. M. (2006). The moderating effect of environmental dynamism on the relationship between entrepreneur leadership behavior and new venture performance. *Journal of Business Venturing, 21*(2), 243–263.

Fisher, G. (2012). Effectuation, causation, and bricolage: A behavioral comparison of emerging theories in entrepreneurship research. *Entrepreneurship Theory and Practice, 36*(5), 1019–1051.

Fisher, G., Kotha, S., & Lahiri, A. (2016). Changing with the times: An integrated view of identity, legitimacy, and new venture life cycles. *Academy of Management Review, 41*(3), 383–409.

Fisher, G., Kuratko, D. F., Bloodgood, J. M., & Hornsby, J. S. (2017). Legitimate to whom? The challenge of audience diversity and new venture legitimacy. *Journal of Business Venturing, 32*(1), 52–71.

Forbes, D. P. (2005). Are some entrepreneurs more overconfident than others? *Journal of Business Venturing, 20*(5), 623–640.

Furr, N. R., Cavarretta, F., & Garg, S. (2012). Who changes course? The role of domain knowledge and novel framing in making technology changes. *Strategic Entrepreneurship Journal, 6*(3), 236–256.

Gartner, W. B., Bird, B. J., & Starr, J. A. (1992). Acting as if: Differentiating entrepreneurial from organizational behavior. *Entrepreneurship Theory and Practice, 16*(3), 13–31.

Gartner, W. B., Gartner, W. C., Shaver, K. G., Carter, N. M., & Reynolds, P. D. (2004). *Handbook of entrepreneurial dynamics: The process of business creation.* Thousand Oaks, CA: Sage.

Gielnik, M. M., Frese, M., Graf, J. M., & Kampschulte, A. (2012). Creativity in the opportunity identification process and the moderating effect of diversity of information. *Journal of Business Venturing, 27*(5), 559–576.

Grimes, M. G. (2012). *To thine own self be true? The process and consequences of "pivoting" during idea-stage entrepreneurship.* Ph.D. Dissertation, Vanderbilt University, Nashville, TN.

Groves, K., Vance, C., & Choi, D. (2011). Examining entrepreneurial cognition: An occupational analysis of balanced linear and nonlinear thinking and entrepreneurship success. *Journal of Small Business Management, 49*(3), 438–466.

Gupta, V., MacMillan, I. C., & Surie, G. (2004). Entrepreneurial leadership: Developing and measuring a cross-cultural construct. *Journal of Business Venturing, 19*(2), 241–260.

Harris, J. D., Sapienza, H. J., & Bowie, N. E. (2009). Ethics and entrepreneurship. *Journal of Business Venturing, 24*(5), 407–418.

Haynes, K. T., Hitt, M. A., & Campbell, J. T. (2015). The dark side of leadership: Towards a mid-range theory of hubris and greed in entrepreneurial contexts. *Journal of Management Studies, 52*(4), 479–505.

Hmieleski, K. M., Cole, M. S., & Baron, R. A. (2012). Shared authentic leadership and new venture performance. *Journal of Management, 38*(5), 1476–1499.

Hoch, J. E., & Dulebohn, J. H. (2017). Team personality composition, emergent leadership and shared leadership in virtual teams: A theoretical framework. *Human Resource Management Review, 27*(4), 678–693.

Hogg, M. A., van Knippenberg, D., & Rast, D. E. (2012). The social identity theory of leadership: Theoretical origins, research findings, and conceptual developments. *European Review of Social Psychology, 23*(1), 258–304.

Huang, L., & Knight, A. P. (2017). Resources and relationships in entrepreneurship: An exchange theory of the development and effects of the entrepreneur-investor relationship. *Academy of Management Review, 42*(1), 80–102.

Ingram, A. E., Lewis, M. W., Barton, S., & Gartner, W. B. (2016). Paradoxes and innovation in family firms: The role of paradoxical thinking. *Entrepreneurship Theory and Practice, 40*(1), 161–176.

Jansen, J. J. P., Vera, D., & Crossan, M. (2009). Strategic leadership for exploration and exploitation: The moderating role of environmental dynamism. *The Leadership Quarterly, 20*(1), 5–18.

Jensen, S. M., & Luthans, F. (2006). Entrepreneurs as authentic leaders: Impact on employees' attitudes. *Leadership & Organization Development Journal, 27*(8), 646–666.

Kerrick, S. A., Cumberland, D. M., & Choi, N. (2016). Comparing military veterans and civilians responses to an entrepreneurship education program. *Journal of Entrepreneurship Education, 19*(1), 9.

Kuratko, D. F. (2007). Entrepreneurial leadership in the 21st century: Guest editor's perspective. *Journal of Leadership & Organizational Studies, 13*(4), 1–11.

Leitch, C. M., & Volery, T. (2017). Entrepreneurial leadership: Insights and directions. *International Small Business Journal: Researching Entrepreneurship, 35*(2), 147–156.

Leonidou, E., Christofi, M., Vrontis, D., & Thrassou, A. (2018). An integrative framework of stakeholder engagement for innovation management and entrepreneurship development. *Journal of Business Research*. Retrieved from https://doi.org/10.1016/j.jbusres.2018.11.054

Lewis, M. W., Andriopoulos, C., & Smith, W. K. (2014). Paradoxical leadership to enable strategic agility. *California Management Review, 56*(3), 58–77.

Lord, R. G., Day, D. V., Zaccaro, S. J., Avolio, B. J., & Eagly, A. H. (2017). Leadership in applied psychology: Three waves of theory and research. *Journal of Applied Psychology, 102*(3), 434.

Lounsbury, M., & Glynn, M. A. (2001). Cultural entrepreneurship: Stories, legitimacy, and the acquisition of resources. *Strategic Management Journal, 22*(6-7), 545–564.

Luthans, F., & Avolio, B. J. (2003). Authentic leadership development. *Positive Organizational Scholarship, 241*, 258.

Mai, Y., Zhang, W., & Wang, L. (2019). The effects of entrepreneurs' moral awareness and ethical behavior on product innovation of new ventures: Evidence from China. *Chinese Management Studies, 13*(2), 421–446.

Martin, R., Guillaume, Y., Thomas, G., Lee, A., & Epitropaki, O. (2016). Leader-member exchange (LMX) and performance: A meta-analytic review. *Personnel Psychology, 69*(1), 67–121.

McDonald, R., & Gao, C. (2019). Pivoting isn't enough? Managing strategic reorientation in new ventures. *Organization Science, 30*(6), 1289–1318.

McKelvie, A., Haynie, J. M., & Gustavsson, V. (2011). Unpacking the uncertainty construct: Implications for entrepreneurial action. *Journal of Business Venturing, 26*(3), 273–292.

McMullen, J. S., & Bergman, B. J. (2017). Social entrepreneurship and the development paradox of prosocial motivation: A cautionary tale. *Strategic Entrepreneurship Journal, 11*(3), 243–270.

Morse, E. A., Fowler, S. W., & Lawrence, T. B. (2007). The impact of virtual embeddedness on new venture survival: Overcoming the liabilities of newness. *Entrepreneurship Theory and Practice, 31*(2), 139–159.

Moser, K. J., Tumasjan, A., & Welpe, I. M. (2017). Small but attractive: Dimensions of new venture employer attractiveness and the moderating role of applicants' entrepreneurial behaviors. *Journal of Business Venturing, 32*(5), 588–610.

Nevid, J. S., & McClelland, N. (2010). Measurement of implicit and explicit attitudes toward Barack Obama. *Psychology & Marketing, 27*(10), 989–1000.

Pierce, J. L., Kostova, T., & Dirks, K. T. (2003). The state of psychological ownership: Integrating and extending a century of research. *Review of General Psychology, 7*(1), 84–107.

Pollack, J. M., Barr, S., & Hanson, S. (2017). New venture creation as establishing stakeholder relationships: A trust-based perspective. *Journal of Business Venturing Insights, 7*, 15–20.

Pontikes, E. G. (2012). Two sides of the same coin: How ambiguous classification affects multiple audiences' evaluations. *Administrative Science Quarterly, 57*(1), 81–118.

Powell, E. E., & Baker, T. (2017). In the beginning: Identity processes and organizing in multi-founder nascent ventures. *Academy of Management Journal, 60*(6), 2381–2414.

Purvanova, R. K., & Bono, J. E. (2009). Transformational leadership in context: Face-to-face and virtual teams. *The Leadership Quarterly, 20*(3), 343–357.

Reid, S. W., Anglin, A. H., Baur, J. E., Short, J. C., & Buckley, M. R. (2018). Blazing new trails or opportunity lost? Evaluating research at the intersection of leadership and entrepreneurship. *The Leadership Quarterly, 29*(1), 150–164.

Renko, M., El Tarabishy, A., Carsrud, A. L., & Brännback, M. (2015). Understanding and measuring entrepreneurial leadership style. *Journal of Small Business Management, 53*(1), 54–74.

Rosing, K., Frese, M., & Bausch, A. (2011). Explaining the heterogeneity of the leadership-innovation relationship: Ambidextrous leadership. *The Leadership Quarterly, 22*(5), 956–974.

Rutherford, M. W., & Buller, P. F. (2007). Searching for the legitimacy threshold. *Journal of Management Inquiry, 16*(1), 78–92.

Rutherford, M. W., Tocher, N., Pollack, J. M., & Coombes, S. M. (2016). Proposing a financial legitimacy threshold in emerging ventures: A multi-method investigation. *Group & Organization Management, 41*(6), 751–785.

Ruvio, A., Rosenblatt, Z., & Hertz-Lazarowitz, R. (2010). Entrepreneurial leadership vision in nonprofit vs. for-profit organizations. *Leadership Quarterly, 21*(1), 144–158.

Ruvio, A., & Shoham, A. (2011). A multilevel study of nascent social ventures. *International Small Business Journal: Researching Entrepreneurship, 29*(5), 562–579.

Sio, U. N., Kotovsky, K., & Cagan, J. (2015). Fixation or inspiration? A meta-analytic review of the role of examples on design processes. *Design Studies, 39*, 70–99.

Smith, W. K., Besharov, M. L., Wessels, A. K., & Chertok, M. (2012). A paradoxical leadership model for social entrepreneurs: Challenges, leadership skills, and pedagogical tools for managing social and commercial demands. *Academy of Management Learning & Education, 11*(3), 463–478.

Stinchcombe, A. L. (1965). Social structure and organizations. In J. G. March (Ed.), *Handbook of organizations* (Vol. 7, pp. 142–193). Chicago: Rand McNally.

Tolbert, P. S., David, R. J., & Sine, W. D. (2011). Studying choice and change: The intersection of institutional theory and entrepreneurship research. *Organization Science, 22*(5), 1332–1344.

Tornikoski, E. T., & Newbert, S. L. (2007). Exploring the determinants of organizational emergence: A legitimacy perspective. *Journal of Business Venturing, 22*(2), 311–335.

Tost, L. P. (2011). An integrative model of legitimacy judgments. *Academy of Management Review, 36*(4), 686–710.

Turner, M. R., McIntosh, T., Reid, S. W., & Buckley, M. R. (2019). Corporate implementation of socially controversial CSR initiatives: Implications for human resource management. *Human Resource Management Review, 29*(1), 125–136.

Überbacher, F. (2014). Legitimation of new ventures: A review and research programme. *Journal of Management Studies, 51*(4), 667–698.

Vecchio, R. P. (2003). Entrepreneurship and leadership: Common trends and common threads. *Human Resource Management Review, 13*(2), 303–327.

Waddock, S., & Steckler, E. (2016). Visionaries and wayfinders: Deliberate and emergent pathways to vision in social entrepreneurship. *Journal of Business Ethics, 133*(4), 719–734.

Welter, C., Mauer, R., & Wuebker, R. J. (2016). Bridging behavioral models and theoretical concepts: Effectuation and bricolage in the opportunity creation framework. *Strategic Entrepreneurship Journal, 10*(1), 5–20.

Welter, F., & Smallbone, D. (2006). Exploring the role of trust in entrepreneurial activity. *Entrepreneurship Theory and Practice, 30*(4), 465–475.

Younkin, P., & Kuppuswamy, V. (2017). The colorblind crowd? Founder race and performance in crowdfunding. *Management Science, 64*(7), 3269–3287.

Yukl, G. (2013). *Leadership in organizations* (8th ed.). Englewood Cliffs, NJ: Prentice Hall.

Zacher, H., & Rosing, K. (2015). Ambidextrous leadership and team innovation. *Leadership & Organization Development Journal, 36*(1), 54–68.

Zhang, Y., Waldman, D. A., Han, Y.-L., & Li, X.-B. (2015). Paradoxical leader behaviors in people management: Antecedents and consequences. *Academy of Management Journal, 58*(2), 538–566.

Zimmerman, M. A., & Zeitz, G. J. (2002). Beyond survival: Achieving new venture growth by building legitimacy. *Academy of Management Review, 27*(3), 414–431.

10

FOUNDER IDENTITY THEORY

Ted Baker & E. Erin Powell

Two Key Theories

Founder Identity Theory[1] has emerged from work applying foundational social psychological theories to the phenomena involved in creating and nurturing new organizations. Two of the most important theories of identity so far brought to bear in entrepreneurship research are Social Identity Theory (Tajfel & Turner, 1979) from psychology and Identity Theory (IDT) (Stryker, 1980) from sociology.[2] The two theories were long considered as competing rather than as complementary (Hogg, Terry, & White, 1995; Stryker, 2008), and until recently (Powell & Baker, 2014, 2017), entrepreneurship scholars had drawn on only one or the other but not both theories.

Nonetheless, as Hogg and colleagues (1995, p. 262) put it,

> [b]oth theories address the structure and function of the socially con-structed self (called identity or social identity) as a dynamic construct that mediates the relationship between social structure or society and individual social behavior. Reciprocal links between society and self are acknowledged by both theories.

These theories are therefore attractive to entrepreneurship researchers in part because they comprehend the intertwining of entrepreneurial agency with the strictures and possibilities provided by the social environments in which founders are embedded.

Social Identity Theory

Tajfel (1978, p. 63) defines social identity as "that part of an individual's self-concept which derives from his knowledge of his membership of a social group (or groups) together with the value and social significance attached to that membership." According to Hogg and colleagues (1995, p. 259),

> [t]he basic idea is that a social category (e.g., nationality, political affiliation, sports team) into which one falls, and to which one feels one belongs, provides a definition of who one is in terms of the defining characteristics of the category . . . People have a repertoire of such discrete category memberships.

This process is guided by what are typically presumed to be a need for self-enhancement as people "assume the perceived prototypical or exemplary characteristics of the category or role as their own" (Ashforth, 2001, p. 25). Social Identity Theory has proved particularly useful in explaining in-group and out-group dynamics.

Social categories—both broad and narrow—are made available as fodder for self-categorization through the social organization of the environments in which people find themselves. For example, self-categorization as a "religious person," or a "liberal" or an "environmentalist," along with images of the prototypical values and behavior of religious people, liberals or environmentalists, are matters of socialization and cultural competence. As Powell and Baker (2014) note, while self-categorization does not require interaction with others in a group or category, it is often shaped by such interactions. Social structure shapes group affiliations and social networks and thereby strongly influences which people will get to know one another and interact as members of groups (Blau & Schwartz, 1984) and how they will self-categorize.

These processes—shaped by both local and broader elements of social structure—in turn, shape organization creation in concrete and practical ways. The interaction of individuals coming together in the formation of a new group—for example, a founding team—can generate new social identity prototypes, in-group/out-group contrasts and social dynamics leading to the formation of a new organization shaped by the emergent social identity the founders come to share (Powell & Baker, 2017). The overall structure and organization of the social environments in which founders are embedded shapes their self-categorizations and their interactions with other founders and stakeholders, which in turn shapes the social identities that emerge in the process of organizing a new venture. Thus, social organization shapes social identities which in turn shape social organization through entrepreneurship.

Identity Theory

In IDT, developed by sociological social psychologists, the linkages between social structure and individual behavior are even stronger (Hogg et al., 1995). The versions of IDT that have supported most founder identity research to date have their roots in the Pragmatism of Dewey and Cooley, especially through their influence on the social psychology of George Herbert Mead (Stryker, 1980). Mead's ideas, and especially his notion of the construction of the self through "taking the role of the other"—in crude terms, coming to understand oneself by drawing on one's sense of how others see and evaluate one—formed the basis for "symbolic interactionism." This process is tied to the practical interactions among individuals in various roles and counter-roles (e.g., parent and child or teacher and student). Early symbolic interactionism paid scant attention to the social environment in which interactions between individuals were embedded (Blumer, 1969). Stryker's (1980), "Structural Symbolic Interactionism"—an early name he gave to IDT—was much more explicit about social structure and organizations. In IDT, social structure affects identity formation, in large part, through the structuring of available roles and the distribution of persons among them (Baker, Gedajlovic, & Lubatkin, 2005).

IDT avoids what some view as the overly conformist imagery of structural role theory (J. A. Turner, 1991) by emphasizing the agentic processes through which individuals may to some extent choose roles, and both choose and negotiate which attendant expectations will most strongly influence their sense of self and behavior (Stryker, 1980). As Stryker argues (1980, pp. 65–66), "[t]o invoke the idea of social structure is to refer to the patterned regularities that characterize most human interaction" and "if the social person is shaped by interaction, it is social structure that shapes the possibilities for interaction and so, ultimately, the person. Conversely, if the social person creatively alters patterns of interaction, those altered patterns can ultimately change social structure."

For example, Mathias and Williams (2017, 2018) demonstrated how the different "hats" (roles and role identities) founders choose to wear shape attention to opportunities and also explored the processes through which founders give up, maintain and take on new roles in their ventures. Stryker also suggested that another pattern of behavior implicated by IDT includes role *creation* behaviors. Powell and Baker (2014, 2017) demonstrate role creation as part of their integration of Social Identity Theory and IDT, showing how social identities can serve as aspirations for the roles and thereby role identities founders create in their organizations, thus shaping both themselves and the social structures in which they are embedded.

Finally, it is important to point out that although Social Identity Theory and IDT provide frameworks that can together support explanations that begin with variations in social organization, explicate how these shape the formation of identities, and, in turn, shape social organization, neither theory has yet to flesh out the full set of processes in any thoroughgoing way.

Multiple Identities Reflect the Complexity, Coherence and Confusion of Social Organization

Scholars have often used "identity" and "self" largely as synonymous. Both IDT and Social Identity Theory are consistent with James's (1890) "vision of a person's having as many selves as there are others, or at least groups of others, to whom that person relates" and thus "posit a multiplicity of selves or a differentiated self composed of multiple aspects rather than a unitary self" (Stryker & Serpe, 1994, p. 16). They build on foundational claims that the complexity of the contemporary social world results in people having many identities. This world is assumed to be complex yet organized but not coherent or rationalized in the sense or to the degree that all the roles or social categories from which people derive their multiple identities fit together well or make sense when considered as a whole. People can be members of groups with contradictory values, and they can have roles with contradictory or otherwise competing behavioral demands. They carry a wealth of identities that sometimes conflict in their implications for individuals' values, for their practical understanding of the world and for their behavior. In particular, people who are embedded in disorganized social environments and networks may have a very messy set of identities.

A well-known quote from the Walt Whitman poem "Song of Myself" provides what might be the most accurate answer many of us could provide to the question, "Who are you?"

Do I contradict myself?
Very well then I contradict myself;
(I am large, I contain multitudes.)

While Social Identity Theory supports the assertion that social identities may be quite malleable as they are cued by changing situations and IDT suggests somewhat greater stability in role identities (Hogg et al., 1995; Stryker & Burke, 2000), they are consistent in the assumption that only subsets of an individual's full set of identities are likely to be invoked or salient in any specific context.

Which identities are invoked or salient in the context of the practical work of entrepreneurship remains an underexplored empirical question. Some authors have studied what they label a singular "entrepreneurial identity." There are likely to be cases in which a founder has a role identity as an "entrepreneur," for example when engaged in a project that requires interacting with potential stakeholders— such as investors—who have expectations of how entrepreneurs should behave. An identity as an "entrepreneur" could instead or also be a social identity if, for example, someone took it on when they self-categorized as such. Murnieks and Mosakowski (2007) point out that such a social identity may well be drawn from popular media depictions and other cultural stereotypes of what it means to be an entrepreneur rather than from accurate descriptions of what most entrepreneurs are actually like. Down and Warren (2008) similarly describe the use of clichés in constructing such an "entrepreneurial identity."

This approach may, however, be *overly* simplifying in a number of ways. First, what it is to be "an entrepreneur" might mean something very different across people who self-categorize this way. Given major differences in definitions among popular commentators and even scholars about what it means to be an entrepreneur (Gartner, 1985; Kim, 2014) and given the differences across contexts in how people understand and value what it means to be an entrepreneur (Welter, Baker, Audretsch, & Gartner, 2017), the meaning of such self-categorizations may not be very clear. In slightly more technical language, the identity prototype (Bartel & Wiesenfeld, 2013; Powell & Baker, 2017) for "entrepreneur" can be very inconsistent across people, time and contexts.

Second, it is not clear that everyone we might as researchers identify as an entrepreneur would self-categorize as such. For example, during fieldwork one of us conducted many years ago (Baker, Miner, & Eesley, 2003), several individuals who had recently founded air pollution control businesses repeatedly objected to the institutional review board-approved informed consent documents that identified our work as a study of "entrepreneurs," saying things like, "Oh, I'm not an entrepreneur, I've only recently started this business," and "An entrepreneur? My bank account looks nothing like that guy from Microsoft." Although social desirability and other demand effects might cause many people to provide answers to questions such as "Tell me about yourself as an entrepreneur" or "Describe who you are as an entrepreneur," or even "What is your identity as an entrepreneur?" it would be a troubling stretch to therefore assume that such an identity is invoked or salient in founders' day-to-day practice.

Third, and more concerning, is any assumption that a single dominant identity is of overwhelming or predominant salience in shaping what entrepreneurs think and do. The close intertwining of life and entrepreneurship make it likely that a number of identities will become salient in the founder's day-to-day work activities. This might be as simple, for example, as a mother or father identity becoming salient to entrepreneurial activities when it keeps the founder from attending children's sports events or throws doubt on a college savings plan. In addition, as Jain, George, and Maltarich (2009) showed in their study of scientist entrepreneurs, expectations attached to distinct work roles can generate conflicts among founders' work identities. Powell and Baker (2014) found that for most of the founders they studied, multiple social and role identities—for example, as a patriot, capitalist and caring boss—affected the structure and strategy of founder-controlled ventures through shaping founders' understanding of the context in which they were trying to maneuver and behave.

Founder Identity Theory—and life—would be simpler if only a singular "entrepreneurial" identity mattered to understanding what founders do. But saying that founders, like other people, are likely to have many identities and that several of them are likely to be salient to their work does not in itself provide much theoretical traction. What are we to do with, for example, the recognition that several different social identities and several different role identities—with substantive content that may not even be consistent across entrepreneurs—are likely to be salient in shaping how founders see and maneuver through their worlds? How do we reduce the empirical complexity to something tractable? To date, entrepreneurship researchers have undertaken a number of theoretical moves that have allowed some simplification of what might otherwise become a theoretically unwieldy set of identities. We briefly review several of these in the following sections and—drawing on our own attachments to pragmatism—look forward to seeing how different lenses provide different sorts of explanatory traction. What is important, at this stage, is to avoid reverting to any oversimplified theoretical presumption that only a single identity—as an "entrepreneur" or as anything else—is all that matters.

Initial Theoretical Tactics to Grapple With Identity Complexity

Salience and Centrality

An established way to see order in a set of identities is through attempting to identify how they are organized in some hierarchy within individuals, which provides "a means of making theoretically-based predictions as to which self-component or which identity, will take precedence in accounting for some self-relevant outcome" (Stryker & Serpe, 1994, p. 18[3]). We focus here on two of the primary ways that this has been conceptualized, in terms of identity "salience" and "centrality."

Stryker and his collaborators conceptualize a salience hierarchy that organizes identities in terms of their relative likelihood of coming into play in a particular situation or across situations. Identities gain their places in the salience hierarchy in the following manner: The greater the loss of valued ties to other people that giving up a role would entail, the greater the commitment to the identity associated with that role and thereby the greater the salience of that identity in the hierarchy. It is important to note that this somewhat indirect process of organizing identities into a hierarchy does not require that the individual be "directly aware of the salience of their identities" (Stryker & Serpe, 1994, p. 19), nor does it assume that identities which are more subjectively valued by a person will play a stronger role in their behavioral choices (Swann, 1983). In contrast, some versions of "centrality[4]" conceive of an identity hierarchy that is structured by individuals' self-aware preferences among their identities while similarly theorizing that the hierarchy predicts the likelihood that an identity will be expressed in any given situation. Various arguments can be made regarding differences in theoretical meaning between these two approaches, as well as in the appropriateness of how they are operationalized. Stryker and Serpe (1994) argue and show some empirical results that favor the theoretical underpinnings of salience, but they suggest that both are valuable. Contributors to Founder Identity Theory continue to make different choices, with some choosing salience and some centrality.

Single Dominant Founder

A simplification useful in the early development of Founder Identity Theory has been the empirical focus on ventures that are dominated by a single founder. The utility of this approach derives from the clarity it provides about the causal connections between a founder's identities and what happens in their venture. For example, Cardon and colleagues (2009) suggested that differences among entrepreneurs in their passion for different functional roles (inventor, founder, developer) influenced their behavior in important ways, supporting predictions of how the founding process and early days of their ventures would unfold. Fauchart and Gruber (2011) studied winter sports equipment manufacturers that were mostly dominated by single founders in building their explanation of striking differences in strategies. Powell and Baker (2014) engaged in theoretical sampling using criteria that included the dominance of a single founder to develop a theory that explained how and why the structure of founders' multiple social identities structured the roles they created in their firms and thereby their responses to adversity. Ahsan and colleagues (2018) reflect a similar focus on single dominant student entrepreneurs in their study of the effects of mentors. Despite the prevalence of ventures founded by more than one person (Klotz, Hmieleski, Bradley, & Busenitz, 2014), the focus on a single dominant founder has been the usual approach in studies tying founder identities to firm outcomes.

Indeed, the picture becomes more complicated when we look at the commonplace circumstance of founding teams. Hamilton (2006) provided insights into the gendered identity dynamics and negotiations in firms founded by spouses, one of the most common forms of a founding team (Ruef, 2010). Cardon, Post and Forster (2017) elaborate a theoretical model that seeks to explain the emergence and some important effects—including team member entry and exit—of what they label "Team Entrepreneurial Passion," tying this to elements of both individual and collective identities. This allows them to describe the interplay of "top-down" and "bottom-up" identity processes. Powell and Baker (2017) showed how groups of founders with seemingly compatible social identities defined around helping their communities engaged in processes of "pragmatic deference," dominance and contestation as they jointly developed a social identity prototype for being part of the founder in-group. These processes shaped whether ventures continued or disbanded as well as shaping individual identities among the founders. Unfortunately, while this study examined multiple identities at the level of the founding team, the complexity of the interplay of identities across individuals in the founding teams forced the authors to focus on a limited number of social and role identities for each founder. Overall, work on groups and teams remains rare.

Focus on Single Type of Identity

Most papers that have built explicitly on the social psychology of identity have engaged in theoretical simplification by examining only one *type* of identity. For example, very few papers have jointly examined role and social identities. Authors have instead focused on one or the other or something close when *no type* of identity or underlying identity theory is mentioned (Alsos, Clausen,

Hytti, & Solvoll, 2016; Barrett & Vershinina, 2017; Clarke & Holt, 2017; Giazit-zoglu & Down, 2017; Gielnik, Uy, Funken, & Bischoff, 2017; Hamilton, 2006). Fauchart and Gruber (2011), while beginning to popularize the use of Social Identity Theory in entrepreneurship research, recognized the value of integrating social and role identities and called for future research to do so. Powell and Baker (2014, 2017) found that they needed both theories to make sense of their data and thereby made progress toward integration. Zuzul and Tripsas (2020, p. 395) built cleverly on this combination in their study of four ventures in the air taxi industry to develop a "framework exploring how, in a nascent industry, a founder's identity can set off self-reinforcing cycles of firm inertia or flexibility." Unfortunately, when researchers force all identities and identity processes into one Procrustean theoretical box, they are at risk of characterizing role (social) identities inappropriately as (social) role identities and, more importantly, of losing the opportunity to further develop founder identity theory by examining the interplay between them.

Functional Roles

Cardon and colleagues (2009) built on Gartner, Starr, and Bhat's (1999) taxonomy of behaviors to theorize three distinct roles undergirding distinct identities for which entrepreneurs can demonstrate different levels of passion. Given the prevalence of notions of a singular "entrepreneurial identity" current at the time of their work, analyzing identity into three distinct role identities represented an important recognition that more than one identity was at play in shaping entrepreneurs' behavior. The three identities—inventor, founder and developer—describe important functions in the emergence of many ventures, perhaps especially those that are technologically innovative. Their approach provides an important and tractable way to anchor sources of passion in role identities. It does not imply that entrepreneurs can only be passionate about a single identity, nor does it imply that their passion could not be for an imagined outcome, with various roles and behaviors perhaps implicated as means and thereby tied to the object of passion (Baker & Powell, 2019; Cardon, Glauser, & Murnieks, 2017). This typology does not, of course, exhaust or encapsulate the myriad other salient founder role identities (e.g., Mathias & Williams, 2017, 2018; Powell & Baker, 2014; Wry & York, 2017) or directly address how entrepreneurial passion might or might not emerge from these or from social identities and their intertwining with role identities. Nonetheless, this foundational work has moved entrepreneurial passion into the mainstream of entrepreneurship scholarship, and it provides a clear foundation for additional theoretical development regarding dynamics that involve founder identity processes and not only passion but other emotional phenomena as well. For example, it seems likely that such an approach might prove useful for examining emotional exhaustion (Zagenczyk, Powell, & Scott, in press in new ventures.

Darwinians, Communitarians, and Missionaries

Brewer and Gardner (1996, p. 84) distinguished three "levels of representation of the self," which they labeled, in increasing order of inclusiveness of others: personal, relational and collective. They identify the highest level or "collective self" as corresponding "to the concept of social identity as represented in social identity theory and self-categorization theory" (Brewer & Gardner, 1996, p. 84). They derive the middle level, corresponding to the "interdependent or relational" self, defined in terms of relationships with others in specific contexts," and in which "self-worth is derived from appropriate role behavior" (Brewer & Gardner, 1996, p. 84) from Sheldon Stryker, the founder of IDT.

Fauchart and Gruber (2011) drew creatively on this framework to help make sense of and theorize their data about recreational equipment entrepreneurs, resulting in their delineation of three categories—Darwinians, Communitarians and Missionaries—distinguished in terms of three primary categorical distinctions building on those suggested by Brewer and Gardner (1996): the basis of self-evaluation, the frame of reference and basic social motivation. In our reading, Darwinian, Communitarian and Missionary are not themselves specific social identities but instead provide a way of understanding differences in how particular social identities may be constructed and for classifying them accordingly. Fauchart and Gruber's (2011) data fit well into these categories or into hybrids of these categories, allowing them to explain important strategic differences among the firms.

Powell and Baker (2017) subsequently drew directly on Fauchart and Gruber's (2011) typology to help make sense of their data about teams of founders engaged in prosocial organizing struggling to work together. Focusing on a single social identity—"community helper"—they theorized a process model of behavior in emerging founder teams, demonstrating the construction of identity prototypes, the emergence of in- and out-groups and the creation of role identities during the founding process. We expect to see substantially greater use of Social Identity Theory in the development of Founder Identity Theory, including the development of typologies and theoretical insights that incorporate additional core elements of social identity theory (Wry & York, 2017, 2019).

Congruent and Incongruent Identity Structures

Powell and Baker (2014) characterized individual founders' multiple identities in a longitudinal study of 13 textile and apparel ventures. Drawing on founders' autobiographical narratives and the intertwining of these with venture histories and current strategies, they observed that the patterning of the identities chronically salient to founders variously reflected the complexity and incomplete integration and coherence of the social worlds in which they were embedded.[5] They characterized the "structure" of identities chronically salient to founders as either singular and therefore congruent, multiple and "congruent" or multiple and "incongruent."

This characterization became the starting point for a process model and theory that explains how and why such differences in identity structures drive differences in how founders enact the adversity they face, leading to distinctive strategic responses and to the creation of role identities in their firms that express their social identities. Identity structures provide a very general way of characterizing the myriad social (and role) identities that may be salient to founders in how they go about doing their work. It is easy to imagine how the processes theorized by Powell and Baker (2014) might be applied to other contexts than the persistent adversity that characterized the textile and apparel founders they studied. It is also possible to imagine additional elements of identity structure—beyond congruence versus incongruence—as well as additional connections between role and social identities that could be explored in the continued development of Founder Identity Theory.

Future Research

This chapter is not an attempt to provide a comprehensive review of the relevant literature but is instead a loosely linked set of descriptions and assessments of the state of the literature. Many interesting papers remain unmentioned. Nonetheless, as part of the writing process, we engaged in some systematic searching and scanning. We searched 27 journals—beginning with the journal's date of first publication through "in press" status—for the phrases "entrepreneurial identity" and "founder identity" (including singular, plural and possessive forms of the phrases). Our search garnered 303 entries. We excluded book reviews, "from the editor" essays and so forth, leaving us with a list of 220 items. What we found matched our perception that work on identity in entrepreneurship has grown quickly over the past 10 years and that much of the increase has occurred during just the past five years. Of the 220 papers, only 20 papers were published in the 2000s; we found 69 papers published during the 2010–2014 time frame, and from 2015 through mid-2019, we found 131 papers. This clearly witnesses burgeoning interest in understanding the identity dynamics of entrepreneurship.

A quick coding of the papers shows that approximately 45% of the papers use qualitative methods, 30% use quantitative methods, 21% are conceptual papers and 4% use mixed methods. As a group, the papers repeatedly cite a number of well-known social psychologists—and especially people associated with IDT, social identity theory and closely related perspectives—including, for example, Burke, Hogg, Serpe, Stryker, Tajfel and J.C. Turner. We took a simple approach to identifying the subset of papers *focusing* on questions involving entrepreneurship and identity by counting the number of times either of our two key phrases were mentioned. Using a cutoff of five times or more left us with 62 papers. We quickly read through each of these papers and read a couple of dozen more carefully.

The results left us excited both by the speed at which the notion of identity as core to understanding entrepreneurship is gaining traction and by the sheer creativity of attempts to apply notions of identity to many different aspects of entrepreneurial behavior and processes. Founder identity is about who I am and who I want to be and about who *we* are and who *we* want to be (Powell & Baker, 2014, 2017); it is about passion for the role one performs and the functions one fulfills in the emergence and growth of ventures (Cardon et al., 2009); it is about wearing many hats and switching hats over time (Mathias & Williams, 2017); it is about orienting oneself not only to oneself but in various ways to others as well (Fauchart & Gruber, 2011; Powell & Baker, 2017); it's about trying to belong while also standing out in positive ways (Shepherd & Haynie, 2009); and it's about making your way in the world when your identities don't fit together any more simply and easily than does the world in which you live (Essers & Benschop, 2009; Jain et al., 2009; Powell & Baker, 2014). It's about being alone and it's about being together (Cardon, Post, & Forster, 2017; Powell & Baker, 2017; Hamilton, 2006).

Less excitingly, research about founder identity is about shallow roots. The bulk of the papers we looked at largely ignore the complex, highly accomplished and deeply relevant bodies of work on identity built up over decades by social psychologists. They either cite none of this work or do so in ways that try one's imagination in attempting to see theoretical connections. Many of the papers cite nothing beyond one or two entrepreneurship papers as their foundations in IDT or they cite nothing relevant at all. We might ask: Why does this matter? Isn't identity largely a matter of commonsense? Can't we all just intuit what it means? No, it is not, and no, we cannot.

Here's a small experiment you might try. As you go about your daily life, try attending for a day or two—or even an hour or two—to the symbols, narratives and ideologies of identities you encounter, for example, simply walking through an urban commercial district or a mall. Advertising for fashion, apparel and "health and beauty products," fairly drip with identity references and resonance. People you see on social media (as well as MBA students looking for jobs) are engaged—often with remarkable clarity about what they are doing—in attempts to construct personal brands and identities using dramaturgical approaches that would bring a twinkle to Erving Goffman's eyes. Perhaps even more than "entrepreneurship," identity is everywhere at the moment. It remains core to the narrative around many social movements and political wrangling; it is a key construct in rapidly evolving public and private dialogues on the meaning and dynamics of gender, race and sexual orientation; it is evoked in concerns about how "addiction" to "likes" on social media may be (mis)shaping users, especially young people. It is at the center of learned debates by public intellectuals about cultural crises and malaise. We suspect that these are all useful applications of the term and that in some cases, there may be core elements of what we mean by "identity" that hold across many forms of political and intellectual discourse.

Nonetheless, the possibilities for ambiguity generated by the combination of "identity" and "entrepreneurship" are mind-boggling. We had initially decided, for example, to include in this chapter a table of the definitions of "entrepreneurial identity" we found. After documenting these definitions for the first 15 papers (alphabetically) we examined, we discovered that nobody (even including in some cases authors with more than one paper) used the same or even very similar definitions. There was in most cases little acknowledgment of the prior usages or explanations for rejecting or ignoring them. The table we envisioned would have, in itself, exceeded our word limit. From our perspective, this swarm of "identity" around us has quashed the usefulness of "commonsense" depictions of identity and instead placed a premium on precision in definitions and on the deliberate use of foundational work in the social psychology of identity. In the comments that follow, we do not call out or point fingers at any researcher or papers in particular but instead describe what we see as some problematic dimensions of the ongoing development of Founder Identity Theory.

Founder Identity Theory researchers have access to an impressive body of theory-driven research on identity accumulated by social psychologists over the last 40 years. To be clear, this work is itself "multi-paradigmatic," and it hardly represents an ideal of communication and integration of theoretical insights across paradigms. Indeed, outside of recent work in entrepreneurship, research on IDT and Social Identity Theory has typically proceeded along noncommunicating parallel paths (Hogg et al., 1995; Stryker, 2008). But the richness of this foundational work provides a great opportunity for entrepreneurship scholars to understand and draw judiciously upon some very thoughtful theory-building that has come before.

From this perspective, we find the commonsense use of "identity," the willy-nilly proliferation of definitions that fail to draw in any explicit way on earlier research, the grazing among theories—picking and choosing ideas and insights built on incompatible underlying theoretical bases—and even the lack of adequate attention and citation to one another among some entrepreneurship researchers, to be troubling. There does not need to be and probably should not be convergence on a single perspective in our journals (Pan, Gruber & Binder, 2019; Wry & York, 2017, 2019). But we suggest that there does need to be ongoing conversation and acknowledgment of work that differs from our own. For one small illustration, at this point when someone doing Founder Identity Theory research says they are studying role or social identities, we think it should be considered incumbent on them to explain why what they are looking at are role identities or social identities (and not the other or both). We suggest that the development of Founder Identity Theory needs approaches that are robust enough to confront and draw insights across the burgeoning but still manageably small body of good work that, as a community, we are producing.

Along these lines, Wry and York (2017) combined role identity theory and notions of "personal identity" to explore configurations of identities supporting social entrepreneurship. In published dialogue in which they were challenged by Pan et al. (2019), they (Wry and York) explained why they did not invoke social identity theory (and, in particular, Fauchart and Gruber's approach) in their theorizing. This is very encouraging: we think that this sort of high-minded scholarly debate, rooted in joint attempts to come to grips with the underlying theories, is a very positive sign for the development of Founder Identity Theory.

Beyond these general comments, we think that researchers should and will gradually begin to both relax and elaborate some of the initial tactics and strategies that have made early research tractable. Perhaps most important, given the prevalence of multi-founder ventures, we need more research and theory that does not require the assumption—or limit its empirical focus to—new organizations with single dominant founders. What are the identity processes that take place among founders in envisioning or creating or nurturing new ventures? Indeed, we suspect that sometimes who we see as dominant founders in existing ventures is the *result* of identity dominance processes rather than the starting point (Powell & Baker, 2017). In addition, work on both dominant founders and teams needs to provide a better understanding of the meandering pathways between founder identity and organizational identity. Our understanding of the role of emotion and affect in entrepreneurship overall remains promising but underdeveloped (Shepherd, 2015). Using the foundational work done over the first few years, we suspect that researchers will not only tie passion to broader sets of identities than those that have anchored prior work but will also explore and theorize connections between identity dynamics and other emotions.

Elements of Founder Identity Theory have been usefully applied in compelling studies examining change, including identity-based effects on willingness to change ideas based on feedback (Grimes, 2018), founders' processes of psychological disengagement from their firms (Rouse, 2016) and the effects of the intertwining of founder–CEO identity and the identity of their firms on the success of CEO turnover (Boeker & Fleming, 2010). These studies cluster around the notion that aspects of founder identity can moderate the pace and outcomes of change processes and, taken as a group, sketch some contours of what is emerging as a key area of research.

Future work is likely to embrace the fact that there are multiple "types" of identities and to explore identity processes that involve role identities, social identities, "personal identities" (a whole additional can of worms across theories and definitions), "narrative identities" and others. Because knowledgeable editors and reviewers will increasingly require that such work be rooted in underlying theoretical perspectives, such combinations may actually help create an integrated and coherent body of work and increase the chances that our work will contribute back to some of the disciplinary underpinnings from which we freely borrow.

Approaches such as the typology of social identities proffered by Fauchart and Gruber (2011) are likely to be elaborated and complemented or challenged by others. The Darwinian, Communitarian and Missionary framework nicely characterizes and integrates three characteristics of social identities. Future work is likely to identify and apply other important social identity characteristics and categories (Wry & York, 2019). See Conger, McMullen, Bergman, Jr, & York.

(2018) for an important extension to "B-Corp" social entrepreneurs' reevaluation of opportunities and their firms' activities. The portrayal of identity structures as "congruent" or "incongruent" helps explain the aspirational effects of suppressed social identities and how they may be expressed as role identities (Farmer, Yao, & Kung–Mcintyre, 2011; Hoang & Gimeno, 2010) when circumstances change. But surely there are many other characteristics of identity structures (Complexity? Integration? Strain?) that will provide the basis for developing a richer theory about the interplay of role, social and other identities.

Building Founder Identity Theory presents countless research opportunities (Eisenhardt, Graebner, & Sonenshein, 2016). The opportunities—and challenges—differ based on the questions we want to ask and answer (Cardon et al., 2009; Cardon, Post & Forster, 2017; Wry & York, 2017) and by the methodological commitments we make as a community of researchers as we embrace admixtures of pictorial tools (Clarke & Holt, 2017), scale development (Alsos et al., 2016; Cardon, Gregoire, Stevens, & Patel, 2013; Sieger, Gruber, Fauchart, & Zell-weger, 2016), inductive approaches (Zuzul & Tripsas, 2020) and the experiments that are more typical of social psychology. This work holds great promise for moving entrepreneurship scholarship forward by bringing together diverse streams of work into powerful and practically useful theories. We should celebrate that an educated entrepreneurship scholar will soon no longer be able to honestly claim ignorance of Founder Identity Theory or of identity theories—as we did when we began working in this area (Powell & Baker, 2014)—or of one another's work.

Notes

1. Although the terms *entrepreneurial identity* and *founder identity* are both in common usage, throughout this chapter, we refer to "Founder Identity Theory" in order to avoid some of the confusion that has long resulted from use of the terms *entrepreneur* and *entrepreneurial* to reference everything from corporate innovation to characteristics of culture (Gartner, 1985). The focus of our attention in this chapter is on the people and processes involved in the creation and nurturing of new organizations. We believe that "Founder Identity Theory" describes this more boundedly and accurately than "Entrepreneur Identity Theory."
2. While other important theories of identity have been developed, including those taking developmental or psychoanalytic approaches, these have not been brought to bear in the development of Founder Identity Theory. Thus, we do not discuss them in this chapter.
3. This section draws heavily on Stryker and Serpe (1994).
4. It will come as no surprise to entrepreneurship scholars that the same word can be used in many different ways: both salience and centrality are used by some social psychologists to mean different things than what we describe here. The meanings we attribute to the constructs here are nonetheless quite mainstream among many identity theorists.
5. It should be noted that some uses of the related construct, "self-concept," refer to individuals' oftentimes artificially coherent and integrated imagery about who they are, thus potentially hiding the messiness, stress, strain, conflict, and incongruence that often characterize the performance demands of multiple identities in day-to-day practice.

References

Ahsan, M., Zheng, C., DeNoble, A., & Musteen, M. (2018). From student to entrepreneur: How mentorships and affect influence student venture launch. *Journal of Small Business Management*, *56*(1), 76–102.

Alsos, G. A., Clausen, T. H., Hytti, U., & Solvoll, S. (2016). Entrepreneurs' social identity and the preference of causal and effectual behaviours in start-up processes. *Entrepreneurship & Regional Development*, *28*(3–4), 234–258.

Ashforth, B. E. (2001). *Role transitions in organizational life: An identity-based perspective*. New York: Psychology Press.

Baker, T., Gedajlovic, E., & Lubatkin, M. (2005). A framework for comparing entrepreneurship processes across nations. *Journal of International Business Studies*, *36*(5), 492–504.

Baker, T., Miner, A. S., & Eesley, D. T. (2003). Improvising firms: Bricolage, account giving and improvisational competencies in the founding process. *Research Policy*, *32*(2), 255–276.

Baker, T., & Powell, E. E. (2019). Entrepreneurship as a new liberal art. *Small Business Economics*, *52*(2), 405–418.

Barrett, R., & Vershinina, N. (2017). Intersectionality of ethnic and entrepreneurial identities: A study of post-war Polish entrepreneurs in an English city. *Journal of Small Business Management*, *55*(3), 430–443.

Bartel, C. A., & Wiesenfeld, B. M. (2013). The social negotiation of group prototype ambiguity in dynamic organizational contexts. *Academy of Management Review*, *38*(4), 503–524.

Blau, P. E., & Schwartz, J. E. (1984). *Crosscutting social circles: Testing a macrostructural theory of intergroup relations*. London, UK: Academic Press.

Blumer, H. (1969). *Symbolic interactionism: Perspective and method*. Englewood Cliffs, NJ: Prentice-Hall.

Boeker, W., & Fleming, B. (2010). Parent firm effects on founder turnover: Parent success, founder legitimacy, and founder tenure. *Strategic Entrepreneurship Journal*, *4*(3), 252–267.

Brewer, M. B., & Gardner, W. (1996). Who is this "we"? Levels of collective identity and self representations. *Journal of Personality and Social Psychology*, *71*(1), 83.

Cardon, M. S., Glauser, M., & Murnieks, C. (2017). Passion for what? Expanding the domains of entrepreneurial passion. *Journal of Business Venturing Insights*, *8*, 24–32.

Cardon, M. S., Gregoire, D. A., Stevens, C. E., & Patel, P. C. (2013). Measuring entrepreneurial passion: Conceptual foundations and scale validation. *Journal of Business Venturing*, *28*(3), 373–396.

Cardon, M. S., Post, C., & Forster, W. (2017). Team entrepreneurial passion (TEP): Its emergence and influence in new venture teams. *Academy of Management Review*, *42*(2), 283–305.

Cardon, M. S., Wincent, J., Singh, J., & Drnovsek, M. (2009). The nature and experience of entrepreneurial passion. *Academy of Management Review*, *34*(3), 511–532.

Clarke, J., & Holt, R. (2017). Imagery of ad-venture: Understanding entrepreneurial identity through metaphor and drawing. *Journal of Business Venturing*, *32*(5), 476–497.

Conger, M., McMullen, J. S., Bergman Jr, B. J., & York, J. G. (2018). Category membership, identity control, and the reevaluation of prosocial opportunities. *Journal of Business Venturing*, *33*(2), 179–206.

Down, S., & Warren, L. (2008). Constructing narratives of enterprise: Clichés and entrepreneurial self-identity. *International Journal of Entrepreneurial Behavior & Research*, *14*(1), 4–23.

Eisenhardt, K. M., Graebner, M. E., & Sonenshein, S. (2016). Grand challenges and inductive methods: Rigor without rigor mortis. *Academy of Management Journal, 59*(4), 1113–1123.

Essers, C., & Benschop, Y. (2009). Muslim businesswomen doing boundary work: The negotiation of Islam, gender and ethnicity within entrepreneurial contexts. *Human Relations, 62*(3), 403–423.

Farmer, S. M., Yao, X., & Kung–Mcintyre, K. (2011). The behavioral impact of entrepreneur identity aspiration and prior entrepreneurial experience. *Entrepreneurship Theory and Practice, 35*(2), 245–273.

Fauchart, E., & Gruber, M. (2011). Darwinians, communitarians, and missionaries: The role of founder identity in entrepreneurship. *Academy of Management Journal, 54*(5), 935–957.

Gartner, W. B. (1985). A conceptual framework for describing the phenomenon of new venture creation. *Academy of Management Review, 10*(4), 696–706.

Gartner, W. B., Starr, J., & Bhat, S. (1999). Predicting new venture survival: An analysis of "anatomy of a start-up" cases from Inc. Magazine. *Journal of Business Venturing, 14*(2), 215–232.

Giazitzoglu, A., & Down, S. (2017). Performing entrepreneurial masculinity: An ethnographic account. *International Small Business Journal: Researching Entrepreneurship, 35*(1), 40–60.

Gielnik, M. M., Uy, M. A., Funken, R., & Bischoff, K. M. (2017). Boosting and sustaining passion: A long-term perspective on the effects of entrepreneurship training. *Journal of Business Venturing, 32*(3), 334–353.

Grimes, M. G. (2018). The pivot: How founders respond to feedback through idea and identity work. *Academy of Management Journal, 61*(5), 1692–1717.

Hamilton, E. (2006). Whose story is it anyway? Narrative accounts of the role of women in founding and establishing family businesses. *International Small Business Journal: Researching Entrepreneurship, 24*(3), 253–271.

Hoang, H., & Gimeno, J. (2010). Becoming a founder: How founder role identity affects entrepreneurial transitions and persistence in founding. *Journal of Business Venturing, 25*(1), 41–53.

Hogg, M. A., Terry, D. J., & White, K. M. (1995). A tale of two theories: A critical comparison of identity theory with social identity theory. *Social Psychology Quarterly, 58*, 255–269.

Jain, S., George, G., & Maltarich, M. (2009). Academics or entrepreneurs? Investigating role identity modification of university scientists involved in commercialization activity. *Research Policy, 38*(6), 922–935.

James, W. (1890). *The principles of psychology.* New York: Henry Holt & Company.

Kim, P. (2014). Action and process, vision and values: Entrepreneurship means something different to everyone. In T. Baker & F. Welter (Eds.), *The Routledge companion to entrepreneurship* (pp. 59–74). New York: Routledge.

Klotz, A. C., Hmieleski, K. M., Bradley, B. H., & Busenitz, L. W. (2014). New venture teams: A review of the literature and roadmap for future research. *Journal of Management, 40*(1), 226–255.

Mathias, B. D., & Williams, D. W. (2017). The impact of role identities on entrepreneurs' evaluation and selection of opportunities. *Journal of Management, 43*(3), 892–918.

Mathias, B. D., & Williams, D. W. (2018). Giving up the hats? Entrepreneurs' role transitions and venture growth. *Journal of Business Venturing, 33*(3), 261–277.

Murnieks, C., & Mosakowski, E. (2007). Who am I? looking inside the "entrepreneurial identity". *Frontiers of Entrepreneurship Research, 27*(5), 1–15.

Pan, N. D., Gruber, M., & Binder, J. (2019). Painting with all the colors: The value of social identity theory for understanding social entrepreneurship. *Academy of Management Review, 44*(1), 213–215.

Powell, E. E., & Baker, T. (2014). It's what you make of it: Founder identity and enacting strategic responses to adversity. *Academy of Management Journal, 57*(5), 1406–1433.

Powell, E. E., & Baker, T. (2017). In the beginning: Identity processes and organizing in multi-founder nascent ventures. *Academy of Management Journal, 60*(6), 2381–2414.

Rouse, E. D. (2016). Beginning's end: How founders psychologically disengage from their organizations. *Academy of Management Journal, 59*(5), 1605–1629.

Ruef, M. (2010). *The entrepreneurial group: Social identities, relations, and collective action*. Princeton, NJ: Princeton University Press.

Shepherd, D. A. (2015). Party on! A call for entrepreneurship research that is more interactive, activity based, cognitively hot, compassionate, and prosocial. *Journal of Business Venturing, 30*(4), 489–507.

Shepherd, D. A., & Haynie, J. M. (2009). Birds of a feather don't always flock together: Identity management in entrepreneurship. *Journal of Business Venturing, 24*(4), 316–337.

Sieger, P., Gruber, M., Fauchart, E., & Zellweger, T. (2016). Measuring the social identity of entrepreneurs: Scale development and international validation. *Journal of Business Venturing, 31*(5), 542–572.

Stryker, S. (1980). *Symbolic interactionism: A social structural version*. San Francisco, CA: Benjamin-Cummings Publishing Company.

Stryker, S. (2008). From mead to a structural symbolic interactionism and beyond. *Annual Review of Sociology, 34*, 15–31.

Stryker, S., & Burke, P. J. (2000). The past, present, and future of an identity theory. *Social Psychology Quarterly, 63*(4), 284–297.

Stryker, S., & Serpe, R. (1994). Identity salience and psychological centrality: Equivalent, overlapping or complementary concepts? *Social Psychology Quarterly, 57*(1), 16–35.

Swann, W. B. (1983). Self-verification: Bringing social reality into harmony with the self. In J. Suls & A. G. Greenwald (Eds.), *Psychological perspectives on the self* (Vol. 2, pp. 33–66). Mahwah, NJ: Lawrence Erlbaum Associates.

Tajfel, H. (1978). *Differentiation between social groups: Studies in the social psychology of intergroup relations* (Vol. 14). London, UK: Academic Press.

Tajfel, H., & Turner, J. C. (1979). An integrative theory of intergroup conflict. In W. Austin & S. Worchel (Eds.), *The social psychology of intergroup relations* (pp. 33–47). Monterey, CA: Brooks-Cole.

Turner, J. A. (1991). *The structure of sociological theory* (5th ed.). Belmont, CA: Wadsworth Publishing.

Welter, F., Baker, T., Audretsch, D., & Gartner, W. (2017, May). Everyday entrepreneurship - A call for entrepreneurship research to embrace entrepreneurial diversity. *Entrepreneurship Theory & Practice*, 311–321.

Wry, T., & York, J. G. (2017). An identity-based approach to social enterprise. *Academy of Management Review, 42*(3), 437–460.

Wry, T., & York, J. G. (2019). Blended colors or black and white? Avoiding dichotomous thinking in identity and entrepreneurship. *Academy of Management Review, 44*(1), 215–219.

Zagenczyk, T. J., Powell, E. E., & Scott, K. L. (in press). How exhausting!? Emotion crossover in organizational social networks. *Journal of Management Studies*, https://doi.org/10.1111/joms.12557.

Zuzul, T., & Tripsas, M. (2020). Start-up inertia versus flexibility: The role of founder identity in a nascent industry. *Administrative Science Quarterly*, *65*(2), 395–433.

11

AN ACTION THEORY APPROACH TO THE PSYCHOLOGY OF ENTREPRENEURIAL ACTIONS AND ENTREPRENEURIAL SUCCESS

Michael Frese

Introduction

This chapter is a completely reworked sequel to the chapter written for the last edition of this book 'Psychology of Entrepreneurship'. I introduce action theory (AT; Frese & Zapf, 1994; Frese, 2009; Zacher & Frese, 2018) by developing propositions for entrepreneurship. There are three subchapters: The first one examines the function of an active and action-oriented approach to entrepreneurship using the theory of personal initiative and its facet model. The second subchapter describes training interventions for entrepreneurship based on AT; the third subchapter discusses what AT can contribute to other behavioral approaches in the realm of entrepreneurship, focusing on McMullen and Shepherd's (2006) approach and Sarasvathy's (2001) theory of effectuation.

AT is an application-oriented meta-theory that attempts to understand, how people regulate their actions to achieve goals using both routines as well as conscious strategies. Much of AT's "charm" is based on its integrative function. I concentrate on individual actions, because individuals' or lead entrepreneurs' actions in are important, particularly at the first stages of a firm's development.

The Facet Model of Personal Initiative

The most general proposition of AT is that entrepreneurs' success depends on whether they are particularly active. Grant and Ashford (2008, p. 9) suggest that any kind of "behavior can be carried out proactively or reactively". Reactive behaviors are nudged, suggested, demanded, commanded, and forced unto the person by their environment. For proactive behavior, Personal Initiative (PI) is central here (Frese, 2009); PI is characterized by being **self-starting**, **future-oriented**, and **overcoming barriers**.

Self-starting means precisely what the word suggests—the entrepreneur starts things him- or herself rather than being triggered, suggested, or commanded from the outside. Self-starting also implies a certain degree of innovation and ambition—a self-starting entrepreneur does something new, at least new to the immediate environment—the action is likely to be started with some degree of boldness. Go-getting is part of self-starting, as well as checking up on the goal and not delegating a task away without active interest in what is happening. Entrepreneurs usually do not have supervisors or bosses (although in some cases investors may act that way). Thus, entrepreneurs are always a tad more self-starting than the general working population. However, entrepreneurs may be also less self-starting when they do things similar to other entrepreneurs or emulate others.

Future-oriented implies that future problems and opportunities are anticipated and converted into goals, cognitive models, plans, and feedback processes that are relevant now.

Overcoming barriers means to protect one's action steps against self-developed barriers (frustration, developing goals too high or too complex) as well as external barriers, like lack of resources, or other problems. Entrepreneurs usually deal with complex and relatively unpredictable environments, and thus, there will be frequent barriers that need to be overcome.

Frese and Fay (2001) described three factors of personal initiative—self-starting, future-oriented, and persistent as a 'syndrome' because there is overlap between them and the factors reinforce each other—future orientation helps to develop self-starting ideas, being self-starting increases persistence, and so on. High persistence may help to be creative and self-starting. In spite of this overlap, the different parts of the PI construct can be discussed separately.

Table 11.1 describes the full facets model which includes the three factors of personal initiative and the action steps (goal setting, information collection, planning, monitoring, and feedback); the action steps are described within AT and each of them can be done actively or not actively (they are defined later). Finally, the table also differentiates the three foci of actions–Task, Self and Others: **Tasks** need to be done as part of one's work or one's role, **Self** relates to one's identity (Chapter 10; sense of consistency and worth that are defended), but the Self can also become tasks in its own right, e.g., developing one's self-discipline); **Others** refer to customers, partners, and patients (again, they may also become tasks, e.g., teaching Others). Not all the facets of this table are equally well studied, indicating gaps for future research.

Active Goals

'Active goals'—the first entry in Table 11.1—sounds like a pleonasm. Are there ever non-active goals? After all, the function of goals is to get people to act. On the other hand, we can differentiate degrees of goals' activeness. Outside tasks need to be interpreted by the acting person; once they are interpreted and infused with specific meaning, they become goals. Depending on the interpretation goals may

TABLE 11.1 Personal Initiative Facets and Action Sequence

Active Goals

Personal initiative element	Task	Self	Others
Self-starting	• Set active goals • High goals • Think of unique selling points • High commitment • Add something interesting and new to the things that you do!	• Develop yourself • Development of expertise • Accentuate your differences to others	• Involve others in innovating ideas • Actively develop networks • Develop goals for others • Push collective actions where individuals cannot succeed
Future-oriented	• Identify future problems and opportunities • Translate them into goals	• Think of what you/your company needs in 2 years! Develop yourself for future	• Develop networks for future opportunities • Develop networks for potential problem solutions
Overcoming barriers	• Protect goals when barriers occur • In case of doubt, keeping the goal more important than plan	• Self-regulation when frustrated • Use problem- instead of emotion-focused coping	• Don't give up innovation if others do not like the idea, try to improve idea or convince others

Active Information Search and Active Mapping

Personal initiative element	Task	Self	Others
Self-starting	• Search actively for information	• Look for several sources of information; go for rare and hard to find information	• Get to know customers and employees actively
Future-oriented	• Collect information on potential future opportunities and problems • Speculate about future technological breakthroughs and prepare actions • Talk to unusual sources of information	• What could be possible threats and opportunities for me/my company in 6 months/2 years?	• Get information on future social trends relevant to your firm

	Task	Self	Others
Overcoming barriers	• Maintain information search even if finding information is difficult	• Push yourself to continue to get information • Get negative information on your ideas even if disagreeable	• Think of other companies that have done what you want to do but improve on them; do not just emulate

Active Plan and execution

Personal initiative element	Task	Self	Others
Self-starting	• Make small plans on conditions and how-to-do and timing • Build flexibility into plan • Develop a doable plan and start soon	• Plan to train yourself to improve	• Make detailed plans on how to introduce innovations • Think about personnel issues • Design and implement plans?
Future-oriented	• Develop backup plans • Develop plans how to seize potential opportunities • Make at least one plan B per barrier on how to overcome barrier and turn it into an opportunity!	• Develop a personal self-development plan	• Develop a plan B in case the first plan for others does not work out or is rejected
Overcoming barriers	• Go back to plan execution as quickly as possible in case of difficulties	• Don't let negative emotions like frustration stop you from following your plan • Ask: What are potential barriers that relate to you that call your skills or strategies into question	• Involve others to become more persistent—e.g., people might encourage you or remind you of your intentions

(Continued)

TABLE 11.1 (Continued)

Active Monitoring and feedback

Personal initiative element	Task	Self	Others
Self-starting	• Search for feedback without waiting for others to provide it • Think of unusual areas in which you can get feedback	• Do not let negative self-thoughts disturb you when you are confronted with your own errors/failures • Search for negative feedback	• Ask colleagues and competitors as well as customers for their feedback, implement feedback sessions on a regular basis, also approach people outside of the company in order to get their unaffected feedback • Approach people in your environment and let them give you their positive and negative feedback
Future-oriented	• Use feedback to detect future problems and opportunities	• Ask: Does my behavior lead to future work success? What exactly should you change?	• Use feedback from others, ask for possible future threats and opportunities
Overcoming barriers	• Continue with feedback search in case of obstacles • Look for at least one alternative to every feedback source that you use!	• Persistently ask for negative feedback • Use small experiments to see which errors you can catch (fast failure forward)	• Keep asking for feedback even if people refuse • Find more suitable time for a feedback • Get Others to compensate for personal weaknesses

Source: Based on Frese & Fay (2001) and Mensmann & Frese (2017) be highly ambitious and high-commitment goals. High ambitiousness implies a stronger 'activeness' (Earley, Wojnaroski, & Prest, 1987). Ambitious and specific goals produce actions that use more sophisticated plans, and feedback is taken more seriously (cf. goal-setting theory Locke & Latham, 2013; Baum, Locke, & Smith, 2001). Higher goal commitment (high activeness) leads to higher goal strivings (Locke & Latham, 2013).

One way to differentiate whether a goal is active or passive is whether the goal comes mainly from the outside or is mainly self-set—this is a difficult area because once a goal is accepted (interpreted), it does not matter much whether it originated from the environment or was self-developed (Latham, Erez, & Locke, 1988). Indeed, it is one of the hallmarks of humans, as social animals, that they take over team tasks easily. My argument here is different than simply differentiating self- versus other-set goals: Entrepreneurial goals should not be derived from mimicking others. Mimicking others implies that goals are taken over ("Let me offer the same product as my competitor").

However, even goals that are taken over from others may be described on the dimension active-reactive. For example, originally, the entrepreneurship literature suggested that there is a "first mover advantage" (Lieberman & Montgomery, 1998) which could be taken to be a self-starting approach and, therefore, successful. However, a meta-analysis found no systematic first-mover advantage (VanderWerf & Mahon, 1997). Instead, examples of second movers being successful exist: for example, Apple's use of metaphorical software design of the original word-processing programs from Xerox Park and the iPhone (taken from Nokia). Some companies rely on a business model to emulate others (e.g., Rocket Internet; https://en.wikipedia.org/wiki/Rocket_Internet). At first sight, such examples would suggest mimicking others to be successful. However, these examples are not based on complete mimicry. Rather the second movers learned from first movers and actively differentiated their products, for example, Apple's iPhone's easy usability differentiated it from Nokia's smartphone. Thus, self-starting does not mean to be the very first—what is proposed here is that entrepreneurs should learn from others but still differentiate their business from others (e.g., which niche to occupy, which marketing instruments chosen, prize and quality differences, or some interesting quirky add-on). In this sense, even Rocket International was self-starting because this company often creatively adapted big business ideas (from the US) to small markets.

Thus, self-started goals imply some innovation. Innovation is useful for the profitability of firms in most markets and nations (Rauch et al., 2013); however, it is particularly useful in dynamic markets (e.g., Asia) and for very small and very large companies (Rauch, Wiklund, Lumpkin, & Frese, 2009; Rosenbusch, Brinckmann, & Bausch, 2011).

Future-oriented thinking about opportunities and problems allows entrepreneurs to proactively prepare for opportunities; this will lead to better use of opportunities appearing in the future (Dimov, 2007).

Overcoming barriers and persistence implies that goals are protected. When entrepreneurs change goals too often, they do not develop expertise in an area. Protection of goals against competing goals or against giving up because of frustration is of primary importance. Overcoming barriers implies not to give up and to develop ideas for how to overcome them; overcoming is significantly related to entrepreneurial success (Glaub, Frese, Fischer, & Hoppe, 2014).

Up to this point, we assumed that goals were oriented towards tasks; however, goals can also be related to the **Self** and to Others. **Self**-related goals may be self-discipline, knowing one's Self, or managing one's personality. Also, entrepreneurs should not concentrate on their emotional state but rather on the problems at hand (Kluger & DeNisi, 1996). There is surprisingly little literature in entrepreneurship to these self-related issues. Mueller, Wolfe, and Syed (2017) suggested the concept of grit to be interesting for understanding persistence and self-regulation in difficult situations. At this moment in the development of the concept, grit may not yet be usable to advance the concept of self-discipline because of the large overlap of 'grit' with the personality variable conscientiousness (Crede, Tynan, & Harms, 2017); further development needs to differentiate grit from conscientiousness.

Developing self-starting, future-oriented, and persistence goals (as well as plans) with regard to **Others** have not been studied much although there is a large literature on correlations between better and larger social networks and entrepreneurial success (Hoang & Antoncic, 2003). Unfortunately, networks are often treated as 'givens' in entrepreneurship research rather than acquired. There is, however, one study on an active PI approach towards social networks; the active approach was related positively to entrepreneurial performance in China (Zhao, Frese, & Giardini, 2010).

Active Information Search and Active Mapping of the Environment (Table 11.1)

Information is usually stored in mental models; however, not every mental model is action-oriented (Gentner & Stevens, 1983). Abstract and general mental models may be unrelated to one's actions. AT assumes that only action-oriented knowledge is useful for entrepreneurs and that the best way to get to know the environment is through active information search and mapping. A good so-called operative (active) mental model is often the result of experimentation and feedback the actors receive getting to know their environment through acting on it.

Memory processes are limited so mapping ought to be parsimonious. Therefore, people sometimes jump to actions prematurely without knowing and analyzing the environment in detail; People use heuristics as shortcuts to being action-oriented (a 'heuristic' a shortcut to the knowledge–action nexus, Miller, Galanter, & Pribram, 1960). However, as environments are often dynamic and their factors interrelated, better mental models may be needed to predict future developments (Dörner, 1996). A strong self-starting approach to get to know the environment is a hallmark of expertise which is related to entrepreneurial success in dynamic environments (Keith, Unger, Rauch, & Frese, 2016).

Note that the preceding points do not just imply developing knowledge on the environment. AT argues for being active vis-à-vis the environment, for entrepreneurs to receive feedback and interacting with the environment to develop good action-oriented mental models. Thus, issues of feedback seeking and developing an active information search are heavily intertwined. One problem is that feedback is often delayed in entrepreneurship or difficult to interpret (e.g., an innovative product may take years until one receives market feedback). Therefore, AT suggests experimentation to receive feedback on the adequacy of an idea (this implies rapid prototyping and frequent potential customer feedback—a feature of 'design thinking' or 'lean entrepreneurship').

Self-starting implies the use of proactive search strategies to get useful information on future developments. Usually there is a knowledge corridor that constrains the innovativeness of entrepreneurs (Shane, 2000); Overcoming these constraints is useful. Indeed, more unusual forms of information lead to more innovative and successful opportunities (Gielnik, Frese, Graf, & Kampschulte, 2012; Gielnik, Krämer, Kappel, & Frese, 2014).

Active information search is useful as long as the information is relevant for the enterprise. Expert entrepreneurs often search for different information than nonexperts; experts are interested in financial indicators for a business idea when searching for opportunities (Baron & Ensley, 2006). Experts usually have a better inventory of signals to understand the environment, and they have a history of actively developing such signals (Hacker, 1992). Complex signals are kept in memory through chunking (Chase & Simon, 1973), allowing expert entrepreneurs to understand complex situations readily.

The **Self** is implicated in the knowledge development of one's personality, role identity, and so on. Surprisingly, the function of **Others** for active information search has not been studied, although team-based entrepreneurial ventures are more successful than single entrepreneur ventures (cf. Chapter 6). In teams, each member can actively involve Others in information search and there is more give and take (feedback) between them to proactively understand their environment. Asking more questions has been shown to be useful in several domains (Morrison, 1993), maybe because the environment is evaluated more realistically. Moreover, the more entrepreneurs take the perspective of Others (potential customers), the better are their business ideas (Prandelli, Pasquini, & Verona, 2016).

Active Plans (Table 11.1)

Without plans, a goal cannot spur an individual into action. A meta-analysis on planning shows the importance of plans for entrepreneurs (Brinckmann, Grichnik, & Kapsa, 2010). Intentions to start a firm do not necessarily predict actions;

however, once intentions are complemented with plans they are powerful predictors of active start-ups (Gielnik et al., 2014; Gielnik, Frese, Kahara-Kawuki et al., 2015). Plans are the 'bridge between thoughts and actions' as they transfer a goal into an executable sequence of operations. Small plans define under which conditions and how intentions can be put into effect, and they make it possible to implement intentions (Gollwitzer, 1999). Plans do not have to be formalized plans like business plans or strategic plans. Rather, plans using AT provide an order for operations (Miller et al., 1960) for the next few seconds, minutes, months, or years. Sometimes plans are developed while acting, for example, improvisation—an important skill in entrepreneurship (Baker & Nelson, 2005). From an AT perspective, plans are mental simulations of actions (*Probehandlung*) and thus 'actions in mind'. Plans can be elaborated and conscious approaches or they can be automatized schemata or frames (e.g., talking to a customer; cf. Miller et al., 1960).

Three characteristics make plans active and self-starting: First, plans need to be doable without long delay. Second, they need to be detailed and future-oriented enough to act even in complex and unpredictable situations. Third, they need to be flexible.

Ad (1) Plans should be 'doable' and to be executed once opportunity arises.[1] Fortunately, plans help in the translation of an intention into action (Gollwitzer, 1999). Once a small plan on the 'how' and 'when' is formed, it will be put into effect. The 'how' implies that actors know which steps to take; the 'when' means that actors think of situations and times that afford actions. A plan converts a 'goal intention' into an 'implementation intention' (Gollwitzer, 1999). Implementation intentions have an automatic cognitive function to propel people into actions (Brandstaetter, Lengfelder, & Gollwitzer, 2001). For entrepreneurs, this means that entrepreneurs should plan for opportunities that may arise when meeting potential customers or in friendship circles—of course, each time the pitch needs to be adequate to the situation. If a plan requires resources, the immediacy of a realistic action plan implies that entrepreneurs should start acquiring resources in due time.

Ad (2) Plans must be elaborated and future-oriented. It does not make much of a difference whether the plan is sketchy (critical point plan) or highly elaborated (complete plan)—as long as entrepreneurs repeatedly use small plans they are likely successful; the opposite—no plan and being reactive—shows negative effects (Frese et al., 2007; van Gelderen, Frese, & Thurik, 2000; van Gelderen, Kautonen, Wincent, & Biniari, 2017). It may be possible that people plan too far into the future, but this is not a typical mistake entrepreneurs make.

Ad (3) Plans must be flexible in the face of surprising events. This implies that entrepreneurs should always have a plan B. Goals should be kept intact rather than sticking to a plan. Plans may change and they often do—there is a certain degree of experimentation necessary to check whether plans work and a certain degree of improvisation when plans are not effective or when resource constraints are high (Baker & Nelson, 2005).

Planning also helps the management of the **Self**, particularly reducing erratic actions and increasing persistence (Diefendorff & Lord, 2004). On the other hand, plans that focus only on the Self and not on the tasks may lead to self-doubts and procrastination (Van Eerde, 2015; Wieber & Gollwitzer, 2010).

Active planning can also relate to **Others**. Others may be involved in active planning or they may be on the receiving end of entrepreneurs' active plans; planning is an important skill of leadership (Mumford, Giorgini, & Steele, 2015). The more entrepreneurs have to deal with employees, the more important planning for and with others becomes. Strategic planning may lead to positive effects because it enhances transparency, co-planning, and commitment by employees. Meta-analytic evidence on strategic planning underlines its relationships with firm performance (Cardinal, Miller, Kreutzer, & TenBrink, 2015).

Active Feedback Development and Processing (Table 11.1)

Without feedback, one does not know where one stands with regard to a goal (Locke & Latham, 2013; Miller et al., 1960). Small firms can process and react to feedback faster than larger firms because they tend to lack hierarchy and formal procedures. However, entrepreneurs need to recognize feedback, to interpret it, and to respond adequately. AT maintains that the most useful feedback is negative feedback, because it provides more learning opportunities (Zacher & Frese, 2018). Positive feedback—a goal has been achieved—may be a motivator to repeat the successful action, but little new learning occurs. In contrast, negative feedback can lead to learning (although this is not always the case; Funken, Gielnik, & Foo, 2020). Negative events stay in memory better, negative emotions are stronger than positive emotions, and negative feedback is processed more deeply than positive feedback (Baumeister, Bratslavsky, Finkenauer, & Vohs, 2001).

Entrepreneurs often do not actively search for negative feedback because they protect their **Self**. Negative feedback tends to generalize and, thus, one's Self and identity may be called into question (negative feedback may lead to the impression to be 'not good at anything' by reducing self-efficacy). Once the focus is on the Self, little learning for task performance takes place (Kluger & DeNisi, 1996).

On the other hand, negative feedback may spur people to work on their self-discipline; one research tradition likens this to practicing a muscle, making sure one is able to deal with ego depletion in the future (Baumeister, Bratslavsky, Muraven, & Tice, 1998). Empirically, self-management has positive effects in employees (Frayne & Latham, 1987) and in entrepreneurship (Neck, Houghton, Sardeshmukh, Goldsby, & Godwin, 2013).

Active Feedback and Error Management

A specific form of negative feedback is action errors and mistakes and a specific form of active feedback-seeking is error management. Errors are usually deviations from goal-directed behaviors that have an element of uncontrolla-bility in them—errors often occur because of unanticipated events or working memory overload (Frese & Keith, 2015). One usually gets to know the error after doing something wrong or omitting to do something. Entrepreneurs act in dynamic environments characterized by other actors (maybe aggressive com-petitors) and they can never prepare for all surprises. They also work on complex tasks with little preparation times. Thus, errors occur frequently and are inherent in actions. Therefore, AT researches how people learn after errors occur (Frese & Keith, 2015). This led to the concept of error management (Frese, 1991) that helps reduce negative error consequences and enhance positive error consequences, such as learning from errors, developing innovations, and improving strategies to deal with errors (Frese & Keith, 2015).

Error management training encourages people to learn from errors (Keith & Frese, 2008). The most important negative effect of errors is related to think-ing about the Self and developing a negative internal dialogue (van der Linden, Sonnentag, Frese, & van Dyck, 2001). Therefore, error management training reduces negative emotions by providing heuristics (error management instruc-tions) of accepting errors. Reducing negative emotions permits individuals to concentrate on the task and to develop a meta-cognitive, reflective approach to understand error occurrence; metacognition and a cool unemotional accept-ance of errors are developed in error management training and lead to higher performance (Keith & Frese, 2005; van der Linden et al., 2001). Experiments show high learning from errors when receiving feedback and accepting errors (Keith & Frese, 2008).

Recently, entrepreneurship research started to be interested in errors, mistakes, action problems, and failures and their consequences leading to an interesting convergence with AT: AT's view of errors is based on learning theories (negative outcomes motivate search processes) and on cognitive theories of errors and cop-ing (working memory resources are clogged up when in addition to a negative event—error or failure—there is also self-blame, a high degree of negative emo-tionality, and little systematic thoughtful analysis). Expressed positively, learning and thoughtful analysis require a person to be motivated (the negative feedback is motivating), to have enough spare capacity of working memory (little self-blame and negative emotions), and to allow meta-cognizing or systematically thinking about (and potentially experimenting on errors to learn; more details, cf. Frese & Keith, 2015). Since AT studied hypotheses in with experiments, causal mecha-nisms could be studied.

Studies on entrepreneurial failures tend to be correlational and often based on self-reported data, but they provide rich results leading to similar conclusions as AT: First, entrepreneurial failure triggers thoughts on potential causes that are often associated with blaming—either the self, others, or the circumstances (Car-don, Stevens, & Potter, 2011). Failure contributes to learning instead of blaming, when entrepreneurs are able to downregulate their negative emotions (Fang He,

Siren, Singh, Solomon, & von Krogh, 2018). Shepherd, Patzelt, and Wolfe (2011) showed that organizational error management culture (called 'perceived normalization' by them) and reducing negative emotions (called 'oscillation after failure') helped learning from failure (Shepherd et al., 2011). Furthermore, it is necessary to reflect or systematically think about the failure, called 'usage of structural alignment processes' by Mueller & Shepherd (2016); this is similar to metacognition in error management research. A direct application of AT to entrepreneurship showed 'error mastery' to moderate the effects of problems appearing as part of the entrepreneurship journey on entrepreneurial learning, leading, in turn, to venture progress over time (Funken et al., 2020). Entrepreneurs also do better when actively searching for negative feedback (Ashford & Stobbelleirm, 2013; Ashford & Tsui, 1991; Peters, 1987), doing experiments, and using errors to improve their business (cf. 'fast failure forward').

Small and mid-sized companies that developed active feedback systems of error management increase their profits in Germany, in the Netherlands, and in China (van Dyck, Frese, Baer, & Sonnentag, 2005). The so-called error management training can be integrated into training for entrepreneurs. The major advantage of this training is that it reduces negative emotionality and enhances meta-cognitive and reflective thinking; we, therefore, integrated error management into trainings for entrepreneurship (Frese, Gielnik, & Mensmann, 2016).

Hierarchical Regulation of Actions

Up to this point, I explained Table 11.1, using the action sequences and PI. In addition, actions are structured hierarchically: The higher levels of the hierarchy of action regulation are conscious thoughts; the lower levels consist of routines; they are specific, and they frequently involve muscle movements. This hierarchy is not neatly organized; sometimes a routine takes over and leads to errors (someone may want to buy bread on the way home, but the routine of the direct way home takes over and the person finds him- or herself at home without bread). Therefore, it is a *weak hierarchy*.

In the following, I discuss why the notion of hierarchy is needed to understand entrepreneurial behaviors. First, a concept of hierarchy is needed to understand how actions are regulated.[2] If actions were not regulated hierarchically, people would learn a specific behavior for every specific situation and repeat this behavior over and over again (as Skinner's, 1953, theory would have it). In contrast, AT argues that upper levels give general commands (e.g., convince customers to buy a product), and the lower levels of regulation then adjust the specific actions to changing circumstances (e.g., uttering a sentence, typing a word, using the appropriate muscles to strike a key, or repeating the pitch), as long as the changes are not drastic (Miller et al., 1960).

Second, commands from upper levels do not necessarily control lower levels; the 'command' structure from upper to lower regulation levels needs to be entrained and practiced. It is not enough to just have a general goal (e.g., start a company) because the general command can 'hit a void'. Therefore, it is not enough to have good intentions—how to put them into effect needs to be learned. The necessary actions do not appear automatically, at least not in the beginning of the learning journey. The lower levels need to be rehearsed; the relationship between the upper and lower levels has to be practiced, as well (e.g., how to formulate a business plan that convinces the bank to give a loan). But once routines are available on the lower level a simply command from the upper level may lead to actions. This differentiates experts from nonexperts in entrepreneurship—as Baron and Ensley (2006) pointed out experts search for different information in comparison to nonexperts, once they get the general command—'opportunity', they immediately think of different (and effective) action ideas.

Third, experts do not just connect upper levels better to lower levels of regulation; they also have more routines available (Hacker, 1992). Why is this advantageous? The answer relates again to the hierarchical levels. Entrepreneurs are often confronted with new situations (uncertain environment) and with new tasks ('jack-of-all-trades'); whenever something is new, it has to be regulated on the upper level of regulation, for example, developing a finance plan for a new product. The upper levels are slow and effortful with little time-sharing between action preparation. Thus, whenever entrepreneurs are engaged in complex tasks, the more quickly they hit their limits of central processing capacity (Kanfer & Ackerman, 1989). Routines (or intuitive processing) are preferred whenever possible because lower levels of processing are fast and processing capacity is nearly limitless (Kahneman, 1973). But routines only come through experience (enhanced via training and coaching; Ericsson & Lehman, 1996). Therefore, expert entrepreneurs tend to rely on routines (Busenitz & Barney, 1997)—thus, entrepreneurs and business investors argue frequently that they decide things 'intuitively' (Huang & Pearce, 2015). 'Intuition' is often a shorthand for lower level regulation (including cognitive routines). Intuition may be efficient under these conditions: (a) The entrepreneur has been in those situations before and developed an effective routine. (b) The deep-level characteristics of the situation now are the same as back when the intuition was acquired; the problem is that surface characteristics may look the same but deep-level characteristics are different; then wrong decisions appear (Adelson, 1984). (c) Entrepreneurs must know the right signals for triggering the right actions. (d) The entrepreneur must be skilled at using feedback on the lower level of regulation (which implies prior exposure and practice with feedback). It follows that whenever a situation is new and requires new thought, intuition is probably bad advice (Kahneman & Klein, 2009).

Fourth, processing on the lower level of regulation is parallel, rapid, and effortless, and this level uses little cognitive resources. Therefore, entrepreneurs who have to deal with uncertainty and with a high degree of tasks prefer routines. The concept of hierarchy could possibly explain why entrepreneurs may give up lofty values of helping society and instead concentrate on 'making the quick buck'. Construal level theory argues that things that are (psychologically) distant in terms of time and space are abstract and regulated on upper levels, while actions of immediate importance are regulated on lower levels and are concrete (Trope & Liberman, 2010). Long-term goals are not (yet) relevant for most actions. In order not to overload central processing capacity, entrepreneurs need to attend the pressing issues first. Once concrete tasks dominate working life, entrepreneurs do not typically think about their life goals or moral issues in everyday activities but on how to get the 'bills paid'. The proposition follows that entrepreneurs change their focus with time and become more hands-on and less idealistic over time.

Fifth, the concept of hierarchy is particularly important for understanding learning processes and entrepreneurship training. All too often learning processes are stuck on the upper level of regulation of knowledge acquisition but are not tied to the routine level that may be important for action effectiveness. But before talking about training interventions, I discuss limits to good performance suggested by AT.

Limits to Good Performance: Mental Resource Constraints, Cognitive Misers, Satisficing Strategy, and Action Styles

Performance is often suboptimal and learning often slow. The most important factors that reduce action optimality relate to resource constraints in attention and memory and on preferences for routines. Thus, concepts like "bounded rationality" (March & Simon, 1958) and "biases" (Kahneman, 2003) have flourished.

One could expect from an AT point of view that learning from feedback leads to efficient and effective approaches. This is not necessarily so. AT suggests five processes responsible for continuous suboptimal performance, all following from resource constraints in central processing capacity: First, people are cognitive misers (Taylor, 1981). They normally prefer the use of lower levels of regulation rather than putting conscious effort into goal analysis, reorienting oneself, developing well thought out plans, or developing new feedback signals (Dörner, 1996). Second, cognitive effort is avoided as long as satisficing routines function half halfway well. This may lead to low levels of aspiration and people preferring satisficing and not necessarily optimizing action strategies (March & Simon, 1958). Thus, the 'next best' solution is preferred instead of an unknown optimal solution. Therefore, entrepreneurs often do not aim 'high' and rather prefer low growth goals (Shane, 2009). Third, suboptimal, satisficing performance may be kept up as a result of action styles. For example, some entrepreneurs may tend towards precise and long-term planning even if that is not necessary. Others may tend to do the opposite even for actions that would certainly profit from a high degree of planfulness (cf. van Gelderen, chapter 12). Since action styles are automatic and general (i.e., they apply to many action areas), we do not consciously think about them (Frese, Stewart, & Hannover, 1987). In the case that we get specific feedback, learning may also be highly specific. Therefore, the person considers only this particular case: 'I will act differently next time in this situation'. In another situation, the entrepreneur may still use the same automatic action styles that got him or her into trouble in the first place. The problem of action styles is aggravated when entrepreneurs have many different tasks to do—again, routine approaches are preferred because of little spare central processing capacity. Fourth, environmental pressures often suggest urgent responses. Here and in danger situations, people prefer their routines (Reason, 1990) even when they are dysfunctional. Fifth, heuristic processing produces fast results that are often right; only in rare circumstances does heuristic processing lead to consistent negative effects; therefore, it makes sense for entrepreneurs to go with their first intuition, at least if they are experienced.

Learning and Interventions From an AT Perspective

Learning takes place on all levels of regulation albeit in different ways. Learning on the lower levels implies that one's skills are adjusted to the particulars of a situation and to improve the coordination of muscles and skills—skill execution becomes smoother, and the skills are better coordinated. Some motor and cognitive skills (e.g., prototyping) are learned on lower levels (Myers & Davids, 1993). In contrast, learning on the conscious level can be transferred to other situations more easily because it is based on developing insights and problem-solving.

The relationship between upper and lower levels of regulation changes with learning. When starting to learn something new, the action is regulated on high (conscious) levels. Over time, regulation of action moves downward so that conscious attention is no longer needed (Kanfer & Ackerman, 1989). An important corollary is that new insights do not usually have regulatory influence over actions. Thus, new insights from training need to be entrained. This is particularly important for entrepreneurship because smooth actions are so important. Therefore, training should be action-oriented right from the start. An example is financial training (Drexler, Fischer, & Schoar, 2014). Most people know that learning to do bookkeeping does not automatically lead to being able to do it well some transfer to lower levels of regulation needs to be done. Bookkeeping knowledge may not have regulatory power, unless entrepreneurs have learned how to use it in practical situations. Therefore, training and teaching have to involve all levels of regulation.

Theoretical Propositions on How to Do AT for PI Training

Trainers should teach an understanding of how all action steps—goals, getting to know the environment, plans, and feedback—can be related to PI with its facets of self-starting, future orientation, and overcoming barriers (PI training is based on a matrix similar to Table 11.1).

These are the requirements of an AT-based training (Mensmann & Frese, 2017; Wolf et al., 2020): First, teaching needs to be related to actions. One way to do that is to teach via action principles (rules of thumb that overcome the knowledge–doing gap by providing teachable, understandable action related ideas that can be adjusted to circumstances). Action principles can be developed on the basis of scientific evidence (Glaub et al., 2014; Locke, 2004). We also suggest providing small case studies of effective and ineffective entrepreneurial actions to elucidate action principles within their respective environment (Frese et al., 2016). Although action principles are action-oriented, in the beginning they still need to be processed on a conscious level of regulation—thus, training needs to tie them to concrete actions. The more entrepreneurs practice these action principles for their business and the more these principles are entrained and internalized, the more entrepreneurs develop a deep action-oriented understanding of entrepreneurship. Entrepreneurs are encouraged to use trained actions between training sessions and report on positive and negative experiences. Group discussions may help here to correct practices and to sharpen understanding of what these principles mean in action.

Another issue involves verbalization: Verbalized instructions for actions have to acquire regulatory power over actions. Learners are instructed to develop shortened verbal instructions to acquire signaling functions for actions (called internationalization; Galperin, 1969): For example, one action principle of PI is 'to be self-starting'; at first, better verbal understanding of the actions involved will be developed. Internationalization happens when entrepreneurs use abbreviated instructions like 'think yourself'; later, the instructions can be further abbreviated and internalized to the signal 'yourself' (Meichenbaum & Deffenbacher, 1988).

In adult training, people enter the training with some 'baggage' of action routines—some of them effective and some ineffective. New action principles may contradict the use of old routines. The trainer will need to convince participants of the long-term effectiveness of the new action principles. However, these new principles may not run smoothly and not easily activated, as long as these new actions have not been rehearsed often enough. Thus, old routines will prevail as long as the new action principles are not routinized at least to some extent; alternatively, clear stop rules for old routines can be rehearsed (again internationalization is important).

Group discussions help with internationalization. Also, the more trainers are able to 'observe' entrepreneurs in action, the better they can discuss (dys)functionality of actions. Re-intellectualization—becoming conscious about how routines are used—is helped by group discussions; moreover, groups may enhance the motivation to change.[3] Errors are also useful for noticing the dysfunctionalities of routines and errors help to make routines conscious. Therefore, trainers should pay attention to errors and use them as learning instruments; we also emphasize the idea of 'fast failure forward' (making errors quickly to see which actions work well and which ones do not). One prerequisite for fast failures is to be open for experimentation and accept action errors as a necessary learning device.

Any training is time-bound; therefore, the transfer of training content to practice is important. Which principles help transfer? Internalization, thinking of different situations in which one can apply these principles, being able to think of principles both consciously and routinizing them, using feedback from others, giving self-feedback, and developing self-correction. Others may help the entrepreneur to stay on track, and therefore, trainers should pair up participants into practice pairs (Frese et al., 2016) who help each other after the training.

Trainers' skills are important (Wolf et al., 2020): Trainers can help getting abstract thoughts connected to concrete actions, providing useful examples, or emphasizing which actions conform to PI principles. Trainers also need to keep participants focused on important action principles, making sure that the action implications are understood and using examples from participants' daily activities as learnings for all. Also, making productive use of errors and encouraging all participants to provide feedback to each other (giving feedback helps internalizing the action principles). Trainers need to articulate learning intentions so as to reinforce action principles; they should also provide examples, make connections between the action principles and PI, encourage participants to practice and actively involve them in giving feedback, use questions, prompts and feedback, plus teaching self-feedback, be positive about errors, celebrate positive actions and deal with misunderstandings.

In one large-scale study, we did a randomized controlled experiment with 1,500 African entrepreneurs using such a training concept to teach PI. Profitability two years after the training increased by approximately 30% for participants in the PI training in comparison to a control group. PI training participants also innovated more, showed more PI behavior, and were more strongly committed to their firms (investing more time and capital). This study also compared PI training with a traditional business training; the latter did not display significant effects (Campos et al., 2017). PI training was successful in other countries as well (Frese et al., 2016); positive effects occurred if trainers had deep knowledge of entrepreneurship (Wolf et al., 2020).

Contributions of AT to Other Behavioral Theories in Entrepreneurship

AT for entrepreneurship provides several advantages: First, its theory of PI offers a useful parsimonious psychological model of entrepreneurship by explicating an active approach to actions. Second, AT can potentially integrate other entrepreneurial behavioral theories. Third, the theory is based on empirical cognitive psychology, as well as on psychological knowledge of motivational and emotional processes. Fourth, by using sophisticated randomized controlled long-term field experimental studies, AT-based PI has been shown to be useful for entrepreneurs.

In the following, I discuss two highly influential theories suggesting ways of how AT can be useful for these theories and vice versa–McMullen and Shepherd's (2006) AT and Sarasvathy's (2001) effectuation theory. Given space constraints, I do not repeat the theories in detail but restrict my comments to potential mutual contributions.

AT by McMullen and Shepherd

McMullen and Shepherd (2006) start out with uncertainty as a crucial environmental characteristic for entrepreneurs; they also argue that in contrast to pure decision-making theories, entrepreneurship is much more about the 'decision to act'—a proposition it shares with AT. According to McMullen and Shepherd, opportunity detection and exploitation are the results of knowledge and motivation. AT's usefulness for this theory is related to active forms of behaviors. For example, AT argues that 'knowledge' is important but it needs to be action-connected—often knowledge is not connected to action. The trick is to make mental models operative and, thus, action-connected. Also, AT suggests that one of the best ways to get to know viable opportunities is to explore actively, to try things out, to fail, to get feedback. Knowledge may help in all of these processes, but more important, one needs to act and get feedback to sharpen these processes.

AT could potentially help to make McMullen and Shepherd's theoretical concepts more dynamic. For example, a given level of uncertainty can be changed as a result of actions because action feedback may decrease uncertainty over time, actively establishing a market niche also reduces uncertainty. Knowledge is dynamic and often a result of actions, not just a prerequisite of actions. Planning is not just the application of knowledge, but it also includes delegation of regulation to lower level routines. Planning also implies simulation of actions and thus sharpens knowledge of opportunities. AT suggests planning to have a dynamic relationship with uncertainty because, first, planning helps to act (implementation intention) and, second, since it simulates action, planning can sharpen ideas on conditions of uncertainty (and thus reduce uncertainty), and planning allows the development of conditional plans (plan Bs), which help individuals stay active and not to be overwhelmed by uncertainty.

McMullen and Shepherd assume that there is a given level of acceptance of uncertainty in individuals and being able to bear uncertainty changes a third-person opportunity into a first-person opportunity (in AT's terminology entrepreneurs develop goals to exploit opportunities). AT suggests that dynamically changing uncertainty reduces uncertainty even if the person's acceptance level stays the same. That may explain why risk acceptance per se is not predictive of success; empirically, a meta-analysis indicated risk acceptance not to be the most important personality factor for explaining entry into entrepreneurship or entrepreneurial success (Rauch & Frese, 2007). In contrast, self-efficacy and need for achievement contribute to entrepreneurship (however, McMullen and Shepherd subsume need for achievement as an indicator of being able to 'bear' uncertainty).

In conclusion, there are large overlaps of AT and McMullen and Shepherd's theory. The potential contributions of AT to McMullen and Shepherd is its dynamic nature (being experimental, changeable action characteristics may reduce subjective uncertainty) and entrepreneurs may change uncertainty and action-oriented knowledge; moreover, the steps of the action sequence and the hierarchical levels may lead to interesting hypotheses (e.g., routines should be much less affected by uncertainty than higher level regulation of actions). In turn, McMullen and Shepherd can help AT to think more precisely about environmental uncertainty and its effects on actions.

Effectuation Theory

I need to briefly discuss Sarasvathy's (2001) effectuation theory. Like AT, effectuation theory is often considered to propagate an active approach to uncertainty (Chandler, DeTienne, McKelvie, & Mumford, 2011). Effectuation theory argues that it is a theory of entrepreneurship par excellence. Therefore, followers of effectuation theory would likely be critical of AT as a theory of entrepreneurship because AT with its emphasis on goals and plans looks like a variant of 'causation logic'.

One central idea of effectuation includes a piecemeal approach of testing available resources interacting with an uncertain and unknowable environment (Sarasvathy, 2004). Resources are available means (what I know, who I am, whom I know) used to develop market opportunities (Sarasvathy, 2001). One of our experimental studies found that creative idea development based on the means approach leads to better and more innovative ideas than a more traditional brainstorming approach (Zhu et al., 2020). Thus, I agree that good ideas are often based on effectuations theory's means approach.

Effectuation also argues that the means approach leads to experiments that need to be affordable, that entrepreneurs should approach others to invest money or buy things, and that contingencies should be leveraged. I find these important points that need to be included into any AT of entrepreneurship. AT's suggestions of active experimentation, of being self-starting and long-term-oriented and overcoming barriers could be dangerous if they are not hedged by keeping losses affordable, by developing knowledge on where resources are constrained and where they are not; obviously, it is necessary to use others' feedback (including inviting them to invest and become partners of firm development); moreover, environmental barriers need be acknowledged and contingencies leveraged (particularly in the sense of a plan B). In many ways then, AT and effectuation theory share concepts, such as error making, action orientation, and experimentation; both theories are process-oriented and emphasize learning in interaction with the environment.

However, not all is well with effectuation theory; it met withering epistemological criticism to be a theory without clear testable concepts, to isolate itself from potential falsification, and to not acknowledge empirical research in relevant areas (Arend, Sarooghi, & Burkemper, 2015). In addition, I see the problem that its core assumption is similar to the now-defunct behaviorist theory by Skinner (1953): Like effectuation, Skinner assumed that situational contingencies determine and shape actions; in the same way, effectuation suggests a highly reactive approach of means testing to see how the environment reacts rather than to think of how entrepreneurs influence the environment. In Sarasvathy's view, the environment shapes entrepreneurial behaviors.

I argue in the following that in spite of many similarities between the theories and AT, Sarasvathy's rejection of goals, plans, and action orientated development of knowledge leads effectuation theory to become a passive and reactive theory of entrepreneurship and thus ignoring active approaches that change the environment as centerpiece of entrepreneurship. Sarasvathy (2001) argues against using concepts of goals and plans in her 'effectuation logic' because the environment is unknowable and unpredictable. Indeed, if the environment were completely unknowable and unpredictable, goals, and plans would most likely prove wrong and would just contribute to misallocation of time, resources, and attention (goals and plans belong to the causation logic in her theory; although a general goal of starting a company is accepted in the theory). Of course, AT acknowledges that it is difficult to set goals and plan well under conditions of *complete* unpredictability (Frese, 1987). However, is there any human-made environment that is completely unpredictable?

There are four major problems of effectuation theory from my perspective. First, uncertainty is relative and not complete. Second, if it were unpredictable, it would not be possible to learn and to do means testing in an incremental way as part of effectuation. Third, it is precisely goals and plans that help reduce uncertainty. Finally, the differentiation of two logics makes little sense because they, indeed, build on each other and cannot be used just by themselves.

Ad First: While it is true that entrepreneurs often deal with a more unpredictable environment than other occupations, the environment is never so chaotic and random that it would invalidate any goal setting and planning. Sarasvathy's concept of uncertainty is categorical—certainty versus uncertainty; this is seldom the case—most often there are degrees and areas of uncertainty. Everyday life teaches us that uncertainty is seldom and specific; people can safely assume that things will not change that much within a certain period—that is also true of entrepreneurship. Most entrepreneurs do well in believing that the building, they live in, the bed they sleep in, the bank they got their loan from, and their suppliers will also be there tomorrow (or at least equivalent functions will exist tomorrow).

Ad Second: Let's do the thought experiment of imagining a situation of very high unpredictability: Such an environment makes it impossible to learn and there is no constancy of resources. Learning assumes that what I learned yesterday is also useful tomorrow. The means approach by Sarasvathy is incremental; this implies that the last increment should be the basis for the next step tomorrow (otherwise, effectuation as a piecemeal would not work). Indeed, if there were no constancies, there would also be no experts, as expertise is knowledge that is applicable tomorrow; paradoxically, Sarasvathy (2001) developed her theory in interviews with experts.

Ad Third: One of the most important implications of AT is that actions change the environment; thus, environments can be made more predictable; moreover, developing specific goals, developing knowledge about the environment, planning, and feedback are instruments to change the environment (although there is, of course, no guarantee that things will work out as planned—therefore, experimentation is necessary as well). Uncertainty can be changed by actions; actions improve knowledge via planning, experimentation, and feedback. In principle, this squares well with other parts of effectuation theory that favor experimentation, failures, and feedback from the environment. Much of this would speak for a chance to combine effectuation and AT; if there were not the curious disconnect in Sarasvathy's theory: Effectuation theory assumes that actions do not affect uncertainty.

At this point a proponent of effectuation theory might argue: People may not be able to predict, but they can influence the environment via control ("Focus on the controllable aspects of an unpredictable future"; Sarasvathy, 2001, p. 251). However, controllability and uncertainty are related although one can in principle differentiate them.[4] The very nature of entrepreneurship implies that time, finances, and other resources are invested with a view that this may turn out positive in the future. This implies that entrepreneurs would prefer a higher degree of predictability and controllability of the environment; both are important and the environment is not binary certain or uncertain. Entrepreneurs need to experiment, they should try things out and see whether there are buyers of their products (or prototypes of their products); they also need to anticipate (and plan for) errors and their plans should include the idea of affordable losses; this implies that one has to learn from the feedback and appropriately change one's product portfolio—all these points are important and are affected and will affect goals, plans, knowledge acquisition, and feedback. Once, routines have been developed, uncertainty is reduced. Certain things may still be uncertain—all the more important to be long term oriented and to attempt to anticipate (predict) potential future barriers, problems, and opportunities and prepare for them now—even if this turns out not to be always correct; it pays off because one's thinking of the environment becomes sharper and more realistic.

Routines appear when there are constancies in the environment. Once a person has developed a number of routines, they do not need to think consciously about their specific goals and plans any more. This may lead to an interesting selection effect: Sarasvathy (2001) interviewed experts—who have many routines available and therefore, no longer consciously think of goals and plans (Sonnentag, 1998); thus, experts may not emphasize and therefore not volunteer reports of their goals and plans in an interview. Novices would probably report a higher amount of planning and goal setting than experts (even though uncertainty is higher for novice entrepreneurs than for experts).

Ad Fourth: Effectuation theory argues that plans and goals belong to one logic (causal thinking) while experimenting on the basis of resources and overcoming barriers belongs to the logic of effectuation; Sarasvathy is actually a bit unclear in her writings whether these logics are opposite or simply independent (Cha,

Ruan, & Frese, 2020). AT would maintain that there are no separate logics and that all of these constructs usually presuppose each other. The very idea of logics as categorical concepts is that they cannot codetermine behavior at the same time. While Sarasvathy (2001) at times seems to also suggest relationships between the two logics, she sharply differentiates them. For example, Table 11.1 (p. 251 of her 2001 paper) clearly conceptualizes them as opposing and contrasting logics. Empirical quantitative work tends to agree with AT. There are positive correlations between causation and effectuation concepts with the possible exception of experimentation (Cha et al., 2020; Chandler et al., 2011). In other words, it makes sense to accept that effectuation requires changeable goals, plans, knowledge parameters, and feedback to tackle the complex environment of the entrepreneurs.[5] There are likely more relationships and contradictions between these two theories; I have tried to show that they can learn from each other.

Conclusion

AT is a general theory of action. However, I believe that it is particularly useful for entrepreneurship because it provides a parsimonious theory of active approaches. This has implications for training and for interventions, which have proved successful.

Notes

1. That may constitute one difference of action plans from business plans—the latter may not necessarily be used as a guide to action but help develop legitimacy. However, developing business plans forces entrepreneurs to think through their business ideas in some detail and develop contingencies and a more explicit business model; thus, formal business plans are not useless (Gielnik, Frese, & Stark, 2015).
2. Action theory is sometimes called action regulation theory—I use the more generic term *action theory* here.
3. Similar ideas have been developed in cognitive behavior therapy (Beck & Clark, 1997; Tang et al., 2005).
4. Psychology has grappled with the issues of control and predictability over aversive events for quite a while. Lack of control may imply that one does not have predictable safety signals (Miller, 1981); from this viewpoint, predictability could be a precondition of control. Usually, control implies that people can decide on how to sequence their actions, their timing and their content as well as on the action conditions (Frese, 1989). Predictability is usually more important in the negative area-only unpredictable negative events are problematic. Given control over action conditions, an actor can influence uncertainty. However, if everything is uncertain, control is not helpful because once an actor has controlled something, conditions may change in unpredictable ways, thus destroying the positivity of actor's past control over it. Arend et al. (2015, p. 641) argue, "One defining characteristic of effectuation is that non-predictive control is not only possible, but advantageous. However, the assumption that the effectual context entails control without- prediction ... appears tenuous. ... Essentially, in the real world, control requires prediction; to control an outcome requires the knowledge of how an input affects an output, where that knowledge is predictive".

5 The fact that these two "logics" are highly related also invalidates a number of qualitative studies that use the coding of effectuation or causation; if the input is based on categorical codes for these two logics; the study and coding design makes it impossible to detect the co-occurrence of both logics—only quantitative studies can show the relationships between these "logics".

References

Adelson, B. (1984). When novices surpass experts: The difficulty of a task may increase with expertice. *Journal of Experimental Psychology: Learning, Memory, and Cognition, 10*, 483–495.

Arend, R., Sarooghi, H., & Burkemper, A. (2015). Effectuation as ineffectual? Applying the 3E theory-assessment framework to a proposed new theory of entrepreneurship. *Academy of Management Review, 40*, 630–651.

Ashford, S. J., & Stobbelleirm, K. E. M. (2013). Feedback, goal setting, and task performance revisited. In E. A. Locke & G. P. Latham (Eds.), *New developments in goal setting and task performance* (pp. 51–64). New York: Routledge.

Ashford, S. J., & Tsui, A. S. (1991). Self-regulation for managerial effectiveness: The role of active feedback seeking. *Academy of Management Journal, 34*, 251–280.

Baker, T., & Nelson, R. E. (2005). Creating something from nothing: Resource construction through entrepreneurial bricolage. *Administrative Science Quarterly, 50*, 329–366.

Baron, R. A., & Ensley, M. D. (2006). Opportunity recognition as the detection of meaningful patterns: Evidence from comparisons of novice and experienced entrepreneurs. *Management Science, 52*, 1331–1344.

Baum, J. R., Locke, E. A., & Smith, K. G. (2001). A multi-dimensional model of venture growth. *Academy of Management Journal, 44*, 292–303.

Baumeister, R. F., Bratslavsky, E., Finkenauer, C., & Vohs, K. D. (2001). Bad is stronger than good. *Review of General Psychology, 5*(4), 323–370.

Baumeister, R. F., Bratslavsky, E., Muraven, M., & Tice, D. M. (1998). Ego depletion: Is the active self a limited resource? *Journal of Personality and Social Psychology, 74*, 1252–1265.

Beck, A. T., & Clark, D. A. (1997). An information processing model of anxiety: Automatic and strategic processes. *Behaviour Research and Therapy, 35*(1), 49–58.

Brandstaetter, V., Lengfelder, A., & Gollwitzer, P. M. (2001). Implementation intentions and efficient action initiation. *Journal of Personality and Social Psychology, 81*, 946–960.

Brinckmann, J., Grichnik, D., & Kapsa, D. (2010). Should entrepreneurs plan or just storm the castle? A meta-analysis on contextual factors impacting the business planning-performance relationship in small firms. *Journal of Business Venturing, 25*, 24–40.

Busenitz, L., & Barney, J. (1997). Differences between entrepreneurs and managers in large organizations: Biases and heuristics in strategic decision-making. *Journal of Business Venturing, 12*, 9–30.

Campos, F., Frese, M., Goldstein, M., Iacovone, L., Johnson, H., McKenzie, D., & Mensmann, M. (2017). Teaching personal initiative beats traditional business training in boosting small business in West Africa. *Science, 357*, 1287–1290.

Cardinal, L. B., Miller, C. C., Kreutzer, M., & TenBrink, C. (2015). Strategic planning and firm performance: Towards a better understaind of a controversial relationship. In M. D. Mumford & M. Frese (Eds.), *The psychology of planning in organizations: Research and applications* (pp. 260–288). New York: Routledge, Taylor & Francis.

Cardon, M. S., Stevens, C. E., & Potter, D. R. (2011). Misfortunes or mistakes? Cultural sensemaking of entrepreneurial failure. *Journal of Business Venturing, 26*(1), 79–92.

Cha, V., Ruan, A.Y., & Frese, M. (2020). Re-visiting effectuation: The relationship of with cuasation, entrepreneurial experience, and innovativeness. In A. Caputo & M. M. Pellegrini (Eds.), *The entrepreneurial behaviour: Unveiling the cognitive and emotional aspect of entrepreneurship*. Bingley, UK: Emerald Group Publishing Limited.

Chandler, G. N., DeTienne, D. R., McKelvie, A., & Mumford, T.V. (2011). Causation and effectuation processes: A validation study. *Journal of Business Venturing, 26*, 375–390.

Chase, W. G., & Simon, H. A. (1973). Perception in chess. *Cognitive Psychology, 4*, 55–81.

Crede, M., Tynan, M. C., & Harms, P. D. (2017). Much ado about grit: A meta-analytic synthesis of the grit literature. *Journal of Personality and Social Psychology, 113*(3), 492.

Diefendorff, J. M., & Lord, R. G. (2004). The volitional and strategic effects of planning on task performance and goal commitment. *Human Performance, 16*, 365–387.

Dimov, D. (2007). From opportunity insight to opportunity intention: The importance of person-situation learning match. *Entrepreneurship Theory & Practice, 31*, 561–583.

Dörner, D. (1996). *The logic of failure*. Reading, MA: Addision Wesley.

Drexler, A., Fischer, G., & Schoar, A. (2014). Keeping it simple: Financial literacy and rules of thumb. *American Economic Journal: Applied Economics, 6*, 1–31.

Earley, P. C., Wojnaroski, P., & Prest, W. (1987). Task planning and energy expended: Exploration of how goals influence performance. *Journal of Applied Psychology, 72*, 107–114.

Ericsson, K. A., & Lehmann, A. C. (1996). Expert and exceptional performance: Evidence of maximal adaptation to task constraints. *Annual Review of Psychology, 47*, 273–305.

Fang He, V., Siren, C., Singh, S., Solomon, G., & von Krogh, G. (2018). Keep calm and carry on: emotion regulation in entrepreneurs' learning from failure. *Entrepreneurship Theory and Practice, 42*(4), 605–630.

Fay, D., & Frese, M. (2001). The concept of personal initiative: An overview of validity studies. *Human Performance, 14*(1), 97–124.

Frayne, C., & Latham, G. (1987). Application of social learning theory to employee self-management of attendance. *Journal of Applied Psychology, 72*, 387–392.

Frese, M. (1987). A theory of control and complexity: Implications for software design and integration of computer system into the work place. In M. Frese, E. Ulich, & W. Dzida (Eds.), *Psychological issues of human-computer interaction at the work place* (pp. 313–337). Amsterdam: North Holland.

Frese, M. (1989). Theoretical models of control and health. In S.L. Sauter, J.J. Hurrel (jr.), & C.L. Cooper (Eds.), *Job control and worker health* (pp. 107–128). Chichester: Wiley.

Frese, M. (1991). Error management or error prevention: Two strategies to deal with errors in software design. In H.-J. Bullinger (Ed.), *Human aspects in computing: Design and use of interactive systems and work with terminals* (pp. 776–782). Amsterdam: Elsevier Science Publication.

Frese, M. (2009). Towards a psychology of entrepreneurship: An action theory perspective. *Foundations and Trends in Entrepreneurship, 5*, 435–494.

Frese, M., & Fay, D. (2001). Personal Initiative (PI): A concept for work in the 21st century. *Research in Organizational Behavior, 23*, 133–188.

Frese, M., Gielnik, M. M., & Mensmann, M. (2016). Psychological training for entrepreneurs to take action: Contributing to poverty reduction in developing countries. *Current Directions in Psychological Science, 25*(3), 196–202.

Frese, M., & Keith, N. (2015). Action errors, error management and learning in organizations. *Annual Review of Psychology, 66*, 661–687.

Frese, M., Krauss, S., Keith, N., Escher, S., Grabarkiewicz, R., Luneng, S.T., . . . Friedrich, C. (2007). Business owners' action planning and Its relationship to business success in three African countries. *Journal of Applied Psychology, 92*, 1481–1498.

Frese, M., Stewart, J., & Hannover, B. (1987). Goal orientation and planfulness: Action styles as a personality concepts. *Journal of Personality and Social Psychology, 52,* 1182–1194.

Frese, M., & Zapf, D. (1994). Action as the core of work psychology: A German approach. In H. C. Triandis, M. D. Dunnette, & J. M. Hough (Eds), *Handbook of industrial and organizational psychology* (2nd ed., Vol. 4, pp. 271–340). Palo Alto, CA: Consulting Psychology Press.

Funken, R., Gielnik, M. M., & Foo, M.-D. (2020). How can problems be turned into something good? The role of entrepreneurial learning and error mastery orientation. *Entrepreneurship Theory and Practice, 44*(2), 315–338.

Galperin, P. Y. (1969). Stages in the development of mental acts. In M. D. Cole & I. Maltzman (Eds.), *A handbook of contemporary Soviet psychology* (pp. 249–273). New York: Basic Books.

Gentner, D. R., & Stevens, A. L. (Eds.). (1983). *Mental models.* Hillsdale, NJ: Lawrence Erlbaum Associates.

Gielnik, M. M., Barabas, S., Frese, M., Namatovu-Dawa, R., Scholz, F. A., Metzger, J. R., & Walter, T. (2014). A temporal analysis of how entrepreneurial goal intentions, positive fantasies, and action planning affect starting a new venture and when the effects wear off. *Journal of Business Venturing, 29,* 755–772.

Gielnik, M. M., Frese, M., Graf, J. M., & Kampschulte, A. (2012). Creativity in the opportunity identification process and the moderating effect of diverse information. *Journal of Business Venturing, 27,* 559–576.

Gielnik, M. M., Frese, M., Kahara-Kawuki, A., Katono, I. W., Kyejjusa, S., Munene, J., . . . Dlugosch, T. J. (2015). Action and action-regulation in entrepreneurship: Evaluating a student training for promoting entrepreneurship. *Academy of Management Learning & Education, 14,* 69–94.

Gielnik, M. M., Frese, M., & Stark, M. S. (2015). Planning and entrepreneurship. In M. D. Mumford & M. Frese (Eds.), *The psychology of planning in organizations: Research and applications* (pp. 289–311). Boston, MA: Routledge, Taylor and Francis Group.

Gielnik, M. M., Krämer, A.-C., Kappel, B., & Frese, M. (2014). Antecedents of business opportunity identification and innovation: Investigating the interplay of information processing and information acquisition. *Applied Psychology: An International Review, 63,* 344–381.

Glaub, M., Frese, M., Fischer, S., & Hoppe, M. (2014). Increasing personal initiative in small business managers/owners leads to entrepreneurial success: A theory-based controlled randomized field intervention for evidence based management. *Academy of Management Learning & Education, 13,* 354–379.

Gollwitzer, P. M. (1999). Implementation intentions: Strong effects of simple plans. *American Psychologist, 54,* 493–503.

Grant, A. M., & Ashford, S. J. (2008). The dynamics of proactivity at work. *Research in Organizational Behavior, 28,* 3–34.

Hacker, W. (1992). *Expertenkönnen: Erkennen und Vermitteln* (Expert knowledge: Recognizing and communicating). Göttingen: Verlag fuer Angewande Psychologie.

Hoang, H., & Antoncic, B. (2003). Network-based research in entrepreneurship: A critical review. *Journal of Business Venturing, 18,* 165–187.

Huang, L., & Pearce, J. L. (2015). Managing the unknowable: The effectiveness of early-stage investor gut feel in entrepreneurial investment decisions. *Administrative Science Quarterly, 60*(4), 634–670.

Kahneman, D. (1973). *Attention and effort.* Englewood Cliffs, NJ: Prentice-Hall.

Kahneman, D. (2003). A perspective on judgment and choice: Mapping bounded rationality. *American Psychologist, 58*, 697–720.

Kahneman, D., & Klein, G. (2009). Conditions for intuitive expertise: A failure to disagree. *American Psychologist, 64*, 515–526.

Kanfer, R., & Ackerman, P. L. (1989). Motivation and cognitive abilities: An integrative/aptitude-treatment interaction approach to skill acquisition. *Journal of Applied Psychology, 74*, 657–690.

Keith, N., & Frese, M. (2005). Self-regulation in error management training: Emotion control and metacognition as mediators of performance effects. *Journal of Applied Psychology, 90*, 677–691.

Keith, N., & Frese, M. (2008). Performance effects of error management training: A meta-analysis. *Journal of Applied Psychology, 93*, 59–69.

Keith, N., Unger, J. M., Rauch, A., & Frese, M. (2016). Informal learning and entrepreneurial success: A longitudinal study of deliberate practice among small business owners. *Applied Psychology: An International Review, 65*, 515–540.

Kluger, A. N., & DeNisi, A. (1996). The effects of feedback interventions on performance: A historical review, a meta-analysis and a preliminary feedback intervention theory. *Psychological Bulletin, 119*, 254–284.

Latham, G. P., Erez, M., & Locke, E. A. (1988). Resolving scientific disputes by the joint design of crucial experiments by the antagonists: Application to the Erez-Latham dispute regarding participation in goal setting. *Journal of Applied Psychology, 73*, 753–772.

Lieberman, M. B., & Montgomery, D. B. (1998). First mover (dis-)advantages: Retrospective and links with the resource-based view. *Strategic Management Journal, 19*, 1111–1125.

Locke, E. A. (Ed.). (2004). *Handbook of principles of organizational behavior.* Oxford: Blackwell.

Locke, E. A., & Latham, G. P. (Eds.). (2013). *New developments in goal setting and task performance.* New York: Routledge.

March, J., & Simon, H. A. (1958). *Organisations.* New York: John Wiley & Sons.

McMullen, J. S., & Shepherd, D. A. (2006). Entrepreneurial action and the role of uncertainty in the theory of the entrepreneur. *Academy of Management Review, 31*, 132–152.

Meichenbaum, D. H., & Deffenbacher, J. L. (1988). Stress inoculation training. *The Counseling Psychologist, 16*, 69–90.

Mensmann, M., & Frese, M. (2017). Proactive behavior training: Theory, design, and future directions. In S. K. Parker & U. K. Bindl (Eds.), *Makings things happen in organizations* (pp. 434–468). New York: Routledge.

Miller, G. A., Galanter, E., & Pribram, K. H. (1960). *Plans and the structure of behavior.* London, UK: Holt.

Miller, S. (1981). Predictability and human stress: Toward a clarification of evidence and theory. In L. Berkowitz (Ed.), *Advances in experimental social psychology* (Vol. 14, pp. 203–256). New York: Academic.

Morrison, E. W. (1993). Longitudinal study of the effects of information seeking on newcomer socialization. *Journal of Applied Psychology, 78*, 173–183.

Mueller, B. A., & Shepherd, D. A. (2016). Making the most of failure experiences: Exploring the relationship between business failure and the identification of business opportunities. *Entrepreneurship Theory and Practice, 40*(3), 457–487.

Mueller, B. A., Wolfe, M. T., & Syed, I. (2017). Passion and grit: An exploration of the pathways leading to venture success. *Journal of Business Venturing, 32*(3), 260–279.

Mumford, M. D., Giorgini, V., & Steele, L. (2015). Planning by leaders: Factors influencing leader planning performance. In M. D. Mumford & M. Frese (Eds.), *The psychology of planning in organizations: Research and applications* (pp. 242–259). New York: Routledge, Taylor & Francis.

Myers, C., & Davids, K. (1993). Tacit skill and performance at work. *Applied Psychology: An International Review, 42*, 117–137.

Neck, C. P., Houghton, J. D., Sardeshmukh, S. R., Goldsby, M., & Godwin, J. L. (2013). Self-leadership: A cognitive resource for entrepreneurs. *Journal of Small Business & Entrepreneurship, 26*(5), 463–480.

Peters, T. (1987). *Thriving on chaos*. New York: Harper & Row.

Prandelli, E., Pasquini, M., & Verona, G. (2016). In user's shoes: An experimental design on the role of perspective taking in discovering entrepreneurial opportunities. *Journal of Business Venturing, 31*(3), 287–301.

Rauch, A., & Frese, M. (2007). Let's put the person back into entrepreneurship research: A meta-analysis on the relationship between business owners' personality traits, business creation, and success. *European Journal of Work & Organizational Psychology, 16*(4), 353–385.

Rauch, A., Frese, M., Wang, Z.-M., Unger, J., Lozada, M., Kupcha, V., & Spirina, T. (2013). National culture and cultural orientations of owners affecting the innovation-growth relationship in five countries. *Entrepreneurship & Regional Development: An International Journal, 25*, 732–755.

Rauch, A., Wiklund, J., Lumpkin, G. T., & Frese, M. (2009). Entrepreneurial orientation and business performance: An assessment of past research and suggestions for the future. *Entrepreneurship Theory & Practice, 33*(3), 761–787.

Reason, J. T. (1990). *Human error*. New York: Cambridge University Press.

Rosenbusch, N., Brinckmann, J., & Bausch, A. (2011). Is innovation always beneficial? A meta-analysis of the relationship between innovation and performance in SMEs. *Journal of Business Venturing, 26*, 441–457.

Sarasvathy, S. D. (2001). Causation and effectuation: Toward a theoretical shift from economic inevitability to entrepreneurial contingency. *Academy of Management Review, 26*, 243–263.

Sarasvathy, S. D. (2004). The questions we ask and the questions we care about: reformulating some problems in entrepreneurship research. *Journal of Business Venturing, 19*(5), 707–717.

Shane, S. (2000). Prior knowledge and the discovery of entrepreneurial opportunities. *Organization Science, 11*, 448–469.

Shane, S. (2009). Why encouraging more people to become entrepreneurs is bad public policy. *Small Business Economics, 33*, 141–149.

Shepherd, D. A., Patzelt, H., & Wolfe, M. (2011). Moving forward from project failure: Negative emotions, affective commitment, and learning from the experience. *Academy of Management Journal, 54*(6), 1229–1259.

Skinner, B. F. (1953). *Science and human behavior*. New York: The Free Press.

Sonnentag, S. (1998). Expertise in professional software design: A process study. *Journal of Applied Psychology, 83*, 703–715.

Tang, T. Z., DeRubeis, R. J., Beberman, R., & Pham, T. (2005). Cognitive changes, critical sessions, and sudden gains in cognitive-behavioral therapy for depression. *Journal of Consulting and Clinical Psychology, 73*(1), 168.

Taylor, S. E. (1981). The interface between cognitive and social psychology. In J. Harvey (Ed.), *Cognition, social behavior, and the environment* (pp. 182–211). Hillsdale, NJ: Erlbaum.

Trope, Y., & Liberman, N. (2010). Construal-level theory of psychological distance. *Psychological Review, 117*(2), 440.

van der Linden, D., Sonnentag, S., Frese, M., & van Dyck, C. (2001). Exploration strategies, performance, and error consequences when learning a complex computer task. *Behaviour and Information Technology, 20*, 189–198.

VanderWerf, P. A., & Mahon, J. F. (1997). Meta-analysis of the impact of research methods on findings of first-mover advantage. *Management Science, 43*(11), 1510–1519.

van Dyck, C., Frese, M., Baer, M., & Sonnentag, S. (2005). Organizational error management culture and its impact on performance: A two-study replication. *Journal of Applied Psychology, 90*, 1228–1240.

Van Eerde, W. (2015). Time management and procrastination. In M. D. Mumford & M. Frese (Eds.), *The psychology of planning in organizations: Research and applications* (pp. 312–333). New York: Taylor & Francis: Routledge.

Van Gelderen, M., Frese, M., & Thurik, R. (2000). Strategies, uncertainty and performance of small business startups. *Small Business Economics, 15*, 165–181.

Van Gelderen, M., Kautonen, T., Wincent, J., & Biniari, M. (2017). Implementation intentions in the entrepreneurial process: Concept, empirical findings, and research agenda. *Small Business Economics*, 1–19.

Wieber, F., & Gollwitzer, P. (2010). Overcoming procrastination through planning. In C. Andreou & M. D. Whilte (Eds.), *The thief of time: Philosophical essays on procrastination* (pp. 185–205). New York: Oxford University Press.

Wolf, K., Papineni, S., Alibhai, S., Buehren, N., Frese, M., & Goldstein, M. (2020). A failed replication of the personal initiative training: Towards understanding the role of trainers. Unpublished manuscript, University of Lueneburg.

Zacher, H., & Frese, M. (2018). Action regulation theory: Foundations, current knowledge, and future directions. In D. S. Ones, N. Anderson, H. K. Sinangil, & C. Viswesvaran (Eds.), *The SAGE handbook of industrial, work, & organizational psychology, Vol.: Organizational psychology* (2nd ed., pp. 122–144). New York: Sage.

Zhao, X.-Y., Frese, M., & Giardini, A. (2010). Business owners' network size and business growth in China: The role of comprehensive social competency. *Entrepreneurship & Regional Development, 22*, 675–705.

Zhu, J., Bischoff, K. M., Kaap, E., Schmidt, D., Gielnik, M. M., & Frese, M. (2020). The effectiveness of effectuation training on business opportunity identification. *Academy of Management: Learning and Education*, in press.

12

ENTREPRENEURS' COMPETENCIES

Marco van Gelderen

Introduction

This chapter offers an overview and integration of theory and research pertaining to the competencies of independent and corporate entrepreneurs. It starts by clarifying the term competency and reviewing types of competencies. It then outlines empirical studies on the effects of competencies: their relations with entrepreneurial emergence and success. Next, the development of entrepreneurial competencies at early and at later ages is discussed. The chapter then offers a few ideas about the competencies of the entrepreneur of the future and concludes with future research suggestions.

The term competency is widely used in the worlds of management, policy, and education. According to Boyatzis (2008), any organization employing 300 people or more somehow involves the competency construct in its HR practices. This practitioner interest in competencies is typically driven by aspirations to improve individual and hence organizational performance (Spencer & Spencer, 1993). For this reason, aspiring and established entrepreneurs (as well as their educators, trainers, mentors, and investors) take an interest in competencies. Competency is an attractive construct for practitioners as a notion of success is implied. Searching *competency definition* on Google gives the result "the ability to do something successfully or efficiently." It makes intuitive sense that if you want to succeed, you should be competent at what you want to succeed in. Adding to the attraction of this construct is that competencies, unlike motives and traits, are considered to be learnable. Thus, even if competencies are currently underdeveloped, they can be improved. A third attractive feature is that competencies have a holistic character that encompasses knowledge, skills, and attitude (KSA), thus capturing in one term a variety of elements involved in high performance (Hayton & Kelley,

2006). In sum, the appeal of competencies is that they are holistic, learnable, and inherently tied to success. At the same time, as the next section elaborates, these very characteristics cause the competency literature to be rather confusing and complex. Thus, this chapter begins with a conceptual clarification.

Conceptual Clarification

I limit this chapter to competencies as attributes of individuals. I disregard applications at the company level as in dynamic capability ("the firm's ability to integrate, build, and reconfigure internal and external competences to address rapidly changing environments," Teece, Pisano, & Shuen, 1997) or the core competencies of the firm (Prahalad & Hamel, 1990). Hence the title of this chapter is "Entrepreneurs' Competencies." Inspired by Hoffmann's (1999) clarification, I distinguish among the antecedents, components, and outcomes of competency (Figure 12.1). The next paragraphs discuss each in turn.

Competency Antecedents

According to Boyatzis (1982, 2008), a competency is a person's underlying characteristic that causes outstanding performance at work. Those who take this approach typically investigate two questions: Who are the most competent performers, and

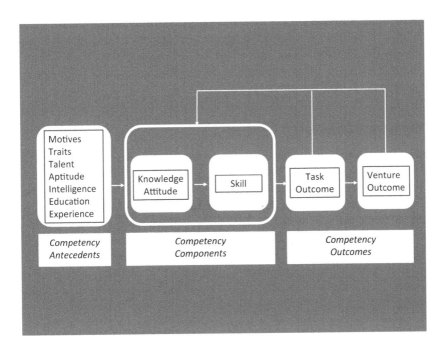

FIGURE 12.1   Competencies: Antecedents, Components, Outcomes

what underlying attributes make them better than others at what they do? In examining these underlying attributes, these authors often take a broad approach. For example, for Spencer and Spencer (1993, p. 4), competencies include

> motives, traits, self-concepts, attitudes or values, content knowledge, or cognitive or behavioral skills—any individual characteristic that can be measured or counted reliably and that can be shown to differentiate significantly between superior and average performers, or between effective and ineffective performers.

For Boyatzis (1982, 2008), competencies might include a "motive, trait, skill, aspect of one's self-image or social role, or a body of knowledge which he or she uses." To which Bird (1995, p. 51), in her application of competency to the entrepreneurship domain, adds: "which result in venture birth, survival and/or growth."

Unfortunately, by labeling *any* underlying individual factor that may contribute to successful individual performance as a competency, the construct becomes a near meaningless container term. A more fruitful approach is to narrow the term. This is commonly done by designating competency as the combined and integrated components of knowledge, skills, and attitudes (KSA; sometimes the "A" refers to ability rather than attitude; I discuss this distinction later). This is the definition used in this chapter. In this manner, constructs such as traits, motives, self-concept, and intelligence are separated from competency and are rather antecedents or inputs into competency (see Figure 12.1). An additional advantage of categorizing characteristics either as part of competency or as an antecedent of competency is that a discussion of the origins of competency thus becomes possible. That is, traits, talent, aptitude, motives are antecedents of competencies (Figure 12.1).

Competency Outcomes

Another confusion stems from using the term competency simultaneously for its components and its outcomes or effects. Several authors (Bird, 1995; Grzeda, 2005; Hoffmann, 1999; Mitchelmore & Rowley, 2010) observed that competencies are often discussed as successful performance, which thus combines actions and the outcomes of those actions into one construct. Outcomes can refer to a standard: If someone achieves beyond a certain standard, that person is said to be "competent." Outcomes can also refer to very high levels of success. For example, Bird (1995) distinguished between competence as a minimum standard—a baseline or threshold—and competence manifested as excellence. The definition by Google referred to earlier—the ability to do something successfully or efficiently—combines proficiency and something to be proficient at. Mixing competencies and positive outcomes is unhelpful, as one can be more or less competent in a particular competency.

When it comes to entrepreneurship, it is important to distinguish between components and outcomes. In particular, it is not advisable to base assessments of competency on venture outcomes or results, because competencies are carried by individuals. The venture of a highly competent entrepreneur can underperform or fail, just like that of an incompetent entrepreneur can succeed, for example, because of luck, coincidence, extreme risk-taking, or contextual factors (Dew, 2009; Görling & Rehn, 2008; Liu & De Rond, 2016). Furthermore, entrepreneurship inherently involves failure (Cacciotti, Hayton, Mitchell, & Giazitzoglu, 2016), so it may be the competency to reflect and to learn that is relevant to entrepreneurial success in the long run (Cope, 2011).

Still, it is necessary to know the goals and the desired outcomes in order to know toward what aims any competencies are directed and thus establish what competencies are relevant. Hence, there are the feedback arrows from Task and Venture Outcomes to Competency in Figure 12.1. It may be more fruitful to proceed from successful task performance, rather than venture performance (Figure 12.1), to arrive at the required competencies involved, even if successful task performance may be more difficult to specify for complex, holistic "jobs" such as being an entrepreneur (Grzeda, 2005). Proceeding from a task analysis has the additional advantage that it makes clear that competencies vary according to task.

Competency Components (Knowledge, Skills, and Attitude)

In this chapter, I define competencies as the combined and integrated components of knowledge, skills, and attitudes (KSA) (Bacigalupo, Kampylis, Punie, & Van den Brande, 2016; Clark, 2005). For example, digital communication competency draws on an individual's knowledge of language, practical information technological skills, and attitudes toward those with whom he or she is communicating. Confusingly, half of the KSA literature refers to attitude and the other half to ability. According to Clark (2005), the A originally stood for attitude, but as later it was deemed politically incorrect to change someone's attitude (competency having widespread usage in education, training, and development practice), attitude started to be replaced by ability. However, seeing ability as a component is problematic as, just like the term competency itself, ability can also be taken as an antecedent or as an outcome. Ability as a competency component is difficult to distinguish from antecedents of competency, such as intelligence, aptitude, or talent, which are also reflections of ability. Moreover, if taken as such, ability is then a fixed characteristic in contrast to skills and knowledge, which are learnable. This conceptualization of ability denies the idea that competencies can be developed (in contrast, attitude is more malleable). If taken as an outcome, ability equates to capability, which implies that one is capable, and as such equates to the effects of a competency, rather than being one of the three (KSA) components making up competency. Attitude—a relatively general and enduring evaluation of an object or concept (Vogel & Wanke, 2016)—does not suffer from these disadvantages. Hence, my definition and Figure 12.1 refer to attitude, rather than ability.

Many authors agree that competencies are best observed and analyzed in their manifestation at a behavioral level (e.g., Bird, 1995; Hayton & Kelley, 2006). By defining competency as the combined and integrated components of knowledge, skills, and attitudes, and by regarding them in their behavioral manifestation, the pitfalls of confusing competency antecedents or outcomes with competencies are avoided. The KSA components can be learned, unlike relatively fixed components such as traits and motives. Moreover, someone can possess favorable competency antecedents, but these are only relevant if they manifest in behavior, a point famously made by Gartner (1988). In addition, by looking at competencies as the behavioral manifestations of KSA, we avoid confusing competencies with the effects of competencies.

Observed behaviors—whether directly or indirectly observed (as in the case of cognitive or emotional (self-regulation) competencies)—are not themselves competencies, as competencies are a latent construct (Hayton & Kelley, 2006; Lans, Baggen, & Ploum, 2018). In terms of behavioral manifestation, skills are a step closer to behavior, as knowledge and attitude are manifest in their application (Figure 12.1). As Campbell, McCloy, Oppler, and Sager (1993) states, declarative knowledge is a prerequisite for procedural skill, and skills are attained when declarative knowledge (knowing what to do) is successfully combined with knowing how to do it. Having clarified that competency concerns the integrated components of attitude, knowledge, and skills, the chapter now reviews various types of competencies.

Types of Competencies

Many authors have attempted to list or categorize the various competencies that entrepreneurs should possess. These approaches differ in terms of how the competencies are selected. Some lists are based on desk research or armchair reasoning (e.g., Kyndt & Baert, 2014; Man, Lau, & Chan, 2002; Mitchelmore & Rowley, 2010). Others are based on the inputs of experts such as practicing entrepreneurs, business developers, or university professors (Chandler & Jansen, 1992; Morris, Webb, Fu, & Singhal, 2013). There also have been attempts to aggregate laundry lists of competencies into higher-level classifications. Sometimes competencies are mapped onto existing higher-level classification schemes, such as "getting ahead" and "getting along" (Hogan & Holland, 2003); "getting ahead," "getting along," and "getting it right" (Lans et al., 2018); or "know-why," "know-how," and "know-whom" (Johannisson, 2016). In other cases, higher-level classifications are proposed by the same authors who initially developed their list. For example, Man et al. (2002) proposed opportunity, relationship, conceptual, organizing, strategic, and commitment competencies. Mitchelmore and Rowley (2010) aggregated their list of competencies in terms of entrepreneurial, business and management, human relations, and conceptual and relationship competencies. The titles of Mitchelmore and Rowley's categories make clear that entrepreneurial competencies are just one out of a range of categories of competencies that entrepreneurs require. Similarly, for skills, Kutzhanova, Lyons, and Lichtenstein (2009) proposed technical, managerial, entrepreneurial, and personal maturity skills. Chandler and Jansen (1992) referred to competencies as entrepreneurial, managerial, and technical-functional roles. These classifications illustrate that entrepreneurs do not only need entrepreneurial competencies but also competencies that are not strictly entrepreneurial or not entrepreneurial at all. The success of the entrepreneur thus also depends on his or her non-entrepreneurial competencies.

Another common contrast is between enterprising and entrepreneurial competencies (Bacigalupo et al., 2016; Draycott & Rae, 2011; Gibb, 1993; Lackéus, 2015, 2018; Mitchelmore & Rowley, 2010; Onstenk, 2003; Neck & Corbett, 2018; Van Gelderen, 2020). Enterprising competencies take on a wider meaning than entrepreneurial competencies and can be decoupled from the commercial business context. These competencies refer to entrepreneurship as a behavioral syndrome, involving risk-taking, proactive, creative, and autonomous behavior in the context of creating value for other people (Lackéus, 2015, 2018; Van Gelderen, 2020). For example, in his enterprising competencies teaching program, Van Gelderen (2020) includes generating ideas for opportunities, taking action, perseverance, teamwork, networking, and convincing others, with the competencies being selected based on achieved learning effects in experiential training formats. Enterprising competencies can express themselves in a wide variety of settings, of which venture creation is only one. Venture creation is thus a special case of enterprising behavior (Lackéus, 2015, 2018; Van Gelderen, 2020). As they are transferable and applicable in a wide range of settings, enterprising competencies are increasingly stressed by entrepreneurship scholars and educators (Kuratko & Morris, 2018; Neck & Corbett, 2018) as well as by scholars who study the skills that will be needed by the generic working population in the near and distant future (www.atc21s.org, www.p21.org).

Beyond the lists and classifications of entrepreneurial competencies, it is important to consider that competencies and their relevance may vary by entrepreneurial task, phase of the business, industry, culture/country, and even historical time period. Even the same tasks can be approached in different manners and thus involve different competencies. For example, in the task of identifying or developing an opportunity, an entrepreneur may use discovery or creation processes (Alvarez, Barney, & Anderson, 2013) or effectual or causation processes (Sarasvathy, 2001). Even more fundamentally, competencies and their level of importance vary by type of entrepreneurship. This applies in terms of the aim (e.g., commercial versus social entrepreneurship (Fauchart & Gruber, 2011), actor (e.g., self-employed, small venture, corporate entrepreneurship), and mode (e.g., lifestyle, small or growth-oriented, innovative or imitative, degree of digitalization, collaborative or competitive). Thus, the notion of fit (Boyatzis, 2008; Markman &

Baron, 2003) is relevant: a competency should be aligned with the task, phase, sector, geography, time period, and type (aim, actor, mode) of entrepreneurship. The next section explores empirical work that addresses these variations.

Empirical Studies Relating Entrepreneurial Competencies to Outcomes

Authors have routinely proposed that competencies are important to venture success (Bacigalupo et al., 2016; Bird, 1995; Lackéus, 2015; Man et al., 2002; Morris et al., 2013; Neck & Corbett, 2018). Unfortunately, the empirical evidence is thinner than the theoretical claim, particularly when it comes to more detailed studies that aim to determine which competencies are relevant to specific industries, tasks, phases, and types of entrepreneurship. In particular, there is little evidence for the impact of enterprising behavior, despite being widely promoted in the EU (e.g., the influential EntreComp framework, Bacigalupo et al., 2016), arguably because of the broad definition and thus diffuse impact (Lackéus, 2015; Lans et al., 2018).

The available empirical research assessing the impact of entrepreneurial competencies tends to rely on self-reports wherein respondents indicate how often they use a particular competency or their self-perceived level of competence. Using a mixture of both, Kyndt and Baert (2014) conducted scale development work with regard to a range of competencies and additionally provided criterion validity for their scales by comparing entrepreneurs with varying levels of experience and investigating the relation with survival over a three- to five-year period. Kyndt and Baert (2014) found that only perseverance and market insight contributed to survival. However, their findings cannot be generalized, as their sample consisted mostly of necessity entrepreneurs; the majority of the participants were unemployed when they completed the initial survey. Chandler and Jansen (1992) based their study on literature that identifies the entrepreneurial, managerial, and technical-functional functions as three roles that founders must competently enact to be successful. Their cross-sectional results indicated that the most successful founders rate themselves as competent in these roles and see themselves as competent generalists.

Another cross-sectional study, now of a specific competency, was conducted by Baron and Markman (2003). They found that the higher the entrepreneurs' social competence (their ability to interact effectively with others based on discrete social skills), the greater their financial success. Baggen et al. (2018) developed the opportunity identification competence assessment test (OICAT) and found proof for its predictive validity. Ploum, Blok, Lans, and Omta (2019) showed that pro-environmental behavior values and moral competencies are important indicators of the ability to recognize opportunities for sustainable development. Volery, Mueller, and von Siemens (2015) studied the competencies of growth-oriented SMEs and found that entrepreneurs of these types of firms divide their time between exploration and exploitation. In this study, successful entrepreneurs were studied to determine their competencies. As such, the predictive validity of such findings should be verified in different samples.

There are many studies on the separate components of various competencies—knowledge, skills, and attitude. It is beyond the scope of this chapter to review these here. Much work has been done, particularly with regard to the skills of opportunity idea generation and evaluation, networking, and pitching. However, the literature sometimes uses the terms *competencies* and *skills* interchangeably, possibly because knowledge and attitude are implied in the behavioral application of skills (Figure 12.1). For this reason, in this section, I selectively include a few studies that refer to skills, rather than competencies, but which are relevant to the study of competencies. First, Unger, Rauch, Frese, and Rosenbusch (2011) conducted a meta-analysis of the relation between human capital and success and provides circumstantial evidence for the relevance of competencies. The authors found that the relationship is higher for what they call outcomes of human capital investments (knowledge/skills) than for human capital itself (education/experience), which can be seen as antecedents of competency (cf. Figure 12.1). Unger et al. (2011) also find the impact of skills or competencies to be higher in developing countries (because of more variation in terms of human capital in the studied sample) and for younger firms (because the emerging firm represents a more challenging situation in which the impact of having the right skills is larger than when the firm is more mature).

Second, a number of researchers have studied the benefits of having a varied set of skills for business performance versus the separate effects of single skills. Lazear (2005) promotes the idea that entrepreneurs are generalists: "Not necessarily superb at anything, entrepreneurs have to be sufficiently skilled in a variety of areas to put together the many ingredients required to create a successful business" (Lazear, 2005, p. 676). Empirical studies supported the hypotheses of Lazear's jack-of-all trades theory, demonstrating the importance of a varied skill set for engaging in entrepreneurship (Wagner, 2006; Åstebro & Thompson, 2011), making progress in the venture creation process (Stuetzer, Obschonka, & Schmitt-Rodermund, 2013), self-employment longevity (Oberschachtsiek, 2012), having higher earnings as an entrepreneur (Hartog, Van Praag, & Van der Sluis, 2010), and the number of businesses owned (Åstebro & Thompson, 2011). With some exceptions (e.g., Hartog et al., 2010), this body of work relied on proxies, usually the breadth of experience, rather than studying the variety of competencies or skills directly, although Stuetzer, Obschonka, Davidsson, and Schmitt-Rodermund (2013) empirically demonstrate that skills derive from experience. Perhaps more importantly, the referenced studies examined individuals rather than teams, although a varied or balanced skill set can obviously be achieved by having a variety of competencies in the start-up team. This issue received more attention in the literature on competencies in corporate entrepreneurship, which is briefly reviewed later in this chapter. In large corporations, it is more common that different specialists cover different tasks and phases.

In evaluating the body of empirical research described above, a first point to observe is that the studies taking a competency approach usually do not systematically specify the components of attitude, knowledge, and skill. Particularly underresearched are the attitude component and the interrelations of the components (e.g., to what extent the components can substitute another).

A second observation is that the validity of self-reported competency ratings can be questioned, as particularly inexperienced entrepreneurs may not yet have a grounded idea about their level of competence, particularly with respect to enterprising (soft) skills. Whereas technical (hard) skills (e.g., programming, language) can be self-rated rather unambiguously, soft skills are relative and thus it may be difficult to determine one's objective skill level. For example, one may believe he or she has competent social skills, but after gaining more entrepreneurial experience, one may discover that there remains a lot to be learned. So identical or even declining self-reported competency scores over time may actually reflect great development, and identical self-reported competency scores between persons may reflect great underlying variety. The literature has suggested ways to make competency scores more valid, for example, by having other individuals assess the observed behavior, such as in the 360-degree feedback and assessment center methodologies (Chen & Naquin, 2006; Hagan, Konopaske, Bernardin, & Tyler, 2006). Bird (1995, Table 11.1) provides an extensive overview of forms of competency assessment.

A third observation is that few studies have related competencies to task outcomes in the setting of actual ventures. Studies on competencies and task outcomes have been conducted in training settings, a few of these studies are covered in the later section in this chapter on competency development. Although task outcomes are more proximal than venture outcomes (Figure 12.1), the relation between competencies and task outcome should not be assumed. Whether competencies relate to successful task performance depends on transfer (Unger et al., 2011) and applicability or fit (Boyatzis, 2008; Grzeda, 2005; Unger et al., 2011). Empirical studies relating entrepreneurial competencies to success in different phases—such as opportunity recognition and idea validation, resource acquisition, launch, growth, and exit—are scarce (an example referring to skills is the discussion of convergent and divergent thinking, as offered by Lex and Gielnik (2017)). Several overviews of the competency literature have suggested that different phases require different competencies (Mitchelmore & Rowley, 2010; Chell, 2013), as do the growth and life cycle models of the firm (Churchill & Lewis, 1983; Greiner, 1972). However, empirical research has been mostly limited to the corporate setting (Rasmussen, Mosey, & Wright, 2011), which will be discussed in the next section.

A fourth observation is that the evidence linking competencies to performance does not extend beyond financial outcomes, despite other motives and outcomes playing important roles in entrepreneurial pursuits (Lackéus, 2015). For example, autonomy is a dominant motive to start and run one's own business, so whether autonomy is actually attained or retained (Van Gelderen, Shirokova, Shchegolev, & Beliaeva, 2020) is an important outcome of entrepreneurial competencies. For enterprising competencies, the relation to success may be even more complex, as enterprising competencies may manifest in a wide range of behaviors, of which starting or running a business is merely one example. As enterprising behavior is more geared to creating value than appropriating value, performance measures should somehow capture the value created for others (Lackéus, 2015).

Entrepreneurial Competencies in Corporate Entrepreneurship

Although corporate entrepreneurship can refer to a broad array of activities or innovations that are adopted in the firm's pursuit of competitive advantage (Kuratko & Morris, 2018), competency research has mostly focused on corporate venturing, that is, the launching of new ventures. In corporate venturing, tasks and phases may be covered by different specialists, who may have no further involvement with the venture beyond that task or phase (O'Connor, Corbett, & Pierantozzi, 2009; Rasmussen et al., 2011). This is uncommon in independent entrepreneurship. Even if roles or tasks are distributed in a team, the team is usually not replaced by an entirely different team when the venture moves into a new phase (Hayton & Kelley, 2006). The authors referenced so far in this section discern more or less similar phases in corporate venturing, even if they use slightly different terminology. The first phase concerns invention, sometimes involving scientists or new technology, and requires the ability to be visionary and creative. Then comes the business building phase, which involves experimenting with technology and business concepts to design a viable business model. This phase also involves selection (deciding which project will be (dis)continued) and championing (promoting the new venture to the mother organization). The last phase concerns the management of growth and the adoption of the venture into the mainstream of the business (or alternatively, to spin off the venture or license IP). As such, the required competencies per phase are quite different and may be carried out by different individuals (Hayton & Kelley, 2006; O'Connor et al., 2009; Rasmussen et al., 2011). Gilsing (2020) argues that the second phase is the most difficult to execute. Capable specialists are in short supply compared to the inventors, creators, and dreamers required in phase 1, and the managers proficient in achieving efficiency, growth, and profit in phase 3. According to Gilsing (2020), the business builders in phase 2 require a hybrid set of seemingly contradictory competencies, such as a willingness to commit as well as to let go, and to be visionary as well as to be hands-on. The role of the phase 2 specialist may be even more difficult nowadays, as a multitude of open innovation formats have emerged that vary in terms of the degree of required corporate involvement (Weiblen & Chesbrough, 2015).

Research on entrepreneurial competencies often looks at individual entrepreneurs, which may be accurate if one person starts a new venture. However, particularly in corporate entrepreneurship, it is unlikely that one individual entrepreneur possesses all of the necessary competencies to make the new venture a success (Rasmussen et al., 2011). Work on competencies in corporate entrepreneurship highlights the varied and temporal role of multiple actors. As Hayton and Kelley (2006) pointed out, an important question is whether these competencies should reside in the organization or can be outsourced or externally acquired, and if they should reside internally, which employees or groups should possess them. Rasmussen et al. (2011) investigate this question and find that if academic entrepreneurs are involved in a new venture (whose competencies pertain more to phase 1, as distinguished earlier), specific competencies for venture creation and growth must be developed or acquired for phases 2 and 3. In their study, the competencies for the latter phases were obtained through accessing competencies from within the corporation as well as externally from industry partners and equity investors. Assessing competencies at the level of the venture has an advantage in that it analyzes competencies from the vantage point of the project for which they are needed. A disadvantage arises if venture level terms like assets and resources are now referred to as competencies (e.g., Rasmussen et al., 2011). By designating anything functional to corporate capability and success as a competency, the competency construct is emptied from having specific meaning. See chapter 7 in this book for further discussion of the role of skills in corporate entrepreneurship.

Competency Development

Early

A number of scholars have investigated the effects of having developed entrepreneurial competencies at an early age. These early entrepreneurial competencies are age-appropriate. For example, Obschonka and colleagues studied early indicators of leadership, self-esteem, social skills, creativity, and proactivity motivation, and find that early competencies feed into later entrepreneurial competencies (Obschonka, Hakkarainen, Lonka, & Salmela-Aro, 2017; Schoon & Duckworth, 2012) and subsequently into entrepreneurial success (Obschonka, Duckworth, Silbereisen, & Schoon, 2012; Obschonka, Silbereisen, Schmitt-Rodermund, & Stuetzer, 2011). Thus, age-appropriate broad competencies are developmental precursors of later, venture-related entrepreneurial competencies. Obschonka et al. (2017) therefore advise that it is better to focus early training on age-appropriate broad competencies, rather than specific venture-related competencies. This conclusion brings us back to the more general enterprising competencies discussed earlier in this chapter. These general competencies can be seen as life competencies (Bacigalupo et al., 2016; Lackéus, 2015), and they can later be applied in a variety of contexts, of which starting a new venture is only one. The development of these intrapersonal and interpersonal competencies can start early, and are based on a foundation of even more basic competencies such as motor skills, reading, writing, etc. In addition, such competencies are primarily directed at value creation rather than value appropriation, which may further their acceptance among both children and their teachers (Lackéus, 2015).

The development of age-appropriate entrepreneurial competencies has a range of antecedents (Figure 12.1). Studies have found evidence that personality influences early competencies (Obschonka et al., 2017; Schmitt-Rodermund, 2004). A warm and supportive parenting style (Schmitt-Rodermund, 2004) relates to entrepreneurial competencies as well as interest, which are both central elements of the enterprising type in John Holland's (1973) well-known career theory (Schmitt-Rodermund, 2004). Thus, early development serves to build not only capability but also motivation. This fits the social cognitive career theory (Lent, Brown, & Hackett, 2002), which postulates that competencies and competence-related beliefs affect vocational behavior via interests (Obschonka et al., 2011). It is worth noting that Obschonka et al. (2017) find that those who pursue entrepreneurial careers are mid-level academic achievers. Training of early age-appropriate entrepreneurial competencies such as leadership, self-esteem, creativity, and proactivity motivation is therefore not necessarily geared at academic achievement per se nor measured by it.

Later

Progression models such as that developed by Martin Lackéus (2018) show competencies both as independent and as dependent variable (in other words, as having antecedents and outcomes). In both capacities, a theory of competency requires a theory of learning (Unger et al., 2011). Competencies should somehow translate into enduring better performance, so entrepreneurial individuals must learn how to apply a competency to a certain situation or problem relevant to the venture. As a dependent variable, competencies require a theory of learning because they need to be acquired and developed.

Education and experience do not necessarily directly translate into advanced competencies (Unger et al., 2011). Evaluations of entrepreneurship education programs have shown that it is possible to develop entrepreneurial competencies (see Chapter 16 in this volume), although more gain is achieved for participants who enter with a lower level of experience, efficacy, or entrepreneurial intention, that is, for those who have more room for improvement (Bae, Qian, Miao, & Fiet, 2014; Lyons & Zhang, 2018; Walter & Block, 2016). This finding potentially indicates a lack of (studies of) training programs for individuals who come in at a higher level of experience, efficacy, or entrepreneurial intention. Generally, success of a training method depends highly on the fit between the program's aims and methods and the participants' needs. As noted in the section on the types of competencies, there is a wide variety of entrepreneurial tasks, phases, types, and so forth. As such, it is imperative to have a training program that is aligned to the specific learning needs and contexts of the participants (Martin, McNally, & Kay, 2013). See Chapter 16 in this book for further discussion on entrepreneurship education and training.

Competencies for the Entrepreneur of the Future

A wave of technological developments is coming to fruition. Multiple concurrent developments in domains such as artificial intelligence/machine learning, genetic sequencing, blockchain, Internet of Things, geo-engineering, cloning, virtual reality, augmented reality, big data, driverless transport, robotics, 3D printing, drones, surveillance/sensors, nanotechnologies, and many more, will affect the conventional ways of working in any industry or market. Therefore, competencies related to learning, such as adaptability and flexibility, are likely to become even more important (Obschonka et al., 2017; Rosa, 2003; Savickas et al., 2009; Van Laar, Van Deursen, Van Dijk, & De Haan, 2017). In addition, meta-competencies, such as reflecting, further facilitate the development of other competencies (Lans et al., 2018). Initiatives such as Act21s and P21 (www.atc21s.org, www.p21.org), which aim to prepare education for the world of work of the future, stress that these competencies do not only pertain to one's actual job but to living in a fast-paced, fast-changing world more generally.

At the same time, the enterprising and entrepreneurial competencies that are relevant today are likely to continue to be so in the future. Just as today, the entrepreneur of the future will still need to be able to discover, create, and evaluate entrepreneurial opportunities, to find resources and mobilize stakeholders, and to organize an emerging venture. In terms of underlying enterprising competencies, the entrepreneur in 2030, just as today, will still need to be able to generate novel ideas, take action, persevere, persuade, network, and work in a team. The importance of enterprising skills is likely to increase because of the increase in the number of self-employed in the so-called gig economy (McKinsey & Company, 2016; World Economic Forum, 2018). Facilitated by online platforms and network-based forms of organizing, many of these freelance "entrepreneurs" may actually be more aptly described as workers looking for work. Yet they may increasingly depend on enterprising competencies, such as proactivity, adaptability, and alertness, to be successful (Uy, Chan, Sam, Ho, & Chernyshenko, 2015), especially in a "job scarce" economy in which more and more human functions are taken over by artificial intelligence (Brynjolfsson & McAfee, 2014; Tegmark, 2017; Wilkinson, 2016). An even more fundamental question concerns the extent to which competencies of the future entrepreneur can be augmented or even completely taken over by AI algorithms.

Conclusion

Scholars have made significant headway in the study of entrepreneurs' competencies, but there remains much work to be done. In doing such work, it is important to clearly distinguish competency and its components from their antecedents and outcomes. Throughout this chapter, research opportunities are identified. I briefly repeat them here. Although the generic competencies of entrepreneurs have been outlined by numerous studies, relatively little work has been done to specify the competencies by phase, sector, approach, time period, and type (aim, actor, mode) of entrepreneurship. In terms of outcome variables, research can examine dependent measures other than firm financial performance. In comparison to the knowledge and skill components of competency, the attitude component and the interrelations of the components (e.g., to what extent the components can substitute another) remain under-researched. Prior work on competencies tended to be directed at the individual, but more can be done to study competencies at the team level (e.g., relating aggregated team-level competency measures to firm performance). We also know little about the early development of entrepreneurial competencies. Enterprising competencies are increasingly seen as important, but future research should systematically evaluate their effects. Given accelerated technological development, the competencies of adaptability, flexibility, and reflection deserve particular attention.

Acknowledgment

I thank the book editors Michael M. Gielnik and Melissa S. Cardon, and Richard Martina of the Amsterdam University of Applied Sciences for their valuable comments.

References

Alvarez, S. A., Barney, J. B., & Anderson, P. (2013). Forming and exploiting opportunities: The implications of discovery and creation processes for entrepreneurial and organizational research. *Organization Science*, *24*(1), 301–317.

Åstebro, T., & Thompson, P. (2011). Entrepreneurs, jacks of all trades or hobos? *Research Policy*, *40*(5), 637–649.

Bacigalupo, M., Kampylis, P., Punie, Y., & Van den Brande, G. (2016). *EntreComp: The entrepreneurship competence framework*. Luxembourg: Publication Office of the European Union.

Bae, T. J., Qian, S., Miao, C., & Fiet, J. O. (2014). The relationship between entrepreneurship education and entrepreneurial intentions: A meta-analytic review. *Entrepreneurship Theory & Practice*, *38*(2), 217–254.

Baggen, Y., Kampen, J. K., Naia, A., Biemans, J. A., Lans, T., & Mulder, M. (2018). Development and application of the opportunity identification competence assessment test (OICAT) in higher education. *Innovations in Education and Teaching International*, *55*(6), 735–745.

Baron, R. A., & Markman, G. D. (2003). Beyond social capital: The role of entrepreneurs' social competence in their financial success. *Journal of Business Venturing, 18*(1), 41–60.

Bird, B. (1995). Towards a theory of entrepreneurial competency. *Advances in Entrepreneurship, Firm Emergence and Growth, 2*(1), 51–72.

Boyatzis, R. E. (1982). *The competent manager: A model for effective performance.* New York: John Wiley & Sons.

Boyatzis, R. E. (2008). Competencies in the 21st century. *Journal of Management Development, 27*(1), 5–12.

Brynjolfsson, E., & McAfee, A. (2014). *The second machine age: Work, progress, and prosperity in a time of brilliant technologies.* New York: W. W. Norton & Company.

Cacciotti, G., Hayton, J. C., Mitchell, R., & Giazitzoglu, A. (2016). A reconceptualization of fear of failure in entrepreneurship. *Journal of Business Venturing, 31*(3), 302–325.

Campbell, J. P., McCloy, R. A., Oppler, S. H., & Sager, C. E. (1993). A theory of performance. In N. Schmitt & W. C. Borman (Eds.), *Personnel selection in organizations* (pp. 35–70). San Francisco, CA: Jossey-Bass.

Chandler, G. N., & Jansen, E. (1992). The founder's self-assessed competence and venture performance. *Journal of Business Venturing, 7*(3), 223–236.

Chell, E. (2013). Review of skill and the entrepreneurial process. *International Journal of Entrepreneurial Behavior & Research, 19*(1), 6–31.

Chen, H. C., & Naquin, S. S. (2006). An integrative model of competency development, training design, assessment center, and multi-rater assessment. *Advances in Developing Human Resources, 8*(2), 265–282.

Churchill, N. C., & Lewis, V. L. (1983, May–June). The five stages of small business growth. *Harvard Business Review,* 30–50.

Clark, D. (2005). What does the "A" in KSA really mean? Retrieved from www.nwlink.com/~donclark/hrd/history/KSA.html, on March 20, 2019.

Cope, J. (2011). Entrepreneurial learning from failure: An interpretative phenomenological analysis. *Journal of Business Venturing, 26*(6), 604–623.

Dew, N. (2009). Serendipity in entrepreneurship. *Organization Studies, 30*(7), 735–753.

Draycott, M., & Rae, D. (2011). Enterprise education in schools and the role of competency frameworks. *International Journal of Entrepreneurial Behavior & Research, 17*(2), 127–145.

Fauchart, E., & Gruber, M. (2011). Darwinians, communitarians, and missionaries: The role of founder identity in entrepreneurship. *Academy of Management Journal, 54*(5), 935–957.

Gartner, W. B. (1988). "Who is an entrepreneur?" is the wrong question. *American Journal of Small Business, 12*(4), 11–32.

Gibb, A. A. (1993). The enterprise culture and education. *International Small Business Journal: Researching Entrepreneurship, 11*(3), 11–34.

Gilsing, V. (2020). From underperformer to worldclass. Book manuscript under review.

Görling, S., & Rehn, A. (2008). Accidental ventures - A materialist reading of opportunity and entrepreneurial potential. *Scandinavian Journal of Management, 24*(2), 94–102.

Greiner, L. (1972, July–August). Evolution and revolution as organizations grow. *Harvard Business Review,* 37–46.

Grzeda, M. M. (2005). In competence we trust? Addressing conceptual ambiguity. *Journal of Management Development, 24*(6), 530–545.

Hagan, C. M., Konopaske, R., Bernardin, H. J., & Tyler, C. L. (2006). Predicting assessment center performance with 360-degree, top-down, and customer-based competency assessments. *Human Resource Management, 45*(3), 357–390.

Hartog, J., Van Praag, M., & Van der Sluis, J. (2010). If you are so smart, why aren't you an entrepreneur? Returns to cognitive and social ability: Entrepreneurs versus employees. *Journal of Economics & Management Strategy, 19*(4), 947–989.

Hayton, J. C., & Kelley, D. J. (2006). A competency-based framework for promoting corporate entrepreneurship. *Human Resources Management, 45*(3), 407–427.

Hoffmann, T. (1999). The meanings of competency. *Journal of European Industrial Training, 23*(6), 275–286.

Hogan, J., & Holland, B. (2003). Using theory to evaluate personality and job-performance relations: A socioanalytic perspective. *Journal of Applied Psychology, 88*, 100–112.

Holland, J. L. (1973). *Making vocational choices: A theory of careers.* Englewood Cliffs, NJ: Prentice-Hall.

Johannisson, B. (2016). Limits to and prospects of entrepreneurship education in the academic context. *Entrepreneurship & Regional Development, 28*(5–6), 403–423.

Kuratko, D. F., & Morris, M. H. (2018). Corporate entrepreneurship: A critical challenge for educators and researchers. *Entrepreneurship Education & Pedagogy, 1*(1), 42–60.

Kutzhanova, N., Lyons, T. S., & Lichtenstein, G. A. (2009). Skill-based development of entrepreneurs and the role of personal and peer group coaching in enterprise development. *Economic Development Quarterly, 23*(3), 193–210.

Kyndt, E., & Baert, H. (2014). Entrepreneurial competencies: Assessment and predictive value for entrepreneurship. *Journal of Vocational Behavior, 90*, 13–25.

Lackéus, M. (2015). *Entrepreneurship in education: What, why, when, how.* Background Paper. Paris: OECD.

Lackéus, M. (2018, May). Classifying entrepreneurial education into five basic types through four questions grounded in definitions of entrepreneurship. Paper presented at *3E Conference*, University of Twente, Netherlands.

Lans, T., Baggen, Y., & Ploum, B. (2018). Towards more synergy in entrepreneurial competence research in entrepreneurship education. In A. Fayolle (Ed.), *A research agenda for entrepreneurship education.* Cheltenham, UK: Edward Elgar Publishing.

Lazear, E. P. (2005). Entrepreneurship. *Journal of Labor Economics, 23*(4), 649–680.

Lent, R. W., Brown, S. D., & Hackett, G. (2002). Social cognitive career theory. *Career Choice and Development, 4*, 255–311.

Lex, M., & Gielnik, M. M. (2017). Creativity and entrepreneurship: A process perspective. In G. Ahmetoglu, T. Chamorro-Premuzic, B. Klinger, & T. Karcisky (Eds.), *The Wiley handbook of entrepreneurship* (pp. 139–172). Hoboken, NJ: John Wiley & Sons.

Liu, C., & De Rond, M. (2016). Good night, and good luck: Perspectives on luck in management scholarship. *Academy of Management Annals, 10*(1), 409–451.

Lyons, E., & Zhang, L. (2018). Who does (not) benefit from entrepreneurship programs? *Strategic Management Journal, 39*(1), 85–112.

Man, T. W., Lau, T., & Chan, K. F. (2002). The competitiveness of small and medium enterprises: A conceptualization with focus on entrepreneurial competencies. *Journal of Business Venturing, 17*(2), 123–142.

Markman, G. D., & Baron, R. A. (2003). Person-entrepreneurship fit: Why some people are more successful as entrepreneurs than others. *Human Resource Management Review, 13*(2), 281–301.

Martin, B. C., McNally, J. J., & Kay, M. J. (2013). Examining the formation of human capital in entrepreneurship: A meta-analysis of entrepreneurship education outcomes. *Journal of Business Venturing, 28*(2), 211–224.

McKinsey & Company. (2016). *Independent work: Choice, necessity, and the gig economy*. San Francisco, CA: McKinsey Global Institute.

Mitchelmore, S., & Rowley, J. (2010). Entrepreneurial competencies: A literature review and development agenda. *International Journal of Entrepreneurial Behavior & Research, 16*(2), 92–111.

Morris, M. H., Webb, J. W., Fu, J., & Singhal, S. (2013). A competency-based perspective on entrepreneurship education: Conceptual and empirical insights. *Journal of Small Business Management, 51*(3), 352–369.

Neck, H. M., & Corbett, A. C. (2018). The scholarship of teaching and learning entrepreneurship. *Entrepreneurship Education & Pedagogy, 1*(1), 8–41.

Oberschachtsiek, D. (2012). The experience of the founder and self-employment duration: A comparative advantage approach. *Small Business Economics, 39*(1), 1–17.

Obschonka, M., Duckworth, K., Silbereisen, R. K., & Schoon, I. (2012). Social competencies in childhood and adolescence and entrepreneurship in young adulthood: A two-study analysis. *International Journal of Developmental Science, 6*, 137–150.

Obschonka, M., Hakkarainen, K., Lonka, K., & Salmela-Aro, K. (2017). Entrepreneurship as a twenty-first century skill: Entrepreneurial alertness and intention in the transition to adulthood. *Small Business Economics, 48*(3), 487–501.

Obschonka, M., Silbereisen, R. K., Schmitt-Rodermund, E., & Stuetzer, M. (2011). Nascent entrepreneurship and the developing individual: Early entrepreneurial competence in adolescence and venture creation success during the career. *Journal of Vocational Behavior, 79*(1), 121–133.

O'Connor, G. C., Corbett, A., & Pierantozzi, R. (2009). Create three distinct career paths for innovators. *Harvard Business Review, 14*, 78–83.

Onstenk, J. (2003). Entrepreneurship and vocational education. *European Educational Research Journal, 2*(1), 74–89.

Ploum, L., Blok, V., Lans, T., & Omta, O. (2019). Educating for self-interest or -transcendence? An empirical approach to investigating the role of moral competencies in opportunity recognition for sustainable development. *Business Ethics: A European Review, 28*(2), 243–260.

Prahalad, C. K., & Hamel, G. (1990). The core competence of the corporation. *Harvard Business Review, 68*(4), 79–91.

Rasmussen, E., Mosey, S., & Wright, M. (2011). The evolution of entrepreneurial competencies: A longitudinal study of university spin-off venture emergence. *Journal of Management Studies, 48*(6), 1314–1345.

Rosa, H. (2003). Social acceleration: Ethical and political consequences of a desynchronized high-speed society. *Constellations, 10*(1), 3–33.

Sarasvathy, S. D. (2001). Causation and effectuation: Toward a theoretical shift from economic inevitability to entrepreneurial contingency. *Academy of Management Review, 26*(2), 243–263.

Savickas, M. L., Nota, L., Rossier, J., Dauwalder, J. P., Duarte, M. E., Guichard, J., . . . Van Vianen, A. E. (2009). Life designing: A paradigm for career construction in the 21st century. *Journal of Vocational Behavior, 75*(3), 239–250.

Schmitt-Rodermund, E. (2004). Pathways to successful entrepreneurship: Parenting, personality, early entrepreneurial competence, and interests. *Journal of Vocational Behavior, 65*(3), 498–518.

Schoon, I., & Duckworth, K. (2012). Who becomes an entrepreneur? Early life experiences as predictors of entrepreneurship. *Developmental Psychology, 48*(6), 1719–1726.

Spencer, L., & Spencer, S. (1993). *Competence at: Model for superior performance*. New York: John Wiley & Sons.

Stuetzer, M., Obschonka, M., Davidsson, P., & Schmitt-Rodermund, E. (2013). Where do entrepreneurial skills come from? *Applied Economics Letters, 20*(12), 1183–1186.

Stuetzer, M., Obschonka, M., & Schmitt-Rodermund, E. (2013). Balanced skills among Nascent entrepreneurs. *Small Business Economics, 41*(1), 93–114.

Teece, D. J., Pisano, G., & Shuen, A. (1997). Dynamic capabilities and strategic management. *Strategic Management Journal, 18*(7), 509–533.

Tegmark, M. (2017). *Life 3.0: Being human in the age of artificial intelligence*. New York: Knopf.

Unger, J. M., Rauch, A., Frese, M., & Rosenbusch, N. (2011). Human capital and entrepreneurial success: A meta-analytical review. *Journal of Business Venturing, 26*(3), 341–358.

Uy, M. A., Chan, K. Y., Sam, Y. L., Ho, M. H. R., & Chernyshenko, O. S. (2015). Proactivity, adaptability and boundaryless career attitudes: The mediating role of entrepreneurial alertness. *Journal of Vocational Behavior, 86*, 115–123.

Van Gelderen, M. W. (2020). Using a comfort zone model and daily life situations to develop enterprising competencies. Manuscript under review.

Van Gelderen, M. W., Shirokova, G., Shchegolev, V., & Beliaeva, T. (2020). Striving for entrepreneurial autonomy: A comparison of Russia and the Netherlands. *Management and Organizational Review, 16*(1), 107–138.

Van Laar, E., Van Deursen, A. J., Van Dijk, J. A., & De Haan, J. (2017). The relation between 21st-century skills and digital skills: A systematic literature review. *Computers in Human Behavior, 72*, 577–588.

Vogel, T., & Wanke, M. (2016). *Attitudes and attitude change*. New York: Psychology Press.

Volery, T., Mueller, S., & von Siemens, B. (2015). Entrepreneur ambidexterity: A study of entrepreneur behaviours and competencies in growth-oriented small and medium-sized enterprises. *International Small Business Journal: Researching Entrepreneurship, 33*(2), 109–129.

Wagner, J. (2006). Are nascent entrepreneurs "jacks-of-all-trades"? A test of Lazear's theory of entrepreneurship with German data. *Applied Economics, 38*(20), 2415–2419.

Walter, S. G., & Block, J. H. (2016). Outcomes of entrepreneurship education: An institutional perspective. *Journal of Business Venturing, 31*(2), 216–233.

Weiblen, T., & Chesbrough, H. W. (2015). Engaging with startups to enhance corporate innovation. *California Management Review, 57*(2), 66–90.

Wilkinson, A. (2016). Using strategic foresight methods to anticipate and prepare for the jobs-scarce economy. *European Journal of Futures Research, 4*(1), 6–12.

World Economic Forum. (2018). *The future of jobs report 2018*. Retrieved from http://www3.weforum.org/docs/WEF_Future_of_Jobs_2018.pdf, on October 8, 2020.

13

A PSYCHOLOGICAL PERSPECTIVE ON RAISING START-UP CAPITAL

Pitching in the Modern Era

Chaim Letwin, Regan Stevenson & Michael P. Ciuchta

Attempts to understand how psychology underpins new venture funding has long been part of the literature on entrepreneurship (Baron & Markman, 2000; Shepherd, 1999). However, technological, social, and legal shifts have altered the ways in which entrepreneurs solicit and secure investment capital (Bruton, Khavul, Siegel, & Wright, 2015). Such changes have also led to the development of new investment vehicles, such as crowdfunding (Ahlers, Cumming, Günther, & Schweizer, 2015; Stevenson, Ciuchta, Letwin, Dinger, & Vancouver, 2019) and distributed ledger technologies (Chen, 2018). These new modes of funding have the potential to fundamentally transform traditional models of capital acquisition over the next decade (Drover et al., 2017).

This chapter provides a brief overview of the most significant recent developments in the venture fundraising landscape, including a discussion of how novel forms of venture funding, particularly crowdfunding, have the potential to alter our understanding of how entrepreneurs raise capital. To organize the review, studies are categorized by theoretical perspective along the broad classification of *theories of persuasion* and *theories of perception*. The way in which these theories have been applied to the capital acquisition process via new funding vehicles is subsequently explored. Where appropriate, how these theories have been applied in traditional funding settings is also discussed (e.g., angel investing). Finally, future research opportunities for scholars interested in the psychological antecedents of raising start-up capital are highlighted.

Recent Developments in the Fundraising Landscape

A key reason for the rapid growth of new venture funding over the past decade is that it has provided access to entrepreneurs and backers who were previously not engaged in the capital acquisition landscape (Mollick & Robb, 2016). This is largely due to the creation of new funding vehicles and an increasingly more diverse spectrum of potential funders. Perhaps most notable is the introduction and mass acceptance of crowd-based funding vehicles.

Prior to investigating this new funding vehicle, it is important to briefly discuss traditional forms of capital. In doing so, we primarily focus on the mechanisms employed in the developed world; therefore, the discussion does not cover finance mechanisms for the bottom of the pyramid in the developing world (Morduch, 1999). However, this distinction is becoming blurred as scholars increasingly use microfinance crowdfunding sites, such as Kiva, in their research (Allison, Davis, Short, & Webb, 2015; Moss, Neubaum, & Meyskens, 2015). Capital investment typically comes in the form of self-funding, debt, and equity. Research has suggested that, due to information asymmetry, a hierarchy of external financing exists, where self-funding is the most preferred followed by debt and then equity (Myers, 1984). Although entrepreneurs often use their personal funds to bootstrap their ventures (Bhide, 1992), self-funding may not be possible for many entrepreneurs. Bootstrapping differs from crowdfunding in that bootstrapping entrepreneurs tend to search only for the funds that they need to overcome immediate financial constraints (Horváth, 2018), whereas crowdfunding entrepreneurs make public appeals for funding that is often used to catapult their ventures beyond their immediate needs. In addition, bootstrapping entrepreneurs typically do not make public appeals for funds; rather, they focus on close relationships and direct personal selling (Bhide, 1992). Furthermore, bootstrapping can limit the speed of and size to which a company can grow (Alhosaini & Abduldaiem, 2016). Debt is a viable alternative for many organizations; however, entrepreneurs frequently must pledge their personal assets to secure a loan (Robb & Robinson, 2014). Traditionally, equity funding comes in the form of angel and venture capital (VC). This type of capital is accompanied by expertise within specific industries in exchange for partial ownership in the venture. Angel rounds typically range upwards of US$750,000, although most individual angels tend to make investments between US$15,000 and US$37,500 (Huang et al., 2017). VC investments are typically larger and can reach up to approximately US$10 million for early-stage deals (Rowley, 2019). Historically, both types of funding have been highly focused on certain geographic regions and toward specific types of entrepreneurs. For instance, recent estimates in the United States show that Massachusetts, California, and New York account for nearly 60% of the VC market, while 29 other states account for less than 5% (Stevenson, Kuratko, & Eutsler, 2019). Furthermore, research shows that women and minorities are much less likely to receive these traditional forms of equity (Kanze, Huang, Conley, & Higgins, 2018).

Crowdfunding is quickly emerging as a viable alternative to traditional funding vehicles. It has been defined as open-sourced fundraising that draws "on relatively small contributions from a relatively large number of individuals using the internet without standard financial intermediaries" (Mollick, 2014, p. 2). There are four general forms of crowdfunding: gift, debt, reward, and equity. Since its emergence about 10 years ago, crowdfunding has exploded in size, with estimates of annual funds raised to be greater than US$34 billion and projections expected to exceed US$300 billion by 2025 (Ma & Liu, 2017; Meyskens & Bird, 2015). These projections are expected to rival if not exceed venture capital and, therefore, drastically change the way entrepreneurs raise capital.

It has been noted that crowdfunding has democratized the landscape of capital acquisition (Stevenson, Kuratko, et al., 2019). This is exemplified by the demographic differences between crowdfunders and traditional venture investors. For instance, approximately 40% of crowdfunders are women, whereas women only make up a quarter of angels and far less venture capitalists (Mollick & Robb, 2016). Furthermore, over 50% of all crowdfunders are younger than the age of 35, whereas the average angel investor is 50 years old (Macht & Weatherston, 2014). Finally, most crowdfunders have significantly less financial and investment experience. Beyond demographical differences, the types of projects funded through crowdfunding also differ from those in traditional capital markets and can be different in terms of product/project type, industry, geographic centrality, and the amount of dollars being raised (Stevenson, Ciuchta, et al., 2019). VC and angel pitches are often face-to-face and in real time, whereas crowdfunding campaigns are conducted through a technological medium, primarily with previously created content (e.g., a video describing the campaign). Furthermore, the ability to understand the information being presented and the motivation to do so may be less in a crowdfunding context, in which investors are not experts and have less money at risk compared with angel investors or venture capitalists.

These significant demographic and structural differences can lead entrepreneurs to adopt different strategies to acquire capital through crowdfunding. As a result, academics have had to consider new and adapt old theoretical perspectives to study how entrepreneurs seek capital and how funders perceive these opportunities.

Theories of Persuasion

The following discussion begins with an explanation of how theories of persuasion have been applied to the resource acquisition process. Here, "persuasion" refers to situations in which entrepreneurs attempt to exert influence over funders with the objective of influencing a funder's opportunity perceptions (i.e., what entrepreneurs do to persuade investors to invest). Theories that we consider include signaling theory (Spence, 1973), impression management theory (Schlenker, 1980), the elaboration likelihood model of persuasion (Petty & Cacioppo, 1986), and entrepreneurial passion (Cardon, Wincent, Singh, & Drnovsek, 2009).

Signaling Theory

Signaling theory (Spence, 1973) is a prominent perspective within the area of entrepreneurial finance. More recently, entrepreneurship and management scholars have broadened the way in which the theory is applied to their unique contexts.[1] Generally, this theory is now invoked when information asymmetries are present between the entrepreneur and the funder, and the entrepreneur must "signal" something to the funder that conveys information about an attribute that is only known or observed by the entrepreneur (Baum & Silverman, 2004; Elitzur & Gavious, 2003). Some prior work has emphasized the types of signals used to convey venture quality and their impact on venture success (Ahlers et al., 2015; Busenitz, Fiet, & Moesel, 2005; Kirsch, Goldfarb, & Gera, 2009).

Some researchers have begun to explore the nuances associated with the signaling process. For example, Clarke and colleagues (2019) demonstrated how mental imagery mediates the effects of gesturing on investors' propensity to invest. Other authors have also examined the boundary conditions in the signaling process. For example, Scheaf and colleagues (2018) distinguished between signals and visual cues. Signals are costly and convey information about underlying quality (e.g., patents), whereas visual cues are low-cost and sensory appealing features that are common on crowdfunding platforms (e.g., eye-catching video transitions). These authors have demonstrated how signals and visual cues interact. Other research on signaling demonstrated that signals are not noticed unless they are combined with other external validations that enhance their value (Plummer, Allison, & Connelly, 2016). Plummer and colleagues (2016) argue that entrepreneurs should align themselves with reliable third parties to increase the efficacy of the quality signals sent to potential investors.

Aside from the signals themselves, research has also explored the influence of certain receiver characteristics on signal viability. For example, the type of signal relied on depends on the receiver's motivation and ability (Allison et al., 2017) or the funding context in which the signal is sent (Anglin et al., 2018). Similarly, signals can also depend on the gender of the entrepreneur. Alsos and Ljunggren (2017) found that the nature of signals conveyed varied by gender and that gender also affected the way the signals were perceived by equity investors. For example, investors appeared to dwell heavily on female entrepreneurs' lack of start-up experience but did not subject their male counterparts to the same level of scrutiny. Eddleston and colleagues (2016) found similar results, noting specifically that positive signals related to venture quality (such as number of employees) were more influential for male entrepreneurs than they were for female entrepreneurs in obtaining bank funding.

In sum, traditional signaling theory research based on economic modeling tends to downplay the importance of text, visual cues, and non-costly signals. In contrast, management researchers have argued that such factors are important, particularly in lower stakes crowdfunding environments. This apparent disconnect and the mixed results noted by these two camps are worthy of further scholarly attention (Steigenberger & Wilhelm, 2018).

Impression Management

Unlike signaling theory, which tends to treat underlying characteristics as given and emphasizes the need for simple communication to the funder, in impression management, entrepreneurs' actions are more strategic in nature. Impression management is a process through which people seek to influence the image others have of them to attain a specific goal (Bolino, 1999). Individuals can employ various tactics to achieve this goal (Mohamed, Gardner, & Paolillo, 1999). Parhankangas and Ehrlich (2014) examined the impact of impression management tactics (such as organizational promotion—presenting the organization in a favorable light) on entrepreneurs' advancement within the application process of an angel group by considering application documents. They found that many of these tactics had curvilinear effects. Nagy and colleagues (2012) found that impression management behaviors of self-promotion, exemplification, and ingratiation increased the cognitive legitimacy of the venture as perceived by potential investors. Most impression management tactics emphasize either the historical or current aspects of the venture. However, in one noteworthy study, Van Balen and colleagues (2019) considered the impact of communicating disruptive visions (defined as the thematic content of vision communication that articulates an intention to disrupt organizations, markets, and ecosystems) on securing early-round funding. They found that more disruptive visions presented in the companies' vision statements increased the chances of obtaining early-round funding, but that the amounts raised were less. One potential reason for this contrasting effect could be that early investors are intrigued by more disruptive visions but at the same time, based on an options mindset, were willing to put smaller bets on them. As this brief review indicates, much of the existing research is situated within traditional funding contexts. Further research on impression management theory in a crowdfunding context would present a meaningful contribution to this body of knowledge.

The Elaboration Likelihood Model of Persuasion

The elaboration likelihood model of persuasion (Petty & Cacioppo, 1986) is a general theory of attitude change resulting from persuasive communications. The elaboration likelihood model suggests there are two distinct routes to persuasion. In the first type (the central route), a person is persuaded by his or her careful and thoughtful consideration of the true merits of the information presented. In the second type (the peripheral route), a person is persuaded by cues presented in the information that generally do not reflect the underlying merits of the issue-relevant information being presented. Elaboration refers to an internal cognitive process by the person being persuaded in which he or she scrutinizes issue-relevant information contained in the communication (Petty & Cacioppo, 1986). When evaluators have the motivation and ability to engage in issue-relevant thinking, elaboration likelihood is said to be high.

The elaboration likelihood model, which has been widely adopted in the marketing literature, has recently been used as a perspective in crowdfunding contexts. Allison and colleagues (2017) examined the impact of both issue-relevant and peripheral cues in crowdfunding campaigns and found that both entrepreneur-specific and product-specific issue-relevant information enhanced crowdfunding performance, as did the presence of peripheral cues, such as "portraying the venture as a personal dream" (Allison et al., 2017, p. 40). Some of these effects were conditional on the funder's ability and motivation to carefully evaluate ventures.

Li and colleagues (2017) conducted a series of studies to examine the processes underlying the persuasiveness of particular cues in a crowdfunding context. The authors reasoned that because crowdfunders are primarily amateur investors with little money at stake, they tend to have both low ability and motivation. As such, they pay considerable attention to peripheral cues. The authors suggested that an entrepreneur's display of passion in a video pitch is an example of such a cue, in that it leads to low-stakes engagement by the backer through a process of passion contagion. The authors found that displayed passion in a video substantially increased funders' enthusiasm for the project, which subsequently made them more willing to contribute funds and share the campaign on social media.

Entrepreneurial Passion

Entrepreneurial passion is generally defined as intense positive feelings that result from performing activities related to roles that are meaningful to an entrepreneur's self-identity (Cardon et al., 2009). Research indicated that displays of passion can be valuable as a means of persuasion (Chen, Yao, & Kotha, 2009). In the past 10 years, passion research related to resource acquisition has primarily focused on affective displays of passion and has found that passion tends to positively influence investors through its contagious nature.

Displays of passion have been shown to be valuable in traditional funding contexts; however, they may be particularly important in crowdfunding, where investors have less motivation and a generally lower ability to consider more complex information (Li, Chen, Kotha, & Fisher, 2017; Mitteness, Sudek, & Cardon, 2012). Crowdfunding research has found displays of passion to positively influence investment. Previously mentioned findings strongly suggest that the contagious nature of passion continues to work in a computer-mediated setting. More specifically, displayed passion has been shown to strengthen the positive influence that a product's creativity has on crowdfunders' affective reactions to a crowdfunding campaign and, in turn, their willingness to fund (Davis, Hmieleski, Webb, & Coombs, 2017). In an even more direct test of the contagious nature of displayed passion, Li and colleagues (2017) found that displays of passion positively influenced the enthusiasm experienced by crowdfunders and in turn the amount that they invested in a campaign and their willingness to tell others about the project. Crowdfunding research has also investigated the type of entrepreneurs who are likely to be viewed as passionate. For example, Oo and colleagues (2019) found that user entrepreneurs (i.e., entrepreneurs who create products to solve their own needs) were more likely to be viewed as passionate and because of this were more likely to be funded.

Theories of Perception

With regard to theories of perception, we focus on theories that have been used to explain why funders react differently to cues provided by different entrepreneurs, their pitches, and their businesses (i.e., how the specific qualities of investors impact their investment decisions). In line with prior research, here, the focus is on theories that consider the psychological underpinnings behind funders' reactions and how they relate to resource acquisition. Current research questions emphasize the factors that impact funder perceptions, with a particular focus on how these perceptions can vary under novel funding contexts. Theories that we consider are regulatory fit theory (Ciuchta, Letwin, Stevenson, & McMahon, 2016), control theory (Stevenson, Ciuchta, et al., 2019), and theories that have a focus on gender, including activist choice homophily (Greenberg & Mollick, 2017) and stereotype content theory (Johnson, Stevenson, & Letwin, 2018).

Regulatory Fit Theory

Regulatory fit theory (Higgins, 2000) explains the action tendencies that occur when a person's regulatory orientation (i.e., their promotion or prevention-focused orientation) matches the contextual framing in which they operate. Promotion-focused individuals experience fit when they are in contexts that emphasize gains, whereas prevention-focused individuals experience fit in contexts that emphasize losses. These regulatory orientations can manifest as traits or states (Zhang, Higgins, & Chen, 2011). Individuals who experience regulatory fit have been shown to feel more enjoyment while pursuing goals (Freitas & Higgins, 2002), which is commonly referred to as the *feeling-right effect* in the regulatory fit literature. Feeling right has previously been demonstrated to enhance engagement, action, and motivation (Cesario, Grant, & Higgins, 2004; Cesario, Higgins, & Scholer, 2008).

Given its parsimony at explaining perception and engagement in response to messaging (Higgins, 2005; Lee & Aaker, 2004), it is surprising that regulatory fit theory has not been used more extensively in the venture fundraising literature. One exception to this is recent research from Ciuchta and colleagues (2016), who used a three-study experimental design with a mock crowdfunding portal to examine funding through a self-regulatory lens. Their findings revealed that participants' willingness to invest was contingent on the interaction between an individual regulatory focus and the social "crowd" context of funding decisions. That is when individual promotion or prevention orientation "matched" that of the crowd, the individual was more likely to follow the crowd and invest. Murnieks and colleagues (2011) investigated the similarity between investors and entrepreneurs based on their decision-making processes, and their findings revealed that similarity moderates the relative importance of other deal attributes as reflected in the venture capitalists' evaluations, and they called for future research to extend their findings by specifically drawing on regulatory fit theory (Higgins, 2000).

Other work in this area has shown a tendency to draw more explicitly on regulatory focus logic rather than fit logic. For example, drawing on regulatory focus theory, Kanze and colleagues (2018) proposed that the regulatory focus of investor questions and entrepreneur responses results in divergent funding outcomes for pitching entrepreneurs, particularly across gender lines. In interactive pitch settings, these authors demonstrated that male entrepreneurs tended to be asked promotion-focused questions, whereas female entrepreneurs tended to be asked prevention-focused questions, and that such questions had a major impact on funding outcomes. In related work, Franić and Drnovšek (2019) demonstrated that promotion-focus increased the likelihood of positively evaluating an investment opportunity, while prevention-focus decreased positive evaluations. They called for further research applying regulatory-fit extensions in this context. Additional opportunities for future research include an examination of the source and emotional mechanisms that induce feeling right in investors.

Control Theory

Another theory that shows promise in explaining the link between individual perceptions and investment decisions is control theory. Control theory explains how individual effort and task performance is influenced by domain-specific self-efficacy and environmental feedback perceived by individuals engaged in decision-making tasks (Schmidt & DeShon, 2009; Vancouver, Thompson, Tischner, & Putka, 2002). This theory suggests that as self-efficacy increases, actors are likely to put forth less effort on a variety of tasks (Vancouver & Kendall, 2006). Stevenson and colleagues (2019a) used control theory and a series of experiments to explain why equity crowdfunders with a high-degree of domain-specific self-efficacy were less likely to perform well when making an investment decision. These authors established that investor search effort mediates the negative relationship between self-efficacy and investment decision-making performance. That is, they found that entrepreneurs with high self-efficacy were less likely to put in the necessary search effort and in turn did not perform as well in making investment decisions. In addition, this research also demonstrated that self-efficacy increases crowd bias—*an individual's tendency to follow the opinions of the crowd despite the presence of contrary objective quality indicators.* Future research rooted in control theory should consider these decision models in other venture investment settings (e.g., VC).

Theories Focusing on Gender

As discussed in the introduction, new capital funding vehicles have democratized the funding landscape. A major effect of this democratization is the increase in female entrepreneurs and funders. Recent research has applied multiple theo-retical perspectives to explore how gender influences funder perceptions in the current funding landscape. These theories include expectation states theory, ste-reotype theories, and activist choice homophily.

Recent research has shown that women are at a disadvantage when rais-ing capital from traditional sources such as VC (Kanze et al., 2018; Malmström, Johansson, & Wincent, 2017) and initial public offering (IPO; Bigelow, Lundmark, McLean Parks, & Wuebker, 2014). In VC, Malmström and colleagues (2017) drew on gender-role congruity theory (Eagly & Karau, 2002) and presented a com-prehensive framework of the gender stereotypes held by venture capitalists. They showed that women received a smaller percentage of their funding request and secured less capital. To explain these findings, they theorized that venture capital-ists tended to favor men over women because they viewed the ideal characteris-tics of an entrepreneur as masculine. In an IPO setting, Bigelow and colleagues (2014) drew on expectation states theory and theories of stereotyping to show that female CEOs were viewed less positively than male CEOs and that their IPO was seen to be less attractive as a result.

Despite these unfortunate findings in VC and IPO settings for women entre-preneurs, more recent research in the crowdfunding setting provides an alternative and more uplifting view. In reward-based crowdfunding, stereotyping theories have been used to explain why women are not necessarily at a disadvantage and can indeed benefit from their gender. Specifically, Johnson and colleagues (2018) utilized the stereotype content model to show that women were viewed as more trustworthy than men that, in turn, made them more likely to be funded. They also found this relationship to be strengthened by the specific crowdfunder's level of implicit gender bias. In explaining why gender yielded different results in the crowdfunding context, the authors noted that trustworthiness was particularly important in crowdfunding due to extreme levels of uncertainty. Greenberg and Mollick (2017) also found women to be more successful in a crowdfunding con-text. They based their findings on activist choice homophily, which suggests that women funders disproportionally support other women entrepreneurs because they view them as disadvantaged. Their findings suggested that activist choice homophily may be of particular benefit to women in a crowdfunding context because a larger percentage of women participate in crowdfunding than in other types of traditional venture financing.

Conclusion and Future Research Directions

This chapter provided a brief overview of the psychological theories that have been used to explore new venture fundraising in recent years with a particular focus on crowdfunding. This overview is not inclusive of all approaches that have been used to date; rather, for simplicity, several impactful theories were identi-fied and were subsequently classified into theories of persuasion or theories of perception. It must be noted that venture fundraising is a dynamic and complex process, and no single perspective or approach is capable of explaining every aspect of the story. Thus, our major calls for future research—which are described in the following—center on theoretical, observational, and methodological integration.

We see three major opportunities for researchers: First, to provide a more comprehensive assessment of the dynamics of venture funding, scholars must juxtapose theoretical perspectives. In particular, we advocate integrating theories of persuasion with theories of perception. Some work has been initiated on this front; for example, Cholakova and Clarysse (2015) integrated self-determination theory with cognitive evaluation theory to assess the extent to which financial and nonfinancial motivations influence equity and rewards-based crowdfunding decisions. Others suggest a juxtaposition between perceptive control theory and persuasive theories of creativity (Stevenson, Ciuchta, et al., 2019). We believe that there are many opportunities for researchers to continue to integrate persuasion and perception perspectives in dynamic and comprehensive models.

Second, our review of the literature revealed that, at present, most of the research that considers the psychological antecedents of venture funding adopts the view of investors. There is good reason for this; the investor is a critical agent in funding transactions. Indeed, the literature is rich in accounts of investor decision criteria, processes, and biases (see Stevenson, Josefy, McMullen, & Shepherd, 2020, for a review of investor decision-making experiments). However, before equity investments occur, entrepreneurs must first decide to pursue funding. Investment transactions are a two-way relationship and entrepreneurs must rely on their own judgments when they decide to transact with discrete types of investors. While some research has suggested that entrepreneurs self-select into the fundraising setting, there is a need for further research on entrepreneurs' perspective to identify the factors that entrepreneurs consider when deciding which types of funding vehicles to pursue. Indeed, in today's evolving private funding environment, entrepreneurs can choose to pursue vastly different types of funding from different types of investors. What factors lead some entrepreneurs to favor equity crowdfunding over angel investment and vice versa? Does experience with one mode of funding influence funding choices for subsequent rounds? Do the new funding options (e.g., crowdfunding) influence what entrepreneurs seek from traditional funding options (e.g., angel capital). Why do some entrepreneurs seek crowdfunding while others prefer to bootstrap? Future work that considers an entrepreneur's unique role in the funding process would complement and extend our understanding of the psychological factors that influence venture fundraising.

Third, methodological scholars have an opportunity to strengthen claims related to internal and external validity by combining methodological approaches. Diverse methods, such as field studies, experiments, and qualitative research, could be combined to unpack difficult-to-observe complexities in the entrepreneurial context. Combining such methods would allow researchers to focus on internal validity and external validity simultaneously (Stevenson & Josefy, 2019).

Moreover, combining methods "can facilitate the identification (and triangulation) of ties between and across levels, such as organizations, unorganized collective groups, individuals, or teams" (Williams & Shepherd, 2017, p. 3). Future research in the domain of venture funding should consider adopting a mixed methodological approach following prior work that has effectively deployed this approach (Chen et al., 2009; Kanze et al., 2018). For instance, with the increased emergence of computer-aided text analysis, researchers can now complement experimental designs and survey-based research with real-world archival data that comes directly from entrepreneurs (spoken and written) and actual entrepreneurial outcomes (e.g., funding, acquisition, survival). Combining this approach with experimentation (particularly developing techniques involving biosensors and functional magnetic resonance imaging) or qualitative work has the potential to increase confidence in both external and internal validity simultaneously.

Note

1. Signaling theory is distinct from signal detection theory (SDT), which has a longer history in psychological science (Green & Swets, 1966). Signal detection theory is a framework for understanding the accuracy of decision processes, particularly the ability to detect a true signal from noise (MacMillan, 2002). Its applicability to entrepreneurship seems limited and to our knowledge, it has not been used in this context.

References

Ahlers, G. K. C., Cumming, D., Günther, C., & Schweizer, D. (2015). Signaling in equity crowdfunding. *Entrepreneurship Theory and Practice*, *39*(4), 955–980. Retrieved from https://doi.org/10.1111/etap.12157

Alhosaini, M. R., & Abduldaiem, A. (2016). *Effects of external funding on the work environment of self-funded firms*. Sweden: Jönköping University. Retrieved from http://urn.kb.se/resolve?urn=urn:nbn:se:hj:diva-30711

Allison, T. H., Davis, B. C., Short, J. C., & Webb, J. W. (2015). Crowdfunding in a prosocial microlending environment: Examining the role of intrinsic versus extrinsic cues. *Entrepreneurship Theory and Practice*, *39*(1), 53–73. Retrieved from https://doi.org/10.1111/etap.12108

Allison, T. H., Davis, B. C., Webb, J. W., & Short, J. C. (2017). Persuasion in crowdfunding: An elaboration likelihood model of crowdfunding performance. *Journal of Business Venturing*, *32*(6), 707–725. Retrieved from https://doi.org/10.1016/j.jbusvent.2017.09.002

Alsos, G. A., & Ljunggren, E. (2017). The role of gender in entrepreneur-investor relationships: A signaling theory approach. *Entrepreneurship Theory and Practice*, *41*(4), 567–590. Retrieved from https://doi.org/10.1111/etp.12226

Anglin, A. H., Short, J. C., Drover, W., Stevenson, R. M., McKenny, A. F., & Allison, T. H. (2018). The power of positivity? The influence of positive psychological capital language on crowdfunding performance. *Journal of Business Venturing*, *33*(4), 470–492. Retrieved from https://doi.org/10.1016/j.jbusvent.2018.03.003

Baron, R. A., & Markman, G. D. (2000). Beyond social capital: How social skills can enhance entrepreneurs' success. *Academy of Management Perspectives*, *14*(1), 106–116. Retrieved from https://doi.org/10.5465/ame.2000.2909843

Baum, J. A. C., & Silverman, B. S. (2004). Picking winners or building them? Alliance, intellectual, and human capital as selection criteria in venture financing and performance of biotechnology startups. *Journal of Business Venturing, 19*(3), 411–436. Retrieved from https://doi.org/10.1016/S0883-9026(03)00038-7

Bhide, A. (1992). Bootstrap finance: The art of start-ups. *Harvard Business Review, 70*(6), 109–117.

Bigelow, L., Lundmark, L., McLean Parks, J., & Wuebker, R. (2014). Skirting the issues: Experimental evidence of gender bias in IPO prospectus evaluations. *Journal of Management, 40*(6), 1732–1759. Retrieved from https://doi.org/10.1177/0149206312441624

Bolino, M. C. (1999). Citizenship and impression management: Good soldiers or good actors? *Academy of Management Review, 24*(1), 82–98. Retrieved from https://doi.org/10.5465/amr.1999.1580442

Bruton, G., Khavul, S., Siegel, D., & Wright, M. (2015). New financial alternatives in seeding entrepreneurship: Microfinance, crowdfunding, and peer-to-peer innovations. *Entrepreneurship Theory and Practice, 39*(1), 9–26. Retrieved from https://doi.org/10.1111/etap.12143

Busenitz, L. W., Fiet, J. O., & Moesel, D. D. (2005). Signaling in venture capitalist–New venture team funding decisions: Does it indicate long-term venture outcomes? *Entrepreneurship Theory and Practice, 29*(1), 1–12. Retrieved from https://doi.org/10.1111/j.1540-6520.2005.00066.x

Cardon, M. S., Wincent, J., Singh, J., & Drnovsek, M. (2009). The nature and experience of entrepreneurial passion. *Academy of Management Review, 34*(3), 511–532. Retrieved from https://doi.org/10.5465/amr.2009.40633190

Cesario, J., Grant, H., & Higgins, E. T. (2004). Regulatory fit and persuasion: Transfer from "feeling right". *Journal of Personality and Social Psychology, 86*(3), 388–404. Retrieved from https://doi.org/10.1037/0022-3514.86.3.388

Cesario, J., Higgins, E. T., & Scholer, A. A. (2008). Regulatory fit and persuasion: Basic principles and remaining questions. *Social and Personality Psychology Compass, 2*(1), 444–463. Retrieved from https://doi.org/10.1111/j.1751-9004.2007.00055.x

Chen, X.-P., Yao, X., & Kotha, S. (2009). Entrepreneur passion and preparedness in business plan presentations: A persuasion analysis of venture capitalists' funding decisions. *Academy of Management Journal, 52*(1), 199–214. Retrieved from https://doi.org/10.5465/amj.2009.36462018

Chen, Y. (2018). Blockchain tokens and the potential democratization of entrepreneurship and innovation. *Business Horizons, 61*(4), 567–575. Retrieved from https://doi.org/10.1016/j.bushor.2018.03.006

Cholakova, M., & Clarysse, B. (2015). Does the possibility to make equity investments in crowdfunding projects crowd out reward-based investments? *Entrepreneurship Theory and Practice, 39*(1), 145–172. Retrieved from https://doi.org/10.1111/etap.12139

Ciuchta, M. P., Letwin, C., Stevenson, R. M., & McMahon, S. R. (2016). Regulatory focus and information cues in a crowdfunding context. *Applied Psychology, 65*(3), 490–514. Retrieved from https://doi.org/10.1111/apps.12063

Clarke, J. S., Cornelissen, J. P., & Healey, M. P. (2019). Actions speak louder than words: How figurative language and gesturing in entrepreneurial pitches influences investment judgments. *Academy of Management Journal, 62*(2), 335–360. Retrieved from https://doi.org/10.5465/amj.2016.1008

Davis, B. C., Hmieleski, K. M., Webb, J. W., & Coombs, J. E. (2017). Funders' positive affective reactions to entrepreneurs' crowdfunding pitches: The influence of perceived product creativity and entrepreneurial passion. *Journal of Business Venturing, 32*(1), 90–106. Retrieved from https://doi.org/10.1016/j.jbusvent.2016.10.006

Drover, W., Busenitz, L., Matusik, S., Townsend, D., Anglin, A., & Dushnitsky, G. (2017). A review and road map of entrepreneurial equity financing research: Venture capital, corporate venture capital, angel investment, crowdfunding, and accelerators. *Journal of Management, 43*(6), 1820–1853. Retrieved from https://doi.org/10.1177/0149206317690584

Eagly, A. H., & Karau, S. J. (2002). Role congruity theory of prejudice toward female leaders. *Psychological Review, 109*(3), 573–598. Retrieved from https://doi.org/10.1037/0033-295X.109.3.573

Eddleston, K. A., Ladge, J. J., Mitteness, C., & Balachandra, L. (2016). Do you see what I see? Signaling effects of gender and firm characteristics on financing entrepreneurial ventures. *Entrepreneurship Theory and Practice, 40*(3), 489–514. Retrieved from https://doi.org/10.1111/etap.12117

Elitzur, R., & Gavious, A. (2003). Contracting, signaling, and moral hazard: A model of entrepreneurs, "angels," and venture capitalists. *Journal of Business Venturing, 18*(6), 709–725. Retrieved from https://doi.org/10.1016/S0883-9026(03)00027-2

Franić, S., & Drnovšek, M. (2019). The role of regulatory focus and cognitive style in business angels' evaluation of an investment opportunity. *Venture Capital, 21*(4), 353–377. Retrieved from https://doi.org/10.1080/13691066.2019.1599191

Freitas, A. L., & Higgins, E. T. (2002). Enjoying goal-directed action: The role of regulatory fit. *Psychological Science, 13*(1), 1–6. Retrieved from https://doi.org/10.1111/1467-9280.00401

Green, D. M., & Swets, J. A. (1966). *Signal detection theory and psychophysics* (Vol. 1). New York: John Wiley & Sons. Retrieved from https://doi.org/10.1016/0022-460x(67)90197-6

Greenberg, J., & Mollick, E. (2017). Activist choice homophily and the crowdfunding of female founders. *Administrative Science Quarterly, 62*(2), 341–374. Retrieved from https://doi.org/10.1177/0001839216678847

Higgins, E. T. (2000). Making a good decision: Value from fit. *American Psychologist, 55*(11), 1217–1230. Retrieved from https://doi.org/10.1037/0003-066X.55.11.1217

Higgins, E. T. (2005). Value from regulatory fit. *Current Directions in Psychological Science, 14*(4), 209–213. Retrieved from https://doi.org/10.1111/j.0963-7214.2005.00366.x

Horváth, K. (2018, September). Financial bootstrapping techniques: A systematic review of the literature. *On Research, 1*, 84–94.

Huang, L., Wu, A., Lee, M. J., Bao, J., Hudson, M., & Bolle, E. (2017). *The American angel: The first in-depth report on the demographics and investing activity of individual American angel investors.* Retrieved from www.theamericanangel.org

Johnson, M. A., Stevenson, R. M., & Letwin, C. R. (2018). A woman's place is in the . . . startup! Crowdfunder judgments, implicit bias, and the stereotype content model. *Journal of Business Venturing, 33*(6), 813–831. Retrieved from https://doi.org/10.1016/j.jbusvent.2018.04.003

Kanze, D., Huang, L., Conley, M. A., & Higgins, E. T. (2018). We ask men to win and women not to lose: Closing the gender gap in startup funding. *Academy of Management Journal, 61*(2), 586–614. Retrieved from https://doi.org/10.5465/amj.2016.1215

Kirsch, D., Goldfarb, B., & Gera, A. (2009). Form or substance: The role of business plans in venture capital decision making. *Strategic Management Journal, 30*(5), 487–515. Retrieved from https://doi.org/10.1002/smj.751

Lee, A. Y., & Aaker, J. L. (2004). Bringing the frame into focus: The influence of regulatory fit on processing fluency and persuasion. *Journal of Personality and Social Psychology, 86*(2), 205–218. Retrieved from https://doi.org/10.1037/0022-3514.86.2.205

Li, J. J., Chen, X.-P., Kotha, S., & Fisher, G. (2017). Catching fire and spreading it: A glimpse into displayed entrepreneurial passion in crowdfunding campaigns. *Journal of Applied Psychology, 102*(7), 1075–1090. Retrieved from https://doi.org/10.1037/apl0000217

Ma, Y., & Liu, D. (2017). Introduction to the special issue on crowdfunding and Fin-Tech. *Financial Innovation, 3*(1), 8. Retrieved from https://doi.org/10.1186/s40854-017-0058-9

Macht, S. A., & Weatherston, J. (2014). The benefits of online crowdfunding for fund-seeking business ventures. *Strategic Change, 23*(1–2), 1–14. Retrieved from https://doi.org/10.1002/jsc.1955

MacMillan, N. A. (2002). Signal detection theory. In *Stevens' handbook of experimental psychology*. New York: John Wiley & Sons. Retrieved from https://doi.org/10.1002/0471214426.pas0402

Malmström, M., Johansson, J., & Wincent, J. (2017). Gender stereotypes and venture support decisions: How governmental venture capitalists socially construct entrepreneurs' potential. *Entrepreneurship Theory and Practice, 41*(5), 833–860. Retrieved from https://doi.org/10.1111/etap.12275

Meyskens, M., & Bird, L. (2015). Crowdfunding and value creation. *Entrepreneurship Research Journal, 5*(2), 155–166. Retrieved from https://doi.org/10.1515/erj-2015-0007

Mitteness, C., Sudek, R., & Cardon, M. S. (2012). Angel investor characteristics that determine whether perceived passion leads to higher evaluations of funding potential. *Journal of Business Venturing, 27*(5), 592–606. Retrieved from https://doi.org/10.1016/j.jbusvent.2011.11.003

Mohamed, A. A., Gardner, W. L., & Paolillo, J. G. P. (1999). A taxonomy of organizational impression management tactics. *Advances in Competitiveness Research, 7*(Annual), 108–130.

Mollick, E. (2014). The dynamics of crowdfunding: An exploratory study. *Journal of Business Venturing, 29*(1), 1–16. Retrieved from https://doi.org/10.1016/j.jbusvent.2013.06.005

Mollick, E., & Robb, A. (2016). Democratizing innovation and capital access: The role of crowdfunding. *California Management Review, 58*(2), 72–87. Retrieved from https://doi.org/10.1525/cmr.2016.58.2.72

Morduch, J. (1999). The microfinance promise. *Journal of Economic Literature, 37*(4), 1569–1614. Retrieved from https://doi.org/10.1257/jel.37.4.1569

Moss, T. W., Neubaum, D. O., & Meyskens, M. (2015). The effect of virtuous and entrepreneurial orientations on microfinance lending and repayment: A signaling theory perspective. *Entrepreneurship Theory and Practice, 39*(1), 27–52. Retrieved from https://doi.org/10.1111/etap.12110

Murnieks, C. Y., Haynie, J. M., Wiltbank, R. E., & Harting, T. (2011). "I like how you think": Similarity as an interaction bias in the investor-entrepreneur dyad. *Journal of Management Studies, 48*(7), 1533–1561. Retrieved from https://doi.org/10.1111/j.1467-6486.2010.00992.x

Myers, S. C. (1984). The capital structure puzzle. *The Journal of Finance, 39*(3), 574–592. Retrieved from https://doi.org/10.1111/j.1540-6261.1984.tb03646.x

Nagy, B. G., Pollack, J. M., Rutherford, M. W., & Lohrke, F. T. (2012). The influence of entrepreneurs' credentials and impression management behaviors on perceptions of new venture legitimacy. *Entrepreneurship Theory and Practice, 36*(5), 941–965. Retrieved from https://doi.org/10.1111/j.1540-6520.2012.00539.x

Oo, P. P., Allison, T. H., Sahaym, A., & Juasrikul, S. (2019). User entrepreneurs' multiple identities and crowdfunding performance: Effects through product innovativeness, perceived passion, and need similarity. *Journal of Business Venturing, 34*(5), 105895. Retrieved from https://doi.org/10.1016/j.jbusvent.2018.08.005

Parhankangas, A., & Ehrlich, M. (2014). How entrepreneurs seduce business angels: An impression management approach. *Journal of Business Venturing, 29*(4), 543–564. Retrieved from https://doi.org/10.1016/j.jbusvent.2013.08.001

Petty, R. E., & Cacioppo, J. T. (1986). The elaboration likelihood model of persuasion. *Advances in Experimental Social Psychology, 19*, 123–205. Retrieved from https://doi.org/10.1016/S0065-2601(08)60214-2

Plummer, L. A., Allison, T. H., & Connelly, B. L. (2016). Better together? Signaling interactions in new venture pursuit of initial external capital. *Academy of Management Journal, 59*(5), 1585–1604. Retrieved from https://doi.org/10.5465/amj.2013.0100

Robb, A. M., & Robinson, D. T. (2014). The capital structure decisions of new firms. *Review of Financial Studies, 27*(1), 153–179. Retrieved from https://doi.org/10.1093/rfs/hhs072

Rowley, J. D. (2019). The Q2 2019 global venture capital report: A market gone sideways. Retrieved from https://news.crunchbase.com/news/the-q2-2019-global-venture-capital-report-a-market-gone-sideways/, on March 30, 2020.

Scheaf, D. J., Davis, B. C., Webb, J. W., Coombs, J. E., Borns, J., & Holloway, G. (2018). Signals' flexibility and interaction with visual cues: Insights from crowdfunding. *Journal of Business Venturing, 33*(6), 720–741. Retrieved from https://doi.org/10.1016/j.jbusvent.2018.04.007

Schlenker, B. R. (1980). *Impression management.* Monterey, CA: Brooks/Cole Publishing Company.

Schmidt, A. M., & DeShon, R. P. (2009). Prior performance and goal progress as moderators of the relationship between self-efficacy and performance. *Human Performance, 22*(3), 191–203. Retrieved from https://doi.org/10.1080/08959280902970377

Shepherd, D. A. (1999). Venture capitalists' introspection: A comparison of "in use" and "espoused" decision policies. *Journal of Small Business Management, 37*(2), 76–87.

Spence, M. (1973). Job market signaling. *The Quarterly Journal of Economics, 87*(3), 355. Retrieved from https://doi.org/10.2307/1882010

Steigenberger, N., & Wilhelm, H. (2018). Extending signaling theory to rhetorical signals: Evidence from crowdfunding. *Organization Science, 29*(3), 529–546. Retrieved from https://doi.org/10.1287/orsc.2017.1195

Stevenson, R. M., Ciuchta, M. P., Letwin, C., Dinger, J. M., & Vancouver, J. B. (2019). Out of control or right on the money? Funder self-efficacy and crowd bias in equity crowdfunding. *Journal of Business Venturing, 34*(2), 348–367. Retrieved from https://doi.org/10.1016/j.jbusvent.2018.05.006

Stevenson, R. M., & Josefy, M. (2019). Knocking at the gate: The path to publication for entrepreneurship experiments through the lens of gatekeeping theory. *Journal of Business Venturing, 34*(2), 242–260. Retrieved from https://doi.org/10.1016/j.jbusvent.2018.10.008

Stevenson, R., Josefy, M., McMullen, J. S., & Shepherd, D. (2020). Organizational and Management Theorizing Using Experiment-Based Entrepreneurship Research: Covered Terrain and New Frontiers. *Academy of Management Annals, 14*, 759–796.

Stevenson, R. M., Kuratko, D. F., & Eutsler, J. (2019). Unleashing main street entrepreneurship: Crowdfunding, venture capital, and the democratization of new venture investments. *Small Business Economics, 52*(2), 375–393. Retrieved from https://doi.org/10.1007/s11187-018-0097-2

Van Balen, T., Tarakci, M., & Sood, A. (2019). Do disruptive visions pay off? The impact of disruptive entrepreneurial visions on venture funding. *Journal of Management Studies*, *56*(2), 303–342. Retrieved from https://doi.org/10.1111/joms.12390

Vancouver, J. B., & Kendall, L. N. (2006). When self-efficacy negatively relates to motivation and performance in a learning context. *Journal of Applied Psychology*, *91*(5), 1146–1153. Retrieved from https://doi.org/10.1037/0021-9010.91.5.1146

Vancouver, J. B., Thompson, C. M., Tischner, E. C., & Putka, D. J. (2002). Two studies examining the negative effect of self-efficacy on performance. *Journal of Applied Psychology*, *87*(3), 506–516. Retrieved from https://doi.org/10.1037/0021-9010.87.3.506

Williams, T. A., & Shepherd, D. A. (2017). Mixed method social network analysis: Combining inductive concept development, content analysis, and secondary data for quantitative analysis. *Organizational Research Methods*, *20*(2), 268–298. Retrieved from https://doi.org/10.1177/1094428115610807

Zhang, S., Higgins, E. T., & Chen, G. (2011). Managing others like you were managed: How prevention focus motivates copying interpersonal norms. *Journal of Personality and Social Psychology*, *100*(4), 647–663. Retrieved from https://doi.org/10.1037/a0021750

14

ENTREPRENEURIAL FAILURE AND EXIT

Anna Jenkins & Orla Byrne

Introduction: Psychological Processes in Entrepreneurial Exit

Entrepreneurial exit—the process by which founder-managers remove themselves from the management and/or ownership of firms they helped create—is an important, yet understudied aspect of the entrepreneurship process (DeTienne, 2010; Shepherd, 2003). Exit can be challenging for entrepreneurs. They invest significant amounts of time, energy and emotional resources into their firms forming strong bonds to their firms (Cardon, Wincent, Singh, & Drnovsek, 2009; Cope, 2005; Yttermyr & Wennberg, 2019). For example, recent studies highlight that entrepreneurs' personal identity and self-worth are strongly coupled with that of their firm (Angel, Jenkins, & Stephens, 2018; Fauchart & Gruber, 2011; Hoang & Gimeno, 2010; Jenkins, Wiklund, & Brundin, 2014; Powell & Baker, 2014) and that how they respond to exit has implications for their well-being and future entrepreneurial behaviour (Singh, Corner, & Pavlovich, 2007). Exit can thus be a challenging process for an entrepreneur. A pertinent question to ask is what psychological processes inform and are triggered by the process of entrepreneurial exit and how do these processes inform our understanding of entrepreneurial exit?

Entrepreneurial exit—successful and unsuccessful—is characterised by a process of psychological and physical disengagement (Rouse, 2016; Shepherd, Wiklund, & Haynie, 2009). To explore and review the psychological processes involved in entrepreneurial exit we focus on understanding the psychological processes that influence the timing of exit, the emotions and well-being of the entrepreneur during the exit process, the ability to appropriate value from the exit and subsequent entrepreneurial behaviour. We adopt a process approach and

---

conceptualise entrepreneurial exit into two broad time frames: the time preceding the physical exit of the entrepreneur from the firm and the time after the physical exit of the entrepreneur from the firm. As exit is a multifaceted phenomenon, we conceptualise entrepreneurial exit into two broad categories, failure and harvest to reflect that failure can involve successful and unsuccessful outcomes. While we focus on both pre-exit and post-exit experiences, we dedicate more time to discussing pre-exit experiences as they are relatively under-explored in the literature relative to post-exit experiences and have potential to explain not only how entrepreneurs experience exit but also how pre-exit experiences influence post-exit experiences.

We organise the chapter by first conceptualising failure and harvest. We then review pre-exit experiences including the different approaches taken to understand this and offer avenues for future research. We then review post-exit experiences and offer avenues for future research before concluding the chapter. Figure 14.1 offers an overview of how we organised the review.

Conceptualising Entrepreneurial Exit

The concept of entrepreneurial exit encompasses the exit of an entrepreneur from both successful and unsuccessful firms (Hessels, Rietveld, Thurik, & Van der Zwan, 2018; Wennberg, Wiklund, DeTienne, & Cardon, 2010). To ensure that we explore the psychological processes involved in both successful and unsuccessful exits we focus on failure and harvest exits. We conceptualise *failure* as exits where

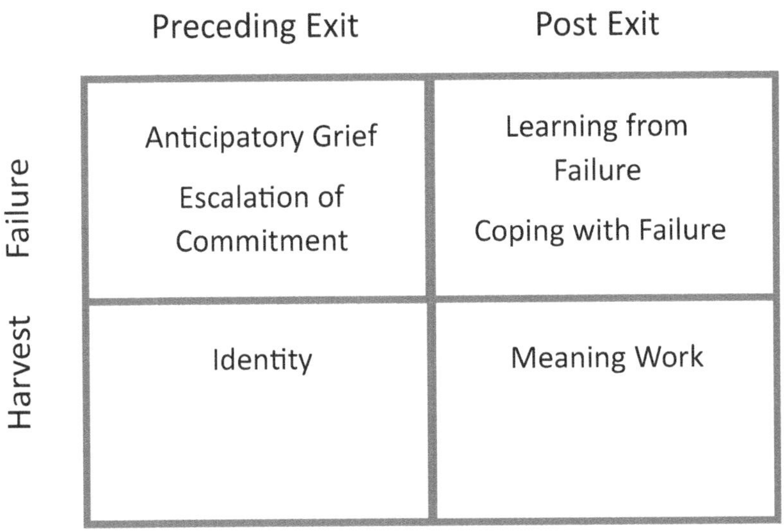

	Preceding Exit	Post Exit
Failure	Anticipatory Grief Escalation of Commitment	Learning from Failure Coping with Failure
Harvest	Identity	Meaning Work

FIGURE 14.1   Psychological Approaches to Studying Entrepreneurial Exit

an entrepreneur closes a firm because it is no longer financially viable and *harvest* as exits where the entrepreneur sells the business and personally profits from doing so (Ucbasaran, Shepherd, Lockett, & Lyon, 2013; Wennberg et al., 2010). The former usually results in the closure of the firm while the latter results in the continuation of the business under new management. We limit our review to the psychological processes involved in founder exit (DeTienne, 2010) as this has been in focus in the literature to date. Future research may attend to psychological processes in entrepreneurial teams (Preller, Patzelt, & Breugst, 2018), or family firms which are known to be distinct with regards to exit and succession (DeTienne & Chirico, 2013; DeTienne, McKelvie, & Chandler, 2015). For a more detailed discussion on how entrepreneurial exit has been conceptualised see (Coad, 2013; DeTienne et al., 2015; Ucbasaran et al., 2013).

Although failure frequently involves negative emotions and financial loss (Cope, 2011; Jenkins et al., 2014; Singh et al., 2007) and harvest economic gain (Mathias, Solomon, & Madison, 2017; Wennberg et al., 2010), both can involve the loss of an important social area and a central aspect of the entrepreneur's identity (Harris & Sutton, 1986; Rouse, 2016). In contrast, processes such as an escalation of commitment are more relevant for understanding failure than harvest (Yamakawa & Cardon, 2017), while forming a new identity through philanthropy is more relevant for understanding harvest than failure (Mathias et al., 2017). Thus, there are likely to be psychological processes which are relevant for understanding failure and harvest and others which are likely to be more relevant for explaining one but not the other. When referring broadly to psychological processes which are relevant for both *harvest* and *failure*, we use the collective term *entrepreneurial exit*, when referring to psychological processes which are relevant for either *harvest* or *failure*, we use these terms explicitly. As there is a more substantial body of literature on the psychological processes involved in failure (Shepherd & Haynie, 2011), this exit route is more prevalent in our review.

Psychological Processes Preceding Entrepreneurial Exit

Most research on the antecedents to entrepreneurial exit focus on firm-level attributes such as firm age or size (e.g. Balcaen, Manigart, & Ooghe, 2011; Headd, 2003) or individual-level attributes such as age, education and entrepreneurial experience (DeTienne & Cardon, 2012; Wennberg et al., 2010). Much less is known about the psychological processes which influence the timeliness of entrepreneurial exit and implications the exit process has for how an entrepreneur responds to exit, including their ability to move on from the venture, what they learn from the experience and their re-entry into self-employment (Balcaen et al., 2011; Jenkins & McKelvie, 2017; Yamakawa & Cardon, 2017).

Recent work taking a psychological perspective on entrepreneurial exit has the starting point that because entrepreneurs form close bonds to their ventures, it can be difficult for them to exit their firm. This work has taken (a) an identity perspective where entrepreneurial exit destabilises an entrepreneur's identity (Rouse, 2016), (b) an anticipatory grief approach where exit creates the need to mourn the loss of the business before physical separation takes place (Shepherd et al., 2009) or (c) drawn on escalation of commitment to explain why an entrepreneur continues to invest resources into a failing firm (Yamakawa & Cardon, 2017). We discuss each of these perspectives before contrasting them and suggesting avenues for future research.

An Identity Perspective

There is a growing interest in identity in entrepreneurship research. Much of this work has focused on the role of identity in explaining how individuals transition into entrepreneurship. Hoang and Gimeno (2010) develop two concepts, identity centrality and identity complexity to look at transitions away from and into an entrepreneurial role. Similarly, Lewis (2016) highlights the role and importance of identity work processes in setting up a new business. Other scholars look at the interplay between founder identity and its impact on the nature and style of firm they establish (Fauchart & Gruber, 2011) and their strategic responses to setbacks (Powell & Baker, 2014, 2017).

With identity playing a central role in the ventures entrepreneurs create (Fauchart & Gruber, 2011; Murnieks, Mosakowski, & Cardon, 2014), it is also likely to play a central role in the exit process. Drawing on the literature from career transition which has found that career transitions can destabilise an individual's identity as they question who they are and who they might be (Ibarra, 2005); Rouse (2016) took an identity perspective to investigate the process of how founders of technology companies exit through a *harvest* strategy. She found two dominant approaches which could explain the psychological processes involved in a *harvest* exit. The first was a sequential process of de-identification with the firm. This began with the founder physically exiting from the firm, followed by a short period of the founder processing the exit, before they eventually identified with a new firm, often in the role of founder. The second approach was a simultaneous process of de-identifying with the firm from which they planned to exit, while also identifying with a new firm. Driving the differences in these approaches was whether the entrepreneur identified strongly with the firm they founded or if they identified strongly with their role as an entrepreneur.

Rouse (2016) found that entrepreneurs who took a sequential approach held an identity which was organisationally based. These entrepreneurs experienced exit as an emotionally challenging experience requiring time after the exit to process the loss of the firm before re-engaging with a new firm. She found these entrepreneurs remained psychologically engaged with their firm during the time leading up to the exit and after it. To disengage from the firm, the entrepreneurs focused on physically disengaging from the firm by, for example hiring replacements, while remaining psychologically committed to the firm and prioritising the longevity of the firm above their personal well-being. As a result, Rouse (2016) found that these entrepreneurs experienced negative emotions at the point of exit as they were leaving an important aspect of their identity as well as an important social arena (Harris & Sutton, 1986; Rouse, 2016), something which they had not prepared for during the exit process. For these entrepreneurs, the physical exit from the firm preceded the psychological exit from the firm. They were slower to re-engage in entrepreneurial behaviour as they needed time to process the exit before they could commit to a new firm.

In contrast, Rouse (2016) found that entrepreneurs who took a simultaneous approach identified strongly with their role as an entrepreneur. While running the firm they planned to exit, these entrepreneurs started a new business, simultaneously disengaging from one firm while engaging in another. For these entrepreneurs, the psychological disengagement preceded the physical exit from the firm. Rather than experiencing a sense of loss and sadness at the time of exit, Rouse (2016) found these entrepreneurs expressed excitement in anticipation of what was to come next.

In a study of emotional responses to *failure*, Jenkins and colleagues (2014) found that not all entrepreneurs expressed strong negative emotions after failure, with portfolio entrepreneurs less likely to express the negative emotions. Drawing on appraisal theory, they found that entrepreneurs who could separate their self-worth from the performance of their firms felt significantly lower levels of negative emotions. One explanation for this is that through running multiple ventures they maintained their entrepreneurial identity and thus did not experience a loss of this identity when their business failed. The findings of Rouse (2016) in the context of *harvest* and Jenkins and colleagues (2014) in the context of *failure* suggest that entrepreneurs who retain their entrepreneurial identity through the exit process, either by transitioning to a firm while exiting or by retaining their entrepreneurial identity by running multiple firms, experience lower levels of negative emotions. They do not experience the loss of an identity which is organisationally based as acutely as entrepreneurs who have this as a central aspect of their identity.

Anticipatory Grief

A second approach to explain the psychological processes of entrepreneurs prior to *failure* is the contextualisation of anticipatory grief by Shepherd and colleagues to explain why entrepreneurs may delay the exit from a failing firm (Shepherd et al., 2009). Anticipatory grief is the emotional preparation for a loss prior to the loss taking place. It has been studied in parents of terminally ill children and with care givers of terminal patients (Fulton & Gottesman, 1980). This body of work has found that individuals start to mourn the loss of a loved one before death, easing their ability to accept the loss (Natterson & Knudson Jr, 1960). By grieving before a loss takes place, the individual starts to work through some of the pending loss, easing the emotional burden when the loss takes place (Bonanno &

Keltner, 1997; Wortman & Silver, 1992). Although predominately used in the context of the loss of a loved one, research has extended the concept to explain other significant losses such as amputation (Wilson, 1977) and divorce (Kitson, Babri, Roach, & Placidi, 1989).

The process of anticipatory grief proposed by Shepherd and colleagues takes as a starting point that once entrepreneurs who have a strong emotional attachment to their firms know that their firms will fail, they start a process of grieving the impending loss of the firm. The entrepreneur grieves the loss of the business, the imminent changes in their lifestyle, or their dreams they had for their business (Shepherd et al., 2009). This mourning process can delay the physical exit from the firm as the entrepreneur mourns the loss of their firm while continuing to run it. An outcome of this mourning process is that the entrepreneur is better prepared emotionally for the failure, facilitating their recovery from the failure. A caveat to the process of anticipatory grieving, however, is that it can be financially costly to delay the exit from a failing firm. Thus, Shepherd and colleagues propose that some delay in exiting a failing business may be beneficial to recovery, provided the entrepreneur balances the emotional and financial costs of failure (Shepherd et al., 2009).

Escalation of Commitment

Escalation of commitment provides an alternative explanation to the gradual process of detachment from a *failing* firm prior to exiting it. Escalation of commitment is the continued investment of resources and time into a losing course of action or project once it is known with certainty that the project will fail (Staw, 1981). Driven by different psychological processes, escalation of commitment has been used to understand why individuals continue to commit resources to a venture despite knowing that it will fail. Like anticipatory grief, this work remains predominately conceptual.

Explanations for escalation of commitment include a sunk-cost agreement, whereby previous investments encourage continued investment in an attempt not to appear wasteful (Arkes & Blumer, 1985) and a preference for risk-seeking behaviour when individuals are in a loss position (Tversky & Kahneman, 1981). When a sequence of decisions needs to be made as opposed to a one-off decision, the likelihood for escalation increases. As a result, situations which are prime candidates for escalation include resource allocation or investment decisions, career decisions and policy decisions (Staw, 1981). As the decision to exit a failing firm combines resource allocation decisions with career decisions it is a situation in which escalation can readily take place.

In a study of entrepreneurs who experienced firm failure and re-entered, Yamakawa and Cardon (2017) found that entrepreneurs who had invested more time and money into their ventures were more likely to delay their exit from a distressed firm and that contingency planning could help mitigate against this delay.

Casas and Hilb (2016) drew on escalation of commitment to explain why entrepreneurs may delay the exit of a failing firm. They suggest that continued injections of time and taking on debt can trap entrepreneurs in running unprofitable businesses—a phenomenon known as the living dead—significantly drawing out the failure process and depleting the entrepreneur's resources in the process. The implications of escalation of commitment is that entrepreneurs delay their exit, deplete their resources and increase their susceptibility to financial loss and emotional hardship when the firm eventually fails. This can restrict the entrepreneur's ability to start again as they have depleted their resource base.

Contrasting the Approaches and Future Research

The three perspectives outlined above offer contrasting psychological processes to explain the timeliness and implications of exit for entrepreneurs' well-being and entrepreneurial behaviour. For example, Rouse (2016) found that entrepreneurs who had strong identity attachments to their firms held these throughout the exit process, experiencing negative emotions at the time of exit and requiring a transitionary period after the exit before starting a new venture. In contrast, Shepherd and colleagues' anticipatory grief argument proposes a process of detachment which is initiated before exiting the firm to enable the entrepreneur to psychologically prepare for life after the firm, easing the emotional strain of the eventual exit. These approaches to explaining exit are likely to be relevant in both harvest and failure contexts for entrepreneurs who strongly identify with their firms, as the processes are driven by attachment to the firm rather than the performance of the firm at the point of exit. However, the drivers of whether an entrepreneur starts the process of letting go as predicated by the anticipatory grief or whether they remain psychologically committed to the firm, as Rouse (2016) found, remains an avenue for future research.

Rouse (2016) also found that in the context of a harvest exit, some entrepreneurs let go of one venture while simultaneously founding a new venture—thus easing the transition from one venture to the next. The extent to which entrepreneurs who experience failure also adopt this strategy is a fruitful avenue for future research. There are some indications that this strategy is used by entrepreneurs as they navigate the failure process. For example, in a representative sample of entrepreneurs who experienced bankruptcy, Jenkins and colleagues (2014) found that 10 per cent of entrepreneurs had paid employment at the time of the bankruptcy, 21 per cent owned and ran another firm and 4 per cent held paid employment and owned and ran another firm. The impact of these alternative forms of employment was that the entrepreneurs were less likely to appraise the bankruptcy as involving loss of self-esteem. Holding such employment prior to exiting a failed business offers an additional explanation for how entrepreneurs may prepare for failure and suggests that they may have also started the process of letting go of the failed firm before physically exiting the firm.

Escalation of commitment involves increased resource commitment to a failing firm, while the other approaches involve some form of de-escalation of commitment to the firm. Although the anticipatory grief argument centres on a process of psychologically letting go, this process results in continued investment of resources into a failing firm as the entrepreneur grieves their loss. Understanding the boundary conditions surrounding escalation of commitment and anticipatory grief thus becomes central to understanding the process of psychologically letting go while continuing to run the business. At what point does a firm become a form of 'living dead' as the entrepreneur grieves it? And at what point does continued investment of time and resources in the failing firm shift from facilitating an entrepreneur's overall recovery to becoming detrimental for it? Persistence is often hailed as critical to entrepreneurial success, yet at what point does persistence become escalation and how can an entrepreneur distinguish between the two? Understanding the antecedents and boundary conditions of these different psychological approaches becomes critical to understanding the process of exit.

New Perspectives to Understand Pre-Failure Experiences

The experience of firm failure has parallels with the experience of divorce. Both are stressful life experiences involving financial loss, emotional strain, social isolation and a sense of failure. Although rates of firm failure are similar to that for marriages, the increase in the rate of divorce, and the well-being implications this has for families, has generated substantial interest from researchers. This has resulted in a substantial body of research taking the starting point that divorce is a stressful life transition which impacts adults and children (Amato, 2000). This body of work provides a potential rich array of approaches to study the process of firm failure.

For example, the divorce literature has focused on divorce as a transition rather than an event, enabling a temporal understanding as to when stress is experienced during a marriage breakdown, acknowledging that the time leading up to a divorce can be more stressful than the time after the divorce (Hewitt & Turrell, 2011). The point at which an individual experiences the pain and stress of divorce can depend on whether they initiated the divorce or whether their partner initiated the divorce. Spouses who initiate divorce are likely to have been considering divorce for some time and have already mourned the end of the marriage before initiating the divorce process (Amato, 2000). In contrast, the non-initiating spouse, who would like to see the marriage continue, is likely to mourn the loss of the marriage after the divorce is finalised. These insights can be used to understand how entrepreneurs experience stress in the time leading up to a failure and the timing of when they experience stress. For example, when anticipatory grief is likely to help explain the failure process and when an escalation of commitment is likely to explain the failure process. It can also be used to understand how entrepreneurs respond to self-initiated exit or when it is necessary to avoid running the business while insolvent or when a creditor initiates the bankruptcy.

More broadly, understanding when stress and strain are experienced in the failure process can provide insights into how entrepreneurs make decisions during the failure process. For example, Hessels and colleagues (2018) found that depression is a relatively strong predictor of exit. Depressed individuals find it harder to plan and problem-solve (Naismith et al., 2003) yet having a plan in place can be important for managing the failure process (Yamakawa & Cardon, 2017), suggesting that important insights can be gained from studying how stress and strain influence how entrepreneurs plan and prepare for exit. Taking these points collectively, potential research questions can include How does the stress of a poorly performing business influence an entrepreneur's ability to make strategic decisions about exiting the venture? How does the timing of stress and strain influence the emotions experienced during the failure process, and what is the interplay between stress and strain and a poorly performing business? It is likely that in some cases, stress and strain can impact the performance of the business, and in other cases, it is the poorly performing business that causes the stress and strain. The relationship between stress, strain and performance is likely to be cyclical, requiring a longitudinal design to capture the relationships among them.

An additional psychological process which could offer new insights into understanding pre-failure experiences is anticipatory coping. Anticipatory coping occurs when an individual knows with certainty that a stressful event will take place and they start to take actions and make plans to reduce the impact of the stressful event (Neupert, Ennis, Ramsey, & Gall, 2015). The role of anticipatory coping is often overlooked in the literature on stressful life events as the event itself demarks the start of the research into responses to it (Neupert et al., 2015). By preparing for the event by for example accumulating resources and information that can help mitigate the extent of the stress experienced, anticipatory coping can minimise the impact of imminent stressful events. This approach offers a complementary explanation to that of anticipatory grieving, while it also focuses on how the entrepreneur prepares for the failure, it is broader in scope covering not just the mourning process but also includes other ways in which the entrepreneur can prepare for failure. For example, entrepreneurs may chase accounts receivable to get their firms' finances in order and sell excess stock (Balcaen et al., 2011). Anticipating the failure also enables the entrepreneur to prepare for what they will do after the failure, minimising the negative impact failure can have on the entrepreneur's well-being (Jenkins et al., 2014). Understanding the extent to which entrepreneurs prepare for failure and the impact that this has on the failure process provides another avenue for future research.

New Perspectives to Understand Pre-Harvest Experiences

While more of the work on psychological processes during exit have focused on failure, the work by Rouse (2016) demonstrates that exiting a business through a *harvest* strategy has some similarities with that of *failure*. Thus, as a starting point for understanding the extent to which entrepreneurs also mourn the leaving of the business, plan for the exit, prepare for their role adjustment or continue their commitment to the venture (even when this continued investment may weaken the potential sale price), can provide insights into the process of exiting through harvest. For example, entrepreneurs often have an exit plan in place (DeTienne, 2010), yet little is known of the contents of these plans and the extent to which entrepreneurs have considered and planned for the psychological impact of exit.

The family business literature also provides a rich body of work on succession, succession planning and the role of emotions and letting go in the succession process (Bertschi-Michel, Kammerlander, & Strike, 2019). In particular, this body of work has uncovered the range of emotions that can be felt in the succession process including feeling intense negative emotions in response to letting go of the business (Shepherd, 2009). Thus, future research could investigate the tensions and range of emotions involved in exiting a successful business.

Studying Exit Empirically–Research and Design Issues

The growing body of empirical work on exit demonstrates that it is possible to identify firms which have recently failed (e.g. Jenkins et al., 2014; Singh et al., 2015) or exited through different routes including harvest (Wennberg et al., 2010). However, identifying firms which are in the process of exiting remains challenging. For example, while it is possible to survey firms to uncover their intended exit strategies (DeTienne et al., 2015), finding firms in the process of exiting is more difficult. In a representative survey of firms, Jenkins and colleagues found that 20 per cent were considering exiting their business within the coming year and 30 per cent were considering exit within the next three years (Jenkins, Steen, & Verreyenne, 2015). Thus, to capture firms in the process of exiting their firms would require a large initial sample frame. Inspiration for this type of data collection could come from the Panel Studies on Entrepreneurial Dynamics studies and their respective counterparts. Alternatively, real-time process studies could be conducted with entrepreneurs as they navigate the exit process—the work by Rouse (2016) provides an exemplar for how this can be done. As it can be difficult to identify firms which are in the process of failing or selling their businesses, cases on these processes may be captured by chance in larger ongoing studies or signs of distress such as poor financial performance could also be used to identify an initial sample frame.

Qualitatively, researchers could deploy a gatekeeper sampling strategy— targeting professionals who work closely with client entrepreneurs and who would be aware of the challenges they faced in their businesses. For example, as with divorce, if an entrepreneur feels their business is in trouble (as is the case with failure) or faces an opportunity for sale (harvest), they may think ahead and seek professional counsel from experts who can advise on legal, financial and tax implications. As such, researchers could make widespread contact with solicitors, accountants, tax consultants, and financial consultants, seeking referrals to clients who may be considering exiting their businesses.

Psychological Processes Post-Entrepreneurial Exit

Entrepreneurs experience greater well-being than individuals in paid work (Nikolaev, Boudreaux, & Wood, 2019; Shir, Nikolaev, & Wincent, 2019). Much of this difference has been explained by entrepreneurs who enjoy 'being independent', in control of their time and scope of work, and experience their work as meaningful (Benz & Frey, 2008). However, the 'peak' of being independent, in control of one's destiny and doing something meaningful also puts entrepreneurs at greater risk of psychological ailment when exiting a venture. It is therefore not surprising that exiting self-employment has been shown to have a greater negative impact on well-being than loss of paid employment. For example using the life satisfaction data from the German Socio-Economic Panel study, Hetschko (2016) found that becoming unemployed after firm exit reduced self-employed workers' satisfaction considerably more than salaried workers' satisfaction.

A range of psychological processes have been used to understand how entrepreneurs manage exit. The literature has predominately focused on psychological processes involved in *failure* with a focus on how entrepreneurs learn from and cope with failure and the impact this has on their well-being. This work takes as a starting point the point at which the firm has failed and focuses on the impact and implications of the failure event. While we discuss the impact of failure in the specific themes: (a) learning from failure, (b) coping with failure and (c) the emotional impact of failure, the all-encompassing impact of failure means that they are often highly intertwined. Recent work on entrepreneurs' experiences after a *harvest* exit focuses on how they find subsequent meaningful work (Mathias et al., 2017).

Learning From Firm Failure

Learning from failure has arguably attracted the most attention in the literature on entrepreneurial failure. One reason for this is the long-held implicit assumption that entrepreneurs learn from a failure experience. This is despite mixed findings on the relationship between prior experience and subsequent firm performance (Frankish, Roberts, Coad, Spears, & Storey, 2012). Qualitative work has identified two broad learning outcomes from failure. First, learning outcomes that focus on how to more effectively manage a business (Cope, 2011; Singh et al., 2007; Stokes & Blackburn, 2002). Cope (2011) found that entrepreneurs learn about the strengths and weaknesses of the venture, about networks and relationships, about the nature and management of relationships and about venture management in general. Second, entrepreneurs achieve personal learning outcomes that relate to the recovery, personal growth (Cope, 2011; Singh , Corner, & Pavlovich, 2015) and resilience (Corner, Singh, & Pavlovich, 2017) of the entrepreneur. For example, Singh et al. (2015) found that failure could transform how an entrepreneur views him- or herself as a result of surviving failure.

> *This was an unexpected finding, but the majority of entrepreneurs described profound realizations and moments of clarity that brought about a fundamental shift in how they perceived their experience of venture failure and themselves as a result of surviving failure.*
>
> *(Singh et al., 2015, p. 158)*

To examine the impact of learning on subsequent entrepreneurial performance, studies have drawn on attribution theory to understand how prior failure experience impacts current firm performance (Eggers & Song, 2015; Yamakawa & Cardon, 2015). Starting with a sample of entrepreneurs who have experienced failure and re-entered, Yamakawa and Cardon (2015) found internal attributions fostered learning and subsequent improvements in performance. Focusing on external attributions, Eggers and Song (2015) suggested that entrepreneurs who experienced failure were more likely to switch industries and perform poorly as they could no longer draw on relevant industry knowledge.

Coping With Failure

The negative impact of failure can cover many aspects of the entrepreneur's life, including marriage breakdowns, sleeplessness, depression, exhaustion and financial loss (Singh et al., 2007; Cope, 2011). Research on the process of coping with failure has focused on how entrepreneurs deal with these stressors. Using in-depth case studies, Cope (2011) breaks down the recovery process into three distinct coping phases: avoidance, confrontation and moving on. He suggests an initial period of avoidance and stepping back from the failure can be important for overcoming the painful emotions associated with failure. He then suggests that confronting the failure can be important for accepting and learning from it and to move on from the failure it is important as to not dwell in the confrontation stage.

Shepherd (2003) proposes that oscillating between a loss orientation coping method—which involves confronting the failure and talking about feelings of grief with friends, family or psychologists—and a restoration coping method—which focuses on avoidance of the loss and focuses on secondary sources of stress—can result in faster recovery from failure. These orientations are similar to Cope's (2011) avoidance and confrontation stages in his recovery process. Singh and colleagues (2007) suggest a similar strategy for coping with failure based on the emotion and problem based coping framework suggested by Lazarus and Folkman (1984). Based on five case studies with entrepreneurs who had recently experienced failure, they found that entrepreneurs use problem-based coping strategies to deal with the financial implications of failure, such as selling assets to help pay debt, and emotional coping strategies, such as talking to friends and family, to deal with the emotional strain from failure (Singh et al., 2007).

The Emotional Impact of Failure

Entrepreneurial exit is an emotional process. The majority of research on emotions in the context of exit relates to the negative emotional impact as a result of failure. These negative emotions, grief, are widely accepted to block an entrepreneur's capacity to learn from failure (Shepherd, 2003; Jenkins et al., 2014). Building on this, Byrne and Shepherd (2015) identify that both negative *and positive* emotions play a complex role in the learning process. Their exploratory qualitative study first identifies that negative emotions, with the assistance of an emotion-focused coping strategy, can motivate sensemaking efforts. Entrepreneurs who showed little sign of negative emotions after failure displayed fewer signs of sensemaking, as they lacked the powerful trigger for reflection. Furthermore, their study identified the powerful role positive emotions played after processing negative emotions. They found that positive emotions both 'undid' negative emotions and informed sensemaking. Together, negative and positive emotions significantly informed the entrepreneurs' sensemaking efforts and stimulated stronger narratives of resilience.

Identity Transition

Similar to pre-exit experiences, an identity lens has been used to understand post-*harvest* experiences. Identity transition has been studied in the context of *harvest* exits. In a study of entrepreneurs who had exited highly successful businesses, Mathias and colleagues (2017) found that entrepreneurs questioned what they should do next after exiting through a harvest, leading them to search for new meaning in their lives through meaningful work. They found that entrepreneurs looked for different ways they could give back to the community through for example philanthropy, volunteer work and mentoring.

Shepherd and Haynie (2009) in the context of *failure* suggest that stigmatised entrepreneurs are more likely to hold negative self-views when they strongly self-identify with the failed firm, blame themselves for the failure or failed in a favourable business environment. Stigma can influence whether an entrepreneur re-enters self-employment and the mode in which they do this (Simmons, Wiklund, & Levie, 2013), even if the stigma experienced is self-imposed (Cope, 2011).

Contrasting the Approaches and Future Research

Most research on post-exit experiences has focused on the impact and influence of *failure* on the entrepreneur. Despite wide interest in the psychological processes associated with entrepreneurial *failure*, there is limited research focused on mechanisms that influence how entrepreneurs learn from failure, how entrepreneurs cope with failure and how entrepreneurs' transition through to new identities after failure. Unlike explanations for pre-failure experiences which offer contrasting explanations for how entrepreneurs' experience the failure process, learning, coping and identity are highly intertwined with reinforcing and tightly coupled explanations for how entrepreneurs respond to failure. With only limited research on entrepreneurs' experiences post a *harvest* exit, there is substantial scope for investigating the impact of a harvest exit on an entrepreneur.

To understand the sometimes complex and intertwined relationships among failure, learning and emotions future research could take inspiration from theories which are rooted in self-regulation which offers insights into how individuals manage their emotions, cognition and behaviour (Baumeister & Vohs, 2004). For example future work could extend the work by Funken, Gielnik, and Foo (2018), who investigated how an entrepreneur's orientation towards errors and problems experienced during the process of establishing a venture influenced the progress of the venture. Understanding how entrepreneurs frame the failure experience and the influence this has their motivation could provide new insights into the relationships among learning, emotion and motivation. Liminality, a period of identity transition where an identity is reconstructed after experiencing a loss of identity (Beech, 2011), offers a potential theoretical lens to investigate identity transitions in both *failure* and *harvest* contexts. Building on the work by Rouse (2016), liminality can be used to understand not just how entrepreneurs prepare for exit but also on how they continue to transition to a new identity after an exit. Liminal experiences are often studied as sequential processes starting with the trigger event, such as unemployment (Daskalaki & Simosi, 2017), whereby an individual detaches from the lost identity to form a new identity. As narratives are often laden with identity references (Humphreys & Brown, 2002), a qualitative narrative approach could offer new insights into how entrepreneurs transition between firms and in and out of self-employment. For example, future research could investigate the extent to which individuals carry hangover identities— residual identities from previous roles (Ebaugh, 1988)—and how this impacts their future endeavours. Studies could consider to what extent entrepreneurs harbour hangover identities and the extent to which they are (a) restrictive and limit an entrepreneur's ability to move on or (b) they channel an entrepreneur's motivation to continue with an entrepreneurial career path.

Most of the research on entrepreneurial exit remains theoretically under-socialised (Cope, 2011) with a focus on the entrepreneur but not on the social context in which they are embedded. Entrepreneurship does not occur in a vacuum, and the same is true for exiting entrepreneurship. Any exit process will involve a range of stakeholders who are likely to influence how the entrepreneur experiences and processes the exit and be influenced by the experience in their own unique way (Mantere, Aula, Schildt, & Vaara, 2013). For example, as alluded to previously entrepreneurs are likely to seek advice from several professionals who may or may not be experienced in dealing with the messy emotional fallout that can surround exit (and failure in particular)—such as a family solicitor providing advice to an entrepreneur knowing the impact that advice will have not only on the firm but on the family too. Likewise, liquidators and bankruptcy experts are visiting the sites of firms undergoing bankruptcy and liaising with entrepreneurs at a highly sensitive time. Other stakeholders affected by exit include staff and family members—who are often one and the same in many small businesses. Failure will mean unemployment for many of these. Furthermore, given the secrecy that typically surrounds the circumstances leading up to exit, family and staff may feel betrayed that they were not alerted to what was happening, especially if their jobs are in danger. A harvest exit can also be shrouded in secrecy, as details are kept concealed until final evaluations and negotiations have been agreed. In the high-growth sector in particular, staff with share options may be alerted of the negotiations, while other colleagues are not. How staff feel they are treated (and rewarded) at the point of harvest may impact their commitment and performance with the newly taken over firm. Future research can consider these ripples of business failure for the wider stakeholder community affected by the firm's exit. Furthermore, future research can consider other social groups who experience exit, such as family businesses and the failure of team-based firms. Studies can build on Shepherd's (2009) model to compare how family and team exit is processed both individually and at the group level and consider what impact the complex interrelationships prevalent in these types of businesses have for learning, coping and identity transition post exit.

Research on entrepreneurial failure has predominately focused on the role of negative emotions for self-worth (Jenkins et al., 2014) and learning (Shepherd, 2003); however, positive emotions also play a role in learning from failure (Byrne & Shepherd, 2015). Extending the literature beyond the dominant focus on negative emotions may uncover new sights into how entrepreneurs respond to failure and build resilience after failure (Corner et al., 2017). Furthermore, studying the role of emotions in a harvest context has the potential to provide new sights into the process of exiting a venture with entrepreneurs likely to be experiencing a mix of emotions as they celebrate what they have accomplished and mourn what they are leaving. Large-scale databases such as the Household, Income and Labour Dynamics in Australia (HILDA) provide opportunities to systematically study exit as a process (Craig, Schaper, & Dibrell, 2007).

Empirical Work

Future research on the psychological processes post exit can take a longitudinal perspective, to map emergence and change over time. While exit studies recognise the importance of a longitudinal perspective (Byrne & Shepherd, 2015; Ucbasaran et al., 2013), few actually adopt this approach. Longitudinal studies mapping entrepreneurs over time would provide much-needed insight into the dynamics of learning, coping and emotions following exit. Future research could also adopt a multi-stakeholder perspective to provide a more balanced and inter-actional insight into how failure unfolds. Finally, exit research would gain from ethnographic studies, where the researcher is situated in the social context and experiencing and observing first-hand the emotions, tensions and celebrations that surround failure. For example, ethnographic work could be carried out at specialised bankruptcy and liquidation firms who deal with harvests and failures on a daily basis.

Conclusion

Psychological perspectives offer a rich array of opportunities for studying the complexities of entrepreneurial exit. This chapter offers an overview of psycho-logical processes underpinning entrepreneurial exit. We conceptualise exit as both successful (in the form of harvest) and unsuccessful (in the form of failure) events (Hessels et al., 2018; Wennberg et al., 2010), and acknowledge that both forms of exit can represent loss of an important part of the entrepreneurs' lives (Harris & Sutton, 1986; Rouse, 2016). By adopting a process perspective, we consider the psychological processes unfolding over two main timeframes—the time preceding the physical exit of the entrepreneur from their firm and the time after exit and suggest that greater focus on pre-exit experiences could offer insights not only into the timing of the exit but also inform how entrepreneurs respond to exit.

References

Amato, P. (2000). The consequences of divorce for adults and children. *Journal of Marriage Family*, *62*(4), 1269–1287.

Angel, P., Jenkins, A., & Stephens, A. (2018). Understanding entrepreneurial success: A phe-nomenographic approach. *International Small Business Journal: Researching Entrepreneur-ship*, *36*(6), 611–636.

Arkes, H. R., & Blumer, C. (1985). The psychology of sunk cost. *Organizational Behavior and Human Decision Processes*, *35*(1), 124–140.

Balcaen, S., Manigart, S., & Ooghe, H. (2011). From distress to exit: Determinants of the time to exit. *Journal of Evolutionary Economics*, *21*(3), 407–446.

Baumeister, R. F., & Vohs, K. D. (2004). *Handbook of self-regulation: Research, theory, and appli-cations*. New York: The Guilford Press.

Beech, N. (2011). Liminality and the practices of identity reconstruction. *Human Relations*, *64*(2), 285–302.

Benz, M., & Frey, B. S. (2008). Being independent is a great thing: Subjective evaluations of self-employment and hierarchy. *Economica*, *75*(298), 362–383.

Bertschi-Michel, A., Kammerlander, N., & Strike, V. M. (2019). Unearthing and alleviating emotions in family business successions. *Entrepreneurship Theory Practice*. Retrieved from https://doi.org/10.1177/1042258719834016

Bonanno, G. A., & Keltner, D. (1997). Facial expression of emotion and the course of con-jugal bereavement. *Journal of Abnormal Psychology*, *106*, 126–137.

Byrne, O., & Shepherd, D. A. (2015). Different strokes for different folks: Entrepreneurial narratives of emotion, cognition, and making sense of business failure. *Entrepreneurship Theory and Practice, 39*(2), 375–405.

Cardon, M. S., Wincent, J., Singh, J., & Drnovsek, M. (2009). The nature and experience of entrepreneurial passion. *Academy of Management Review, 34*(3), 511–532.

Casas, T., & Hilb, M. (2016). Founders in the living-dead trap: A theoretical exploration at entrepreneurship's dark core. *Entrepreneurship Research Journal, 6*(4), 401–423.

Coad, A. (2013). Death is not a success: Reflections on business exit. *International Small Business Journal: Researching Entrepreneurship, 32*(7), 721–732.

Cope, J. (2005). Toward a dynamic learning perspective of entrepreneurship. *Entrepreneurship Theory and Practice, 29*(4), 373–397.

Cope, J. (2011). Entrepreneurial learning from failure: An interpretative phenomenological analysis. *Journal of Business Venturing, 26*(6), 604–623.

Corner, P. D., Singh, S., & Pavlovich, K. (2017). Entrepreneurial resilience and venture failure. *International Small Business Journal: Researching Entrepreneurship, 35*(6), 687–708.

Craig, J. B., Schaper, M., & Dibrell, C. (2007). *Life in small business in Australia: Evidence from the HILDA Survey: Mimeo.* Paper presented at the HILDA Survey Research Conference, University of Melbourne.

Daskalaki, M., & Simosi, M. (2018). Unemployment as a liminoid phenomenon: Identity trajectories in times of crisis. *Human Relations, 71*(9), 1153–1178.

DeTienne, D. R. (2010). Entrepreneurial exit as a critical component of the entrepreneurial process: Theoretical development. *Journal of Business Venturing, 25*(2), 203–215.

DeTienne, D. R., & Cardon, M. S. (2012). Impact of founder experience on exit intentions. *Small Business Economics, 38*(4), 351–374.

DeTienne, D. R., & Chirico, F. (2013). Exit strategies in family firms: How socioemotional wealth drives the threshold of performance. *Entrepreneurship Theory and Practice, 37*(6), 1297–1318.

DeTienne, D. R., McKelvie, A., & Chandler, G. N. (2015). Making sense of entrepreneurial exit strategies: A typology and test. *Journal of Business Venturing, 30*(2), 255–272.

Ebaugh, H. R. F. (1988). *Becoming an ex: The process of role exit.* Chicago, IL: University of Chicago Press.

Eggers, J., & Song, L. (2015). Dealing with failure: Serial entrepreneurs and the costs of changing industries between ventures. *Academy of Management Journal, 58*(6), 1785–1803.

Fauchart, E., & Gruber, M. (2011). Darwinians, communitarians, and missionaries: The role of founder identity in entrepreneurship. *Academy of Management Journal, 54*(5), 935–957.

Frankish, J. S., Roberts, R. G., Coad, A., Spears, T. C., & Storey, D. J. (2012). Do entrepreneurs really learn? Or do they just tell us that they do? *Industrial and Corporate Change, 22*(1), 73–106.

Fulton, R., & Gottesman, D. J. (1980). Anticipatory grief: A psychosocial concept reconsidered. *The British Journal of Psychiatry, 137*(1), 45–54.

Funken, R., Gielnik, M. M., & Foo, M.-D. (2018). How can problems be turned into something good? The role of entrepreneurial learning and error mastery orientation. *Entrepreneurship Theory and Practice, 4*(2), 315–338.

Harris, S. G., & Sutton, R. I. (1986). Functions of parting ceremonies in dying organizations. *The Academy of Management Journal, 29*(1), 5–30.

Headd, B. (2003). Redefining business success: Distinguishing between closure and failure. *Small Business Economics, 21*, 51–61.

Hessels, J., Rietveld, C. A., Thurik, A. R., & Van der Zwan, P. (2018). Depression and entrepreneurial exit. *Academy of Management Perspectives, 32*(3), 323–339.

Hetschko, C. (2016). On the misery of losing self-employment. *Small Business Economics*, *47*(2), 461–478.

Hewitt, B., & Turrell, G. (2011). Short-term functional health and well-being after marital separation: Does initiator status make a difference? *American Journal of Epidemiology*, *173*(11), 1308–1318.

Hoang, H., & Gimeno, J. (2010). Becoming a founder: How founder role identity affects entrepreneurial transitions and persistence in founding. *Journal of Business Venturing*, *25*(1), 41–53.

Humphreys, M., & Brown, A. D. (2002). Narratives of organizational identity and identification: A case study of hegemony and resistance. *Organization Studies*, *23*(3), 421–447.

Ibarra, H. (2005). Identity transitions: Possible selves, liminality and the dynamics of career change. *INSEAD Working Paper Series* INSEAD, Fontainebleu Cedex France.

Jenkins, A., & McKelvie, A. (2017). Is this the end? Investigating firm and individual level outcomes post-failure. *Journal of Business Venturing Insights*, 8, 138–143.

Jenkins, A., Steen, J., & Verreyenne, M. L. (2015). Growing business in Redlands. *Technical Report*.

Jenkins, A. S., Wiklund, J., & Brundin, E. (2014). Individual responses to firm failure: Appraisals, grief, and the influence of prior failure experience. *Journal of Business Venturing*, *29*(1), 17–33.

Kitson, G. C., Babri, K. B., Roach, M. J., & Placidi, K. S. (1989). Adjustment to widowhood and divorce: A review. *Journal of Family Issues*, *10*(1), 5–32.

Lazarus, R. S., & Folkman, S. (1984). *Stress, appraisal, and coping.* New York, NY: Springer.

Lewis, K. V. (2016). Identity capital: An exploration in the context of youth social entrepreneurship. *Entrepreneurship & Regional Development*, *28*(3–4), 191–205.

Mantere, S., Aula, P., Schildt, H., & Vaara, E. (2013). Narrative attributions of entrepreneurial failure. *Journal of Business Venturing*, *28*(4), 459–473.

Mathias, B. D., Solomon, S. J., & Madison, K. J. (2017). After the harvest: A stewardship perspective on entrepreneurship and philanthropy. *Journal of Business Venturing*, *32*(4), 385–404.

Murnieks, C. Y., Mosakowski, E., & Cardon, M. S. (2014). Pathways of passion: Identity centrality, passion, and behavior among entrepreneurs. *Journal of Management*, *40*(6), 1583–1606.

Naismith, S. L., Hickie, I. B., Turner, K., Little, C. L., Winter, V., Ward, P. B., . . . Parker, G. (2003). Neuropsychological performance in patients with depression is associated with clinical, etiological and genetic risk factors. *Journal of Clinical Experimental Neuropsychology*, *25*(6), 866–877.

Natterson, J. M., & Knudson Jr, A. G. (1960). Observations concerning fear of death in fatally ill children and their mothers. *Psychosomatic Medicine*, *22*(6), 456–465.

Neupert, S. D., Ennis, G. E., Ramsey, J. L., & Gall, A. A. (2015). Solving tomorrow's problems today? Daily anticipatory coping and reactivity to daily stressors. *The Journals of Gerontology Series B: Psychological Sciences and Social Sciences*, *71*(4), 650–660.

Nikolaev, B., Boudreaux, C. J., & Wood, M. (2019). Entrepreneurship and subjective well-being: The mediating role of psychological functioning. *Entrepreneurship Theory and Practice*. Retrieved from https://doi.org/10.1177/1042258719830314.

Powell, E. E., & Baker, T. (2014). It's what you make of it: Founder identity and enacting strategic responses to adversity. *Academy of Management Journal*, *57*(5), 1406–1433.

Powell, E. E., & Baker, T. (2017). In the beginning: Identity processes and organizing in multi-founder nascent ventures. *Academy of Management Journal*, *60*(6), 2381–2414.

Preller, R., Patzelt, H., & Breugst, N. (2018). Entrepreneurial visions in founding teams: Conceptualization, emergence, and effects on opportunity development. *Journal of Business Venturing, 35*(2).

Rouse, E. D. (2016). Beginning's end: How founders psychologically disengage from their organizations. *Academy of Management Journal, 59*(5), 1605–1629.

Shepherd, D. (2003). Learning from business failure: Propositions about the grief recovery process for the self-employed. *Academy of Management Review, 282*, 318–329.

Shepherd, D. (2009). Grief recovery from the loss of a family business: A multi- and meso-level theory. *Journal of Business Venturing, 24*(1), 81–97.

Shepherd, D. A., & Haynie, J. M. (2011). Venture failure, stigma, and impression management: A self-verification, self-determination view. *Strategic Entrepreneurship Journal, 5*(2), 178–197.

Shepherd, D. A., Wiklund, J., & Haynie, J. M. (2009). Moving forward: Balancing the financial and emotional costs of business failure. *Journal of Business Venturing, 24*(2), 134–148.

Shir, N., Nikolaev, B. N., & Wincent, J. (2019). Entrepreneurship and well-being: The role of psychological autonomy, competence, and relatedness. *Journal of Business Venturing, 34*(5), 105875.

Simmons, S., Wiklund, J., & Levie, J. (2013). Stigma and business failure: Implications for entrepreneurs' career choices. *Small Business Economics*, 1–21.

Singh, S., Corner, P., & Pavlovich, K. (2007). Coping with entrepreneurial failure. *Journal of Management and Organization, 13*, 331–344.

Singh, S., Corner, P., & Pavlovich, P. (2015). Failed, not finished: A narrative approach to understanding venture failure stigmatization. *Journal of Business Venturing, 30*(1), 150–166.

Staw, B. (1981). The escalation of commitment to a course of action. *The Academy of Management Review (pre-1986)*, 577.

Stokes, D., & Blackburn, R. (2002). Learning the hard way: The lessons of owner-managers who have closed their businesses. *Journal of Small Business and Enterprise Development, 9*(1).

Tversky, A., & Kahneman, D. (1981). The framing of decisions and the psychology of choice. *Science, 211*(4481), 453–458.

Ucbasaran, D., Shepherd, D. A., Lockett, A., & Lyon, S. J. (2013). Life after business failure: The process and consequences of business failure for entrepreneurs. *Journal of Management, 39*(1), 163–202.

Wennberg, K., Wiklund, J., DeTienne, D. R., & Cardon, M. S. (2010). Reconceptualizing entrepreneurial exit: Divergent exit routes and their drivers. *Journal of Business Venturing, 25*(4), 367–375.

Wilson, J. (1977). Anticipatory grief in response to threatened amputation. *Maternal-Child Nursing Journal, 6*(3), 177–186.

Wortman, C. B., & Silver, R. C. (1992). Reconsidering assumptions about coping with loss: An overview of current research. In L. Montada, S. H. Filipp, & M. Lerner (Eds.), *Life crises and experience of loss in adulthood*. Hillsdale, NJ: Erlbaum.

Yamakawa, Y., & Cardon, M. S. (2015). Causal ascriptions and perceived learning from entrepreneurial failure. *Small Business Economics, 44*(4), 797–820.

Yamakawa, Y., & Cardon, M. S. (2017). How prior investments of time, money, and employee hires influence time to exit a distressed venture, and the extent to which contingency planning helps. *Journal of Business Venturing, 32*(1), 1–17.

Yttermyr, O., & Wennberg, K. J. (2019, July). Psychological ownership development in new venture teams. In *Academy of Management Proceedings* (Vol. 2019, No. 1, p. 14550). Briarcliff Manor, NY: Academy of Management.

15

GEOGRAPHICAL CONTEXTS OF ENTREPRENEURSHIP

Spaces, Places and Entrepreneurial Agency

Erik Stam & Friederike Welter

Introduction

Whatever definition of entrepreneurship we apply, it mainly focuses on what individuals do. Agency is the starting point for entrepreneurship. However, entrepreneurship does not take place in a vacuum, but in particular circumstances, that is contexts. These circumstances, structures, and other agents are formative for entrepreneurship: they enable and constrain entrepreneurship, and they are constructed and enacted by entrepreneurs. The role and relevance of geographical contexts are not self-evident. For some, globalization means the end of geography (Cairncross, 2001; O'Brien, 1992), because processes of time-space compression have dramatically decreased the relevance of spatial distance. You can much more easily fly to locations on the other side of the world than ever, and communication with people around the world, regardless of the distance between them, has never been so easy. Acting globally as an entrepreneur seems less constrained than ever. However, in contradiction, place is said to become more important in the current period of globalization: most of the world's venture capital and unicorns (start-ups valued at US$1 billion, before public offering) are concentrated in a few places, with Silicon Valley standing out of the crowd. There are huge differences in self-employment rates between countries, and large cities, in general, are becoming more and more important concentrations of talent, entrepreneurial talent included. It is these new articulations of the local and the global that make the geographies of entrepreneurship such a fascinating field of studies.

This chapter focuses on contexts of entrepreneurship, in particular geographical contexts, and entrepreneurial agency. We start this chapter with the twin terms *space* and *place* that are key in understanding geographical contexts and how they are used in relation to entrepreneurship before we turn to present a model of entrepreneurial ecosystems that allows us to focus simultaneously on the geographical contexts for entrepreneurship and the agency of entrepreneurs within those. We then discuss entrepreneurial agency in relation to places in more detail. At the end of the chapter, we focus on new articulations that are currently emerging and outline a future research agenda.

Space and Place

Understanding Space and Place

In everyday language, *space* and *place* are often regarded as synonymous with terms including *region, area, location, geography,* and *landscape*. For geographers, however, space and place are distinctive key concepts to understand geography (Hubbard, Kitchin, & Valentine, 2004). Space refers to objective and place to subjective geographical contexts. Space has traditionally been conceived as a surface on which the relationship between things are played out, with distance and connection as concepts capturing spatial differences. Examples of space being the physical space in which entrepreneurship takes place, range from accessibility via plane, car, and train, to the workspace in a building, and the connectivity of nodes in social spaces. Place is subjectively defined. What constitutes a place is largely individualistic: simply put, a place means different things to different people. Examples of subjective place are the sense of place entrepreneurs have, place-specific cultures, and formal institutions, including politics and language. In reality, spaces devoid of subjective elements, and places devoid of objective elements are rare. The objective and subjective elements can overlap: countries and regions often having both objective physical and subjective institutional demarcations. They may also be disconnected: diaspora entrepreneurs' feeling of belonging, largely reflects a socially constructed view of the home country, and in social contexts, you can be physically proximate to certain persons while affectively being at a large distance.

This chapter focuses on geographical contexts, because for understanding entrepreneurship one has to take into account multiple geographical contexts. Even though one could say that entrepreneurship takes place in one geographical context, for example the 'world context', the geographical contexts that are relevant for entrepreneurship are multiple, ranging from the individual workspace to the world and perhaps outer space to the geographical location of the household of the entrepreneurs, their place identity, and the local and national institutions that enable and constrain the business activities of the entrepreneur. These contexts can be nested, reflecting different spatial scales (ranging for example from daily commuting/travel-to-work regions to nations to continents), potentially reinforced by political and economic hierarchical powers (municipalities, provinces, nations, supranational entities like the European Union).

Putting Space Back Into Place

Place does not exist without physical space. Research that has emphasized 'other' places for entrepreneurship or 'other' forms of entrepreneurship in relation to contexts has started to re-connect place and space, albeit in some instances more implicitly than explicit. We have identified the following discussions as important in this regard: the role of gendered places and spaces for entrepreneurship; research that brings household, family and neighbourhood perspectives to entrepreneurship; and research exploring new spaces for entrepreneurship.

Welter, Brush, & De Bruin (2014) provide a review on research that looks into how *spaces and places are gendered*, illustrating the close interactions between space as the physical business site and place as social and institutional spatial contexts and their impact on the nature and extent of women's entrepreneurship (Hanson, 2003, 2009). Physical space directly influences venture survival and development. Because women often start home-based they are frequently trapped in low-growth and low-performance activities (Thompson, Jones-Evans, & Kwong, 2009). However, women entrepreneurs also cluster spatially when working outside the home and in high-tech entrepreneurship. Mayer (2008) investigated high-tech female entrepreneurship in two established (Silicon Valley, Boston) and two emerging high-tech regions (Washington, Oregon) in the U.S. Women entrepreneurs tended to be located in suburban areas rather than the downtown locations whilst men-owned tech companies did not show such a spatial concentration. That implies that women select their business location based on more than business considerations.

Entrepreneurs may start from home, not only because they require the flexibility that space can provide but also because they lack resources. *Households and families* are important sites and places for entrepreneurship (Welter, 2011). Family, for example, impacts on entrepreneurship to a much greater extent than is implied in the literature on family businesses which puts the business into focus. Other perspectives focus on the wider family and their role for entrepreneurship in providing material and immaterial resources and support or in constraining entrepreneurial activities. Research has included a family embeddedness of entrepreneurship (e.g., Aldrich & Cliff, 2003), drawing on findings from family sciences (Jaskiewicz, Combs, Shanine, & Kacmar, 2017) or introducing the concept of family entrepreneurship (Bettinelli, Fayolle, & Randerson, 2014; Randerson, Bettinelli, Fayolle, & Anderson, 2015). Researchers also argue that households be studied as spatial sites of entrepreneurial activities. Entrepreneurial households can facilitate business growth, as has been shown for rural farm businesses in Norway and Scotland (Alsos, Carter, & Ljunggren, 2014): Business and households are nested within each other; family and kinship simultaneously are resources for business development and can impose restrictions onto business growth. Research therefore suggests a circular household–entrepreneurship interdependence model (Mwaura & Carter, 2015) to model the complex relations between business impact on the lives, well-being and fortunes of the household (Carter, Kuhl, Marlow, & Mwaura, 2017). Research on urban neighbourhoods and communities expands this spatial perspective on entrepreneurial households to their embeddedness in local places (Mason, Reuschke, Syrett, & van Ham, 2015; Van Ham, Reuschke, Kleinhans, Mason, & Syrett, 2017), drawing attention to the interplay of social and spatial contexts. Such local neighbourhoods and communities are the primary domains of many young ventures.

Not all households and families, however, are spatially close, and they may act entrepreneurial even though spatially disconnected which has been studied for the example of enterprising families living on both sides of a border, in this case the border between Belarus, Lithuania and Latvia (Welter et al., 2014). Family involvement came in two patterns. The first pattern reflects typical family participation in entrepreneurial ventures: Some family was directly involved in trading activities; some took over household responsibilities and the like. The second pattern of family involvement resulted from the border context. Family visits across the hard border between Belarus, Lithuania and Latvia, were possible because cross-border families were subject to favourable border-crossing regulations, especially if pensioners were involved. Family members living across the border triggered new opportunities for Belarussian entrepreneurs, asking for specific goods to be brought along on visits; they used their connections to market surplus brought along, thus reducing the risks and constraints connected with the informal trading activities; and they also helped to access products that, at that time, were scarce in Belarus and could be (oftentimes semi-legally) reimported to Belarus. This pattern of family involvement reflects the interplay of specific spatial, institutional and historical contexts (i.e., the border contexts during the transition from socialist to market economies in Eastern Europe in the late 1990s and early 2000s) with entrepreneurship, highlighting the importance of a spatial perspective on entrepreneurial families and households.

Recent work has started to pay attention to *new spaces of entrepreneurship* where social context is a constitutive element of space. For example, co-working places are gaining importance for entrepreneurs who may share office space, together with the social context inherent in co-working, and they oftentimes are used by freelancers or solo entrepreneurs (e.g., Fuzi, 2015; Gandini, 2016; Gerdenitsch, Scheel, Andorfer, & Korunka, 2016). Bouncken and Reuschl (2018) suggest that co-working emphasizes community building despite its pronounced focus on entrepreneurial autonomy. They point to co-working spaces as fostering entrepreneurial self-efficacy and trust which, in turn, will positively impact on entrepreneurial learning and performance. Other studies look at so-called makerspaces as spaces for (new) entrepreneurship. Making is commonly understood as "small-scale, integrated design and production of physical goods using low-cost equipment" (Eisenburger, Doussard, Wolf-Powers, Schrock, & Marotta, 2019, p. 1), makerspaces as physical spaces that are "shared fabrication facilities, representing a local manifestation of the movement and functioning as vertically integrated settings in which members benefit from co-located activities" (Browder, Aldrich, & Bradley, 2019). The authors model the maker movement as based on social exchange, the availability of technology resources, and with knowledge exchange and sharing as constitutive elements.

However, users of such new spaces may have similar attitudes to these flexible and open-space working arrangements, which indicates the potentially dark sides of such spaces. Even where these spaces have been constructed with openness in mind and foster social relations, the similarity of those using them may result, over time, in lock-in effects and a loss of openness, thus being detrimental to the region's development. Many of the new spaces for entrepreneurs are white and male-dominated, also because the built environment implicitly acts as additional constraint, excluding some and favoring others (Welter & Baker, 2020). Research on women entrepreneurs in high-technology business incubators (Marlow & McAdam, 2012) and makerspaces (Rosner, 2014, p. 67) suggests a highly gendered culture of these spaces in terms of who gets access and is supported. All this already points to the complexities of the interactions between entrepreneurship, place and space which we explore next from an ecosystems perspective.

Reconnecting Entrepreneurship to Geographical Contexts: An Ecosystems Perspective

Even though entrepreneurship is first and foremost about agency, there is growing recognition amongst entrepreneurs and other stakeholders in the entrepreneurial process about the role of place and space. This recognition is most strongly articulated with the new concept of entrepreneurial ecosystems. Just like it takes a village to raise a child, it is recognized that it takes an entrepreneurial ecosystem to create and grow a business. The entrepreneurial ecosystem comprises a set of interdependent actors and factors that are governed in such a way that they enable productive entrepreneurship (Stam, 2015). This set of interdependent actors and factors enable and constrain entrepreneurship within a particular territory (Stam & van de Ven, 2020). Entrepreneurship is an emergent property of the interactions of the elements and actors in the entrepreneurial ecosystem (Arthur, 2013; Fuller, Warren, & Welter, 2008; McKelvey, 2004). An entrepreneurial ecosystem includes both space and place. It is often spatially delineated, includes a physical infrastructure and has a spatial distance to actors and factors outside its territory. It also includes subjective elements like place-based culture and leadership.

Building on prior academic studies (Stam, 2015; Stam & Spigel, 2018), an integrative model of entrepreneurial ecosystems consisting of ten elements and entrepreneurial outputs has been developed. These ten elements are operational constructs of the broader concepts of institutions and resources of an entrepreneurial ecosystem. An entrepreneurial ecosystem includes institutional arrangements and resource endowments. The institutional arrangements component is captured by the formal institutions, culture and network elements, what has been called socio-cultural factors (Thornton, Ribeiro-Soriano, & Urbano, 2011). The resource endowment component is captured by the physical infrastructure, finance, leadership, talent, knowledge, intermediate services and demand elements. Entrepreneurship is the outcome of the ecosystem. Table 15.1 summarizes and relates these concepts, constructs and elements of entrepreneurial ecosystems.

The presence of these elements and their interactions are crucial for the success of the ecosystem. Institutions provide the fundamental preconditions for economic action to take place (Granovetter, 1992) and for resources to be used

TABLE 15.1 Constructs of Entrepreneurial Ecosystem Elements and Outputs

Concept	Construct	Definition	Element
Institutions	Formal institutions	The rules of the game in society	Formal institutions
	Informal institutions	Cultural context	Culture
	Social networks	The social context of actors, especially the degree to which they are socially connected	Networks
Resources	Physical resources	The physical context of actors that enables them to meet other actors in physical proximity	Physical infrastructure
	Financial resources	The presence of financial means to invest in activities that do not yet deliver financial means	Finance
	Leadership	Leadership that provides guidance for, and direction of, collective action	Leadership
	Human capital	The skills, knowledge, and experience possessed by individuals	Talent
	Knowledge	Investments in (scientific and technological) knowledge creation	Knowledge
	Means of consumption	The presence of financial means in the population to purchase goods and services	Demand

Concept	Construct	Definition	Element
	Producer services	The intermediate service inputs into proprietary functions	Intermediate services
New value creation	Productive entrepreneurship	Any entrepreneurial activity that contributes (in) directly to net output of the economy or to the capacity to produce additional output	Productive entrepreneurship

Source: Stam and Van de Ven (2020)

productively (Acemoglu, Johnson, & Robinson, 2005). Institutions also affect the way entrepreneurship is pursued and the welfare consequences of entrepreneurship (Baumol, 1990). Networks of entrepreneurs provide an information flow, enabling both the creation and effective distribution of resources. A highly developed physical infrastructure is a key element of the context to enable economic interaction and entrepreneurship in particular. Access to financing—preferably provided by investors with entrepreneurial knowledge—is crucial for investments in uncertain entrepreneurial projects with a long-term horizon. Leadership provides direction and instigates collective action for the entrepreneurial ecosystem. Perhaps the most important element of an effective entrepreneurial ecosystem is the presence of a diverse and skilled group of workers ('talent'). An important source of opportunities for entrepreneurship can be found in knowledge, from both public and private organizations. The supply of support services by a variety of intermediaries (including business services, incubators, accelerators) can substantially lower entry barriers for new entrepreneurial projects and reduce the time to market of innovations.

The proposed Entrepreneurial Ecosystem model (see Table 15.1 and Figure 15.1) extends insights from the geography of entrepreneurship literature by travelling the ladder of abstraction from theoretical constructs to observable elements of an entrepreneurial ecosystem. Specifically, the entrepreneurial ecosystem causal model is based on three propositions (Stam & van de Ven, 2020). First, the co-evolutionary proposition that the entrepreneurial ecosystem elements are mutually interdependent and co-evolve in a territory. Second, the upward causation proposition that the 10 observable entrepreneurial ecosystem elements explain the levels of entrepreneurial activity in a territory. Third, the downward causation proposition that prior entrepreneurial activities feedback into entrepreneurial ecosystem elements in a territory.

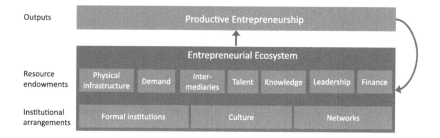

FIGURE 15.1 Entrepreneurial Ecosystem Model

Source: Based on Stam and Van de Ven (2020)

The growing interest in entrepreneurial ecosystems signals yet another shift of the entrepreneurship field in its consideration of geographical contexts for entrepreneurship and in contextualizing entrepreneurship. Entrepreneurial ecosystems are said to be defined and demarcated by a particular territory, mainly because many of the actors and factors enabling entrepreneurship need to be in spatial proximity of entrepreneurs but also because stakeholders of the ecosystem have a jurisdictional responsibility (public stakeholders) or identify themselves with the place in which the ecosystem is situated.

Whilst the entrepreneurial ecosystem approach emphasizes the structures enabling and constraining entrepreneurship, it also puts entrepreneurial agency centre stage in the governance and change of the ecosystem, via leadership and feedback effects of entrepreneurship on the nature of the entrepreneurial ecosystem. It thus combines agency—the 'doing contexts' perspective (Baker & Welter, 2018) we turn to next, and the geographical contexts of space and place. Entrepreneurial agency can be an output and input to the system: entrepreneurship emerges as a product of the ecosystem ('emergent property'), enabled and constrained by its elements and their interactions, but entrepreneurial agents can also change the ecosystem by infusing their knowledge and networks and by acting as a role model or even as a leader, enforcing collective action, changing formal institutions and cultures ('institutional entrepreneurship').

The Agency of Entrepreneurs in and Towards Geographical Contexts

Entrepreneurs can influence geographical contexts, as they enact, talk about and visualize their contexts (Baker & Welter, 2020). Entrepreneurial activities and actions impact on and change the geographical contexts, as Feldman (2014, p. 10) observes: "What matters most is human agency—the building of institutions and the myriad public and private decisions that determine the character of place". In describing a case of a locally rooted company with broad global sales which, by settling locally in the hometown of the entrepreneur, helped reviving a peripheral town and region, Feldman (2014) points to that his entrepreneurial actions do not fit existing explanations of what makes places entrepreneurial. However, her example clearly illustrates that and how entrepreneurs engage with and enact their spatial contexts—they 'do context' (Baker & Welter, 2017). Research has explored entrepreneurship as change-making for and in a variety of places. In this section, we draw on selected elements of the model set out in the previous section to briefly discuss the facets of entrepreneurial agency in relation to spaces and places.

Institutional Change and Entrepreneurship

Places change because formal and informal institutions change. Entrepreneurship is one of the mechanisms through which such change can happen. Some research identifies differences in the importance attributed to spatial factors between family and non-family start-ups (Bird & Wennberg, 2014): Family start-ups were less concerned about economic factors but put higher emphasis on non-economic factors like favourable place attitudes towards entrepreneurship. The authors suggest that this may reflect the long-term orientation of family firms and their strong regional embeddedness, which favours them locating in regions they are familiar with and where they can easily establish long-term oriented relationships with relevant stakeholders—even if those regions may not prosper economically. Socio-spatial links and a strong past in the region apparently help family firms to overcome (temporary) resource scarcities and, in turn, influence the enterprise community within the region.

This points to the role of regional traditions and mentalities that may foster or hamper entrepreneurial agency within places. For example, Fritsch, Obschonka, and Wyrwich (2019) show a link between historical differences in regional levels of self-employment (as a measure for entrepreneurial activities), favourable cultural attitudes towards entrepreneurship and new firm formation rates in the present. Where regional entrepreneurship levels historically have been high, the authors observe a positive relation to the current entrepreneurial personality fit. Variations in the average entrepreneurial personality fit across regions that result from these historical differences positively affect current new business formation. The authors conclude that entrepreneurial place traditions matter, as they foster place-based role models which are transmitted across generations.

Such entrepreneurial place traditions even survive disruptive political shocks, as has been demonstrated for Kaliningrad, a former Soviet, now Russian exclave (Fritsch, Sorgner, Wyrwich, & Zazdravnykh, 2019). Historically, Kaliningrad was part of East Prussia until the Second World War, before the German population was expelled and the exclave came under Soviet rule. But despite the fundamental shocks the exclave Kaliningrad experienced over the past century, historical entrepreneurial attitudes still influence today's entrepreneurship, as reflected in the positive relationship between industry-specific self-employment rates in

1925 and industry-specific share of small firms in 2010 (Fritsch, Sorgner, et al., 2019, p. 791). The authors identify a place-specific awareness of entrepreneurial traditions as helpful transmission mechanism throughout periods of high uncertainty. Similarly, research has illustrated how entrepreneurs creatively use, re-use and recombine spatially demarcated resources and institutions, as, for example, the shared cultural and historical backgrounds of the population both sides of a national border, to circumvent and adjust border regulations in their favour (Cassidy, 2011; Fadahunsi & Rosa, 2002; Polese & Rodgers, 2011; Welter, Xheneti, & Smallbone, 2018).

Some research also suggests that maker entrepreneurship could assist in reviving regional manufacturing in the U.S. (Wolf-Powers et al., 2017). Makers certainly can change local places, not least because of their 'unruliness' and the grass-roots nature of the movement. For example, Lin (2019) shows in which ways the maker-space movement in Taipei draws on socio-spatial strategies across multiple spaces as alternative strategies for urban development but which contradict existing official policies that focus on the makers' potential contribution to local development.

Such behaviour has been labelled 'institutional entrepreneurship' (Li, Feng, & Jiang, 2006). However, that concept has been criticized for its lack of attention to contexts (Clegg, 2010) and to the emergent nature of entrepreneurship (Aldrich, 2010) respectively the dominant focus on intentional agency (Welter, 2012). Welter and Smallbone (2015) therefore suggest the concept of institutional change-makers to also capture institutional change as an unintended by-product of entrepreneurial actions. Much research on entrepreneurship in turbulent political or economic contexts shows entrepreneurs acting as rule-breakers or rule-avoiders (e.g., Mair & Marti, 2009; Welter & Smallbone, 2011), thus—unintentionally—contributing to institutional change over time.

More in line with the core concept of 'institutional entrepreneurship', that is intentional entrepreneurial agency directed towards institutional change is the dealmaker, introduced by Feldman and Zoller (2012) as a key change agent: The dealmaker is someone who is deeply embedded in a place and intentionally and actively builds local capacity, thus demonstrating place-based leadership through assuming "a constitutive role" and demonstrating "regional stewardship by making connections in purposeful ways" (p. 26). Their empirical results for 12 exemplary U.S. regions suggest that the presence of many dealmakers, signalling a highly networked regional economy is a more suitable indicator to assess successful entrepreneurial regions than high rates of firm birth. Also, firms that are connected to at least one dealmaker can improve their business performance, as reflected in employment and sales (Kemeny, Feldman, Ethridge, & Zoller, 2016).

Networking for Community Development

Focusing on the person and their networks, Johannisson (1990) introduced the community entrepreneur as someone who acts in favour of the community, who networks for local development (Johannisson & Nilsson, 1989) and who "also takes pride in making him/herself redundant by building a self-organizing community" (Johannisson, 1990, p. 78). In its original understanding, community-based entrepreneurship has a distinctive geographical connotation and is linked to disadvantaged places, with the community acting collectively as entrepreneur and enterprise (Peredo & Chrisman, 2006, 2017). Much research on community-based entrepreneurship focuses on investigating the role of entrepreneurs for (disadvantaged) communities. For example, depleted places which are characterized by low economic prospects, but high social and place attachments, have been shown to offer unique opportunities for community-based entrepreneurship—opportunities that allow entrepreneurs to doing good to the place while doing business (Johnstone & Lionais, 2004): The entrepreneurs that initiated social community change were both anchored in their local and in the outside world. Business leaders had acquired their education outside of the place of business and held high-status employment positions prior to their community business whilst at the same time they had no problems stepping outside their status and roles and challenging community perceptions.

Marti, Courpasson and Dubard Barbosa's (2013) study looks into how a local community in Argentina becomes entrepreneurial. They identify the interactions between a close-knit local community, with values like mutuality, care and belonging, and community members who are outgoing, emancipated and provide individual leadership, as vital for its entrepreneurization. Similarly, for rural entrepreneurship, Korsgaard, Ferguson, and Gaddefors (2015) suggest that local thick social ties matter as does the willingness and ability of entrepreneurs to communicate and interact beyond the region their business is located in. Not surprisingly, those that are not fully embedded in local communities and economies are quicker in relocating outside of their place, creating bridges between spatial contexts (Korsgaard, Müller, & Tanvig, 2015). Accessing resources outside the region also will support regional development, because entrepreneurs contribute to openness and prevent lock-ins.

Jennings, Greenwood, Lounsbury, and Suddaby (2013) suggest a classification of community entrepreneurship that goes beyond the geographical, social and disadvantaged notion of community but includes also well-off spatial community contexts as well as industry and sector, national and transnational contexts. They emphasize the various ways beyond community-based entrepreneurship that entrepreneurs profit from being embedded in place and simultaneously can contribute to spatial change by leveraging various elements of the entrepreneurial ecosystem as resources.

Leveraging Human Capital, Knowledge and Social Networks as Spatial Resources

Where a place-bound knowledge infrastructure such as higher education organizations has existed for a long time, this positively impacts on today's entrepreneurship, drawing attention to the interplay of historical and social contexts as spatial resources for entrepreneurship. For German regions, Fritsch and Wyrwich (2018) can identify a clear impact of regional historical knowledge trajectories, entrepreneurial traditions (especially of science-based businesses) on innovative business activities today. Del Monte and Pennacchio (2019) expand this, showing for Italian regions that not only the place-bound historical knowledge base is positively related to current innovative entrepreneurship but also past place-related creativity as reflected by the presence of scientists and inventors in past times.

Also, communities of practices as spatially bounded networks that are based on trust, spatial and relational proximity, have been shown to assist small firms, especially in peripheral regions, to leverage knowledge and other resources. For knowledge-intensive business services, Schmidt (2015) illustrates the role of spatial knowledge spillovers in improving strategic decision-making within the firm and the quality of services offered. Brinks and Ibert (2015) focus on the relational spaces of such communities. However, such communities of practice also rely on members being able and willing to engage and develop their spatial community. And not all entrepreneurs show the same commitment to the places their business is located in as has been shown by Crowley, McAdam, Cunningham and Hilliard (2018), who suggest a link between the networking identity of owner-managers and their willingness to participate in developing their community of practice.

Social capital, as reflected in networks and such communities of practice, also fosters knowledge transfer between enterprises and other organizations residing within a place. Such collective learning needs spatial and social proximity, because it emerges from conversations and interactions among individuals within a regional context. However, social capital also has its dark sides in this regard: for Poland, Kaminska (2010) shows how bonding social capital changed its role and impact on regions over time: it contributed to local economic development in the early 1990s but became more harmful over time, restricting learning and de-learning within the region as well as negatively impacting on cooperative behaviour. Research for enterprises in Russia (Batjargal, 2003, 2006) illustrates a differentiated picture of inert social capital in relation to business and regional development: Extensive and resource-rich networks which however are relationally inert, improved business performance. Old-tie networks that are not renewed create stability in turbulent economic and institutional contexts, although over time they contribute to firm-level and regional lock-in effects.

Advancing a Future Research Agenda on Geographical Contexts for Entrepreneurship

In the final section, we briefly outline avenues for future research on geographical contexts for entrepreneurship, that build on and could extend current perspectives on the geographical contexts of entrepreneurship.

Expanding Entrepreneurial Agency: The Construction of Entrepreneurial Places and Spaces

The mechanisms through which geographical changes happen are not only entrepreneurial actions but also the way we make sense of the world, through our cognitions (Brännback & Carsrud, 2016), as well as the words and images we use to describe our world (Welter, 2019). High-tech entrepreneurial identities are influenced by potentially contradictory place-based discourses whilst entrepreneurs simultaneously engage in 'place-making' through their own storytelling (Gill & Larson, 2014), entrepreneurial ecosystems also are narrated (Roundy & Bayer, 2019), regional institutions are lived and interpreted experiences (Lowe & Feldman, 2017), and entrepreneurship is influenced by the materiality of places and the role of place-specific artefacts (Muñoz & Kimmitt, 2019). We suggest this focus on the various mechanisms of context construction as fruitful future research themes, because it can provide novel insights into why entrepreneurship differs across regions and why some places are more entrepreneurial than others.

Entrepreneurship, New and Old Forms of Spatiality

Digitization potentially changes the role and impact of spatial proximity for entrepreneurship and it creates a new form of spatiality. Entrepreneurial networks no longer need spatial proximity to emerge although relational proximity may still be required; hybrid virtual communities afford social dynamics and entrepreneurial learning which does not happen in face-to-face contexts (Grabher & Ibert, 2013). Still, there is an ongoing discussion as to whether entrepreneurship networks can only operate in digital space or whether they need face-to-face contacts as well. The recent emergence of new physical spaces for entrepreneurship such as co-working spaces or makerspaces appears to reconfirm the importance of real-world contacts beyond the virtual exchange possibilities the new technologies offer. Research could explore the good and bad sides of spatial proximity and distance in relation to physical, virtual and hybrid spaces for entrepreneurship.

Digital technologies also contribute to a revival of home-based business, allowing entrepreneurs to easily connect from home to the world, thus bridging local sites for business with global spaces. Is this indeed a part of a process connecting economy back with society as has been suggested by some (Luckman, 2015, p. 146)? Which are the social and individual consequences of the further intrusion of economic considerations in spaces and places that have been considered private, thus further blurring the boundaries between work and private lives? Overall, we need more studies that uncover the complexities of the new spaces and places, their impact on entrepreneurship respectively the agency of entrepreneurs in shaping these geographical contexts the ways they want and need them.

Developing the Entrepreneurial Ecosystem Approach

Entrepreneurial ecosystem research has the promise to provide a science-based framework for improving the conditions of entrepreneurship and to ultimately improve aggregate welfare. In order to achieve this, we need to better understand both the elements of ecosystems and the interactions within and between these elements, in other words, their interdependence and co-evolution. The entrepreneurial ecosystem approach provides a new lens to study the geographical contexts of entrepreneurship. An improved and expanded analysis of space and place is needed. Space not only includes the territorial bounds of the ecosystem but also refers to the nestedness and multiple spatial scales that are relevant for the actors and key mechanisms driving entrepreneurship. Space also includes the role of physical infrastructures enabling interaction, the movement of bodies, artefacts and data. The latter currently is being revolutionized by digitization. However, the effects of space on entrepreneurship are often mediated or moderated by the nature of place that is the meanings people give to and derive from their geographical context. Studying these interactions within and between elements of entrepreneurial ecosystems, their interdependence and co-evolution, necessitates a rich set of quantitative and qualitative methodologies and a large research program to integrate and accumulate the findings of how entrepreneurial ecosystems work around the world.

References

Acemoglu, D., Johnson, S., & Robinson, J. A. (2005). Institutions as a fundamental cause of long-run growth. In P. Aghion & S. Durlauf (Eds.), *Handbook of economic growth* (Vol. 1, pp. 385–472). Amsterdam: Elsevier.

Aldrich, H. E. (2010). Beam me up, Scott(ie)! Institutional theorists' struggles with the emergent nature of entrepreneurship. *Research in the Sociology of Work, 21,* 329–364.

Aldrich, H. E., & Cliff, J. E. (2003). The pervasive effects of family on entrepreneurship: Toward a family embeddedness perspective. *Journal of Business Venturing, 18*(5), 573–596.

Alsos, G. A., Carter, S., & Ljunggren, E. (2014). Kinship and business: How entrepreneurial households facilitate business growth. *Entrepreneurship & Regional Development, 26*(1–2), 97–122. Retrieved from https://doi.org/10.1080/08985626.2013.870235

Arthur, W. B. (2013). *Complexity economics.* New York: Oxford University Press.

Baker, T., & Welter, F. (2017). Come on out of the ghetto, please! - Building the future of entrepreneurship research. *International Journal of Entrepreneurial Behaviour & Research, 23*(2), 170–184. Retrieved from https://doi.org/10.1108/ijebr-02-2016-0065

Baker, T., & Welter, F. (2018). Contextual entrepreneurship: An interdisciplinary perspective. *Foundations and Trends in Entrepreneurship, 14*(4), 357–426. Retrieved from https://doi.org/10.1561/0300000078

Baker, T., & Welter, F. (2020). *Contextualizing entrepreneurship theory.* New York: Routledge.

Batjargal, B. (2003). Social capital and entrepreneurial performance in Russia: A longitudinal study. *Organization Studies, 24,* 535–556.

Batjargal, B. (2006). The dynamics of entrepreneurs' networks in a transitioning economy: The case of Russia. *Entrepreneurship & Regional Development, 18*(4), 305–320. Retrieved from https://doi.org/10.1080/08985620600717448

Baumol, W. J. (1990). Entrepreneurship - Productive, unproductive, and destructive. *Journal of Political Economy, 98*(5), 893–921. <Go to ISI>://A1990EE96700001

Bettinelli, C., Fayolle, A., & Randerson, K. (2014). Family entrepreneurship: A developing field. *Foundations and Trends® in Entrepreneurship, 10*(3), 161–236. Retrieved from https://doi.org/10.1561/0300000049

Bird, M., & Wennberg, K. (2014). Regional influences on the prevalence of family versus non-family start-ups. *Journal of Business Venturing, 29*(3), 421–436. Retrieved from https://doi.org/10.1016/j.jbusvent.2013.06.004

Bouncken, R. B., & Reuschl, A. J. (2018). Coworking-spaces: How a phenomenon of the sharing economy builds a novel trend for the workplace and for entrepreneurship. *Review of Managerial Science, 12*(1), 317–334.

Brännback, M., & Carsrud, A. (2016). Understanding entrepreneurial cognitions through the lenses of context. In F. Welter & W. B. Gartner (Eds.), *A research agenda on entrepreneurship and context* (pp. 16–27). Cheltenham, UK: Edward Elgar Publishing.

Brinks, V., & Ibert, O. (2015). Mushrooming entrepreneurship: The dynamic geography of enthusiast-driven innovation. *Geoforum, 65*, 363–373.

Browder, R. E., Aldrich, H., & Bradley, S. W. (2019). The emergence of the maker movement: Implications for entrepreneurship research. *Journal of Business Venturing, 34*(3), 459–476.

Cairncross, F. (2001). *The death of distance 2.0.* London, UK: Texere.

Carter, S., Kuhl, A., Marlow, S., & Mwaura, S. (2017). Households as a site of entrepreneurial activity. *Foundations and Trends in Entrepreneurship, 13*(2), 81–190. Retrieved from https://doi.org/10.1561/0300000062

Cassidy, K. (2011). Performing the cross-border economies of post-socialism. *The International Journal of Sociology and Social Policy, 31*(11-12), 632–647. Retrieved from https://doi.org/10.1108/01443331111177841

Clegg, S. (2010). The state, power, and agency: Missing in action in institutional theory? *Journal of Management Inquiry, 19*(1), 4–13. Retrieved from https://doi.org/10.1177/1056492609347562

Crowley, C., McAdam, M., Cunningham, J. A., & Hilliard, R. (2018). Community of practice: A flexible construct for understanding SME networking roles in the Irish artisan cheese sector. *Journal of Rural Studies, 64*, 50–62.

Del Monte, A., & Pennacchio, L. (2019). Historical roots of regional entrepreneurship: The role of knowledge and creativity. *Small Business Economics*, 1–22.

Eisenburger, M., Doussard, M., Wolf-Powers, L., Schrock, G., & Marotta, S. (2019). Industrial inheritances: Makers, relatedness and materiality in New York and Chicago. *Regional Studies, 53*(11), 1625–1635. Retrieved from https://doi.org/10.1080/00343404.2019.1588460

Fadahunsi, A., & Rosa, P. (2002). Entrepreneurship and illegality: Insights from the Nigerian cross-border trade. *Journal of Business Venturing, 17*(5), 397–429.

Feldman, M. P. (2014). The character of innovative places: Entrepreneurial strategy, economic development, and prosperity. *Small Business Economics, 43*(1), 9–20.

Feldman, M. P., & Zoller, T. D. (2012). Dealmakers in place: Social capital connections in regional entrepreneurial economies. *Regional Studies, 46*(1), 23–37. Retrieved from https://doi.org/10.1080/00343404.2011.607808

Fritsch, M., Obschonka, M., & Wyrwich, M. (2019). Historical roots of entrepreneurship-facilitating culture and innovation activity: An analysis for German regions. *Regional Studies*, 1–12. Retrieved from https://doi.org/10.1080/00343404.2019.1580357

Fritsch, M., Sorgner, A., Wyrwich, M., & Zazdravnykh, E. (2019). Historical shocks and persistence of economic activity: Evidence on self-employment from a unique natural experiment. *Regional Studies, 53*(6), 790–802. Retrieved from https://doi.org/10.1080 /00343404.2018.1492112

Fritsch, M., & Wyrwich, M. (2018). Regional knowledge, entrepreneurial culture, and innovative start-ups over time and space-an empirical investigation [journal article]. *Small Business Economics, 51*(2), 337–353. Retrieved from https://doi.org/10.1007/ s11187-018-0016-6

Fuller, T., Warren, L., & Welter, F. (2008). An emergence perspective on entrepreneurship: Processes, structure and methodology. *Centre for Operational Research, Management Science and Information Systems Working Papers* (CORMSIS-08-02). Southampton University: School of Management.

Fuzi, A. (2015). Co-working spaces for promoting entrepreneurship in sparse regions: The case of South Wales. *Regional Studies, Regional Science, 2*(1), 462–469.

Gandini, A. (2016). *The reputation economy: Understanding knowledge work in digital society.* London, UK: Palgrave MacMillan.

Gerdenitsch, C., Scheel, T. E., Andorfer, J., & Korunka, C. (2016). Coworking spaces: A source of social support for independent professionals. *Frontiers in Psychology, 7.* Retrieved from https://doi.org/10.3389/fpsyg.2016.00581

Gill, R., & Larson, G. S. (2014). Making the ideal (local) entrepreneur: Place and the regional development of high-tech entrepreneurial identity. *Human Relations, 67*(5), 519–542. Retrieved from https://doi.org/10.1177/0018726713496829

Grabher, G., & Ibert, O. (2013). Distance as asset? Knowledge collaboration in hybrid virtual communities. *Journal of Economic Geography, 14*(1), 97–123. Retrieved from https:// doi.org/10.1093/jeg/lbt014

Granovetter, M. (1992). Economic institutions as social constructions – A framework for analysis. *Acta Sociologica, 35*(1), 3–11. <Go to ISI>://A1992HM40200001

Hanson, S. (2003). Geographical and feminist perspectives on entrepreneurship. *Geographische Zeitschrift, 91*(1), 1–23.

Hanson, S. (2009). Changing places through women's entrepreneurship. *Economic Geography, 85*(3), 245–267. Retrieved from https://doi.org/10.1111/j.1944-8287.2009.01033.x

Hubbard, P., Kitchin, R., & Valentine, G. (Eds.). (2004). *Key thinkers on space and place.* Thousand Oaks, CA: Sage.

Jaskiewicz, P., Combs, J. G., Shanine, K. K., & Kacmar, K. M. (2017). Introducing the family: A review of family science with implications for management research. *Academy of Management Annals, 11*(1), 309–341. Retrieved from https://doi.org/10.5465/ annals.2014.0053

Jennings, P. D., Greenwood, R., Lounsbury, M. D., & Suddaby, R. (2013). Institutions, entrepreneurs, and communities: A special issue on entrepreneurship. *Journal of Business Venturing, 28*(1), 1–9. Retrieved from https://doi.org/10.1016/j. jbusvent.2012.07.001

Johannisson, B. (1990). Community entrepreneurship-cases and conceptualization. *Entrepreneurship & Regional Development, 2*(1), 71–88.

Johannisson, B., & Nilsson, A. (1989). Community entrepreneurs: Networking for local development. *Entrepreneurship & Regional Development, 1*(1), 3–19.

Johnstone, H., & Lionais, D. (2004). Depleted communities and community business entrepreneurship: Revaluing space through place. *Entrepreneurship & Regional Development, 16*(3), 217–233. Retrieved from https://doi.org/10.1080/0898562042000197117

Kaminska, M. E. (2010). Bonding social capital in a postcommunist region. *American Behavioral Scientist, 53*(5), 758–777. Retrieved from https://doi.org/10.1177/0002764209350836

Kemeny, T., Feldman, M., Ethridge, F., & Zoller, T. (2016). The economic value of local social networks. *Journal of Economic Geography, 16*(5), 1101–1122. Retrieved from https://doi.org/10.1093/jeg/lbv043

Korsgaard, S., Ferguson, R., & Gaddefors, J. (2015). The best of both worlds: How rural entrepreneurs use placial embeddedness and strategic networks to create opportunities. *Entrepreneurship & Regional Development, 27*(9–10), 574–598. Retrieved from https://doi.org/10.1080/08985626.2015.1085100

Korsgaard, S., Müller, S., & Tanvig, H. W. (2015). Rural entrepreneurship or entrepreneurship in the rural-between place and space. *International Journal of Entrepreneurial Behavior & Research, 21*(1), 5–26.

Li, D. D., Feng, J., & Jiang, H. (2006). Institutional entrepreneurs. *The American Economic Review, 96*(2), 358–362. Retrieved from https://doi.org/10.1257/000282806777211775

Lin, C.-Y. (2019). The hybrid gathering of maker communities in Taipei makerspaces: An alternative worlding practice. *City, Culture and Society, 19*, 100282. Retrieved from https://doi.org/10.1016/j.ccs.2019.01.001

Lowe, N. J., & Feldman, M. P. (2017). Institutional life within an entrepreneurial region. *Geography Compass, 11*(3), e12306. Retrieved from https://doi.org/10.1111/gec3.12306

Luckman, S. (2015). Women's micro-entrepreneurial homeworking: A "magical solution" to the work–life relationship? *Australian Feminist Studies, 30*(84), 146–160. Retrieved from https://doi.org/10.1080/08164649.2015.1038117

Mair, J., & Marti, I. (2009). Entrepreneurship in and around institutional voids: A case study from Bangladesh. *Journal of Business Venturing, 24*(5), 419–435. Retrieved from https://doi.org/10.1016/j.jbusvent.2008.04.006

Marlow, S., & McAdam, M. (2012). Analyzing the influence of gender upon high-technology venturing within the context of business incubation. *Entrepreneurship Theory and Practice, 36*(4), 655–676.

Marti, I., Courpasson, D., & Dubard Barbosa, S. (2013). "Living in the fishbowl": Generating an entrepreneurial culture in a local community in Argentina. *Journal of Business Venturing, 28*(1), 10–29. Retrieved from https://doi.org/10.1016/j.jbusvent.2011.09.001

Mason, C., Reuschke, D., Syrett, S., & van Ham, M. (Eds.). (2015). *Entrepreneurship in cities: Neighbourhoods, households and homes*. Cheltenham, UK: Edward Elgar Publishing.

Mayer, H. (2008). Segmentation and segregation patterns of women-owned high-tech firms in four metropolitan regions in the United States. *Regional Studies, 42*(10), 1357–1383. Retrieved from https://doi.org/10.1080/00343400701654194

McKelvey, B. (2004). Toward a complexity science of entrepreneurship. *Journal of Business Venturing, 19*(3), 313–341.

Muñoz, P., & Kimmitt, J. (2019). Rural entrepreneurship in place: An integrated framework. *Entrepreneurship & Regional Development*, 1–32. Retrieved from https://doi.org/10.1080/08985626.2019.1609593

Mwaura, S., & Carter, S. (2015). Entrepreneurship as the business of the household. In C. Mason, D. Reuschke, S. Syrett, & M. Van Ham (Eds.), *Entrepreneurship in cities: Neighbourhoods, households and homes* (pp. 201–222). Cheltenham, UK: Edward Elgar Publishing.

O'Brien, R. (1992). *Global financial integration: The end of geography*. London, UK: Pinter.

Peredo, A. M., & Chrisman, J. J. (2006). Toward a theory of community-based enterprise. *Academy of Management Review, 31*(2), 309–328.

Peredo, A. M., & Chrisman, J. J. (2017). Conceptual foundations: Community-based enterprise and community development. In M. Van Ham, D. Reuschke, R. Kleinhans, C. Mason, & S. Syrett (Eds.), *Entrepreneurial neighbourhoods* (pp. 151–178). Cheltenham, UK: Edward Elgar Publishing.

Polese, A., & Rodgers, P. (2011). Surviving post-socialism: The role of informal economic practices. *The International Journal of Sociology and Social Policy, 31*(11-12), 612–618. Retrieved from https://doi.org/10.1108/01443331111177896

Randerson, K., Bettinelli, C., Fayolle, A., & Anderson, A. (2015). Family entrepreneurship as a field of research: Exploring its contours and contents. *Journal of Family Business Strategy, 6*(3), 143–154.

Rosner, D. K. (2014). Making citizens, reassembling devices: On gender and the development of contemporary public sites of repair in Northern California. *Public Culture, 26*(1 (72)), 51–77.

Roundy, P. T., & Bayer, M. A. (2019). Entrepreneurial ecosystem narratives and the microfoundations of regional entrepreneurship. *International Journal of Entrepreneurship and Innovation, 20*(3), 194–208. Retrieved from https://doi.org/10.1177/1465750318808426

Schmidt, S. (2015). Balancing the spatial localisation "tilt": Knowledge spillovers in processes of knowledge-intensive services. *Geoforum, 65*, 374–386. Retrieved from https://doi.org/10.1016/j.geoforum.2015.05.009

Stam, E. (2015). Entrepreneurial ecosystems and regional policy: A sympathetic critique. *European Planning Studies, 23*(9), 1759–1769.

Stam, E., & Spigel, B. (2018). Entrepreneurial ecosystems. In R. Blackburn, D. De Clercq, & J. Heinonen (Eds.), *The SAGE handbook of small business and entrepreneurship* (pp. 407–422). Thousand Oaks, CA: Sage.

Stam, E., & van de Ven, A. (2020). Entrepreneurial ecosystems: A systems perspective. *Small Business Economics*. Retrieved from https://doi.org/doi:10.1007/s11187-019-00270-6

Thompson, P., Jones-Evans, D., & Kwong, C. (2009). Women and home-based entrepreneurship evidence from the United Kingdom. *International Small Business Journal: Researching Entrepreneurship, 27*(2), 227–239.

Thornton, P. H., Ribeiro-Soriano, D., & Urbano, D. (2011). Socio-cultural factors and entrepreneurial activity: An overview. *International Small Business Journal: Researching Entrepreneurship, 29*(2), 105–118. Retrieved from https://doi.org/10.1177/0266242610391930

Van Ham, M., Reuschke, D., Kleinhans, R., Mason, C., & Syrett, S. (Eds.). (2017). *Entrepreneurial neighbourhoods: Towards an understanding of the economies of neighbourhoods and communities*. Cheltenham, UK: Edward Elgar Publishing.

Welter, F. (2011). Contextualizing entrepreneurship: Conceptual challenges and ways forward. *Entrepreneurship Theory and Practice, 35*(1), 165–184. Retrieved from https://doi.org/10.1111/j.1540-6520.2010.00427.x

Welter, F. (2012). Breaking or making institutions? A closer look at (institutional) change agents. *Rencontres de St-Gall 2012: In search of a dynamic equilibrium: Exploring and managing tensions in entrepreneurship and SMEs*, University of St. Gallen, St. Gallen.

Welter, F. (2019). The power of words and images – Towards talking about and seeing entrepreneurship and innovation differently. In D. Audretsch, E. Lehmann, & A. N. Link (Eds.), *A research agenda for entrepreneurship and innovation* (pp. 179–196). Cheltenham, UK: Edward Elgar Publishing.

Welter, F., & Baker, T. (2020). Moving contexts onto new roads – Clues from other disciplines. *Entrepreneurship Theory and Practice*. Retrieved from https://journals.sagepub.com/doi/10.1177/1042258720930996

Welter, F., Brush, C., & De Bruin, A. (2014). The gendering of entrepreneurship context. *Working Paper*, IfM Bonn.

Welter, F., & Smallbone, D. (2011). Institutional perspectives on entrepreneurial behavior in challenging environments. *Journal of Small Business Management, 49*(1), 107–125. Retrieved from https://doi.org/10.1111/j.1540-627X.2010.00317.x

Welter, F., & Smallbone, D. (2015). Creative forces for entrepreneurship: The role of institutional change agents. *Working Paper*, No. 1/15, IfM Bonn.

Welter, F., Smallbone, D., Slonimski, A., Linchevskaya, O., Pobol, A., & Slonimska, M. (2014). Enterprising families in a cross-border context: The example of Belarus. In M. T. T. Thai & E. Turkina (Eds.), *Internationalization of firms from economies in transition* (pp. 276–302). Cheltenham, UK: Edward Elgar Publishing.

Welter, F., Xheneti, M., & Smallbone, D. (2018). Entrepreneurial resourcefulness in unstable institutional contexts: The example of European Union borderlands. *Strategic Entrepreneurship Journal, 12*(1), 23–53. Retrieved from https://doi.org/10.1002/sej.1274

Wolf-Powers, L., Doussard, M., Schrock, G., Heying, C., Eisenburger, M., & Marotta, S. (2017). The maker movement and urban economic development. *Journal of the American Planning Association, 83*(4), 365–376.

16

ENTREPRENEURSHIP TRAINING AND TRANSFER

K. Jakob Weers & Michael M. Gielnik

Introduction

Practitioners still debate whether entrepreneurs are born or whether entrepreneurs can learn their trade (e.g. The Guardian, 2017). In this regard, the last decade of research on entrepreneurship education and training (EET) has provided some answers. Meta-analytical evidence suggests that EET can be effective in increasing short- and long-term outcomes in entrepreneurship (Martin, McNally, & Kay, 2013). However, the same meta-analysis also shows that the effects significantly vary across studies, suggesting that EET interventions substantially differ in their effectiveness. In this chapter, we give an overview of the meta-analytic findings and point out that a lot of heterogeneity exists in the effect sizes of EET interventions. To explain the heterogeneity, we argue that a more detailed investigation of different teaching methodologies (i.e. the pedagogical approach of training elements) is needed to advance the understanding of how and why entrepreneurship education is effective. Furthermore, we argue that the rigor of the evaluation study accounts for additional heterogeneity in effect sizes. To provide a detailed discussion of the two factors that explain differences in EET effectiveness (i.e., training methodology and methodological rigor of the evaluation studies), we present the results of the most rigorous evaluation studies and discuss the effectiveness of different EET interventions based on trustworthy effect sizes. Moreover, we develop a framework of training methodologies to better understand the effectiveness of different types of EET interventions. The framework is based on a review of the literature on EET and the psychological literature on training and complex skill acquisition. Finally, to acknowledge that outcomes of EET interventions, such as business creation, usually unfold over long periods (i.e., months or years), we give an overview of our current understanding of long-term transfer of EET and point out directions for future research in this area.

Meta-Analyses on the Effectiveness of Entrepreneurship Education and Training

We present the meta-analytical evidence on the effectiveness of EET and differentiate between learning outcomes, behavior, and results. Within the category of learning outcomes, we focus on cognitive and motivational outcomes (Kraiger, Ford, & Salas, 1993). Regarding behavior and results, we present findings on entrepreneurial behavior and success.

Learning: Motivational and Cognitive Outcomes of EET Interventions

Motivational Outcomes

Motivational outcomes have been at the center of interest in both training research in general (e.g. Blume, Ford, Baldwin, & Huang, 2010) and EET research specifically. In EET research, motivational factors are, for example, entrepreneurial (goal) intentions, entrepreneurial self-efficacy and action planning. Of the 42 independent samples Martin et al. (2013) used for their meta-analysis, 19 used entrepreneurial intention as an outcome to measure the effectiveness of the intervention. It is therefore the most used outcome to evaluate EET interventions. The theoretical argument for using motivational outcomes to evaluate the effectiveness of EET interventions is based on the theory of planned behavior (Ajzen, 1991). The reasoning is that entrepreneurial intention leads to entrepreneurial behavior in the long term, making it a useful tool for evaluating the short-term effectiveness of EET interventions (e.g. Fayolle & Gailly, 2015; Krueger & Carsrud, 1993; Rauch & Hulsink, 2015; Souitaris, Zerbinati, & Al-Laham, 2007; von Graevenitz, Harhoff, & Weber, 2010). The idea that short-term changes in motivational outcomes predict long-term behavior also applies to entrepreneurial self-efficacy. However, despite being used extensively to evaluate training interventions in other contexts (Blume et al., 2010; Colquitt, LePine, & Noe, 2000), entrepreneurial self-efficacy has received less attention as a learning outcome in entrepreneurship (e.g., Gielnik et al., 2015; Gielnik, Uy, Funken, & Bischoff, 2017; Huber, Sloof, & Van Praag, 2014; Piperopoulos & Dimov, 2015). Similarly, theoretical approaches like action regulation theory (e.g., Frese & Zapf, 1994) and respective motivational learning outcomes like action planning have also not been used extensively to measure the effectiveness of EET interventions (for exceptions, see Campos et al., 2017; Gielnik et al., 2015, Glaub, Frese, Fischer, & Hoppe, 2014).

Overall, the meta-analytical evidence suggests that EET interventions are effective in increasing motivational outcomes related to entrepreneurship. Martin et al. (2013) report small, but significant effects of EET interventions on positive perceptions of entrepreneurship ($r = .109$), as well as on entrepreneurial intentions ($r = .137$). Bae, Qian, Miao, and Fiet (2014), who focused in their meta-analysis on the effects of EET interventions on entrepreneurial intentions, also found a significant positive effect ($r = .143$). However, it is important to note that, when controlling for pre-intervention levels of entrepreneurial intentions, the effect of the EET intervention was substantially reduced (Bae et al., 2014), suggesting that the effects can be explained to some extent by selection effects. To conclude, while effect sizes are small, there is a significant positive effect of EET interventions on motivational outcomes.

Cognitive Outcomes

Cognitive outcomes relevant to entrepreneurship are declarative knowledge, for example, about the entrepreneurial process (Martin et al., 2013), as well as entrepreneurial skills and competencies. Skills required for entrepreneurship include, for example, identifying business opportunities, planning or negotiation skills (see Chapter 12 for a more detailed discussion of entrepreneurial competencies). The theoretical argument for using cognitive outcomes to evaluate EET interventions is mostly based on human capital theory. Specifically, increases in cognitive outcomes reflect increases in entrepreneurship-related human capital, which may translate into entrepreneurial success (Unger, Rauch, Frese, & Rosenbusch, 2011). The meta-analytical evidence shows that there is a small to medium-sized effect of EET interventions on entrepreneurial knowledge and skills ($r = .237$; Martin et al., 2013).

Entrepreneurial Behavior and Success

The goal in most EET interventions is to increase the number of new ventures started amongst the participants of the intervention. Long-term training outcomes therefore include entrepreneurial behavior, such as activities to start and successfully manage a business, as well as entrepreneurial success, for example, in terms of venture growth and survival.

Meta-analytical evidence suggests that EET has a positive effect on behavior and results related to entrepreneurship, reporting significant effects on both entrepreneurial behavior (i.e. start-up and nascent behavior; $r = .124$) and entrepreneurial success (i.e. financial success of the business, survival, and personal income; $r = .166$; Martin et al., 2013). Similarly, Walter and Block (2016) find that participation in EET interventions significantly predicts entrepreneurial activity ($B = .18$, $p < .001$). Although their study is not a meta-analysis, their sample includes 11,320 individuals from 32 countries, which is comparable to the combined sample size of the data sets used in other meta-analyses. Overall, the results suggest that entrepreneurship education can increase entrepreneurial behavior and success.

Factors Important for Explaining Differences in the Effectiveness of EET

Effectiveness Based on Rigorous Evaluation Studies

The results of the meta-analysis by Martin et al. (2013) show that the effect sizes of EET interventions are heterogeneous, indicating considerable variance in the effectiveness of EET interventions. A factor that can explain the heterogeneity is the methodological rigor of the evaluation study. The meta-analysis included 42 studies, of which only six used an experimental approach (11 studies used at least pre- and post-measurements and a control group, but five of these did not use randomization; that is, they used only a quasi-experimental design). Comparing the effects of the 31 studies that did not meet the rigor threshold of at least a quasi-experimental design to the effects of the 11 studies that met the threshold showed significant differences in effect sizes. Less rigorous studies showed significantly higher effect sizes of EET interventions (r = .246) compared to more rigorous studies (r = .142).

We present an overview of nine studies to examine the effectiveness of EET interventions within the subset of most rigorous evaluation studies. We included the studies that Martin et al. (2013) used for their meta-analysis and additional rigorous studies on EET that were published since then. We included studies that met the highest methodological rigor thresholds, that is, have an experimental design and pre- and posttest measurements (with the exception of Oosterbeek, van Praag, & Ijsselstein, 2010, and Solomon, Frese, Friedrich, and Glaub, 2013, who used a quasi-experimental design). Table 16.1 gives an overview of the studies and their outcomes.

The effect of EET interventions on short-term learning outcomes remains heterogeneous in the subset of the rigorous studies, further supporting the notion of differences in the effectiveness of EET interventions. While positive effects on various short-term learning outcomes were observed by three studies (Gielnik et al., 2015; Glaub et al., 2014; Solomon et al., 2013), one study observed mixed results (Huber et al., 2014), and one observed negative effects (Oosterbeek et al., 2010). The remaining four studies did not report short-term learning outcomes. Positive effects were found for goal-setting knowledge (Solomon et al., 2013), entrepreneurial knowledge (Gielnik et al., 2015; Glaub et al., 2014; Huber et al., 2014), action planning and goal intentions (Gielnik et al., 2015) and entrepreneurial self-efficacy (Gielnik et al., 2015; Huber et al., 2014). Huber et al. (2014) and Oosterbeek et al. (2010) reported negative effects on entrepreneurial intention, further validating findings that EET interventions do not necessarily have a significant positive effect on entrepreneurial intentions (Bae et al., 2014).

TABLE 16.1 Overview of Rigorous Studies Evaluating EET Interventions

Authors & Year		N	Short-term Outcomes	Long-term Outcomes	Results/Success
			Learning Outcomes	*Behavioral Outcomes*	
Berge, Bjorvatn, and Tungodden. (2015)[1]		430	NR	Record keeping[1]; Marketing[1]	Sales[1]; Profit[1]
Solomon et al. (2013)		57	Goal setting knowledge	Innovation; Personal initiative; Proactive goal setting and planning	Sales[†];
Oosterbeek et al. (2010)		250	*Negative:* Entrepreneurial skills, creativity and entrepreneurial intentions	NR	NR
Drexler, Fischer, and Schoar (2014)	Standard Training	1,193	NR	NS	NS
	Rule of Thumb Training		NR	Business and personal finance practices	Sales in bad weeks
Gielnik et al. (2015)		406	Action planning; Goal intentions; Action knowledge; Self-efficacy	Entrepreneurial action; Opportunity identification	Business creation
Campos et al. (2017)	Business Training	1,500	NR	Business practices; Personal initiative; Capital & labor inputs; Innovation; Product diversification; Access to finance	NS
	Psychological Training		NR	Business practices; Personal initiative; Capital & labor inputs; Innovation; Product diversification; Access to finance	Sales; Profit

Glaub et al. (2014)	100	Knowledge about training content	Initiative behavior; Overcoming barriers	Sales; Employees
Anderson, Chandy, and Zia (2018)[2]	852	NR	Financial practices[2]; Marketing practices[2]	Profit
Huber, Sloof, and Van Praag (2014)	2413	*Negative:* Entrepreneurial intentions; *Positive:* Non-cognitive entrepreneurial skills	NR	NR

Note. If not indicated otherwise, a significant positive difference in the listed outcome was stated (experimental vs. control group). NR = not reported, NS = nonsignificant effects reported; † = marginally significant (p < .10).

[1] The effects were only positive for male participants that received a grant in addition to the training;

[2] Positive effects on profit for two different training interventions (marketing training and finance training). Behavioral outcomes dependent on the type of training.

Six of the seven rigorous studies that reported long-term outcomes found positive effects on behavioral outcomes and success measures. The success measures included significant increases in sales levels (five studies; increases ranging from 17% to 69%), profits (three studies; increases ranging from 30% to 63%) and the number of employees (two studies; increases ranging from 31% to 35%). Only the study by Berge et al. (2015) did not report positive effects of an EET intervention on long-term outcomes. In their study, the intervention was only effective when paired with a grant and only for male participants.

It is important to note that two of the six studies reporting positive effects on long-term outcomes tested different methodological approaches to EET interventions. The studies by Campos et al. (2017) and Drexler et al. (2014) both examined two interventions that differed in terms of the teaching methodology. In both studies, only one of the interventions resulted in significant increases in long-term success measures. This highlights that while the most rigorous studies on EET interventions find positive long-term effects, there is still heterogeneity in effect sizes, in particular when taking into consideration that different methodologies in training were compared with each other. This indicates that EET interventions substantially vary in their effects on entrepreneurship. In conclusion, the meta-analytical findings and the findings of the most rigorous studies suggest that EET interventions can be effective. However, the heterogeneity in the findings suggests that there is a need to further analyze EET interventions to get a better understanding of how and why some of the EET interventions are more or less effective. We therefore propose a framework to describe different teaching methodologies used in EET interventions, which might help to understand differences in their effectiveness.

Teaching Methodologies of EET Interventions: Developing a Framework

Previous meta-analyses have combined very different types of EET interventions to determine effect sizes. The EET interventions included in the meta-analyses range from short training interventions to MBA courses on entrepreneurship. They can follow different methodological approaches or target different groups of participants. Both Martin et al. (2013) and Bae et al. (2014) include the type of intervention as a moderator in their respective meta-analyses. However, they used only one characteristic of EET interventions for their moderator analyses, and the characteristic they used is not based on a comprehensive theoretical foundation. Martin et al. (2013) find that academic interventions are more effective than training interventions. A possible reason for the difference in effectiveness could be self-selection biases in academic interventions, i.e. students who are already interested are more likely to choose an entrepreneurship program (cf., Bae et al., 2014). Also examining differences between different methodologies in training, Bae et al. (2014) report a nonsignificant difference between interventions focused on writing a business plan and interventions focused on new venture creation.

In the following, we develop a framework to describe and categorize EET interventions. We took two avenues to develop this framework. First, we reviewed the literature on EET to identify the methodological elements that are frequently used in EET. We particularly focused on the last ten years and identified 36 studies, describing EET interventions in various contexts. We note that this is not a systematic review, and we do not claim to present an exhaustive list of the research on EET interventions. Second, we reviewed the psychological literature on training and complex skills acquisition. Entrepreneurship is a complex skill, because starting a business requires a diverse set of different skills to deal with tasks under uncertain conditions. Furthermore, entrepreneurs need to quickly adapt to unforeseen events and problems (e.g., McMullen & Shepherd, 2006). The psychological literature on the acquisition of complex skills can therefore inform the design of EET interventions.

We identified four dimensions that provide a framework to differentiate between the teaching methodologies of EET interventions: *Level of Process Orientation, Level of Contact, Level of Action Learning Orientation*, and *Level of Fidelity*. Table 16.2 gives an overview of the four dimensions. Two of the dimensions in this framework are the result of the review of the literature on EET (*Level of Process Orientation and Level of Contact*). The other two dimensions are based on the review of both literatures, EET and the psychological training literature of complex skills acquisition (*Level of Action Learning Orientation and Level of Fidelity*). Additionally, we provide examples for high scores and low scores in the four dimensions based on the nine rigorous studies discussed earlier and presented in Table 16.1.

We consider the dimensions as tools for comparison. This framework has not yet been evaluated. Therefore, ranking low on one of the dimensions is not a sign of a qualitatively low intervention. Instead, interventions with a low ranking should be systematically compared to those with higher ranks in this dimension to determine whether differences in this dimension affect the outcomes of the intervention. We formulate propositions for each of the dimensions based on previous research on entrepreneurship and training interventions.

Level of Process Orientation

Entrepreneurship is defined as the process of identifying, evaluating and exploiting opportunities (Shane & Venkataraman, 2000). Baron (2007) describes the entrepreneurial process in three phases: The pre-launch phase, the launch phase and the post-launch phase. Each phase requires performing different actions for the business to be successful. During the pre-launch phase, the entrepreneur has to identify and evaluate business opportunities, develop an intention to proceed with the exploitation of the identified opportunity, and assemble the required resources (e.g., find starting capital, identify suppliers, etc.). In the launch phase of the business, the entrepreneur needs to choose the legal form for the new venture,

TABLE 16.2 Overview of the Four Methodological Dimensions of EET Interventions

	Low Level	Medium Level	High Level
Level of Process Orientation (= the extent to which EET interventions cover the whole entrepreneurial process and emphasize that entrepreneurship is a recursive and iterative process)	The intervention focusses on one phase of the entrepreneurial process and does not emphasize that the process is recursive and iterative	The intervention focusses on at least two phases of the entrepreneurial process or emphasizes that entrepreneurship is a recursive and iterative process	The intervention covers the whole entrepreneurial process and emphasizes that entrepreneurship is a recursive and iterative process
Level of Contact (= the extent to which participants in an EET intervention are in contact with experts in the field of entrepreneurship)	Little to no contact to experts in the field of entrepreneurship	Experts in the field of entrepreneurship play a minor role in the intervention (e.g. as guest speakers)	Experts in the field of entrepreneurship are conducting the intervention or are acting as coaches or mentors and the participants have access to entrepreneurial networks
Level of Action Learning Orientation (= the extent to which the intervention uses active and exploratory learning, explicitly encourages errors and uses action principles to build action-oriented mental models)	The intervention only relies on classroom activities (lecture type interventions) and emphasizes theoretical knowledge presented in a deductive way	The intervention uses action learning elements in parts of the intervention	The intervention has an active and exploratory learning approach, encourages errors and uses action principles
Level of Fidelity (= the extent to which the intervention environment resembles the real-world environment)	The participants operate in a purely fictional environment and do not use real-world materials	The participants operate in a detailed, realistic simulation of the real-world environment	The participants operate in a real-world environment (e.g., by having real customers and competitors) and use real-world materials (e.g., starting capital)

protect the new product or service from competitors, and develop marketing plans and strategy. In the post-launch phase, the entrepreneur needs to manage the business, including attracting and retaining quality employees, influencing and motivating them and other stakeholders, conducting negotiations, and handling conflicts. It is important to note that this does not imply that this process is necessarily linear. Rather, researchers emphasized that entrepreneurship is a recursive and iterative process (McMullen & Dimov, 2013). Throughout the whole process, entrepreneurs refine and readjust business ideas based on the feedback that they receive (McMullen & Dimov, 2013). Taking the three phases and that iterative process into consideration, we conceptualize the *Level of Process Orientation* to include two facets. First, the extent to which EET interventions cover the whole entrepreneurial process including all three phases as described by Baron (2007). Interventions have a high level of process orientation if they involve all phases of the entrepreneurial process and a low level of process orientation if they only deal with a single phase. Second, the extent to which EET interventions emphasize this process to be recursive and iterative. This means that in interventions with high levels of process orientation, participants are encouraged to iteratively change business ideas based on feedback from the environment. Conversely, interventions that propose a linear view on entrepreneurship have a low level of process orientation.

When reviewing the literature on EET interventions, we were only able to assess the level to which interventions covered the whole entrepreneurial process. The second facet of process-orientation, the extent to which interventions included a recursive and iterative view on the entrepreneurial process was typically not reported. We therefore chose to only focus on the first facet of process orientation for identifying examples of interventions with high and low levels of process orientation. An example of an EET intervention that has a high level of process orientation is the Junior Achievement Company Project described by Oosterbeek et al. (2010). This study covers all phases of the entrepreneurial process, starting with identifying a business opportunity to pursue, raising starting capital, making sales, and closing down the company after the intervention. In contrast, some EET interventions focus only on one specific phase of the entrepreneurial process, for example, the two interventions described by Anderson et al. (2018), which focused only on marketing and managing finances (i.e., only on the post-launch phase).

Several interventions have medium levels of process orientation by taking into account two of the three phases. An example of an intervention with a medium score is the BizWorld training intervention (Huber et al., 2014). While the program covers the process of launching and managing a hypothetical business, it seems to have little focus on the identification of opportunities. The participants are with materials for business opportunities that have a limited range of applications and they are not required to assemble the resources necessary to start the business.

We expect interventions with a high level of process orientation to be more effective than interventions with a low level of process orientation. Prior research suggested that changing and adapting business opportunities in a recursive and iterative process based on feedback is necessary to develop a viable business opportunity (Dimov, 2007; McMullen & Dimov, 2013; Shepherd & Gruber, 2020) Indeed, empirical findings suggest that this iterative change can have a positive function in entrepreneurship (Hmieleski & Baron, 2008).

Level of Contact

EET interventions vary in their level of contact with experts in the field of entrepreneurship, such as experienced entrepreneurs, who serve as coaches or mentors, or venture capitalists. Reasons to include experts in EET are to provide human and social capital, advice, inspiration, or access to capital. Specifically, research showed that social capital has a significant effect on entrepreneurial success and that social capital is particularly important for nascent entrepreneurs or entrepreneurs in the early parts of the entrepreneurial process (Stam, Arzlanian, & Elfring, 2014). Furthermore, research showed that experienced entrepreneurs can inspire participants of EET interventions (Souitaris et al., 2007). Finally, research showed that social capital can increase access to financial capital (e.g., Florin, Lubatkin, & Schulze, 2003).

We define *Level of Contact* as the extent to which participants in an EET intervention are in contact with experts in the field of entrepreneurship. An intervention with high levels of contact includes experts in the field of entrepreneurship, either as a part of the knowledge transfer (i.e., as a trainer, lecturer, mentor, or coach), or through other forms of interaction (e.g. participants having to pitch ideas to experienced entrepreneurs or investors). In contrast, an intervention with low levels of contact does not include experienced entrepreneurs or other experts of entrepreneurship as part of the program.

Of the nine rigorous studies, none included a high level of contact. There are, however, other studies that describe programs with high levels of contact, for example, the interventions described by Rauch and Hulsink (2015) or Lyons and Zhang (2018) mentoring by entrepreneurs and pitching business ideas to real venture capitalists and experienced entrepreneurs. The STEP Program (Gielnik et al., 2015) is an example of an intervention that has low levels of contact. The training sessions are held by university staff without explicit entrepreneurial experience and the training does not include any other form of contact with entrepreneurs or experts in the field of entrepreneurship.

We expect that the level of contact does not have a consistent positive or negative effect. EET interventions can increase social capital through including experts (e.g., potential funders). Social capital promotes success in entrepreneurship (Stam et al., 2014). However, including experts for the purpose of inspiring participants or boosting their confidence through verbal persuasion can potentially also yield negative effects. While confidence plays an important role in developing entrepreneurial goals (e.g., Baron, Mueller, & Wolfe, 2016), confidence can negatively impact venture creation and survival if it is too high and leads to unrealistic expectations and complacency (Gielnik, Bledow, & Stark, 2020; Koellinger, Minniti, & Schade, 2007).

Level of Action Learning Orientation

Traditionally, training and educational interventions treated the learner as a passive recipient of knowledge and instruction. For example, social cognitive theory suggests that tightly structured training eliminates errors and therefore removes unnecessary inefficiency (Bandura, 1986; Latham & Saari, 1979). However, more recent work on training and the acquisition of complex skills have explored more active approaches to learning (e.g., Bell & Kozlowski, 2002; Debowski, Wood, & Bandura, 2001; Keith & Frese, 2005). Action learning approaches were shown to be successful in enhancing learning of complex tasks (Kozlowski et al., 2001). This is especially true for contexts that are complex and dynamic and therefore require adaptive expertise, which is the ability to adapt the learning outcomes to new problems or situations (Bell, Tannenbaum, Ford, Noe, & Kraiger, 2017; Keith & Frese, 2008; Smith, Ford, & Kozlowski, 1997).

Action learning approaches have two main features, trainee control and inductive learning (Bell & Kozlowski, 2008). Trainee control means that learners take responsibility for their learning (e.g., setting learning goals and monitoring and evaluating their progress). Inductive learning means that trainees explore the task and develop their own strategies and principles via experimentation (Smith et al., 1997). In action learning, active and exploratory learning is explicitly encouraged, which means that trainees learn via experimenting with the task. This can be free or guided (e.g., Bell & Kozlowski, 2002; Debowski et al., 2001; Keith & Frese, 2005; Kozlowski et al., 2001). Free exploration means that trainees receive no or minimal guidance during training. Guided exploration means that while the participants are still learning through exploration, external guidance is provided to encourage systematic and preplanned exploration. Exploratory learning positively impacts participants' metacognition, which enhances adaptive expertise and transfer (Bell & Kozlowski, 2008; Keith & Frese, 2005; Smith et al., 1997). Adaptive transfer means adapting the knowledge and skills acquired in the intervention to new situations and problems (Ivancic & Hesketh, 2000). Adaptive transfer is important for EET interventions, because of the uncertainty inherent in entrepreneurship and the constant need to adapt to changing situations and unforeseen problems (McMullen & Shepherd, 2006) and EET interventions cannot include all potential problems that can arise during the venture creation process.

Some interventions based on action learning also emphasize the role of errors in the process of exploration. Error management training for example goes beyond exploratory learning by emphasizing the importance of making errors and framing them as a learning opportunity (Keith & Frese, 2005). The meta-analysis by Keith and Frese (2008) showed that error management training leads to higher adaptive transfer than proceduralized training interventions that avoid making errors by giving detailed instructions.

In addition to the mode of instruction, the way theoretical input is delivered in training sessions can also impact the acquisition of skills. Trainees need an action-oriented mental model (Frese, Beimel, & Schoenborn et al., 2003). An action-oriented mental model is a "cognitive representation of the starting situation, the goal state, and how the present situation can be transferred into a future state" (Frese et al., 2003, p. 677). Such a model can be developed through action principles. Action principles are "rules of thumb" that break down theoretical concepts into simple principles that the participants of the intervention can easily understand (Drexler et al., 2014). An example of an action principle is "*Set yourself SMART goals*". The students learn how to formulate goals in a way that maximizes the chance of accomplishing these goals, instead of learning about the underlying theory (e.g., goal setting theory; Locke & Latham, 1990). These "rules of thumb" are geared towards direct application. Accordingly, this form of presenting the training content has higher action learning orientation than presenting theories and theoretical knowledge (Gielnik et al., 2015; Glaub et al., 2014).

The role of action plays a prominent role in EET. Action is a key element in new venture creation (Frese, 2009), and scholars have recommended EET to be action-oriented (Edelman, Manolova, & Brush, 2008; Rasmussen & Sørheim, 2006). In the context of EET interventions, action learning means that students are not passive recipients of knowledge but engage in (guided) exploratory learning in terms of experimenting with entrepreneurial tasks. This means that EET interventions high in action learning orientation involve engagement in activities that resemble the actions performed by nascent entrepreneurs. Additionally, interventions with high levels of action learning orientation can include explicit encouragement of errors and use action principles to present the training content.

An example of an intervention from the list of the most rigorous studies that has a high level of action learning orientation is the STEP training (Gielnik et al., 2015). During the intervention, the participants actively engage in exploration by applying the content learned in a classroom setting to small-scale businesses they start at the beginning of the training. The training offers guidance by sequencing the tasks through the order of sessions but encourages the students to actively explore the task themselves. Additionally, the training incorporates encouragement of making and learning from errors. In contrast, EET interventions that solely rely on theoretical or passive approaches toward learning (e.g., lecture-type interventions) have low levels of action orientation. An example is the intervention described by Berge et al. (2015) that uses lecture-style sessions in a classroom setting. The study by Anderson et al. (2018) also focuses on lecture-style elements. However, the participants were also encouraged to apply what they have learned in class outside the training context. Accordingly, this study ranks on a medium level of action learning orientation.

Previous studies have provided empirical evidence that EET interventions with high levels of action learning orientation are more effective in increasing short- and long-term outcomes. In their meta-analysis, Bae et al. (2014) compared effect sizes of EET interventions that focus on new venture creation (i.e. high levels of action learning orientation) to those that focus on learning how to draft a business plan (i.e., low or medium levels of action learning orientation). They reported a tendency of interventions focusing on new venture creation to be more effective in increasing participants' entrepreneurial intentions ($r = .269$) than those focusing on business planning ($r = .153$). However, the difference in effect sizes was not significant. Other evidence from a primary study shows that EET interventions with action-based pedagogy yielded positive effects on entrepreneurial intentions compared to EET interventions with lecture-based pedagogy suggesting that action learning orientation is beneficial in EET (Varamäki, Joensuu, Tornikoski, & Viljamaa, 2015).

We expect that EET interventions with a high level of action learning orientation are more effective in increasing outcomes related to entrepreneurship than those that have lower levels of action learning orientation. This proposition is based on previous findings about action learning orientation in the context of EET (Bae et al., 2014; Varamäki et al., 2015) as well as on the findings on the use of action principles in EET (Drexler et al., 2014). Additionally, findings on training effectiveness in general suggest that an exploratory learning approach and explicit encouragement of errors positively affect adaptive transfer and the long-term outcomes of training interventions (Keith & Frese, 2005; Kozlowski et al., 2001).

Level of Fidelity

The level of fidelity is the level to which an intervention reflects or happens in a real-world setting. The differentiation between high- and low-fidelity simulations has mainly been used in the context of personnel selection (Motowidlo, Dunnette, & Carter, 1990), but can be translated to an educational or training setting. A high-fidelity environment very closely resembles the real environment, for example by using realistic equipment and materials. A low-fidelity environment is a verbal description of a hypothetical situation (e.g., a trainer in an EET intervention verbally describes a typical pitch to venture capitalists). In the context of training, the level of fidelity describes the extent to which the training tasks match real-world tasks. High-fidelity training is likely to increase the EET transfer (Baldwin & Ford, 1988; Frese & Zapf, 1994; Gielnik & Frese, 2013).

In the context of EET, a high-fidelity intervention involves using real materials (e.g., starting capital, raw materials) in a real-world environment (e.g., by having real competitors, customers, etc.). In contrast, a low-fidelity intervention is when students come up with a business plan for a hypothetical business in a classroom setting. In such an intervention, students are working on a business plan but do not use any concrete materials (e.g., not building prototypes) and are only required to describe their planned behavior. An intervention that qualifies as having a medium level of fidelity is, for example, an intervention that uses a detailed simulation of a real-world environment and materials.

An example of an high-fidelity EET intervention from the list of the most rigorous evaluation studies is the STEP Training (Gielnik et al., 2015). The participants operate in a real-world business environment with real materials, competing with real competitors. The Junior Achievement Company Program (Oosterbeek et al., 2010) or the BizWorld training (Huber et al., 2014) both have a medium level of fidelity. In both cases, the participants operate in a detailed simulation of the real-world environment and use real materials. During the Junior Achievement Company Program, the students produce their own goods and sell them at specific trade fairs. However, they only compete with other participants of the program. The students who participate in the BizWorld training are provided with materials they use to produce goods and sell them to other students in exchange for a fictional currency. There was no example of a low-fidelity simulation among the nine studies we examined. However, outside this list, there are a number of interventions that fit this description. An example is the intervention described by von Graevenitz et al. (2010), where participants worked on business plans for hypothetical businesses, that is, a verbal description of what they plan to do.

We propose that EET interventions with a high level of fidelity are more effective than interventions with low levels of fidelity. In a high-fidelity intervention, the training tasks match the real-world tasks, resulting in sophisticated mental models and enhancing training transfer (Baldwin & Ford, 1988; Frese & Zapf, 1994).

Using the Framework to Assess the Effectiveness of EET: An Example on Action Learning Orientation

We used the framework on EET methodologies to assess the level of action learning orientation of the nine rigorous studies described in Table 16.1. We focused on action learning orientation for two reasons. First, research has suggested that action learning orientation is the most important teaching methodology to train entrepreneurship (Nabi, Liñán, Fayolle, Krueger, & Walmsley, 2017). Second, the relatively small sample of rigorous studies limited us in applying the framework. For example, none of the nine studies featured elements of a high level of contact (contrary to some EET interventions that were not evaluated as rigorously) or low levels of fidelity.

The nine studies tested a total of twelve different training interventions. Of those, six had high levels of action learning orientation (the psychological training in Campos et al., 2017; Gielnik et al., 2015; Glaub et al., 2014; Huber et al., 2014; Oosterbeek et al., 2010; Solomon et al., 2013). Three had medium levels of action learning orientation (both trainings in Anderson et al., 2018; the rule-of-thumb training in Drexler et al., 2014). Three had low levels of action learning orientation (the business training in Campos et al., 2017; the accounting training in Drexler et al., 2014; Berge et al., 2015).

Interventions with at least medium levels of action learning orientation reported positive effects on behavioral outcomes or success. Three interventions that had low levels of action learning orientation reported nonsignificant results. Berge et al., (2015) reported significant results but only for male participants, who additionally received a grant. Therefore, it is likely that their positive effects can be attributed to financial factors. Accordingly, we conclude that interventions using action learning orientation are more effective than interventions low on action learning orientation. The conclusion is in line with our proposition and demonstrates the usefulness of our framework to understand the effectiveness of EET interventions.

We suggest that assessing interventions on dimensions of our framework and comparing effect sizes of the interventions on different outcomes contributes to understanding *how* EET interventions work. For each dimension, research needs to assess whether (a) differences on the dimension have an impact on the effectiveness of the interventions, (b) which levels on the dimensions are optimal, and (c) whether the optimal level varies for different conditions (e.g., level of contact could be more important for some target groups than for others). Additionally, future research needs to assess whether and how the dimensions interact; for example, high levels in one dimension can compensate for low levels in other dimensions. Future meta-analyses on EET interventions can take this methodological framework into consideration when testing moderation effects to provide insights into effective training methodologies in EET.

The Transfer of Entrepreneurship Education and Training Outcomes

Typically, EET interventions aim at increasing venture creation. The process of venture creation usually happens after the intervention. Therefore, to fully understand the effects of EET interventions, we discuss how outcomes of EET interventions are maintained over time.

Maintenance in the Context of EET

The "transfer problem" is one of the main challenges of the literature on training and human resource development in general (Baldwin, Kevin Ford, & Blume, 2017). Transfer refers to the generalization and maintenance of training outcomes over time (Baldwin & Ford, 1988).

Generalization means that trainees translate what they have learned into behavior outside the training context. In EET, generalization means that participants show entrepreneurial behavior after the intervention. Meta-analytical evidence as well as the analysis of the most rigorous studies suggest that EET can be effective in increasing entrepreneurial behavior (Martin et al., 2013). *Maintenance* refers to the retention of training outcomes over time. In general, training effects tend to decay over time (Blume et al., 2010). Nevertheless, some studies show that training effects can be maintained over extensive periods. Elert, Andersson, and Wennberg (2015) found significant effects of an EET intervention 10 years after the intervention. While we still lack profound knowledge on how and why outcomes are maintained in the context of EET, research in the last five years has produced initial findings on underlying mechanisms that facilitate the maintenance of outcomes. Findings suggest that entrepreneurial behavior and success can be generalized via action regulatory constructs like action planning or action knowledge (Gielnik et al., 2015), personal initiative (Campos et al., 2017; Glaub et al., 2014), improved business practices (Anderson, Chandy, & Zia, 2018; Campos et al., 2017), and entrepreneurial intentions (Rauch & Hulsink, 2015). Additionally, entrepreneurial self-efficacy can facilitate the maintenance of entrepreneurial passion, which, in turn, increases the likelihood of business creation (Gielnik et al., 2017). Furthermore, Mensmann and Frese (2019) showed that the need for cognition facilitates the maintenance of proactive behavior. However, despite those insights, we lack a coherent theoretical model that explains transfer in the context of EET.

A Dynamic Model of Transfer in the Context of EET

So far, the general literature on training transfer has produced a number of theories that could be integrated into EET research. An example of a theoretical model on the transfer of training that could be used in the context of EET is the Dynamic Transfer Model (DTM; Blume, Ford, Surface, & Olenick, 2019). The DTM understands transfer as a dynamic process that unfolds from the start of the training up to the point where the behavioral outcomes are generalized and maintained. During the training, the participants gain knowledge, skills, and change their attitudes (KSAs) towards a certain behavioral outcome. The participants then evaluate the newly developed KSAs and form the intention to transfer if the participants deem the KSA useful. The intention to transfer then leads to a first attempt at training transfer and the acquired KSAs are used in a real-world setting (e.g., performing start-up activities). The application of the KSAs leads to feedback, which informs the trainee on whether the application of the new KSAs was successful. The feedback will either be integrated, leading to an adoption of the KSAs for a second attempt to transfer, or the new KSAs are discarded. These feedback loops are repeated and form early transfer experiences. These early transfer experiences determine whether the training outcomes are maintained over time.

While the DTM has not been explicitly used in EET research, Gielnik et al. (2017) adopted a similar view on the maintenance of training outcomes over time. In their evaluation study, varying levels of entrepreneurial self-efficacy at three measurements after the training explained the long-term maintenance of passion over time. Successful maintenance then predicted new venture creation. Based on the idea that self-efficacy is a result of experiencing mastery of a specific domain (Bandura, 1997), the findings suggest that the development of entrepreneurial self-efficacy is a result of successful initial attempts at transfer, giving us a first indication that the DTM could be useful in the context of EET. An entrepreneurship specific DTM would offer a dynamic view on training transfer. The DTM includes feedback loops and self-regulatory processes that are essential to the entrepreneurial process (Frese, 2009) and could therefore be a starting point for developing a transfer theory specific to EET.

Conclusion–The "Knowns" and the "Unknowns"

The meta-analytical evidence presented in the first part of this chapter suggests that EET can be effective in increasing motivational and cognitive outcomes in the short term and behavioral outcomes related to entrepreneurship in the long term. Additionally, empirical findings suggest that these outcomes can be maintained over time. However, there are a lot of questions remaining. Research has not yet provided sufficient evidence on *how* and *why* EET is effective. To identify which types of interventions are more effective than others, research needs to assess which characteristics of EET interventions determine their effectiveness. We propose a framework with four dimensions that can be used to compare the effectiveness of interventions (see Table 16.2). We used the framework to draw a first conclusion that EET interventions are more effective when having high levels of action learning orientation. However, this effect has to be validated using a wider range of studies (e.g., in a meta-analytical study testing moderation effects). This also requires future research to describe the methodology of the evaluated EET intervention in more detail. Additionally, to understand the mechanisms behind the maintenance of EET outcomes, research needs to work towards a theory of EET transfer and/or use existing theory, like the DTM, to analyze the mechanisms.

Future research should shift its focus from trying to answer the question whether EET *can* work to *why* and *how* it works. The questions about EET require future research to incorporate more rigorous study designs. Longitudinal studies with multiple measurements, as well as rigorous evaluation designs (i.e., experimental studies comparing different interventions and/or interventions and control groups), are needed to answer these questions.

References

Ajzen, I. (1991). The theory of planned behavior. *Organizational Behavior and Human Decision Processes, 50*(2), 179–211. Retrieved from https://doi.org/10.1016/0749-5978(91)90020-T

Anderson, S. J., Chandy, R., & Zia, B. (2018). Pathways to profits: The impact of marketing vs. finance skills on business performance. *Management Science*, *64*(12), 5559–5583. Retrieved from https://doi.org/10.1287/mnsc.2017.2920

Bae, T. J., Qian, S., Miao, C., & Fiet, J. O. (2014). The relationship between entrepreneurship education and entrepreneurial intentions: A meta-analytic review. *Entrepreneurship Theory and Practice*, *38*(2), 217–254. Retrieved from https://doi.org/10.1111/etap.12095

Baldwin, T. T., & Ford, J. K. (1988). Transfer of training: A review and directions for future research. *Personnel Psychology*, *41*(1), 63–105. Retrieved from https://doi.org/10.1111/j.1744-6570.1988.tb00632.x

Baldwin, T. T., Kevin Ford, J., & Blume, B. D. (2017). The state of transfer of training research: Moving toward more consumer-centric inquiry. *Human Resource Development Quarterly*, *28*(1), 17–28. Retrieved from https://doi.org/10.1002/hrdq.21278

Bandura, A. (1986). *Social foundations of thought and action*. Englewood Cliffs, NJ: Prentice Hall.

Bandura, A. (1997). *Self-efficacy: The exercise of control*. New York: W. H. Freeman and Co.

Baron, R. A. (2007). Entrepreneurship: A process perspective. In J. R. Baum, M. Frese, & R. A. Baron (Eds.), *The psychology of entrepreneurship* (pp. 19–39). New York: Psychology Press.

Baron, R. A., Mueller, B. A., & Wolfe, M. T. (2016). Self-efficacy and entrepreneurs' adoption of unattainable goals: The restraining effects of self-control. *Journal of Business Venturing*, *31*(1), 55–71. Retrieved from https://doi.org/10.1016/j.jbusvent.2015.08.002

Bell, B. S., & Kozlowski, S. W. J. (2002). Adaptive guidance: Enhancing self-regulation, knowledge, and performance in technology-based training. *Personnel Psychology*, *55*(2), 267–306. Retrieved from https://doi.org/10.1111/j.1744-6570.2002.tb00111.x

Bell, B. S., & Kozlowski, S. W. J. (2008). Active learning: Effects of core training design elements on self-regulatory processes, learning, and adaptability. *Journal of Applied Psychology*, *93*(2), 296–316. Retrieved from https://doi.org/10.1037/0021-9010.93.2.296

Bell, B. S., Tannenbaum, S. I., Ford, J. K., Noe, R. A., & Kraiger, K. (2017). 100 years of training and development research: What we know and where we should go. *Journal of Applied Psychology*, *102*(3), 305–323. Retrieved from https://doi.org/10.1037/apl0000142

Berge, L. I. O., Bjorvatn, K., & Tungodden, B. (2015). Human and financial capital for microenterprise development: Evidence from a field and lab experiment. *Management Science*, *61*(4), 707–722. Retrieved from https://doi.org/10.1287/mnsc.2014.1933

Blume, B. D., Ford, J. K., Baldwin, T. T., & Huang, J. L. (2010). Transfer of training: A meta-analytic review. *Journal of Management*, *36*(4), 1065–1105. Retrieved from https://doi.org/10.1177/0149206309352880

Blume, B. D., Ford, J. K., Surface, E. A., & Olenick, J. (2019). A dynamic model of training transfer. *Human Resource Management Review*, *29*(2), 270–283. Retrieved from https://doi.org/10.1016/j.hrmr.2017.11.004

Campos, F., Frese, M., Goldstein, M., Iacovone, L., Johnson, H. C., McKenzie, D., & Mensmann, M. (2017). Teaching personal initiative beats traditional training in boosting small business in West Africa. *Science*, *357*(6357), 1287–1290. Retrieved from https://doi.org/10.1126/science.aan5329

Colquitt, J. A., LePine, J. A., & Noe, R. A. (2000). Toward an integrative theory of training motivation: A meta-analytic path analysis of 20 years of research. *Journal of Applied Psychology*, *85*(5), 678–707. Retrieved from https://doi.org/10.1037/0021-9010.85.5.678

Debowski, S., Wood, R. E., & Bandura, A. (2001). Impact of guided exploration and enactive exploration on self-regulatory mechanisms and information acquisition through electronic search. *Journal of Applied Psychology, 86*(6), 1129–1141. Retrieved from https://doi.org/10.1037//0021-9010.86.6.1129

Dimov, D. (2007). From opportunity insight to opportunity intention: The importance of person-situation learning match. *Entrepreneurship Theory and Practice, 31*(4), 561–583. Retrieved from https://doi.org/10.1111/j.1540-6520.2007.00188.x

Drexler, A., Fischer, G., & Schoar, A. (2014). Keeping it simple: Financial literacy and rules of thumb. *American Economic Journal: Applied Economics, 6*(2), 1–31. Retrieved from https://doi.org/10.1257/app.6.2.1

Edelman, L. F., Manolova, T. S., & Brush, C. G. (2008). Entrepreneurship education: Correspondence between practices of nascent entrepreneurs and textbook prescriptions for success. *Academy of Management Learning & Education, 7*(1), 56–70. Retrieved from https://doi.org/10.5465/amle.2008.31413862

Elert, N., Andersson, F. W., & Wennberg, K. (2015). The impact of entrepreneurship education in high school on long-term entrepreneurial performance. *Journal of Economic Behavior & Organization, 111,* 209–223. Retrieved from https://doi.org/10.1016/j.jebo.2014.12.020

Fayolle, A., & Gailly, B. (2015). The impact of entrepreneurship education on entrepreneurial attitudes and intention: Hysteresis and persistence. *Journal of Small Business Management, 53*(1), 75–93. Retrieved from https://doi.org/10.1111/jsbm.12065

Florin, J., Lubatkin, M., & Schulze, W. (2003). A social capital model of high-growth ventures. *Academy of Management Journal, 46*(3), 374–384. Retrieved from https://doi.org/10.2307/30040630

Frese, M. (2009). Towards a psychology of entrepreneurship: An action theory perspective. *Foundations and Trends® in Entrepreneurship, 5*(6), 437–496. Retrieved from https://doi.org/10.1561/0300000028

Frese, M., Beimel, S., & Schoenborn, S. (2003). Action training for charismatic leadership: Two evaluations of studies of a commercial training module on inspirational communication of a vision. *Personnel Psychology, 56*(3), 671–698. Retrieved from https://doi.org/10.1111/j.1744-6570.2003.tb00754.x

Frese, M., & Zapf, D. (1994). Action as the core of work psychology: A German approach. In H. C. Triandis, M. D. Dunnette, & L. M. Hough (Eds.), *Handbook of industrial and organizational psychology* (4th ed., pp. 271–340). Palo Alto, CA: Consulting Psychology Press.

Gielnik, M. M., Bledow, R., & Stark, M. S. (2020). A dynamic account of self-efficacy in entrepreneurship. *Journal of Applied Psychology, 105*(5), 487–505. Retrieved from https://doi.org/10.1037/apl0000451

Gielnik, M. M., & Frese, M. (2013). Entrepreneurship and poverty reduction: Applying IO psychology to microbusiness and entrepreneurship in developing countries. In J. Olson-Buchanan, L. Koppes Bryan, & L. Foster Thompson (Eds.), *Using industrial-organizational psychology for the greater good: Helping those who help others* (pp. 394–438). London, UK: Routledge.

Gielnik, M. M., Frese, M., Kahara-Kawuki, A., Wasswa Katono, I., Kyejjusa, S., Ngoma, M., . . . Dlugosch, T. J. (2015). Action and action-regulation in entrepreneurship: Evaluating a student training for promoting entrepreneurship. *Academy of Management Learning & Education, 14*(1), 69–94. Retrieved from https://doi.org/10.5465/amle.2012.0107

Gielnik, M. M., Uy, M. A., Funken, R., & Bischoff, K. M. (2017). Boosting and sustaining passion: A long-term perspective on the effects of entrepreneurship training. *Journal of Business Venturing*, *32*(3), 334–353. Retrieved from https://doi.org/10.1016/j.jbusvent.2017.02.003

Glaub, M. E., Frese, M., Fischer, S., & Hoppe, M. (2014). Increasing personal initiative in small business managers or owners leads to entrepreneurial success: A theory-based controlled randomized field intervention for evidence-based management. *Academy of Management Learning & Education*, *13*(3), 354–379. Retrieved from https://doi.org/10.5465/amle.2013.0234

The Guardian. (2017, January 20). Can you learn to be an entrepreneur? *The Guardian*. Retrieved from www.theguardian.com/professional-supplements/2017/jan/20/can-you-learn-to-be-an-entrepreneur

Hmieleski, K. M., & Baron, R. A. (2008). Regulatory focus and new venture performance: A study of entrepreneurial opportunity exploitation under conditions of risk versus uncertainty. *Strategic Entrepreneurship Journal*, *2*(4), 285–299. Retrieved from https://doi.org/10.1002/sej.56

Huber, L. R., Sloof, R., & Van Praag, M. (2014). The effect of early entrepreneurship education: Evidence from a field experiment. *European Economic Review*, *72*, 76–97. Retrieved from https://doi.org/10.1016/j.euroecorev.2014.09.002

Ivancic, K., & Hesketh, B. (2000). Learning from errors in a driving simulation: Effects on driving skill and self-confidence. *Ergonomics*, *43*(12), 1966–1984. Retrieved from https://doi.org/10.1080/00140130050201427

Keith, N., & Frese, M. (2005). Self-regulation in error management training: Emotion control and metacognition as mediators of performance effects. *Journal of Applied Psychology*, *90*(4), 677–691. Retrieved from https://doi.org/10.1037/0021-9010.90.4.677

Keith, N., & Frese, M. (2008). Effectiveness of error management training: A meta-analysis. *Journal of Applied Psychology*, *93*(1), 59–69. Retrieved from https://doi.org/10.1037/0021-9010.93.1.59

Koellinger, P., Minniti, M., & Schade, C. (2007). "I think I can, I think I can": Overconfidence and entrepreneurial behavior. *Journal of Economic Psychology*, *28*(4), 502–527. Retrieved from https://doi.org/10.1016/j.joep.2006.11.002

Kozlowski, S. W. J., Toney, R. J., Mullins, M. E., Weissbein, D. A., Brown, K. G., & Bell, B. S. (2001). 2: Developing adaptability: A theory for the design of integrated-embedded training systems. In *Advances in human performance and cognitive engineering research* (Vol. 1, pp. 59–123). Bingley, UK: Emerald Group Publishing Limited (MCB UP). Retrieved from https://doi.org/10.1016/S1479-3601(01)01004-9

Kraiger, K., Ford, J. K., & Salas, E. (1993). Application of cognitive, skill-based, and affective theories of learning outcomes to new methods of training evaluation. *Journal of Applied Psychology*, *78*(2), 311–328. Retrieved from https://doi.org/10.1037/0021-9010.78.2.311

Krueger, N. F., & Carsrud, A. L. (1993). Entrepreneurial intentions: Applying the theory of planned behaviour. *Entrepreneurship & Regional Development*, *5*(4), 315–330. Retrieved from https://doi.org/10.1080/08985629300000020

Latham, G. P., & Saari, L. M. (1979). Importance of supportive relationships in goal setting. *Journal of Applied Psychology*, *64*(2), 151–156. Retrieved from https://doi.org/10.1037/0021-9010.64.2.151

Locke, E. A., & Latham, G. P. (1990). *A theory of goal setting & task performance*. Englewood Cliffs, NJ: Prentice-Hall.

Lyons, E., & Zhang, L. (2018). Who does (not) benefit from entrepreneurship programs? *Strategic Management Journal*, *39*(1), 85–112. Retrieved from https://doi.org/10.1002/smj.2704

Martin, B. C., McNally, J. J., & Kay, M. J. (2013). Examining the formation of human capital in entrepreneurship: A meta-analysis of entrepreneurship education outcomes. *Journal of Business Venturing, 28*(2), 211–224. Retrieved from https://doi.org/10.1016/j.jbusvent.2012.03.002

McMullen, J. S., & Dimov, D. (2013). Time and the entrepreneurial journey: The problems and promise of studying entrepreneurship as a process. *Journal of Management Studies,* 1481–1512. Retrieved from https://doi.org/10.1111/joms.12049

McMullen, J. S., & Shepherd, D. A. (2006). Entrepreneurial action and the role of uncertainty in the theory of the entrepreneur. *Academy of Management Review, 31*(1), 132–152. Retrieved from https://doi.org/10.5465/amr.2006.19379628

Mensmann, M., & Frese, M. (2019). Who stays proactive after entrepreneurship training? Need for cognition, personal initiative maintenance, and well-being. *Journal of Organizational Behavior, 40*(1), 20–37. Retrieved from https://doi.org/10.1002/job.2333

Motowidlo, S. J., Dunnette, M. D., & Carter, G. W. (1990). An alternative selection procedure: The low-fidelity simulation. *Journal of Applied Psychology, 75*(6), 640–647. Retrieved from https://doi.org/10.1037/0021-9010.75.6.640

Nabi, G., Liñán, F., Fayolle, A., Krueger, N., & Walmsley, A. (2017). The impact of entrepreneurship education in higher education: A systematic review and research agenda. *Academy of Management Learning & Education, 16*(2), 277–299. Retrieved from https://doi.org/10.5465/amle.2015.0026

Oosterbeek, H., van Praag, M., & Ijsselstein, A. (2010). The impact of entrepreneurship education on entrepreneurship skills and motivation. *European Economic Review, 54*(3), 442–454. Retrieved from https://doi.org/10.1016/j.euroecorev.2009.08.002

Piperopoulos, P., & Dimov, D. (2015). Burst bubbles or build steam? Entrepreneurship education, entrepreneurial self-efficacy, and entrepreneurial intentions. *Journal of Small Business Management, 53*(4), 970–985. Retrieved from https://doi.org/10.1111/jsbm.12116

Rasmussen, E. A., & Sørheim, R. (2006). Action-based entrepreneurship education. *Technovation, 26*(2), 185–194. Retrieved from https://doi.org/10.1016/j.technovation.2005.06.012

Rauch, A., & Hulsink, W. (2015). Putting entrepreneurship education where the intention to act lies: An investigation into the impact of entrepreneurship education on entrepreneurial behavior. *Academy of Management Learning & Education, 14*(2), 187–204. Retrieved from https://doi.org/10.5465/amle.2012.0293

Shane, S., & Venkataraman, S. (2000). The promise of entrepreneurship as a field of research. *Academy of Management Review, 25*(1), 217–226. Retrieved from https://doi.org/10.5465/amr.2000.2791611

Shepherd, D. A., & Gruber, M. (2020). The lean startup framework: Closing the academic-practitioner divide. *Entrepreneurship Theory and Practice.* Retrieved from https://doi.org/10.1177/1042258719899415

Smith, E. M., Ford, J. K., & Kozlowski, S. W. (1997). Building adaptive expertise: Implications for training design strategies. In M. A. Quiñones & A. Ehrenstein (Eds.), *Training for a rapidly changing workplace: Applications of psychological research* (pp. 89–118). Washington, DC: American Psychological Association.

Solomon, G., Frese, M., Friedrich, C., & Glaub, M. (2013). Can personal initiative training improve small business success? A longitudinal South African evaluation study. *The International Journal of Entrepreneurship and Innovation, 14*(4), 255–268. Retrieved from https://doi.org/10.5367/ijei.2013.0129

Souitaris, V., Zerbinati, S., & Al-Laham, A. (2007). Do entrepreneurship programmes raise entrepreneurial intention of science and engineering students? The effect of learning, inspiration and resources. *Journal of Business Venturing, 22*(4), 566–591. Retrieved from https://doi.org/10.1016/j.jbusvent.2006.05.002

Stam, W., Arzlanian, S., & Elfring, T. (2014). Social capital of entrepreneurs and small firm performance: A meta-analysis of contextual and methodological moderators. *Journal of Business Venturing, 29*(1), 152–173. Retrieved from https://doi.org/10.1016/j.jbusvent.2013.01.002

Unger, J. M., Rauch, A., Frese, M., & Rosenbusch, N. (2011). Human capital and entrepreneurial success: A meta-analytical review. *Journal of Business Venturing, 26*(3), 341–358. Retrieved from https://doi.org/10.1016/j.jbusvent.2009.09.004

Varamäki, E., Joensuu, S., Tornikoski, E., & Viljamaa, A. (2015). The development of entrepreneurial potential among higher education students. *Journal of Small Business and Enterprise Development, 22*(3), 563–589. Retrieved from https://doi.org/10.1108/JSBED-02-2012-0027

von Graevenitz, G., Harhoff, D., & Weber, R. (2010). The effects of entrepreneurship education. *Journal of Economic Behavior & Organization, 76*(1), 90–112. Retrieved from https://doi.org/10.1016/j.jebo.2010.02.015

Walter, S. G., & Block, J. H. (2016). Outcomes of entrepreneurship education: An institutional perspective. *Journal of Business Venturing, 31*(2), 216–233. Retrieved from https://doi.org/10.1016/j.jbusvent.2015.10.003

17

ENTREPRENEURSHIP ACROSS THE LIFE SPAN

Mona Mensmann & Hannes Zacher

This chapter deals with the universal process of aging, which entails individual development across the life span, and its impact on entrepreneurship. Although the process of aging has been studied for a long time (Baltes, Reese, & Lipsitt, 1980; Baltes, Rudolph, & Zacher, 2019), scholarly interest in the effects of aging on entrepreneurship, and particularly the interest in older entrepreneurs, has significantly increased over the past decade (for recent reviews, see Ratten, 2019; Matos, Amaral, & Baptista, 2018; Zacher, Mensmann, & Gielnik, 2019; Zhao, O'Connor, Wu, & Lumpkin, 2020). This interest is partly rooted in the growing importance of entrepreneurship for different age groups. For younger members of the workforce, employment has become increasingly unstable in times of demographic change, globalization, and technological advancement, while new business opportunities arise continuously. The global rate of youth unemployment is currently estimated at 13% (UN, 2018), with some extreme records, especially in developing countries (e.g., 57.4% in South Africa; UN, 2018). At the same time, small and medium-sized enterprises (SMEs) create between 60% and 70% of new jobs in developed countries (OECD, 2000) and 80% of jobs in developing countries (World Bank, 2015). Even for employed young people, entrepreneurial thinking becomes more and more important as an expected key work competence (Obschonka, Silbereisen, Schmitt-Rodermund, & Stuetzer, 2011).

For older adults, entrepreneurship provides a chance to continue to be an active member of the workforce. Due to increased life expectancies and decreased fertility rates, the world population is aging, especially in developed countries (e.g., in the UK, where one sixth of the population is older than 65 years) but also in developing countries (e.g., China, India; Hertel & Zacher, 2018). In many countries, the mandatory retirement age has increased (e.g., to 67 years in Germany) or the timing of retirement has become more flexible. Consequently, the global workforce is aging and becoming more age-diverse. For older workers, the opportunity to start a business has become increasingly attractive. Starting a business may constitute a source of financial security, autonomy, and meaning in later life (Halvorsen & Morrow-Howell, 2017; Kean, Van Zandt, & Maupin, 1993). At the societal level, older entrepreneurs take away some pressure from social security systems, as they contribute to social security and retirement funds (Pilkova, Holienka, & Rehak, 2014).

In light of the importance of entrepreneurship for people from different age groups, we aim to describe how aging influences physical, cognitive, and socioemotional abilities, as well as motivation, and how these factors, in turn, affect entrepreneurial decision-making, behavior, and success. Based on the entrepreneurship and the life-span development literature, we make two fundamental assumptions, which both require the adoption of a process perspective on the impact of aging on entrepreneurship. First, entrepreneurship is not a stable condition or final outcome. Instead, it constitutes a dynamic process with different entrepreneurial stages (Baron, 2007; Shane & Venkataraman, 2000). Second, life-span development constitutes a continuous process of adaptation to personal and contextual changes, in which no phase is superior to other phases (Baltes, 1987).

We combine these two assumptions by linking intraindividual psychological processes that go along with aging with the process of entrepreneurship, providing insights into how aging affects each entrepreneurial stage. We first describe entrepreneurship from a process perspective, highlighting the key tasks and characteristics of each stage of the process. We subsequently present key tenets of the life-span developmental perspective, emphasizing different psychological processes that go along with the aging process. We then link the two topics by summarizing current evidence on the effects of aging on each of the phases of entrepreneurial action. We conclude the chapter with theoretical and practical implications resulting from our life-span perspective on aging and entrepreneurship and outline suggestions for future research.

Entrepreneurship as a Process

Entrepreneurship is an agentic endeavor that is highly dependent on the actions of the entrepreneur (Frese, 2009; McMullen & Shepherd, 2006). However, entrepreneurship does not require one central action that needs to be constantly maintained; in contrast, it constitutes a process involving different stages with each requiring unique actions to successfully deal with the specific tasks at hand (Baron, 2007; Gartner, 1988). Therefore, entrepreneurs' characteristics that impact their action (such as their age) might be beneficial for the success in one stage of the entrepreneurial process but insignificant or even detrimental to another (Gartner, 1988). Accordingly, a closer examination of the entrepreneurial process should contribute to more fine-grained insights into the influence of entrepreneurs' characteristics on the entrepreneurial process and success (see also Gielnik, Zacher, & Wang, 2018).

The entrepreneurial process starts with a pre-launch phase (Baron, 2007). The dominant task of this phase is opportunity identification. Entrepreneurs have to recognize and evaluate possible opportunities to start a business and subsequently develop those opportunities. To do so, they do not only need to detect possible third-person opportunities (i.e., opportunities that someone with the necessary knowledge and motivation might be able to seize), but also transform them into first-person opportunities (i.e., opportunities that entrepreneurs consider a business opportunity for themselves; Shepherd, McMullen, & Jennings, 2007). In addition, entrepreneurs need to detect and assemble resources they may need to seize detected opportunities (Baron, 2007).

The second phase of the entrepreneurial process—the launch phase—typically includes the first 12 to 18 months of business start-up (Baron, 2007). In this phase, the dominant task is the transition from mainly cognitive and motivational preparatory work and formed intentions to first "real" business action. Entrepreneurs craft and develop initial business strategies, form first marketing plans, and decide on the legal form of their business. The task of transforming entrepreneurial intention into action is not trivial, as identified first-person opportunities and resulting entrepreneurial intentions do not automatically result in entrepreneurial action. Changes in preferences of the entrepreneurs or external restrictions may hinder the transition, creating an intention-action gap that characterizes human behavior in different domains of life (Gollwitzer, 1999; Miller, Gallanter, & Pribram, 1960).

In the last stage of the entrepreneurial process—the post-launch stage—the entrepreneurs' primary task is to run the established company. Interpersonal skills that allow the entrepreneur to communicate, resolve conflicts, negotiate, and influence and motivate others (e.g., employees, customers) become increasingly relevant (Baron, 2007). Although entrepreneurs' decision-making and action clearly differ from those of managers in many respects (e.g., Busenitz & Barney, 1997), managerial actions like leading employees are part of this stage of the entrepreneurial process. In addition, given that numerous businesses eventually fail (Shepherd, 2003), many entrepreneurs need to develop possible business exit strategies in the post-launch stage.

Aging as a Process of Development Across the Life Span

Age has been shown to be one of the characteristics that affects entrepreneurial behavior and success differently depending on the stage of the entrepreneurial process (Gielnik et al., 2018). Whereas age refers to the time a person has lived since birth (typically measured in years), aging and life-span development describe a continuous process of adaptation to internal and external changes. Aging takes place from conception until death and does not give priority to any particular age or life stage (Baltes, 1987; Schwall, 2012). The life span theoretical perspective introduced and formalized by Paul Baltes (e.g., Baltes et al., 1980) aims to describe the nature of individual development (called ontogenesis) and to understand which person and contextual factors influence different developmental pathways and outcomes (see also Zacher, Rudolph, & Baltes, 2019). The life-span developmental perspective is a meta-theoretical framework that has been used to develop and integrate more specific theories, for instance theories of cognitive aging and personality maturation (Baltes, Staudinger, & Lindenberger, 1999), motivation and action regulation (Baltes & Baltes, 1990), as well as regulation of emotions and social relationships (Carstensen, Isaacowitz, & Charles, 1999; Charles & Carstensen, 2010).

Empirical research based on the life-span perspective has uncovered various age-related normative trends in the general population, interindividual differences in development, and intraindividual plasticity or the range and boundaries of modifiability of experience and behavior (see Figure 17.1). Importantly, psychological characteristics can follow different developmental trajectories over time. While some of these age-related trends are linear, others have a nonlinear pattern (e.g., lower or higher levels in a characteristic at both younger and older ages and a peak or dip around middle-age, respectively).

First, there is solid evidence that, on average, physical abilities (e.g., muscle strength, flexibility) and fluid cognitive abilities (e.g., working memory, speed of information processing) decline with age, whereas crystallized cognitive abilities (e.g., experiential knowledge and judgment, wisdom) stabilize or even increase across the life span (Fisher, Chacon, & Chaffee, 2019; Maertens, Putter, Chen, Diehl, & Huang, 2012; Salthouse, 2012).

Second, people generally tend to become more mature and socially competent as they get older, which is indicated by increases in conscientiousness,

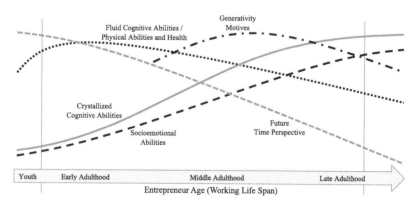

FIGURE 17.1   Important Normative Age-Related Changes in Person Characteristics

Source: Based on Kanfer, Beier, & Ackerman (2013)

agreeableness, and emotional stability (Nye & Roberts, 2019). Meta-analytic research on age and work motives has shown that growth and extrinsic motives (e.g., challenging work, advancement, compensation) decrease across the adult life span, whereas intrinsic motives (e.g., autonomy, accomplishment, use of skills, helping people, and contributing to society) increase with age (Kooij, De Lange, Jansen, Kanfer, & Dikkers, 2011). The generativity motives (i.e., establishing and supporting the next generation) is thought to peak in middle-age (i.e., approximately 40–60 years), with correspondingly lower levels at younger and older ages (McAdams & de St. Aubin, 1992; Zacher, Schmitt, & Gielnik, 2012).

Third, according to socioemotional selectivity theory (Carstensen et al., 1999), people's future time perspective decreases with age, which leads to the prioritization of positive emotional experiences at higher ages, as compared to a more important role of growth in knowledge and social networks at younger ages (e.g., Lang & Carstensen, 2002). Thus, the life-span perspective acknowledges that development is both multidimensional and multidirectional, including dynamic patterns of growth, maintenance (including recovery and resilience), and loss over time (Baltes, 1987). Based on Kanfer et al. (Kanfer & Ackerman, 2004; Kanfer et al., 2013), Figure 17.1 summarizes several important normative, age-related changes in person factors, which we link with the entrepreneurship process in the next section.

With regard to interindividual differences in development, there is evidence that enriched (work) environments (e.g., high levels of complexity and autonomy) as well as more frequent participation in physical, mental, and social activities can buffer cognitive decline at higher ages (Hertzog, Kramer, Wilson, & Lindenberger, 2009; Schallberger, 1988). Moreover, research based on the life-span perspective suggests that older adults can maintain high levels of well-being and functioning by using so-called successful aging strategies, including voluntary and loss-based goal selection, optimization of goal pursuit, and compensation of losses (Baltes & Baltes, 1990; Moghimi, Zacher, Scheibe, & Von Yperen, 2017). For example, instead of pursuing multiple goals and business opportunities at once, an older entrepreneur could focus on a smaller set of the most important goals related to the start-up process (selection) and invest a greater amount of time and energy into these selected goals (optimization). When confronted with barriers that exceed available personal resources, the older entrepreneur could ask others for help or adjust the initial time plan (compensation).

Finally, research on plasticity shows that developmental pathways are not predetermined and that older adults are not "set in their ways", but that their experience and behavior can be changed in meaningful ways, for instance through social and intergenerational interactions (Kessler & Staudinger, 2007), as well as interventions such as job crafting training (Kooij, van Woerkom, Wilkenloh, Dorenbosch, & Denissen, 2017) and self-distancing exercises (Kross & Grossman, 2012). Overall, the life-span perspective views aging as a dynamic and "open" process that is shaped by individual characteristics and behavior as well as contextual factors, ranging from daily work experiences and events over social relationships and institutions to historical and cultural influences (Settersten, 2017).

Merging Two Processes: The Effects of Aging on Entrepreneurship

Table 17.1 summarizes our review of the effect of aging on the entrepreneurial context.

TABLE 17.1 Research Topics on Aging Across the Entrepreneurial Process

	Pre-Launch	*Launch*	*Post-Launch*
Age-related differences	**A** Motivation to start a business • Perceived opportunity costs • Risk aversion • Future time perspective • (Internalized) age stereotypes • Search for bridge employment • Financial needs • Intrinsic vs. extrinsic start-up motivation	**C** Capital • Human capital: Crystallized cognitive abilities (e.g., knowledge, wisdom) • Social capital: Time to acquire social capital, personality development	**E** Effects of entrepreneurship on aging • Quality of life • Cognitive decline • Increased wisdom **F** Managerial behavior • Leadership: Legacy beliefs • Growth orientation: Focus on opportunities • Business failure: Human, social, and financial capital, trial and error mentality, intrinsic motivation • Succession: Generativity
Factors impacting the influence of age on entrepreneurship	**B** • Perceived age norms • Age discrimination of older workers • Work socialization • Culture	**D** • Perception of "aging well"	**G** • Support/exclusion based on age stereotypes

Aging and the Pre-Launch Phase of Entrepreneurship

In the pre-launch phase of entrepreneurship, entrepreneurs do not only need to identify opportunities but also consider the first-person opportunities they want to exploit themselves in order to start the entrepreneurial process (Shepherd et al., 2007). Age may influence this stage in the entrepreneurial process through a change in motivation that determines whether individuals take the decision to engage in entrepreneurship and the type of business they are interested in.

While scholars agree on the fact that becoming an entrepreneur constitutes an attractive opportunity for both younger people and people in later life stages, research provides contradictory evidence on whether aging might increase or decrease the motivation for opportunity identification and business start-up. Some evidence suggests that younger individuals are more interested in new venture foundation (Blanchflower, Oswald, & Stutzer, 2001), with start-up rates of people at "prime age" (i.e., between 20 and 49 years) being twice as high as those of people at "third age" (i.e., over 50 years; Kautonen, 2008). Adding to this, a study finds that only 14% of older workers show intentions to become self-employed (Curran & Blackburn, 2001). In contrast, some research indicates higher rates of entrepreneurial interest at higher vs. lower ages and emphasizes the constantly increasing start-up rates among people in later life stages (Halvorsen & Morrow-Howell, 2017). More recent evidence points to a curvilinear relationship between age and entrepreneurial intentions with a peak at between the age of 40 and 50 years (Kautonen, Down, & Minniti, 2014). From a life-span developmental perspective, an explanation for the curvilinear relationship between age and entrepreneurial intention might be that middle-aged adults have already experienced increases in psychological characteristics as well as personal resources important for entrepreneurship (e.g., experience, maturity, funding), while they have not yet experienced age-related declines that could reduce their entrepreneurial intentions (e.g., information processing skills, future time perspective).

Research has provided several findings regarding the development of entrepreneurial motivation across the life span (see Table 17.1, Part A, for an overview of motivational factors in the pre-launch phase). These findings reveal that the influence of aging on opportunity identification and entrepreneurial intentions is complex. One explanation for lower entrepreneurial intentions at a higher age is that older individuals perceive higher opportunity costs due to generally higher accumulated wealth and that they show higher risk aversion (Josef et al., 2016; Lévesque & Minniti, 2006; Mamerow, Frey, & Mata, 2016; Mata, Josef, & Hertwig, 2016). Risk propensity, however, is a personality dimension that has been associated with increased entrepreneurial intentions (Rauch & Frese, 2007; Zhao, Seibert, & Lumpkin, 2010). The decreased future time perspective of older individuals (Carstensen et al., 1999) may also explain why the likelihood of turning identified business opportunities into entrepreneurial intentions decreases with age, as the relative return of entrepreneurship decreases (Gielnik et al., 2018; Zacher & Gielnik, 2014). The fact that entrepreneurship is generally associated with youth (Ainsworth & Hardy, 2008; De Bruin & Dupuis, 2003; Down & Reveley, 2004) might further demotivate older individuals to become entrepreneurs; they may feel "too old" to start up a business (Curran & Blackburn, 2011). However, retirees may also consider temporary self-employment as a form of "bridge employment" on their way back to late employment (Singh & DeNoble, 2003; von Bonsdorff, Zhan, Song, & Wang, 2017). Shrinking retirement funds and age discrimination in recruiting processes also lead some older individuals into starting a business (De Bruin & Dupuis, 2003; Kautonen, Tornikoski, & Kibler, 2011; Zacher & Gielnik, 2014).

The interaction of age and contextual factors across the life span (Settersten, 2017) also applies to the context of forming entrepreneurial intentions in the pre-launch phase (see Table 17.1, Part B). Perceived age norms regarding whether entrepreneurial behavior is a behavior that is appropriate in later life play an important role in this regard (Kautonen et al., 2011). The more these perceived age norms support entrepreneurial behavior of older people, the more social support older entrepreneurs receive and the more positive their attitude toward entrepreneurship and their own perceived entrepreneurial ability. In contrast, if there is low age discrimination and a high demand for older workers in a society, older people show decreased levels of motivation to start a business (Kautonen, 2012). Socialization across the life span also affects the decision to start up a business. Research for example suggests that older workers who have spent their occupational life in blue-collar jobs show lower entrepreneurial intentions than younger colleagues in comparable positions. The lower intentions are driven by a decreased belief in own entrepreneurial abilities and a perceived lack of support by the immediate environment (Kautonen, Luoto, & Tornikoski, 2010). Prior work experience in business, in contrast, does not impact or even increases older people's decision to start up a business (Ainsworth, 2015; Kautonen et al., 2010). Finally, cultural dimensions like uncertainty avoidance, institutional collectivism, and performance orientation, have also been found to affect the effect of age on the motivation to start a business (Minola, Criaco, & Obschonka, 2016).

In line with findings on decreasing extrinsic motives of older workers (Kooij et al., 2011), research suggests that older entrepreneurs start businesses out of intrinsic motives, such as personal interest, rather than extrinsic motives, such as monetary benefits (Kautonen, 2008), in case they are not forced into entrepreneurial action by financial needs and a lack of alternatives (Singh & DeNoble, 2003; Weber & Schaper, 2004).

Aging and the Launch Phase of Entrepreneurship

Entrepreneurial intentions formed in the pre-launch phase are a necessary, but not a sufficient, condition for entrepreneurial action. In addition, entrepreneurs need to detect and assemble necessary resources to move from intention to action. Existing research on the effect of age in the launch phase of entrepreneurship mainly focuses on the transition from intention to action, that is, on the transition from the pre-launch to the launch phase of entrepreneurship. Older entrepreneurs have an advantage here, as human, social, and financial capital increase over the life span (Rogoff, 2007; Weber & Schaper, 2004) and because these forms of capital are critical drivers of start-up behavior (Davidsson & Honig, 2003). Table 17.1, Part C, summarizes capital-related age effects in the launch phase.

Higher human capital at older age partly results from the entrepreneur gathering experience over the life course. Age goes along with a rise in crystallized cognitive abilities such as knowledge gained from life experience (Fisher et al., 2019; Maertens et al., 2012; Salthouse, 2012), as well as wise reasoning about complex life problems, such as social conflicts (Grossman , Varnum, Park, Kitayama, & Nisbett, 2010). This experiential knowledge, in turn, has been shown to increase the probability to turn entrepreneurial intentions into start-up actions (Gielnik et al., 2018). Social capital also grows with age, as age comes along with more time to build up supportive networks. This effect might be reinforced by the general increase in social competence over the life span reflected in higher conscientiousness, agreeableness, and emotional stability levels (Nye & Roberts, 2019), also known as the "maturity principle" or "dolce vita effect" (Lucas & Donnellan, 2011; Marsh, Nagengast, & Morin, 2010). In addition, due to increasing life experience and expertise, people might become more attractive business and personal contacts with age. As a result, older entrepreneurs possess bigger networks with more strong and weak ties, which are crucial support factors for business start-up (Davidsson & Honig, 2003).

Critically, the availability of more human, social, and financial capital alone does not lead older individuals to start businesses. Potential entrepreneurs also need to feel ready to take action. One important driver of this perceived readiness is the perception of the entrepreneur to "age well" (see Table 17.1, Part D), meaning that they feel younger than their chronological age (Kautonen & Minniti, 2014). Potential entrepreneurs who enter the midlife stage (between 40 and 50) and feel that they have aged well are more likely to transform their entrepreneurial intentions into business action. This is even more important in view of the fact that perceived opportunities and perceived skills for entrepreneurship seem to stop older individuals from showing entrepreneurial activity (Bohlmann, Rauch, & Zacher, 2017).

Aging and the Post-Launch Phase of Entrepreneurship

The last phase of the entrepreneurial process is characterized by managerial action that is necessary to run an established business and actions taken in case of business failure (Baron, 2007). Importantly, much research on age and the post-launch phase of entrepreneurship concentrates on the role that entrepreneurial behavior plays for the process of aging instead of the effect that aging has on entrepreneurial behavior (see Table 17.1, Part E). This research is in line with life-span theories emphasizing the role of enriched work environments for buffering the effect of aging on health and well-being (Hertzog et al., 2009). Kautonen, Kibler, and Minniti (2017), for example, could show that the transition from employment to entrepreneurship in late careers positively affects older people's quality of life (despite overall negative effects on income). In general, the intellectual work and social embeddedness that come along with engaging in entrepreneurship should prevent cognitive decline at older age (Hertzog et al., 2009; Zacher, 2015). Dealing with complex and challenging personal and work-related issues, such as financial insecurity or social conflicts, may also contribute to the development of wisdom with age (Zacher & Kunzmann, 2019).

Research also provides some insights into the impact of age on business management (see Table 17.1, Part F). Some of this research has been conducted in areas other than entrepreneurship but may be applied to the entrepreneurial context. A study by Zacher, Rosing, and Frese (2011), for example, suggests that older leaders only show transformational and transactional leadership in case of high legacy beliefs, that is, beliefs that oneself and ones actions will be remembered far beyond death. Consequently, older entrepreneurs may be more motivated to actively lead their employees (either by showing transformational behaviors, such as coaching employees, or by showing transactional behaviors, such as rewarding employees for their effort), if they think that their actions as entrepreneurs will be remembered by others in the future. Other motives that drive leadership behavior at younger ages, such as own career advancement, may lose their influence as leaders age, supporting the thought that personal development motives decline over the life span (e.g., Lang & Carstensen, 2002). Although the study by Zacher et al. (2011) has been conducted in the academic context, it may indicate that entrepreneurs' leadership behavior may be dependent on age-related motivational changes.

The likelihood *that* entrepreneurs will hire employees and need to lead, however, decreases with age; older entrepreneurs are less likely to employ workers and if they do, the number of employees is lower than in businesses led by younger entrepreneurs (Curran & Blackburn, 2001; De Kok, Ichou, & Verheul, 2010; Kautonen et al., 2014). In general, businesses led by younger business owners tend to be higher in growth; one possible explanation may be that the focus on future business opportunities decreases with age (Gielnik, Zacher, & Schmitt, 2017). A recent meta-analytic review on age and entrepreneurial success, however, showed that age is only very weakly related to overall entrepreneurial success ($\rho = .02$, based on K = 102 studies with a total of N = 65,753 participants; Zhao et al., 2020). This effect size is somewhat stronger when more women are included in the sample, but is not influenced by entrepreneurs' company tenure. Interestingly, when differentiating between different indicators of entrepreneurial success, the meta-analysis found that age is weakly and negatively related to growth

($\rho = -.05$), but weakly and positively related to subjective success ($\rho = .09$), firm size ($\rho = .07$), and financial success ($\rho = .04$; Zhao et al., 2020).

Age also has an impact on the likelihood that businesses fail in the post-launch phase. Businesses led by older versus younger entrepreneurs are more likely to survive the first years (Ainsworth, 2015; Robb & Reedy, 2012), possibly due to the higher level of human, social, and financial capital of older entrepreneurs (Ainsworth, 2015; Singh & DeNoble, 2003; Weber & Schaper, 2004). In case business owners fail, their age also impacts the likelihood of business reentry. The relationship between age and reentry is positive in the younger age early-career stage, negative in the middle-age mid-career stage, and positive in the old-age late-career stage (Baù, Sieger, Eddleston, & Chirico, 2017). Younger entrepreneurs may still possess a trial and error mentality and reentry is facilitated by the fact that failing in entrepreneurship is less stigmatized for young entrepreneurs. Older entrepreneurs may show a higher probability for reentry as they are more emotionally stable and therefore better able to cope with the emotions involved with business failure. In addition, they have a clearer self-concept and deeply enjoy the entrepreneurial experience, which may foster reentry. In contrast, people in their mid-careers face a desire to progress in their careers and may be more prone to question past career choices, which should lead them to ultimately leave the entrepreneurial path after failure (Baù et al., 2017).

In case entrepreneurs do not fail and establish a successful enterprise, they may wish to pass on their family business to the next generation one day. In this case, their age may impact the family succession process, that is, those actions that facilitate the takeover of the business by a younger generation family member (Sharma, 2004). Research suggests that starting in middle-age (i.e., around 50 or 60 years), business owners are more likely to make succession plans than younger owners, as they show higher levels of generativity, which makes them more interested in supporting and guiding the next generation (Zacher et al., 2012). At the same time, researchers have suggested that, after a peak in middle-age, the generativity motive declines at older ages (McAdams & de St. Aubin, 1992), which might lead to problems in the family succession process (i.e., not "letting go").

Interactions between age and social factors have also been researched in the post-launch phase of entrepreneurship. A study by Kibler, Wainwright, Kautonen, and Blackburn (2015), for example, shows that social influences (in form of either support or exclusion based on age stereotypes) influence the development of older entrepreneurs' businesses by affecting their entrepreneurial confidence and fostering or hindering access to resources, support, and information (see Table 17.1, Part G).

Implications for Theory, Research, and Practice

Our review of the extant literature on aging and entrepreneurship has a number of important implications for theory development, future empirical research, and practical applications. First, it suggests that the field needs to move away from a static examination of age on entrepreneurship. Instead, both age and entrepreneurship should be theoretically conceptualized as processes that influence each other over time. This thought is in line with a recent call for a stronger consideration of time as a critical influence factor in entrepreneurship (Lévesque & Stephan, 2019). Critically, the relationship between aging and the entrepreneurial process should be examined as a bidirectional process, with influences of age on entrepreneurship but also with subsequent influences of entrepreneurial action on the process of aging (e.g., prevention of cognitive decline through activity, development of wisdom). Future research may pay tribute to this reciprocal relationship that unfolds over time and try to integrate the so far scattered field of age and entrepreneurship.

Second, empirical studies should adopt more rigorous longitudinal designs and statistical analyses. Consistent with recommendations of methodologists (Ployhart & Vandenberg, 2010), studies on the processes of aging and entrepreneurship should include at least three, ideally more, measurement points which are separated by appropriate time intervals (e.g., Gielnik et al., 2018, use intervals of six months between three measurement waves). Moreover, it is important that future research does not only use chronological age as a "catchall" proxy but operationalizes the most important assumed age-related mechanisms (e.g., experience, future time perspective, abilities; see Bohlmann, Rudolph, & Zacher, 2018). At the same time, the entrepreneurial process needs to be rigorously investigated by using true longitudinal designs (e.g., through panel data) and adequate statistical analyses (e.g., structural equation modeling; see Levesque & Stephan, 2019, for further suggestions), and operationalized by using measures that can distinguish the behavior of different stages of the entrepreneurial process (e.g., start-up vs. growth behavior).

Finally, research on aging and entrepreneurship has implications for the selection of individuals into entrepreneurship development programs, training interventions, and governmental programs. Specifically, these interventions could take the age-related strengths and challenges of participants into account, for instance by providing additional information and "reality checks" to younger, less experienced participants or by allowing older participants to capitalize on their greater knowledge and experience gained over the years or to make use of their generativity motive by starting social businesses. Moreover, practical applications should be designed in such a way that negative age stereotypes are not applied or reinforced and that positive age-related views are facilitated (e.g., aging-friendly climate, open-ended future time perspective). This type of research may also lead to insights into how to build and sustain diverse entrepreneurial teams that use the strengths of team members in an optimal way and compensate for potential age-related weaknesses.

Conclusion

The goal of this chapter was to examine links between the aging process and the process of entrepreneurship. We set out by describing three entrepreneurial phases as well as key propositions and findings of research based on the life-span developmental perspective. Our review of the empirical literature on aging and entrepreneurship suggests that, although much progress has been made over the past few decades, more and enhanced theory development and research is needed to adequately guide practical applications in this area. Precarious employment among young adults and extended and more flexible employment among older adults are key challenges for individuals, organizations, and society that require an evidence-based approach to the role of aging in entrepreneurship.

References

Ainsworth, S. (2015). Aging entrepreneurs and volunteers: Transition in late career. In P. M. Bal, D. T. A. M. Kooi, & D. M. Rousseau (Eds.), *Aging workers and the employee-employer relationship* (pp. 243–260). New York: Springer.

Ainsworth, S., & Hardy, C. (2008). The enterprising self: An unsuitable job for an older worker. *Organization, 15*(3), 389–405. doi:10.1177/1350508408088536

Baltes, P. B. (1987). Theoretical propositions of life-span developmental psychology: On the dynamics between growth and decline. *Developmental Psychology, 23*(5), 611–626.

Baltes, P. B., & Baltes, M. M. (1990). Psychological perspectives on successful aging: The model of selective optimization with compensation. In P. B. Baltes & M. M. Baltes (Eds.), *Successful aging: Perspectives from the behavioral sciences* (pp. 1–34). New York: Cambridge University Press.

Baltes, P. B., Reese, H. W., & Lipsitt, L. P. (1980). Life-span developmental psychology. *Annual Review of Psychology, 31*(1), 65–110. doi:10.1146/annurev.ps.31.020180.000433

Baltes, P. B., Rudolph, C. W., & Zacher, H. (2019). *Work across the lifespan.* London, UK: Academic Press.

Baltes, P. B., Staudinger, U. M., & Lindenberger, U. (1999). Lifespan psychology: Theory and application to intellectual functioning. *Annual Review of Psychology, 50*, 471–507. doi:10.1146/annurev.psych.50.1.471

Baron, R. A. (2007). Entrepreneurship: A process perspective. In J. R. Baum, M. Frese, & R. A. Baron (Eds.), *The psychology of entrepreneurship* (pp. 19–39). Mahwah, NJ: Lawrence Erlbaum Associates.

Baù, M., Sieger, P., Eddleston, K. A., & Chirico, F. (2017). Fail but try again? The effects of age, gender, and multiple-owner experience on failed entrepreneurs' reentry. *Entrepreneurship Theory & Practice, 41*(6), 909–941. doi:10.1111/etap.12233

Blanchflower, D. G., Oswald, A., & Stutzer, A. (2001). Latent entrepreneurship across nations. *European Economic Review, 45*(4–6), 680–691. doi:10.1016/S0014-2921(01)00137-4

Bohlmann, C., Rauch, A., & Zacher, H. (2017). A lifespan perspective on entrepreneurship: Perceived opportunities and skills explain the negative association between age and entrepreneurial activity. *Frontiers in Psychology, 8*, 2015. doi:10.3389/fpsyg.2017.02015

Bohlmann, C., Rudolph, C. W., & Zacher, H. (2018). Methodological recommendations to move research on work and aging forward. *Work, Aging and Retirement, 4*(3), 225–237. doi:10.1093/workar/wax023

Busenitz, L. W., & Barney, J. B. (1997). Differences between entrepreneurs and managers in large organizations: Biases and heuristics in strategic decision-making. *Journal of Business Venturing, 12*(1), 9–30. doi:10.1016/S0883-9026(96)00003-1

Carstensen, L. L., Isaacowitz, D. M., & Charles, S. T. (1999). Taking time seriously: A theory of socioemotional selectivity. *American Psychologist, 54*(3), 165–181. doi:10.1037/0003-066X.54.3.165

Charles, S. T., & Carstensen, L. L. (2010). Social and emotional aging. *Annual Review of Psychology, 61*, 383–409. doi:10.1146/annurev.psych.093008.100448

Curran, J., & Blackburn, R. A. (2001). Older people and the enterprise society: Age and self-employment propensities. *Work, Employment and Society, 15*(4), 889–902.

Davidsson, P., & Honig, B. (2003). The role of social and human capital among Nascent entrepreneurs. *Journal of Business Venturing, 18*(3), 301–331. doi:10.1016/S0883-9026(02)00097-6

De Bruin, A., & Dupuis, A. (2003). *Entrepreneurship: New perspectives in a global age*. Aldershot: Ashgate Publishing, Ltd.

De Kok, J. M., Ichou, A., & Verheul, I. (2010). New firm performance: Does the age of founders affect employment creation. *Zoetermeer: EIM Research Reports, 12*, 42–63.

Down, S., & Reveley, J. (2004). Generational encounters and the social formation of entrepreneurial identity: "Young guns" and "old farts". *Organization, 11*(2), 233–250. doi:10.1177/1350508404030381

Fisher, G. G., Chacon, M., & Chaffee, D. S. (2019). Theories of cognitive aging and work. In B. B. Baltes, C. W. Rudolph, & H. Zacher (Eds.), *Work across the lifespan* (pp. 17–45). London, UK: Academic Press.

Frese, M. (2009). Towards a psychology of entrepreneurship – An action theory perspective. *Foundations and Trends® in Entrepreneurship, 5*(6), 437–496. doi:10.1561/0300000028

Gartner, W. B. (1988). "Who is an entrepreneur?" is the wrong question. *Entrepreneurship Theory & Practice, 12*(4), 11–32. doi:10.1177/104225878801200401

Gielnik, M. M., Zacher, H., & Schmitt, A. (2017). How small business managers' age and focus on opportunities affect business growth: A mediated moderation growth model. *Journal of Small Business Management, 55*(3), 460–483. doi:10.1111/jsbm.12253

Gielnik, M. M., Zacher, H., & Wang, M. (2018). Age in the entrepreneurial process: The role of future time perspective and prior entrepreneurial experience. *Journal of Applied Psychology, 103*(10), 1067–1085. doi:10.1037/apl0000322

Gollwitzer, P. M. (1999). Implementation intentions: Strong effects of simple plans. *American Psychologist, 54*(7), 493–503.

Grossmann, I., Na, J., Varnum, M. E. W., Park, D. C., Kitayama, S., & Nisbett, R. E. (2010). Reasoning about social conflicts improves into old age. *Proceedings of the National Academy of Science, 107*(16), 7246–7250. doi:10.1073/pnas.1001715107

Halvorsen, C. J., & Morrow-Howell, N. (2017). A conceptual framework on self-employment in later life: Toward a research agenda. *Work, Aging and Retirement, 3*(4), 313–324. doi:10.1093/workar/waw031

Hertel, G., & Zacher, H. (2018). Managing the aging workforce. In D. S. Ones, C. Anderson, C. Viswesvaran, & H. K. Sinangil (Eds.), *The Sage handbook of industrial, work and organizational psychology* (2nd ed., Vol. 3, pp. 396–428). Thousand Oaks, CA: Sage.

Hertzog, C., Kramer, A. F., Wilson, R. S., & Lindenberger, U. (2009). Enrichment effects on adult cognitive development: Can the functional capacity of older adults be preserved and enhanced? *Psychological Science in the Public Interest, 9*(1), 1–65. doi:10.1111/j.1539-6053.2009.01034.x

Josef, A. K., Richter, D., Samanez-Larkin, G. R., Wagner, G. G., Hertwig, R., & Mata, R. (2016). Stability and change in risk-taking propensity across the adult life span. *Journal of Personality and Social Psychology, 111*(3), 430–450. doi:10.1037/pspp0000090

Kanfer, R., & Ackerman, P. L. (2004). Aging, adult development, and work motivation. *Academy of Management Review, 29*(3), 440–458. doi:10.5465/AMR.2004.13670969

Kanfer, R., Beier, M. E., & Ackerman, P. L. (2013). Goals and motivation related to work in later adulthood: An organizing framework. *European Journal of Work and Organizational Psychology, 22*(3), 253–264. doi:10.1080/1359432X.2012.734298

Kautonen, T. (2008). Understanding the older entrepreneur: Comparing third age and prime age entrepreneurs in Finland. *International Journal of Business Science Applied Management, 3*(3), 3–13.

Kautonen, T. (2012). Do age-related social expectations influence entrepreneurial activity in later life? *The International Journal of Entrepreneurship and Innovation, 13*(3), 179–187. doi:10.5367/ijei.2012.0083

Kautonen, T., Down, S., & Minniti, M. (2014). Ageing and entrepreneurial preferences. *Small Business Economics, 42*(3), 579–594.

Kautonen, T., Kibler, E., & Minniti, M. (2017). Late-career entrepreneurship, income and quality of life. *Journal of Business Venturing, 32*(3), 318–333. doi:10.1016/j.jbusvent.2017.02.005

Kautonen, T., Luoto, S., & Tornikoski, E. T. (2010). Influence of work history on entrepreneurial intentions in "prime age" and "third age": A preliminary study. *International Small Business Journal: Researching Entrepreneurship, 28*(6), 583–601. doi:10.1177/0266242610368592

Kautonen, T., & Minniti, M. (2014). "Fifty is the new thirty": Ageing well and start-up activities. *Applied Economics Letters, 21*(16), 1161–1164. doi:10.1080/13504851.2014.914138

Kautonen, T., Tornikoski, E. T., & Kibler, E. (2011). Entrepreneurial intentions in the third age: The impact of perceived age norms. *Small Business Economics, 37*(2), 219–234.

Kean, R. C., Van Zandt, S., & Maupin, W. (1993). Successful aging: The older entrepreneur. *Journal of Women & Aging, 5*(1), 25–42. doi:10.1300/J074v05n01_03

Kessler, E.-M., & Staudinger, U. M. (2007). Intergenerational potential: Effects of social interaction between older adults and adolescents. *Psychology and Aging, 22*(4), 690–704.

Kibler, E., Wainwright, T., Kautonen, T., & Blackburn, R. (2015). Can social exclusion against "older entrepreneurs" be managed? *Journal of Small Business Management, 53*(S1), 193–208. doi:10.1111/jsbm.12194

Kooij, D. T. A. M., De Lange, A. H., Jansen, P. G. W., Kanfer, R., & Dikkers, J. S. E. (2011). Age and work-related motives: Results of a meta-analysis. *Journal of Organizational Behavior, 32*(2), 197–225. doi:10.1002/job.665

Kooij, D. T. A. M., van Woerkom, M., Wilkenloh, J., Dorenbosch, L., & Denissen, J. J. (2017). Job crafting towards strengths and interests: The effects of a job crafting intervention on person-job fit and the role of age. *Journal of Applied Psychology, 102*(6), 971–981. doi:10.1037/apl0000194

Kross, E., & Grossmann, I. (2012). Boosting wisdom: Distance from the self enhances wise reasoning, attitudes, and behavior. *Journal of Experimental Psychology: General, 141*(1), 43–48. doi:10.1037/a0024158

Lang, F. R., & Carstensen, L. L. (2002). Time counts: Future time perspective, goals, and social relationships. *Psychology and Aging, 17*(1), 125–139. doi:10.1037/0882-7974.17.1.125

Lévesque, M., & Minniti, M. (2006). The effect of aging on entrepreneurial behavior. *Journal of Business Venturing, 21*(2), 177–194. doi:10.1016/j.jbusvent.2005.04.003

Lévesque, M., & Stephan, U. (2019). It's time we talk about time in entrepreneurship. *Entrepreneurship Theory & Practice, 44*(2), 163–184. doi: 10.1177/1042258719839711

Lucas, R. E., & Donnellan, M. B. (2011). Personality development across the life span: Longitudinal analyses with a national sample from Germany. *Journal of Personality and Social Psychology, 101*(4), 847–861. doi:10.1037/a0024298

Maertens, J. A., Putter, S. E., Chen, P.Y., Diehl, M., & Huang,Y.-H. (2012). Physical capabilities and occupational health of older workers. In J. W. Hedge & W. C. Borman (Eds.), *The Oxford handbook of work and aging* (pp. 215–235). New York: Oxford University Press.

Mamerow, L., Frey, R., & Mata, R. (2016). Risk taking across the life span: A comparison of self-report and behavioral measures of risk taking. *Psychology and Aging, 31*(7), 711–723. doi:10.1037/pag0000124

Marsh, H. W., Nagengast, B., & Morin, A. J. S. (2010). Testing measurement invariance and latent mean differences of the Big-Five factor structure over age, gender, and their interaction: Exploratory structural equation modeling tests of plasticity, maturity and La Dolce Vita effects. Unpublished manuscript, Oxford University. Oxford, UK.

Mata, R., Josef, A. K., & Hertwig, R. (2016). Propensity for risk taking across the life span and around the globe. *Psychological Science, 27*(2), 231–243. doi:10.1177/095679761 5617811

Matos, S. C., Amaral, M., & Baptista, R. (2018). Senior entrepreneurship: A selective review and a research agenda. *Foundations and Trends® in Entrepreneurship, 14*(5), 427–554. doi:10.1561/0300000084

McAdams, D. P., & de St. Aubin, E. (1992). A theory of generativity and its assessment through self-report, behavioral acts, and narrative themes in autobiography. *Journal of Personality and Social Psychology, 62*(6), 1003–1015. doi:10.1037/0022-3514.62.6.1003

McMullen, J. S., & Shepherd, D. A. (2006). Entrepreneurial action and the role of uncertainty in the theory of the entrepreneur. *Academy of Management Review, 31*(1), 132–152. doi:10.5465/amr.2006.19379628

Miller, G. A., Gallanter, E., & Pribram, K. H. (1960). *Plans and the structure of behavior.* London, UK: Holt.

Minola, T., Criaco, G., & Obschonka, M. (2016). Age, culture, and self-employment motivation. *Small Business Economics, 46*(2), 187–213.

Moghimi, D., Zacher, H., Scheibe, S., & Von Yperen, N. W. (2017). The selection, optimization, and compensation model in the work context: A systematic review and meta-analysis of two decades of research. *Journal of Organizational Behavior, 38*(2), 247–275. doi:10.1002/job.2108

Nye, C., & Roberts, B. W. (2019). A neo-socioanalytic model of personality development. In B. B. Baltes, C. W. Rudolph, & H. Zacher (Eds.), *Work across the lifespan* (pp. 47–79). London, UK: Academic Press.

Obschonka, M., Silbereisen, R. K., Schmitt-Rodermund, E., & Stuetzer, M. (2011). Nascent entrepreneurship and the developing individual: Early entrepreneurial competence in adolescence and venture creation success during the career. *Journal of Vocational Behavior, 79*(1), 121–133.

OECD. (2000, June). Small and medium-sized enterprises: Local strength, global reach. *OECD Policy Brief,* Paris. Retrieved from www.oecd.org/cfe/leed/1918307.pdf

Pilkova, A., Holienka, M., & Rehak, J. (2014). Senior entrepreneurship in the perspective of European entrepreneurial environment. *Procedia Economics and Finance, 12*, 523–532. doi:10.1016/S2212-5671(14)00375-X

Ployhart, R. E., & Vandenberg, R. J. (2010). Longitudinal research: The theory, design, and analysis of change. *Journal of Management, 36*(1), 94–120. doi:10.1177/0149206309352110

Ratten, V. (2019). Older entrepreneurship: A literature review and research agenda. *Journal of Enterprising Communities: People and Places in the Global Economy, 13*(1-2), 178–195. doi:10.1108/JEC-08-2018-0054

Rauch, A., & Frese, M. (2007). Let's put the person back into entrepreneurship research: A meta-analysis on the relationship between business owners' personality traits, business creation, and success. *European Journal of Work and Organizational Psychology, 16*(4), 353–385. doi:10.1080/13594320701595438

Robb, A., & Reedy, E. J. (2012). An overview of the Kauffman firm survey: Results from 2010 business activities. Retrieved from SSRN 2055265.

Rogoff, E. (2007). Opportunities for entrepreneurship in later life. *Generations, 31* (1), 90–95.

Salthouse, T. A. (2012). Consequences of age-related cognitive declines. *Annual Review of Psychology, 63*, 201–226. doi:10.1146/annurev-psych-120710-100328

Schallberger, U. (1988). Berufsausbildung und Intelligenzentwicklung (Vocational training and the development of intelligence). In K. Huafeli, U. Kraft, & U. Schallberger (Eds.), *Berufsausbildung und Persönlichkeitsentwicklung: Eine Längsschnittuntersuchung* (Occupational education and personality development: A longitudinal study) (pp. 146–167). Bern: Huber.

Schwall, A. R. (2012). Defining age and using age-relevant constructs. In J. W. Hedge & W. C. Bormann (Eds.), *The Oxford handbook of work and aging* (pp. 169–186). New York: Oxford University Press.

Settersten, R. A. (2017). Some things I have learned about aging by studying the life course. *Innovation in Aging, 1*(2), 1–7. doi:10.1093/geroni/igx014

Shane, S., & Venkataraman, S. (2000). The promise of entrepreneurship as a field of research. *Academy of Management Review, 25*(1), 217–226. doi:10.5465/amr.2000.2791611

Sharma, P. (2004). An overview of the field of family business studies: Current status and directions for the future. *Family Business Review, 17*(1), 1–36. doi:10.1111/j.1741-6248.2004.00001.x

Shepherd, D. A. (2003). Learning from business failure: Propositions of grief recovery for the self-employed. *Academy of Management Review, 28*(2), 318–328. doi:10.5465/amr.2003.9416377

Shepherd, D. A., McMullen, J. S., & Jennings, P. D. (2007). The formation of opportunity beliefs: Overcoming ignorance and reducing doubt. *Strategic Entrepreneurship Journal, 1*(1-2), 75–95. doi:10.1002/sej.3

Singh, G., & DeNoble, A. (2003). Early retirees as the next generation of entrepreneurs. *Entrepreneurship Theory & Practice, 27*(3), 207–226. doi:10.1111/1540-8520.t01-1-00001

UN. (2018). *World youth report: Youth and the 20130 agenda for sustainable development*. United Nations: Department of Economic and Social Affairs Youth.

von Bonsdorff, M. E., Zhan, Y., Song, Y., & Wang, M. (2017). Examining bridge employment from a self-employment perspective - Evidence from the health and retirement study. *Work, Aging and Retirement, 3*(3), 298–312. doi:10.1093/workar/wax012

Weber, P., & Schaper, M. (2004). Understanding the grey entrepreneur. *Journal of Enterprising Culture, 12*(2), 147–164. doi:10.1142/s0218495804000087

World Bank. (2015). *Small and medium enterprises (SMEs) finance: Improving SMEs' access to finance and finding innovative solutions to unlock sources of capital*. Washington, DC: World Bank. Retrieved from www.worldbank.org/en/topic/smefinance

Zacher, H. (2015). Successful aging at work. *Work, Aging and Retirement, 1*(1), 4–25. doi:10.1093/workar/wau006

Zacher, H., & Gielnik, M. (2014). Organizational age cultures: The interplay of chief executive officers' age and attitudes toward younger and older employees. *International Small Business Journal: Researching Entrepreneurship, 32*(3), 327–349. doi:10.1177/0266242 612463025

Zacher, H., & Kunzmann, U. (2019). Wisdom in the workplace. In R. J. Sternberg, H. C. Nusbaum, & J. Glück (Eds.), *Applying wisdom to contemporary world problems* (pp. 255–292). Cham, Switzerland: Palgrave Macmillan.

Zacher, H., Mensmann, M., & Gielnik, M. M. (2019). Aging and entrepreneurship: A psychological perspective. In M. Karlsson, M. Backman, & O. Kekezi (Eds.), *Handbook on entrepreneurship and aging.* Cheltenham, UK: Edward Elgar Publishing.

Zacher, H., Rosing, K., & Frese, M. (2011). Age and leadership: The moderating role of legacy beliefs. *Leadership Quarterly, 22*(1), 43–50. doi:10.1016/j.leaqua.2010.12.006

Zacher, H., Rudolph, C. W., & Baltes, P. B. (2019). An invitation to lifespan thinking. In P. B. Baltes, C. W. Rudolph, & H. Zacher (Eds.), *Work across the lifespan* (pp. 1–14). London, UK: Academic Press.

Zacher, H., Schmitt, A., & Gielnik, M. M. (2012). Stepping into my shoes: Generativity as a mediator of the relationship between business owners' age and family succession. *Ageing and Society, 32*(4), 673–696. doi:10.1017/S0144686X11000547

Zhao, H., O'Connor, G., Wu, J., & Lumpkin, G. T. (2020). Age and entrepreneurial career success: A review and a meta-analysis. *Journal of Business Venturing.* doi:10.1016/j. jbusvent.2020.106007

Zhao, H., Seibert, S. E., & Lumpkin, G. T. (2010). The relationship of personality to entrepreneurial intentions and performance: A meta-analytic review. *Journal of Management, 36*(2), 381–404. doi:10.1177/0149206309335187

18

EVIDENCE-BASED ENTREPRENEURSHIP

An Extended Approach

Andreas Rauch & Michael M. Gielnik

Introduction

Evidence-based entrepreneurship (EBE) is the science-informed practice of entrepreneurship (Frese, Bausch, Schmidt, Rauch, & Kabst, 2012). Similar to evidence-based management (Pfeffer & Sutton, 2006), it is based on the general concept of evidence-based practices, which deals with the explicit use of current best evidence in making decisions and guiding practices in a field (Hesse-Biber, 2012). Accordingly, an important prerequisite is the systematic accumulation of evidence to establish valid theories about entrepreneurship (Frese & Gielnik, 2014). Accumulation of evidence means that a solid body of evidence is generated based on multiple studies and sources, not on a single study only. The accumulated evidence and theories should then be used to develop practices that can be applied to increase the likelihood of success in entrepreneurship. Furthermore, it is useful to assess the effectiveness of the applied practices in order to advance the theories regarding the mechanisms and boundary conditions of these practices (Reay, Berta, & Kohn, 2009). Accordingly, EBE involves (1) accumulating systematically the best scientific evidence in entrepreneurship, (2) establishing theories to explain entrepreneurship, (3) developing practices to inform and guide entrepreneurs' decisions and actions, and, finally, (4) evaluating the effectiveness of the practices, using for example randomized controlled trials (RCT; Frese et al., 2012).

EBE is useful because it provides stakeholders in entrepreneurship with practices and guidance in decision-making. For example, such practices and guidance can inform entrepreneurs how to grow the business venture, policy makers how to stimulate entrepreneurship, investors how to avoid biased investment decisions, and training institutions how to develop an effective syllabus. Thereby, EBE raises the practical relevance of scientific findings and emphasizes practical significance.

Furthermore, EBE acknowledges that there is variation in study findings. EBE aims at investigating the reasons for variations in study findings and thereby arrives at a best estimate of a relationship. In this way, EBE also contributes to addressing issues with replicability of scientific studies (Camerer et al., 2016; Open Science Collaboration, 2015).

EBE has recently gained momentum in entrepreneurship research (Frese & Gielnik, 2014). In particular, the systematic accumulation of evidence in terms of quantitative meta-analyses has increased considerably. Meta-analytic evidence has established magnitudes of important relationships in the field, set standards for theory validation, and solved several debates in the field, such as whether planning is harmful or beneficial (it's beneficial!) (Brinckmann, Grichnik, & Kapsa, 2010), whether quitting school or college increases the chances of success (no!) (Unger, Rauch, Frese, & Rosenbusch, 2011), and what role personality plays (considerable if the traits match entrepreneurship; Rauch & Frese, 2007). In Table 18.1, we provide an overview of the large number of published meta-analyses in the psychology of entrepreneurship. Researchers need to continue pursuing this important method of research, because it provides a robust foundation for developing evidence-based practices.

In this chapter, we do not aim to summarize the evidence and conclusions derived from quantitative meta-analyses (see reviews for these aims (Frese et al., 2012; Frese & Gielnik, 2014)), but to use the existing research as a starting point for extending the methodological approach underlying EBE. Specifically, we seek to look at evidence in a broader way, including quantitative and qualitative methods, to advance our understanding of entrepreneurship from an evidence-based perspective.

Evidence-Based Entrepreneurship: An Extended Perspective

The core of EBE is the systematic accumulation and interpretation of the scientific evidence on entrepreneurship (Frese, Rousseau, & Wiklund, 2014; Rauch & Frese, 2006). Evidence provides empirical corroboration and thus helps to determine the truth of an assertion. However, in times of fake news, it is important to reiterate briefly what constitutes the best or most credible evidence available (Lazer et al., 2018). The medical literature was early in trying to establish criteria for good evidence, classifying meta-analysis as the highest form of evidence, followed by randomized control trials, cohort/longitudinal studies, case-control studies, cross-sectional studies, and case studies (Edwards, Russell, & Stott, 1998; Greenhalgh, 2010). Thus, the quality of evidence depends on the research design and credible evidence can be established with meta-analyses and RCT. It is important to note, however, that the pure presence of one of these designs does not guarantee credible evidence. For example, meta-analyses that are based on primary studies with poor research designs are limited in their validity and even

TABLE 18.1 Meta-Analytical Studies on the Psychology of Entrepreneurship

Reference	Topic	Mag-nitude	Bi- or multi-variate	Conceptual approach	Method[2]	Test of publication bias	Number of citations/ per year[3]	Notes	Heterogeneity
Unger et al., 2011	Human capital	yes	bi	theory testing	H&S	file save N, published versus unpublished analysis	1,200/150		yes
Martin et al., 2013	Entrepreneurship education outcomes	yes	bi	theory testing	H&S	published versus unpublished analysis	761/127		yes
Bae et al., 2014	Entrepreneurship education and intentions	yes	bi	theory testing	H&S	published versus unpublished analysis	662/132	test of causality included	yes
van der Sluis et al., 2005	Schooling, selection, performance	no	multi	explorative	–	yes	349/25	strong focus on regressions	yes
Zhao & Seibert, 2006	Personality and entrepreneurial status	yes	multi	theory testing	H&S	no	1,370/105	meta-regression based on a small number of studies	yes
Zhao, Seibert, & Lumpkin, 2010	Personality and performance	yes	multi	theory testing	H&S	no	1,012/112	N of meta-regressions not reported	not reported

(Continued)

TABLE 18.1 Continued

Reference	Topic	Mag-nitude	Bi- or multi-variate	Conceptual approach	Method[2]	Test of publication bias	Number of citations/per year[3]	Notes	Heterogeneity
Rauch & Frese, 2007	Personality, emergence, performance	yes	bi	theory testing	H&S	published versus unpublished analysis	1,356/113		yes
Collins, Hanges, & Locke, 2004	Need for achievement	yes	bi	theory testing	H&O	no	783/52	tests a number of moderators	not reported
Stewart & Roth, 2001	Risk-taking entrepreneurs vs. managers	yes	bi	explorative	H&S	no	1,044/58	d values	no, results are homogeneous
Stewart & Roth, 2007	Need for achievement, entrepreneurs vs. manager	yes	bi	explorative	H&S	no	322/27	d values	yes
Miao, Qian, & Ma, 2017	Self-efficacy and performance	yes	bi	theory testing	H&S	published versus unpublished analysis	42/21		yes
Sarooghi, Libaers, & Burkemper, 2015	Creativity and innovation	yes	multi	theory testing	H&S	fail save N and publication status	189/47	magnitude very high, N not reported in meta-regression	yes
Brinckmann et al., 2010	Planning and performance	yes	multi	theory testing	L&W	fail save N	664/74	d values; test of common method bias; N for regressions not reported	yes

Study	Topic					fail save N and publication status funnel plot		post-hoc analyses reported	not reported
Brinckmann, Dew, Mayer-Haug, & Grichnik, 2019[1]	Planning and human capital	yes	bi	theory testing	H&S	fail save N and publication status funnel plot	2/2	post-hoc analyses reported	not reported
Stam, Arzlanian, & Elfring, 2014	Networking	yes	multi	theory testing	H&S	no	504/101	no N reported for regressions	yes
Andreas Rauch, Rosenbusch, Unger, & Frese, 2016	Networking	yes	multi	theory testing	H&S	file save N, published versus unpublished analysis	27/9		yes
Jin et al., 2017	Venture team composition and performance	yes	bi	theory testing	H&S	no	45/23		not reported
Fodor & Pintea, 2017	Affect and performance	yes	bi	theory testing	H&S	Begg and Mazumdar's rank correlation test	13/7		yes
Alferaih, 2017	Predictors of entrepreneurial intentions	yes	bi	explorative	H&S	no	2/1	combined meta-analysis with weight analysis	yes
Schlaegel & Koenig, 2014	Prediction of entrepreneurial intentions	yes	multi	theory testing	H&S	published versus unpublished analysis	471/94	MASEM and MARA	yes
Read, Song, & Smit, 2009	Effectuation and performance	yes	bi	theory testing	H&S	no	379/38		not reported

Note: H&S = Hunter & Schmidt, 2004; MARA = meta-analytical regression analysis; MASEM = meta-analytical structural regression analysis.

RCT face the risk of biases. The Cochrane Collaboration's tool for assessing risk of bias in RCTs addresses seven potential sources of bias in RCT (Higgins et al., 2011). For example, participants' knowledge of an intervention might affect the outcomes of RCT.

One critical aspect is that evidence is derived from internally and externally valid studies. Internal validity refers to the causality underlying a relationship between an independent and dependent variable. Lab studies often establish internal validity through using an experimental design in which the cause precedes the effect, the cause and effect systematically covary, and alternative explanations are controlled for by holding all other factors constant (cf., Mill, 1843). Establishing causality in field studies is more challenging but can be done, for example with the help of randomized controlled trials that test interventions in the field (e.g., Campos et al., 2017). However, field studies often employ a design to investigate systematic covariation of the independent and dependent variables, but they do not control for all other possible alternative explanations. Accordingly, these designs cannot preclude that a significant covariation between the independent and dependent variables is spurious and the result of an omitted variable. This issue even prevails when employing a lagged longitudinal design, investigating the systematic covariation over time. Therefore, field studies are often approaching rather than testing causal explanations.

External validity refers to the generalizability of findings to other people and situations. External validity can be established through studying phenomena in field studies and in natural settings. Lab studies have more problems establishing external validity, although there are tools available to do so, such as increasing the ecological validity of the setting, study materials, and experimental tasks (Gregoire, Binder, & Rauch, 2019). A certain degree of both internal and external validity can be achieved, for example by conducting randomized control trials in a natural setting. Evidently, the degree of validity of findings can be further increased by conducting quantitative meta-analyses of several randomized control trials.

The validity of findings can also be increased by mixing different methods in studying the same phenomenon, for example, by applying different operationalizations of constructs and establishing convergence in findings across operationalizations (Campbell & Fiske, 1959). Another form of mixed-methods approach is to combine quantitative and qualitative methods (Jick, 1979). This approach seeks to exploit the assets and neutralize the weaknesses of each method to achieve corroboration as well as breadth and depth in understanding (Johnson, Onwuegbuzie, & Turner, 2007; Molina-Azorin, Bergh, Corley, & Ketchen, 2017; Molina-Azorin, Lopez-Gamero, Pereira-Moliner, & Perusa-Ortega, 2012).

In the following, we discuss how such mixed-methods involving quantitative and qualitative research adds to the accumulation of credible evidence, and thus complements current methodologies in evidence-based entrepreneurship, such as quantitative meta-analyses and RCTs. This discussion allows us to conclude that a broader view on EBE can advance our understanding of entrepreneurship,

TABLE 18.2 An Extended Model of Evidence-Based Entrepreneurship

	Primary / replication studies	Aggregation of primary/replication studies
Single method	RCT	Meta-analysis
		Synthesis of qualitative studies
Mixed methods	RCT+	Integrative synthesis

resulting in more effective practices. Table 18.2 illustrates our extended methodological model of EBE. The table shows that credible evidence can be established via primary replication studies and via aggregation of primary studies, and it can rely on a single method or on mixed-methods study. In the next sections, we address the elements of our model.

Randomized Controlled Trial

An RCT is a primary study using a quantitative method to assess the consequences of a treatment in comparison to a control group in a randomized design. Because of the randomized and controlled design, an RCT has high internal validity, enabling researchers to draw causal conclusions. Oftentimes, internal validity is achieved at the expense of external validity, resulting in a trade-off between the two types of validity. To avoid this trade-off, evidence-based entrepreneurship advocated applying RCTs in the field, which achieve internal validity because of their experimental design, and external validity because they take place outside the artificial setting of a laboratory (Frese & Gielnik, 2014). Recently, studies that focused on psychological success factors in entrepreneurship adopted such a design to provide robust evidence for the effect of personal initiative and action-regulatory factors on business growth and new venture creation (Campos et al., 2017; Gielnik et al., 2015; Glaub, Frese, Fischer, & Hoppe, 2014). These studies used an experimental design with random assignment to a training intervention and followed up the participants of the training and control groups to assess their long-term success as entrepreneurs. These studies provided credible evidence because of the demonstrated link between cause and effect, which was observed over time outside the context of the intervention.

Notably, there is no perfect single study and, among other problems (cf. Rauch & Frese, 2006), any single study carries the risk of weak construct, internal, or external validity (Gregoire et al., 2019). For example, the RCT field studies on personal initiative and action-regulatory factors cited earlier took place in developing countries, potentially limiting the generalizability of the findings to other contexts. Therefore, replication is a critical element to provide support for the generalizability of findings (Davidsson, 2015). In replication studies, it can be useful to vary the study design, as this provides further support for the generalizability and thus contributes to the external validity of findings (Davidsson, 2015).

Mixed-Methods RCT: RCT+

Following previous research, we use the label RCT+ to refer to RCTs with a qualitative component (Bakhshi et al., 2015; Bamberger, Tarsilla, & Hesse-Biber, 2016). The qualitative component can be integrated at all stages of an RCT. A particularly interesting way of integrating the qualitative component into an RCT is using in-depth interviews at the end of the intervention to corroborate and explore the findings from the quantitative assessment of the short- and long-term effects of the intervention. To corroborate the findings, researchers can use the findings from the qualitative interviews to verify and illustrate the hypothesized factors and processes leading to the intended outcomes. Furthermore, qualitative methods are useful for describing and explaining differences in the effectiveness of the intervention within- or between participants (Hesse-Biber, 2012; O'Cathain, Thomas, Drabble, Rudolph, & Hewison, 2013). For example, Bakhshi et al. (2015) conducted an RCT+ to examine how SMEs benefitted differently from an innovation program in the short and long run. The qualitative interviews showed that learning new technical or marketing skills as a by-product of the innovation program could be an explanation for long-term benefits for some enterprises but not others. Also, qualitative methods can provide insights into boundary conditions that explain why the intervention might have only worked for certain subgroups, even though the intervention might not have had an overall effect. These results can then be used to refine the intervention.

Furthermore, the qualitative part can reveal unanticipated insights, thus overcoming the limitation of examining the outcomes of interventions primarily through predefined and standardized quantitative instruments (Hesse-Biber, 2012). For example, Bamberger et al. (2016) reported several cases that illustrate how qualitative interviews revealed unintended outcomes of interventions, for example in terms of increased infidelity after a program aimed at improving sexual health knowledge and safer sex practices. These unintended outcomes were not anticipated and thus not accounted for in the quantitative evaluation, but accidentally detected in the qualitative interviews. The qualitative findings thus helped to contextualize the findings, contribute to a better understanding of the overall effectiveness of the program, and help address negative side effects of the program (Bamberger et al., 2016). In a similar vein, qualitative methods can provide novel insights into the effectiveness of interventions by examining in detail anecdotes from those who either benefited greatly or not at all from an intervention. Such research might borrow from the field of medicine, which examines so-called exceptional responders[1] to better understand the causes and mechanisms of diseases and remedies. Classical examples are people who were not infected with HIV despite multiple-exposure because of a defect in the genetic code (Liu et al., 1996). Similarly, a mutation in the genetic code of patients with lung cancer determines whether they experience a rapid clinical response when being administered a specific drug. However, this is only the case for about 10% of the patients (Lynch et al., 2004). Nevertheless, these findings provide insights into the differential effects and boundary conditions of treatments, changing the way interventions are designed and applied. Exceptional responders are rare by definition and therefore quantitative methods are not well-suited to deal with such outliers. Accordingly, qualitative methods can complement and go beyond quantitative methods to gather evidence that corroborates and extends findings from quantitative analyses. In entrepreneurship, Glaub et al. (2014) complemented the results from their quantitative analyses by reporting qualitative observations made one year after having administered a personal initiative training to business owners in Uganda. Glaub et al. (2014) described how training participants showed personal initiative and improved their business practices to achieve exceptional performance. For example, the business owners obtained quality certification, changed the product portfolio, or expanded to foreign markets, yielding higher sales and profits. These cases illustrate the specific mechanisms and practices through which the personal initiative intervention positively influenced business owners' success. Similarly, Bischoff, Gielnik, and Frese (2014) reported two cases to illustrate how participants of an entrepreneurship training program in Uganda pursued an entrepreneurial career after graduation from university. The two cases demonstrate that young entrepreneurs in Uganda use very naturally and extensively the strategy of portfolio and/or serial entrepreneurship to overcome resource constraints and mitigate risks. This finding is interesting because this strategy corresponds to the idea of entrepreneurship as a career and is in contrast to the more common idea of entrepreneurship as creating and growing a single business (Rosa, 2019). Needless to say that a single RCT+ cannot provide evidence-based best practices as even the best experiments might suffer from biases (Higgins et al., 2011), and it is important to navigate the tradeoffs of different types of validity (Gregoire et al., 2019). Aggregating RCT+ may allow researchers to identify some of these issues and, therefore results in more credible evidence.

Meta-Analysis

Meta-analysis combines the results of empirical studies using statistical methods for the synthesis of the literature (Rauch, 2020). Table 18.1 depicts 22 meta-analyses conducted in the domain of psychological entrepreneurship research (see also Frese et al., 2012; Frese & Gielnik, 2014). It is interesting that these meta-analyses are well recognized in the literature; seven meta-analyses are cited more than 100 times per year and between 504 and 1,370 times in total according to Google Scholar. A standard meta-analysis on simple relationships is valuable in entrepreneurship research as it provides meaningful information about the presence and the magnitude of effects. All meta-analyses on the psychology of entrepreneurship shown in Table 18.1 reported the magnitude of effects. Moreover, 21 of these meta-analyses used bivariate analysis to establish the magnitude of effect sizes. While valuable, however, such bivariate analyses cannot test multivariate models that are important for advancing the theoretical understanding of mechanisms underlying the relationship between cause and effect. Two more recent developments in meta-analysis allow then to contribute to both theory-building and practice implications: Meta-analytical regression analysis (MARA) (Gonzalez-Mulé & Aguinis, 2018) and meta-analytical structural equation modeling (MASEM) (Visweswaran & Ones, 1995). Both are important for evidence-based entrepreneurship as the former specifies under which conditions practices and interventions are promising, while the latter explains through which mechanisms the practices and interventions work.

We found eight meta-analyses using a MARA providing information about the boundary conditions of effects, thus, information about the circumstances under which practices and interventions do or do not work. Notably, 13 meta-analyses relied on a classical subgroup analysis. Such a bivariate moderator analysis can only partially accomplish the aim to specify boundary conditions of theories as the Type I error is becoming inflated if there are multiple interrelated moderators present. MARA accounts for this problem by analyzing multiple moderators at the same time (Aguinis, Dalton, Bosco, Pierce, & Dalton, 2011). Moreover, a MARA can include both control variables and moderator variables. One issue that is often overlooked in MARA is that the same rigid assumptions apply as those of linear regression analysis. Therefore, MARA cannot be applied in analyses that are based on a small number of studies as the number of studies limits the number of predictors that can be included in the regression equation (Schmidt, 2017). Violating assumptions of regression analysis might lead to nonreplicable findings and, thus, does not serve the aim to establish credible evidence regarding the boundary conditions of theories. Moreover, while MARA is useful for detecting sources of residual variance, it is hardly possible to interpret beta weights. The reason is that there are always omitted variables in MARA as it allows only for inclusion of those variables that have been studied frequently. Therefore, researchers should always report meta-analytic correlations along with MARA results. Finally, one aim of a moderator analysis is to explain residual variance, which is variance that is not accounted for by sampling error variance. We found only one study (Stewart & Roth, 2001) in which the residual variance was reduced to such an extent that results became homogeneous and differences in effect sizes could be explained by differences in sample sizes. All other studies reported heterogeneous results even after conducting a moderator analysis and there was unexplained variation in reported relationships. Since the source of this variation is unknown, the heterogeneity creates challenges to the validity of results making it difficult to establish boundary conditions of theories. Therefore, it is inevitable in meta-analysis to assess whether the amount of heterogeneity is acceptable, to search for the sources of heterogeneity (e.g., study-level covariates), and to decide on the most appropriate way to analyze the heterogeneous results (e.g., by using a random effect model).

A second multivariate approach that has been used more recently in meta-analyses on the psychology of entrepreneurship is MASEM (Viswesvaran & Ones, 1995). MASEM has a number of advantages. The most important one is that it allows researchers to test mediators, thus the mechanisms through which practices and interventions affect outcomes. Such mechanisms are not only important for testing and developing verifiable theories, but they also provide leverage points for developing interventions helping entrepreneurs in their venture practices. For example, discovering that the environment (e.g., in terms of environmental munificence or dynamism) influences firm performance through entrepreneurial orientation (Rosenbusch, Rauch, & Bausch, 2013), suggests that interventions could target at firms' entrepreneurial orientation and not necessarily at the firms' environment to increase their performance. We identified only one study on the psychology of entrepreneurship reporting MASEM results (Schlaegel & Koenig, 2014). However, such meta-analyses are very important and need to be performed more often. Notably, MASEM is not free from challenges (Combs, Crook, & Rauch, 2019), such as small numbers of studies included in some subsets of the analysis or MASEM analyses that are based on heterogeneous effect sizes, challenging the interpretation of MASEM results. Fortunately, there are extended MASEM techniques available to address such methodological challenges (Yu, Downes, Carter, & O'Boyle, 2016). An additional observation is that while 17 meta-analyses aimed to test theories, the method is hardly applied for developing theory.

Mixed-Methods Meta-Analyses: Considering the Synthesis of Qualitative Studies (Qualitative Meta-Analysis)

The synthesis of qualitative studies (qualitative meta-analyses) is a very recent methodological advancement. In this section, we therefore present the method of qualitative meta-analysis before we discuss mixed-methods meta-analyses. Given the substantial body of qualitative studies in entrepreneurship research, researchers might feel unease about not including such results into an evidence-based approach. This type of EBE is particularly useful for addressing issues that cannot be easily addressed via quantitative studies, such as business failure or other complex processes and context conditions (Rauch, 2020). Notably, qualitative information can be synthesized just as meta-analysis synthesizes quantitative information. Recently, researchers introduced the methods suitable to accumulate and interpret qualitative studies (Habersang, Küberling-Jost, Reihlen, & Seckler, 2019; Hoon, 2013; Rauch, van Doorn, & Hulsink, 2014). The method of qualitative meta-analysis refers to the systematic accumulation of qualitative evidence from multiple case studies about a particular phenomenon. Such qualitative meta-analyses can provide rich and contextualized descriptions of relationships and underlying processes. In an evidence-based approach, this type of analysis relies on the same principles as any quantitative meta-analysis as findings are synthesized in a transparent, explicit, and replicable way (Briner & Denyer, 2012). These criteria necessarily exclude interpretative syntheses of qualitative research such as, for example, ethnographic approaches, but it allows researchers to develop generalizable phenomena and to test and develop new theoretical insights (Rauch et al., 2014). Notably, there is not one single method of the synthesis of qualitative research and researchers began to describe systematically the various approaches towards the synthesis of qualitative research (Dixon-Woods, Agarwal, Young, Jones, & Sutton, 2004; Habersang & Reihlen, 2018). Interestingly, some of these approaches, such as content analysis and cumulative case studies, also allow quantifying the information collected (e.g., Crayne & Hunter, 2017; Rauch et al., 2014). The synthesis of qualitative research requires thorough coding and, therefore, researchers need to explain the coding procedure in detail to allow replicability.

Following our logic of mixed-methods approaches to advance EBE, it is possible to aggregate evidence that is based on primary studies relying on different (e.g., qualitative and quantitative) designs by using integrative forms of research synthesis (Rousseau, Manning, & Denyer, 2008). Unfortunately, there is, to our knowledge no standardized methodology available and replication is, therefore, difficult. Moreover, such an approach has not yet been used in the psychology of entrepreneurship. Nevertheless, we encourage researchers to develop and use such an approach in order to make full use of the methodological toolbox that helps to enhance our understanding of entrepreneurship.

Conclusion

The different evidence-based methodologies (see Table 18.2) discussed in this chapter should not be seen in isolation, but they form a framework of the evidence-based best practice approaches in the psychology of entrepreneurship. Ultimately, science has to establish knowledge and an evidence-based approach can help to develop and apply this knowledge. Theories on the psychology of entrepreneurship can be tested in individual studies as well as in studies aggregating individual studies. Primary studies should be replicated and phenomena should be examined using a mixed-methods approach. This mixed-methods approach can be used to demonstrate that the phenomenon can be explained by the underlying causes and processes,[2] not by the method used (Johnson et al., 2007). It is important to note, however, that different methods might not necessarily lead to convergence but inconsistency or contradiction. In the case of convergence, the results based on the various methods help to illustrate and clarify the phenomenon. In case of inconsistency or contradiction, the results potentially lead to new insights about mechanisms and outcomes. Meta-analyses can then help to synthesize the heterogeneous empirical evidence by identifying boundary conditions that facilitate making sense of inconsistent or contradictory findings. Finally, the empirical evidence is used to develop practice recommendations and interventions. These recommendations and interventions are again tested relying on robust impact assessment studies, such as RCTs. Depending on the results of such intervention studies, theories need to be altered. This starts the evidence-based cycle anew, and thus, theories are not static but change given the scientific evidence.

We suggested a mix of different methods that can and should be used for developing evidence-based entrepreneurship. Importantly, we want to stress that the methodological fit of these approaches needs to be considered as well. For example, Edmondson and McManus (2007) stated that the methodological fit depends on the state of prior theory and research. According to these authors, established theories such as human capital theory require the use of quantitative research designs (Unger et al., 2011). Qualitative research is more useful to study nascent theories, and mixed-method designs are useful for investigating intermediate theories, which would require more explorative research. The lean start-up method might represent such an intermediate concept that calls for a mixed-methods approach (Ries, 2011). In line with Edmondson and McManus (2007), we want to emphasize that our extended EBE approach does not allow a discretionary choice of methods for establishing evidence but rather that the choice of the methodology depends on the research question and the stage of prior theory and research.

In conclusion, we think that the scientific evidence about the psychology of entrepreneurship is in some areas very strong (see Table 18.1). Indeed, entrepreneurship research has gone through the whole evidence-based entrepreneurship process of theory, meta-analytical evidence, and impact assessment through RCTs in some areas. An example is the literature about entrepreneurship education, where we have meta-analytical evidence indicating what works (Martin, McNally, & Kay, 2013), and we have studies using RCT design to test the interventions based on psychological theories and meta-analytical findings. As a matter of fact, these studies showed that a psychological entrepreneurship training enhancing participants' personal initiative is more effective than a traditional business training (Campos et al., 2017). Thus, the psychology of entrepreneurship is a powerful approach to entrepreneurship. Yet we need more credible evidence using multiple methods to arrive at strong evidence-based best practice recommendations.

Note

1. We note that sometimes entrepreneurs themselves are considered as exceptional responders, because the prevalence of entrepreneurs worldwide can be as low as 3.9% (Cyprus; Bosma & Kelley, 2018).

References

Aguinis, H., Dalton, D. R., Bosco, F. A., Pierce, C. A., & Dalton, C. M. (2011). Meta-analytic choices and judgment calls: Implications for theory building and testing, obtained effect sizes, and scholarly impact. *Journal of Management, 37*(1), 5–38.

Alferaih, A. (2017). Weight- and meta-analysis of empirical literature on entrepreneurship: Towards a conceptualization of entrepreneurial intention and behaviour. *The International Journal of Entrepreneurship and Innovation, 18*(3), 195–209.

Bae, T. J., Qian, S., Miao, C., & Fiet, J. O. (2014). The relationship between entrepreneurship education and entrepreneurial intentions: A meta-analytic review. *Entrepreneurship Theory and Practice, 38*(2), 217–254.

Bakhshi, H., Edwards, J. S., Roper, S., Scully, J., Shaw, D., Morley, L., & Rathbone, N. (2015). Assessing an experimental approach to industrial policy evaluation: Applying RCT+ to the case of Creative Credits. *Research Policy, 44*(8), 1462–1472.

Bamberger, M., Tarsilla, M., & Hesse-Biber, S. (2016). Why so many "rigorous" evaluations fail to identify unintended consequences of development programs: How mixed methods can contribute. *Evaluation and Program Planning, 55,* 155–162.

Bischoff, K. M., Gielnik, M. M., & Frese, M. (2014). Entrepreneurship training in developing countries. In W. Reichman (Ed.), *Industrial and organizational psychology help the vulnerable: Serving the underserved* (pp. 92–119). Houndmills, UK: Palgrave Macmillan.

Bosma, N., & Kelley, D. J. (2018). *Global entrepreneurship monitor: 2018/2019 Global Report.* London, UK: The Global Entrepreneurship Research Association (GERA).

Brinckmann, J., Dew, N., Read, S., Mayer-Haug, K., & Grichnik, D. (2019). Of those who plan: A meta-analysis of the relationship between human capital and business planning. *Long Range Planning, 52*(2), 173–188.

Brinckmann, J., Grichnik, D., & Kapsa, D. (2010). Should entrepreneurs plan or just storm the castle? A meta-analysis on contextual factors impacting the business planning-performance relationship in small firms. *Journal of Business Venturing, 25*(1), 24–40.

Briner, R. B., & Denyer, D. (2012). Systematic review and evidence synthesis as a practice and scholarship tool. In D. Rousseau (Ed.), *The Oxford handbook of evidence-based management* (pp. 112–129). New York: Oxford University Press.

Camerer, C. F., Dreber, A., Forsell, E., Ho, T.-H., Huber, J., Johannesson, M., . . . Wu, H. (2016). Evaluating replicability of laboratory experiments in economics. *Science, 351*(6280), 1433–1436.

Campbell, D. T., & Fiske, D. W. (1959). Convergent and discriminant validation by the multitrait-multimethod matrix. *Psychological Bulletin, 56*(2), 81–105.

Campos, F., Frese, M., Goldstein, M., Iacovonne, L., Johnson, H. C., McKenzie, D., & Mensmann, M. (2017). Teaching personal initiative beats traditional training in boosting small business in West Africa. *Science, 357*(6357), 1287–1290.

Collins, C. J., Hanges, P. J., & Locke, E. A. (2004). The relationship of achievement motivation to entrepreneurial behavior: A meta-analysis. *Human Performance, 17*(1), 95–117.

Combs, J. G., Crook, T. R., & Rauch, A. (2019). Meta-analytic research in management: Contemporary approaches, unresolved controversies, and rising standards. *Journal of Management Studies, 56*(1), 1–18.

Crayne, M. P., & Hunter, S. T. (2017). Historiometry in organizational science: Renewed attention for an established research method. *Organizational Research Methods, 21*(1), 6–29.

Davidsson, P. (2015). Data replication and extension: A commentary. *Journal of Business Venturing Insights, 3,* 12–15.

Dixon-Woods, M., Agarwal, S., Young, B., Jones, D., & Sutton, A. (2004). *Integrative approaches to qualitative and quantitative evidence.* London, UK: Health Development Agency.

Edmondson, A. C., & McManus, S. E. (2007). Methodological fit in management field research. *Academy of Management Review, 32*(4), 1155–1179.

Edwards, A. G., Russell, I. T., & Stott, N. C. (1998). Signal versus noise in the evidence base for medicine: An alternative to hierarchies of evidence? *Family Practice, 15*(4), 319–322.

Fodor, O. C., & Pintea, S. (2017). The "emotional side" of entrepreneurship: A meta-analysis of the relation between positive and negative affect and entrepreneurial performance. *Frontiers in Psychology, 8,* 310.

Frese, M., Bausch, A., Schmidt, P., Rauch, A., & Kabst, R. (2012). Evidence-based entrepreneurship: Cumulative science, action principles, and bridging the gap between science and practice. *Foundations and Trends in Entrepreneurship, 8*(1), 1–62.

Frese, M., & Gielnik, M. M. (2014). The psychology of entrepreneurship. *Annual Review of Organizational Psychology and Organizational Behavior, 1,* 413–438.

Frese, M., Rousseau, D. M., & Wiklund, J. (2014). The emergence of evidence-based entrepreneurship. *Entrepreneurship Theory and Practice, 38*(2), 209–216.

Gielnik, M. M., Frese, M., Kahara-Kawuki, A., Katono, I. W., Kyejjusa, S., Ngoma, M., . . . Dlugosch, T. J. (2015). Action and action-regulation in entrepreneurship: Evaluating a student training for promoting entrepreneurship. *Academy of Management Learning & Education, 14*(1), 69–94.

Glaub, M. E., Frese, M., Fischer, S., & Hoppe, M. (2014). Increasing personal initiative in small business managers or owners leads to entrepreneurial success: A theory-based controlled randomized field intervention for evidence-based management. *Academy of Management Learning & Education, 13*(3), 354–379.

Gonzalez-Mulé, E., & Aguinis, H. (2018). Advancing theory by assessing boundary conditions with metaregression: A critical review and best-practice recommendations. *Journal of Management, 44*(6), 2246–2273.

Greenhalgh, T. (2010). *How to read a paper: The basics of evidence-based medicine* (6th ed.). Hoboken, NJ: Wiley-Blackwell.

Gregoire, D. A., Binder, J. K., & Rauch, A. (2019). Navigating the validity tradeoffs of entrepreneurship research experiments: A systematic review and best-practice suggestions. *Journal of Business Venturing, 34*(2), 284–310.

Habersang, S., Küberling-Jost, J., Reihlen, M., & Seckler, C. (2019). A process perspective on organizational failure: A qualitative meta-analysis. *Journal of Management Studies, 56*(1), 19–56.

Habersang, S., & Reihlen, M. (2018). Advancing qualitative meta-analyses: A realist and a constructivist approach. *Academy of Management Proceedings, 2018*(1). Retrieved from doi.org/10.5465/AMBPP.2018.129Hesse-Biber, S. (2012). Weaving a multimethodology and mixed methods praxis into randomized control trials to enhance credibility. *Qualitative Inquiry, 18*(10), 876–889.

Higgins, J. P. T., Altman, D. G., Gotsche, P. C., Juni, P., Moher, D., Oxman, A. D., . . . Sterne, J. A. C. (2011). The Cochrane Collaboration's tool for assessing risk of bias in randomised trials. *British Medical Journal, 343,* d5928.

Hoon, C. (2013). Meta-synthesis of qualitative case studies: An approach to theory building. *Organizational Research Methods, 16*(4), 522–556.

Hunter, J. E., & Schmidt, F. L. (2004). *Methods for meta-analysis: Correcting error and bias in research findings.* Newbury Park, CA: Sage.

Jick, T. D. (1979). Mixing qualitative and quantitative methods: Triangulation in action. *Administrative Science Quarterly, 24*(4), 602–611.

Jin, L., Madison, K., Kraiczy, N. D., Kellermanns, F. W., Crook, T. R., & Xi, J. (2017). Entrepreneurial team composition characteristics and new venture performance: A meta-analysis. *Entrepreneurship Theory and Practice, 41*(5), 743–771.

Johnson, R. B., Onwuegbuzie, A. J., & Turner, L. A. (2007). Toward a definition of mixed methods research. *Journal of Mixed Methods Research, 1*(2), 112–133.

Lazer, D. M. J., Baum, M. A., Benkler, Y., Berinsky, A. J., Greenhill, K. M., Menczer, F., . . . Zittrain, J. L. (2018). The science of fake news. *Science, 359*(6380), 1094–1096.

Liu, R., Paxton, W. A., Choe, S., Ceradini, D., Martin, S. R., Horuk, R., . . . Landau, N. R. (1996). Homozygous defect in HIV-1 coreceptor accounts for resistance of some multiply-exposed individuals to HIV-1 infection. *Cell, 86*(3), 367–377.

Lynch, T. J., Bell, D. W., Sordella, R., Gurubhagavatula, S., Okimoto, R. A., Brannigan, B. W., . . . Haber, D. A. (2004). Activating mutations in the epidermal growth factor receptor underlying responsiveness of non-small-cell lung cancer to Gefitinib. *The New England Journal of Medicine, 350*(21), 2129–2139.

Martin, B. C., McNally, J. J., & Kay, M. J. (2013). Examining the formation of human capital in entrepreneurship: A meta-analysis of entrepreneurship education outcomes. *Journal of Business Venturing, 28*(2), 211–224.

Miao, C., Qian, S., & Ma, D. (2017). The relationship between entrepreneurial self-efficacy and firm performance: A meta-analysis of main and moderator effects. *Journal of Small Business Management, 55*(1), 87–107.

Mill, J. S. (1843). *A system of logic.* New York: Harper.

Molina-Azorin, J. F., Bergh, D. D., Corley, K. G., & Ketchen, D. J. (2017). Mixed methods in the organizational sciences: Taking stock and moving forward. *Organizational Research Methods, 20*(2), 179–192.

Molina-Azorin, J. F., Lopez-Gamero, M. D., Pereira-Moliner, J., & Perusa-Ortega, E. M. (2012). Mixed methods studies in entrepreneurship research: Applications and contributions. *Entrepreneurship & Regional Development, 24*(5–6), 425–456.

O'Cathain, A., Thomas, K. J., Drabble, S. J., Rudolph, A., & Hewison, J. (2013). What can qualitative research do for randomised controlled trials? A systematic mapping review. *British Medical Journal Open, 3*, 1–15.

Open Science Collaboration. (2015). Estimating the reproducibility of psychological science. *Science, 349*(6251), 1–7.

Pfeffer, J., & Sutton, R. I. (2006). Evidence-based management. *Harvard Business Review, 84*(1), 62–74.

Rauch, A. (2020). Opportunities and threats in reviewing entrepreneurship theory and practice. *Entrepreneurship Theory and Practice, 44*(5):847–860. Retrieved from https://doi.org/10.1177/1042258719879635

Rauch, A., & Frese, M. (2006). Meta-analysis as a tool for developing entrepreneurship research and theory. In J. Wiklund, D. Dimov, J. A. Katz, & D. A. Shepherd (Eds.), *Advances in entrepreneurship, firm emergence and growth* (Vol. 9, pp. 29–51). Oxford: JAI Press.

Rauch, A., & Frese, M. (2007). Let's put the person back into entrepreneurship research: A meta-analysis on the relationship between business owners' personality traits, business creation, and success. *European Journal of Work and Organizational Psychology, 16*(4), 353–385.

Rauch, A., Rosenbusch, N., Unger, J., & Frese, M. (2016). The effectiveness of cohesive and diversified networks: A meta-analysis. *Journal of Business Research, 69*(2), 554–568.

Rauch, A., van Doorn, R., & Hulsink, W. (2014). A qualitative approach to evidence-based entrepreneurship: Theoretical considerations and an example involving business clusters. *Entrepreneurship Theory and Practice, 38*(2), 333–368.

Read, S., Song, M., & Smit, W. (2009). A meta-analytic review of effectuation and venture performance. *Journal of Business Venturing, 24*(6), 573–587.

Reay, T., Berta, W., & Kohn, M. K. (2009). What's the evidence on evidence-based management? *Academy of Management Perspectives, 23*(4), 5–18.

Ries, E. (2011). *The lean startup.* New York: Crown Business.

Rosa, P. (2019). Entrepreneurial growth through portfolio entrepreneurship: The entrepreneurial career ladder. In M. Rautiainen, P. Rosa, T. Pihkala, M. Parada, & A. Cruz (Eds.), *The family business group phenomenon.* London, UK: Palgrave Macmillan.

Rosenbusch, N., Rauch, A., & Bausch, A. (2013). The mediating role of entrepreneurial orientation in the task environment-performance relationship: A meta-analysis. *Journal of Management*, *39*(3), 633–659.

Rousseau, D. M., Manning, J., & Denyer, D. (2008). Evidence in management and organizational science: Assembling the field's full weight of scientifc knowledge through syntheses. *Academy of Management Annals*, *2*(1), 475–515.

Sarooghi, H., Libaers, D., & Burkemper, A. (2015). Examining the relationship between creativity and innovation: A meta-analysis of organizational, cultural, and environmental factors. *Journal of Business Venturing*, *30*(5), 714–731.

Schlaegel, C., & Koenig, M. (2014). Determinants of entrepreneurial intent: A meta-analytic test and integration of competing models. *Entrepreneurship Theory and Practice*, *38*(2), 291–332.

Schmidt, F. L. (2017). Statistical and measurement pitfalls in the use of meta-regression in meta-analysis. *Career Development International*, *22*(5), 469–476.

Stam, W., Arzlanian, S., & Elfring, T. (2014). Social capital of entrepreneurs and small firm performance: A meta-analysis of contextual and methodological moderators. *Journal of Business Venturing*, *29*(1), 152–173.

Stewart, W. H., & Roth, P. L. (2001). Risk propensity differences between entrepreneurs and managers: A meta-analytic review. *Journal of Applied Psychology*, *86*(1), 145–153.

Stewart, W. H., & Roth, P. L. (2007). A meta-analysis of achievement motivation differences between entrepreneurs and managers. *Journal of Small Business Management*, *45*(4), 401–421.

Unger, J. M., Rauch, A., Frese, M., & Rosenbusch, N. (2011). Human capital and entrepreneurial success: A meta-analytical review. *Journal of Business Venturing*, *26*(3), 341–358.

van der Sluis, J., van Praag, C. M., & Vijverberg, W. (2005). Entrepreneurship, selection and performance: A meta-analysis of the role of education. *World Bank Economic Review*, *19*(2), 225–261.

Viswesvaran, C., & Ones, D. S. (1995). Theory testing: Combining psychometric meta-analysis and structural equation modeling. *Personnel Psychology*, *48*(4), 865–885.

Yu, J. (J.), Downes, P. E., Carter, K. M., & O'Boyle, E. H. (2016). The problem of effect size heterogeneity in meta-analytic structural equation modeling. *Journal of Applied Psychology*, *101*(10), 1457–1473.

Zhao, H., & Seibert, S. E. (2006). The Big Five personality dimensions and entrepreneurial status: A meta-analytical review. *Journal of Applied Psychology*, *91*(2), 259–271.

Zhao, H., Seibert, S. E., & Lumpkin, G. T. (2010). The relationship of personality to entrepreneurial intentions and performance: A meta-analytic review. *Journal of Management*, *36*(2), 381–404.

19

THE WELL-BEING OF ENTREPRENEURS AND THEIR STAKEHOLDERS

James Bort, Ute Stephan & Johan Wiklund

Introduction[1]

Over the past decades, research on individual well-being has flourished (Diener, Oishi, & Tay, 2018; Ryff & Keyes, 1995; Kahneman, 1999; Ryan, Huta, & Deci, 2008). In turn, evolving empirical evidence and corresponding theoretical developments have ushered in two dominant views on well-being. The hedonic approach to well-being highlights 'feeling well'—including cognitive (evaluative) and affective (emotional) components of well-being, while the eudaimonic approach focuses on 'living well'—including self-directed actions, personal growth, and connections with others.

Entrepreneurship scholars show increasing interest in the relationship between entrepreneurship and well-being (see, e.g., Stephan, 2018. for a review or Wiklund, Nikolaev, Shir, Foo, & Bradley, 2019, for a research agenda). Although current entrepreneurship research focuses mostly on hedonic well-being, entrepreneurship offers an interesting context for both theoretical lenses because of the salience of well-being issues. The entrepreneurial process is rife with challenges (Cardon & Patel, 2015). Failure is common and it can be emotionally draining (Shepherd, Wiklund, & Haynie, 2009). At the same time, entrepreneurs have the opportunity to self-actualize as they craft their jobs to their own idiosyncratic needs (Wiklund, Hatak, Patzelt, & Shepherd, 2018) and thus will draw nonpecuniary benefits (Gimeno, Folta, Cooper, & Woo, 1997). For instance, some ask whether entrepreneurs are happier (hedonic focus) with their career than employees (e.g., Benz & Frey, 2008; Kautonen, Kibler, & Minniti, 2017), and whether they draw greater personal fulfillment (eudaimonic focus) from entrepreneurship (e.g. Shir , Nikolaev, & Wincent, 2018).The hedonic and eudaimonic approaches to well-being are complementary and not mutually exclusive (Ryff,

2019), creating ample opportunities for entrepreneurship research to leverage the unique nature of entrepreneurship and push theory forward.

To date, entrepreneurship well-being research has focused on the founder(s) (Stephan, 2018), yet many stakeholders are crucial to the entrepreneurial process and their well-being is rarely considered. Although still in its infancy, a small number of studies concerning stakeholder well-being within entrepreneurship highlight the potential ahead. For example, entrepreneurs show concern for their *employees* well-being as they grow their firms (Wiklund, Davidsson, & Delmar, 2003), which also impacts the firm's ability to recruit talent (Moser, Tumasjan, & Welpe, 2015). Despite the important role entrepreneurial firms play in the labor market (Haltiwanger, Jarmin, & Miranda, 2013) and the expansive literature on employee well-being (Bliese, Edwards, & Sonnentag, 2017), very little is known about whether employees of new ventures enjoy their jobs. *Resource providers* also play a critical role in the new venture, sharing in the success and failures of the firms they choose to invest in (Drover et al., 2017). Recent studies examining crowdfunding lenders (see Letwin et al., this volume) suggest that the process of investing influences the lenders' affective state (Davis, Hmieleski, Webb, & Coombs, 2017), and has the potential to fulfill psychological needs associated with well-being (Allison, Davis, Short, & Webb, 2015).

The remainder of this chapter takes a holistic view of the entrepreneurial process and explores the ways in which entrepreneurship can impede or enhance well-being not only of entrepreneurs but also of stakeholders, such as employees and investors. Figure 19.1 provides a visual depiction. We begin with an overview of the scholarly traditions foundational to well-being research, followed by a review of the current body of knowledge explicitly concerned with the well-being of entrepreneurs and their stakeholders. We conclude with future research

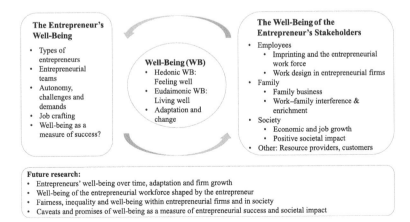

FIGURE 19.1   Well-Being of Entrepreneurs and Their Stakeholders

opportunities including a reflection on whether well-being should be considered an alternative metric for entrepreneurial success.

A Brief History of Assessing Individual Well-Being

Well-being research falls primarily into two conceptualizations—hedonic and eudaimonic.[1] Both approaches were in part inspired by the tendency of psychological research to focus on negative, rather than positive states (Diener, Lucas, & Smith, 1999; Ryff, 1989). Though they are viewed as complementary, studies highlight that hedonic and eudaimonic well-being are not necessarily correlated (Keyes, Shmotkin, & Ryff, 2002) and that individuals differentiate them subjectively (Adler, Dolan, & Kavetsos, 2017). As such, the literature on hedonic and eudaimonic well-being have evolved somewhat independently of each other.

The hedonic approach, commonly referred to as subjective well-being (SWB), assesses overall life satisfaction, pleasant or unpleasant affective experience, and domain satisfaction, such as job or marital satisfaction (Diener et al., 1999). Researchers have used numerous techniques to measure the dimensions of SWB. These include broad measures such as the satisfaction with life scale (Diener, Emmons, Larsen, & Griffin, 1985) and the subjective happiness scale (Lyubomirsky & Lepper, 1999), along with domain-specific scales like the Minnesota job satisfaction questionnaire (Weiss, Dawis, & England, 1967), and the couples satisfaction index (Funk & Rogge, 2007). These instruments vary depending on the context, but each measures an outcome (e.g., positive feelings) rather than the process leading up to the outcome. Interventions that manipulate SWB often only have a temporary effect, leading to questions if there is value in the 'pursuit of happiness' as an end in itself. For instance, in their classic study on hedonic adaptation, Brickman, Coates, and Janoff-Bulman (1978) noted the lottery winners and accident victims initially experienced significant changes in how they assessed life satisfaction but returned to their previous levels of happiness as time elapsed (dubbed the hedonic treadmill adaptation effect). More recently, Sheldon and Lyubomirsky (2012) proposed the hedonic adaptation model that highlights mechanisms that erode gains in well-being and identifies moderators that reduce the impact of this erosion.

The eudaimonic approach, also referred to as psychological well-being (PWB), is an assessment of positive psychological functioning. In contrast to the hedonic theories of well-being, eudaimonic theories focus on areas like personal growth and living with purpose—pursuits that might at times even impair hedonic well-being. While this tradition is centered on what it means to be a fully functioning person, leading theories offer differing ideas on which elements lead to PWB (Martela & Sheldon, 2019). As highlighted by Ryan et al. (2008), conceptualizations of PWB are prescriptive in nature and outline pragmatic ways to be fully functioning. For example, Ryff's (1989) theory suggests that if an individual resists social pressures (autonomy) and continuously realizes their potential (personal growth), they will score high in PWB. Ryan and Deci (2001) emphasize that the eudaimonic well-being is fostered by the satisfaction of basic psychological needs of autonomy, relatedness, and competence. Thus, scholars offer different configurations of elements that make up the fully functioning human (Ryan & Deci, 2000; Ryff, 1989; Waterman et al., 2010).

Despite the developments of assessing well-being highlighted earlier, the context of entrepreneurship offers numerous opportunities to further refine the ways that scholars assess well-being (cf. Ryff, 2019), using both formulations. For example, examining the length of time between promotions in high growth new ventures and its influence on job satisfaction is likely to glean new insights into domain-specific forms of hedonic adaptation, and with potential implications for adaptation prevention. Furthermore, the balance between social and economic motivations vary between entrepreneurs (Moss, Renko, & Bort, 2019) and is likely to influence how different dimensions of PWB are valued and fulfilled. For example, entrepreneurs who place greater emphasis on social good might value personal connection over personal growth or environmental mastery. Next, we explore the contributions the field of entrepreneurship has offered thus far.

Well-Being and the Entrepreneur

Entrepreneurs enjoy a great amount of autonomy in terms of how they design their jobs (Baron, 2010), giving the entrepreneur a unique ability to craft their daily work in a way that capitalizes on their unique differences (e.g., Wiklund Hatak, Patzelt, & Shepherd, 2018). The motivations behind entrepreneurial pursuits also vary considerably, ranging from the opportunity-based start-ups that rise to industry leadership (Coad, Daunfeldt, Holzl, Johansson, & Nightingale, 2014) and social entrepreneurs that seek to change society (Stephan, Patterson, Kelly, & Mair, 2016) to necessity-based start-ups that may never gain institutional legitimacy (Webb, Bruton, Tihanyi, & Ireland, 2013). Thus, the experience of the entrepreneur is not only different from paid employment but is also different between entrepreneurs.

There is some evidence that on average entrepreneurship leads to higher cognitive evaluations of well-being, for example, job and life satisfaction. For example, utility derived from the independence associated with self-employment increases job satisfaction (Benz & Frey, 2008). Advanced matching methodologies allow ruling out systematic differences between entrepreneurs and paid employees (e.g., in demographic, income, and health variables) by creating counterfactual comparison cases. Such studies demonstrate higher life satisfaction among entrepreneurs (Binder & Coad, 2013; Kautonen et al., 2017). However, some contingencies are important to note.

Necessity entrepreneurs tend to experience lower well-being than opportunity entrepreneurs (Stephan, 2018). Cross-country comparisons suggest that institutions hostile towards entrepreneurship negate any positive relationship between well-being and entrepreneurship (Fritsch, Sorgner, & Wyrwich, 2019). Previous entrepreneurial experience also plays a role in well-being—inexperienced entrepreneurs have more difficulty recovering from day-to-day job stress (Kollmann, Stöckmann, & Kensbock, 2019). Perceptions of firm performance, either financial (e.g., Laguna & Razmus, 2019) or social (Kibler, Wincent, Kautonen, Cacciotti, & Obschonka, 2019) also enhance or impede well-being. Poor firm performance is also emotionally taxing (Shepherd et al., 2009) and impedes an entrepreneur's autonomy (van Gelderen, 2016).

Autonomy is a key component of positive psychological functioning (Ryff, 2019) and fundamental to entrepreneurship (Covin & Wales, 2019). The autonomy of entrepreneurs allows a great deal of latitude in what tasks they perform (Baron, 2010). For example, Craig Newmark the founder of Craigslist remained in a customer-facing role instead of becoming chief executive. A prevailing theme in the work design literature is that individuals place great value on autonomy and utilizing their skills (Parker, 2014). Entrepreneurs generally score high on need for achievement (Frese & Gielnik, 2014) and find many opportunities to fulfill this need inside their firm (Baron & Henry, 2010). Thus, so long as entrepreneurs retain autonomy and focus on tasks they enjoy, they can fulfill other key psychological needs that lead to higher assessments of well-being (Shir et al., 2018).

However, autonomy in entrepreneurship is not guaranteed (van Gelderen, 2016; Van Gelderen, Shirokova, Shchegolev, & Beliaeva, 2019). Entrepreneurs are typically portrayed as the archetypical 'lone hero', but in practice, they are beholden to their stakeholders, including investors, customers, employees, and external regulators. The entrepreneur's ability to focus on autonomous and enjoyable tasks is largely contingent on their ability to manage these relationships effectively. As firms mature, the role of the entrepreneur evolves (Mathias & Williams, 2018) and they become increasingly dependent on finding the right people to fill roles within the firm (Forbes, Borchert, Zellmer–Bruhn, & Sapienza, 2006). Entrepreneurs also face issues like conflict with early investors (Collewaert, 2012), conflict with family (Carr & Hmieleski, 2015), and corrupt regulators (Baron, J. Tang, Z. Tang, & Zhang, 2018). In sum, the entrepreneur's stakeholders influence the entrepreneur's well-being. Next we highlight that this relationship is reciprocal—the entrepreneur also plays an important role in the well-being of their stakeholders.

Well-Being and the Stakeholders of Entrepreneurial Firms

Entrepreneurs at the helm of successful new ventures have a widespread impact (Coad et al., 2014). They are a key driver of job creation (Haltiwanger et al., 2013), and change the nature of work by pioneering innovative practices not found in established firms, such as unlimited vacation (e.g., Netflix) and work time allocated to pursue passion projects (e.g., Google). Compassion-driven entrepreneurs introduce innovative business models focused on helping those in need (Miller, Grimes, McMullen, & Vogus, 2012), such as creating meaningful work for those who are marginalized through work-integration business models. Family-owned firms provide opportunities for the current generation of family members as well as subsequent generations (Shepherd & Zacharakis, 2000), potentially in perpetuity (e.g., Wegmans). As such, the impact of entrepreneurship on well-being extends beyond the entrepreneur, impacting numerous stakeholders as well (cf. Wiklund et al., 2019). Next, we discuss this impact on the new venture employees, family members, and society at large.

Entrepreneurial firms are intimate environments (Ensley, Pearce, & Hmieleski, 2006). As opposed to established firms with large bureaucracies, work at new ventures is largely defined by the preferences of the entrepreneurs (Baron, 2010). Thus, the experiences of those working within a new venture—the entrepreneurial workforce—are unique and idiosyncratically shaped by the needs of the firm and its founder(s) (Aldrich & Ruef, 2006). The imprint on the firm left by the entrepreneur is significant but can be a double-edged sword in terms of employee well-being.

There is ample evidence that the behavioral traits of leaders impact the well-being of their subordinates in both positive and negative ways (Inceoglu, Thomas, Chu, Plans, & Gerbasi, 2018). These impacts are amplified in new ventures due to their lack of formality (Sine, Mitsuhashi, & Kirsch, 2006) and human resources functions (Rauch & Hatak, 2016). For example, the entrepreneur can help employees find meaning and personal growth in their work, key components of eudaimonic well-being (Keyes et al., 2002), via charisma (Arnold, Turner, Barling, Kelloway, & McKee, 2007) and passion (Cardon, 2008; Hubner, Baum, & Frese, 2019). However, dark personality traits, such as narcissism, can be prevalent among entrepreneurs (Hmieleski & Lerner, 2016), and they can fuel toxic work environments (Mathieu, Neumann, Hare, & Babiak, 2014). Such toxic work environments are often only resolved after the founder is removed from the firm, highlighted in cases like Uber and WeWork.

There is also a strong link between the work of the entrepreneur and their families' well-being, especially when their firms incorporate family members directly, be it as co-owners or supporting family members (Miller, Wiklund, & Yu, 2019; Nordstrom & Jennings, 2018). Similarly, research on the work–family interface of entrepreneurs whose businesses are not co-owned by or employ family members suggest a potential for work–family conflict as well as enrichment (Nguyen & Sawang, 2016). The potential for conflict arises from entrepreneurs' varied work demands, for example, long work hours or use of family assets to secure business loans. Work–family enrichment is not as well understood and accounts often focus on the social support provided by family members (see Stephan, 2018). Yet the benefits might be broader, for instance, family duties can increase employee's focus at work (Dumas & Perry-Smith, 2018), suggesting that the entrepreneurs' family might also be an indirect source of firm productivity.

Entrepreneurship impacts society by contributing to economic growth (van Praag & Versloot, 2007). However, the scope of these benefits remains an open question (Wiklund et al., 2019). Some evidence suggests that small and medium-sized ventures are partially responsible for growing wealth inequality (Carney & Nason, 2018), while others highlight that entrepreneurial firms reduce wealth inequality by breaking down monopolies and spreading opportunities across more individuals (Packard & Bylund, 2018). At the same time, entrepreneurial firms can also stimulate positive social change through the mitigation of health and social inequalities, increasing the well-being of individuals and communities beyond their firms' boundaries (Stephan et al., 2016).

Future Research: The Entrepreneur

Research concerning entrepreneurship and well-being is steadily increasing, although much remains unknown. As highlighted earlier, the majority of studies thus far assess the subjective well-being of the entrepreneur (cf. Stephan, 2018) and may be a key reason for mixed results regarding whether entrepreneurs are happier than those in paid employment. Entrepreneurship can offer substantial autonomy yet is demanding and stressful. The balance between autonomy and demands shifts over time as the firms grows, relationships with new stakeholders are formed or existing relationships renegotiated. For instance, investors often seek controlling shares in new firms thereby limiting entrepreneurs' autonomy; they will force particular strategies upon the entrepreneur especially during times of setbacks that may threaten their investment (Reymen et al., 2015). In other words, entrepreneurs' levels of hedonic and eudaimonic well-being may wax and wane depending on the inner and outer workings of their firms. More generally, ups and downs are common during the venturing process, which hardly ever has a linear trajectory (McMullen & Dimov, 2013). Yet research on entrepreneurs' well-being hardly considers such dynamics. Future studies can better illuminate the impact of the entrepreneurial process on the well-being of entrepreneurs and their stakeholders over time (Lévesque & Stephan, 2019).

Adaptation theories (cf. Brickman, Coates, & Janoff-Bulman, 1978) of well-being might be particularly suited to provide insights into the ups and downs of the entrepreneurial process. Hedonic or potentially eudaimonic (Waterman, 2007) adaptation highlights that the effect of a major life event on well-being wanes over time. Similar to Brickman and colleagues' (1978) findings on lottery winners and accident victims where changes in well-being due to major events were temporary, the highs (lows) from entrepreneurial success (failure) are likely to be temporary in nature and dependent on how entrepreneurs appraise these events (Jenkins et al., 2014). Adaptation may also lead to self-reinforcing processes. For instance, entrepreneurs may adapt to the well-being 'highs' they derive from achievements, influencing their hedonic baseline (Diener, Lucas, & Scollon, 2006).

This may lead them to seek out ever-greater challenges over time to experience personal growth and happiness, ultimately leading to exhaustion.

Next, the entrepreneur's role within the firm changes as the firm grows (Mathias & Williams, 2018; Wiklund et al., 2003). This change has upsides and downsides for the entrepreneur, in particular along the well-being dimensions of competence and relatedness. For example, the expansion of available resources is likely to enhance an entrepreneurs' ability to deliver their product or service. However, as the firm grows the entrepreneur has little choice but to delegate, which could be challenging (Wiklund et al., 2003) and turn them from doing the actual job to managing others (Kuhn & Galloway, 2015). Thus, their sense of mastery and competence may be reduced as the firm expands (Wiklund et al., 2003). As the firm grows, it must also professionalize (Flamholtz & Randle, 2012), and many entrepreneurs believe that growth will impede the sense of familiarity within the firm (Wiklund et al., 2003), which could reduce their sense of relatedness with other employees. In fact, the fear of losing that level of relatedness within the firm is the single most important factor that deters entrepreneurs from wanting to expand their businesses (Wiklund et al., 2003).

Future Research: Stakeholders

Although employees are critical to the success of a new venture, virtually nothing is known about the entrepreneurial workforce and more specifically, their well-being and how that may be influenced by the entrepreneur's well-being. Given the small size of most firms, especially in their infancy, the behavior of the entrepreneur is likely to have a direct impact on the well-being of employees. As highlighted earlier, the experience of working within a new venture is a distinct context and offers several important avenues for exploration, including influences from the characteristics of the entrepreneur, from the nature of job design, and from that of the performance and direction of the firm.

First, the attributes of the entrepreneur permeate throughout the firm, and often with a lasting effect. For example, previous studies highlight positive relationships between narcissism and firm performance (Wales et al., 2013). However, as noted by Miller (2015), what is positive for the firm, may not be positive for all stakeholders. Evidence suggests that the effects of narcissistic leadership on followers is dependent on how 'close' followers are to those leaders. For employees with more opportunities for direct observation, narcissistic leaders have negative impacts on employees (Nevicka et al., 2018). This suggests that entrepreneurs who exhibit the 'dark triad' traits (Hmieleski & Lerner, 2016) are likely to inflict psychological harm on the people around them especially those that they are in direct contact with. Furthermore, new ventures vary in the quality of the human resource practices (Rauch & Hatak, 2016), leaving employees further exposed to poor and even abusive behavior, such as seen at Uber (Edelman, 2017). Future research in this area can advance entrepreneurship research while also contributing to the rapidly emerging research on leadership and well-being (Inceoglu et al., 2018).

Second, entrepreneurs not only craft their own job but also design the jobs of their employees. Future research could usefully draw on research on work characteristics, which are an important influence on employee well-being, innovation, and performance (Parker, 2014). Research on how entrepreneurs are designing the work of their employees would contribute both to research on entrepreneurship and stakeholder well-being, as well as offer new insights to work design research, which only very recently has begun to investigate how laypeople design work. On one hand, research on work design shows that those without dedicated training in this area privilege individual extrinsic incentives and rewards instead of designing intrinsically motivating work (Heath, 1999; Parker et al., 2019). On the other hand, reports in the media suggest that work design in a new firm can have intrinsically motivating features such as giving employees autonomy, flexibility, and challenging tasks. Due to their lack of legitimacy, small and young firms may have to offer such enriched work to attract talent. Moreover, smaller firm size means that there is ample opportunity for employees to utilize a variety of skills due to lack of specialization and division of labor that typically can only be created when firms grow. In sum, research is needed to advance our understanding of on the nature of good work design in the entrepreneurial firms.

Third, studies suggest a strong link between perceptions of fairness and well-being (Ford et al., 2018). This is likely to be the case of highly successful start-ups—where the distribution of stock options can yield astronomical wealth for those who obtain them. Yet employee well-being may be more effectively stimulated through enhancing employees' perception of participation in organizational decision-making, which is the critical ingredient through which employee ownership schemes (including stock options) impact well-being (Weber et al., 2019). This is not only an underexplored area of research but is also a practically relevant one for new firms where resources are limited. Moreover, equal distribution of ownership across the firm might not have the expected effects either as such structural mechanisms do not necessarily translate into perceived participation opportunity and thus fairness for employees (Weber et al., 2019), for example, when interests of minority employees get sidelined. The related aspect of pay inequalities within new firms also lack systematic study. Pay inequalities within new firms might be large as entrepreneurs see them as an effective way of motivating employees. However, the effectiveness of such inequalities in motivating performance and enhancing employee well-being is far from clear and can be negative (Breza et al., 2018)

Fourth, entrepreneurship has positive and negative implications for society as a whole. For example, some of the most successful start-ups within the last decade ushered a new era of connectedness via social media platforms, bringing with it public criticism on the very nature of entrepreneurship and their power. Indeed, platform-based new firms such as Taskrabbit and Uber create self-employment, the nature of which has been alternatively lauded as a new avenue to self-realization and flexible work or as precarious work where the pressure to obtain positive ratings lead to free labor, low pay, and diminished well-being of the platform workers (Prassl, 2018).

Conclusion

Finally, should well-being be used as a metric for success? Entrepreneurs value their own well-being and that of their employees, and consider both as indicators of their success (Wach et al., 2016). Thus, future research could consider entrepreneurs' and employees' well-being alongside economic firm performance (e.g., profitability, market share, revenue, and employee growth) to offer a more holistic understanding of performance in line with what matters to entrepreneurs. Research is needed to explore when and how the two align and diverge. Interventions to support micro-entrepreneurs have already started to apply dual metrics of well-being and financial performance. For example, a randomized control trial showed that a microcredit intervention increased the financial performance but not the well-being of entrepreneurs (e.g. Karlan & Zinman, 2011). One reading of these findings is the need to pay attention to the type of well-being. The intervention might have raised the aspiration of the entrepreneurs, and thus, they do not necessarily feel happy and content (hedonic well-being) but now start to strive for fulfillment and eudaimonic well-being. Efforts to assess the social impact of enterprises through the well-being of beneficiaries may meet similar challenges. For instance, social enterprises that empower their beneficiaries to lead lives that are more autonomous and to make their own choices may appear unsuccessful if their social impact is accessed through beneficiaries' life satisfaction (hedonic well-being). Indeed, empowerment may enable these beneficiaries to question their life situation and to strive for personal growth instead of being content with what they have (Mair et al., 2012). Moreover, if well-being is used as a success metric, we also need to devote more research attention to understanding the processes and consequences of entrepreneurs' well-being for their stakeholders and their firms.

Disclaimer

We have no known conflicts of interest to disclose.

Note

1. Seligman (2018) offers a combination of the two approaches via the PERMA (Positive Emotion, Engagement, Relationships, Meaning, and Accomplishment) model.

References

Adler, M. D., Dolan, P., & Kavetsos, G. (2017). Would you choose to be happy? Trade-offs between happiness and the other dimensions of life in a large population survey. *Journal of Economic Behavior & Organization, 139*, 60–73. Retrieved from https://doi.org/10.1016/j.jebo.2017.05.006

Aldrich, H. E., & Ruef, M. (2006). *Organizations evolving.* Thousand Oaks, CA: Sage.

Allison, T. H., Davis, B. C., Short, J. C., & Webb, J. W. (2015). Crowdfunding in a prosocial microlending environment: Examining the role of intrinsic versus extrinsic cues. *Entrepreneurship Theory and Practice, 39*(1), 53–73. Retrieved from https://doi.org/10.1111/etap.12108

Arnold, K. A., Turner, N., Barling, J., Kelloway, E. K., & McKee, M. C. (2007). Transformational leadership and psychological well-being: The mediating role of meaningful work. *Journal of Occupational Health Psychology, 12*(3), 193–203. Retrieved from https://doi.org/10.1037/1076-8998.12.3.193

Baron, R. A. (2010). Job design and entrepreneurship: Why closer connections = mutual gains. *Journal of Organizational Behavior, 31*(2–3), 370–378. Retrieved from https://doi.org/10.1002/job.607

Baron, R. A., & Henry, R. A. (2010). How entrepreneurs acquire the capacity to excel: Insights from research on expert performance. *Strategic Entrepreneurship Journal, 4*(1), 49–65. Retrieved from https://doi.org/10.1002/sej.82

Baron, R. A., Tang, J., Tang, Z., & Zhang, Y. (2018). Bribes as entrepreneurial actions: Why underdog entrepreneurs feel compelled to use them. *Journal of Business Venturing, 33*(6), 679–690. Retrieved from https://doi.org/10.1016/j.jbusvent.2018.04.011

Benz, M., & Frey, B. S. (2008). The value of doing what you like: Evidence from the self-employed in 23 countries. *Journal of Economic Behavior & Organization, 68*(3), 445–455. Retrieved from https://doi.org/10.1016/j.jebo.2006.10.014

Binder, M., & Coad, A. (2013). Life satisfaction and self-employment: A matching approach. *Small Business Economics, 40*(4), 1009–1033. Retrieved from https://doi.org/10.1007/s11187-011-9413-9

Bliese, P. D., Edwards, J. R., & Sonnentag, S. (2017). Stress and well-being at work: A century of empirical trends reflecting theoretical and societal influences. *Journal of Applied Psychology, 102*(3), 389–402. Retrieved from https://doi.org/10.1037/apl0000109

Breza, E., Kaur, S., & Shamdasani, Y. (2018). The morale effects of pay inequality*. *The Quarterly Journal of Economics, 133*(2), 611–663. Retrieved from https://doi.org/10.1093/qje/qjx041

Brickman, P., Coates, D., & Janoff-Bulman, R. (1978). Lottery winners and accident victims: Is happiness relative? *Journal of Personality and Social Psychology, 36*(8), 917–927. Retrieved from https://doi.org/10.1037/0022-3514.36.8.917

Cardon, M. S. (2008). Is passion contagious? The transference of entrepreneurial passion to employees. *Human Resource Management Review, 18*(2), 77–86. Retrieved from https://doi.org/10.1016/j.hrmr.2008.04.001

Cardon, M. S., & Patel, P. C. (2015). Is stress worth it? Stress-related health and wealth trade-offs for entrepreneurs: Entrepreneurial stress. *Applied Psychology, 64*(2), 379–420. Retrieved from https://doi.org/10.1111/apps.12021

Carney, M., & Nason, R. S. (2018). Family business and the 1%. *Business & Society, 57*(6), 1191–1215. Retrieved from https://doi.org/10.1177/0007650316661165

Carr, J. C., & Hmieleski, K. M. (2015). Differences in the outcomes of work and family conflict between family and nonfamily businesses: An examination of business founders.

Entrepreneurship Theory and Practice, *39*(6), 1413–1432. Retrieved from https://doi.org/10.1111/etap.12174

Coad, A., Daunfeldt, S.-O., Holzl, W., Johansson, D., & Nightingale, P. (2014). High-growth firms: Introduction to the special section. *Industrial and Corporate Change*, *23*(1), 91–112. Retrieved from https://doi.org/10.1093/icc/dtt052

Collewaert, V. (2012). Angel investors' and entrepreneurs' intentions to exit their ventures: A conflict perspective. *Entrepreneurship Theory and Practice*, *36*(4), 753–779. Retrieved from https://doi.org/10.1111/j.1540-6520.2011.00456.x

Covin, J. G., & Wales, W. J. (2019). Crafting high-impact entrepreneurial orientation research: Some suggested guidelines. *Entrepreneurship Theory and Practice*, *43*(1), 3–18. Retrieved from https://doi.org/10.1177/1042258718773181

Davis, B. C., Hmieleski, K. M., Webb, J. W., & Coombs, J. E. (2017). Funders' positive affective reactions to entrepreneurs' crowdfunding pitches: The influence of perceived product creativity and entrepreneurial passion. *Journal of Business Venturing*, *32*(1), 90–106. Retrieved from https://doi.org/10.1016/j.jbusvent.2016.10.006

Diener, E., Emmons, R. A., Larsen, R. J., & Griffin, R. (1985). The satisfaction with life scale. *Journal of Personality Assessment*, *49*(1), 71–75.

Diener, E., Lucas, R. E., & Scollon, C. N. (2006). Beyond the hedonic treadmill: Revising the adaptation theory of well-being. *American Psychologist*, *61*(4), 305–314. Retrieved from https://doi.org/10.1037/0003-066X.61.4.305

Diener, E., Oishi, S., & Tay, L. (2018). Advances in subjective well-being research. *Nature Human Behaviour*, *2*(4), 253–260. Retrieved from https://doi.org/10.1038/s41562-018-0307-6

Diener, E., Suh, E. M., Lucas, R. E., & Smith, H. L. (1999). Subjective well-being: Three decades of progress. *Psychological Bulletin*, *125*(2), 276–302.

Drover, W., Busenitz, L., Matusik, S., Townsend, D., Anglin, A., & Dushnitsky, G. (2017). A review and road map of entrepreneurial equity financing research: Venture capital, corporate venture capital, angel investment, crowdfunding, and accelerators. *Journal of Management*, *43*(6), 1820–1853. Retrieved from https://doi.org/10.1177/0149206317690584

Dumas, T. L., & Perry-Smith, J. E. (2018). The paradox of family structure and plans after work: Why single childless employees may be the least absorbed at work. *Academy of Management Journal*, *61*(4), 1231–1252. Retrieved from https://doi.org/10.5465/amj.2016.0086

Edelman, B. (2017, June 21). Uber can't be fixed - It's time for regulators to shut it down. *Harvard Business Review*. Retrieved from https://hbr.org/2017/06/uber-cant-be-fixed-its-time-for-regulators-to-shut-it-down

Ensley, M. D., Pearce, C. L., & Hmieleski, K. M. (2006). The moderating effect of environmental dynamism on the relationship between entrepreneur leadership behavior and new venture performance. *Journal of Business Venturing*, *21*(2), 243–263. Retrieved from https://doi.org/10.1016/j.jbusvent.2005.04.006

Flamholtz, E. G., & Randle, Y. (2012). *Growing pains: Transitioning from an entrepreneurship to a professionally managed firm*. New York: John Wiley & Sons.

Forbes, D. P., Borchert, P. S., Zellmer–Bruhn, M. E., & Sapienza, H. J. (2006). Entrepreneurial team formation: An exploration of new member addition. *Entrepreneurship Theory and Practice*, *30*(2), 225–248. Retrieved from https://doi.org/10.1111/j.1540-6520.2006.00119.x

Ford, M. T., Agosta, J. P., Huang, J., & Shannon, C. (2018). Moral emotions toward others at work and implications for employee behavior: A qualitative analysis using critical incidents. *Journal of Business and Psychology*, *33*(1), 155–180. Retrieved from https://doi.org/10.1007/s10869-016-9484-3

Frese, M., & Gielnik, M. M. (2014). The psychology of entrepreneurship. *Annual Review of Organizational Psychology and Organizational Behavior, 1*(1), 413–438. Retrieved from https://doi.org/10.1146/annurev-orgpsych-031413-091326

Fritsch, M., Sorgner, A., & Wyrwich, M. (2019). Self-employment and well-being across institutional contexts. *Journal of Business Venturing, 34*(6), 105946. Retrieved from https://doi.org/10.1016/j.jbusvent.2019.105946

Funk, J. L., & Rogge, R. D. (2007). Testing the ruler with item response theory: Increasing precision of measurement for relationship satisfaction with the Couples Satisfaction Index. *Journal of Family Psychology, 21*(4), 572–583. Retrieved from https://doi.org/10.1037/0893-3200.21.4.572

Gimeno, J., Folta, T. B., Cooper, A. C., & Woo, C. Y. (1997). Survival of the fittest? Entrepreneurial human capital and the persistence of underperforming firms. *Administrative Science Quarterly, 42*(4), 750–783. JSTOR. Retrieved from https://doi.org/10.2307/2393656

Haltiwanger, J., Jarmin, R. S., & Miranda, J. (2013). Who creates jobs? Small versus large versus young. *Review of Economics and Statistics, 95*(2), 347–361. Retrieved from https://doi.org/10.1162/REST_a_00288

Heath, C. (1999). On the social psychology of agency relationships: Lay theories of motivation overemphasize extrinsic incentives. *Organizational Behavior and Human Decision Processes, 78*(1), 25–62. Retrieved from https://doi.org/10.1006/obhd.1999.2826

Hmieleski, K. M., & Lerner, D. A. (2016). The dark triad and Nascent entrepreneurship: An examination of unproductive versus productive entrepreneurial motives. *Journal of Small Business Management, 54*, 7–32. Retrieved from https://doi.org/10.1111/jsbm.12296

Hubner, S., Baum, M., & Frese, M. (2019). Contagion of entrepreneurial passion: Effects on employee outcomes. *Entrepreneurship Theory and Practice.* Retrieved from https://doi.org/10.1177/1042258719883995

Inceoglu, I., Thomas, G., Chu, C., Plans, D., & Gerbasi, A. (2018). Leadership behavior and employee well-being: An integrated review and a future research agenda. *The Leadership Quarterly, 29*(1), 179–202. Retrieved from https://doi.org/10.1016/j.leaqua.2017.12.006

Jenkins, A. S., Wiklund, J., & Brundin, E. (2014). Individual responses to firm failure: Appraisals, grief, and the influence of prior failure experience. *Journal of Business Venturing, 29*(1), 17–33. Retrieved from https://doi.org/10.1016/j.jbusvent.2012.10.006

Kahneman, D. (1999). Objective happiness. In D. Kahneman, E. Diener, & N. Schwarz (Eds.), *Well-being: The foundations of hedonic psychology* (pp. 3–25). New York: Russell Sage Foundation.

Karlan, D., & Zinman, J. (2011). Microcredit in theory and practice: Using randomized credit scoring for impact evaluation. *Science, 332*(6035), 1278–1284. Retrieved from https://doi.org/10.1126/science.1200138

Kautonen, T., Kibler, E., & Minniti, M. (2017). Late-career entrepreneurship, income and quality of life. *Journal of Business Venturing, 32*(3), 318–333. Retrieved from https://doi.org/10.1016/j.jbusvent.2017.02.005

Keyes, C. L. M., Shmotkin, D., & Ryff, C. D. (2002). Optimizing well-being: The empirical encounter of two traditions. *Journal of Personality and Social Psychology, 82*(6), 1007–1022. Retrieved from https://doi.org/10.1037//0022-3514.82.6.1007

Kibler, E., Wincent, J., Kautonen, T., Cacciotti, G., & Obschonka, M. (2019). Can prosocial motivation harm entrepreneurs' subjective well-being? *Journal of Business Venturing, 34*(4), 608–624. Retrieved from https://doi.org/10.1016/j.jbusvent.2018.10.003

Kollmann, T., Stöckmann, C., & Kensbock, J. M. (2019). I can't get no sleep - The differential impact of entrepreneurial stressors on work-home interference and insomnia among experienced versus novice entrepreneurs. *Journal of Business Venturing, 34*(4), 692–708. Retrieved from https://doi.org/10.1016/j.jbusvent.2018.08.001

Kuhn, K. M., & Galloway, T. L. (2015). With a little help from my competitors: Peer networking among artisan entrepreneurs. *Entrepreneurship Theory and Practice, 39*(3), 571–600. Retrieved from https://doi.org/10.1111/etap.12053

Laguna, M., & Razmus, W. (2019). When I feel my business succeeds, I flourish: Reciprocal relationships between positive orientation, work engagement, and entrepreneurial success. *Journal of Happiness Studies, 20*(8), 2711–2731. Retrieved from https://doi.org/10.1007/s10902-018-0065-1

Lévesque, M., & Stephan, U. (2019). It's time we talk about time in entrepreneurship. *Entrepreneurship Theory and Practice.* Retrieved from https://doi.org/10.1177/1042258719839711

Lyubomirsky, S., & Lepper, H. S. (1999). A measure of subjective happiness: Preliminary reliability and construct validation. *Social Indicators Research, 46*, 137–155.

Mair, J., Martí, I., & Ventresca, M. J. (2012). Building inclusive markets in rural Bangladesh: How intermediaries work institutional voids. *Academy of Management Journal, 55*(4), 819–850. Retrieved from https://doi.org/10.5465/amj.2010.0627

Martela, F., & Sheldon, K. M. (2019). Clarifying the concept of well-being: Psychological need satisfaction as the common core connecting eudaimonic and subjective well-being. *Review of General Psychology, 23*(4), 458–474. Retrieved from https://doi.org/10.1177/1089268019880886

Mathias, B. D., & Williams, D. W. (2018). Giving up the hats? Entrepreneurs' role transitions and venture growth. *Journal of Business Venturing, 33*(3), 261–277. Retrieved from https://doi.org/10.1016/j.jbusvent.2017.12.007

Mathieu, C., Neumann, C. S., Hare, R. D., & Babiak, P. (2014). A dark side of leadership: Corporate psychopathy and its influence on employee well-being and job satisfaction. *Personality and Individual Differences, 59*, 83–88. Retrieved from https://doi.org/10.1016/j.paid.2013.11.010

McMullen, J. S., & Dimov, D. (2013). Time and the entrepreneurial journey: The problems and promise of studying entrepreneurship as a process: Time and the entrepreneurial journey. *Journal of Management Studies.* Retrieved from https://doi.org/10.1111/joms.12049

Miller, D. (2015). A downside to the entrepreneurial personality? *Entrepreneurship Theory and Practice, 39*(1), 1–8. Retrieved from https://doi.org/10.1111/etap.12130

Miller, D., Wiklund, J., & Yu, W. (2019). Mental health in the family business: A conceptual model and a research agenda. *Entrepreneurship Theory and Practice.* Retrieved from https://doi.org/10.1177/1042258719837987

Miller, T. L., Grimes, M. G., McMullen, J. S., & Vogus, T. J. (2012). Venturing for others with heart and head: How compassion encourages social entrepreneurship. *Academy of Management Review, 37*(4), 616–640. Retrieved from https://doi.org/10.5465/amr.2010.0456

Moser, K., Tumasjan, A., & Welpe, I. M. (2015). Small, but attractive: The effect of employer branding and legitimacy on startup attractiveness. *Academy of Management Proceedings, 2015*(1), 10528. Retrieved from https://doi.org/10.5465/ambpp.2015.105

Moss, T. W., Renko, M., & Bort, J. (2019). The story behind the story: Microfoundations of hybrid communication by microenterprises. *Academy of Management Proceedings, 2019*(1), 13052. Retrieved from https://doi.org/10.5465/AMBPP.2019.196

Nevicka, B., Van Vianen, A. E. M., De Hoogh, A. H. B., & Voorn, B. C. M. (2018). Narcissistic leaders: An asset or a liability? Leader visibility, follower responses, and group-level absenteeism. *Journal of Applied Psychology*, *103*(7), 703–723. Retrieved from https://doi.org/10.1037/apl0000298

Nguyen, H., & Sawang, S. (2016). Juggling or struggling? Work and family interface and its buffers among small business owners. *Entrepreneurship Research Journal*, *6*(2). Retrieved from https://doi.org/10.1515/erj-2014-0041

Nordstrom, O., & Jennings, J. E. (2018). Looking in the other direction: An ethnographic analysis of how family businesses can be operated to enhance familial well-being. *Entrepreneurship Theory and Practice*, *42*(2), 317–339. Retrieved from https://doi.org/10.1177/1042258717749236

Packard, M. D., & Bylund, P. L. (2018). On the relationship between inequality and entrepreneurship. *Strategic Entrepreneurship Journal*, *12*(1), 3–22. Retrieved from https://doi.org/10.1002/sej.1270

Parker, S. K. (2014). Beyond motivation: Job and work design for development, health, ambidexterity, and more. *Annual Review of Psychology*, *65*(1), 661–691. Retrieved from https://doi.org/10.1146/annurev-psych-010213-115208

Parker, S. K., Andrei, D. M., & Van den Broeck, A. (2019). Poor work design begets poor work design: Capacity and willingness antecedents of individual work design behavior. *Journal of Applied Psychology*. Retrieved from https://doi.org/10.1037/apl0000383

Prassl, J. (2018). *Humans as a service: The promise and perils of work in the gig economy*. New York: Oxford University Press.

Rauch, A., & Hatak, I. (2016). A meta-analysis of different HR-enhancing practices and performance of small and medium sized firms. *Journal of Business Venturing*, *31*(5), 485–504. Retrieved from https://doi.org/10.1016/j.jbusvent.2016.05.005

Reymen, I. M. M. J., Andries, P., Berends, H., Mauer, R., Stephan, U., & Burg, E. van. (2015). Understanding dynamics of strategic decision making in venture creation: A process study of effectuation and causation. *Strategic Entrepreneurship Journal*, *9*(4), 351–379. Retrieved from https://doi.org/10.1002/sej.1201

Ryan, R. M., & Deci, E. L. (2000). Self-determination theory and the facilitation of intrinsic motivation, social development, and well-being. *American Psychologist*, 67.

Ryan, R. M., & Deci, E. L. (2001). On happiness and human potentials: A review of research on hedonic and eudaimonic well-being. *Annual Review of Psychology*, *52*(1), 141–166. Retrieved from https://doi.org/10.1146/annurev.psych.52.1.141

Ryan, R. M., Huta, V., & Deci, E. L. (2008). Living well: A self-determination theory perspective on eudaimonia. *Journal of Happiness Studies*, *9*(1), 139–170. Retrieved from https://doi.org/10.1007/s10902-006-9023-4

Ryff, C. D. (1989). Happiness is everything, or is it? Explorations on the meaning of psychological well-being. *Journal of Personality and Social Psychology*, *57*(6), 1069–1081. Retrieved from https://doi.org/10.1037/0022-3514.57.6.1069

Ryff, C. D. (2019). Entrepreneurship and eudaimonic well-being: Five venues for new science. *Journal of Business Venturing*, *34*(4), 646–663. Retrieved from https://doi.org/10.1016/j.jbusvent.2018.09.003

Ryff, C. D., & Keyes, C. L. M. (1995). The structure of psychological well-being revisited. *Journal of Personality and Social Psychology*, *69*(4), 719–727.

Seligman, M. (2018). PERMA and the building blocks of well-being. *The Journal of Positive Psychology*, *13*(4), 333–335. Retrieved from https://doi.org/10.1080/17439760.2018.1437466

Sheldon, K. M., & Lyubomirsky, S. (2012). The challenge of staying happier: Testing the hedonic adaptation prevention model. *Personality and Social Psychology Bulletin, 38*(5), 670–680. Retrieved from https://doi.org/10.1177/0146167212436400

Shepherd, D. A., Wiklund, J., & Haynie, J. M. (2009). Moving forward: Balancing the financial and emotional costs of business failure. *Journal of Business Venturing, 24*(2), 134–148. Retrieved from https://doi.org/10.1016/j.jbusvent.2007.10.002

Shepherd, D. A., & Zacharakis, A. (2000). Structuring family business succession: An analysis of the future leader's decision making. *Entrepreneurship Theory and Practice, 24*(4), 25–39. Retrieved from https://doi.org/10.1177/104225870002400402

Shir, N., Nikolaev, B. N., & Wincent, J. (2018). Entrepreneurship and well-being: The role of psychological autonomy, competence, and relatedness. *Journal of Business Venturing*. Retrieved from https://doi.org/10.1016/j.jbusvent.2018.05.002

Sine, W. D., Mitsuhashi, H., & Kirsch, D. A. (2006). Revisiting burns and stalker: Formal structure and new venture performance in emerging economic sectors. *Academy of Management Journal, 49*(1), 121–132. Retrieved from https://doi.org/10.5465/amj.2006.20785590

Stephan, U. (2018). Entrepreneurs' mental health and well-being: A review and research agenda. *Academy of Management Perspectives, 32*(3), 290–322. Retrieved from https://doi.org/10.5465/amp.2017.0001

Stephan, U., Patterson, M., Kelly, C., & Mair, J. (2016). Organizations driving positive social change: A review and an integrative framework of change processes. *Journal of Management, 42*(5), 1250–1281. Retrieved from https://doi.org/10.1177/0149206316633268

Van Gelderen, M. (2016). Entrepreneurial autonomy and its dynamics: Entrepreneurial autonomy. *Applied Psychology, 65*(3), 541–567. Retrieved from https://doi.org/10.1111/apps.12066

Van Gelderen, M., Shirokova, G., Shchegolev, V., & Beliaeva, T. (2019). Striving for entrepreneurial autonomy: A comparison of Russia and the Netherlands. *Management and Organization Review*, 1–32. Retrieved from https://doi.org/10.1017/mor.2019.24

Van Praag, C. M., & Versloot, P. H. (2007). What is the value of entrepreneurship? A review of recent research. *Small Business Economics, 29*(4), 351–382. Retrieved from https://doi.org/10.1007/s11187-007-9074-x

Wach, D., Stephan, U., & Gorgievski, M. (2016). More than money: Developing an integrative multi-factorial measure of entrepreneurial success. *International Small Business Journal: Researching Entrepreneurship, 34*(8), 1098–1121. Retrieved from https://doi.org/10.1177/0266242615608469

Wales, W. J., Patel, P. C., & Lumpkin, G. T. (2013). In pursuit of greatness: CEO narcissism, entrepreneurial orientation, and firm performance variance: In pursuit of greatness. *Journal of Management Studies, 50*(6), 1041–1069. Retrieved from https://doi.org/10.1111/joms.12034

Waterman, A. S. (2007). On the importance of distinguishing hedonia and eudaimonia when contemplating the hedonic treadmill. *American Psychologist, 62*(6), 612–613. Retrieved from https://doi.org/10.1037/0003-066X62.6.612

Waterman, A. S., Schwartz, S. J., Zamboanga, B. L., Ravert, R. D., Williams, M. K., Bede Agocha, V., . . . Brent Donnellan, M. (2010). The questionnaire for eudaimonic well-being: Psychometric properties, demographic comparisons, and evidence of validity. *The Journal of Positive Psychology, 5*(1), 41–61. Retrieved from https://doi.org/10.1080/17439760903435208

Webb, J. W., Bruton, G. D., Tihanyi, L., & Ireland, R. D. (2013). Research on entrepreneurship in the informal economy: Framing a research agenda. *Journal of Business Venturing*, *28*(5), 598–614. Retrieved from https://doi.org/10.1016/j.jbusvent.2012.05.003

Weber, W. G., Unterrainer, C., & Höge, T. (2019). Psychological research on organizational democracy: A meta-analysis of individual, organizational, and societal outcomes. *Applied Psychology*. Retrieved from https://doi.org/10.1111/apps.12205

Weiss, D. J., Dawis, R. V., & England, G. W. (1967). Manual for the Minnesota satisfaction questionnaire. *Minnesota Studies in Vocational Rehabilitation*, *22*, 120–120.

Wiklund, J., Davidsson, P., & Delmar, F. (2003). What do they think and feel about growth? An expectancy-value approach to small business managers' attitudes toward growth. *Entrepreneurship Theory and Practice*, *26*(3), 247–270. Retrieved from https://doi.org/10.1111/1540-8520.00014

Wiklund, J., Hatak, I., Patzelt, H., & Shepherd, D. A. (2018). Mental disorders in the entrepreneurship context: When being different can be an advantage. *Academy of Management Perspectives*, *32*(2), 182–206. Retrieved from https://doi.org/10.5465/amp.2017.0063

Wiklund, J., Nikolaev, B., Shir, N., Foo, M.-D., & Bradley, S. (2019). Entrepreneurship and well-being: Past, present, and future. *Journal of Business Venturing*. Retrieved from https://doi.org/10.1016/j.jbusvent.2019.01.002

20

PSYCHOLOGY, PROCESS, AND THE ENTREPRENEURIAL ARTIFACT

Per Davidsson

Introduction

Entrepreneurship research has undergone phenomenal quantitative and qualitative development over the last couple of decades (Aldrich, 2012; Davidsson, 2016a; Meyer et al., 2014). This development includes top entrepreneurship journals rising to ratings that stand well in any comparison (McMullen, 2019) as well as an increased presence of entrepreneurship research within disciplines, including psychology (Gorgievski & Stephan, 2016). It also includes a drift toward regarding the core of entrepreneurship research as explaining how new businesses emerge; the journey from nonexistence to existence. This is a domain that other business research subfields do not necessarily cover because they typically take existing firms, industries, and markets as the vantage point. Thus, in this area entrepreneurship research can make unique contributions to the broader domain of economic and organizational studies.

However, two core ideas that Shane and Venkataraman (2000) raised in their otherwise highly influential 'Promise' article are still in dire need of further theoretical and empirical development today. This is despite the widespread agreement-in-principle that has evolved around their importance. The first is that entrepreneurship is best seen as a process (Davidsson & Grünhagen, 2020; McMullen & Dimov, 2013). Venture creation is not instantaneous, and what happens during the process can be even more important for explaining entrepreneurial action and success than are the conditions and resources present at the outset of the journey. The second is that characteristics of the emerging entrepreneurial artifact—the elements that eventually become a fully functional venture—are as important as those of the entrepreneurial agent. Thus, the conceptualization and operationalization of the entrepreneurial artifact become central. This chapter outlines some ideas about how researchers in psychology can contribute to developing these two, essential areas of entrepreneurship research.

Before continuing, it may be useful to clarify the author's background. I took my PhD in Economic Psychology within an organizational unit where figures like Amos Tversky and Daniel Kahneman (cognitive psychology) and Robert Cialdini (social psychology) were local heroes and occasional guests. This said, I do not hold a degree in psychology proper, and starting from my dissertation study, the focus of my work has been the phenomenon of entrepreneurship, approached from a variety of theoretical vantage points. This means that my connections with the discipline of psychology have been piecemeal and patchy. As a consequence, in developing the below ideas I stand on much firmer ground with my entrepreneurship leg than with my psychology leg. Therefore, some omissions and misconceptions are likely to occur as I dabble in psychology. My hope is that some of my ideas will still have value and that this value can be further enhanced as readers add to them their own, richer, and more refined insights from psychology.

The Entrepreneurial Artifact

Entrepreneurial Opportunities and the Entrepreneurship Nexus

If we follow serial entrepreneurs over time, we will likely find that they engage in a variety of business ventures with tremendously variable outcomes. This strongly suggests that not just the qualities of the entrepreneurial agent but also the inherent qualities of 'that, on which they act'—the entrepreneurial artifact—has an important influence on outcomes. The entrepreneurial artifacts that entrepreneurs create are new business ventures. These may be small and only employ a single person, but they do have some tangible features that separate them from the individuals who created them, giving them their own identity (Katz & Gartner, 1988). Once fully created, the entrepreneurial artifact has, among other things, its own resources, routines, and recurring exchange relationships. The characteristics of the artifact, like those of its human agents, will influence outcomes.

In an attempt to steer entrepreneurship research away from an exaggerated focus on heroic entrepreneurs, Shane and Venkataraman (2000) wanted to give the artifact the same weight as that given to the entrepreneurial agent. Consistent with the view that the core of entrepreneurship is the journey from nonexistence to sustainable existence, they discussed the entrepreneurial artifact not as realized new ventures, but as potential ones. They labeled these potentials 'opportunities' and cast their framework as the 'individual-opportunity nexus'. In short, they argued that entrepreneurial action and outcomes are the fruit of entrepreneurial individuals, entrepreneurial opportunities, and the fit between the two. Opportunities were conceptualized as objective, preexisting, and actor-independent, consisting of combinations of favorable conditions in the environment.

Their framework spawned a rapidly growing research stream using 'entrepreneurial opportunity' in a central role. Within that literature, psychological research on the identification and evaluation of 'opportunities' has been one of the most vibrant and successful branches (Davidsson, 2015; Shepherd & Grégoire, 2012). However, many have found Shane and Venkataraman's notion of objective, preexisting opportunities philosophically objectionable and empirically inoperable (Alvarez & Barney, 2010; Dimov, 2011) and therefore drifted to radically different uses of the opportunity concept (Davidsson, 2015). Moreover, although the research has pinpointed some characteristics of agents that make them better at identifying, evaluating, and/or realizing 'opportunities' (generally or, in particular, domains), there is little accumulation of knowledge around agreed on, abstracted characteristics of 'opportunities' and how they influence such identification, evaluation, and realization across agents. The choice and labeling of opportunity characteristics to include in the design of empirical research tend to be rather ad hoc.

One reason for limited progress may be that Shane and Venkataraman's (2000) notion of opportunity is quite demanding. For one thing, opportunities were cast as favorable by definition, although admittedly their favorability—and therefore their identity as opportunities—cannot be known for certain until a favorable outcome has ensued (Eckhardt & Shane, 2010, p. 49). Among other complications, this makes it impossible to sample opportunities in real time and poses the question, What are those entrepreneurs who do not steer the process to a favorable outcome are working on?[1] Defining the emerging artifact as objectively favorable would seem to clash with the nexus idea that outcomes are determined by the opportunity, the agent, and the fit between the two. If the opportunity part of the nexus is favorable by definition, it can only be failure by the agent to correctly identify and/or exploit the opportunity that explains a negative outcome; opportunities as defined cannot cause failure (Davidsson, 2016b, p. 231).

It has later been realized that Shane and Venkataraman (2000) actually confounded two phenomena in their discussion of entrepreneurial opportunity (Davidsson, 2015; Shane, 2012). On one hand, there is—as per their definition of opportunity—the constellation of objective, actor-independent circumstances that make the new venture possible and help in its success. We will come back to in what sense this can be viewed as (part of) the entrepreneurial artifact. On the other hand, there are subjective ideas about the design and operations of an imagined, future venture—ideas that can be of any quality and which may make more or less use of favorable, external circumstances. These two phenomena are very different and have a high degree of spatial and temporal independence from each other. A given venture idea can be implemented in different geographical environments with different external conditions, leading to varying levels of success. Furthermore, during the venture creation process the idea and the external conditions may change without these changes being temporally coordinated or causally connected (Davidsson, 2017, p. 67).

However, both phenomena may underpin relevant representations of the (emerging) entrepreneurial artifact, that is, what eventually may become an up-and-running business venture. Of course, in observational studies of entrepreneurs pursuing their own ideas, the agent and the emerging artifact can never be fully independent (Sarason, Dillard, & Dean, 2010). We do not randomly assign entrepreneurs to emerging ventures or vice versa; the entrepreneurs choose the idea and/or set of circumstances to act on. Yet, the outcome variability across ventures initiated by the same individuals suggests that the nexus idea remains highly relevant for entrepreneurship research, that is, that trying to fulfill Shane and Venkataraman's promise remains a worthwhile pursuit.

The following elaborates on how psychologists can contribute to research on the entrepreneurial artifact, discussing first the subjective-imaginative side under the label *new venture ideas* (NVI) and then offering an alternative take on the objective, actor-independent circumstances under the rubric of *external enablers* (EE). These labels were first introduced in Davidsson (2015) where I suggest a radical re-conceptualization of what had previously been referred to as entrepreneurial opportunity.

Research on New Venture Ideas

In Davidsson (2015, p. 683) I defined 'NVI' as "[a]n 'imagined future venture'; i.e., an imaginary combination of product/service offering, markets, and means of bringing the offering into existence". Hence, it is the mental image of the-business-to-be.[2] Note that unlike definitions of 'opportunity', this definition does not say anything about objectively or subjectively perceived quality. NVIs can objectively be anything from exceedingly bad to unbelievably good. Similarly, observers may rate one and the same idea anywhere on a favorability spectrum. The challenge is to conceptualize the variance in NVIs that determine the variance in their objective and subjective favorability.

Psychology is a large and well-establish discipline. As such, it offers a vast catalogue of theoretical constructs to describe characteristics of and variance across human individuals and collectives. These constructs are often linked to validated operationalizations as well as theoretical propositions and empirical evidence on how the characteristics relate to antecedents and outcomes. Despite its recent growth in quantity and quality, entrepreneurship research is but a moderately sized research field and community rather than a large and well-developed discipline. Entrepreneurship researchers can borrow from various disciplines as well as develop their own research tools, but when it comes to doing research on NVIs, the entrepreneurship research community has very little of firmly established conceptualizations, operationalizations, theory, and effectively accumulated empirical evidence to build on. This leaves the conditions for research on the entrepreneurship nexus, using the NVI as the entrepreneurial agent's counterpart, far short of ideal.

Psychologists' familiarity with strong conceptualizations of traits and other well-defined personal characteristics, as well as with multidimensional assessment of these, can make important contributions to rectify this deficiency. These potential contributions can take at least two distinct forms. The first concerns the conceptualization and operationalization of characteristics on NVIs. This work is likely best done in collaboration with experienced entrepreneurship researchers with other backgrounds. The second concerns how characteristics of NVIs, characteristics of entrepreneurial agents, and the matching of the two, influence entrepreneurial action and outcomes.

Varying characteristics are undoubtedly an important part of what makes NVIs more or less attractive to entrepreneurs and investors; more or less likely to lead to a realized venture and more or less likely to yield above-average financial returns and other positive outcomes later in their existence. Would it be possible to develop something akin to the Big Five personality characteristics applied to NVIs? That is, a small set of abstracted and coarse-grained yet validated and broadly applicable concepts that can capture most of the relevant variance in NVIs? This would be a monumental contribution from psychologists to entrepreneurship research!

It is, of course, a goal for the long term; the Big Five were certainly not developed quickly or in a single study (John & Srivastava, 1999). But the work would not start entirely from scratch. Past research on 'opportunities' or new venture ideas offers some leads, such as recurring references to various aspects of novelty/newness/innovativeness (e.g., Dahlqvist & Wiklund, 2012), scope (e.g., Davidsson, Hunter, & Klofsten, 2006; Reymen et al., 2015), and appropriability (e.g., Eckhardt & Shane, 2010). Other literature that might provide leads are those on innovation characteristics that speed up diffusion (e.g., Rogers, 1995); business model design (e.g., George & Bock, 2011; Zott, Amit, & Massa, 2011); investors' decision criteria (e.g., Mason & Stark, 2004) and creative artifacts in other domains (e.g., Maher, 2011). There is some overlap between NVI and psychological notions of *plan* and *goal* (Austin & Vancouver, 1996; Elavsky, Doerksen, & Conroy, 2012), so these literatures could also prove useful in this endeavor.

As regards how the characteristics of the NVI match those of the entrepreneurial agent, this variant of Shane and Venkataraman's (2000) individual–opportunity nexus idea is just a special case of a familiar theme in industrial-organizational psychology: *fit* between individuals and their context (Kristof-Brown, Zimmerman, & Johnson, 2005). Psychologists can apply such fit approaches to match agent characteristics as conceptualized in psychological theories with sufficiently well conceptualized and operationalized characteristics of NVIs in studying how idea characteristics, agent characteristics, and their interactions influence entrepreneurial action and outcomes. Presumably, this can be done both in observational and experimental studies.

As regards observational studies, accomplished psychologists who are new-comers to entrepreneurship are well advised to avoid some of the design mistakes entrepreneurship researchers have learned the hard way over the last few decades (cf. Davidsson, 2016b). One thing to have in mind is the balance between sample size and statistical representativeness on the one hand, and theoretical relevance and avoidance of unmeasured heterogeneity on the other. A random sample—if possible to achieve at all (Davidsson & Steffens, 2011; Reynolds, 2009)—will be very heterogeneous and dominated by low-ambition/low-potential ventures (Davidsson & Gordon, 2012). Apart from heterogeneity in terms of size; type of product/service offered, and the qualities of the entrepreneurs, there is temporal heterogeneity. That is, the ventures are at varying stages of development at the time of capture, and they progress forward at an unequal pace. We revisit these important considerations in the following section on process research. Depending on what the research aims to achieve, a theory-driven sample that is more homogenous along dimensions that are not the focus of the research may be preferable even if sample size needs to be reduced (Davidsson & Gordon, 2012; Shugan, 2007). Also to be avoided is the assumption that one individual equates one venture. The agent side of the research may be better represented on the team level (Klotz, Hmieleski, Bradley, & Busenitz, 2014), or the sample may need to be restricted to solo ventures (cf. Dimov, 2010). Conversely, the focal individual may be investing their money, effort, and emotions in a different venture than the sampled one (Wiklund & Shepherd, 2008). These are design issues that relate to observational entrepreneurship research in general and not just research on the role of new venture ideas.

Experimentation is increasingly welcomed in entrepreneurship (Hsu, Simmons, & Wieland, 2017; Williams, Wood, Mitchell, & Urbig, 2019) and much prior research on NVIs is experimental or quasi-experimental, usually appearing under the 'entrepreneurial opportunities' banner. That is, the research presents some researcher-controlled stimuli that essentially describe, reflect, or imply NVIs, and assesses whether the participants identify promising ideas, and/or how they evaluate them. Psychologists can improve on such research by applying the most sophisticated and up-to-date psychological theories as well as by adhering to the high design standards of experimental research in psychology (Davis, 2008). As mentioned earlier, they can also help in providing stronger conceptualizations and operationalizations of NVI characteristics, and theorizing how idea and person characteristics interact in perception and evaluation of NVIs (Grégoire, & Shepherd, 2012; Wood, McKelvie, & Haynie, 2014; Wood & Williams, 2014).

Important in this context is to observe the distinction between third-person and first-person assessments (McMullen & Shepherd, 2006). The former concerns belief in the idea as such—whether it would be a good idea for *someone [suitable]* to try to implement it—whereas the latter concerns whether pursuing the idea would be a good opportunity for the evaluator *him- or herself*. Past research has often been ambiguous on this point, or implicitly favored a first-person perspective but done so with an ad hoc and often single-item measure. Both of these alternatives make it hard to fully tease out the extent to which favorable evaluations are attributable to the characteristics of the idea and those of the agent, respectively. Recently, instruments focusing squarely on evaluation and being clear about third- versus first-person stance have been developed and validated (Davidsson, Grégoire, & Lex, 2018; Scheaf, Loignon, Webb, Heggestad, & Wood, 2020), so that part of the toolbox should no longer be a reason for a lack of progress.

Research on External Enablers

Although the idea of 'objective opportunity' as the full set of external circumstances that make a new venture viable is simply too demanding to be useful for research purposes (Davidsson, 2016b, Ch. 8), the emphasis on actor-independent external circumstances is not only justified but needed (Davidsson, 2019). As an alternative way of making room for these, I introduced the notion of *external enabler* (EE; Davidsson, 2015). This refers to significant changes to the business environment such as new technology, regulatory shifts, sociocultural trends, and demographic, macro-economic, or natural-environmental changes. The EE concept thus includes a broader set of changes than what can be comfortably viewed as 'institutional change', 'external shock', or 'environmental jolt', to mention a few extant theoretical notions that the EE concept envelopes. The changes can be good or bad for existing businesses and for the economy as a whole, and unlike 'objective opportunities' they are never a complete success recipe for any new venture. They have in common, however, that they change the balance of some part of the economic system. It is a rather safe theoretical assumption that this improves the prospects for *some* conceivable and not-yet-existing ventures. It is this potential of being a salient element in the design and success of *some* new ventures that earns them the EE label.

Before continuing, it may be worth clarifying on what basis environmental changes can be considered part of the entrepreneurial artifact. To illustrate this, consider the following, admittedly simplified and compressed reasoning behind launching an electronic scooter rental business (cf. Davidsson, 2019):

> Batteries have become so much better. OK, this means electric scooters with some oomph and reach are now possible. Let's have people rent them, building on the recently developed 'sharing economy' mentality of not necessarily owning what you use. But if we drop them here and there around cities, won't local authorities just ban them? No, not necessarily. The scooters are *green;* both users and policy-makers will love a contribution to saving the planet. By the way, they help ease increasing congestion resulting from ever-increasing urban populations. Moreover, the bikeway infrastructure that many cities have recently invested in partly for these reasons make the scooters an even more attractive commuting alternative. But how do we

organize this? Well, everybody has a smartphone in their pocket these days. We can use them for both users and re-chargers to locate the scooters; for making sure they are legally parked in suitable areas at the end of trips; for making payments; for distributing incentives, and for collecting feedback.

In this example, benefits from a number of different types of EEs (technological, sociocultural, and natural-environmental) are strategically used in the design of the entrepreneurial artifact. In other cases, the influence of identifiable EEs may be less pronounced or less strategic. Sometimes entrepreneurs benefit from EEs automatically and perhaps even without realizing it; in other cases, it may take considerable ingenuity and much hard work to identify and realize the benefits EEs can offer.

Davidsson, Recker, and von Briel (2020) recently expanded the EE idea into a framework that looks beyond the classification of types of enablers to instead focus on their inherent *characteristics* (their *scope* in spatial, temporal, sectoral, and sociodemographic terms, and their *onset* in terms of suddenness and predictability); the varied range of enabling *mechanisms* they offer that can improve supply or increase either demand or the appropriation of the value created; the *opacity* and *agency-intensity* of these mechanisms (i.e., how demanding they are to identify and activate), and the *roles* these mechanisms have in, e.g., shaping the product offered, the organization of the venture, and in facilitating the process of its creation.

This new framework is virgin and potentially fertile ground for important contributions from multiple disciplinary vantage points, including psychology. How do entrepreneurs identify external enablers and their mechanisms? How does this differ between types of entrepreneurial agents (e.g., experts vs. novices; individuals vs. teams; entrepreneurs vs. investors)? How do agent characteristics and experiences influence and perhaps bias what mechanisms and roles are easily identified and which tend to remain unexploited? Which existing psychological theories, measures, and empirical designs can be used to address these questions?

There is great potential for important contributions from psychology here. Much of this would likely be experimental or at least 'laboratory' research. Compared to past research on 'entrepreneurial opportunities' the framework can be helpful in thinking through what characteristics are truly objective and how they can be represented in the research. This would serve to avoid, for example, assigning 'objective' characteristics like '75 percent chance of success', which in real life can only be a subjective assessment. Furthermore, the framework encourages much more detailed assessment of the stimulus (idea description; scenario) than just an overall evaluation of the degree to which it represents an opportunity. For example, the research can probe into what particular mechanisms for what particular ventures more and less qualified participants identify in an EE, as well as what role this mechanism has, and at what stage of the venture's development.

The reader is probably better equipped than I am for suggesting precisely how to integrate interesting ideas from psychological theory into such research. Although it predated the EE concept, the exemplary study by Grégoire and Shepherd (2012), described in Exhibit 20.1, can provide some inspiration.

The article *Technology-market combinations and the identification of entrepreneurial opportunities: An investigation of the opportunity-individual nexus* is exemplary in a number of ways. It addresses variance in both 'opportunities' and agents, explicitly building on Shane and Venkataraman's (2000) nexus idea. In addressing opportunity variance the authors do not – like some other 'opportunity recognition' research – represent this as variance in a common-sense-based, ad hoc selection of characteristics of hypothetical opportunities. Instead, the relevant opportunity variance is derived from cognitive psychological theory and empirically represented as *structural* vs. *superficial alignment* of supply and demand elements that may indicate opportunities. Alignment is systematically manipulated with the use of actual human needs and real, new technologies – e.g., increased diagnosing of ADHD in children and improved knowledge about their learning needs on the demand side, and new technology developed for other purposes as a potential way of addressing this on the supply side. These demand and supply representations can be seen as examples of external enablers. Identifying these real-world materials to use in the experiments is in itself a research feat.

The authors develop hypotheses about how structural and superficial alignment relate to the development of positive opportunity beliefs. On the agent-side they test moderating effects of entrepreneurial intentions and prior knowledge. In so doing, they build directly on prior entrepreneurship research (e.g., Shane, 2000). They test the hypotheses with a rigorous, within-subject experimental design and use entrepreneurially experienced individuals – not students or some other easily accessible group – as participants. Despite pre-dating the reproducibility crisis they test their hypotheses in two experiments rather than one. Throughout, the research is indicative of a careful, thoughtful research process geared toward finding meaningful truths about the phenomenon rather than aiming for the fastest way to a successful publication. Nevertheless, the work was eventually published in a top, mainstream outlet, giving it the chance to attain the influence it deserves.

Within and beyond what is directly addressed in the experiments the focus on varying type and degree of alignment opens up for non-obvious insights that are likely to be teach- and learnable. Akin to the notion of opacity in the external enabler framework (Davidsson, Recker & von Briel, 2020) the research highlights the possibility that new venture ideas based on structurally aligned enablers require more knowledge, effort and creativity to be identified, but it also seems quite plausible that they would be inherently more valuable and become part of ventures that stand out more from the competition. If this is the case, and if identification of structural alignment (and some caution against 'mere' superficial alignment) can be trained, this would seem a major opportunity at the heartland of entrepreneurship education. In all, Grégoire & Shepherd (2012) is an inspiring example of applying psychological theory to core, under-researched entrepreneurship issues in creatively conceived experiments, leading to non-obvious insights that appear teach- and learnable and which might offer competitive advantages for those who learn and apply them. However, the study does not provide all the answers needed to reach these conclusions; a follow-on program of research would be needed for these speculations to evolve into a reliable evidence-base.

EXHIBIT 20.1 Exemplary Psychological Research on External Enablers: Grégoire and Shepherd (2012)

Entrepreneurship as Process

Taking a Process Perspective

A process perspective on new venture creation highlights issues of timing and temporality, recursion, sequence, causal order, critical events, pivoting, and path-dependence as well as demarcations of start- and endpoints and the stages, milestones, and transitions between them. At the time of this writing, the author is involved in a comprehensive review of process-focused entrepreneurship research.[3] On the basis of this ongoing work, it can be said that despite much agreement on the soundness and importance of a process perspective on new venture creation, theoretical ideas, and empirical evidence on these issues remain rather thin. As yet, there does not really exist a unified stream and paradigm of research on entrepreneurship as process. So there is much interesting work still to be done!

In their short note, Shane and Venkataraman (2000) mentioned but did not have much room to elaborate on the process nature of entrepreneurship. Their simple depiction of the process as consisting of *discovery* followed by *exploitation* conjured the image of a particular type of orderly process where the entrepreneurial artifact (to be) is precisely defined at the outset of the journey. Subsequent research has portrayed a more dynamic and iterative process (Alvarez & Barney, 2007; Furr, Cavarretta, & Garg, 2012; Sarasvathy, 2001; Wood & McKinley, 2010) but these attempts often remain insular and descriptive whereas quantitative research with few exceptions (e.g., Lichtenstein, Carter, Dooley, & Gartner, 2007) mainly relate initial conditions to eventual outcomes without much attention to the process itself. Although the use of longitudinal data has grown significantly, entrepreneurship research has not yet 'nailed' how to deal with process conceptually, that is, how to ask pertinent research questions about the process and how to conceptualize and measure characteristics of the process itself (McMullen & Dimov, 2013).

The most obvious way in which psychological researchers can contribute to entrepreneurship process research is to apply psychological theory and methods to address how characteristics of and events occurring in the process affect the psychological states of founders and how these state changes in turn affect the continuation of the journey. Such research can follow venture creation processes in real time, for example, with Experience Sampling Methodology (Uy, Foo, & Aguinis, 2010). Given the central role of experimentation in psychological research and the increased appetite for it in entrepreneurship, multiperiod experiments are another interesting alternative. An exemplar of psychological entrepreneurship process research is presented in Exhibit 20.2. Another exemplar worth mentioning is Grimes (2018) case-based study of the sometimes painful wrestling with psychological ownership, identity, and making feedback-based changes to the new venture idea during the new venture creation process.

Delineating the Venture Creation Process and Identifying Its Method Challenges

When doing research on the entrepreneurial process, a good starting point is to define what one means by that expression. Our ongoing review shows that many studies are exceedingly vague in defining this, to the detriment of knowledge

Just like the article in Exhibit 1, the exemplary process research article was published in a top, mainstream management journal, securing for it the influence it deserves. In *"I put in effort, therefore I am passionate": Investigating the path from effort to passion in entrepreneurship,* Gielnik et al. (2015) address the process issues of sequence and causal order. Starting from the increasingly popular notion of entrepreneurial passion (Cardon, Wincent, Singh, & Drnovsek, 2009) the article's vantage point is a non-obvious and mildly provocative research question: does the received view, i.e., that passion drives effort, which drives outcomes, really tell the whole story? Could it perhaps be that effort leads to passion rather than the other way around? It is a thought reminiscent of a classic idea from the early days of psychology as an academic discipline, namely William James' turning things around with the assertion "I am afraid because I run away" (Myers, 1969).

Building on psychological theories of self-regulation and self-perception, the authors outline an alternative causal sequence in which entrepreneurial effort leads to a feeling of passion for the entrepreneurial endeavor – but only if the effort is rewarded with making tangible progress in the process. That is, new venture progress acts as mediator between effort and passion. In addition, the authors theorize that this mediated effect is stronger if entrepreneurship is a free choice, i.e., it should be weaker for so called 'necessity entrepreneurs' (Block & Wagner, 2010). To test this model, they conduct a weekly field study with 54 entrepreneurs over eight weeks. This type of intense, process study remains rare in entrepreneurship research (cf. Foo, Uy, & Baron, 2009). Consistent with the notion that the core of entrepreneurship is the journey from non-existence to existence, the participants' ventures were early-stage efforts not yet operating in the market on a regular basis. As expected of well-trained psychologists, considerable attention was given to the quality of operationalizations of the studied research variables. A fully cross-lagged design was used in the data collection. The results supported a causal flow from effort to passion with a one-week time lag, whereas no significant effect of passion on effort was found.

Studying real entrepreneurs pursuing their own ventures over time gives the study credibility, but as the authors are aware, the evidence for causation is tentative and the causal mechanisms not tested directly. Therefore, they undertake a second study in which the mechanisms are quite cleverly manipulated in an experimental–causal–chain design. Adding this second study they achieved full support for their theorized model, including mediation by progress and moderation by free choice. On the downside, the experimental study used undergraduate students as participants. However, in combination the two studies build quite convincing evidence in support of the hypothesized model.

Sorting out the causal order of passion, effort and outcomes is important and has direct implications for entrepreneurial strategy and training. It also points to something that may have much more general applicability. For example, is it as important as we sometimes think that PhD students select a topic they are passionate about? Isn't it often the case that what one commits to becomes interesting and even absorbing (i.e., a matter of passion) once one starts to devote serious effort to it?

While the study is processual and set within the venture creation process, Gielnik et al. (2015) do not address the 'whole process' from initiation to 'final' outcome. Instead, Gielnik and collaborators wisely address other aspects of the role of passion in the venture creation process in another, related study (Gielnik, Funken & Bischoff, 2017).

EXHIBIT 20.2   Exemplary Psychological Research on Entrepreneurship as Process: Gielnik, Spitzmuller, Schmitt, Klemann, and Frese (2015) accumulation across studies and often to the detriment of the individual studies themselves. If we take as the starting point that entrepreneurship is about the journey from nonexistence of new business ventures, then we can make the label for the research a bit more precise and call it 'the venture creation process.' I would recommend this, because 'entrepreneurial process' can justifiably be understood in many different ways.

But when does the venture creation process begin and end? When does something start to move from nonexistence to new venture existence, and when is that process completed? In the constant flow of reality, there is no indisputable right way of making such distinctions. For research purposes, it is nevertheless useful to make them (cf. McMullen & Dimov, 2013; Pentland, 1999).

I have come to the conclusion that it is fruitful to consider the venture creation process started when someone both has the *intent* of starting a new venture and is taking *concrete action* toward its realization. This dual emphasis on intent and action was observed in an early, insightful article by Katz and Gartner (1988) and its importance was further highlighted in an early and influential process study by Bhave (1994). The latter found, contrary to widespread belief at the time, that business founders often did not start with a wish to start a business, followed by a search for the right idea on which to base it. Instead, they first identified and solved a problem related to their work, hobby, medical condition, or life situation and only then realized that the solution was needed by others and could be the basis of a business (cf. Shah & Tripsas, 2007). If one were to take the first action these people took to solve their problem as the start of the venture creation process, then one should also include every other hobbyist or other potential 'user entrepreneur' on the basis that they *might* turn their solution into a business at some future point. This is untenable.

At the other end of the spectrum, those who express a dream, ambition, aspiration, willingness, or intention to start a business without ever doing anything to bring this to realization hardly deserve to be included in a sample of new venture creation processes. Intentions predict behavior and do so also in the domain of entrepreneurship (Kautonen, van Gelderen, & Fink, 2015) but not with near enough precision to consider every case of an expressed intention the start of a venture creation process. For these reasons, the dual criteria of intent and action are needed.

Past research within the Panel Study of Entrepreneurial Dynamics (PSED) and Global Entrepreneurship Monitor (GEM) paradigms has developed detailed protocols for distinguishing among underqualified, qualified, and overqualified cases of being in the venture creation process (Davidsson & Steffens, 2011; Reynolds, 2009). These protocols are useful vantage points that can be adapted and applied in future research. Although the PSED and GEM projects aimed at nationally representative samples, a similar type of screening procedure can be applied to more homogenous and theory-driven samples.

Except for processes ending in abandonment of the venture creation process, defining the endpoint of the journey can be even more contentious. It is, after all, an ongoing activity where the business will continue to develop and 'become' after it has fulfilled some criterion for having graduated from emerging to established business. But the field of entrepreneurship should not try to appropriate all of 'business'—there are other subfields that study the strategies and management of established organizations—and empirical studies cannot continue forever. The venture creation process endpoint that I find conceptually most appealing is the point where the venture has recouped all its development costs with revenue from its product market (Davidsson, 2016b, p. 203). Running the business from that point forward is arguably more a matter of management and strategy than of entrepreneurship. However, this criterion has yet to be operationalized and applied in empirical research. What prior empirical research has used is either the entrepreneurs' subjective assessment that the business is now 'up and running' or some more objective criterion indicating the regular and sustainable presence in the market such as having revenues that cover running costs on a regular basis (Lichtenstein et al., 2007).

The emphasis I have here given process start- and endpoints are not to suggest that every psychological study of venture creation processes should capture the entire process. Although we need research with such a broad perspective as well, we know that research focusing on some sub-process within that process can be more manageable and easier to succeed with. In fact, the two process studies singled out as exemplary earlier do not address 'the new venture creation as a whole'. Rather, they study a sub-process of the venture creation journey or add some temporality-based insight to a variable relationship within it, and such 'partial' process coverage is what our ongoing review suggests is becoming the norm.

However, sub-process research on, for example, networking and social capital strongly suggests that there is a strong interdependence between what happens and what is critical in the sub-process and the stage of development of the venture overall (Hayter, 2016; Hung, 2006; Larson & Starr, 1993). Focusing on a sub-process thus does not imply permission to ignore the progression of the overall process. Moreover, without stringent criteria for start- and endpoints, a study might come to include cases that are either under- or overqualified compared to one's theoretical definition of the venture creation process. This typically leads to weaker and perhaps confusing results. Furthermore, nonnegligible temporal heterogeneity will remain even if all cases adhere to the theoretical definition; it is simply not possible to include all cases on the day they first show both intention and behavioral evidence of qualifying. Experience has shown that this heterogeneity is best controlled through the inclusion of an assessment of how many essential activities have already been undertaken or milestones have been completed, not with the mere passage of time (Davidsson & Gordon, 2012).

Furthermore, closely related to the questions of start- and endpoints is the question of duration. There are two important method issues related to this. First, the sampling of 'currently ongoing venture creation processes' will lead to an oversampling of processes that are long in duration, because each of the long processes is eligible for sampling over a longer period and therefore more of these are eligible at any given time. However, this can be corrected for (Shim & Davidsson, 2018). Second, ventures starting with higher ambition and/or higher potential may take longer to complete (Samuelsson & Davidsson, 2009). This means that within the study's time window, high-potential ventures can appear less successful, although they may, in fact, become the group showing superior outcomes further down the line. Psychological research may be able to avoid this issue by focusing on psychological effects rather than business outcomes, but it cannot be ruled out that similar method artifacts stemming from temporal heterogeneity may pertain to psychological outcomes as well.

The Substantive Content of the Research

Many different process characteristics and events and many types of psychological states are conceivable foci for venture creation process research. Regarding the former, the methods challenges mentioned earlier suggest that process characteristics such as *duration* and *pace* are important. Few previous studies have been built around such abstracted process notions, that is, concepts capturing how the process pans out over time without getting into detail of the behavioral content of the process. An interesting example that has attracted some following is provided by Lichtenstein et al. (2007), who focus on the *timing, rate*, and *concentration* of 'gestation activities' without regard to what specific activities were undertaken.

Prior research has shown that a focus on manifest actions makes the research end up overly descriptive (of possibly idiosyncratic cases) or leads to the unhelpful conclusion that 'the process is messy' (cf. Liao & Welsch, 2008). Even without going to Lichtenstein et al.'s extreme, abstracted conceptualizations that meaningfully group actions into categories are preferable, as they allow effective knowledge accumulation. Previously tried distinctions include 'discovery' versus 'exploitation' (Shane & Venkataraman, 2000) and 'intentionality-resources-boundaries-exchange' (Katz & Gartner, 1988). These and others have been rewarded with some level of success, compared to the messy picture that emerges when manifest behaviors are sequenced. However, the grouping labels have often been assigned in arrears to an eclectic collection of actions captured by the research. Future research can do better by tightly aligning the conceptualizations and operationalizations from the very start.

Concerning what psychological phenomena to research and what psychological theories to apply, the reader may have better ideas than what I can suggest. This said, of central interest would be how the process affects and is affected by changes to the entrepreneur's or team's entrepreneurial self-efficacy (Bandura, 1982; Elorriaga Rubio, Mors, & Lerner, 2018; McGee, Peterson, Mueller, & Sequeira, 2009) and their opportunity confidence (Davidsson, 2015). The former refers to belief in one's ability as an entrepreneur, the latter to belief in the new venture idea (the entrepreneurial artifact in the making) in and of itself.

This distinction between confidence in oneself and confidence in one's idea (or emerging venture) has not been made in prior research, and neither concept has been applied in a process context, despite calls for such research. For example, Wood & McKinley (2010, 2017) discuss and present detailed theoretical ideas of how confidence in the idea can wax and wane over time in interaction with stakeholders. To take but one example of the importance of the difference between belief in oneself and belief in one's new venture idea: depending on the nature of feedback from various stakeholders, entrepreneurial self-efficacy and opportunity confidence should be differentially affected. The type and direction of influence should, in turn, influence decisions to increase or decrease resource investments in the venture, making changes to the team or to the new venture idea, the propensity to abandon the start-up, and the inclination to try again with a new idea at a later point in time, among a whole lot else. Of course, entrepreneurs may either over- or underestimate their own entrepreneurial ability, the merits of their idea, or both (Frey & Heggli, 1989; Kruger & Dunning, 1999; Invernizzi, Menozzi, Passarani, Patton, & Viglia, 2017), but as psychology is more geared toward explaining human behavior than business outcomes, the perceptions may be more important than the true qualities.

Conclusion

In this chapter, I have offered some ideas about how researchers with a solid grounding in psychology can contribute to two central yet underdeveloped areas of entrepreneurship research, where entrepreneurship is understood as the creation of new business ventures. The first area concerns the conceptualization of the entrepreneurial artifact, especially before it has become a tangible and sustainable business venture, and how characteristics of that artifact together with those of the entrepreneurial agent determine entrepreneurial action and outcomes. The second area is new venture creation conceived and studied as a process. This entails conceptualizing features of the process itself and studying how psychological factors influence and are influenced by the process.

The two issues are related. Because entrepreneurship is a process of moving from nonexistence to existence, the entrepreneurial artifact is a moving target. During the process, it may evolve from a vague, initial idea and/or external state of conditions into a functional new venture, and this rarely happens in a linear fashion. This malleable nature of the artifact adds interesting research challenges. However, it would be a mistake to believe that the agent is necessarily much more stable. Individuals learn over time, and their confidence in themselves and their project may grow and shrink as the process progresses. Furthermore, many ventures are created by teams that may add and lose members over time as well as being subject to evolving, internal dynamics (Klotz et al., 2014). Moreover, the entire venture may be absorbed by another organization before its creation journey has been completed.

New venture creation is thus a phenomenon that is both fascinating and challenging. I am convinced that as long as they build on the lessons about the phenomenon that entrepreneurship researchers have gained rather than starting from the naïve or otherwise incorrect assumptions about it, psychologists drawing on the treasure trove of their discipline can deal with the challenges and make great contributions to these two core areas of entrepreneurship while at the same time breaking new ground that is appreciated within the psychological discipline.

Notes

1. Shane (2012, p. 15) argues that the definition of opportunities as objectively favorable should be interpreted as only implying that success chances exceed zero. This triggers, on one hand, the question how we can know *that* as an objective fact at the outset, and on the other hand the question what, that is not against the laws of nature, is actually excluded with such a weak criterion? (0.0000001% chance of success is above zero).
2. There is some overlap between NVI and psychological notions of *plan* and *goal* (Austin & Vancouver, 1996; Elavsky, Doerksen, & Conroy, 2012).
3. During production of the present manuscript the review was published as Davidsson & Grünhagen (2020).

References

Aldrich, H. E. (2012). The emergence of entrepreneurship as an academic field: A personal essay on institutional entrepreneurship. *Research Policy, 41*(7), 1240–1248.

Alvarez, S. A., & Barney, J. (2007). Discovery and creation: Alternative theories of entrepreneurial creation. *Strategic Entrepreneurship Journal, 1*(1–2), 11–26.

Alvarez, S. A., & Barney, J. B. (2010). Entrepreneurship and epistemology: The philosophical underpinnings of the study of entrepreneurial opportunities. *Academy of Management Annals, 4*(1), 557–583.

Austin, J. T., & Vancouver, J. B. (1996). Goal constructs in psychology: Structure, process, and content. *Psychological Bulletin, 120*(3), 338.

Bandura, A. (1982). Self-efficacy mechanism in human agency. *American Psychologist, 37*, 122–147.

Bhave, M. P. (1994). A process model of entrepreneurial venture creation. *Journal of Business Venturing, 9*, 223–242.

Block, J. H., & Wagner, M. (2010). Necessity and opportunity entrepreneurs in Germany: Characteristics and earning s differentials. *Schmalenbach Business Review, 62*(2), 154–174.

Cardon, M. S., Wincent, J., Singh, J., & Drnovsek, M. (2009). The nature and experience of entrepreneurial passion. *Academy of Management Review, 34*(3), 511–532.

Dahlqvist, J., & Wiklund, J. (2012). Measuring the market newness of new ventures. *Journal of Business Venturing, 27*(2), 185–196.

Davidsson, P. (2015). Entrepreneurial opportunities and the entrepreneurship nexus: A re-conceptualization. *Journal of Business Venturing, 30*(5), 674–695.

Davidsson, P. (2016a). The field of entrepreneurship research: Some significant developments. In D. Bögenhold, J. Bonnet, M. Dejardin, & D. Garcia Pérez de Lema (Eds.), *Contemporary entrepreneurship* (pp. 17–28). New York: Springer.

Davidsson, P. (2016b). *Researching entrepreneurship: Conceptualization and design* (2nd ed.). New York: Springer.

Davidsson, P. (2017). Reflections on misgivings about "dismantling" the opportunity construct. *Journal of Business Venturing Insights*, 7(C), 65–67.

Davidsson, P. (2019). Guidepost: Look out! See change? Sea change ahead! *Academy of Management Discoveries*. Retrieved from doi.org/10.5465/amd.2019.0141

Davidsson, P., & Gordon, S. R. (2012). Panel studies of new venture creation: A methods-focused review and suggestions for future research. *Small Business Economics*, *39*(4), 853–876.

Davidsson, P., & J. Grünhagen, J. (2020). Fulfilling the process promise: A review and agenda for new venture creation process research. *Entrepreneurship Theory and Practice*. https://doi.org/10.1177/1042258720930991

Davidsson, P., Grégoire, D., & Lex, M. (2018, June). Developing validating and testing a new measure of opportunity confidence. Paper presented at the *BCERC Conference*, Waterford, Ireland.

Davidsson, P., Hunter, E., & Klofsten, M. (2006). Institutional forces: The invisible hand that shapes venture ideas? *International Small Business Journal: Researching Entrepreneurship*, *24*(2), 115–131.

Davidsson, P., Recker, J., & von Briel, F. (2020). External enablement of new venture creation: A framework. *Academy of Management Perspectives*, *34*(3), 311–332.

Davidsson, P., & Steffens, P. (2011). Comprehensive Australian study of entrepreneurial emergence (CAUSEE): Project presentation and early results. In P. D. Reynolds & R. T. Curtin (Eds.), *New business creation* (pp. 27–51). New York: Springer.

Davis, S. F. (Ed.). (2008). *Handbook of research methods in experimental psychology*. Hoboken, NJ: John Wiley & Sons.

Dimov, D. (2010). Nascent entrepreneurs and venture emergence: Opportunity confidence, human capital, and early planning. *Journal of Management Studies*, *47*(6), 1123–1153.

Dimov, D. (2011). Grappling with the unbearable elusiveness of entrepreneurial opportunities. *Entrepreneurship Theory and Practice*, *35*(1), 57–81.

Eckhardt, J. T., & Shane, S. (2010). An update to the individual-opportunity nexus. In Z. J. Acs & D. B. Audretsch (Eds.), *Handbook of entrepreneurship research* (2nd ed., pp. 47–76). New York, NY: Springer.

Elavsky, S., Doerksen, S. E., & Conroy, D. E. (2012). Identifying priorities among goals and plans: A critical psychometric reexamination of the exercise goal-setting and planning/scheduling scales. *Sport, Exercise, and Performance Psychology*, *1*(3), 158.

Elorriaga Rubio, M., Mors, M. L., & Lerner, D. (2018). Collective efficacy and risk-taking in the context of entrepreneurial team competition. *Academy of Management Proceedings*, *18*(1). Retrieved from https://doi.org/ 10.5465/AMBPP.2018.10924abstract

Foo, M.-D., Uy, M. A., & Baron, R. A. (2009). How do feelings influence effort? An empirical study of entrepreneurs' affect and venture effort. *Journal of Applied Psychology*, *94*(4), 1086–1094.

Frey, B. S., & Heggli, B. (1989). An ipsative theory of business behaviour. *Journal of Economic Psychology*, *10*(1), 1–20.

Furr, N. R., Cavarretta, F., & Garg, S. (2012). Who changes course? The role of domain knowledge and novel framing in making technology changes. *Strategic Entrepreneurship Journal*, *6*(3), 236–256.

George, G., & Bock, A. J. (2011). The business model in practice and its implications for entrepreneurship research. *Entrepreneurship Theory and Practice*, *35*(1), 83–111.

Gielnik, M. M., Spitzmuller, M., Schmitt, A., Klemann, D. K., & Frese, M. (2015). "I put in effort, therefore I am passionate": Investigating the path from effort to passion in entrepreneurship. *Academy of Management Journal*, *58*(4), 1012–1031.

Gielnik, M. M., Uy, M. A., Funken, R., & Bischoff, K. M. (2017). Boosting and sustaining passion: A long-term perspective on the effects of entrepreneurship training. *Journal of Business Venturing, 32*(3), 334–353.

Gorgievski, M. J., & Stephan, U. (2016). Advancing the psychology of entrepreneurship: A review of the psychological literature and an introduction. *Applied Psychology, 65*(3), 437–468.

Grégoire, D. A., & Shepherd, D. A. (2012). Technology-market combinations and the identification of entrepreneurial opportunities: An investigation of the opportunity-individual nexus. *Academy of Management Journal, 55*(4), 753–785.

Grimes, M. G. (2018). The pivot: How founders respond to feedback through idea and identity work. *Academy of Management Journal, 61*(5), 1692–1717.

Hayter, C. S. (2016). Constraining entrepreneurial development: A knowledge-based view of social networks among academic entrepreneurs. *Research Policy, 45*(2), 475–490.

Hsu, D. K., Simmons, S. A., & Wieland, A. M. (2017). Designing entrepreneurship experiments: A review, typology, and research agenda. *Organizational Research Methods, 20*(3), 379–412.

Hung, H. (2006). Formation and survival of new ventures: A path from interpersonal to interorganizational networks. *International Small Business Journal: Researching Entrepreneurship, 24*(4), 359–378.

Invernizzi, A. C., Menozzi, A., Passarani, D. A., Patton, D., & Viglia, G. (2017). Entrepreneurial overconfidence and its impact upon performance. *International Small Business Journal: Researching Entrepreneurship, 35*(6), 709–728.

John, O. P., & Srivastava, S. (1999). The Big Five trait taxonomy: History, measurement, and theoretical perspectives. In L. A. Pervin & O. P. John (Eds.), *Handbook of personality: Theory and research* (Vol. 2, pp. 102–138). Amsterdam: Elsevier.

Katz, J., & Gartner, W. B. (1988). Properties of emerging organizations. *Academy of Management Review, 13*(3), 429–441.

Kautonen, T., van Gelderen, M., & Fink, M. (2015). Robustness of the theory of planned behavior in predicting entrepreneurial intentions and actions. *Entrepreneurship Theory and Practice, 39*(3), 655–674.

Klotz, A. C., Hmieleski, K. M., Bradley, B. H., & Busenitz, L. W. (2014). New venture teams: A review of the literature and roadmap for future research. *Journal of Management, 40*(1), 226–255.

Kristof-Brown, A. L., Zimmerman, R. D., & Johnson, E. C. (2005). Consequences of individuals' fit at work: A meta-analysis of person-job: Person-organization, person-group and person-supervisor fit. *Personnel Psychology, 58*(2), 281–342.

Kruger, J., & Dunning, D. (1999). Unskilled and unaware of it: How difficulties in recognizing one's own incompetence lead to inflated self-assessments. *Journal of Personality and Social Psychology, 77*(6), 1121–1134.

Larson, A., & Starr, J. A. (1993). A network model of organization formation. *Entrepreneurship Theory and Practice, 17*(2), 5–15.

Liao, J., & Welsch, H. (2008). Patterns of venture gestation process: Exploring the differences between tech and non-tech Nascent entrepreneurs. *Journal of High Technology Management Research, 19*(2), 103–113.

Lichtenstein, B. B., Carter, N. M., Dooley, K. J., & Gartner, W. B. (2007). Complexity dynamics of nascent entrepreneurship. *Journal of Business Venturing, 22*(2), 236–261.

Maher, M. (2011). Design creativity research: From the individual to the crowd. In T. Taura & Y. Nagai (Eds.), *Design creativity 2010*. London, UK: Springer.

Mason, C., & Stark, M. (2004). What do investors look for in a business plan? A comparison of the investment criteria of bankers, venture capitalists and business angels. *International Small Business Journal: Researching Entrepreneurship, 22*(3), 227–248.

McGee, J. E., Peterson, M., Mueller, S. L., & Sequeira, J. M. (2009). Entrepreneurial self-efficacy: Refining the measure. *Entrepreneurship Theory and Practice, 33*(4), 965–988.

McMullen, J. S. (2019). A wakeup call for the field of entrepreneurship and its evaluators. *Journal of Business Venturing, 34*(3), 413–417.

McMullen, J. S., & Dimov, D. (2013). Time and the entrepreneurial journey: The problems and promise of studying entrepreneurship as a process. *Journal of Management Studies, 50*(8), 1481–1512.

McMullen, J. S., & Shepherd, D. (2006). Entrepreneurial action and the role of uncertainty in the theory of the entrepreneur. *Academy of Management Review, 31*(1), 132–152.

Meyer, M., Libaers, D., Thijs, B., Grant, K., Glänzel, W., & Debackere, K. (2014). Origin and emergence of entrepreneurship as a research field. *Scientometrics, 98*(1), 473–485.

Myers, G. E. (1969). William James's theory of emotion. *Transactions of the Charles S. Peirce Society, 5*(2), 67–89.

Pentland, B. T. (1999). Building process theory with narrative: From description to explanation. *Academy of Management Review, 24*(4), 711–724.

Reymen, I. M., Andries, P., Berends, H., Mauer, R., Stephan, U., & Van Burg, E. (2015). Understanding dynamics of strategic decision making in venture creation: A process study of effectuation and causation. *Strategic Entrepreneurship Journal, 9*(4), 351–379.

Reynolds, P. D. (2009). Screening item effects in estimating the prevalence of Nascent entrepreneurs. *Small Business Economics, 33*(2), 151–163.

Rogers, E. M. (1995). *Diffusion of innovations* (4th ed.). New York: The Free Press.

Samuelsson, M., & Davidsson, P. (2009). Does venture opportunity variation matter? Investigating systematic process differences between innovative and imitative new ventures. *Small Business Economics, 33*(2), 229–255.

Sarason, Y., Dillard, J. F., & Dean, T. (2010). How can we know the dancer from the dance? Reply to "Entrepreneurship as the structuration of individual and opportunity: A response using a critical realist perspective" (Mole and Mole, 2008). *Journal of Business Venturing, 25*(2), 238–243.

Sarasvathy, S. D. (2001). Causation and effectuation: Toward a theoretical shift from economic inevitability to entrepreneurial contingency. *Academy of Management Review, 26*(2), 243–263.

Scheaf, D. J., Loignon, A. C., Webb, J. W., Heggestad, E. D., & Wood, M. S. (2020). Measuring opportunity evaluation: Conceptual synthesis and scale development. *Journal of Business Venturing, 35*(2). Retrieved from doi.org/10.1016/j.jbusvent.2019.04.003

Shah, S. K., & Tripsas, M. (2007). The accidental entrepreneur: The emergent and collective process of user entrepreneurship. *Strategic Entrepreneurship Journal, 1*(1-2), 123–140.

Shane, S. A. (2000). Prior knowledge and the discovery of entrepreneurial opportunities. *Organization Science, 11*(4), 448–469.

Shane, S. A. (2012). Reflections on the 2010 AMR Decade Award: Delivering on the promise of entrepreneurship as a field of research. *Academy of Management Review, 37*(1), 10–20.

Shane, S. A., & Venkataraman, S. (2000). The promise of entrepreneurship as a field of research. *Academy of Management Review, 25*(1), 217–226.

Shepherd, D. A., & Grégoire, D. A. (2012). *Entrepreneurial opportunities.* Cheltenham, UK: Edward Elgar Publishing.

Shim, J., & Davidsson, P. (2018). Shorter than we thought: The duration of venture creation processes. *Journal of Business Venturing Insights, 9*, 10–16.

Shugan, S. M. (2007). Errors in the variables, unobserved heterogeneity, and other ways of hiding statistical error. *Marketing Science, 25*(3), 203–216.

Uy, M. A., Foo, M.-D., & Aguinis, H. (2010). Using experience sampling methodology to advance entrepreneurship theory and research. *Organizational Research Methods, 13*(1), 31–54.

Wiklund, J., & Shepherd, D. A. (2008). Portfolio entrepreneurship: Habitual and novice founders, new entry, and mode of organizing. *Entrepreneurship Theory and Practice, 32*(4), 701–725.

Williams, D. W., Wood, M. S., Mitchell, J. R., & Urbig, D. (2019). Applying experimental methods to advance entrepreneurship research: On the need for and publication of experiments. *Journal of Business Venturing, 34*(2), 215–223.

Wood, M. S., McKelvie, A., & Haynie, J. M. (2014). Making it personal: Opportunity individuation and the shaping of opportunity beliefs. *Journal of Business Venturing, 29*(2), 252–272.

Wood, M. S., & McKinley, W. (2010). The production of entrepreneurial opportunity: A constructivist perspective. *Strategic Entrepreneurship Journal, 4*(1), 66–84.

Wood, M. S., & McKinley, W. (2017). After the venture: The reproduction and destruction of entrepreneurial opportunity. *Strategic Entrepreneurship Journal, 11*(1), 18–35.

Wood, M. S., & Williams, D. W. (2014). Opportunity evaluation as rule-based decision making. *Journal of Management Studies, 51*(4), 573–602.

Zott, C., Amit, R., & Massa, L. (2011). The business model: Recent developments and future research. *Journal of Management, 37*(4), 1019–1042.

21

THE PSYCHOLOGY OF ENTREPRENEURSHIP

Looking 10 Years Back and 10 Years Ahead

Melissa S. Cardon, Dean A. Shepherd & Robert Baron

When reading the chapters leading up to this one, it is clear that research in the space broadly defined as the "psychology of entrepreneurship" has come quite a long way in the past 10 years since the first volume of this book was published. While many topics remain relevant (competencies, cognition, action-orientation, leadership, training, and innovation), the conversation has also shifted to include new topics such as emotions and affect, psychological disorders, biology, identity, well-being, and teams. Our methodological sophistication in terms of what we can accomplish with web scraping, python, and modeling complicated dynamic, multilevel, and recursive relationships has grown exponentially. The next 10 years will likely demonstrate equally unparalleled growth in what we are thinking about, how we are thinking about it, and how we develop, operationalize, and test our models through inductive, abductive, and deductive processes (O'Kane, Smith, & Lerman, 2019). What we find most fascinating in both looking back at the progress we have made in the past 10 years as a field, as well as looking ahead to the next 10 years and beyond, are the commonalities and streams of ideas that transcend past, present, and future, as well as the specific topic areas of research being described in this volume and elsewhere. We comment first on the ties that bind our work together before exploring topics, ideas, and questions that we might explore well into the future.

The Ties That Bind Our Work Together

Entrepreneurship is about people within unique and critical contexts. Over 20 years ago, Gartner (1989) challenged us all to think beyond "who is the entrepreneur" to understand more complex phenomenon of what entrepreneurs do and why, how they act, think, and feel, and how these may rely upon what it is that they are trying to accomplish. In each of the chapters in this volume, the message is clear that it is not just about who the entrepreneur is in terms of traits or static characteristics that helps us understand their world, but a combination of who the entrepreneur is within their social world, the tasks they need to accomplish, the stakeholders with whom they interact, the goals they strive to achieve, and the ventures that they form and/or work within.

Entrepreneurs are incredibly heterogeneous in who they are and the types of firms they are part of. For many years, the fascination of our field was on the high-tech, high-performing "gazelles" (Birch, Haggerty, & Parsons, 1995), while in the past decade, the very broad definition of entrepreneurship (Shane & Venkataraman, 2000; Venkataraman, 1997) has been more wholly embraced in our research. In 2016, Welter, Baker, and Audretsch (2017), encouraged us to "embrace entrepreneurial diversity" in order to improve our theoretical and practical insights concerning why and how entrepreneurship emerges, and with what effects. Evidence of the broadened reach of what we consider "entrepreneurship" is the explosion of studies on individuals who put nascent ideas and unproven products on social internet sites and end up receiving considerable funding, at best, and valuable market feedback, at worst (see Chapter 12 on Crowdfunding; also the ET&P Virtual Special Issue on Crowd-Funded Entrepreneurial Opportunities). The stream of work on entrepreneurial opportunities (e.g., McMullen & Shepherd, 2006; Wood, McKelvie, & Haynie, 2014; Wood & McKinley, 2010; Wood & Williams, 2014) is also evidence that previous notions of entrepreneurs being just those that found firms have broadened (see also Chapter 7 in this volume). In Chapter 20, Davidsson explains how the emerging entrepreneurial artifact—the elements of what eventually may become a fully functional venture—are as important as those of the entrepreneurial agent him- or herself. Thus, entrepreneurship not only is about entrepreneurs, very broadly defined, but is also about the processes they go through, the opportunities they create, discover, and/or evaluate, and the firms that may (or may not) eventually form.

This framework is also important in another respect—it helps us answer a question often asked by our colleagues in other branches of management: "What makes entrepreneurship unique? What does it provide that we don't already have?" One answer to this question, and one that fits closely with the focus of our research, is this: Entrepreneurship focuses on the emergence and early development of new businesses. In contrast, other branches of management direct their attention primarily to events and processes occurring in existing, often large and mature organizations. It is this focus on what could be termed "beginnings" that makes entrepreneurship unique, and also a foundation for other branches of management.

New Research Areas That Have Arisen in the Last 10 Years and the Courses They May Take

While many of the same topics discussed in the previous edition of this book are also discussed in this volume since they are still prevalent and important conversations in the literature, many topics have emerged and risen in focus and prominence in the last ten years. We touch on a few of them here, including identity, affect, nonfinancial outcomes such as well-being, psychological diversity, biology, and entrepreneurial teams.

Identity

The topic of identity does not appear in the original edition of this book on the psychology of entrepreneurship. Although research on social identity theory (Tajfel & Turner, 1979) and role identity theory (Stryker, 1980) has been ongoing for over 40 years in psychology and sociology, respectively, its incorporation into entrepreneurship has been much more recent (Cardon, Wincent, Singh, & Drnovsek, 2009; Fauchart & Gruber, 2011; Murnieks, 2007; Powell & Baker, 2014, 2017; Tripathi, Zhu, Jacob, Frese, & Gielnik, in press). Yet the explosion of work has been profound, with over 175 papers published about the identity of entrepreneurs in the past two decades (Mmbaga, Mathias, Williams, & Cardon, 2020). As Baker and Powell point out in Chapter 10 of this volume, this rapid increase of work has unfortunately had "shallow roots", where researchers are not always full attending to the deep and complex psychological and sociological origins of identity theories. As a result, the definitions used are often inconsistent and sometimes contradictory. Yet despite these challenges, we have also made large advancements as a field in understanding the multiple different identities that may exist for entrepreneurs (e.g., Fauchart & Gruber, 2011; Mathias & Williams, 2018) and entrepreneurial teams (Powell & Baker, 2017), how they are formed through identity work (e.g., Crosina, 2018; Grimes, 2018), how they are expressed through identity narratives (e.g., Martens, Jennings, & Jennings, 2007), and the impact of identities on social entrepreneurship (e.g., Conger, McMullen, Bergman, & York, 2018), emotional experiences (e.g., Cardon et al., 2009), and responses to adversity (Powell & Baker, 2014), among other critical aspects of entrepreneurship. We encourage those interested in understanding and building deeper roots in identity theory to read Chapter 10 by Baker and Powell.

Although research on identity and entrepreneurs has grown considerably, we see several avenues for development in the next 10 years. First, while we might argue about the definition of entrepreneurship (because it reflects who we are as scholars), we also know that how people see themselves as entrepreneurs and how people see others as entrepreneurs differs across contexts, and these differences matter. Future research will help advance the field of entrepreneurship by exploring the role of identity on actions that they believe to be entrepreneurial whether others from other contexts believe it to be entrepreneurial or not. For example, we appreciate identity research moving beyond resource-abundant high-tech start-ups to investigating entrepreneurship in resource-constrained environments (Powell & Baker, 2014; Shepherd, Saade, & Wincent, 2020). We look forward to future research further exploring the role of identity on entrepreneurial action in highly adverse environments. Such research could also examine the fact that individuals often construct their self-identities out of the views about them expressed by others. For instance, in many countries, there is a very positive stereotype of entrepreneurs: they are seen as creative, energetic, willing to accept high risks, and, often, as the 'heroic figure' who succeeds against all odds and despite strong rejection of their ideas. An example is Elon Musk, who is widely viewed as an entrepreneur who possesses all these characteristics. Upon reflecting on these views, Musk and many other entrepreneurs, including ones who are not highly successful or famous, may come to accept these stereotypes and develop very positive self-identities. The way the world views them, in short, influences how they view themselves (e.g., Ellemers, Spears, & Doosje, 2002). Yet in other countries, such positive views of entrepreneurs may not exist, and this likely impacts individuals and activities they engage in. We see great promise in further exploration of how reflected identities (how others see us; Stryker, 2008) and identity prototypes based on famous highly successful entrepreneur influence aspiring entrepreneurs' self-identities and identity work during new venture creation.

Second, and consistent with the exploration of entrepreneurial identities in resource-constrained (and adverse) environments, is the need to theorize about identity on different levels of analysis (or across levels of analysis). For example, rather than focus on the role of an individual's identity in the creation of a new organization, there are research opportunities to build on the notion of the community as the entrepreneurial actor (Peredo & Chrisman, 2006). How do communities differ in their entrepreneur-related identities, how are a community's multiple identities managed to facilitate its entrepreneurial actions, and to what effect? Cross-level research can explore how these community-level identities are created, developed, and propagated (individuals, organizations, and/or national culture) and how they impact the identity of members (individuals and organizations) of that community. There is much to learn about the role of community in fostering entrepreneurial action, especially in developing economies, and identity researchers are well positioned to generate important new insights.

Finally, as more scholars recognize entrepreneurial action as both a tool for good and for bad, hopefully greater scholarly attention will be focused on explaining the bad. How does identity enable (or fail to obstruct) entrepreneurial actions that destroy nature and harm others? It could be that identity focuses attention on financial performance (e.g., Darwinians [Fauchart and Gruber, 2011])—away from the environment and community—such that the environment and community are collateral damage. However, perhaps identity plays a more direct role on entrepreneurial actions that cause harm to nature and community, for example, an entrepreneurial identity as villain or notorious or countercultural or science-denier and so on. It is only by understanding the dark side of identities that we can begin to gain a full understanding of their implications for entrepreneurship.

Affect

While emotions have always been an important aspect of the entrepreneurial journey, this topic was also not explicitly included in the previous edition of *The Psychology of Entrepreneurship* published in 2007. Yet an "affect revolution" seems to have mounted with the publication of Baron's 2008 paper on the role of affect in the entrepreneurial process, which was followed by theoretical (Cardon et al., 2009) and empirical (Chen, Yao, & Kotha, 2009; Foo, Uy, & Baron, 2009) work encouraging the study of different types of affect (positive affect, negative affect, and passion, among others) and their influences and antecedents related to different aspects of entrepreneurship. As noted in the review of this literature provided in Chapter 3 (Huang et al., this volume), research on both experienced affect and displayed affect has burgeoned in the past decade and a half, yielding at least 70 journal articles across top journals, the majority of which are empirical. Also noteworthy is the large literature we now have on grief, failure, and exit, which has expanded substantially since Shepherd's (2003) paper on grief associated with firm failure, and DeTienne's and Wennberg's work on exit (DeTienne, 2010; Wennberg, Wiklund, DeTienne, & Cardon, 2010). Action theory (Chapter 11) also emphasizes the important role of errors. As Jenkins and Byrne explain in Chapter 14 of this volume, failure and exit are distinct ideas, and the emotional and other psychological processes preceding and subsequent to each can be profound.

Despite the rapidly growing body of research on affect of entrepreneurs, several areas remain unexplored. First, we hope future research continues to explore affect at the team level. We have all worked in teams; some of which were good, some were bad, and some were like a roller-coaster ride. How is the team affect different from the aggregate of each members' specific affect (e.g., team entrepreneurial passion; Boone, Adries, & Clarysse, 2019; Cardon, Post, & Forster, 2017; Santos & Cardon, 2019) or diversity of that affect among team members (e.g., passion diversity; de Mol, Cardon, de Jong, Khapova, & Elfring, 2019)? Why is this team-member affect gap greater in some teams than others, and to what effect? It is important to theoretically and empirically investigate the creation of a team's affect, the maintenance of that affect and changes in team affect. Cross-level research is going to be important to explore the individual-level antecedents (affective, cognitive, decision-making, and so on) of team-level affect and how team-level affect impacts individual-level variables (affect, cognitive processing, decision-making, and so on). We hope cross-level research will continue to build and test theories across three levels of affect—the individual, team, and organization.

Second, as research focuses on entrepreneurs engaging communities of inquiry to co-construct potential opportunities (Seyb, Shepherd, & Williams, 2019; Shepherd et al., 2020), scholarly attention within this stream of research will begin to move beyond the cognitive aspects of engagement to explore the interactive effects of affect and cognition (hot cognition). For example, how do entrepreneurs generate positive emotional reactions amongst potential users of a new technology? Fortunately, such research on interpersonal affective reactions can build on the "transmission" of affect in successful crowdfunding campaigns (Davis, Hmieleski, Webb, & Coombs, 2017; Li, Chen, Kotha, & Fisher, 2017) or with employees (Breugst, Domurath, Patzelt, & Klaukien, 2012; Hubner, Baum, & Frese, 2019). Furthermore, while it is important to understand affect within an entrepreneurial team and how an entrepreneurial team can generate positive affect in a community of inquiry or community of practice, future research can also focus more exclusively on the community of inquiry itself. Does the community of inquiry experience or display affect separately from its members, and if so, how does that affect influence the community members' affect, the community's actions toward the entrepreneurial venture, and the entrepreneurial team's subsequent affect? Entrepreneurs are embedded in communities in which they interact with many stakeholders, and there is benefit in studying the affect of people that are not entrepreneurs but are nonetheless involved in the entrepreneurial process.

Third, future research can also continue to examine the interplay between entrepreneurs' affect and cognition. Many studies (primarily in the field of social psychology) have investigated this issue, and the general conclusion is, not surprisingly, that our thoughts influence our feelings, and our feelings, in turn, influence our thoughts (Baron & Branscombe, 2017). Applied to entrepreneurs, for instance, if they have very strong positive feelings (i.e., positive affect) about their ideas for new products or services, this my lead them to hold high, perhaps unrealistic, expectations about the appeal of these products to potential customers (entrepreneurs are sometimes in love with their own ideas). These strong positive feelings then shape their expectations—an important aspect of their cognition. Similarly, an entrepreneur who thinks over and over again (i.e., ruminates) about the consequences of potential failure may experience strong negative affect that may then, in turn, interfere with her or his ability to make effective presentations to venture capitalists or potential customers. Future studies could investigate the complex but intimate relationships between affect and cognition to provide new insights into such processes as entrepreneurs' decision-making, developing strategies for gaining competitive advantage, and many other important aspects of entrepreneurship.

Finally, while there are some hints that positive emotions are not always positive for entrepreneurial outcomes (Baron, Hmieleski and Henry, 2012) and that negative emotions are not always negative for entrepreneurial outcomes (Shepherd, 2003; Shepherd, Patzelt, & Wolfe, 2011), much more research is needed on this topic. For example, high creativity can result when a person experiences negative affect followed by an "affective shift", where negative affect is decreased and positive affect is increased (Bledow, Rosing, & Frese, 2013). Research on "dual-tuning" (George & Jing, 2007; George, Jing, & Zhou, 2002) and "dual pathways" (De Dreu, Baas, & Nijstad, 2008) also suggests positive outcomes can occur from both positive and negative affective experiences. This work leads to questions, such as: When is an entrepreneur's positive affect a liability, why, and how can this liability be managed to minimize its negative consequences? When is an entrepreneur's negative affect an asset, why, and how can this asset best be accessed and deployed for entrepreneurial benefit? Furthermore, given the ups and downs of the entrepreneurial journey, there are future research opportunities to explore the relationship between positive and negative affect. Some scholars suggest that positive emotions can undo negative emotions (Fredrickson, Mancuso, Branigan, & Tugade, 2000), but this would not be a good outcome for those instances when negative emotions are an asset. Even when entrepreneurs want their positive emotions to undo negative emotions, how are some able to generate positive emotions (to undo negative emotions) when facing adversity that generated the negative emotions in the first place? There is much important research required on this topic.

Nonfinancial Outcomes

The last decade of research has seen much more emphasis on outcomes of entrepreneurship other than, or in addition to, financial success. The notion that entrepreneurship has a substantial impact on much more than pursuing or achieving financial gain or rapid growth is mentioned in several chapters in this volume, such as those on competencies (van Gelderen, Chapter 12) and affect (Huang et al., Chapter 3), and is particularly discussed in Chapter 19 by Bort and colleagues. Entrepreneurship has substantial impacts on individual well-being, including both feeling well (the hedonic approach) and living well (the eudaimonic approach; Bort et al., this volume; Stephan, 2018). As is pointed out in Chapter 19, the well-being of entrepreneurs also has a substantial symbiotic relationship with the well-being of other stakeholders such as employees, family members, resource providers, customers, and society at large. Recognizing this, scholars have turned their attention to critical issues such as how entrepreneurs manage their stress (Lerman, Munyon, & Carr, in press), the trade-offs between physical health and financial health (Cardon & Patel, 2015), and mental health (Wiklund, Hatak, Patzelt, & Shepherd, 2018) as both input to and outcome from entrepreneurial activity.

We fully endorse this research movement toward nonfinancial outcomes from entrepreneurial activity. Of note is that non-financial outcomes are often very important to entrepreneurs; we cannot really get a full understanding of entrepreneurship without including the outcomes entrepreneurs themselves seek. Attaining these nonfinancial goals is how, in a way, entrepreneurs evaluate their own success, although we as outside observers often tend to evaluate that success in financial terms. Future research will hopefully continue this trend of assessing both financial and nonfinancial motives and outcomes from entrepreneurship. Not to deviate from (or contradict) this message, we note that critics could argue that such research leads to a fragmented body of knowledge that obstructs knowledge accumulation. The same argument of fragmentation and generalizability can be targeted at more contextualized research and other middle-range theories. To such arguments we suggest that future research begin to theorize across "similar" nonfinancial outcomes to begin to develop and test more general theories of entrepreneurship, to offer "literature review"–style papers that seek to elucidate patterns across finer-grained studies and perform meta-analyses that accommodate different operationalizations of nonfinancial outcomes. By providing such synthesized knowledge, future research could contribute to our understanding of nonfinancial outcomes of entrepreneurship on two fronts—continuing to develop and extend middle-range theories (i.e., with more specific dependent variables) and reviewing and/or theorizing across these studies (e.g., see Chapter 18) to elucidate the bigger picture.

Psychological Disorders and Their Potential Unexpected Positive Benefits

Related to mental health as an important nonfinancial outcome from entrepreneurship is the evolution of research into how psychological and mental health may enhance or inhibit entrepreneurial action and outcomes. Insights from clinical psychology and other fields have been integrated into entrepreneurship research in complex and unanticipated ways. As Lerner and colleagues explore in Chapter 4, a number of clinical conditions such as attention-deficit/hyperactivity disorder (ADHD), depression, and other personality disorders can be associated with constructs such as impulsivity, disinhibition, and the dark triad of personality (narcissism, psychopathy, and Machiavellianism), which may be both positively and negatively related to engagement and performance in entrepreneurship. Importantly, they point out that conditions and characteristics that may seem dysfunctional in some contexts may, in fact, be particularly functional in other contexts, including entrepreneurship. For example, although often considered a disorder, positive links have been found between ADHD symptoms and opportunity recognition (Wiklund, Yu, Tucker, & Marino, 2017), entrepreneurial intention, entrepreneurial orientation (Lerner, Verheul, & Thurik, 2019), and performance (Yu, Wiklund, & Pérez-Luño, in press). This line of research delving more deeply into other fields such as clinical psychology to determine the linkages and applications of that work in the unique context of entrepreneurship have revealed insights important to our research, teaching, and practical support of would-be entrepreneurs. This work has also underscored the need to embrace psychological and other forms of diversity in our research and practice.

Yet questions remain concerning psychological diversity in entrepreneurship. Future research needs to continue to investigate outliers to enhance knowledge of entrepreneurial phenomena. What is most interesting in this stream of research is the finding that an individual's attributes that are at a disadvantage in society and employment can be an advantage in entrepreneurship. To what extent do those creating entrepreneurial teams consider individuals who are societally undervalued but have valued skills for the entrepreneurial context? How are such individuals selected, and why are some ventures more effective at capitalizing on these individuals' (outliers') skills than other new ventures?

Indeed, as we acknowledge the importance of future research on identity, affect, and nonfinancial outcomes, future research can explore how these constructs are impacted by psychological diversity. For example, does adding psychological diversity to an entrepreneurial team slow identity formation; that is, how identity is formed, propagated, and maintained for psychological diverse teams vis-à-vis less psychologically diverse teams? How does the different cognitive processing of more psychologically diverse entrepreneurial teams impact the teams' affective responses to progress, setbacks, and changes in team composition? While there are arguments and some evidence that psychological diversity has a positive impact on ventures' financial performance, this should not be the sole criterion for assessing the role of psychological diversity—we need to explore nonfinancial outcomes, as well. How does psychological diversity impact the individual providing the diversity (i.e., the outlier)—does it enhance their psychological well-being, social skills and integration, and feelings of independence? How does psychological diversity impact the "typical" members of the entrepreneurial team—does it enable new perspectives that facilitate creativity, generate positive and negative affect, and improve psychological well-being? Furthermore, we hope that just as entrepreneurial ventures benefit from psychological diversity, more established organizations may potentially also learn of its benefits and how to manage this diversity to change their human resource management practices.

Biology—Genetics, Physiology, and Neuroscience

The work reviewed in Chapter 5 also embraces the integration of knowledge from other fields outside of management to the unique entrepreneurial context. Nafal, Nicolaou, and Shane (Chapter 5, this volume) examine the ways in which human biology and specifically, genetics, physiology, and neuroscience have an influence on entrepreneurship and entrepreneurs. Over 80 papers have been published based on biological research within entrepreneurship, the majority of which focus on genetics. Interestingly, the research shows that genetic factors explain 48% of the variance in self-employment, 40% of the variance in starting a new business, and 43% of the variance in engaging in a firm start-up process (see Chapter 5 for citations and explanations of these findings). In addition to genetic influences, entrepreneurial activity has also been linked to hormones such as testosterone (related to risk-taking) and cortisol (related to stress). Nafal and colleagues point out that there is also quite a bit of emerging work applying neuroscience to entrepreneurship (de Holan, 2014; Nicolaou & Shane, 2014), which examines how different parts of an entrepreneur's brain are engaged in different decision tasks, with implications for emotions and cognitions (Laureiro-Martínez, Brusoni, Canessa, & Zollo, 2015). Researchers have also been integrating data from wearable medical devices (e.g., Fitbit trackers, Empatica E4) with traditional survey and interview techniques in order to better understand the connection between entrepreneur's mental, physical, and behavioral functioning (e.g., Arenius, Aslam, Brough, & Huq, 2019; Cardon, Murnieks, & Winsted, 2018). New technologies such as portable functional magnetic resonance imaging and electrocochleograms make research into the neurology of entrepreneurs more accessible and affordable, which promises fascinating insights in the years to come.

We are excited by experts in biology, physiology, and genetics entering the field of entrepreneurship. Welcome. We are also excited about technological innovations (current and anticipated) that enable research on these topics to occur with dramatically lower costs, less intrusion on participants, and with data collection outside the lab. Future research can use genetics, physiology, and neurology to support previous research on the antecedents of entrepreneurial action, offer new antecedents to the currently known set, introduce new mechanisms of established or newly theorized relationships and processes, and potentially offer the field a new set of dependent variables to consider.

Greater Focus on Teams

Finally, despite the reality that ventures are more likely to be founded by a team of people rather than a solo entrepreneur (Klotz, Hmieleski, Bradley, & Busenitz, 2014), our research has only recently begun to fully embrace studying the dynamics of such teams. As Breugst and Preller explain in Chapter 6 (this volume), while existing work has provided important insights into entrepreneurial team inputs such as human capital and capabilities and their relationship to important venture outcomes, very little is known about how entrepreneurial teams translate these inputs into outcomes. The research they review (just 26 papers, demonstrating the need for more work in this area) focuses on how the ways in which teams engage in task-related and interpersonal processes impact their cognitive and affective emergent states. The idea of team affect is also touched on in Chapter 3 by Huang and colleagues. Not surprisingly, Breugst and Preller emphasize the complexity of studying team dynamics within entrepreneurial teams, both conceptually and methodologically, particularly from a process perspective. Yet with their suggestions as well as topic-specific grounding provided by authors of other chapters in this volume, we are confident that researchers will embrace novel methodologies and deep thinking to more fully understand the complexities involved with the psychology of teams of entrepreneurs in the future.

Many questions remain concerning entrepreneurial teams. In particular, despite research demonstrating that teams should be diverse in several ways (optimism/pessimism, regulatory focus, etc.), some types of diversity are problematic (e.g., passion diversity; de Mol et al., 2019; Uy et al., in press), and teams are more likely to form based on similarity and liking rather than optimizing potential positive effects of diversity. Such similarity, in turn, could increase the likelihood of the "risky shift"—a move toward extreme decisions as discussions between the group members continue. Holding similar views and attitudes, or simply being similar in background, education, or other ways (e.g., teams consisting of all engineers), team members may, essentially, convince themselves that the view with which they started—perhaps a fairly moderate one—is correct, so why not adopt it more strongly? The result may be a tendency for the team to go "off the deep end", rather than choose more moderate ways forward. Understanding how individuals make decisions about entrepreneurial partners, and with what effects, warrants further investigation.

While we have discussed future research on teams in most of the sections earlier, we acknowledge the challenges of conducting such research. However, we are optimistic that with the recognition of the importance of teams and with recent (and forthcoming) innovations in data-collection devices, techniques, and experiments, there will be a surge in the number of entrepreneurial-team studies. For example, the novel technologies in neuroscience, wearable medical devices, and portable technologies may be combined in ways not previously used to understand the formation and functioning of entrepreneurial teams.

While it is understandable to initially focus on the formation of entrepreneurial teams and why some are more successful than others, we hope that future research also explores the termination of teams and why some teams become dysfunctional. For example, failure is a common occurrence for entrepreneurial projects (Shepherd, Patzelt, & Wolfe, 2011) and entrepreneurial firms (Shepherd, 2003), which can lead to the disbanding of a team. This termination or disbanding of entrepreneurial teams is a topic that has considerable potential to make important contributions to the entrepreneurship field. Similarly, and consistent with the notion of counterproductive work behaviors in established organizations, why do some entrepreneurial teams become destructive—to individual members, the team, the venture, or others (i.e., the environment and community)? We look forward to future research on entrepreneurial teams that incorporates research questions related to their disbanding and also their potentially dark and destructive sides.

Ideas That Might Take Us Into New Ways of Understanding Entrepreneurship

Entrepreneurship is not a simple or static phenomenon. Theoretically, we echo the sentiment of many authors in this volume that the most interesting ideas in the future are those that are more complex and dynamic (see, e.g., Chapter 11). Yet, as Davidsson points out in Chapter 20, although there is considerable agreement on the importance of taking a process-based view of entrepreneurship, "theoretical ideas and empirical evidence on these issues remain rather thin" perhaps due to the many challenges to engaging in process research. Papers that have taken a process perspective are often on disparate topics within our field, and there is not yet a cohesive and coherent framework in which to connect this work. This strikes us as an important opportunity that we hope scholars will pursue in the coming years. Given that processes unfold over different time spans (e.g., Foo et al., 2009; Lex, Gielnik, Spitzmuller, Jacob, & Frese, 2020), different methodological tools and approaches might be helpful depending on the specific time frames of most interest. For example, experience sampling methodology (ESM; Uy, Foo, & Aguinis, 2010) and daily diary studies are useful for examining changes that occur during days or weeks. Longitudinal designs are useful for capturing processes that unfold over longer time frames, such as months or years. Moreover, entrepreneurial processes may unfold differently based on one's age (Gielnik, Zacher, Mo, & Wang, 2018; see also Chapter 17), self-regulation skill (e.g., Gielnik et al., 2015; Van Gelderen, Kautonen, & Fink, 2015), or other factors.

Furthermore, although entrepreneurship is distinct in important ways from other contexts, it is not so distinct that core ideas from psychology, sociology, social psychology, or management are not applicable. Just as our field evolves, so do other fields that can inform our work in important ways and that we can inform through our own discoveries. As scholars examining issues that fall at the intersections of fields, we can pursue research that is deeply rooted in existing psychological theories, such as those on cognition (e.g., Chapter 2), leadership (Chapter 9), and affect (Chapter 3). Or we can develop new theories that are particularly suited for the context of entrepreneurship, such as theories on action (McMullen & Shepherd, 2006), bricolage (Baker & Nelson, 2005), or effectuation (Sarasvathy, 2001). We would be well served to not just use ideas already within the management or entrepreneurial fields and not just to borrow ideas superficially from other disciplines but to read deeply to understand foundational ideas, conceptual nuances, and current developments in thinking and methodologies in other fields as well as our own and to develop new ideas that can contribute back to other disciplines. I (Melissa here) will be the first one to note that it is challenging to stay up to date with work going on in multiple fields, especially those outside my core discipline. Yet some of the most interesting advancements and understanding come through conversations with people outside of entrepreneurship or even management, as they see the phenomenon I am interested in from a unique angle and their perspective helps inform my own. Moreover, each of the authors of this chapter has extensive professional networks in other countries and disciplines, and this is essential to the ability to think broadly and to keep an open mind to our work, rather than risk becoming more myopic or entrenched in our preferred way of thinking. Such open-mindedness allows for stronger development of work, such as through examining cultural issues of entrepreneurship (Chapter 8), and enhances our knowledge concerning interactions of entrepreneurs and factors in their environments (Chapter 15). The quality of research on the psychology of entrepreneurs in the future depends on broadening our conversations and integrating ideas across typical boundaries.

We likely have not even conceived of the methodologies we will be using 10 years from now. ESM (Uy et al., 2010) was a brand-new practice 10 years ago, and since then, wearable/trackable technologies that allow us to study sleep, stress, physical activity, and other biometric evidence have opened a plethora of research possibilities. Similarly, the use of artificial intelligence (AI), machine learning, and other techniques that vastly increase our ability to process large quantities of data to test hypotheses and draw conclusions is fantastic. We encourage pursuit of such opportunities to help us learn what we can about entrepreneurship and other phenomenon. Yet we suggest that we should also keep an eye to the ethical implications of more invasive and saturated access to details of individual people's lives. For example, if researchers utilize medical wearable technology to study entrepreneurial physiological reactions to stress, team members, investors, and researchers may be able to see medical diagnoses before the study subject. What are the implications for "informed consent", obligations to inform our participants, and so on? Yes, we are doctors but not medical professionals, and we urge caution as risks of invasion of privacy and other ethical quandaries we have yet to discover are likely going to increase over the next 10 years.

We also encourage research that studies how responses to major environmental and health risks such as earthquakes (Williams & Shepherd, 2018) and COVID-19 have been and continue to be entrepreneurial. At the start of the COVID-19 global pandemic that began in 2020, there were many examples of rapidly created groups on various social media platforms organized to help higher education and K–12 teachers quickly pivot their courses to online learning platforms, to help companies create productive work-from-home policies, and to create online collaborations designed to bring together people fired up about creating companies to address problems stemming from the pandemic (e.g., Indiana University's start-up weekend). We wonder about entrepreneurial opportunities that exist to help the people "left behind by innovation" such as those whose jobs have been eliminated by technology such as robots or AI, or those who lose jobs during major health crises because their technological infrastructure or nature of work does not allow them to work or attend classes from home. Research has emerged rapidly on the economic factors and outcomes of such situations, and we encourage work on the psychological processes that are also involved, such as loss of hope, increased feelings of inequity, substantial challenges to in-home work/life balance, and others. There are many examples (e.g., Shepherd & Williams, 2019) of Shepherd's (2015) discussion of how to better integrate work on compassion organizing into our own research. We encourage our field to continue to explore how entrepreneurial actions, and, in particular, spontaneous venturing, can help alleviate human suffering and improve the human condition. More broadly, we encourage the continued focus on the psychology of entrepreneurship, which can involve action, emotion, cognition, identity, learning, individuals, teams, employees, investors, and so much more. We look forward to the third edition of this book to see what strides we have made 10 more years down the line.

References

Arenius, P., Aslam, N., Brough, A., & Huq, A. (2019). Exploration of the positive and negative emotional states related to entrepreneurial actions and the link to sustained entrepreneurial performance. Paper presented at the *Babson College Entrepreneurship Research Conference*, Wellesley, MA.

Baker, T., & Nelson, R. E. (2005). Creating something from nothing: Resource construction through entrepreneurial bricolage. *Administrative Science Quarterly, 50*(3), 329–366. doi:10.2189/asqu.2005.50.3.329

Baron, R. A., & Branscombe, N. (2017). *Social psychology* (14th ed.). New York, NY: Pearson.

Baron, R. A., Hmieleski, K. M., & Henry, R. A. (2012). Entrepreneurs' dispositional positive affect: The potential benefits – and potential costs – of being "up". *Journal of Business Venturing, 27*(3), 310–324. doi:10.1016/j.jbusvent.2011.04.002

Birch, D. L., Haggerty, A., & Parsons, W. (1995). *Who's creating jobs*. Boston, MA: Cognetics Inc.

Bledow, R., Rosing, K., & Frese, M. (2013). A dynamic perspective on affect and creativity. *Academy of Management Journal, 56*(2), 432–450. doi:10.5465/amj.2010.0894

Boone, S., Adries, P., & Clarysse, B. (2019). Does team entrepreneurial passion matter for relationship conflict and team performance? On the importance of fit between passion focus and venture development stage. *Journal of Business Venturing, 35*(5): 1–20.

Breugst, N., Domurath, A., Patzelt, H., & Klaukien, A. (2012). Perceptions of entrepreneurial passion and employees' commitment to entrepreneurial ventures. *Entrepreneurship: Theory & Practice, 36*(1), 171–192. doi:10.1111/j.1540-6520.2011.00491.x

Cardon, M. S., Murnieks, C. Y., & Winsted, K. (2018). Well-being challenges from dual identities of hybrid entrepreneurs. Paper presented at the *Babson College Entrepreneurship Research Conference*, Warwick, Ireland.

Cardon, M. S., & Patel, P. C. (2015). Is stress worth it? Stress-related health and wealth trade-offs for entrepreneurs. *Applied Psychology: An International Review, 64*(2), 379–420. doi:10.1111/apps.12021

Cardon, M. S., Post, C., & Forster, W. R. (2017). Team entrepreneurial passion: Its emergence and influence in new venture teams. *Academy of Management Review, 42*(2), 283–305. doi:10.5465/amr.2014.0356

Cardon, M. S., Wincent, J., Singh, J., & Drnovsek, M. (2009). The nature and experience of entrepreneurial passion. *Academy of Management Review, 34*(3), 511–532. doi:10.5465/AMR.2009.40633190

Chen, X.-P., Yao, X. I. N., & Kotha, S. (2009). Entrepreneur passion and preparedness in business plan presentations: A persuasion analysis of venture capitalists' funding decisions. *Academy of Management Journal, 52*(1), 199–214. doi:10.5465/AMJ.2009.36462018

Conger, M., McMullen, J. S., Bergman, B. J., & York, J. G. (2018). Category membership, identity control, and the reevaluation of prosocial opportunities. *Journal of Business Venturing, 33*(2), 179–206. doi:10.1016/j.jbusvent.2017.11.004

Crosina, E. (2018). On becoming an entrepreneur: Unpacking entrepreneurial identity. In P. G. Greene & C. G. Brush (Eds.), *A research agenda for women in entrepreneurship: Identity through aspirations, behaviors and confidence* (pp. 93–113). Cheltenham, UK: Edward Elgar Publishing.

Davis, B. C., Hmieleski, K. M., Webb, J. W., & Coombs, J. E. (2017). Funders' positive affective reactions to entrepreneurs' crowdfunding pitches: The influence of perceived product creativity and entrepreneurial passion. *Journal of Business Venturing, 32*(1), 90–106. doi:10.1016/j.jbusvent.2016.10.006

De Dreu, C. K. W., Baas, M., & Nijstad, B. A. (2008). Hedonic tone and activation level in the mood-creativity link: Toward a dual pathway to creativity model. *Journal of Personality & Social Psychology, 94*(5), 739–756. doi:10.1037/0022-3514.94.5.739

De Holan, P. M. (2014). It's all in your head: Why we need neuroentrepreneurship. *Journal of Management Inquiry, 23*(1), 93–97. doi:10.1177/1056492613485913

De Mol, E., Cardon, M. S., de Jong, B. A., Khapova, S. N., & Elfring, T. (2019). Entrepreneurial passion diversity in new venture teams: An empirical investigation of short- and long-term performance implications. *Journal of Business Venturing*, 1–18.

DeTienne, D. R. (2010). Entrepreneurial exit as a critical component of the entrepreneurial process: Theoretical development. *Journal of Business Venturing, 25*(2), 203–215. doi:10.1016/j.jbusvent.2008.05.004

Ellemers, N., Spears, R., & Doosje, B. (2002). Self and social identity. *Annual Review of Psychology, 53*(1), 161. doi:10.1146/annurev.psych.53.100901.135228

Fauchart, E., & Gruber, M. (2011). Darwinians, communitarians, and missionaries: The role of founder identity in entrepreneurship. *Academy of Management Journal, 54*(5), 935–957. doi:10.5465/amj.2009.0211

Foo, M.-D., Uy, M. A., & Baron, R. A. (2009). How do feelings influence effort? An empirical study of entrepreneurs' affect and venture effort. *Journal of Applied Psychology, 94*(4), 1086–1094. doi:10.1037/a0015599

Fredrickson, B. L., Mancuso, R. A., Branigan, C., & Tugade, M. M. (2000). The undoing effect of positive emotions. *Motivation and Emotion, 24*(4), 237–258. doi:10.1023/A:1010796329158

Gartner, W. B. (1989). "Who is an entrepreneur?" is the wrong question. *Entrepreneurship Theory & Practice, 13*(4), 47–68. doi:10.1177/104225878901300406

George, J. M., & Jing, Z. (2007). Dual tuning in a supportive context: Joint contributions of positive mood, negative mood, and supervisory behaviors to employee creativity. *Academy of Management Journal, 50*(3), 605–622. doi:10.5465/AMJ.2007.25525934

George, J. M., Jing, Z., & Zhou, J. (2002). Understanding when bad moods foster creativity and good ones don't: The role of context and clarity of feelings. *Journal of Applied Psychology, 87*(4), 687–697. doi:10.1037/0021-9010.87.4.687

Gielnik, M. M., Frese, M., Kahara-Kawuki, A., Katono, I. W., Kyejjusa, S., Ngoma, M., . . . Dlugosch, T. J. (2015). Action and action-regulation in entrepreneurship: Evaluating a student training for promoting entrepreneurship. *Academy of Management Learning & Education, 14*(1), 69–94. doi:10.5465/amle.2012.0107

Gielnik, M. M., Zacher, H., Mo, W., & Wang, M. (2018). Age in the entrepreneurial process: The role of future time perspective and prior entrepreneurial experience. *Journal of Applied Psychology, 103*(10), 1067–1085. doi:10.1037/apl0000322

Grimes, M. G. (2018). The pivot: How founders respond to feedback through idea and identity work. *Academy of Management Journal, 61*(5), 1692–1717. doi:10.5465/amj.2015.0823

Hubner, S., Baum, M., & Frese, M. (2019). Contagion of entrepreneurial passion: Effects on employee outcomes. *Entrepreneurship Theory & Practice*. doi: 10.1177/1042258719883995

Klotz, A. C., Hmieleski, K. M., Bradley, B. H., & Busenitz, L. W. (2014). New venture teams: A review of the literature and roadmap for future research. *Journal of Management, 40*(1), 226–255. doi:10.1177/0149206313493325

Laureiro-Martínez, D., Brusoni, S., Canessa, N., & Zollo, M. (2015). Understanding the exploration-exploitation dilemma: An fMRI study of attention control and decision-making performance. *Strategic Management Journal (John Wiley & Sons, Inc.), 36*(3), 319–338. doi:10.1002/smj.2221

Lerman, M. P., Munyon, T. P., & Carr, J. C. (2020). Stress events theory: A theoretical framework for understanding entrepreneurial behavior. In P. L. Perrewé, P. D. Harms, & C. -H. Chang (Eds.), *Entrepreneurial and small business stressors, experienced stress, and well-being. Research in occupational stress and well being* (Vol. 18, pp. 35–63). Emerald Publishing Limited. Retrieved from https://doi.org/10.1108/S1479-355520200000018003

Lerner, D. A., Verheul, I., & Thurik, R. (2019). Entrepreneurship and attention deficit/hyperactivity disorder: A large-scale study involving the clinical condition of ADHD. *Small Business Economics, 53*(2), 381–392. doi:10.1007/s11187-018-0061-1

Lex, M., Gielnik, M. M., Spitzmuller, M., Jacob, G. H., & Frese, M. (2020). How passion in entrepreneurship develops over time: A self-regulation perspective. *Entrepreneurship Theory and Practice.* doi:10.1177/1042258720929894

Li, J., Chen, X.-P., Kotha, S., & Fisher, G. (2017). Catching fire and spreading it: A glimpse into displayed entrepreneurial passion in crowdfunding campaigns. *Journal of Applied Psychology, 102*(7), 1075–1090. doi:10.1037/apl0000217

Martens, M. L., Jennings, J. E., & Jennings, P. D. (2007). Do the stories they tell get them the money they need? The role of entrepreneurial narratives in resource acquisition. *Academy of Management Journal, 50*(5), 1107–1132. doi:10.5465/AMJ.2007.27169488

Mathias, B. D., & Williams, D. W. (2018). Giving up the hats? Entrepreneurs' role transitions and venture growth. *Journal of Business Venturing, 33*(3), 261–277. doi:10.1016/j.jbusvent.2017.12.007

McMullen, J. S., & Shepherd, D. A. (2006). Entrepreneurial action and the role of uncertainty in the theory of the entrepreneur. *Academy of Management Review, 31*(1), 132–152. doi:10.5465/AMR.2006.19379628

Mmbaga, N. A., Mathias, B. D., Williams, D. W., & Cardon, M. S. (in press). A review of and future agenda for research on identity in entrepreneurship.

Murnieks, C. Y. (2007). *Who am I? The quest for an entrepreneurial identity and an investigation of its relationship to entrepreneurial passion and goal-setting.* Boulder, CO: University of Colorado Press.

Nicolaou, N., & Shane, S. (2014). Biology, neuroscience, and entrepreneurship. *Journal of Management Inquiry, 23*(1), 98–100. doi:10.1177/1056492613485914

O'Kane, P., Smith, A. D., & Lerman, M. P. (2019). Building transparency and trustworthiness in inductive research through computer aided qualitative data analysis software. *Organizational Research Methods.* doi: 10.1177/1094428119865016

Peredo, A. M., & Chrisman, J. J. (2006). Toward a theory of community-based enterprise. *Academy of Management Review, 31*(2), 309–328. doi:10.5465/AMR.2006.20208683

Powell, E. E., & Baker, T. E. D. (2014). It's what you make of it: Founder identity and enacting strategic responses to adversity. *Academy of Management Journal, 57*(5), 1406–1433. doi:10.5465/amj.2012.0454

Powell, E. E., & Baker, T. E. D. (2017). In the beginning: Identity processes and organizing in multi-founder Nascent ventures. *Academy of Management Journal, 60*(6), 2381–2414. doi:10.5465/amj.2015.0175

Santos, S. C., & Cardon, M. S. (2019). What's love got to do with it? Team entrepreneurial passion and performance in new venture teams. *Entrepreneurship Theory & Practice, 43*(3), 475–504. doi:10.1177/1042258718812185

Sarasvathy, S. D. (2001). Causation and effectuation: Toward a theoretical shift from economic inevitability to entrepreneurial contingency. *Academy of Management Review*, 26(2), 243–263. doi:10.5465/AMR.2001.4378020

Seyb, S. K., Shepherd, D. A., & Williams, T. A. (2019). Exoskeletons, entrepreneurs, and communities: A model of co-constructing a potential opportunity. *Journal of Business Venturing*, 34(6). doi:10.1016/j.jbusvent.2019.105947

Shane, S., & Venkataraman, S. (2000). The promise of entrepreneurship as a field of research. *Academy of Management Review*, 25(1), 217–226. doi:10.5465/AMR.2000.2791611

Shepherd, D. A. (2003). Learning from business failure: Propositions of grief recovery for the self-employed. *Academy of Management Review*, 28(2), 318–328. doi:10.5465/AMR.2003.9416377

Shepherd, D. A. (2015). Party on! A call for entrepreneurship research that is more interactive, activity based, cognitively hot, compassionate, and prosocial. *Journal of Business Venturing*, 30(4), 489–507. doi:10.1016/j.jbusvent.2015.02.001

Shepherd, D. A., Patzelt, H., & Wolfe, M. (2011). Moving forward from project failure: Negative emotions, affective commitment, and learning from the experience. *Academy of Management Journal*, 54(6), 1229–1259. doi:10.5465/amj.2010.0102

Shepherd, D. A., Saade, F. P., & Wincent, J. (2020). How to circumvent adversity? Refugee-entrepreneurs' resilience in the face of substantial and persistent adversity. *Journal of Business Venturing*, 35(4). doi:10.1016/j.jbusvent.2019.06.001

Shepherd, D. A., & Williams, T. A. (2019). *Spontaneous venturing: An entrepreneurial approach to alleviating suffering in the aftermath of a disaster*. Cambridge, MA: Massachusetts Institute of Technology Press.

Stephan, U. (2018). Entrepreneurs' mental health and well-being: A review and research agenda. *Academy of Management Perspectives*, 32(3), 290–322. doi:10.5465/amp.2017.0001

Stryker, S. (1980). *Symbolic interactionism: A social structural version*. San Francisco, CA: Benjamin-Cummings Publishing Company.

Stryker, S. (2008). From mead to a structural symbolic interactionism and beyond. *Annual Review of Sociology*, 34, 15–31. doi:10.1146/annurev.soc.34.040507.134649

Tajfel, H., & Turner, J. C. (1979). An integrative theory of intergroup conflict. In W. Austin & S. Worchel (Eds.), *The social psychology of intergroup relations* (pp. 33–47). Monterey, CA: Brooks-Cole.

Tripathi, N., Zhu, J., Jacob, G. H., Frese, M., & Gielnik, M. M. (in press). Intraindividual variability in identity centrality: Examining the dynamics of perceived role progress and identity centrality. *Journal of Applied Psychology*.

Uy, M. A., Foo, M.-D., & Aguinis, H. (2010). Using experience sampling methodology to advance entrepreneurship theory and research. *Organizational Research Methods*, 13(1), 31–54. doi:10.1177/1094428109334977

Uy, M. A., Jacob, G. H., Gielnik, M. M., Frese, M., Antonio, T., Wonohadidjojo, D. M., & Christina, C. (in press). When passions collide: Passion convergence in entrepreneurial teams. *Journal of Applied Psychology*.

Van Gelderen, M., Kautonen, T., & Fink, M. (2015). From entrepreneurial intentions to actions: Self-control and action-related doubt, fear, and aversion. *Journal of Business Venturing*, 30(5), 655–673. doi:10.1016/j.jbusvent.2015.01.003

Venkataraman, S. (1997). The distinctive domain of entrepreneurship research. In J. A. Katz (Ed.), *Advances in entrepreneurship, firm emergence and growth* (Vol. 3, pp. 119–138). Oxford: JAI Press.

Welter, F., Baker, T., Audretsch, D. B., & Gartner, W. B. (2017). Everyday entrepreneurship - A call for entrepreneurship research to embrace entrepreneurial diversity. *Entrepreneurship Theory & Practice, 41*(3), 311–321. doi:10.1111/etap.12258

Wennberg, K., Wiklund, J., DeTienne, D. R., & Cardon, M. S. (2010). Reconceptualizing entrepreneurial exit: Divergent exit routes and their drivers. *Journal of Business Venturing, 25*(4), 361–375. doi:10.1016/j.jbusvent.2009.01.001

Wiklund, J., Hatak, I., Patzelt, H., & Shepherd, D. A. (2018). Mental disorders in the entrepreneurship context: When being different can be an advantage. *Academy of Management Perspectives, 32*(2), 182–206. doi:10.5465/amp.2017.0063

Wiklund, J., Yu, W., Tucker, R., & Marino, L. D. (2017). ADHD, impulsivity and entrepreneurship. *Journal of Business Venturing, 32*(6), 627–656. doi:10.1016/j.jbusvent.2017.07.002

Williams, T. A., & Shepherd, D. A. (2018). To the rescue!? Brokering a rapid, scaled and customized compassionate response to suffering after disaster. *Journal of Management Studies (John Wiley & Sons, Inc.), 55*(6), 910–942. doi:10.1111/joms.12291

Wood, M. S., McKelvie, A., & Haynie, J. M. (2014). Making it personal: Opportunity individuation and the shaping of opportunity beliefs. *Journal of Business Venturing, 29*(2), 252–272. doi:10.1016/j.jbusvent.2013.02.001

Wood, M. S., & McKinley, W. (2010). The production of entrepreneurial opportunity: A constructivist perspective. *Strategic Entrepreneurship Journal, 4*(1), 66–84. doi:10.1002/sej.83

Wood, M. S., & Williams, D. W. (2014). Opportunity evaluation as rule-based decision making. *Journal of Management Studies (John Wiley & Sons, Inc.), 51*(4), 573–602. doi:10.1111/joms.12018

Yu, W., Wiklund, J., & Pérez-Luño, A. (in press). ADHD symptoms, entrepreneurial orientation (EO), and firm performance. *Entrepreneurship Theory and Practice.* doi:10.1177/1042258719892987

INDEX

Note: Page numbers in italic indicate a figure and page numbers in bold indicate a table on the corresponding page. Page numbers followed by "n" indicate a note.

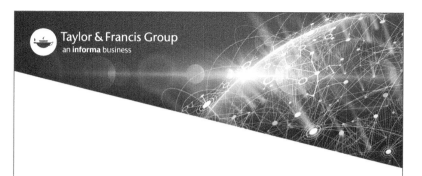